Seaweed Resources
in Europe:
Uses and Potential

Seaweed Resources in Europe: Uses and Potential

Edited by

Michael D. Guiry

Department of Botany, University College Galway
The National University of Ireland, Galway, Ireland

and

Gerald Blunden

School of Pharmacy and Biomedical Sciences
Portsmouth Polytechnic, UK

JOHN WILEY & SONS

Chichester · New York · Brisbane · Toronto · Singapore

Other Wiley Editorial Offices

John Wiley & Sons, Inc., 605 Third Avenue,
New York, NY 10158-0012, USA

Jacaranda Wiley Ltd, G.P.O. Box 859, Brisbane,
Queensland 4001, Australia

John Wiley & Sons (Canada) Ltd, 22 Worcester Road,
Rexdale, Ontario M9W 1L1, Canada

John Wiley & Sons (SEA) Pte Ltd, 37 Jalan Pemimpin   05-04,
Block B, Union Industrial Building, Singapore 2057

Library of Congress Cataloging-in-Publication Data:

Seaweed resources in Europe: uses and potential/edited by M.D. Guiry and
    G. Blunden.
        p. cm.
    Includes bibliographical references and indexes.
    ISBN 0 471 92947 6
    1. Marine algae—Europe—Utilization.
    2. Marine algae culture—Europe.
    I. Guiry, Michael, D.   II. Blunden, G.
    SH390.7.S44   1991
    333.95'3—dc20   90-24343
                                                               CIP

British Library Cataloguing in Publication Data:

Seaweed resources in Europe.
    1. Seaweeds. Use
    I. Guiry, M. D.   II. Blunden, G.
    589.392

    ISBN 0 471 92947 6

Typeset by Acorn Bookwork, Salisbury, Wiltshire
Printed in Great Britain by Biddles Ltd, Guildford

This book is dedicated to Dr E.H. Schulte, Scientific Secretary of the COST Action Programme 48 from 1985 to 1990. The success of this programme owes much to his hard work and enthusiasm, which has been appreciated greatly by everybody who has collaborated with him.

Contents

Contributors

Dr G. Blunden
School of Pharmacy and Biomedical Sciences, Portsmouth Polytechnic, Park Building, King Henry I Street, Portsmouth PO1 2DZ, UK

Dr X. Briand
Société des Englais Composés Minéraux et Amendements (SECMA), BP 65, F-22260 Pontrieux, France

Dr B. Carpentier
Laboratoire des Sciences et Technologies Brassicoles, Louvain-la-Neuve, Belgium

Dr R.H. Charlier
SA SOPEX NV, Antwerp, Belgium

Dr B.E. Christensen
Division of Biotechnology, Laboratory for Marine Biochemistry, The Norwegian Institute of Technology, University of Trondheim, N-7034 Trondheim-NTH, Norway

Dr Y. De Roeck-Holtzhauer
Centre Atlantique d'Études en Cosmetologie, Université de Nantes, 68 Boulevard Eugène Orieux, F-44000 Nantes, France

Dr D. de Waart
CIVO-Instituten TNO, PO 360, 3700 AJ Zeist, The Netherlands

Dr D.J. Garbary
Department of Biology, St. Francis Xavier University, Antigonish, Nova Scotia, B2G 1C0, Canada

Dr M.D. Guiry
Department of Botany, University College Galway, The National University of Ireland, Galway, Ireland

Dr M. Indergaard
Division of Biotechnology, Laboratory for Marine Biochemistry, The Norwegian Institute of Technology, University of Trondheim, N-7034 Trondheim-NTH, Norway

Dr J.M. Kain (Jones)
University of Liverpool, Department of Marine Biology, Port Erin, Isle of Man, UK

Dr A. Martinsen
Division of Biotechnology, Laboratory for Marine Biochemistry, The Norwegian Institute of Technology, University of Trondheim, N-7034 Trondheim-NTH, Norway

Dr J. Mazé
Centre d'Aide par le Travail de Quatre-Vaulx, Saint-Cast-Le Guildo, France

Dr J. Minsaas
SINTEF, Trondheim, Norway

Dr P. Morand
Centre de Recherche en Ecologie Marine et Aquaculture, CNRS-IFREMER, L'Houmeau, Case 5, Nieul-sur-mer, France

Dr M. Orlandini
Istituto di Chimica Applicata e Industriale, Universitá di Trieste, I-34127 Trieste, Italy

Dr K. Østgaard
Division of Biotechnology, Laboratory for Marine Biochemistry, The Norwegian Institute of Technology, University of Trondheim, N-7034 Trondheim-NTH, Norway

Dr B.A. Plunkett
Department of Chemistry, Portsmouth Polytechnic, White Swan Road, Portsmouth PO1 2DT, UK

Dr W. Schramm
Institute für Meereskunde, Universität Kiel, Düsternbrooker Weg 20, D-2300 Kiel, Germany

Dr G. Skjåk-Bræk
Division of Biotechnology, Laboratory for Marine Biochemistry, The Norwegian Institute of Technology, University of Trondheim, N-7034 Trondheim-NTH, Norway

Dr O. Smidsrød
Division of Biotechnology, Laboratory for Marine Biochemistry, The Norwegian Institute of Technology, University of Trondheim, N-7034 Trondheim-NTH, Norway

Preface

This book has resulted from the efforts of many people associated with the COST action programme 48 on Aquatic Primary Biomass (Marine Macroalgae). During informal discussions at one of the Management Committee meetings in Brussels, several members expressed the view that although there was a lot of information known about the current and potential uses of seaweeds in Europe, this had never been collected together in a readily available form. The idea of pursuing this aim was raised formally at the committee meeting and the project was launched. It was the intention to keep a European perspective for the book, although it is readily accepted that vast amounts of work on seaweed utilization have been conducted in other areas of the World, in particular Asia and North America. Also, the decision was taken to discuss work on marine macroalgae only, even though it is realized that considerable effort has been expended on the investigation of microalgae. Other topics could have been included in the volume, but the decision was taken for the book to reflect the major lines of research and development being undertaken in the COST action programme 48.

The editors wish to thank the authors of the chapters, the referees and the members of the Management Committee for their help. Special thanks go to Dr E.H. Schulte, Scientific Secretary of the COST action programme 48 from its inception in 1985 until 1990, and to Mrs Deirdre Murphy for secretarial assistance at University College Galway. Without their assistance and patience neither the book nor the COST 48 programme would have advanced very far. Thanks are due also to Mrs Wendy Guiry for translation of one of the chapters from French into English.

M.D. Guiry
G. Blunden

xi

1 A Geographical and Taxonomic Guide to European Seaweeds of Economic Importance

MICHAEL D. GUIRY[1] and DAVID J. GARBARY[2]
[1]*Department of Botany, University College, Galway, Ireland and*
[2]*Department of Biology, St Francis Xavier University, Antigonish, Canada*

INTRODUCTION

Europe is bounded to the west by the Atlantic Ocean, to the south by the Mediterranean Sea, and to the north by the Arctic Ocean and North Sea; it also includes two large, almost land-locked seas, the Baltic and the Adriatic. Of these sea areas, the Atlantic and the Mediterranean are most productive in terms of seaweed diversity and biomass. The largest proportion of the biomass is found as brown algae growing in the lower intertidal and shallow subtidal zones on Atlantic coasts. Although the red algae are responsible for most of the diversity on European coasts, their biomass is considerably lower than that of the brown algae.

Even after more than two centuries of scientific study of seaweeds on European coasts, the taxonomy and nomenclature of marine algae remain in a state of flux, largely as a result of the extreme complexity of these variable organisms and an overall waning of interest in systematics.

No overall Mediterranean flora or checklist exists, although there are useful floristic accounts and lists for particular areas. A very helpful checklist and distributional index of the benthic marine algae of the North Atlantic was recently compiled by South and Tittley (1986). This list includes the Baltic and North Seas and reference should be made to it for the more recent taxonomic and nomenclatural changes.

The biogeography and factors controlling distribution of marine algae in the North Atlantic basin and in the Mediterranean are discussed by Hoek and Donze (1967), Hoek (1982a,b) and Lüning (1985, 1990).

A brief guide to the literature on identification, distribution and taxonomy of marine algae of actual or potential economic importance is presented here. Table 1 is a guide to the primary distributional and taxonomic literature based on geographical area. A brief discussion of selected families that include

Seaweed Resources in Europe: Uses and Potential. Edited by M. D. Guiry and G. Blunden
© 1991 John Wiley & Sons Ltd

Table 1. Guide to the literature for the marine algae of Europe and adjacent waters

Country/Region	References	Comments
EUROPE		
Sweden and the Baltic Sea	Levring (1935)	Algae of the Swedish west coast
	Kylin (1944, 1947, 1949)	Algae of the Swedish west coast
	Levring (1937)	Flora of the Swedish west coast
	Ravanko (1968)	Marine algae of Finland
	Waern (1952)	Algae of eastern Sweden
	Pankow (1971)	Algae of the southern Baltic
	Starmach (1977)	Brown and red algae from the southern Baltic
	Wallentinius (1979)	Ecology of marine algae in the Baltic proper
Norway	Kylin (1910)	Algae of the Norwegian west coast
	Jorde (1966)	Ecology of seaweeds of the Bergen area
	Jorde & Klavestad (1963)	Ecology of seaweeds of the Hardangerfjord
	Jaasund (1965)	Algae of northern Norway
	Rueness (1977)	Algae of Norway
Denmark	Rosenvinge (1909, 1917, 1924, 1931)	Red algae of Denmark
	Rosenvinge & Lund (1941, 1943, 1947)	Brown algae of Denmark
	Christensen *et al.* (1985)	Distribution and list of Danish marine algae
Germany	Kornmann & Sahling (1977, 1983)	Flora of Helgoland
The Netherlands	den Hartog (1959)	Ecological account of algal communities
	Nienhuis (1980)	Epilithic algal vegetation
	Stegenga & Mol (1983)	Marine algal flora
Belgium	Coppejans (1982a, 1982b)	Marine algal flora
	Coppejans & Ben (1980)	Keys to marine algae
UK and Ireland	Newton (1931)	Illustrated flora with keys
	Knight & Parke (1931)	Ecology of the algae of the Isle of Man
	Parke & Dixon (1976)	Checklist of marine algae
	Dixon *et al.* (1966)	Guide to literature
	Dixon & Irvine (1977)	Illustrated flora with keys to species of red algae
	Irvine (1983)	Illustrated flora with keys to species of red algae
	Christensen (1987)	Illustrated flora with keys to species of marine and brackish Tribophyceae

Table 1. (*continued*)

Country/Region	References	Comments
EUROPE		
UK and Ireland (*continued*)	Fletcher (1987)	Illustrated flora with keys to species of brown algae
	Guiry (1978a)	List and distributional guide for Ireland
	Hiscock (1986)	Illustrated keys to marine flora
	Tittley & Price (1978)	Ecology and distribution of Channel coast algae
Atlantic France	Gayral (1966)	Seaweed flora
	Hamel (1930, 1931, 1935, 1937, 1938, 1939)	Accounts of selected groups
	Feldmann & Hamel (1936)	Taxonomy of Gelidiales
	Tittley & Price (1978)	Floristics of eastern English Channel
	Feldmann (1954)	List of the marine algae of the Roscoff area with notes on distribution in Brittany
	Feldmann & Magne (1964)	Additional species for the Roscoff area
	Hoek & Donze (1966)	Algal list from Biarritz
	De Virville (1962)	Studies on seaweeds from Normandy
	Dizerbo (1971a, 1971b, 1975)	Distributional records from Brittany
Iberian Peninsula	Gallardo *et al.* (1985)	Checklist of marine algae
	Donze (1968)	Algae of north-eastern Spain
	Ardré (1970)	Flora of Portugal
	Seoane-Camba (1965)	Algae from the Cadiz area
Azores	Martins (1990)	Bibliography of marine flora
Mediterranean France	Feldmann (1937a, 1937b, 1939, 1942a, 1942b)	Flora of the Côte des Albères
	Boudouresque & Perret (1977)	Inventory of Corsican flora
	Boudouresque (1971)	Phytosociology of marine flora
	Coppejans (1983)	Illustrations of marine algae
Italy	Giaccone (1969)	Checklist of marine flora
	Giaccone *et al.* (1985)	List and distribution in Sicily
	Giaccone (1978)	List of Adriatic seaweeds
Greece	Gerloff & Geissler (1971)	Annotated list of seaweeds
	Haritonidis & Tsekos (1975)	List from the northern coasts

(continued)

Table 1. (*continued*)

Country/Region	References	Comments
EUROPE		
Greece (*continued*)	Haritonidis & Tsekos (1976)	List from the western coasts
	Athanasiadis (1987)	Flora of the Aegean Sea
ADJACENT COASTS		
Black Sea	Zinova (1967)	Seaweed flora
Iceland	Caram & Jónsson (1972)	Annotated checklist
	Munda (1979)	List of seaweed flora
Macaronesia	Børgesen (1927, 1929, 1930)	Red algae of the Canary Islands
	Levring (1974)	List of seaweeds from Madeira
	Weisscher (1983)	List from the Salvage Islands
Morocco	Gayral (1958)	Seaweed flora

economically important species, or those that have potential for human utilization, is presented below.

SYSTEMATIC GUIDE

CHLOROPHYTA

A reclassification of the Chlorophyta into five classes has been proposed (Mattox & Stewart 1984); this new arrangement has not been universally accepted, but is likely to be (see also Hoek *et al.* 1988). Most marine green algae included in this volume are referred to as either the Ulvophyceae or the Chlorophyceae. The families below are those used by South and Tittley (1986).

Percursariaceae

Percursaria percursa (C. Agardh) Bory is a brackish water species used in sewage treatment experiments (Chapter 12); Bliding (1963) has given an account of the morphology and systematics of this species.

Monostromataceae

Nine species of *Monostroma* are listed by South and Tittley (1986) from the North Atlantic. Some taxonomic uncertainty exists as to the correct generic placement of these species, some authors referring species to the genera *Ulvaria*, *Ulvopsis* and *Protomonostroma*. Blade-like algae referred to the Monostromataceae are occasionally used as food (Madlener 1977).

Ulvaceae

Two large and systematically difficult genera belonging to this family are of economic importance: *Ulva* and *Enteromorpha*. Bliding (1963, 1968) provided monographic accounts for Europe as a whole, whereas Koeman and Hoek (1980, 1982a, 1982b, 1984) have studied in detail species of these genera occurring in the Netherlands, and these papers should be consulted for literature on identification. Species of *Enteromorpha* and *Ulva* are important in the treatment of waste waters (Chapter 6), as fouling organisms (Fletcher 1980), and as food organisms (Madlener 1977; Boisvert 1987, 1988).

Cladophoraceae

Cladophora is a large and widespread genus in the North Atlantic and Mediterranean. Söderström (1963) and Hoek (1963) have made the only comprehensive studies of the genus in the North Atlantic. A synoptic key to the species of *Cladophora* that occur in marine and brackish waters in France is given by Jónsson et al. (1989). Some species of *Cladophora* are fouling organisms (Fletcher 1980).

Codiaceae

About nine species of *Codium* are found in the North Atlantic, many of which also occur in the Mediterranean. Several subspecies of *Codium fragile* have been introduced into the Atlantic in historical times; it is likely that these originated in the Pacific. Descriptions of and keys to the species of *Codium* in the Atlantic may be found in Silva (1955, 1957, 1960, 1962); they are sometimes a nuisance in harbours and shellfish beds, but it is possible that some can be used as human food.

Codium species have been used as food elsewhere in the world (Abbott & Williamson 1974), but there would appear to be no such usage in Europe.

PHAEOPHYTA

Phaeophyta is often included in the Chromophyta as the Phaeophyceae or Fucophyceae (see Christensen 1980). Many of the supposedly primitive brown algae are of economic importance as fouling organisms in maricultural operations, harbours and submerged marine structures (Fletcher 1980), but their generic status and placement at the ordinal and familial level is in a state of almost continual change (see Pedersen 1984; Fletcher 1987). At the moment, these latter two accounts are the most useful guides to the identification of brown algae in the North Atlantic and in the Mediterranean; unfortunately, neither is comprehensive in coverage.

The Laminariales and the Fucales are the two most important orders economically, largely as a result of their food potential (Madlener 1977; Boisvert 1987, 1988) and polysaccharide contents (Chapters 7 and 9).

Ectocarpaceae

This family includes a large number of uniseriate, branched or unbranched filamentous algae, variously placed in the genera *Ectocarpus, Pilayella, Giffordia* and *Feldmannia*, among others. Systematic accounts of these algae have been given by Cardinal (1964) and Pedersen (1984). Filamentous brown algae are a considerable nuisance in algal cultivation and shellfish mariculture, and cause both ship and harbour fouling (Fletcher 1980).

Scytosiphonaceae

Colpomenia species are represented in the Atlantic by two entities: *C. peregrina* Sauvageau and *C. sinuosa* (Roth) Derbès et Solier in Castagne. The former species appears to have undergone a natural geographical range extension in the early part of the present century, which was probably aided by increased shellfish mariculture and shipping activities. *Colpomenia* is reputed to have caused problems in the latter industry by attaching to the shells of the molluscs, gradually filling with gas, and floating away with the animal still attached; this has given rise to the name 'oyster thief'.

Scytosiphon is a tubular, annual alga of some small potential as a food organism.

Chordaceae

The primitive genus *Chorda* with two species in the North Atlantic has been used for food, but may also be a nuisance in small harbours during the summer.

Alariaceae

Alaria, with a single species, *A. esculenta* (Linnaeus) Greville, in the northern part of the North Atlantic, has been used as fodder and for human consumption.

Undaria pinnatifida (Harvey) Suringar, a Pacific species, has been introduced recently into the Mediterranean (Pérez *et al.* 1981) and the Atlantic around France. This species is used extensively for food in Japan, Korea and, to a lesser extent, China. It is being cultivated experimentally in France for food production.

Laminariaceae

Laminaria is probably the most economically important genus of the order in Europe; five or six species occur in the Atlantic (see Kain 1979; South & Tittley 1986) with an additional deep-water species in the Mediterranean (*Laminaria rodriguezii* Bornet).

Exhaustive studies of the biology and ecology of *Laminaria hyperborea* (Gunnerus) Foslie, the most important species of the genus economically, have been made (reviewed in Kain 1979). Stipes and laminae of *L. hyperborea* are collected in the British Isles, northern France and Norway for alginate extraction. *Laminaria digitata* (Hudson) Lamouroux is gathered in Brittany for alginate extraction and for the manufacture of cosmetics. *Laminaria saccharina* (Linnaeus) Lamouroux has been used in the British Isles, Norway and France as a soil conditioner, animal feed and, more recently, human food (Boisvert 1988). Stipes of *Laminaria* species are also utilized during obstetrical procedures requiring cervical dilatation (Feochari 1979).

Saccorhiza polyschides (Lightfoot) Batters, an annual kelp endemic to the north eastern Atlantic (Norton & Burrows 1969; Norton 1970), is not harvested for alginate production at present, but may ultimately be of interest as it has a rapid growth rate.

Fucaceae

Ascophyllum nodosum (Linnaeus) Le Jolis is the most important member of the family economically. It is most common in the northern part of the North Atlantic. Plants harvested in Ireland, Scotland and Norway are used for the extraction of alginates and for the manufacture of seaweed meal for animal and human consumption. Biological and harvesting data for this species were compiled by Baardseth (1970).

Fucus species, although they dominate the intertidal over much of the North Atlantic, have not been used commercially to any great extent, mainly because of relatively low alginate content and poor food value. Isolated reports of their use as animal feed and as a soil conditioner do however exist in the British Isles (Brennan 1950; Newton 1951). *Fucus* farms in which stones are placed in the intertidal of sheltered embayments and the plants harvested by hand (Cotton 1912; Brennan 1950) are no longer in use in Ireland (Wilkins 1989). Similarly, *Pelvetia canaliculata* (Linnaeus) Decaisne et Thuret, also used sporadically as animal feed (Brennan 1950), is no longer in use.

Himanthaliaeceae

The receptacles of *Himanthalia elongata* (Linnaeus) S.F. Gray are used for certain crops in Brittany (Chapman & Chapman 1980), but their use is restricted.

Sargassaceae

Sargassum muticum (Yendo) Fensholt, an adventive species in the North Atlantic and the Mediterranean (Farnham *et al.* 1973; Critchley *et al.* 1983; Critchley & Dijkema 1984; Belsher & Pommellec 1988), has spread extensively since its arrival in Europe from the Pacific. It is said to have caused problems in the fouling of fixed and floating structures in harbours.

RHODOPHYTA

The red algae are the most diverse group of seaweeds in the North Atlantic and the Mediterranean. There have been extensive taxonomic revisions of the Rhodophyta in recent years, particularly at the ordinal level (see reviews in Garbary *et al.* 1980; Gabrielson & Garbary 1986; Garbary & Gabrielson 1991). In addition to the ordinal changes proposed in Guiry (1987b) and Pueschel and Cole (1982), several other changes have taken place recently. The Gelidiaceae, previously referred to the Nemaliales (Dixon & Irvine 1977; Dixon 1982), have now been unequivocally placed in the Gelidiales (Hommersand & Fredericq 1988). The Corallinaceae, previously placed in the Cryptonemiales, are now referred to the Corallinales (Silva & Johansen 1986). The Gracilariaceae, formerly placed in the Gigartinales, have been made the basis for a new order, the Gracilariales (Fredericq & Hommersand 1989a). Similarly, the genus *Ahnfeltia* has been removed from the Phyllophoraceae and referred to a new order, the Ahnfeltiales (Maggs & Pueschel 1989). Critical taxonomic and nomenclatural changes at the generic and specific level are indicated below.

Bangiaceae

This family contains the most economically important genus of red algae, *Porphyra*, of which there are more than six species found in northern Europe (South & Tittley 1986). There is a large aquaculture industry in the Orient, particularly in Japan, China and Korea, of *Porphyra* species that are used for human consumption (see Chapters 2 and 11); and they are gathered as the basis of a cottage industry in Wales. Some areas of the north eastern Atlantic may be environmentally suitable for *Porphyra* aquaculture development using oriental methodology.

Palmariaceae

Palmaria palmata (Linnaeus) Kuntze (previously known as *Rhodymenia palmata*; Guiry 1974) is widespread in the colder waters of the North Atlantic (see Lüning 1985, 1990 for distribution maps), and is used for human food and animal fodder.

Gelidiaceae

Gelidium sesquipedale (Turner) Thuret (also known as *G. cartilagineum*) is collected for agar extraction in Spain, Portugal and the Azores (Gallardo *et al.* 1990). There is still considerable nomenclatural and taxonomic confusion regarding the Atlantic and Mediterranean species of this genus, much of which remains to be resolved.

Bonnemaisoniaceae

In addition to three native species, two species have been introduced into the Atlantic and the Mediterranean from the Pacific: *Bonnemaisonia hamifera* Hariot and *Asparagopsis armata* Harvey. Although members of this family have not been the cause of any identifiable economic effect, they do produce a diversity of chemical substances, especially halogenated compounds, which may be of pharmaceutical interest as antibiotics (Glombitza 1979).

Dumontiaceae

Dilsea carnosa (Schmidel) Kuntze is said to have been eaten in Britain and Ireland, but such reports may be the result of confusion with *Palmaria palmata* (Newton 1931).

   Pikea californica Harvey, a Pacific species from Japan and North America, has recently been reported from the Scilly Isles, off south-west Britain (Maggs & Guiry 1987), but no economic repercussions have been reported.

   Several genera of this family from the Pacific were reported to have strong antiviral properties, particularly in experiments with herpes virus (Ehresmann *et al.* 1977; Hatch *et al.* 1979). European species should be examined from a similar perspective so that resource utilization can be evaluated.

Halymeniaceae

Cryptonemia hibernica Guiry et L. Irvine known only in the North Atlantic from the south coast of Ireland, is likely to have been introduced from the Pacific (Guiry & Irvine 1974).

   Grateloupia doryphora (Montagne) Howe, apparently introduced to the south coast of England (Farnham 1980) and Mediterranean France (Riouall *et al.* 1985), and *G. filicina* var. *luxurians* A. Gepp et E.S. Gepp, also an adventive species on the south coast of England (Farnham 1980), do not appear to have caused any economic problems. *Grateloupia* species have been used as food in Hawaii (Abbott & Williamson 1974; Abbott 1978), but no reports of their use exist in Europe.

Corallinaceae

Species of *Phymatolithon* and *Lithothamnion* form beds of detached plants in the subtidal of Ireland, the UK, France, Spain and the western Mediterranean (see Chapter 3). In England and northern France these 'maërl' beds are dredged, and the plants are dried and ground and sold as a soil conditioner (Blunden *et al.* 1975; Chapter 3).

  Corallina officinalis Linnaeus was used in various places in Europe as a vermifuge. However, it no longer appears to be gathered for this purpose (Michanek 1979).

Gracilariaceae

Species of *Gracilaria* produce agar of varying quality (see Chapter 8). There is, however, much taxonomic and nomenclatural confusion in the genus. The species previously referred to as *Gracilaria verrucosa* (Hudson) Papenfuss in the North Atlantic includes two entities: *Gracilaria verrucosa sensu stricto* and *Gracilariopsis lemanaeiformis* (Bory) Dawson, Acleto et Foldvik (Fredericq & Hommersand 1989b), which are difficult to distinguish without close examination of the development of the cystocarp. The species previously known in the north-eastern Atlantic and western Mediterranean as *Gracilaria foliifera* var. *foliifera* (Forsskål) Børgesen has been shown to represent *G. multipartita* (Clemente) Harvey (Guiry & Freamhainn 1986). In the western Atlantic, the entity variously known as *G. foliifera* and *G. foliifera* var. *angustissima* W.R. Taylor has been referred to *G. tikvahiae* McLachlan (McLachlan 1979). Similar problems with applying specific epithets are apparent in the Mediterranean (Tripodi *et al.* 1989). Further taxonomic and nomenclatural studies of this difficult genus are needed on a worldwide basis.

Furcellariaceae

An unattached form of *Furcellaria lumbricalis* (Hudson) Lamouroux, previously known as *F. fastigiata*, is harvested in the Baltic for carrageenan (furcellaran) production, and this species is harvested in eastern Canada for processing in Denmark (McLachlan 1985).

Phyllophoraceae

Species of *Gymnogongrus*, *Phyllophora*, *Schottera* and *Stenogramme* contain carrageenan (McCandless *et al.* 1982), but none of these is used commercially in either the Atlantic or the Mediterranean, largely because of the small quantities available for harvesting. *Phyllophora truncata* (Pallas) A. Zinova and two other putative species of the genus are used in the Black Sea as a source of a type of carrageenan (Michanek 1975; Chapman & Chapman 1980, see especially McCandless *et al.* 1982).

Petrocelidaceae

Mastocarpus stellatus (Stackhouse in Withering) Guiry, previously known as *Gigartina stellata* (Stackhouse) Batters, is now referred to the Petrocelidaceae (Guiry *et al.* 1984). This is the only recognized species of the genus in the North Atlantic; it occurs in quantity in the intertidal of semi-exposed shores around the North Atlantic basin (Guiry & West 1983). It contains carrageenan (McCandless *et al.* 1983), but is not used for commercial extraction to any great extent. This species, together with *Chondrus crispus*, is collected in Ireland as Carrageen Moss or Irish Moss (Barwell *et al.* 1989).

Gigartinaceae

Chondrus crispus Stackhouse, a common lower intertidal species in the North Atlantic basin, is collected commercially in the Maritime Provinces of Canada for carrageenan production. In Europe, quantities are too small to make harvesting for industrial purposes cost-effective (see Chapter 10), but small quantities (often mixed with *Mastocarpus stellatus*) are collected in Ireland and France as Carrageen Moss or Irish Moss. Plants are dried, frequently bleached, and sold either whole or ground as a health food or as a thickener in cooking. Some commercial extracts are sold as cough mixtures or general tonics (Waaland 1981).

Several species of *Gigartina* occur in the Atlantic and Mediterranean; these also contain carrageenan (McCandless *et al.* 1983), but do not occur in sufficient quantities on most European shores to make harvesting economically feasible. *Gigartina acicularis* (Roth) Lamouroux and *G. teedii* (Roth) Lamouroux are collected with *C. crispus* in Spain for carrageenan extraction (Gallardo *et al.* 1990).

Solieriaceae

Agardhiella subulata (C. Agardh) Kraft et Wynne is referred to in many papers as *Agardhiella baileyi* and *Neoagardhiella baileyi*. Kraft and Wynne (1979) and Gabrielson (1985) have commented on its present nomenclatural status. This entity has been widely used in North America for maricultural studies. It has also been found in southern Britain (Farnham 1980), where it may be adventive. *Solieria chordalis* (C. Agardh) J. Agardh has also been discovered in south-western Britain recently (Hiscock & Maggs 1984).

ACKNOWLEDGEMENTS

Dr J. Kain (Jones) kindly read the manuscript, which was written while M.G. held the James Chair of Pure and Applied Science in the Department of Biology, St Francis Xavier University, Antigonish, Nova Scotia, Canada.

REFERENCES

Abbott I.A. 1978. The uses of seaweed as food in Hawaii. *Econ. Bot.* **32**: 409–12.

Abbott I.A. & Williamson E.H. 1974. *Limu An Ethnobotanical Study of Some Edible Hawaiian Seaweeds*. Hawaii: Pacific Tropical Botanical Garden.

Ardré F. 1970. Contribution à l'étude des algues marines du Portugal. I. La flore. *Port. Acta Biol. (B)* **10**: 137–555.

Athanasiadis A. 1987. *A Survey of the Seaweeds of the Aegean Sea with Taxonomic Studies on Species of the Tribe Antithamnieae (Rhodophyta)*. Published Ph.D. thesis, University of Gothenburg.

Baardseth, E. 1970. Synopsis of biological data on Knobbed Wrack *Ascophyllum nodosum* (Linnaeus) Le Jolis. *Fish. Synop. FAO* no. 38, Rev. 1.

Barwell C.J., Canham C.A. & Guiry M.D. 1989. Hordenine content of the marine alga *Mastocarpus stellatus* and the algal food product Carrageen. *Phytotherapy Res.* **3**: 67–9.

Belsher T. & Pommellec S. 1988. Expansion de l'algue d'origine japonaise *Sargassum muticum* (Yendo) Fensholt, sur les côtes françaises, de 1983 à 1987. *Cah. Biol. Mar.* **29**: 221–31.

Bliding C. 1963. A critical survey of European taxa in Ulvales. Part I. *Capsosiphon, Percursaria, Blidingia, Enteromorpha. Opera Bot.* **8**: 1–160.

Bliding C. 1968. A critical survey of European taxa in Ulvales. II. *Ulva, Ulvaria, Monostroma, Kornmannia. Bot. Not.* **121**: 535–629.

Blunden G., Binns W.W. & Perks F. 1975. Commercial collection and utilization of maërl. *Econ. Bot.* **29**: 140–5.

Boisvert C. 1987. *La Cuisine des Plantes Sauvages*. 2nd edn. Paris: Dargaud Éditeur.

Boisvert C. 1988. *Les Jardins de la Mer du Bon Usage des Algues* Paris: Terre Vivante.

Børgesen F. 1927. Marine algae from the Canary Islands especially from Tenerife and Gran Canaria. III. Rhodophyceae Part I: Bangiales and Nemalionales. *K. Danske Vidensk. Selks. Biol. Meddel.* **6**: 1–97.

Børgesen F. 1929. Marine algae from the Canary Islands especially from Tenerife and Gran Canaria III. Rhodophyceae Part II: Cryptonemiales, Gigartinales and Rhodymeniales. *K. Danske Vidensk. Selsk. Biol. Meddel.* **8**: 1–97.

Børgesen F. 1930. Marine algae from the Canary Islands especially from Tenerife and Gran Canaria. III. Rhodophyceae Part III: Ceramiales. *K. Danske Vidensk. Selsk. Biol. Meddel.* **9**: 1–159.

Boudouresque C.-F. 1971. Contribution a l'étude phytosociologique des peuplements algaux des côtes varoisses. *Vegetatio* **22**: 83–184.

Boudouresque C.-F. & Perret M. 1977. Inventaire de la Flore Marine de Corse (Méditerranée): Rhodophyceae, Phaeophyceae, Chlorophyceae et Bryopsidophyceae. *Bibliotheca Phycol.* **25**: 1–171.

Brennan A.T. 1950. *Notes on some Common Irish Seaweeds*. Dublin: Stationery Office.

Caram B. & Jónsson S. 1972. Nouvel inventaire des algues marines de l'Islande. *Acta Bot. Isl.* **1**: 5–31.

Cardinal A. 1964. Étude sur les Ectocarpacées de la Manche. *Beih. Nova Hedwigia* **15**: 1–86.

Chapman V.J. & Chapman D.J. 1980. *Seaweeds and their Uses*. 3rd edn. London: Chapman & Hall.

Christensen T. 1980. *Algae, A Taxonomic Survey. Fasc. 1.* Odense: AiO Trykas.

Christensen T. 1987. *Seaweeds of the British Isles. Vol. 4. Tribophyceae (Xanthophyceae)*. London: British Museum (Natural History).

Christensen T., Koch C. & Thomsen H.A. 1985. *Distribution of Algae in Danish Salt and Brackish Waters*. Copenhagen: Institut for Sporeplanter.

Coppejans E. 1982a. *Zeewierengids voor de Belgische en Noordfanse Kust. Deel II: Beschrijvingen Groen- en Brun-wieren* Gent: Wetenschappelijk Tijdschrift van de Belgische Jeugbond voor Natuurstudie 17 (extra number): 157–254.

Coppejans E. 1982b. *Zeewierengids voor de Belgische en Noordfanse Kust. Deel III: Beschrijvingen Roodwieren*. Gent: Wetenschappelijk Tijdschrift van de Belgische Jeugbond voor Natuurstudie 18 (extra number): i, 255–392.

Coppejans E. 1983. Iconographie d'Algues Méditerranéennes. *Bibliotheca Phycol.* **63**: xxviii, 317 pls.

Coppejans E. & Ben D. van der. 1980. *Zeewierengids voor de Belgische en Noordfanse Kust*. Gent: Belgische Jeugbond voor Natuurstudie.

Cotton A.D. 1912. Marine algae. In: A biological survey of Clare Island in the county of Mayo, Ireland and of the surrounding district. (Ed. R.L. Praeger) *Proc. R. Ir. Acad.* **31**, section 1: 1–178.

Critchley A.T. & Dijkema R. 1984. On the presence of the introduced brown alga *Sargassum muticum*, attached to commercially imported *Ostrea edulis* in the S. W. Netherlands. *Botanica Mar.* **27**: 211–16.

Critchley A.T., Farnham W.F. & Morrell S.L. 1983. A chronology of new European sites of attachment for the invasive brown alga, *Sargassum muticum*, 1973–1981. *J. Mar. Biol. Ass. UK* **63**: 799–811.

De Virville A.D. 1962. Contribution à l'étude de la flore marine des Îles Anglo-Normandes. Première partie: Guernsey, Herm, Jethou, Serq, Burhou, Aurigny, les Casquets. *Rev. Gén. Bot.* **70**: 5–66.

Dixon P.S. 1982. Life histories in the Florideophyceae with particular reference to the Nemaliales *sensu lato*. *Botanica Mar.* **25**: 611–21.

Dixon P.S. & Irvine L.M. 1977. *Seaweeds of the British Isles. Vol. 1. Rhodophyta. Part I: Introduction, Nemaliales, Gigartinales*. London: British Museum (Natural History).

Dixon P.S., Irvine D.E.G. & Price J.H. 1966. The distribution of benthic marine algae: a bibliography for the British Isles. *Br. Phycol. Bull.* **3**: 87–142.

Dizerbo A.G. 1971a. Les limites géographique de quelques algues de la Manche occidentale entre l'Île de Bréhat et Saint-Vaast-la-Houge. *Bull. Soc. Phycol. Fr.* **16**: 21–4.

Dizerbo A.H. 1971b. Note sur la végétation marine du Cap Fréhel en Plévenon (Côtes-du-Nord). *Bull. Soc. Scient. Bretagne* **45**: 171–6.

Dizerbo A.H. 1975. La végétation et la flore des algues marines de la presqu'île de Crozon et de la baie de Douarnenez (du goulet de Breste à l'anse du Ris). *Bull. Soc. Scient. Bretagne* **50**: 83–100.

Donze M. 1968. The algal vegetation of the Ria de Arosa (NW Spain). *Blumea* **16**: 159–83.

Ehresmann D.W., Deig E.F., Hatch M.T., DiSalvo L.H. & Vedros N.A. 1977. Antiviral substances from California marine algae. *J. Phycol.* **13**: 37–40.

Farnham W.F. 1980. Studies on aliens in the marine flora of southern England. In *The Shore Environment. Vol. 2. Ecosystems*. (Eds. J.H. Price, D.E.G. Irvine & W.F. Farnham) pp. 875–914. London: Academic Press.

Farnham W.F., Fletcher R.L. & Irvine L.M. 1973. Attached *Sargassum* found in Britain. *Nature Lond.* **243**: 231–2.

Feldmann J. 1937a. Recherches sur la végétation marine de la Méditerranée: la côte des Albères. *Rev. Algol.* **10**: 1–339.

Feldmann J. 1937b. Les algues marine de la côte des Albères. I–III. Cyanophycées, Chlorophycées, Phéophycées. *Rev. Algol.* **9**, 141–335.

Feldmann J. 1939. Les algues marine de la côte des Albères. IV. Rhodophycées. *Rev. Algol.* **11**: 247–330.

Feldmann J. 1942a ('1941'). Les algues marine de la côte des Albères. IV. Rhodophycées (suite). *Rev. Algol.* **12**: 77–100.

Feldmann J. 1942b. Les algues marine de la côte des Albères. IV. Rhodophycées (fin). *Rev. Algol.* **13**: 29–113.

Feldmann J. 1954. Inventaire de la flore marine de Roscoff: algues, champignons, lichens et spermatophytes *Trav. Stat. Biol. Roscoff* Supplément **6**: 1–151.

Feldmann J. & Hamel G. 1936. Floridées de France VII: Gélidiales. *Rev. Algol.* **9**: 85–140.

Feldmann J. & Magne F. 1964. *Additions à l'Inventaire de la Flore Marine de Roscoff.* Éditions de la Station Biologique de Roscoff.

Feochari K. 1979. The use of *Laminaria* tent in obstetrical practice. In *Marine Algae in Pharmaceutical Science.* (Eds. H.A. Hoppe, T. Levring & Y. Tanaka) pp. 663–7. Berlin: Walter de Gruyter.

Fletcher R.L. 1980. *Catalogue of Main Marine Fouling Organisms. Vol. 6. Algae.* pp. 61. Bruxelles: ODEMA.

Fletcher R.L. 1987. *Seaweeds of the British Isles. Vol. 3. Fucophyceae (Phaeophyceae) Part 1.* London: British Museum (Natural History).

Fredericq S. & Hommersand M.H. 1989a. Proposal of the Gracilariales ord. nov. (Rhodophyta) based on an analysis of the reproductive development of *Gracilaria verrucosa. J. Phycol.* **25**: 213–27.

Fredericq S. & Hommersand M.H. 1989b. Comparative morphology and taxonomic status of *Gracilariopsis* (Gracilariales, Rhodophyta). *J. Phycol.* **25**: 228–41.

Gabrielson P.W. 1985. *Agardhiella* versus *Neoagardhiella* (Solieriaceae, Rhodophyta): another look at the lectotypification of *Gigartina tenera. Taxon* **34**: 275–80.

Gabrielson P.W. & Garbary D. 1986. Systematics of red algae (Rhodophyta). *CRC Crit. Rev. Pl. Sci.* **3**: 325–66.

Gallardo T., Gómez Garreta A., Ribera M.A., Alvarez M. & Conde F. 1985. *A Preliminary Checklist of Iberian Benthic Marine Algae.* Madrid: Real Jardín Botanico.

Gallardo T., Alvarez Cobelas M. & Alvarez de Meneses A. 1990. Current state of seaweed resources in Spain. *Proc. Intl Seaweed Symp.* **14**: 287–92.

Garbary D.J. & Gabrielson P.W. 1991 Taxonomy and evolution. In *Biology of the Red Algae* (Eds. K.M. Cole & R.G. Sheath) pp. 477–498. Cambridge: University Press.

Garbary D., Hansen G.I. & Scagel R.F. 1980. A revised classification of the Bangiophyceae (Rhodophyta). *Nova Hedwigia* **33**: 145–66.

Gayral P. 1958. *Algues de la Côte Atlantique Marocaine.* Rabat: Société des Sciences Naturelles et Physiques du Maroc.

Gayral P. 1966. *Les Algues des Côtes Françaises.* Paris: Doin-Deren & Cie.

Gerloff J. & Geissler U. 1971. Eine revidierte Liste der Meeresalgen Griechenlands. *Nova Hedwigia* **22**: 721–93.

Giaccone G. 1969. Raccolte di phytobenthos sulla banchina continentale Italiana. *Giorn. Bot. Ital.* **103**: 485–514.

Giaccone G. 1978 Revisione della flora marina del mare Adriatico: parco marino di Miramare. *Staz. Controllo Trieste* **6**: 5–118.

Giaccone G., Colonna P., Graziano C., Mannino A.M., Tornatore E., Cormaci M., Furnari G. & Scammacca B. 1985. Revisione della flora marine di Sicilia e isole minori. *Boll. Acc. Gioenia Sci. Nat.* **18**: 537–781.

Glombitza K.-W. 1979. Antibodies from algae. In *Marine Algae in Pharmaceutical*

Science. (Eds. H.A. Hoppe, T. Levring & Y. Tanaka) pp. 303–42. Berlin: Walter de Gruyter.
Guiry M.D. 1974. A preliminary consideration of the taxonomic position of *Palmaria palmata* (Linnaeus) Stackhouse = *Rhodymenia palmata* (Linnaeus) Greville. *J. Mar. Biol. Ass. UK* **54**: 509–28.
Guiry M.D. 1978a. *A Consensus and Bibliography of Irish Seaweeds*. Vaduz: J. Cramer.
Guiry M.D. 1978b. The importance of sporangia in the classification of the Florideophyceae. In *Modern Approaches to the Taxonomy of Red and Brown Algae Systematics Association Special Vol. 10*. (Eds. D.E.G. Irvine & J.H. Price) pp. 111–44. London: Academic Press.
Guiry M.D. & Freamhainn M.T. 1986. Biosystematics of *Gracilaria foliifera* (Forsskål) Børgesen (Gigartinales, Rhodophyta). *Nordic J. Bot.* **5**: 629–37.
Guiry M.D. & Irvine L.M. 1974. A species of *Cryptonemia* new to Europe. *Br. Phycol. J.* **9**: 225–37.
Guiry M.D. & West J.A. 1983. Life history and hybridization studies on *Gigartina stellata* and *Petrocelis cruenta* (Rhodophyta) in the north eastern Atlantic. *J. Phycol.* **19**: 474–94.
Guiry M.D., West J.A., Kim D.-H. & Masuda M. 1984. Reinstatement of the genus *Mastocarpus* Kützing (Rhodophyta). *Taxon* **33**: 53–63.
Hamel G. 1930. Floridées de France VI. *Rev. Algol.* **5**: 61–109.
Hamel G. 1931. *Phéophycées de France*. Fasc. I, pp. 1–80. Paris: privately published.
Hamel G. 1935. *Phéophycées de France*. Fasc. II, pp. 81–176. Paris: privately published.
Hamel G. 1937. *Phéophycées de France*. Fasc. III, pp. 177–240. Paris: privately published.
Hamel G. 1938. *Phéophycées de France*. Fasc. IV, pp. 241–366. Paris: privately published.
Hamel G. 1939. *Phéophycées de France*. Fasc. V, pp. 337–432, i–xlvii. Paris: privately published.
Haritonidis S. & Tsekos I. 1975. Marine algae of northern Greece. *Botanica Mar.* **18**: 203–21.
Haritonidis S. & Tsekos I. 1976. Marine algae of the Greek west coast. *Botanica Mar.*, **19**: 273–86.
Hartog C. den 1959. The epilithic algal communities occurring along the coast of the Netherlands. *Wentia* **1**: 3–241.
Hatch M.T., Ehresmann D.W. & Deig E.F. 1979. Chemical characterization and therapeutic evaluation of anti-herpesvirus polysaccharides from species of Dumontiaceae. In *Marine Algae in Pharmaceutical Science*. (Eds. H.A. Hoppe, T. Levring & Y. Tanaka) pp. 343–63. Berlin: Walter de Gruyter.
Hiscock S. 1986. A field key to the British red seaweeds. *Occ. Publ. Field Stud. Council*, no. 13, 1–101.
Hiscock S. & Maggs C.A. 1984. Notes on distribution and ecology of some new and interesting seaweeds from south-west Britain. *Br. Phycol. J.* **19**: 73–87.
Hoek C. van den. 1963. *Revision of the European species of Cladophora*. Leiden: Brill.
Hoek C. van den. 1982a. Phytogeographic distribution groups of benthic marine algae in the North Atlantic Ocean: a review of experimental evidence from life history studies. *Helgol. Meeresunters.* **35**: 153–214.
Hoek C. van den. 1982b. The distribution of benthic marine algae in relation to the temperature regulation of their life histories. *Biol. J. Linn. Soc.* **18**: 81–144.

Hoek C. van den & Donze M. 1966. The algal vegetation of the rocky Côte Basque (SW France). *Bull. Cent. Étud. Rech. Sci. Biarritz* **6**: 289–319.

Hoek C. van den & Donze M. 1967. Algal phytogeography of the European Atlantic coasts. *Blumea* **15**: 63–89.

Hoek C. van den, Stam W.T. & Olsen J.L. 1988. The emergence of a new chlorophytan system and Dr Kornmann's contribution thereto. *Helgol. Meeresunters.* **42**: 339–83.

Hommersand M.H. & Fredericq S. 1988. An investigation of cystocarp development in *Gelidium pteridifolium* with a revised description of the Gelidiales (Rhodophyta). *Phycologia* **27**: 254–72.

Irvine L.M. 1983. *Seaweeds of the British Isles. Vol. 1 Rhodophyta. Part 2A Cryptonemiales (sensu stricto), Palmariales, Rhodymeniales.* London: British Museum (Natural History).

Jaasund E. 1965. Aspects of the marine algal vegetation of North Norway. *Bot. Gothoburg.* **4**: 1–174.

Jónsson S., Hoek C. van den & Bot P.V.M. 1989. Clé de détermination des *Cladophora* des côtes Françaises. *Crypt. Algol.* **10**: 15–22.

Jorde I. 1966. Algal associations of a coastal area south of Bergen, Norway. *Sarsia* **23**: 1–52.

Jorde I. & Klavestad N. 1963. The natural history of the Hardangerfjord 4: the benthonic algal vegetation. *Sarsia* **9**: 1–99.

Kain J.M. 1979. A view of the genus *Laminaria*. *Oceanogr. Mar. Biol. Ann. Rev.* **17**: 101–61.

Knight M. & Parke M. 1931. Manx algae: an algal survey of the south end of the Isle of Man. *Mem. Typ. Br. Mar. Pl. Anim. Liverpool Mar. Biol. Comm.* **30**: 1–155.

Koeman R.P.T. & Hoek C. van den. 1980. The taxonomy of *Ulva* (Chlorophyceae) in the Netherlands. *Br. Phycol. J.* **16**: 9–53.

Koeman R.P.T. & Hoek C. van den. 1982a. The taxonomy of *Enteromorpha* Link, 1820 (Chlorophyceae) in the Netherlands. I. The section *Enteromorpha*. *Acta Hydrobiol.* **63** (*Algol Stud.* **32**): 279–330.

Koeman R.P.T. & Hoek C. van den. 1982b. The taxonomy of *Enteromorpha* Link, 1820 (Chlorophyceae) in the Netherlands. II. The section *Prolifera*. *Crypt. Algol.* **3**: 37–70.

Koeman R.P.T. & Hoek C. van den. 1984. The taxonomy of *Enteromorpha* Link, 1820 (Chlorophyceae) in the Netherlands. III. The sections Flexuosae and *Clathratae* and an addition to the section *Proliferae*. *Crypt. Algol.* **5**: 21–61.

Kornmann P. & Sahling P.-H. 1977. Meeresalgen von Helgoland: benthische Grün-, Braun- und Rotalgen. *Helgol. Wiss. Meeresunters.* **29**: 1–289.

Kornmann P. & Sahling P.-H. 1983. Meeresalgen von Helgoland: Ergänzung. *Helgol. Meeresunters.* **36**: 1–65.

Kraft G.T. & Wynne M.J. 1979. An earlier name for the Atlantic North American red alga *Neoagardhiella baileyi* (Solieriaceae, Gigartinales). *Phycologia* **18**: 325–9.

Kylin H. 1910. Zur Kenntnis der norwegischen Westküste. *Ark. Bot.* **10**: 1–37.

Kylin H. 1944. Die Rhodophyceen der schwedischen Westküste. *Acta Univ. Lund* N.F. Avd. 2, **40**: 1–104.

Kylin H. 1947. Die Phaeophyceen der schwedischen Westküste. *Acta Univ. Lund* N.F. Avd. 2, **43**: 1–99.

Kylin H. 1949. Die Chlorophyceen der schwedischen Westküst. *Acta Univ. Lund* N.F. Avd. 2, **45**: 1–79.

Levring T. 1935. Zur Kenntnis der Algenflora von Kullen und der schwedischen Westküste. *Acta Univ. Lund* Avd. 2, **31**: 1–63.

Levring T. 1937. Zur Kenntnis der algenflora der norwegischen Westküste. *Acta Univ. Lund* Avd. 2, **33**: 1–63.

Levring T. 1974. The marine algae of the archipelago of Madeira. *Bol. Mus. Mun. Funchal* **28**: 1–111.

Lüning K. 1985. *Meeresbotanik*. Stuttgart & New York: George Thieme Verlag.

Lüning K. 1990. *Seaweed Biogeography and Ecophysiology*. New York: Wiley.

McCandless E.L., West J.A. & Guiry M.D. 1982. Carrageenan patterns in the Phyllophoraceae. *Biochem. Syst. Ecol.* **10**: 275–84.

McCandless E.L., West J.A. & Guiry M.D. 1983. Carrageenan patterns in the Gigartinaceae. *Biochem. Syst. Ecol.* **11**: 175–82.

McLachlan J. 1979. *Gracilaria tikvahiae* sp. nov. (Rhodophyta, Gigartinales, Gracilariaceae), from the northwestern Atlantic. *Phycologia* **18**: 19–23.

McLachlan J. 1985. Macroalgae (seaweeds): industrial resources and their utilization. *Plant Soil* **89**: 137–57.

Madlener J.C. 1977. *The Seavegetable Book*. New York: Clarson N. Potter Inc.

Maggs C.A. & Guiry M.D. 1987. An Atlantic population of *Pikea californica* (Dumontiaceae, Rhodophyta). *J. Phycol.* **23**: 170–6.

Maggs C.A. & Pueschel C.M. 1989. Morphology and development of *Ahnfeltia plicata* (Rhodophyta): proposal of Ahnfeltiales ord. nov. *J. Phycol.* **25**: 333–51.

Martins H.R. 1990. A selected bibliography of the marine flora and fauna of the Azores. *Arquipélago* no. 8: 35–44.

Mattox K.R. & Stewart K.D. 1984. Classification of the green algae: a concept based on comparative cytology. In *Systematics of the Green Algae*, Systematics Association Special Vol. No. 27 (Eds. D.E.G. Irvine & D.M. John) pp. 29–72. London: Academic Press.

Michanek G. 1975. Seaweed resources of the Ocean. *Fish. Tech. Pap. FAO* no. 138: v + 127.

Michanek G. 1979. Seaweed resources for pharmaceutical uses. In *Marine Algae in Pharmaceutical Science* (Eds. H.A. Hoppe, T. Levring & Y. Tanaka) pp. 203–302. Berlin: Walter de Gruyter.

Munda I.K. 1979. Additions to the check-list of benthic marine algae from Iceland. *Botanica Mar.* **22**: 459–63.

Newton L. 1931. *A Handbook of the British Seaweeds*. London: British Museum (Natural History).

Newton L. 1951. *Seaweed Utilisation*. London: Sampson Low.

Nienhuis P.H. 1980. The epilithic algal vegetation of the SW Netherlands. *Nova Hedwigia* **33**: 1–94.

Norton T.A. 1970. Synopsis of biological data on *Saccorhiza polyschides*. *Fish. Synopsis F.A.O.* no. 83: v + 29.

Norton T.A. & Burrows E.M. 1969. Studies on the marine algae of the British Isles. 7. *Saccorhiza polyschides* (Lightf.) Batt. *Br. Phycol. J.* **4**: 19–53.

Pankow H. 1971. *Algenflora der Ostsee. I. Benthos (Blau-, Grün-, Braun- und Rotalgen)*. Stuttgart: Gustav Fischer Verlag.

Parke M. & Dixon P.S. 1976. Check-list of British marine algae: third revision. *J. Mar. Biol. Ass. UK* **56**: 527–94.

Pedersen P.M. 1984. Studies on primitive brown algae (Fucophyceae). *Opera Bot.* **74**: 1–76.

Pérez R., Lee J.Y. & Juge C. 1981. Observations sur la biologie de l'algue *Undaria pinnatifida* (Harvey) Suringar introduite accidentallement dans l'Étang de Thau. *Science et Pêche, Bull. Inst. Pêches Marit.* **315**: 1–12.

Pueschel C.M. & Cole K.M. 1982. Rhodophycean pit plugs: an ultrastructural survey with taxonomic implications. *Am. J. Bot.* **69**: 703–20.

Ravanko O. 1968. Macroscopic green, brown, and red algae in the southwestern archipelago of Finland. *Acta Bot. Fennica* **79**: 1–50.

Riouall R., Guiry M.D. & Codomier L. 1985. Introduction d'une espèce foliacée de

Grateloupia dans la flore marine de l'Etang de Thau (Hérault, France). *Crypt. Algol.* **6**: 91–8.

Rosenvinge L.K. 1909. The marine algae of Denmark. Contributions to their natural history. Part I. Introduction. Rhodophyceae I. (Bangiales and Nemaliales). *K. Danske Vidensk. Selsk. Skr.* 7 Raekke *Nat. Math. Afd.* **7**: 1–151.

Rosenvinge L.K. 1917. The marine algae of Denmark. Contributions to their natural history Part II. Rhodophyceae, II (Cryptonemiales). *K. Danske Vidensk. Selsk. Skr.* 7 Raekke *Nat. Math. Afd.* **7**: 153–284.

Rosenvinge L.K. 1924. The marine algae of Denmark. Contributions to their natural history. Part II. Rhodophyceae, III. (Ceramiales) *K. Danske Vidensk. Selsk. Skr.* 7 Raekke *Nat. Math. Afd.* **7**: 285–488.

Rosenvinge L.K. 1931. The marine algae of Denmark. Contributions to their natural history. Part IV. Rhodophyceae, IV (Gigartinales, Rhodymeniales, Nemastomatales). *K. Danske Vidensk. Selsk. Skr.* 7 Raekke *Nat. Math. Afd.* **7**: 489–628.

Rosenvinge L.K. & Lund S. 1941. The marine algae of Denmark. Vol. II. Phaeophyceae. I. Ectocarpaceae and Acinetosporaceae. *K. Dansk. Vidensk. Selsk. Biol. Skr.* **1**: 1–79.

Rosenvinge L.K. & Lund S. 1943. The marine algae of Denmark. Vol. II. Phaeophyceae. II. Corynophleaceae, Chordariaceae, Acrotrichaceae, Spermatochnaceae, Sporochnaceae, Desmarestiaceae, Arthrocladiaceae, with supplementary comments on Elachistaceae. *K. Dansk. Vidensk. Selsk. Biol. Skr.* **2**: 5–59.

Rosenvinge L.K. & Lund S. 1947. The marine algae of Denmark. Vol. II. Phaeophyceae. III. Encoeliaceae, Myriotrichiaceae, Giraudiaceae, Striariaceae, Dictyosiphonaceae, Chordaceae and Laminariaceae. *K. Dansk. Vidensk. Selsk. Biol. Skr.* **4**: 1–99.

Rueness J. 1977. *Norsk Algeflora*. Oslo: Universitetsforlaget.

Seoane-Camba J. 1965. Estudios sobre las algas bentónicas en la costa sur la Península Ibérica (littoral de Cádiz). *Inv. Pesqu.* **29**: 3–216.

Silva P.C. 1955. The dichotomous species of *Codium* in Britain. *J. Mar. Biol. Ass. UK* **34**: 565–77.

Silva P.C. 1957. *Codium* in Scandinavian waters. *Svensk Bot. Tidskr.* **51**: 117–34.

Silva P.C. 1960. *Codium* (Chlorophyta) of the tropical western Atlantic. *Nova Hedwigia* **1**: 497–536.

Silva P.C. 1962. Comparison of algal floristic patterns in the Pacific with those in the Atlantic and Indian oceans, with special reference to *Codium*. *Proc. Ninth Pac. Sci. Congr. 1957* **4**: 201–16.

Silva P.C. & Johansen H.W. 1986. A reappraisal of the order Corallinales (Rhodophyceae). *Br. Phycol. J.* **21**: 245–54.

Söderström J. 1963. Studies in *Cladophora*. *Bot. Gothoburg.* **1**: 1–147.

South G.R. & Tittley I. 1986. *A Checklist and Distributional Index of the Benthic Marine Algae of the North Atlantic Ocean*. St Andrews & London: Huntsman Marine Laboratory & British Museum (Natural History).

Starmach K. 1977. *Flora Slodkowodna Polski, Vol. 14, Phaeophyta, Rhodophyta*. Warsaw: Panstwowe Wydanictwo Naukowe.

Stegenga H. & Mol I. 1983. *Flora van der Nederlandse Zeewieren*. Hoogwoud: Koninklijke Nederkandse Natuurhistorische Vereniging.

Tittley I. & Price J.H. 1978. The benthic marine algae of the eastern English Channel: a preliminary floristic and ecological account. *Botanica Mar.* **21**: 499–512.

Tripodi G., Garguilo G.M. & De Masi F. 1989. Osservazioni sulla tassonomia del genere '*Gracilaria*' (Gigartinales, Rhodophyta) nel Mediterraneo (Ed. Anonymous) pp. 57–63. In *Alghe e Loro Utilizzazione Convegno Nazionale*. Lecce: Camera di Commēcio.

Waaland J.R. 1981. Commercial utilization. In *The Biology of Seaweeds* (Eds. C.S. Lobban & M.J. Wynne) pp. 726–41. Oxford: Blackwell Scientific Publications.

Waern M. 1952. Rocky-shore algae in the Öregrund Archipelago. *Acta Phytogeograph. Suecica* **30**: xvi + 1–298.

Wallentinius I. 1979. Environmental influences on benthic macrovegetation in the Trosa-Ascö area, northern Baltic proper. II. The ecology of macroalgae and submersed phanerograms. *Contrib. Ascö Lab. Univ. Stockholm* **25**: 1–210.

Weisscher F.C.M. 1983. Marine algae from Selvagem Pequena (Salvage Islands). *Bol. Mus. Mun. Funchal* **35**: 41–8.

Wilkins N.P. 1989. *Ponds, Passes and Parcs: Aquaculture in Victorian Ireland*. Dublin: Glendale Press.

Zinova A.D. 1967. *A Guide to the Green, Brown and Red Algae of the Southern Seas of the USSR*. Moscow & Leningrad: V.L. Komarov Botanical Institute, Academy of Science USSR (in Russian).

2 Animal and Human Nutrition

MENTZ INDERGAARD[1] AND JOHANNES MINSAAS[2]
[1]*Norwegian Institute of Technology, Trondheim, Norway and* [2]*The Foundation for Scientific and Industrial Research at the Norwegian Institute of Technology (SINTEF), Trondheim, Norway*

INTRODUCTION

Although algae were known and prized for nutritional purposes at a very early date in the Orient, several centuries went by before mention was made of the use of seaweeds in the West. The unknown author of *Bellum Africanum* (written *ca.* 45 BC) records that 'in times of scarcity, they [the Greeks] collected seaweed from the shore and, having washed it in fresh water, gave it to their cattle and thus prolonged their lives' (Newton 1951 p. 31). In this chapter only animal nutrition as it relates to domestic animals will be considered. Ecologically important grazing by sea urchins on kelp beds and similar marine herbivorous activities in the wild is not discussed (Pearse & Hines 1979; Duggins 1980; Pringle *et al.* 1980; Bernstein *et al.* 1983; Hagen 1983; Scheibling 1986; Witman 1987).

One of the earliest records of the use of algae for human nutrition in Europe is given in the saga of Egil Skalla-Grimsson (Skalla-Grimsson 1950 p. 253). Egil was tricked into eating *Palmaria palmata* (soll) to create a thirst for milk when he threatened to starve himself to death. He lived from 910 to 990, so this must have taken place in Iceland around AD 950. Even earlier than that, some 1400 years ago, St Columba's monks were diligent harvesters of dulse (*P. palmata*). Their gathering of it for the poor is recorded in a Gaelic poem attributed to St Columba (Newton 1951 p. 102). Further historical uses are reviewed in Chapman (1950), Chapman and Chapman (1980) and Jensen (1978).

Economic development and declining coastal populations (connected to industrialization and reduced dependence and knowledge of local resources) have caused most of Europe's traditional uses of seaweeds to disappear. Today's uses of seaweeds for nutrition in Europe are rather modest. In contrast, more seaweeds are now eaten by the Japanese than ever before (Arasaki & Arasaki 1983; Olsen 1985; Nisizawa *et al.* 1987).

Sea plants are in the popular press often spoken of as future saviours of a starving world. A hard look at the consequences of ingesting large amounts of seaweed, especially the brown algae, will lead to a realization that such an

Seaweed Resources in Europe: Uses and Potential. Edited by M. D. Guiry and G. Blunden
© 1991 John Wiley & Sons Ltd

optimistic statement must be moderated. In any case, the food problem of the world is one of distribution, not one of production. This is evident from the food surplus problems of Europe (milk, butter and fruit) and North America (grains).

It is sometimes stated that a regular intake of seaweed will help develop an intestinal bacterial flora capable of breaking down and making possible the digestion of the unfamiliar polysaccharides that seaweeds contain. Regarding humans, this statement still lacks hard evidence, and Mori *et al.* (1981) stated bluntly that 'seaweeds contain alginic acid, laminaran, fucoidan, agar and other polysaccharides which belong to indigestible polysaccharides'. Nevertheless, the seaweed-eating sheep in North Ronaldsay in the Orkneys are indeed intriguing.

Considering the rather low digestibility and high mineral content of seaweeds, the general impression most people have of them for nutrition is one of fodder supplement and sea vegetables.

RAW MATERIAL

SPECIES AND THEIR SUPPLY

A global survey has shown that 107 genera and 493 species are being utilized by humans (Tseng 1981). Most are collected locally in small quantities as foodstuffs in the Far East and the Pacific region.

In Europe a very small number of species are processed for use in either animal or human nutrition (Table 1). The heaviest users of seaweed products are naturally the producing countries, whereas other countries are roughly estimated to import each year only a few tonnes of processed seaweeds, for fodder supplement and the (health) food market. Only a minor part of the brown algal seaweed meal production ends up being used for nutritional purposes. The dominant use is still for the production of phycocolloids such as alginates from brown algae.

CHEMICAL COMPOSITION OF SOME SPECIES

Only one major review includes the inorganic chemical content of macroalgae (Vinogradov 1953). Levring *et al.* (1969) subsequently compiled a bibliography of chemical composition by species. The chemical composition of a few macroalgae representing the three macroalgal classes is given in Table 2. The quantitative ranges for the various components are probably mostly due to seasonal variations, but may also vary with tissue of varying age and type, harvesting location, preprocessing treatment and analytical methods. The most used species for nutritional purposes today, mainly as a fodder supplement, is the brown alga *Ascophyllum nodosum*. The chemical composition of this species is given in Table 3.

Table 1. Estimated seaweed production for actual and potential direct use in animal or human nutrition

Producing country	Species	Product	Volume per year[a] (t)
France[b,c]	*Laminaria digitata*	Seaweed meal, alginate (also dried whole as 'Kombu Breton')	≈2500
Iceland[d]	*Laminaria* spp.	Kelp meal	356
	Ascophyllum nodosum	Seaweed meal, alginates	2312
Ireland[e]	*Ascophyllum nodosum*	Seaweed meal, alginates	≈5000
	Chondrus crispus	Dried plants; food	50–200
	Palmaria palmata	Dried plants; food	≈5
	Fucus vesiculosus	Dried plants; health food	≈5
	Laminaria digitata	Iodine tablets	≈1
Norway[f]	*Ascophyllum nodosum*	Seaweed meal, alginates	≈6000
	Laminaria digitata	Kelp meal and tablets	1–3
UK[g,h]	*Porphyra* sp.	Laver/laverbread	216 (1954)
	Ascophyllum nodosum	Seaweed meal, alginates	≈3000

[a]Commercial dry weight (water content 10–15%).
[b]Brault and Briand (1987); Briand (1987).
[c]France's Embassy in Denmark from French official statistics for 1987.
[d]Iceland's Embassy in Norway from Icelandic official statistics for 1987.
[e]Guiry and Blunden (1980, 1981). The latest information is that the seaweed meal production from *A. nodosum* has declined drastically with possibly only one seaweed meal factory still in operation.
[f]Minsaas (1985). Minor quantities of meal from *A. nodosum* are also sold as health food in tablets or gelatin capsules.
[g]Hampson (1957).
[h]Baardseth (1970).

ANIMAL NUTRITION

Domesticated animals have few opportunities to graze seaweeds in a natural way. Only in coastal areas with either shallow, sheltered waters with good and frequent low tides or shores that regularly receive fresh cast weed can the animals be acquainted regularly with this fodder resource.

This section will mostly deal with industrially processed seaweed meal from *Ascophyllum nodosum*, largely based on Norwegian reports. It is by far the most common seaweed source in animal nutrition in Europe today, and the one whose uses are best documented.

ASCOPHYLLUM NODOSUM MEAL

All *Ascophyllum nodosum* is harvested from wild populations. This is done both by hand-cutting and by use of special boats (see Chapter 10). In the early years, *A. nodosum* was taken to suitable drying grounds close to the harvesting area and sun-dried either on the cliffs or sometimes on hay-drying frames. Rain and long periods of bad weather gave a washed-out, rotten brown-black

Table 2. Chemical composition of some seaweeds with present or future European commercial potential in nutrition

	Brown algae			Red algae			Green alga
	Ascophyllum nodosum	Laminaria digitata (lamina)	Alaria esculenta	Palmaria palmata	Porphyra sp.	Porphyra yezoensis	Ulva sp.
References	1	2,3,5	2,4,5	6	7,10–12	11	7,11,12
Water (%)	70–85	73–90	73–86	79–88	86	n.d.	78
Ash	15–25	21–35	14–32	15–30	8–16	7.8	13–22
Total carbohydrates	—	—	—	—	40	44.4	42–46
Alginic acid	15–30	20–45	21–42	0	0	0	0
Xylan (pentoses)	0	0	0	29–45	0	0	0
Laminaran	0–10	0–18	0–34	0	0	0	0
Mannitol	5–10	4–16	4–13	0	0	0	0
Fucoidan	4–10	2–4	n.d.	0	0	0	0
Floridoside	0	0	—	2–20	n.d.	n.d.	0
Fibre	5	6–8	5–7	1.5–3.5	4–7	2.0	4–5
Other carbohydrates	ca. 10	1–2	1–2	n.d.	n.d.	n.d.	n.d.

Protein[a]	5–10	8–15	9–18	8–25	33–47	43.6	15–25
Fat	2–7	1–2	1–2	0.3–3.8	0.7	2.1	0.6–0.7
Tannins	2–10	ca. 1	0.5–6[h]	n.d.	n.d.	n.d.	n.d.
Potassium	2–3	1.3–3.8	n.d.	7–9	3.3	2.4	0.7
Sodium	3–4	0.9–2.2	n.d.	2–2.5	n.d.	0.6	3.2
Magnesium	0.5–0.9	0.5–0.8	n.d.	0.4–0.5	2.0	n.d.	n.d.
Iodine	0.01–0.1	0.3–1.1	0.05[i]	0.01–0.1	0.0005	n.d.	n.d.

All figures except percentage water as g/100 g dry matter; n.d. no data.

[a] The commonly accepted factor of 6.25 in the conversion of total nitrogen to protein should be treated with caution as, among other factors, content of free nitrate will influence the total nitrogen level. Free nitrate is found in varying amounts both in brown and red algae (See text).

[b] The values for fibre for *Porphyra* sp. are most probably mannan. For reviews of the highly diverse polysaccharides in macroalgae, see Turvey (1978), McCandless (1981) and Painter (1983).

1, Baardseth (1970).
2, Haug and Jensen (1954).
3, Gayral and Cosson (1973).
4, Baardseth and Haug (1953).
5, Estimated from Jensen (1956a, b).
6, Averaged from Morgan et al. (1980).
7, Arasaki and Arasaki (1983).
8, Steinberg 1984 (*Alaria marginata*).
9, Jensen (1959).
10, Johnston (1972).
11, Nisizawa et al. (1987).
12, Levring et al. (1969).

SEAWEED RESOURCES IN EUROPE

Table 3. Minerals, trace elements and vitamins in the brown alga *Ascophyllum nodosum*

Minerals	% dry wt.	Reference	Trace elements[a]	ppm	Reference
Potassium	2–3	1	Iron	101–176	2
Phosphorus	0.1–0.15	1	Manganese	10–15	2
Magnesium	0.5–0.9	1	Zinc	70–240	2
Calcium	1–3	1	Copper	18–35	2
Sodium	3–4	1	Molybdenum	1–2	2
Chlorine	3.1–4.4	1	Iodine	700–1200	1
Sulphur	2.5–3.5	1	Cobalt	0.4–0.7	2
			Selenium	0.06–0.09	2
			Fluorine	25.5	3
			Chromium	n.d.	
			Barium	15–50	1
			Nickel	2–5	1
			Arsenic	22–44	2
			Antimony	0.19–0.53	2
			Vanadium	1.5–3	1

Vitamins	mg kg^{-1} dry wt. (ppm)	Reference
Carotene (provitamin A)	35–80	7
Ascorbic acid (C)	550–1650	5
Thiamine (B_1)	1–5	1
Riboflavin (B_2)	5–10	1
Niacin (B group)	10–30	6
Folic acid (B group)	0.1–0.5	1
Folinic acid (B group)	0.1–0.5	1
Cobalamine (B_{12})	0.0008–0.003	4
Tocopherols (E)	260–450	9
Biotin (H)	0.1–0.4	8
Menadione (K_3)	10	1

The values are both from analysis of seaweed meal from *A. nodosum* and whole *A. nodosum* plants. The ranges are mostly due to seasonal variations.

[a]Essential elements found in the human body in smaller quantities than iron ($\approx$ 50 mg/kg body weight) are considered trace elements (i.e. iodine, fluorine, zinc, cobalt, chromium, selenium, molybdenum, manganese, silicon, nickel, tin, vanadium, arsenic).

1, Jensen *et al.* (1968).
2, Lunde (1970).
3, Siebert and Trautner (1985).
4, Karlström (1963). Ericson and Lewis (1953) suggested that B_{12} stems from an exogeneous source, possibly from closely associated bacteria.
5, Jensen (1963a).
6, Larsen (1958).
7, Haug and Larsen (1957). In simultaneous feeding experiments with rats they found that the vitamin A was 80–100% of the value corresponding to the carotene content.
8, Larsen (1961).
9, Jensen (1969).

product, that would also develop large amounts of mould during storage. Cast weed should never be used, as it is low in minerals and will inevitably become infected with mould within a week. In summers with sufficient wind and sun the product may be good, but, as often as not, it will be in a condition such that one would be fortunate if it did not cause any harm. This practice lasted well into the 1960s.

Some harvesting methods rely on storing the cut *A. nodosum* afloat in nets until it can be picked up by freight vessels. The quality will be maintained for 1–3 weeks if the seaweed is kept in a fresh stream of seawater, and for shorter times when the sea temperatures are high. The following steps in the production of seaweed meal were described by Jensen (1960):

1. Hammer-milling with 14 mm sieve pores.
2. Repeated milling with 8–10 mm sieve pores.
3. Transport screw.
4. Through heating in an adequately filled drying drum at an entrance temperature of 700–800 °C and a maximum exit temperature of 70 °C.
5. Milling before packing, using cyclone and bag filters to eliminate dust.
6. Packaging in bags.

The packaged seaweed meal should be stored at low temperature with an optimal moisture content of about 15%. As seaweed meal is very hygroscopic, airtight paper sacks must be used. At 5°C and 15% moisture content, the packaged seaweed meal quality was unchanged after 1 year of storage. First-class seaweed meal should be green, not caramel-coloured (Jensen 1960). As subsequent data will show, it is extremely important to make sure that the seaweed meal to be used satisfies the analytical requirements, and one should always keep in mind that the content of vitamins will decrease on storage of the meal (Nebb & Jenson 1966). Being foodstuffs, the processing and further handling should be the same as for any kind of nutritional substance in order to avoid contamination (Sieburth & Jensen 1967; Kazanas 1987).

Seaweed meal from *A. nodosum* first came into use in Norway in 1937. For several years after this the consensus was that seaweed meal from *A. nodosum* would be a good source of minerals. The fact that it contains all the elements present in seawater promoted a belief that the meal had the ability to prevent certain pathological conditions in domestic animals where the cause–effect relationships were not clear at the time. However, there had already been some work in Norway (Isaachsen *et al.* 1917; Ringen 1939; Engdahl & Ulvesli 1942) concluding that no positive effects were evident from the inclusion of seaweed meal from species of the order Fucales into animal fodder. The expanded use through the 1950s and 1960s of standardized compound feeds to complement the use of grass and other fodder plants turned the production of fodder supplements into a major business. Thus, interest in seaweed meal as a fodder additive gained new momentum.

The quality requirements for seaweed meal from large brown seaweeds (i.e. species of *Fucus*, *Ascophyllum*, *Laminaria* and *Alaria*) have been specified by the Norwegian authorities in a law of 1973: 'For the production of seaweed meal only the use of freshly cut raw material is allowed. No castweed or blackweed is permitted. All types of artificially dried meal products from seaweed ('kelp') that are to be sold for animal consumption shall contain a declaration of chemical content with regard to dry matter, ash, iodine and fibre. If the product is not declared regarding chemical content, it shall carry a statement saying that it satisfies the actual requirements regarding dry matter, ash, iodine and fibre. The requirements for chemical content and quality are:

Dry matter	min. 86.0%
Iodine	max. 0.7%
Fibre	max. 10.0%
Ash	15.0–25.0%

Sand should not be present in larger amounts than 0.5 g per 100 g.' In addition, the following specifications regarding meal from grass and seaweeds to be used in fodder are made: 'In almost all kinds of compound feeds marketed, an inclusion of up to a total of 3% of grass meal and seaweed meal is allowed. In protein concentrates an addition of grass meal and seaweed meal is allowed in quantities so that the ready-to-use compound feeds are within the aforementioned 3% limit.' In an additional listing of the maximum allowed contents of unwanted elements and compounds, arsenic is set at a limit of 50 mg kg^{-1}; this is the only compound that might be of relevance for seaweed meal derived from *A. nodosum* (Tables 3 and 7).

Use in Feeding Stuffs and as a Supplemental Fodder

Feeding stuffs

In Europe, the products of the feed-compounding industry in general are requried to have a declaration of content. Either a guarantee concerning the content of nutrients and net energy or a statement of energy available for animal metabolism and a certain lower threshold of these factors is also required. This should be stated either as a per kilogram value or as a percentage.

For farmers to be competitive they need to be able to combine the available components of a compound feedstuff so that the price per unit usable energy and nutrients is as low as possible. Thus there is an advantage in the optimal use of raw materials. It follows, therefore, that the value of a component depends on the contribution it may make to the creation of an optimum quality fodder mixture. The price per kilogram, as such, is not the decisive factor for a component's possible inclusion. Of foremost interest to the farmer is the digestibility and overall nutritive value of the seaweed meal.

Larsen and Hawkins (1961) collected spring–summer samples and made alkali extracts from *Chondrus crispus* (Rhodophyta) and *Laminaria digitata* (Phaeophyta) and isopropanol extracts of *C. crispus*. These were incorporated into diets at levels of 7–10% crude protein. The digestibility of the nitrogenous constituents, if any, was considerably lower than that of egg albumen. The biological value, as measured by the retention of absorbed nitrogen, was 75% that of egg albumen for the *L. digitata* preparations and about the same as that of egg albumen for the *C. crispus* preparations. None of the preparations supported an adequate rate of growth. In the case of *L. digitata* this could be explained by a combination of poor digestibility and low biological value. In the case of *C. crispus* it was probably the result of poor digestibility. Dried preparations of *A. nodosum* and *Fucus vesiculosus* gathered late in the spring of 1959 were treated in the same way as the preparation of *L. digitata*. The original nitrogen content of these plants was lower than those of *C. crispus* and *L. digitata*, and the residual nitrogen content in the final extracts was not sufficiently high to allow the preparation of diets suitable for testing. The debate about methods for quantifying digestibility is still continuing, as indicated by Ryu *et al.* (1982).

Until the early 1970s the nutritive value of seaweed meal from *A. nodosum* was set by Norwegian agriculture authorities at *ca.* 0.65 feeding units in energy, with a positive content of digestible protein, so that 1 kg meal of *A. nodosum* equalled about 0.6 kg of grains like barley, durra, yellow corn and wheat. Then a new calculation method led to a drastically lowered estimate of the nutritive value of seaweed meal from *A. nodosum*, and to a decline in its use in the compounding industry. The energy value was reduced to 65% of the previous value as fodder for pigs, chickens and hens, and the digestibility of protein was reduced to zero. The actual value of seaweed meal was thus reduced to less than 30% of the feeding value of grains. A simultaneous major price increase of the seaweed meal made its continued use too expensive for the feed business. Only price subsidies are keeping seaweed meal on the Norwegian food-additive market.

The digestibility value is slightly higher when the meal is used for cattle than when used for pigs, chickens and hens. Material for a series of new experiments (Table 4) was cut both from an area with low salinity (close to an estuary) and from the usual coastal oceanic regions. Larsen and Haug (1956, 1958) found that the reducing power of *A. nodosum* varied between 0.2 and 2.2 mEq per g dry matter, with the low values recorded for the weed collected in the estuarine locations (Haug & Larsen 1958). The variation in reducing power corresponded to a variation in the tannin content of 4–13 g per 100 g dry matter. They also found a strong positive correlation between reducing power and dry matter content. Plants from the low salinity area had a lower than normal content of phenols, which may explain its better performance (Table 4). It is very likely that this is due to the protein of the seaweed being bound to phenols to form insoluble compounds. These cannot be decomposed either by microbial stomach processes or by intestinal enzymes. It has been stated that, if a simple method for removing phenols from brown algae could be found, it would make brown algal seaweed meal much more

Table 4. Chemical analyses, as percentage commercial dry weight, of two batches of seaweed meal from *Ascophyllum nodosum*

Component	Harvested at an oceanic location	Harvested at a low-salinity location
Crude protein (nitrogen × 6.25)	5.4	8.1
Fat	2.1	3.7
Water	10.7	9.0
Ash	20.1	14.5
Fibre	4.1	5.3
Salt	4.0	1.3
Nitrogen-free extracts	57.6	59.3
Iodine	0.07	0.04
Digestibility coefficients as determined for sheep		
Organic material	30	48
Dry matter	37	50
Feeding units/100 kg meal	23	47
Feeding units/100 kg dry matter	26	52

From Minsaas (1985), with permission of SINTEF, Trondheim.

attractive as a feed supplement. Larsen and Hawkins (1961) also found a negative digestibility for protein, which means that protein has to be supplied from other fodder components to have the seaweed meal digested and its nutritive components physiologically utilized.

Steinberg (1985) investigated the feeding practice of an intertidal gastropod (*Tegula funebralis*) on macroalgae. He found that relative levels of phenolic compounds, which are known to deter grazing by herbivorous snails, differed greatly between the six most preferred macroalgal species (average 0.83% of dry weight) and the seven non-preferred species (average 4.53% of dry weight). He concluded that high levels of phenolic compounds in brown algae are generally an effective deterrent against many marine invertebrate herbivores. Algae in the order Laminariales are typically low in phenolic content, whereas those in Fucales are uniformly high. Paul and Hay (1986) found that several common reef seaweeds appeared to resist herbivorous animals by relying primarily on chemical deterents. Such findings expand on earlier speculations that plant tissue carbon and nitrogen levels were mainly responsible for their attraction as food for marine herbivores (Paine & Vadas 1969); higher carbon : nitrogen ratios indicated more indigestible carbohydrates and less proteinaceous matter.

To compensate for the protein requirement for digestion and utilization of the energy content of *A. nodosum* seaweed meal, it would be necessary to add about 40 g protein per kg seaweed meal. The additional cost for this protein just about equals the value of the minerals in 1 kg of seaweed meal. It is, however, not possible to achieve the full effect of these minerals in the final composition of the fodder.

Fodder supplement

Fodder supplements are usually considered to be vitamins, minerals and trace elements. They may also be, for example, pharmaceuticals, antioxidants and preservatives. Fodder supplements will also include carriers for these compounds. In modern animal husbandry there is a considerable market for supplemental fodder. Compound feeds usually contain 2.5–3% feed supplements, thus limiting the possibilities of using seaweed meal as a fodder additive. Seaweed meal is a superb carrier for supplemental fodder compounds, and the consumption of such supplemental fodder mixtures to be used with roughages has secured a small but steady market niche for seaweed meal. However, in Norway this relies partly on government subsidies.

The supplemental compound feeds described are such a minor part of a total fodder that the carrier's feed value is not decisive. Thus the producers of supplemental compound feeds have been able to pay the market price for seaweed meal. As can be seen in Table 3, the content of minerals and trace elements, except iodine, is moderate. In animal nutrition iodine is the main uncertain factor. The basic requirements are well known, but factors affecting metabolism in the thyroid gland are uncertain. The supply of iodine to animals is therefore of considerable interest in connection with the composition of an optimal diet.

Poultry Seaweed meal from *A. nodosum* has been tested in extensive feeding experiments conducted in a collaborative project between the then Norwegian Institute of Seaweed Research at The Norwegian Institute of Technology, Trondheim, and The Agricultural College of Norway (Høie & Sandvik 1955; Høie & Sannan 1960). The results have been reviewed by Minsaas (1985), who concluded:

1. Meal from *A. nodosum* could not be attributed any single effect when used as an addition to an otherwise fully composed feeding stuff.
2. The impact of the vitamins in the meal of *A. nodosum* was about the same as that of grass meal. The same was observed for the effect of seaweed meal on the colour of egg yolks (connected to the meal's content of carotenoids, which has been treated in depth by Jensen (1963b)). There is, however, some uncertainty regarding the quality of the grass meal used in these studies.
3. Hatching results were improved when laying hens that received insufficient animal protein received a diet of meal of *A. nodosum*. This might be due to the cobalamins (vitamin B_{12}) in the seaweed meal. The use of large quantities of *A. nodosum* meal, as much as 10–15% of the total feed,

resulted in diarrhoea. When the fodder was adjusted for the low net energy content of the meal of *A. nodosum*, this could be added to the compound feed in a quantity of up to 7% without negative effects.

4. Mixing *A. nodosum* meal into the fodder increased the iodine content of the eggs without affecting their storage properties.

Pigs The observations by Ringen (1939) were discouraging as digestibility was low, the protein value negative, and the *A. nodosum* meal had a low net energy content. Jensen and Minsaas (1960) carried out two feeding experiments with bacon pigs. The *A. nodosum* meal was used as a fodder additive replacing up to 3% of the fodder. In one experiment the pigs were fed compound feeds either with or without seaweed meal. In the second experiment the animals were fed boiled potatoes supplemented with a protein concentrate, either with or without seaweed meal, and with seaweed meal also acting as a source of vitamins. Growth, feed efficiency and carcass quality were not significantly different for any of the total of eight groups in the two experiments. The conclusion was, therefore, that 3% *A. nodosum* seaweed meal in the feeding of pigs did not affect the meat yield. As the seaweed meal replaced more expensive compounds, feed costs were reduced by 2–6% per kg dressed weight in the groups that received seaweed meal of *A. nodosum*. In the experimental group the number of livers that were discarded after veterinary inspection was greatly reduced; the reason for this is not clear.

Homb (1961), however, found that seaweed meal of *A. nodosum* used in amounts of 3–6% of the fodder given to bacon pigs resulted in reduced growth when used in a compound feed with marginal protein content. This is probably related to the phenol content of the seaweed meal.

Whittemore and Percival (1975) tested the residual material after alginate extraction from *A. nodosum* as a fodder supplement. When fed at a level of 50% of the diet, the dried residue was found to cause diarrhoea in pigs within 7 days. Digestibility coefficients for a diet containing 50% seaweed residue, 20% barley, 19% wheat and 10% fish meal were 0.47 for energy and 0.52 for nitrogen. By difference calculation the digestible energy and digestible crude protein values of the seaweed residue were determined to be 2.2 MJ kg^{-1} and -30 g kg^{-1} dry matter.

Aas (1982) added 1% *A. nodosum* seaweed meal to compound feeds for bacon pigs in an attempt to reduce the goitrogenous effect of glucosinolates in solvent-extracted rape seed meal. *A. nodosum* meal used in this context had no effect on the weight of the thyroid gland and the liver when it was added to a feedstuff containing 20% rape seed meal. It is generally known, however, that extra supply of iodine in the feed may counteract the effect of some of the harmful compounds that are being formed by the degradation of glucosinolates.

Cattle In an experiment lasting 3 years with the addition of 300 g *A. nodosum* meal per animal per day to dairy cows, Ørud *et al.* (1964) found no effect on either milk yield or the fertility of the cows. Jensen *et al.* (1968) carried out an experiment over 7 years with lactating cows (seven pairs of identical, homozygous twins). The results included more than 46 lactation periods. A group containing one of the twins of each pair received 200 g mineral-enhanced *A. nodosum* meal (78.74% *A. nodosum* meal + 20% $Ca_2P_2O_7$ + 1.2% MgO + 0.06% $CuSO_4$) every day. The control group received the same feeding, with 100 g per day of standard mineral mixture substituted for the seaweed meal. General fertility was better for the seaweed meal group, which also averaged a milk yield 6.8% above that of the control group over the whole experimental period. The addition of *A. nodosum* meal gave a highly increased content of iodine in the milk. The mean of milk samples from the group that received *A. nodosum* meal was 0.6 mg iodine l^{-1} while the control group gave milk that contained only 0.1 mg iodine l^{-1}. In the autumn–spring period, when the animals were kept indoors, the seaweed meal group showed an insignificant increase in body weight, simultaneously producing 150 kg milk more per animal. The body weight of the control group, however, increased by an average of 16 kg from autumn to spring. The 6.8% higher milk yield following the feeding of seaweed meal increased income by 13%, because of unchanged basic expenses.

Sheep After 2 years of trials, Sæter and Jensen (1957) found that addition of seaweed meal had no effect on either breeding or sterility. All offspring showed an increased winter wool production. The effects of *A. nodosum* meal were more pronounced after a dry summer with a consequent reduction in hay quality.

In the mid-1950s there was a major investigation using supplements of *A. nodosum* meal to sheep during the winter (Jensen 1958). A daily supplement of 35 g *A. nodosum* meal was given to 900 ewes and this group was compared with 900 ewes of the same stock which did not receive seaweed meal. The ewes receiving seaweed meal maintained their body weight much better during indoor winter feeding, and had a greater wool production. There was also a tendency to improved fertility and also a significantly higher growth rate in lambs born by mothers receiving *A. nodosum* meal. However, no definite effects on other health parameters were noted.

Sæter's (1960) report of a visit to North Ronaldsay, the Orkneys, is interesting in this connection. There is a local breed of small black sheep which graze entirely on seaweed. The whole island is surrounded by a wall so that the animals are confined to the foreshore. Orpin *et al.* (1985) reported that the sheep population in the intertidal was about 10 per hectare. They are allowed to enter a pasture only when in lamb or just before slaughter. Even if the farmers had virtually no fodder expenses, Sæter (1960) commented that this husbandry was not an example to follow. It might be regarded as a large-scale feeding experiment that has been going on for a very long time, and it proves that sheep can feed on seaweed alone without any evident deficiencies and without being chronically poisoned. He added, however: 'One must admit that the sheep at North Ronaldsay were a miserable sight. Usually they are wet; they are small, skinny and scruffy as they are seldom cut, not even once a year.' The seaweed species preferred by the animals when available were *Palmaria palmata*, *Odonthalia dentata*, *Delesseria sanguinea*, *Chondrus crispus* and *Mastocarpus stellatus*. Ranked lower by the sheep were *Ptilota plumosa*, *Corallina officinalis* and *Codium* sp. Sæter's impression was that 80% of the sheep's diet consisted of *Laminaria digitata* and *L. hyperborea*. An ironic observation was '. . . The people said the sheep would rather starve to death than eat *Ascophyllum* . . . one must remember here that seaweed to these animals is the *only* feed available . . . sheep brought in from other places will manage if they can graze grass in the summer. If not, they die within a year.' Orpin *et al.* (1985) confirmed the above diet, adding *Alaria esculenta* and *L. saccharina* to the preferred species. They also noted that some rough pasture was available on the foreshore, but that this was often ignored as a food source by the animals. As a control group in their investigation they used grass-fed animals of the same breed from neighbouring islands. They concluded that the two groups had both qualitative and quantitative differences in the dominant microbial populations in the rumen. Of interest is their observation that few of the bacteria isolated from seaweed-fed animals grew well on alginate and fucoidan. Despite the seaweed diet being chemically dissimilar to that of pasture, the majority of the identified bacteria were species found in other ruminants. An absence of cellulolytic bacteria from the seaweed-fed sheep was not surprising. The rumen microbiology seemed more adapted to decomposing xylans, which are a major component of the red alga *Palmaria palmata* (McCandless 1981).

Hallsson (1964) found that sheep grazing on cast weed in Iceland selectively chose species like *Palmaria palmata* and *Alaria esculenta*. Young fronds of *L. saccharina* were eaten by horses.

Use as a Source of Iodine in Animal Nutrition

In Pen-Tsao Teng's treatise on herbs and roots, *Sargassum* sp. (Phaeophyta) is mentioned as an effective agent against endemic goitre (Michanek 1981). In Europe kelp was certainly used for this purpose by Roger of Salerno in the 12th century. Iodine was first isolated from kelp by Bernard Courtois in 1811, and a few years later it was recommended as a means of combating goitre (Booth 1979). According to Haug (1956), 60–70% of iodine in brown seaweed is inorganic, occurring mostly as free iodide (Shaw 1962), with the rest found as monoiodotyrosine and diiodotyrosine, and triiodothyronine (Shaw 1962; Ragan 1981).

Iodine is the only essential element for which brown algal meal is an important source (Table 9). In human and animal nutrition iodine affects many aspects of the metabolism. To examine expectations of the use of seaweed meal from *A. nodosum* as a good source of iodine in animal fodder, we will first have to look at the physiology of iodine nutrition. Then it will be easier to see the importance of its necessity and supply, both in quantity and in a suitable chemical form. Meat, milk and eggs from domesticated animals are regarded as vital for human nutrition, so it is important that these products have an iodine content that suits human metabolic requirements; both too little and too much are dangerous.

Physiology

About 20% of all iodine in humans and animals is found in the thyroid gland. Smaller amounts occur in the kidneys, the salivary glands, the ovaries, the milk-producing glands, the chorion, the small intestines, and the skin and hair. Iodine compounds are rapidly degraded and absorbed from the digestive tract into the blood. Free iodine and iodate are reduced to iodide in the intestinal wall. In the blood, iodide has diffusion properties similar to those of sodium chloride. In the thyroid, iodide is oxidized, converted to organic iodine by coupling to the amino acid L-tyrosine, and incorporated into hormones like 3,5,3'5'-tetraiodothyronine (thyroxin) and 3,5,3'-triiodothyronine. The same reaction occurs, but to a lesser degree, in the milk glands of milk-producing animals and in the eggs of poultry before ovulation.

According to Morrison (1951), no difference has been demonstrated in the effect of inorganic iodine and organically bound iodine in kelp in the treatment of goitre. This is to be expected from the chemistry of the digestive process. The relationship might, however, be viewed differently when taking into account the stability of iodine during storage. Simple iodine compounds, such as potassium iodide, are very unstable under some conditions as iodine is liberated through sublimation.

Hemken *et al.* (1981) showed that organically bound iodine might give higher values of iodine in milk than the same amount of iodine added to the fodder as simple, inorganic compounds. Potassium iodide gave a higher content of iodine in blood serum, but lower levels in milk compared with an organic compound (ethylenediaminedihydroiodide) used to combat hoof-rot in cattle.

The thyroid influences many functions of an organism (Scott *et al.* 1976):

1. Intensity of the metabolism, i.e. energy turnover in the cells.
2. Psychic and mental development, and differentiation and maturation of tissue.
3. Other internal secretory glands, especially the pituitary and sexual glands (the ovaries and testicles).
4. Muscle functions.
5. The cardiovascular system.
6. Skin, hair/fur, growth of feathers.
7. Metabolism of a range of nutrients, including minerals.

It is evident that iodine nutrition directly influences many aspects of economic importance in animal husbandry: the vital energy efficiency, reproduction and fertility performance (sexual activity and embryonic deaths), and the development of fur. With iodine deficiency there is a reduction in the production of hormones from the thyroid, which results in the development of simple goitre; this is demonstrated by abnormal growth of the thyroid gland. The reason for this is that the pituitary gland produces a hormone which stimulates the thyroid to increase its hormonal production. When iodine is lacking the thyroid seeks to compensate for this by increasing the mass of gland tissue. The requirement for iodine is low in absolute weight, and is defined as the amount necessary to ensure normal functioning of the thyroid gland. The US Food and Nutrition Board recommends for human adults a daily intake of 0.15 mg iodine (Food and Nutrition Board 1980).

Overdoses

Excess intake of iodine may produce fatal effects in both humans and animals. Goitre (thyrotoxicosis) was demonstrated as a consequence of a *high* intake of kelp products both in children in Japan (Zuzuki 1965) and in adults in Finland (Liewendahl 1972). Similar incidents have been reported from Australia and other countries (Wheeler *et al.* 1982). The cause was, among other things, milk for consumption with an extremely high content of iodine caused by contamination with disinfectants containing iodine, which had been used on the udders and teats, and especially the milking machines. This resulted in up to 2.5 mg iodine l^{-1} milk.

In the USA, milk and dairy products are considered the most important sources of iodine for human nutrition (Hemken *et al.* 1981). It is therefore important to ensure that milk contains sufficient amounts of iodine, but not so much that it might be harmful. The normal content of iodine in milk should be 0.1–0.3 mg l^{-1}. Iodine contents lower than 0.05–0.025 mg l^{-1} indicate iodine deficiency. The content of iodine in fodder affects the iodine content of milk (Convey *et al.* 1977). Cows receiving 164 mg iodine per day in the fodder produced milk with 2.2 mg iodine l^{-1}, while the content of iodine in milk from cows receiving 16 mg iodine per day was only 0.37 mg l^{-1}. Horses, especially thoroughbreds, are notably sensitive to overdoses of iodine. Their requirement is lower than that of other domesticated animals, being about 0.1–0.2 mg kg^{-1} dry weight of the fodder. Overdoses may lead to goitre, lowered fertility and lowered physical capacity (Baker & Lindsey 1968; Bridget *et al.* 1975).

The milk gland regulates and limits the milk's content of, for example, heavy metals like iron, copper and cadmium within rather narrow limits. This mechanism does not operate for iodine. An increase in the iodine content of feed quickly results in an increase in the iodine content of the milk. A high content of iodine in the fodder combined with careless use of sterilizing agents containing iodine may therefore result in a seriously high content of iodine in the milk. In recent years there have been a number of reports about the effect of disinfectants and cleaning agents containing iodine on the iodine content of milk. Several countries have registered an alarmingly high content of iodine in milk. These findings have led to a reduction in the addition of iodine to dairy feeds in California (Bruhn et al. 1983). The 1980 mean level of iodine in milk was 0.5 mg l^{-1}, later falling to 0.25 mg l^{-1} as a consequence of the reduction of iodine in the fodder. The use of iodine-containing disinfectants and cleaning agents should be considerate and careful. Important as they are to the hygiene and prevention of the spread of diseases, they must be used with the utmost care. Lewis et al. (1980) showed that iodine in liquids for cleaning udders and teats might be absorbed through the skin and thus increase the content of iodine in the blood, serum and milk.

Considering the content of iodine to be 0.7–1.2 g kg^{-1} in meal from A. nodosum (Table 3) and 4–8 g kg^{-1} in meal from Laminaria sp. (Haug & Jensen 1954), it seems obvious that the overdoses may be massive in relation to the daily minimum requirement of 0.5–2 mg for horses and 2–5 times that amount for lactating cows. With a daily ration of 100 g seaweed meal for horses, the intake of iodine will be 10–20 times the minimum requirement, but still far below any damaging amounts. From the observations by Sæter (1960) of the seaweed-eating sheep at North Ronaldsay, one would have expected to see thyrotoxicosis in these sheep, as the seaweed intake was estimated as 1 kg dry matter per day per animal with a body weight of about 30 kg. If 80% was Laminaria sp. this would mean a daily intake of 3–7 g iodine per animal. Two sick animals were autopsied, but no abnormality of the thyroid was observed.

Increased need for iodine

A range of brassicaceous forages, like rape and pithy cabbage, contain glucosinolates. Similar compounds are also found in other plants grown for use as fodder, like clover. The glucosinolates yield fission products (e.g. vinyloxazolidinthion) that compete with, reduce or inhibit the incorporation of iodine in animal metabolism. The result is an enlarged thyroid gland and goitre, similar to conditions with lowered activity of thyroxin in the blood plasma (Homb 1981). It has been suggested (Astrup 1982) that an increased occurrence of chronic milk fever in lactating cows may be connected to failures in the hormone production of the thyroid gland. It has also been shown that the glucosinolates reduce the transfer of the iodine in the fodder to the milk (Lindell & Knutsson 1976).

The plants mentioned above are important for grazing and silage, constituting important feed crops for cattle. Seed and seed-based products from rape are also important protein supplements in concentrates for all domestic animals, particularly in northern Europe and Canada. New and improved varieties of rape have a lower content of glucosinolates, but still enough to affect the size of the thyroid gland in pigs fed with high percentages of rape meal (Aas 1982). Addition of *A. nodosum* meal at 1% did not seem to counter the effect of the fission products of the glucosinolates. Both Homb (1981) and Astrup (1982) suggest, however, the possibility that an increased amount of iodine may counter the goitrogenous effect of the glucosinolates. This mechanism has led to an upwards adjustment of the norms for the addition of iodine to feeding stuffs in both Norway and Sweden to a standard of $2\,mg\,kg^{-1}$ of compound feeds for cows. It has also generated renewed interest in research concerning the role of iodine in animal nutrition. Norwegian cows receive on average 5–10 mg iodine per day from ordinary feed. The minimum requirement is definitely lower, but the optimal amount is not known as it depends on the composition of the fodder. There is also an antagonistic relationship between milk quality and iodine content. Two major problems regarding the quality of the milk are the oxidation defect (metallic taste) and an acrid taste from the milk. The thyroid gland hormone is involved in the oxidation defect, but counteracts the acrid taste. It is also being suggested that low fertility rate and increased occurrence of chronic milk fever in cows may be related to hormone production failure in the thyroid.

Pointing to what has been said about iodine requirements, Astrup (1982) called for more research on iodine and iodine compounds in animal nutrition, especially with regard to milk-producing cows. Simultaneously, Homb (1981) mentioned that 'the weak point when trying to evaluate the effects of using rape seed and rape meal in large quantities in animal feeding, is the long-term effect on health and fertility'. Cattle are far more sensitive to the damaging effects of the fission compounds of glucosinolates than poultry and pigs.

Long-term storage effects

Some simple tests were carried out using various sources of iodine (Table 5). The method used is reputedly very accurate and sensitive, but will only allow very small sample volumes. The varying values are recorded from homogenized material and sample volumes of 0.8–1 g. Small samples create problems when they contain seaweed meal, as uneven distribution of small particles with a high iodine content may strongly influence the results. Samples containing finely distributed mineral components in the compound feeds showed a more even distribution of iodine, although none of them reached the expected value of $2\,mg\,iodine\,kg^{-1}$. Only the feeding stuff mixtures with seaweed meal from *A. nodosum* were close to or above this level, if calculated as averages. It is then reasonable to suppose that the values in Table 6 express the stability of the seaweed meal as a source of iodine. The results from the three milk samples (Table 5) demonstrate the accuracy and reproducibility of the method. Table 6 shows the iodine content of seaweed meal after storage

Table 5. Elemental iodine content in Norwegian standard compound feed for dairy cows (type A) with the addition of 2 mg kg^{-1} of two different iodine compounds, and the iodine content of three milk samples

Sample	Iodine (mg kg^{-1})	
	November 13 1981	April 15 1982
Feeding stuffs		
No extra iodine	0.36	0.46
With Ca(IO$_3$)$_2$	1.11	1.19
With oceanic seaweed meal		
I	1.39	3.99
II	2.09	1.96
With estuarine seaweed meal		
I	4.24	1.76
II	2.53	1.87
With commercial micromineralmix	0.59	0.87
With standard mineral additives	0.88	1.01
Milk		
From Trondheim (fjord region)		
I	n.d.	0.13
II	n.d.	0.13
From Alvdal (mountain region)		
I	n.d.	0.35
II	n.d.	0.37
From Hamar (inland region)		
I	n.d.	0.21
II	n.d.	0.22

The analytical procedure was according to Johansen and Steinnes (1976). n.d., not determined.
From Minsaas (1985), with permission of SINTEF, Trondheim.

for a considerable period. However, evidence for deciding whether it is advantageous to use seaweed meal as a stable iodine source is still lacking.

NUTRITIONAL USE OF SEAWEEDS FOR FARMED MARINE ORGANISMS

Montgomery and Gerking (1980) reported that two species of fish tested from the Gulf of California grazed red and green algae but ignored brown and calcareous species. According to stomach samples, *Eupomacentrus rectifraenum* (Cortez damselfish) absorbed approximately 88% of the available protein, 56% of the available lipid and only 2% of the available carbohydrate, whereas the other species (*Microspathodon dorsalis*, giant blue damselfish) absorbed 57% of the algal protein, 47% of the lipid and 37% of the carbohydrate. The diets of the two species were different. This points to a

Table 6. Iodine content in stored samples of seaweed meal of *Ascophyllum nodosum*

Sampling date	Iodine (mg kg^{-1} dry meal)	
	Original values	Values at March 1980
August 1950	450	580
2 May 1951	1000	600
2 February 1955	800	900
5 May 1955	800	600

Samples analysed in 1980 according to Larsen (1978). Original analyses according to Baggesgaard-Rasmussen and Bjerresø (1941). The meal had been stored in tin cans with tightly secured, removable lids. All analyses were performed in triplicate.

major problem in the digestion of algae: the hydrolysis of the algal polysaccharides. It was also suggested that conditions of temperature, pH and residence time in the fish stomach would be insufficient to allow significant digestion. Again we encounter indirect arguments that seaweeds should be regarded as a feed additive. Yone *et al.* (1986) stated that the nutritive value of diets for red sea bream (*Chrysophrys major*) was improved by the addition of wakame (*Undaria pinnatifida*), and attributed this effect to an increased feed efficiency through a delaying action of the seaweed feed additive. Using the presence of lipoproteins in serum as an assay, Nakagawa *et al.* (1986) found that a 10% addition of meal from *Ulva pertusa* increased the albumin content, but did not affect body weight gain or feed efficiency. Appler and Jauncey (1983) found that the weight gain and protein utilization of *Tilapia* (milk-fish) decreased as the level of the green alga *Cladophora glomerata* increased in the diet, although the protein digestibility was the same in diets with 0, 5 and 10% of the algal meal.

Besides fish, there are many commercially valuable marine organisms that are well adapted to utilize seaweed in their diet. However, proposing large-scale farming or sea-ranching in European waters of seaweed-grazing sea urchins for exotic, high-priced food uses, for example, will probably be met with firm resistance from the local alginate industries.

USE OF CRUDE ALGINATES AND FINELY GROUND SEAWEED MEAL AS BINDERS AND VISCOSIFIERS IN FEEDS FOR FARMED FISH AND FUR ANIMALS

Wet fodder is largely used for fish farming and the raising of fur-yielding animals. This is partly sterilized waste from the meat industry, and fish and fish wastes that are in part fresh, but are usually either frozen or acid-preserved (fish silage). The wet wastes are mixed with dry concentrates containing supplementing nutrients to produce a firm, dough-like consistency.

In fur farming the dough-like fodder is placed directly onto the netting cages. The waste of fodder is considerable if it is not solid enough. If the fodder releases water, drops may cause permanent damage to the furs of both minks and foxes. Crude alginates are now regularly added to the fodder in concentrations of 0.25–1% of viscosifiers at certain times of the year, when the inclusion of gelatinized grains is low for physiological reasons. Alginates have the required physical properties, but do not affect digestibility (Loftsgaard, personal communication).

A similar dough-like feed is used in fish farming. If it lacks an adequate texture, the feed will 'dissolve' on entering the water. This is corrected by adding either alginates or other viscosifiers. Alginates must be added in a concentration of about 1–2% to give an effective binding. Higher amounts of alginate may lead to unwanted side-effects, like removal of physiologically essential divalent cations (like Zn^{2+}) from the diet.

So far, guar gum is the main competitor to alginates in fish fodder, even though it reduces the digestibility of protein and fats by 30–40% (Utne *et al.* 1981). The price of the binding agent may constitute 20–40% of the total fodder price: an expense that has been justified only by the high price of the finished product, the fish. The use of cheaper alginates, which in this context may also include finely ground seaweed meal, may help to shift this price balance in their favour. The potential is considerable because the Norwegian fish-farming industry alone will exceed 100 000 t year^{-1} in 1990, providing a potential market of several thousand tonnes of alginates per year for use as a binding agent. The trend is, however, to use more dry fodder.

OTHER REPORTS

A dramatically toxic effect was reported when substituting 5–10% of rabbit fodder with meal from *A. nodosum* (Blunden & Jones 1972; Jones *et al.* 1981). As many as two-thirds of the animals died during the 100-day test period, but rats and pigs were not affected. The biochemical mechanism causing this effect was not determined, and neither has there been any similar report of toxicity.

Reports on the use of other seaweed species are few. Administration of fresh or frozen, well macerated samples of the green alga *Cladophora* sp. (Chlorophyceae) to poultry was said to give the egg yolk a more intense colour, and to improve both the appearance and the colour of the chicken meat (Stadniciuc & Calotoiu 1972). Feeding trials have also been reported with the green alga *Ulva* sp. given to chicks. Wong and Leung (1979) reported optimal body weight responses after supplementing 10–15% dry weight of the fodder mixture with dried seaweed, but reported negative effects for additions as high as 25%. The kelp *Alaria esculenta* has a favourable historical reputation as a fodder additive. As supplements to an incomplete mixture without addition of vitamins A, E and B_2, meal of *A. esculenta* had better effect than meal of *Laminaria hyperborea* and *Ascophyllum nodosum* when given as 5% of the ration of young chicks, particularly with regard to body weight increase and mortality (Seterlund *et al.* 1968). Meal made in the spring was superior to that made in the autumn.

HUMAN NUTRITION

SEAWEEDS AS SEA VEGETABLES

In the western world the use of seaweeds for human consumption is very limited. Uses exist as the remnants of a long tradition in some coastal communities, as an additive said to be of general interest, and for people with special tastes and interests, as in so-called healthfoods. Since 1970, there has been an enthusiastic activity in France called *algue alimentaire* (Brault & Briand 1987). France is now the European country where the drive to use seaweed for human nutrition seems to be greatest. The culinary aspects of seaweeds as exciting new vegetables and spices is emphasized, looking to the Far Eastern uses as a model. Until recently, the seaweeds used in human foods in Europe have been almost entirely imported from Japan. In 1988, the French National Council for Health (CNSH) lifted the restriction on the use of native seaweed species as foodstuffs, and set new limits on maximum levels of selected heavy metals (Table 7). At present there is a burgeoning industry with 15 employees and a volume of 3 million francs utilizing ten native species. The species being used are *L. saccharina*, *A. nodosum*, *Himanthalia elongata*, *Fucus vesiculosus*, *Ulva* spp., *Enteromorpha* sp., *Palmaria palmata*, *Porphyra umbilicalis*, *Chondrus crispus*, *Lithothamnion* sp., and the culti-vated adventive species *Undaria pinnatifida*. Of further immediate potential are *Fucus serratus*, *Sargassum muticum*, *Alaria esculenta* and *Gracilaria verrucosa*. In addition, the product groups listed in Table 7 are imported. Total production of seaweeds in France was about 60 000 t in 1985, including raw material for phycocolloid production, which still provides most of the volume. France is now exporting its products, selling them on the healthfood market and using them in the cosmetics industry (see Chapter 4). A special feature of the French cultivation industry is the growth in European waters of introduced species like *Undaria pinnatifida* (Perez *et al.* 1984). *Undaria pinnatifida* (wakame) is a high-volume human foodstuff species in Japan (Table 9).

Eating seaweeds is considered an unusual activity in most of Europe. It might thus be fruitful first to look at the whole concept of human nutrition. For energy we need carbohydrates and fat; for amino acids we need proteins. Why then do we pay so much attention to cucumber and lettuce? They consist

Table 7. The maximum content of heavy metals allowed in macroalgae for human consumption in France, Japan and the USA

Country	Maximum content allowed (ppm)				
	Lead	Cadmium	Arsenic	Mercury	Zinc
France	5	0.5	3	0.1	100
Japan	0.9	0.1	0.2	0.1	15
USA	10	3			
Palmaria palmata[a]	0.7–3.5	1.0–2.7	5.5–7.5	< 0.02	57–84

From Sirota and Uthe (1979), Brault and Briand (1987), Mabeau personal communication.
[a]The values for dulse lie well within the safety values established for a foodstuff by the Canadian Food and Drug Act (Sirota & Uthe 1979).

almost entirely of water, with no protein to speak of and hardly any carbohydrates for energy (Table 8). So why do we not add some seaweed to the daily diet?

The polysaccharides in sea vegetables are different from those in terrestrial vegetables (Painter 1983). The ease of their hydrolysis is linked to the nature of the glycosidic linkages between the monomers; α-linkages, as found in starch, are more susceptible to amylases than are β-linkages. Enzymes capable of degrading β-linked polymers such as cellulose and its analogues are not found in humans. The brown algae are characterized by carbohydrates that are β-linked polymers of glucose and uronic acids. In contrast, green algae store starch, an α-linked polymer of glucose, but the cell walls contain highly resistant polymers of glucose, mannose and xylose (Painter 1983). Because they are 'filling', seaweeds are a good diet food. Their soft cell walls regulate bowel action without damaging intestinal walls. In terms of amino acids, seaweed protein is similar to that of egg whites and legumes (Table 11 and Morgan *et al.* 1980). Sea vegetables are low in fats, and have a competitive content of vitamins and minerals (Tables 2, 3 and 8). Results from experiments with sea vegetable protein digestibility in humans and animals over a long period of time have, however, provided no conclusive results. Kimura (1952, cited in Boney 1965) measured digestibility in terms of absorption rate for polished rice when mixed with the brown algae *Laminaria japonica* or *Undaria pinnatifida* and the red alga *Porphyra tenera*. The results indicated that the carbohydrate and fat values were higher in *L. japonica* and *U. pinnatifida*, and the protein value higher in *P. tenera*. However, Arasaki and Arasaki (1983) compared the values of Kimura (1952) with later studies and reduced Kimura's digestibility values by 30–50%; only the values for *P. tenera* were roughly the same, with a digestibility of 50% of its carbohydrates and 70% of its protein. The commonly accepted conversion factor of 6.25 for calculating total nitrogen into protein was challenged by, among others, Ryu *et al.* (1982). They proposed using the factor method: first multiplying the quantity of each amino acid by its molecular nitrogen factor, then summing the weighted nitrogen values to provide an amino acid nitrogen content based on amino acid composition, and finally dividing the total amino acid content by this total amino acid nitrogen value to obtain a nitrogen conversion factor. This resulted in a range of values from a low of 5.83 for a brown alga (*Hizikia fusiforme*) to a high of 6.52 for a red alga (*Porphyra tenera*). Their *in vitro*

Table 8. Content of nutritional components per 100 g edible product in vegetables and as g per 100 g dry wt in seaweeds

	Water (g)	Protein (g)	Fat (g)	Carbohydrates (g)	Energy (kcal)	Ca (mg)	Fe (mg)	Carotene (mg)
Cucumber	96	0.8	0.1	2.4	14	15	0.4	0.22
Curly kale	85	5.0	0.6	6.3	51	200	3.0	5.10
Carrot	88	0.9	0.2	9.2	42	40	0.7	11.0
Garden beans	74	7.0	0.3	16.8	98	20	1.7	0.55
Yellow corn	73	3.5	1.0	21.4	109	3	0.7	—
Lettuce	94	1.3	0.2	2.8	18	25	1.3	1.60
Spinach	92	2.2	0.3	3.1	24	100	3.0	4.40
Palmaria palmata						560	50	
Porphyra tenera						470	23	
Porphyra yezoensis						440	13	
Ulva sp.						730	87	
Laminaria sp.						800	15	

	Vit. A (IU[a])	Thiamine (mg)	Riboflavine (mg)	Niacin (mg)	Vit. C (mg)	Vit. B$_{12}$ (g)	Reference
Cucumber	145	0.02	0.02	0.2	8	0	1
Curly kale	3 400	0.15	0.29	2.8	150	0	1
Carrot	4 400	0.05	0.04	1.0	5	0	1
Garden beans	370	0.31	0.13	2.2	25	0	1
Yellow corn	—	0.15	0.12	1.7	12	0	1
Lettuce	1 070	0.08	0.10	0.5	15	0	1
Spinach	2 950	0.09	0.24	0.7	20	0	1
Palmaria palmata	26 600	0.4	0.5	4	200	10	2
Porphyra tenera	38 400	0.21	1.00	3.0	20	20	2
Porphyra yezoensis	16 000	1.3	3.8	11.0	112	0.03	3
Ulva sp.	960	0.06	0.03	8.0	10	6.3	2,3
Laminaria sp.	430	0.08	0.32	1.8	11	0.3	2

For water, protein, fat and carbohydrate contents of seaweeds, see Table 2.
[a]IU vitamin A = 1 μh retinol or 6 μg β-carotene or 1.2 μg α-carotene (Eeg-Larsen and Nes 1984). Vitamin A content of *P. palmata* calculated on the basis of $\alpha/\beta = 2.0$ (Morgan *et al.* 1980).
1, Wielgolaski (1979).
2, Arasaki and Arasaki (1983).
3, Nisizawa *et al.* (1987).

digestibility experiments showed about 80% digestibility, with almost double the trypsin inhibitor content in the brown algae as compared with the reds.

The difference in the phenolic content of algae is vital, low contents favouring the protein digestibility of green and especially red algae at the expense of the browns. In addition, red algal species generally have higher protein levels than the other two macroalgal classes.

The use of seaweed vegetables has been treated for various audiences by Madlener (1977), Arasaki and Arasaki (1983), Xia and Abbott (1987) and Nisizawa *et al.* (1987). The outstanding region for human seaweed consumption is the Far East, particularly Japan, China and Korea. Detailed references to the enormous volume of Far Eastern literature in this field is, however, beyond the scope of the present review. In the Far East, the population eat more seaweed than is utilized in the West for both nutritional and industrial purposes combined. Table 9 gives the volumes and prices for the common species used in Japan. Olsen (1985, 1986) has treated this subject extensively. The Japanese utilize 50 species from 29 genera. The Japanese harvest in 1982/83 was about 370 000 t fresh red algae and a similar quantity of brown algae. Almost all the catch was used for human consumption. Of the total, 3% was exported, and imports accounted for 8% of consumption, making a total annual consumption of about 800 000 t fresh weight, with a yearly consumption per citizen of about 6.7 kg fresh weight, which has doubled over the last 30 years. The first-hand value averaged in 1982 US$ $1.2 \, \text{kg}^{-1}$, a total of more than US$ 1 billion (10^9). The end-user dry weight price of high-quality products was US$ $15–70 \, \text{kg}^{-1}$, for products from both red and brown algae. Total end-product sales value in 1983/84 was about US$ 3×10^9. Seaweed production volume was 50% of the total marine culture of shellfish, fish and algae, which added up to 1 million t. Algal production was 6% of total marine tonnage (wild and cultivated), but in value it was 8%, in other words fetching a 35% higher price per weight unit. Some 80 000 people were employed in seaweed cultivation, excluding those involved in final processing and sale.

Table 9. Volume and value of seaweeds produced for human nutrition in Japan in 1982/83

	Species (Product name)		
	Porphyra spp. (nori)	*Laminaria* spp. (kombu)	*Undaria* spp. (wakame)
Harvested volume (t fresh wt year^{-1})	360 000	160 000	180 000
Percentage from cultivation	91–100	25	90
Product value (US$ $\times 10^6$)	1800	600	600

Data from Olsen (1985, 1986).

The main species used for nori in Japan has shifted from *Porphyra tenera* to *P. yezoensis* (Nisizawa *et al.* 1987). Some 50 600 people were employed in 1982/83 in the provision of nori: 22 000 production units each with an average of 2.3 employees. The gross sales income per unit in 1983 was about US$ 30 000. About 55% of the total income covered operational costs, so net annual income was about US$ 15 000 per family, depending on locality, and thus the quality of the product. Average cultivated area per production unit was 3500 m^2, with a total cultivated *Porphyra* spp. area of about 650 km^2. The yield of nori was about 0.6 kg m^{-2} $year^{-1}$ with a landed first-hand value of US$ 1.2–2 per kg fresh weight. There are 70 different price groups, and the best quality is 20–30 times more expensive than the poorest quality.

The harvest volume of kombu (kelp) in Japan has remained unchanged since 1945. About 15 000 people were employed in 1982/83 in harvesting wild *Laminaria*, and about 6000 in its cultivation. Total cultivated area was 200 km^2, producing 2 kg m^{-2}. The finest quality kombu comes from natural kelp beds and is sold for as much as US$ 30 per kg dry weight. The Japanese use about 1.3 kg fresh weight per capita in a year, and fresh algae is priced at about US$ 1 per kg. Cultivated plants were 80% of the price of wild material.

For wakame (*Undaria pinnatifida*) the cultivation area covered 110 km^2, with an average yield of 1 kg fresh weight m^{-2}. In 1982/83 about 21 000 people were involved in wakame cultivation, and the landed value was about US$ 0.8 per kg. Japan also imported some 80 000 t from Korea. Total consumption increased five-fold compared with that in 1950. It is priced in the same range as kombu, with the usual large price difference between high- and low-grade material.

Terrestrial vegetables are eaten because of their content of minerals and vitamins and because of their taste. To this the Far Eastern users of sea vegetables would certainly add colour, flavour, texture, chewiness and chewing sounds (Olsen 1986), the latter being considered in good taste in Japan. In the Far East, seaweed products are considered as vegetables and herbs, the highest qualities being luxury commodities. In addition to aesthetic values, seaweeds add vitamins and minerals to the diet. A few red algae, like *Porphyra* sp., have a reasonably high content of protein, and may thus provide a small protein supplement. But, even in Japan, the daily consumption is only about 10 g per person (360 000 t $year^{-1}$), and this equals no more than 2–4 g pure protein per day. Eating large amounts of macroalgae to obtain protein may result in the ingestion of an excessive amount of minerals or, rather, ash, leading to diarrhoea for most digestive systems.

The energy content of foodstuffs is determined by the content of carbohydrates, fat and proteins. Energy values of various seaweeds are given by Paine and Vadas (1969). The chemical energy is measured in a bomb calorimeter. The average physical heat of combustion, according to Eeg-Larsen and Nes

(1984), is:

Carbohydrates 17.2 kJ (4.1 kcal) g^{-1}
Fat   39.4 kJ (9.4 kcal) g^{-1}
Protein   23.5 kJ (5.6 kcal) g^{-1}

But these values cannot be thought of as physiological energy before the digestibility of the various compounds is determined.

Bioavailability is still a much-disputed topic, both for the major compounds such as protein and carbohydrates, and also for the inorganic compounds. Johnston (1972) fractionated the elements of seaweeds into available and unavailable elements. He found calcium availability to be higher in the red alga *P. yezoensis* than in the brown alga *Analipus japonica* (= *Heterochordaria abietina*), although iron appeared to be moderately available from both sources. Kim and Zemel (1986) found the solubility of calcium from *Undaria pinnatifida* in an *in vitro* digestive system to be comparable to that of calcium in spinach and milk when gastric acid concentrations were varied. However, reducing the acidity by 50% caused a significant reduction in calcium solubility from *U. pinnatifida*, and complete elimination of the acid caused a further reduction. They did not discuss the probable interaction between calcium and the brown alga's polysaccharides. Similarly, the brown algae should not be used as the only source of trace elements, because the alginate they contain binds divalent cations *strongly* (cf. Chapters 8 and 9). In the light of such studies, one should treat with caution the data in Table 10 in which some rough calculations are given of the possible contribution of some elements and vitamins from seaweed meal. Manganese, molybdenum and silicon have proved essential in studies of animals, but so far no deficiency effects have been described for humans. Human physiological deficiencies have been described for iron, fluorine, zinc, chromium, selenium and copper.

Table 11 summarizes some of the data that exist about bound amino acids in seaweeds. The content of free amino acids is fairly high, being up to 10–20% of the total nitrogen content (when free nitrate is excluded). In 'hoshi-nori' from *Porphyra* sp. the contents of free alanine, glutamic acid and taurine are each about 15 mg g^{-1} dry weight. The characteristic, faintly sweet taste of 'hoshi-nori' is caused by the coexistence of relatively large amounts of alanine, glutamic acid and glycine (Nisizawa *et al.* 1987).

SPECIES USED

The following information is largely based on Madlener (1977), except where otherwise stated.

Table 10. Recommended daily intake for adults of some minerals and vitamins compared with their content in *Ascophyllum nodosum* meal

Element vitamin	Recommended daily adult intake (mg)	Approx. amount of *A. nodosum* seaweed meal containing this amount (g)
Iron		
Men	10	33
Women	18	60
Fluorine	1.4–4	55–160
Chromium	0.05–0.2	n.d.
Zinc	15	60–200
Copper	2–3	50–150
Iodine	0.05–0.3	0.1–0.6
Selenium	0.05–0.2	500–2000
Manganese	2.5–5	80–160
Molybdenum	0.15–0.5	300–1000
Vitamin A	0.8–1.0	10–30
Thiamin (B$_1$)	1.0≈100 μg MJ^{-1} energy intake	≈200–1000
Riboflavin (B$_2$)	140 μg MJ^{-1} energy intake	≈140–280
Niacin (B group)	1000 μg MJ^{-1} energy intake	≈1000–3000
Folic acid	0.4	800–2000
Pyridoxin (B$_6$)	2.0	n.d.
Pantothenic acid	No deficiencies reported	—
Biotin (H)	No deficiencies reported	—
Ascorbic acid (C)	30–75	0.02–0.14
Calciferol (D)	5–10 μg	n.d.
Tocopherols (E)	8–10 μg (as α–tocopherol)	0.04–0.14

Calculated from Food and Nutrition Board (1980) and Table 3. n.d., no data available.

European Species with Dietary Tradition

Chondrus crispus (Irish moss)

This species is perhaps the most famous seaweed used in Europe for food purposes, although it is mostly used indirectly (see carrageenan, Chapter 5). It is used in Brittany, Ireland and the UK, where it is boiled to utilize its thickening properties. The commercial supply is from Ireland and Brittany.

Palmaria palmata (= Rhodymenia palmata) (dulse, dillisk)

As mentioned earlier in this chapter the use of this species was recorded as one of the earliest in Europe, tradition recording its saltiness, which promotes thirst. In North America and Europe (Brittany, Ireland, Iceland) the frond is

Table 11. Amino acid composition (g amino acid nitrogen/100 g crude protein) of crude protein from various algae

	Green alga		Brown alga	Red algae		
	Ulva	sp.	*Laminaria hyperborea*	*Palmaria palmata*	*Porphyra tenera*	Whole egg
Reference	2	4	1	3	4	5
Essential amino acids						
Histidine (for children)	1.2	4.0	0.0[a]	1.2	1.4	n.d.
Isoleucine	n.d.	3.5	0.7	3.5	4.0	6.6
Leucine	5.2	6.9	7.0	5.9	8.7	8.8
Lysine	0.0	4.5	3.7	5.0	4.5	6.4
Methionine	0.0	1.6	0.9	4.5	1.7	3.1
Phenylalanine	2.3	3.9	1.1	4.4	3.9	5.8
Threonine	n.d.	3.1	3.1	4.1	4.0	5.1
Tryptophan	0.3	0.3	Traces[a]	3.0	1.3	1.6
Valine	5.2	4.9	3.5	5.1	6.4	7.3
Non-essential amino acids						
Alanine	6.5	6.1	8.5	6.3	7.4	
Arginine	7.5	14.9	12.3	4.6	16.4	
Aspartic acid	4.1	6.5	7.9	8.5	7.0	
Cystine	1.8	1.2	Traces[a]	1.4	0.3	
Glycine	0.8	5.2	3.1	4.9	7.2	
Glutamic acid	7.6	6.9	3.4	6.7	7.2	
Proline	7.0	4.0	3.9	4.4	6.4	
Serine	n.d.	3.0	3.2	4.0	2.9	
Tyrosine	0.0	1.4	0.9	1.3	2.4	

[a]For *Laminaria japonica* (Nisizawa *et al.* 1987) these occur in about the same amount: 1 g amino acid nitrogen per 100 g crude protein.
1, Frond (Coulson 1955).
2, Fowden (1962).
3, Averaged selected values from Morgan *et al.* (1980).
4, Arasaki and Arasaki (1983) (*Ulva pertusa*)
5, World Health Organization values (Anon. 1965) cited in Morgan *et al.* (1980).

eaten raw as a vegetable substitute or is dried and eaten as a condiment, or in a powdered form. Dulse is a good source of both minerals and vitamins compared with ordinary vegetables (Tables 2 and 8), as it contains all trace elements recognized in human physiological processes. It also has a high protein content (Morgan *et al.* 1980). Dulse had the highest protein quality of several marine algae examined by Larsen and Hawkins (1961). In Ireland, small quantities are collected by a company for drying and sale, either powdered or whole (Guiry & Blunden 1981). In Iceland, Hallsson (1964) stated that 'nowadays sól (= *P. palmata*) is only occasionally collected and dried [for human consumption]'.

Porphyra spp. *(red laver/purple laver)*

This is one of the few seaweed food staples currently in everyday use in Western Europe. It is particularly popular in parts of South Wales, but is also eaten elsewhere along the western coast of the UK and Ireland. The weed is washed four times to remove all traces of sand, and boiled for 8–12 h with salt and sufficient water to allow cooking without burning. When the frond has been reduced almost to a pulp the laver is sufficiently cooked. It is then taken out of the boiler and allowed to stand overnight, usually on a wooden table which allows any surplus liquid to drain away. Next day it is minced. The final blackish colour of laverbread is due to added colour. The prepared product looks like a dark (almost black) shiny gelatinous mass which has a pleasant flavour identical with the smell of seaweed on the shore (Hampson 1957). 'Laverbread' is prepared by warming it in bacon fat (or butter in Ireland), and it may first be made into small cakes coated with oatmeal. It normally takes the place of eggs, etc., with bacon for a breakfast dish and it is usually eaten during the weekend. The convention is that it should only be eaten in months with an 'r' (October–April), possibly due to deterioration of the plants in the hot weather (Hampson 1957, Moyse personal communication). Although a Welsh speciality, in 1965 60% of the raw material was collected in Stranraer, Scotland and Cumbria, England (Booth 1975). Swansea is, however, the only place where processing takes place. This is now generally done by one-man businesses, and the product is marketed in 0.5 or 1 lb packs weighed out in cellophane or polythene. The bulk of laverbread is eaten in the South Wales industrial region centred on Swansea, but there is now an increasing sale of canned laver to Welsh expatriates in North America, Australia and New Zealand (Moyse personal communication).

Ulva lactuca (sea lettuce)

This is locally used in Scotland, where it is added to soups or used in salads.

Alaria esculenta (wing kelp/honeyware/dabberlocks)

Of the kelps, *A. esculenta* is thought to be the best protein source, possibly because of its low phenol content. It also has a reasonably low amount of iodine. The sporophylls are considered a special treat, being very low in phenolic compounds (Steinberg 1984). *Alaria* is used either fresh or cooked, in Greenland, Iceland, Scotland and Ireland, but is not available commercially. Large-scale cultivation of this species off the Isle of Man is now under way with the intention of marketing the alga (and also *L. saccharina*) for human nutrition, for example, as a French-fry snack (Kain & Dawes 1987; Chapter 10).

Ascophyllum nodosum (egg wrack/knotted wrack/knobbed wrack)

This species had no previous tradition in Europe for human nutrition before the industrial production of seaweed meal (Table 1).

Fucus vesiculosus (bladderwrack)

The boiled broth has found use as a health drink.

Laminaria digitata (fingered tangle)

Used dried and rehydrated, and marketed under the name 'Kombu Breton', *L. digitata* is a newcomer to human nutrition in Northern France (Brault & Briand 1987).

Laminaria saccharina (sugar wrack)

Young stipes are used fresh. Otherwise the alga is eaten in various forms as a vegetable in coastal Western Europe.

European Species with no Dietary Traditions, but with Reported Use in Human Nutrition on Other Continents

Petalonia fascia (flower seaweed) is used fresh or dried in Japan.

Bangia atropurpurea (= *B. fuscopurpurea*) (cow hair) has been used in vegetarian recipes in the Far East.

Chorda filum (mermaid's fishing line/mermaid's tresses) is used fresh in Japan.

Codium fragile is used fresh or boiled in Korea and Japan.

Enteromorpha intestinalis (green nori) is used fresh, dried or steamed in the Far East.

Gracilaria verrucosa is used fresh or, as it is an agarophyte, as a thickening agent.

Scytosiphon lomentaria is used dried, either eaten directly or mixed into soups.

In a rather special position is the previously mentioned Far Eastern species *Undaria pinnatifida* (wakame/sea mustard), which is being experimentally cultivated in France for potential human consumption (Perez *et al.* 1984; Vinot *et al.* 1987).

Other Aspects of Seaweeds and Human Nutrition

Some aspects of the dietary use of seaweeds are in the border area between preventive medicine and nutrition. For further information see Hoppe *et al.* (1979), Hoppe and Levring (1982), and Stein and Borden (1984).

A bulk use of seaweeds as a food material with obvious therapeutic benefits is found in the brown algae which contain iodine to combat endemic goitre. More than 200 million people around the world are said to suffer from goitre (Anon. 1981). Kelp as a diet iodine source finds its most widespread use in the inland distribution of 'haidai' (made from *L. japonica*) in the People's Republic of China (Michanek 1981). However, ingestion of large amounts of seaweeds leading to excess iodine in the body may itself be the cause of goitre (Wolff 1969), although rats fed with eggs from hens supplied with food containing seaweeds rich in iodine did not display any negative effects (Katamine *et al.* 1987; see p. 36).

The polysaccharides of the macroalgae, especially those of the Phaeophyceae, have some very special ion-exchange affinities for divalent cations such as Ca^{2+} (Tsytsugina *et al.* 1975, and Chapter 7). This might be both an advantage and a source of possible contamination when ingested. A major problem with the proposed use of alginates to cleanse the body of unwanted heavy metals (like ^{90}Sr) is that the algal polysaccharides must be ingested simultaneously with the contaminant (Tanaka *et al.* 1972).

The intake of fish and seafood (including macroalgae) is very much higher in Japan than in inland countries like Germany and Finland, with a corresponding 20-fold increase in intake of both cadmium and lead in Japan. This may reflect both possible environmental conditions and differences in the basic concentration of heavy metals in the different food ingredients for the different regions (Louekari & Salminen 1986). Consuming large amounts of seaweed is thought to be a potential cause of human arsenic poisoning (Walkiw & Douglas 1975), but Watanabe *et al.* (1979, cited in Teas 1983) found that arsenic was in a form in the seaweed that was not assimilable. Only the Far Eastern species *Hizikia fusiforme* is reported to contain large amounts of the inorganic toxic form (As^{3+}) (Nisizawa *et al.* 1987). Investigating kelp-containing dietary supplements on sale in the UK in 1986, Norman *et al.* (1988) found that the levels of reducible arsenic were generally low, and ingestion of the products was unlikely to exceed the daily tolerance levels set by the Joint Expert Committee on Food Additives (JECFA).

Of the macroalgae, Russell (1984) lists *Caulerpa* sp. (Chlorophyceae) as being reported in association with kills of marine organisms, and *Turbinaria ornata* (Phaeophyceae) as creating gastrointestinal distress in humans. Hashimoto (1979, cited in Stein & Bordern 1984) listed the macroscopic algae *Nemacystis decipiens*, *Cladosiphon okamuranus* (Chordariales, Phaeophyceae) and *Caulerpa* spp. (Caulerpales, Chlorophyceae) as producing toxic reactions. Neurotoxins from *Caulerpa* sp. were reported by Schantz (1970) to cause dizziness, but without well defined symptoms. In comparison with the more than 1200 toxic marine organisms that were included in Russell's review, one must conclude that the macroalgae as a group are more or less non-toxic. None of the species mentioned above is found in Europe; they are all tropical and subtropical in distribution and not usual diet ingredients.

With a few exceptions, mutagenic agents are carcinogenic (Sugimura & Nagao 1979), and when found in cooked food their presence should be a basis for corrective action. Mower (1983) listed more than a hundred low-molecular-weight halogenated alkanes and alkenes, of which many are supposedly mutagenic, found in the red algal genus *Asparagopsis*. *Asparagopsis taxiformis* is eaten in Hawaii (Abbott 1978) and may contribute to a number of cancer incidences there. When food is either broiled or fried, pyrolysis effects may yield new classes of mutagenic compounds. This may also be the case for seaweeds, but Sugimura and Nagao (1979) also stated that food material with a low water content yielded mutagens at 300 °C, while materials with a high water content (like fresh seaweeds) needed 400 °C to yield mutagens. Furthermore, it was stated that the degree of mutagenicity was closely related to the protein content; foodstuffs containing less than 10% protein did not yield significant amounts of mutagenic agents.

As seaweeds are used very little in the European diet, they do not usually enter the human food chain. However, because of the practice of eating laverbread (from *Porphyra* spp.) in Wales, *Porphyra* spp. are being monitored for content of radionuclides. Off the coast of Cumbria, activity levels were a maximum of 1100 Bq kg^{-1} wet weight, 90% of which originated from ^{106}Ru (Hunt 1986a). In laverbread the total β count was only 92 Bq kg^{-1} at most, with a calculated exposure of critical laverbread consumers at less than 0.01 mSv, suggesting little difficulty with this pathway. In a later report in the same year (Hunt 1986b), the effects of the Chernobyl Reactor accident in the USSR were included. Although levels in *Porphyra* spp. of 1000–3000 Bq kg^{-1} were found in the first few weeks after the accident, by the end of June 1986 levels were no more than about 100 Bq kg^{-1}, with no significant differences between brown and red algae. Peak levels were found in places where *Porphyra* spp. were not normally harvested for human consumption. In addition, red algae do not contain polysaccharides with the same extreme ability to incorporate divalent heavy metals as those from brown algae (see Chapter 7).

Even though European usage of whole seaweed in everyday cooking is minimal, the use of phycocolloids in the food industry is quite considerable. We eat a small volume of algal polysaccharides every day, for example through ready-made dressings, ice-cream, mayonnaise and ketchup (see Chapter 5; Glicksman 1983, 1987; King 1983).

Commercially, recognition as GRAS (Generally Recognized As Safe) by the US Food and Drug Administration is critical. In 1978, the brown alga *Macrocystis pyrifera* was accepted, but the terms 'Algae, brown' 'Algae, red' 'Dulse' and 'Kelp (see algae, brown)' were rejected as these group terms were too ill-defined, and there was hardly any written information about their use in the USA (Food and Drug Administration 1978). The Select Committee carrying out this investigation concluded, however, that 'there is no available information on the brown algae (*Laminaria* sp. and *Nereocystis* sp.), also

referred to as kelp, and the red algae *Porphyra* sp. and *Rhodymenia palmata*
(L.) Grev. [now known as *Palmaria palmata* (L.) Kuntze], also referred to as
dulse, and the materials derived from these species, that demonstrates or
suggests reasonable grounds to suspect a hazard to the public when they are
used at levels that now seem to be current or that might reasonably be
expected in the future if their use is confined to ingredients of spices,
seasonings, and flavorings.'

A vibrantly positive view of dietary intake of algae is taken by Teas (1983),
when she speculates about the possible positive influence of eating *Laminaria*
spp. for cancer prevention (see Stein & Borden 1984). This, she argues, might
be due to its content of indigestible fibre, antibiotic effects or content of β-
1,3-glucans, which alter the enzymatic activity of the faecal flora and stimulate the host-mediated immune response. She concluded that, on the basis of
current information, the brown seaweeds seem to be neither carcinogenic nor
toxic.

A relatively modest amount of specially produced meal from *Laminaria*
spp., and some seaweed meal from *Ascophyllum nodosum*, is used for human
consumption. This is sold on the basis of the content of fibre, minerals and
vitamins. It may be taken mixed with water or a few spoonfuls may be added
to the dough when making bread. Its use in bread for a slimming diet is even
part of a French patent (Leriche 1971). Seaweeds are now also firmly
anchored in the healthfood market. Many humdrum oriental seaweeds and
seaweed products are thus resold in Europe as specialities. One can also find
neatly packaged seaweed meal in gelatin capsules fetching high prices. But
even if this market increased many times it would hardly register as a major
volume increase in the total seaweed consumption in Europe.

CONCLUSIONS AND OUTLOOKS

ANIMAL NUTRITION

When performing feeding experiments it is vital to keep in mind that even
small reductions in the protein content of the diet may cause considerable
decrease in growth rates, especially at relatively low protein levels. The
chemical composition of seaweed meal, as from *Ascophyllum nodosum*,
immediately characterizes the material as being low in energy, especially for
non-ruminants. The overall content of vitamins and minerals is also too low to
contribute significantly as a sole source of these substances. The only exception is an iodine content that will cover the needs of domesticated animals.
Iodine requirements vary with various animals, in the range $0.2\text{--}0.6$ mg kg^{-1}
dry matter. With about 500 mg iodine kg^{-1} seaweed meal, $1\text{--}3$ g seaweed
meal kg^{-1} dry matter of fodder will suffice.

Under Norwegian law, up to 3% grass meal and seaweed meal addition in feedstuff mixtures may be used. The actual use is limited to 0.5–1% in some fodder mixtures for poultry and 1–2% in horse fodder. In mineral mixtures a maximum of 50% may be of organic origin as carried. In Norway, about 40 000 t minerals are used annually for mixing into various compounded feedstuffs. In the standardized mineral mixtures, 3.5–6% *A. nodosum* meal is used as carrier. About 30% *A. nodosum* meal may be used in some other fodder supplements. In Norway in the late 1970s, the total use of *A. nodosum* meal for this purpose was 700–1000 t year^{-1}. There is an official recommendation in Norway that seaweed meal should be used instead of inorganic iodine in compound feeds. Mineral mixtures for domestic animals must contain 60–80 mg iodine kg^{-1}, and today 2% of compound feeds are minerals. If this was substituted with *A. nodosum* meal with an average content of 500 mg iodine kg^{-1}, the annual requirement in Norway would result in a demand for 3500–4000 t seaweed meal each year.

However, at present it seems to be the price of the seaweed meal that prevents its further use as a fodder component instead of grass meal and other mineral additives. Norwegian authorities state that compound feeds should be as cheap as possible, and they are reluctant to make addition of seaweed meal to animal fodder mandatory.

Is *A. nodosum* the best choice of a seaweed for animal supplemental feed? Neither the analytical data nor the feeding experiments gives it any advantage over other seaweed species. The main reason for its wide usage is that it is in an easily accessible part of the intertidal zone (Jensen 1960). Added to this is its use as a raw material for the extraction of certain alginates. A survey of earlier peasant uses of seaweeds in coastal Norway for supplemental feed suggests that the most sought after species were *Alaria esculenta* (cattle-kelp) and *Palmaria palmata* (Høegh 1975) (described by an early Norwegian botanist as *Fucus ovinus*; sheepwrack). It was, however, found necessary to steep the algae in hot water in order to remove laxative substances before it was given as roughage to animals. Baardseth (1970) claimed that *A. nodosum* treated in this way resulted in an inferior type of fodder.

Why not take a closer look at other species that might have a more favourable composition, for example containing a minimum of phenols? In terrestrial agriculture, expanded availability of desirable species has always been effected by cultivation. Agriculture is subsidized in many national economies to provide citizens with products from plants that are often not indigenous to the country and thus need to be manipulated in order to survive. As for human nutrition, the choice of species will then be much wider, and the recognition of the species diversity more easily accepted.

If, for example, *A. esculenta* was available in sufficient quantities, perhaps through cultivation, this could mean an improved use both in quality and in quantity. Norway, like many other countries, has to import high-carbohydrate fodder (about 400 000 t every year). If only 10% of this could be substituted with a seaweed meal better than that made from *A. nodosum*, it would mean saving 40 000 of imported fodder per year.

The making of yeast protein from seaweed carbohydrates may be one way to utilize the fodder potential of the macroalgae (Nadson *et al.* 1923, cited in Seshadri & Sieburth 1975). This may become essential to cover the increasing need for fodder in the fish-farming business.

HUMAN NUTRITION

The addition of seaweed meal as a source of iodine and other minerals to the diets of fast-growing children and pregnant women may be advisable even in countries with otherwise rationally balanced diets. However, one may argue that a better means of introducing these elements into the diet would be to use seaweed meal as animal feed or to fertilize the plants whose products are eventually consumed by humans. This would correct deficiencies in humans, animals and plants. In many countries a significant number of cattle suffer iodine deficiency and produce milk that is very low in iodine. Intensive European agriculture, both plant and animal, is not balanced from the aspect of mineral supply and removal. The positive effects resulting from the use of a small amount of seaweeds in the daily food of animals, by increasing the mineral content of the diet, is fairly well documented. Used as a supplement of 3–7%, no negative effects could be found, and conventional mineral and vitamin mixtures may be substituted by seaweed meal according to the quantity of each substance in the seaweed. One would expect that this would also hold true for human physiology. The case for seaweeds as a well balanced, harmless, natural source with a high degree of bioavailability of trace elements is strongly advocated by Booth (1964). He pointed to the seaweed meal content of iron, copper, iodine, cobalt, zinc, magnesium and boron.

As already stated, the use of sea vegetables in the same way as terrestrial vegetables seems to be the natural way to proceed. This will, however, require a change in the use of vegetables. Unfamiliar and exotic fruits and vegetables increasingly find their way into European households, so attitudes towards sea vegetables may change rapidly. It seems to be mostly a question of proper marketing, which would help in revising the myths about the benefits of seaweeds and give them their proper place in nutrition. If, for example, the same market volume for seaweed was attained as we now have for cucumber and lettuce, this would result in an explosion in the demand for seaweeds. As in agriculture, cultivation would be required to supply the right species of the best quality at the right time. This maricultural work is already under way, both with classical agriculture methods for plant selection (Fang 1983; Miura *et al.* 1979), and through modern biotechnical approaches (Cheney 1986).

ACKNOWLEDGEMENTS

One of the authors (M.I.) thanks the Bioenergy Programme of the Norwegian Research Council for Agriculture for financial support of this work.

REFERENCES

Aas T. 1982. Forsøk med rapsmel til slaktegris, Staur 1981/82. Bilag IV/8 til orienteringsmøte, Institutt for Husdyrernæring og Fôringslære, Norges Landbrukshøyskole, Ås, may 1982. (In Norwegian.)

Abbott I.A. 1978. The uses of seaweed as food in Hawaii. *Econ. Bot.* **32**: 409–12.

Anon. 1965. *Protein Requirements*. World Health Organization Tech. Rep. Ser. 301.

Anon. 1981. *Sci. News*, 4 April.

Appler H.N. & Jauncey K. 1983. The utilization of a filamentous green alga (*Cladophora glomerata* (L.) Kützing) as a protein source in pelleted feeds for *Sarotherodon (Tilapia) niloticus* fingerlings. *Aquaculture* **30**: 21–30.

Arasaki S. & Arasaki T. 1983. *Vegetables from the sea*. Tokyo: Japan Publ. Inc.

Astrup H.N. 1982. Får kua nok jod? Bilag 57, Samrådingsmøte, Inst. for Husdyrernæring og Fôringslære, Norges Landbrukshøyskole, Ås. (In Norwegian.)

Baardseth E. 1970. Synopsis of biological data on knobbed wrack *Ascophyllum nodosum* (L.) Le Jolis. *Fish. Synop. FAO* No. 38 Rev. **1**: v + 44.

Baardseth E. & Haug A. 1953. *Individual Variation of Some Constituents in Brown algae, and Reliability of Analytical Results*. Rep. Norw. Inst. Seaweed Res. No. 2.

Baggesgaard-Rasmussen H. & Bjerresø G. 1941. Om jodingdoldet i tang, samt lidt om tangens øvrige indholdsstoffer. 2. Bestemmelse av jodmængder i alger. *Dansk Tidsskr. Farmaci* **15**: 132–43. (In Danish.)

Baker H.J. & Lindsey J.R. 1968. Equine goiter due to excess dietary iodine. *J. Am. Vet. Med. Assoc.* **153**: 1618–30.

Bernstein B.B., Schroeter S.C. & Mann K.H. 1983. Sea urchin (*Strongylocentrotus droebachiensis*) aggregating behavior investigated by a subtidal multifactorial experiment. *Can. J. Fish. Aquat. Sci.* **40**: 1975–86.

Blunden G. & Jones R.T. 1972. Toxic effects of *Ascophyllum nodosum* as a rabbit food additive. *Proceedings of the Marine Technology Society: Food–Drugs from the Sea.* **1972**: 267–73.

Boney A.D. 1965. Aspects of the biology of the seaweeds of economic importance. In *Advances in Marine Biology*. Vol. 3. (Ed. F.S. Russell) pp. 105–253. London: Academic Press.

Booth E. 1964. Trace elements and seaweeds. In *Proceedings of the 4th International Seaweed Symposium*. (Eds. A.D. De Virville & J. Feldmann) pp. 385–93. London: Macmillan.

Booth E. 1975. Seaweeds in industry. In *Chemical Oceanography*. Vol. 4. (Eds. J.D. Riley & G. Skirrow) pp. 219–68. London: Academic Press.

Booth E. 1979. The history of the seaweed industry. Part 3. The iodine industry. *Chem. Ind.* **1979**: 52–5.

Brault D. & Briand X. 1987. L'algue alimentaire humaine, perspectives de développement en France. *Equinoxe* **16**: 4–13. (In French.)

Briand X. 1987. *L'Industrie 'Algue alimentaire': Une realité economique. Symposium sur les Algues/Brest le 19 novembre 1987*. Brest: Université de Bretagne Occidentale.

Bridget D., Barber W.P. & Williams D.G. 1975. The effect of dietary iodine on pregnant mares and foals. *Vet. Rec.* **97**: 93–4.

Bruhn J.C., Franke A.A., Bushnell R.B., Weisheit H., Hutton G.H. & Gurtle G.C. 1983. Sources and content of iodine in California milk and dairy products. *J. Food Protection* **46**: 41–6.

Chapman V.J. 1950. *Seaweeds and their Uses.* London: Methuen.

Chapman V.J. & Chapman D.G. 1980. *Seaweeds and their Uses.* 2nd edn. London: Chapman and Hall.

Cheney D.P. 1986. Genetic engineering in seaweeds: applications and current status. In *Algal Biomass Technologies.* (Eds. W.R. Barclay & R.P. McIntosh) pp. 22–30. Berlin: J. Cramer.

Convey E.M., Chapin L., Kesner J.S., Hillman D. & Curtis A.R. 1977. Serum thyroprotein and thyroxine after thyrotropin releasing hormone in dairy cows fed varying amounts of iodine. *J. Dairy Sci.* **60**: 975–80.

Coulson C.B. 1955. Plant proteins. 1. Proteins and amino-acids of marine algae. *J. Sci. Food Agric.* **6**: 674–82.

Duggins D.O. 1980. Kelp beds and sea otters: an experimental approach. *Ecology* **61**: 447–53.

Eeg-Larsen N. & Nes M. 1984. *Ernæringslære.* Oslo: Landsforeningen for kosthold og helse. (In Norwegian.)

Engdahl O.T. & Ulvesli O. 1942. Forsøk med mineraltilskudd til lam. (Experiments on mineral supplements for lambs.) Ås: Institutt for Husdyrernæring og Fôringslære, Norges Landbrukshøyskole, Beretn. nr. 52 (In Norwegian with English Summary.)

Ericson L.-E. & Lewis L. 1953. On the occurrence of vitamin B$_{12}$-factors in marine algae. *Ark. Kemi* **6**: 427–42.

Fang T.C. 1983. A summary of the genetic studies of *Laminaria japonica* in China. In *Proceedings of the Joint China-US Phycology Symposium.* (Ed. C.K. Tseng) pp. 123–37. Beijing: Science Press.

Food and Drug Administration 1978. Certain brown and red algae and their extractives. Proposed affirmation of GRAS status of a brown alga, with specific limitations as a direct human food ingredient. *Federal Register* **43**(151): 34500–3.

Food and Nutrition Board 1980. *Recommended dietary allowances.* 9th edn. Washington DC: National Academy of Sciences.

Fowden L. 1962. Amino acids and proteins. In *The Physiology and Biochemistry of Algae.* (Ed. R.A. Lewin) pp. 189–206. New York: Academic Press.

Gayral P. & Cosson J. 1973. Exposé synoptique des données biologiques sur la laminaire digitée *Laminarta digitata. Fish. Synop. FAO* No. 89: v + 45. (In French.)

Glicksman M. 1983. Red seaweed extracts (agar, carrageenan, furcellaran). *Food Hydrocoll.* **2**: 73–113.

Glicksman M. 1987. Utilization of seaweed hydrocolloids in the food industry. In *Proceedings of the 12th International Seaweed Symposium.* (Eds. M.A. Ragan & C.J. Bird) pp. 31–49. Dordrecht: Dr. W. Junk Publ.

Guiry M.D. & Blunden G. 1980. What hope for Irish seaweed? *Technology Ireland* September: 38–43.

Guiry M.D. & Blunden G. 1981. The commercial collection and utilisation of seaweeds in Ireland. In *Proceedings of the 10th International Seaweed Symposium.* (Ed. T. Levring) pp. 675–80. Berlin: de Gruyter.

Hagen N.T. 1983. Destructive grazing of kelp beds by sea urchins in Vestfjorden, Northern Norway. *Sarsia* **68**: 177–90.

Hallsson S.V. 1964. The uses of seaweeds on Iceland. In *Proceedings of the 4th International Seaweed Symposium.* (Eds. A.D. de Virville & J. Feldmann) pp. 398–405. Oxford: Pergamon Press.

Hampson M.A. 1957. The laverbread industry in South Wales and the laverweed. *Fish. Invest.* Ser. II, **21**: 1–8.

Hashimoto Y. 1979. *Marine Toxins and other Bioactive Marine Metabolites.* Tokyo: Japan Scientific Societies Press. (Cited in Stein & Borden 1984.)

Haug A. 1956. Nyere undersøkelser over tang- og tare-artenes kjemi. *Tidsskr. Kjemi, Bergvesen Metallurgi* **1**: 1–8. (In Norwegian.)

Haug A. & Jensen A. 1954. *Seasonal Variations in the Chemical Composition of* Alaria esculenta, Laminaria saccharina, Laminaria hyperborea *and* Laminaria digitata *from Northern Norway.* Rep. Norw. Inst. Seaweed Res. No. 4.

Haug A. & Larsen B. 1957. *Carotene Content of Seaweed and Seaweed Meal.* Rep. Norw. Inst. Seaweed Res. No. 15.

Haug A. & Larsen B. 1958. Chemical composition of the brown alga *Ascophyllum nodosum* (L.) Le Jol: influence of habitat on the chemical composition of *Ascophyllum nodosum. Nature Lond.* **181**: 1225.

Hemken R.W., Fox J.D. & Hicks C.L. 1981. Milk iodine content as influenced by feed sources and sanitizer residues. *J. Food Protection* **44**: 476–9.

Høegh O.A. 1975. *Planter og tradisjon.* Oslo: Universitetsforlaget. (In Norwegian.)

Høie J. & Sandvik Ø. 1955. *Forsøk med tang- og taremjøl som sikringsfôr til kyllinger og høner.* (Experiments with seaweed meals as supplements to rations for chicks and laying hens. 8th Report from the Institute of Poultry and Fur Animals. The Agricultural College of Norway). Ås: Norges Landbrukshøyskole, Intitutt for Fjørfe og Pelsdyr, Melding nr. 8. (In Norwegian with English Summary.)

Høie J. & Sannan F. 1960. *Forsøk med tang- og tare-mjøl som sikringsfôr til kyllinger og høner (II).* (Experiments with seaweed meals as supplements to rations for chicks and laying hens (II). *Scientific Reports from The Agricultural College of Norway.* Vol. **39**(19)). Ås: Norges Landbrukshøyskole, *Meldinger fra Norges Landbrukshøyskole* **39**(19). (In Norwegian with English Summary.)

Homb T. 1961. *Forsøk med tilskudd av tangmel til slaktesvin.* (Experiments on seaweed meal as an ingredient in feed mixtures for bacon pigs). Ås: Institutt for Husdyrernæring og Fôringslære, Norges Landbrukshæyskole. Beretn. nr. 106. (In Norwegian with English Summary.)

Homb T. 1981. Rapsfrø og ekstrahert rapsmel i norsk drøvtyggerernæring. Unpublished lecture manuscript. (In Norwegian.)

Hoppe H.A. & Levring T. 1982. *Marine Algae in Pharmaceutical Science.* Vol. 2. Berlin: de Gruyter.

Hoppe H.A., Levring T. & Tanaka Y. 1979. *Marine Algae in Pharmaceutical Science.* Berlin: de Gruyter.

Hunt G.J. 1986a. *Radioactivity in Surface and Coastal Waters of the British Isles, 1985.* Aquatic Environment Monitoring Report No. 14, Ministry of Agriculture, Fisheries and Food, Directorate of Fisheries Research, Lowestoft, 48 pp.

Hunt G.J. 1986b. *Radioactivity in Surface and Coastal Waters of the British Isles. Monitoring of Fallout from the Chernobyl Reactor Accident.* Aquatic Environment Monitoring Report No. 15, Ministry of Agriculture, Fisheries and Food, Directorate of Fisheries Research, Lowestoft, 39 pp.

Isaachsen H., Fridrichsen E., Aafhamar O., Bangsandmo F. 1917. *Forsøk med tørket tang til melkefe.* Ås: Norges Landbrukshøyskole, Institutt for Husdyrernæring og Fôringslære, Beretn. nr. 10. (In Norwegian.)

Jensen A. 1956a. *Component Sugars of Some Common Brown Algae.* Rep. Norw. Inst. Seaweed Res. No. 9.

Jensen A. 1956b. *Preliminary Investigation of the Carbohydrates of* Laminaria digitata *and* Fucus serratus. Rep. Norw. Inst. Seaweed Res. No. 10.

Jensen A. 1958. *Experiments on the Feeding of Seaweed Meal to Domestic Animals.* Rep. Norw. Inst. Seaweed Res. No. 20, pp. 25–8.

Jensen A. 1959. Tang og tare. Forekomster, kjemi og anvendelse. *Tidsskr. Kjemi, Bergvesen Metallurgi* **3**: 51–6. (In Norwegian).

Jensen A. 1960. *Produksjon av tangmel.* Rep. Norw. Inst. Seaweed Res. No. 24. (In Norwegian).

Jensen A. 1963a. Ascorbic acid in *Ascophyllum nodosum, Fucus serratus*, and *Fucus vesiculosus*. In *Proceedings of the 4th International Seaweed Symposium*. (Eds. A.D. de Virville & J. Feldmann) pp. 319–25. Oxford: Pergamon Press.

Jensen A. 1963b. The effect of seaweed carotenoids on egg yolk coloration. *Poultry Sci.* **42**: 912–16.

Jensen A. 1969. Tocopherol content of seaweed and seaweed meal. II. Individual, diurnal and seasonal variations in some Fucaceae. *J. Sci. Food Agric.* **20**: 454–8.

Jensen A. 1978. Industrial utilization of seaweeds in the past, present and future. In *Proceedings of the 9th International Seaweed Symposium*. (Eds. A. Jensen & J.R. Stein) pp. 17–34. Princeton: Science Press.

Jensen A. & Minsaas J. 1960. Forsøk med tangmel som tilskuddsfôr til slaktesvin. (Experiments with Seaweed Meal in Rations for Growing Fattening Pigs). *Tidsskr. Det Norske Landbruk* **67**: 81–96 (In Norwegian with English Summary).

Jensen A., Nebb H. & Sæter E.A. 1968. *The Value of Norwegian Seaweed Meal as Mineral Supplement for Dairy Cows*. Rep. Norw. Inst. Seaweed Res. No. 32.

Johansen O. & Steinnes E. 1976. Determination of iodine in plant material by a neutron-activation method. *Analyst* **101**: 455–7.

Johnston H.W. 1972. Analysis of edible Japanese seaweeds. In *Proceedings of the 7th International Seaweed Symposium*. (Ed. K. Nisizawa) pp. 429–35. Tokyo: University of Tokyo Press.

Jones R.T., Blunden G. & Probert A.J. 1981. Effects of dietary *Ascophyllum nodosum* on blood parameters of rabbits, rats and pigs. In *Proceedings of the 8th International Seaweed Symposium*. (Eds. G.E. Fogg & W.E. Jones) pp. 718–23. Menai Bridge: The Marine Science Laboratory.

Kain J.M. & Dawes C.P. 1987. Useful European seaweeds: past hopes and present cultivation. In *Proceedings of the 12th International Seaweed Symposium*. (Eds. M.A. Ragan & C.J. Bird) pp. 173–81. Dordrecht: Junk.

Karlström O. 1963. *The Vitamin B_{12} Content of Marine Algae*. Rep. Norw. Inst. Seaweed Res. No. 29.

Katamine S., Tanaami S., Sekimoto K., Hoshino N., Totsuka K. & Suzuki M. 1987. Nutritional implications of high-iodine egg diet in rats: effects on lipid metabolism and thyroid function. *Drugs Exp. Clin. Res.* **13**: 1–4.

Kazanas N. 1987. Pathogenic fungi isolated from desiccated mushrooms, seaweed, anchovies and rice sticks imported from the Orient. *J. Food Protection* **50**: 933–9.

Kim H. & Zemel M.B. 1986. *In vitro* estimation of the potential bioavailability of calcium from sea mustard (*Undaria pinnatifida*), milk, and spinach under simulated normal and reduced gastric acid conditions. *J. Food Sci.* **51**: 957–9.

Kimura T. 1952. Japanese Foods – 8. Digestibility of some seaweeds. *J. Jap. Soc. Food Nutr.* **5**: 176–9. (In Japanese; cited in Boney 1965).

King A.H. 1983. Brown seaweed extracts (alginates). *Food Hydrocoll.* **2**: 155–88.

Larsen B. 1958. *The Influence of Season, Habitat and Age of Tissue on the Niacin Content of Some Brown Algae*. Rep. Norw. Inst. Seaweed Res. No. 19.

Larsen B. 1961. *The Biotin Content of Marine Algae*. Rep. Norw. Inst. Seaweed Res. No. 26.

Larsen, B. 1978. Brown seaweeds: analysis of ash, fiber, iodine, and mannitol. In *Handbook of Phycological Methods. Physiological and Biochemical Methods*. (Eds. J.A. Hellebust & J.S. Craigie) pp. 181–9. Cambridge: Cambridge University Press.

Larsen B. & Haug A. 1956. *The Influence of Habitat on the Chemical Composition of*

Ascophyllum nodosum *(L.) Le Jol.* Rep. Norw. Inst. Seaweed Res. No. 20, pp. 29–38.

Larsen B. & Haug A. 1958. Chemical composition of the brown alga *Ascophyllum nodosum* (L.) Le Jol. Presence of reducing compounds in *Ascophyllum nodosum*. *Nature Lond.* **181**: 1224.

Larsen B.A. & Hawkins W.W. 1961. Nutritional value as protein of some of the nitrogenous constituents of two marine algae, *Chondrus crispus* and *Laminaria digitata. J. Sci. Food Agric.* **12**: 523–9.

Leriche R.R.L. 1971. Pain spécial pour régime amaigrissant. French Patent 2 076 436 (Copy no. 70.01328). (In French).

Levring T., Hoppe H.A. & Schmid O.J. 1969. *Marine Algae – A Survey of Research and Utilization.* Hamburg: Cram, de Gruyter.

Lewis P.A., Hemken R.W. & Crist W.L. 1980. Effect of teat dip viscosity on milk iodine levels. *J. Dairy Sci.* **63**(Suppl. 1): 182–3.

Liewendahl T. 1972. Iodine induced goiter and hypothyroidism in a patient with chronic, lymphocytic thyroiditis. *Acta Endocrinol.* **71**: 289–96.

Lindell L. & Knutsson P.G. 1976. Rapeseed meal for dairy cows. 1. Comparison of three levels of rapeseed meal. *Swed. J. Agric. Res.* **6**: 55–63.

Louekari K. & Salminen S. 1986. Intake of heavy metals from foods in Finland, West Germany and Japan. *Food Addit. Contam.* **3**: 355–62.

Lunde G. 1970. Analysis of trace elements in seaweed. *J. Sci. Food Agric.* **21**: 416–18.

Madlener J.C. 1977. *The Seavegetable Book.* New York: Clarkson N. Potter Inc.

McCandless E.L. 1981. Polysaccharides of the seaweeds. In *The Biology of Seaweeds.* (Eds. C.S. Lobban & M.J. Wynne) pp. 559–88. Oxford: Blackwell.

Michanek G. 1981. Getting seaweed to where it's needed. *Ceres* January–February: 41–4.

Minsaas, J. 1985. *Markedsforhold og utviklingsmuligheter i tangmelindustrien.* Trondheim: Selskapet for Industriell og Teknisk Forskning Rapport STF21 A85010. (In Norwegian).

Miura A., Fuijo Y. & Suto S. 1979. Genetic differentiation between the wild and cultured populations of *Porphyra yezoensis. Tohoku J. Agric. Res.* **30**: 114–25.

Montgomery W.L. & Gerking S.D. 1980. Marine macroalgae as foods for fishes: an evaluation of potential food quality. *Environ. Biol. Fishes* **5**: 143–53.

Morgan K.C., Wright J.L.C. & Simpson F.J. 1980. Review of chemical constituents of red alga *Palmaria palmata* (dulse). *Econ. Bot.* **34**: 27–50.

Mori B., Kusima K., Iwasaki T. & Okiya H. 1981. Dietary fiber content of seaweed. *Nippon Nōgeikagaku Kaishi* **55**: 787–91.

Morrison F.B. 1951. *Feeds and Feeding.* 21st edn. Ithaca: Morrison.

Mower H.F. 1983. Mutagenic compounds contained in seaweeds. In *Carcinogens and Mutagens in the Environment.* Vol. 3. (Ed. H.F. Stich) pp. 81–5. Boca Raton: CRC.

Nadson G., Konokotina A.G. & Burgwitz G.K. 1923. Marine algae as source for the cultivation of yeasts, fats and alcohol. *Izv. Glav. Bot. Sada RSFSR.* (In Russian; cited in Seshadri & Sieburth 1975).

Nakagawa H., Kasahara S. & Sugiyama T. 1986. Influence of *Ulva* meal supplement to diet on plasma lipoprotein of Black Sea Bream. *J. Fac. Appl. Biol. Sci. Hiroshima Univ.*, **25**: 11–18.

Nebb H. & Jensen A. 1966. Seaweed meal as a source of minerals and vitamins in rations for dairy cows and bacon pigs. In *Proceedings of the 5th International Seaweed Symposium.* (Eds. E.G. Young & J.L. McLachlan; pp. 387–93. Oxford: Pergamon Press.

Newton L. 1951. *Seaweed Utilisation.* London: Sampson Low.

Nisizawa K., Noda H., Ryo K. & Watanabe T. 1987. The main seaweed foods in

Japan. In *Proceedings of the 12th International Seaweed Symposium*. (Eds. M.A. Ragan & C.J. Bird) pp. 5–29. Dordrecht: Junk.

Norman J.A., Pickford C.J., Sanders T.W. & Waller M. 1988. Human intake of arsenic and iodine from seaweed-based food supplements and health foods available in the UK. *Food Addit. Contam.* **5**: 103–9.

Olsen B.E. 1985. *Konsum av sjøplanter i Japan. Del I: Anvendelse.* Tromsø: Rapport Fiskeriteknologisk Forskn. Inst. (In Norwegian).

Orpin C.G., Greenwood Y., Hall F.J. & Paterson I.W. 1985. The rumen microbiology of seaweed digestion in Orkney sheep. *J. Appl. Bacteriol.* **58**: 585–96.

Ørud I., Homb T., Johnsgård K. & Skjerven O. 1964. Tangmeltilskudd til melkekyr. I. Virkningen på melkeavdråtten. II. Virkningen på fruktbarhet og sunnhetstilstand. *Tidsskr. Det Norske Landbruk* **111**: 137–50. (In Norwegian).

Paine R.T. & Vadas R.L. 1969. Calorific values of benthic marine algae and their postulated relation to invertebrate food preference. *Mar. Biol.* **4**: 79–86.

Painter T.J. 1983. Algal polysaccharides. In *The Polysaccharides*. Vol. 2. (Ed. G.O. Aspinall) pp. 196–286. London: Academic Press.

Paul V.J. & Hay M.E. 1986. Seaweed susceptibility to herbivory: chemical and morphological correlates. *Mar. Ecol. Prog. Ser.* **33**: 255–64.

Pearse J.S. & Hines A.H. 1979. Expansion of a Central California kelp forest following the mass mortality of sea urchins. *Mar. Biol.* **51**: 83–91.

Perez R., Kaas R. & Barbaroux O. 1984. Culture expérimentale de l'algue *Undaria pinnatifida* sur les côtes de France. *Sci. Pêche* **343**: 3–15.

Pringle, J.D., Sharp G.J. & Caddy J.F. 1980. *Proceedings of the workshop on the relationship between sea urchin grazing and commercial plant/animal harvesting.* Halifax: Department of Fisheries and Oceans Canada.

Ragan M.A. 1981. Chemical constituents of seaweeds. In *The Biology of Seaweeds*. (Eds. C.S. Lobban & M.J. Wynne) pp. 589–626. Oxford: Blackwell.

Ringen H. 1939. *Fôrverdien av tangmel.* (The nutritive value of seaweed). Ås: Norges Landbrukshøyskole, Institutt for Husdyrernæring og Fôringslære, Beretn. nr. 47. (In Norwegian with English Summary).

Russell F.E. 1984. Marine toxins and venomous and poisonous marine plants and animals. In *Advances in Marine Biology*. Vol. 21. (Eds. J.H.S. Blaxter, F.S. Russel & M. Yonge) pp. 60–233. London: Academic Press.

Ryu H.-S., Satterlee L.D. & Lee H.-H. 1982. Nitrogen conversion factors and *in vitro* protein digestibility of some seaweeds. *Bull. Korean Fish. Soc.* **15**: 263–70.

Sæter E.A. 1960. *Rapport over en reise til Skottland, Orknøyene, Shetlandsøyene og Færøyene fra 9/7 til 13/8-59.* Prelim. Rep. Norw. Inst. Seaweed Res. No. 97. (In Norwegian).

Sæter E.A. & Jensen A. 1957. *Forsøk med tangmel som tilskuddsfôr til sau.* Rep. Norw. Inst. Seaweed Res. No. 17. (In Norwegian with English Summary).

Schantz E.J. 1970. Algal toxins. In *Properties and Products of Algae*. (Ed. J.E. Jajic) pp. 83–96. New York: Plenum Press.

Scheibling R. 1986. Increased macroalgal abundance following mass mortalities of sea urchins (*Strongylocentrotus droebachiensis*) along the Atlantic coast of Nova Scotia. *Oecologia (Berlin)* **68**: 186–98.

Scott M.L., Nesheim M.C. & Young R.J. 1976. *Nutrition of the Chicken.* 2nd edn. Ithaca: M.L. Scott.

Seshadri R. & Sieburth J. McN. 1975. Seaweeds as a reservoir of *Candida* yeasts in inshore waters. *Mar. Biol.* **30**: 105–17.

Seterlund W., Høie J., Sannan F. & Raastad N. 1968. Forsøk med butare (*Alaria esculenta*) som sikringsfôr til kyllinger. (Experiments with Dabberlocks (*Alaria esculenta*) as supplement to rations for chicks). *Meld. Norges Landbrukshøgskole* **47**: 1–18. (In Norwegian with English Summary).

Shaw T.I. 1962. Halogens. In *Physiology and Biochemistry of Algae*. (Ed. R.A. Lewin) pp. 247–53. New York: Academic Press.

Siebert G. & Trautner K. 1985. Fluoride content of selected human food, pet food and related materials. *Z. Ernährungswiss*. **24**: 54–66.

Sieburth J. McN. & Jensen A. 1967. Effect of processing on the microflora of Norwegian seaweed meal, with observations on *Sporendonema minutum* (Høye) Frank and Hess. *Appl. Microbiol*. **15**: 830–8.

Sirota G.R. & Uthe J.F. 1979. Heavy metal residues in dulse, an edible seaweed. *Aquaculture* **18**: 41–4.

Skalla-Grimsson E. 1950. Egils Saga Skalla-Grimssonar. In *Islendinga sögur*. Vol. 4. (Ed. S. Bergsveinsson). Reykjavik: Bókaverzlun Sigurðar Kristjánssonar. (In Old Norwegian).

Stadniciuc M. & Calotoiu E. 1972. *Certain Aspects Regarding the Use of Marine Algae for Poultry Fodder*. Rep. Romanian Inst. Mar. Res. nr. 3, pp. 163–70.

Stein J.R. & Borden C.A. 1984. Causative and beneficial algae in human disease conditions: a review. *Phycologia* **23**: 485–501.

Steinberg P.D. 1984. Algal chemical defense against herbivores: allocation of phenolic compounds in the kelp *Alaria marginata*. *Science* **223**: 405–7.

Steinberg P.D. 1985. Feeding preferences of *Tegula funebralis* and chemical defenses of marine brown algae. *Ecol. Monogr*. **55**: 333–49.

Sugimura T. & Nagao M. 1979. Mutagenic factors in cooked foods. *CRC Crit. Rev. Toxicol*. **6**: 189–209

Tanaka Y., Hurlburt A.J., Angeloff L., Skoryna S.C. & Stara J.F. 1972. Application of algal polysaccharides as *in vivo* binders of metal pollutants. In *Proceedings of the 7th International Seaweed Symposium*. (Ed. K. Nisizawa) pp. 602–7. Tokyo: University of Tokyo Press.

Teas J. 1983. The dietary intake of *Laminaria*, a brown seaweed, and breast cancer prevention. *Nutr. Cancer* **4**: 217–22.

Tseng C.K. 1981. Commercial cultivation. In *The Biology of Seaweeds*. (Eds. C.S. Lobban & M.J. Wynne) pp. 680–725. Oxford: Blackwell.

Tsytsugina V.G., Risik N.S. & Lazorenko G.E. 1975. Extraction of radionuclides by alginic acid from seawater. In *Artificial and Natural Radionucleides in Marine Life* (Ed. G.G. Polikarpov) pp. 68–77. Jerusalem: Keter. (Translated from Russian).

Turvey J.R. 1978. Biochemistry of algal polysaccharides. In *Biochemistry of Carbohydrates*. Vol. II. (Ed. D.J. Manners) pp. 151–77. Baltimore: University Park Press.

Utne F., Gulbrandsen K.E., Rosenlund G. & Fosseide J.E. 1981. *Bindemidler i våtfôr til fisk*. Rep. Norw. Fish. Res. Council No. 1 711.17.

Vinogradov A.P. 1953. *The Elementary Chemical Composition of Marine Organisms*. New Haven: Sears Foundation for Marine Research.

Vinot C., Durand P., Leclercq M. & Bourgeay-Causse M. 1987. Étude de la composition biochimique d'*Undaria pinnatifida* en vue de son utilisation en alimentation humaine. (Studies on the biochemical composition of *Undaria pinnatifida* with a view to its utilisation in human feeding). *Sciences des Aliments* **7**: 589–601. (In French with English Summary).

Walkiw O. & Douglas D.E. 1975. Health-food supplements prepared from kelp: A source of elevated urinary arsenic. *Clin. Toxicol*. **8**: 325–31.

Watanabe T., Hirayama T., Takahashi T., Kokubu T. & Ikeda M. 1979. Toxicological evaluation of arsenic in edible seaweed *Hizikia* species. *Toxicology* **14**: 1–22. (Cited in Teas 1983).

Wheeler S.M., Fleet G.H. & Ashley R.J. 1982. The contamination of milk with iodine from iodophors used in milking machine sanitation. *J. Sci. Food Agric*. **33**: 987–95.

Whittemore C.T. & Percival J.K. 1975. A seaweed residue unsuitable as a major source of energy or nitrogen for growing pigs. *J. Sci. Food Agric*. **26**: 215–17.

Wielgolaski F.E. 1979. *Anvendt botanikk*. Oslo: Universitetsforlaget. (In Norwegian).

Witman J.D. 1987. Subtidal coexistence: storms, grazing, mutualism, and the zonation of kelps and mussels. *Ecol. Monogr*. **57**: 167–87.

Wolff J. 1969. Iodide goiter and the pharmacologic effects of excess iodine. *Am. J. Med*. **47**: 101–24.

Wong W.H. & Leung K.L. 1979. Sewage sludge and seaweed (*Ulca* sp.) as supplementary feed for chicks. *Environ. Poll*. **20**: 93–101.

Xia B. & Abbott I.A. 1987. Edible seaweeds of China and their place in the Chinese diet. *Econ. Bot*. **41**: 341–53.

Yone Y., Furuichi M. & Urano K. 1986. Effects of wakame *Undaria pinnatifida* and *Ascophyllum nodosum* on absorption of dietary nutrients, and blood sugar and plasma amino-N levels of red sea bream. *Bull. Jap. Soc. Sci. Fish*. **52**: 1817–19.

Zuzuki A. 1965. Endemic coast goiter in Hokkaido, Japan. *Acta Endocrinol*. **50**: 161–76.

3 Agricultural Uses of Seaweeds and Seaweed Extracts

G. BLUNDEN
Portsmouth Polytechnic, UK

Seaweeds have been collected and used as fertilisers and soil conditioning agents in Europe for many years. However, utilisation has been restricted mainly to coastal areas because of the high costs involved in collection, drying and transportation. As a result, very little trade has developed in the supply of seaweeds as fertilisers, and most of the material employed for this purpose is collected by farmers for their own use.

Usually in Europe seaweed cast up by tides and storms ('total drift') is used. The composition of this will vary from region to region and with the time of year, but the predominant species will be brown algae. *Fucus* and *Laminaria* species and *Ascophyllum nodosum* would usually form the bulk of the drift weed in countries like the UK, Norway, France and Ireland, but several other brown algal species, as well as many green and red algae, are likely to be present.

In some areas specific algal species have been collected, for example in Brittany, where large quantities of *Himanthalia elongata* have been harvested for use in the growing of artichokes (Chapman & Chapman 1980). In other areas, for example Jersey, brown algae (mainly *Fucus* species) are collected in the autumn and spread out on fields in which it is intended to grow early potatoes (Chapman & Chapman 1980). In very barren areas, for example the Aran Islands off the west coast of Ireland, seaweed is layered with either soil or sand for the production of vegetables, in particular potatoes (Guiry 1989).

The manurial value of seaweed is difficult to assess because the material used is variable in composition. Analysis of fresh algae will give results that may differ markedly from the seaweed applied to the soil, particularly if drift weed is used. Significant quantities of water-soluble constituents can be removed by exposure to rain when the weed is either on the beach or stored in piles after collection. Similarly, washing the collected weed to remove excess 'salt' will remove other water-soluble compounds.

Comparison of farmyard manure with an equivalent weight of fresh seaweed showed that the nitrogen contents of both were similar, but the potassium level was higher and the phosphorus level lower in the seaweed (Chapman & Chapman 1980). Comparison of analyses has to be viewed with

Seaweed Resources in Europe: Uses and Potential. Edited by M. D. Guiry and G. Blunden
© 1991 John Wiley & Sons Ltd

caution, however, because the availability to plants of the nutrients may be different. Some are readily available, but others will form part of complex molecules and will be released only after microbial breakdown of these complexes in the soil. This process may occur rapidly with some algae, but may be slow with others. For example, many species of brown algae, such as *Fucus* species and *Ascophyllum nodosum*, have high contents of polyphenols (see Indergaard & Minsaas, Chapter 2), which have antimicrobial activity. As a result, the breakdown of these algae can be slow, whereas *Laminaria* species either lack or have very low levels of polyphenols and hence are readily broken down in the soil.

As stated earlier, most of the seaweeds used as fertilisers and soil-conditioning agents in Europe are species of brown algae. These contain a number of polysaccharides, the most important of which are the alginates. These compounds are known to be adsorbed by clays and to stabilise clay suspensions (Zavorkhina & Ben'kovskii 1958), and thus the addition of seaweeds to the soil may improve its structure by causing flocculation of the native clays. Also, other algal components, for example fucoidan (Zavor-khina & Ben'kovskii 1958) and the polyphenols, may help to stabilise the soil aggregates. A number of products containing seaweed derivatives have been patented for use as soil conditioners (France 1980; Primo 1981), to correct nutritional imbalances (Shinkyo Sangyo Co. Ltd 1982) and to prevent soil erosion (Weeks & Wilson 1960). The erosion-control product was formulated as a suspension containing 0.25% sodium alginate and 2.25% bentonite and it was shown to significantly decrease soil losses that resulted from run-off.

Purified alginates are expensive and the use of either whole or modified seaweeds in soil conditioners and erosion-control products should give equally good results, especially if compounds other than the alginates are involved in stabilising the soil. The trace elements present in whole algae have been claimed to encourage plant growth, but the contribution to plant nutrition made by the addition of seaweed to the soil is very small and unlikely to be critical for the establishment of plants in subsoils. Fresh marine algae have been shown to contain small quantities of plant growth-regulatory compounds, but it is unlikely that the algal products used in land reclamation contain such materials in sufficient quantities to have any significant biological activity.

A product based on composted *Ascophyllum nodosum* has been used successfully in landscaping and reclamation projects. When dried, this alga contains the equivalent of about 20–30% sodium alginate (Chapman & Chapman 1980) and, like most members of the Fucaceae, it has a high polyphenol content. The soil conditioner is produced by allowing dried, powdered *Ascophyllum* to compost under controlled conditions for 11–12 days. This process is believed to cause partial degradation of the alginates, probably reducing their molecular weights and gel strengths. The final product is a dark brown, granular material containing 20–25% water, and the soil conditioner can be easily stored and handled in this form.

The method used to apply the soil conditioner will depend on the nature of the site. Where topsoil is available, composted *Ascophyllum* is mixed with the soil at a rate of 1.5 kg m^{-3}, and then the area is cultivated as usual. However, in many cases no topsoil is used and the seaweed product must be applied to subsoils. If the site is relatively flat, the soil conditioner is worked into the top 50 mm of subsoil at a rate of 75 g m^{-2}, and then appropriate fertilisers and seeds are added using ordinary horticultural techniques. Often, the area to be treated includes steep slopes which are impossible to cultivate using conventional equipment and are more liable to suffer soil loss due to run-off than flat sites. A number of methods have been used to stabilise such slopes and to encourage the growth of plants on them. Hand-planting, often using netting stretched over the soil to hold it in place, has been tried, but this is expensive because it uses mature plants and is labour intensive. Bitumen-based and synthetic polymer sprays which bind the soil together have met with some success, although they do not always encourage plant growth. Spraying with a mixture containing composted *Ascophyllum*, together with clay, fertiliser, seed, a mulch (either cellulose pulp or peat) and water has given satisfactory results, even on bare rock. Plants rapidly become established, and a topsoil layer develops after a number of years. The spray is formulated as a thixotropic gel containing about 60% solid material. Under conditions of high shear, as found in mixing and spraying equipment, it is relatively fluid and will give an even coating over the sprayed area, but when the shearing force is removed the gel becomes very viscous and will adhere to vertical surfaces. The spray can be applied in most weather conditions, although heavy rain may wash the gel away before it has thickened completely. Once applied, the material acts as a physical barrier which holds the soil in place and retains sufficient moisture to allow the seeds to germinate.

This algal product has been used in Britain and Europe for the reclamation of industrial sites, including sand pits and quarries, and also for various landscaping schemes, for instance the area around the Tower of London, England, and in the Olympic village and stadia in Munich, West Germany. In tropical and subtropical areas, heavy rains make the problem of erosion due to run-off more acute than in the temperate zones and, since the layer of topsoil is often very thin, the use of imported soil is not feasible. Composted *Ascophyllum* has been used after the construction of roads in a number of countries, including Tanzania and Malaysia, and the results have been very encouraging. The seaweed product has performed at least as well as the alternative techniques of hand-planting, netting and spraying with either bitumen derivatives or synthetic polymers.

Composted *Ascophyllum* has been used on a small scale to improve soil structure in parks and gardens. When applied as a top dressing on established turf, for instance in sports grounds and on golf courses, it is claimed to help prevent compaction of the ground and thus to improve the quality of the grass. The product is also used as a root dip for the treatment of bare-rooted trees and shrubs during transplantation. The root dip contains finely ground composted seaweed, clay and water and it is supplied as a very viscous concentrate, which is diluted to a suitable consistency before use. The gel is applied to the roots of trees and shrubs after they are removed from the nursery beds, and it is believed to protect the root hairs from physical damage. Preliminary investigations have shown that use of the root dip reduces water losses from plants during storage, and the rate of successful transplantation is said to be higher for treated plants than for untreated ones.

Although the seaweeds used as fertilisers and soil-conditioning agents are mainly species of brown algae, several crustose, calcareous red algae of the family Corallinaceae (Fig. 1), known collectively as maërl, are used, primarily on acid soil (Blunden et al. 1975). Maërl has been collected from the Cornish coast of England for use in agriculture from at least the 18th century, but it would appear that it was not utilised in this way in France until the beginning of the 19th century. Commercial supplies of maërl are obtained by dredging from around the coasts of Brittany in France and off Falmouth Harbour in England. Chemical analysis of maërl shows that it is composed almost entirely of calcium and magnesium carbonates, with the calcium content, calculated as Ca^{2+}, varying from 25.5 to 33.3% of the dry weight, and the magnesium content, calculated as Mg^{2+}, varying from 1.7 to 3.3%. The major component is calcite, with magnesium carbonate present as a solid solution in the calcite structure at a concentration of about 8%. Aragonite was shown to form about 10–15% of the total material (Blunden et al. 1977). The chemical analyses were very similar regardless of the area of collection (Blunden et al. 1977, 1981). The cost of maërl to the farmer is high compared with lime, but it has

Table 1. Average trace element content of maërl

Sulphur	0.60%	Lead	50 ppm
Phosphorus	0.35%	Fluorine	50 ppm
Chlorine	0.20%	Titanium	25 ppm
Potassium	0.20%	Copper	15 ppm
Sodium	0.17%	Zinc	15 ppm
Iron	2500 ppm	Nickel	10 ppm
Iodine	1200 ppm	Arsenic	5 ppm
Aluminium	500 ppm	Chromium	5 ppm
Manganese	480 ppm	Bromine	3 ppm
Tin	200 ppm	Cobalt	1.5 ppm
Indium	200 ppm	Silver	1 ppm
Strontium	150 ppm	Molybdenum	1 ppm
Boron	80 ppm		

From Blunden et al. (1975).

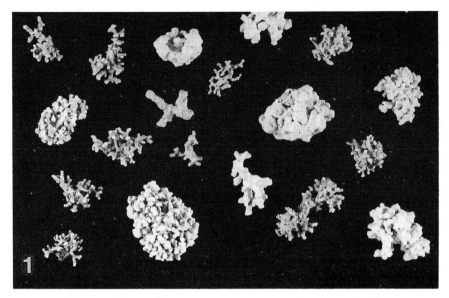

Figure 1. Maërl (mainly *Phymatolithon calcareum* and *Lithothamnion corallioides*) collected from Falmouth Harbour, UK and the Glenan Islands, France (× 0.7)

been claimed by the producers that the seaweed product has the advantage over lime in having a relatively large amount of trace elements (Table 1). However, the difference in cost seems difficult to justify in terms of trace elements alone.

Maërl is marketed in many western European countries for use in agriculture and horticulture as a soil conditioner. The effects produced are claimed to be dependent on the particle size of the applied material, which differs from product to product from approximately 50 to 300 mesh. A typical application rate of the finer mesh maërl is 100 kg per hectare every three years. In addition to products composed only of powdered calcified seaweed, others are available which contain added materials, in particular phosphate.

SEAWEED EXTRACTS AND SUSPENSIONS

Seaweed extracts and suspensions derived from marine brown algae are marketed for use in agriculture and horticulture. In Europe and North America, the alga most commonly utilised is *Ascophyllum nodosum* (for example, Maxicrop – Maxicrop International Ltd, Tonbridge, UK; Seamac – Seamac Agricultural Ltd, Chippenham, UK; Goëmill – Goëmar SA, Saint Malo, France;) Alginex – Thorverk HF, Rykhólum, Iceland; Algifert – Algea Produkter AS, Kristiansund, Norway), although other species are used in addition, for example *Fucus serratus* and *Laminaria* species (SM3 – Chase Organics Ltd, Weybridge, UK; Cytex – Atlantic & Pacific Research Inc, North Palm Beach, Florida, USA). Outside Europe other brown algae are employed; for example, *Ecklonia maxima* (Kelpak 66 – Kelp Products Ltd, Cape Town, South Africa) in South Africa and *Durvillea potatorum* (Seasol) in Australia. The products available are either true extracts or suspensions of finely divided alga. The former (Maxicrop, SM3, Seamac, Alginex, Algifert, Seasol) are produced by extraction of the seaweeds with either water or an aqueous alkali (sodium carbonate or potassium hydroxide). Examples of the latter type of product are Kelpak 66 and Goëmill.

The process used to produce Goëmill can be summarised as follows. Fresh seaweed is rinsed quickly in water and rapidly deep frozen into blocks at −25 °C before cryo-microcrushing. After various other procedures, including homogenisation and micropartition, a liquid seaweed extract is obtained with a creamy consistency and containing small particles of about 6–10 μm diameter (Pellegrini *et al.* 1987). Various additives may be blended with the seaweed products, as in Goëmill.

In the case of Kelpak 66 the seaweed concentrate is prepared by a cell-burst process. *Eklonia maxima* plants are harvested by excising them at the base of the stipe above the holdfast. After hand washing, the plants are progressively reduced in particle size. These reduced particles finally pass, under extremely high pressure, into a low-pressure chamber wherein they shear and disintegrate, resulting in the liquid concentrate (Featonby-Smith & Van Staden 1983a).

A wide range of beneficial effects has been reported from the use of seaweed extracts, including increased crop yields, increased resistance of plants to frost, increased uptake of inorganic constituents from the soil, increased resistance to stress conditions, reduced incidence of fungal and insect attack, reduced storage losses of fruit, and improved seed germination. These effects have been reviewed by Blunden (1977) and Abetz (1980).

Subsequent to these reviews other papers have appeared in which details are given of beneficial effects produced with the use of seaweed products. Much of this work has involved the use of Kelpak 66. Featonby-Smith and Van Staden (1983b) showed that foliar application of the product to Swiss chard plants (*Beta vulgaris*) improved their growth significantly, irrespective of whether the seaweed material was applied on its own as a foliar spray, or to the soil mixed with a chemical fertiliser. The same authors (1983a) also reported that application of low dilutions of the product to tomato plants significantly improved root growth and that, associated with this, was a reduction in root knot nematode infection. Another trial, by Nelson and Van Staden (1984) showed that the culm diameters of wheat plants were increased significantly when Kelpak 66 was used either as a root drench or as a foliar spray. Abetz and Young (1983) reported that the use of Maxicrop on lettuce and cauliflower plants produced beneficial results. In the case of the former there was a significant decrease in the number of plants failing to form hearts, and significant increases in the weight of marketable lettuces and in their mean heart diameter. In the case of cauliflower plants significant increases in curd diameters were recorded.

One of the reported effects produced with the use of seaweed extracts is the increase in uptake of inorganic constituents from the soil. As a result, it has been stated by some manufacturers that the use of their products will improve the utilisation of applied fertiliser. De Villiers *et al.* (1983) tested this hypothesis using two different seaweed products, which were applied to apple and peach trees and to vines. They found that the treatment did lead to significantly higher contents of some elements in the leaves of the treated plants, but these increases were of little practical significance as the elements were already present in adequate amounts. Moreover, in cases involving apple trees and vines in which analyses indicated mineral deficiencies, the use of the seaweed sprays did not improve uptake.

De Villiers *et al.* (1983) found no clear trend in the effects produced by the seaweed extracts used by them as foliar sprays. The results obtained varied with the product, the concentration used and the crop being tested. The authors showed that ion uptake can be altered by using seaweed extracts, but the effects produced were not significant and hence the products could not be recommended for use on deciduous trees.

Ketring and Schubert (1981) tested the possible effect on the enhancement of reproduction of peanuts (*Arachis hypogaea*) with the use of a seaweed extract (Cytex). Three varieties of peanut plants were used, as well as different application times and application rates. In one year a significant increase in yield of Tamnut 74 peanuts was obtained with the use of the seaweed extract, but a repeat trial in the following year did not produce any significant difference between the test and control plants.

Featonby-Smith and Van Staden (1987) conducted pot trials to determine the effect of Kelpak 66 on the yield of peanuts. Significant increases were obtained, particularly from the plants treated twice, 3 and 8 weeks after emergence of the seedlings.

Aldworth and Van Staden (1987) found that significantly improved seedling growth of cabbage (*Brassica oleracea*) and dwarf marigolds (*Tagetes patula*) was produced when the roots of the plants were soaked in Kelpak 66 at the time of transplantation. In the case of dwarf marigolds, foliar application of the seaweed product also produced a beneficial effect, but this was not so pronounced as that brought about by soaking the roots.

BIOLOGICALLY ACTIVE COMPOUNDS IN SEAWEED EXTRACTS

In the past it was claimed that the effects produced by seaweed extracts could be explained by their content of trace elements. However, the quantities of dissolved solids in seaweed extracts that would be applied annually to one

Table 2. Quantities of certain inorganic elements supplied in 1 year to 1 hectare by seaweed extract and the estimated annual requirement of these elements for hay

Element	Weight (g) per hectare from seaweed extract application	Estimation of possible annual requirement per hectare (g)
Iron	22	280
Manganese	0.3	140
Zinc	0.7	140
Copper	0.3	140
Boron	0.006	56
Molybdenum	0.07	1.4
Cobalt	0.03	1.4

From Blunden (1977).

hectare are very small and it has been shown that the amounts of trace elements form an insignificant proportion of the annual requirement of a crop (Blunden 1977) (Table 2).

CYTOKININS

Because of the small amount of material applied to a hectare, the substances in seaweed exacts responsible for the agriculturally beneficial results must be capable of having an effect in very low concentrations. As a result, consideration was given to the presence of plant hormones. Following the suggestion of Booth (1965) that cytokinins might be one of the active constituents of seaweed extracts, as many of the results reported for each were similar, Brain *et al.* (1973) demonstrated the high cytokinin-like activity of one commercially available product (SM3). Later work showed that all the products tested gave similar responses, although the level of activity varied from batch to batch of the same product (Williams *et al.* 1981). It was suggested that the quantities of cytokinins present in the seaweed extracts were sufficient to produce biological effects when applied to plants, even at the low rates of application used in the field.

Field trials were undertaken by Blunden and co-workers to determine whether cytokinins could be the active substance in seaweed extracts. In an initial trial with SM3, both new and established varieties of sugar beet were used, which were grown in randomised blocks, replicated six times. At harvest, the roots were weighed and analysed for sugar content, and the juice was analysed for amino-nitrogen, potassium and sodium (Table 3). No significant difference was found in root weight between control and treated plants. However, the sugar content of the seaweed-extract-treated plants was significantly higher and the amino-nitrogen and potassium contents of the

Table 3. Mean values of collected root weight, root sugar content, and juice contents of sodium, potassium and amino-nitrogen from control and seaweed-extract-treated plants of varieties of sugar beet

Sugar beet variety	Collected root weight (kg)		Root sugar content (%)		Juice content (mEq)					
					Amino-nitrogen		Potassium		Sodium	
	C	T	C	T	C	T	C	T	C	T
Monobel	52.2	51.7	15.6	16.5	4.10	2.23	8.79	8.30	0.40	0.53
Amono	49.9	47.6	15.5	16.4	4.42	3.02	9.10	7.58	0.45	0.58
Tribel	54.4	58.1	16.0	16.7	3.57	2.72	9.02	7.85	0.82	0.50
Hybrid 4	58.9	59.2	15.0	16.3	5.72	4.40	8.92	6.77	0.70	0.52
Monohil	63.7	74.1	15.9	16.4	4.25	3.52	6.85	6.32	0.72	0.65

C, control plants; T, seaweed-extract-treated plants.
From Blunden *et al.* (1979).

extracted juice significantly lower than the corresponding values for the control roots. No significant difference was found between the sodium contents of the extracted juice of the control and treated plants (Blunden *et al.* 1979).

Important effects of cytokinins are those on cell division, cell enlargement, the delaying of senescence and the related transport of nutrients. Although there is no direct evidence for the stimulation of any of these processes by seaweed extract application in this trial, the results seemed consistent with cytokinin-like activity. During leaf senescence, some substances, especially those containing nitrogen and phosphorus, are broken down into soluble forms and translocated back into the stem and root before the leaf abscisses. Delaying senescence would decrease the amount of soluble amino-nitrogen, and possibly potassium, entering the beet roots and would therefore reduce the content of these substances in the juice.

In subsequent trials, seaweed extracts of known cytokinin activities and a reference cytokinin, kinetin (6-furfurylaminopurine), were used. The seaweed extracts were assayed using the radish leaf expansion bioassay with kinetin as the reference compound. In one trial on potatoes, the seaweed extract (SM3) was applied at a rate of 11 litres per hectare, which resulted in a cytokinin application rate equivalent to 1.4 g per hectare of kinetin. This treatment resulted in a significant increase in the yield of potatoes of the variety King Edward, but produced no significant effect with Pentland Dell. Application of an aqueous solution of kinetin, also at a rate equivalent to 1.4 g per hectare, resulted in a significant increase in the weight of King Edward potatoes obtained, there being no significant difference in the results from the kinetin application and those from the application of seaweed extract (Table 4). This close correlation suggested that the beneficial result

Table 4. Yields from potato plants of the varieties King Edward and Pentland Dell treated with either aqueous seaweed extract or kinetin solutions

Treatment	Tuber yield (% of control)	
	King Edward	Pentland Dell
Seaweed extract (cytokinin content equivalent to 1.4 g ha^{-1} kinetin)	112.9[a]	112.2 (n.s.)
Kinetin (1.4 g ha^{-1})	110.8[a]	113.2 (n.s)

[a]$P = 0.05$; n.s., no significant difference.
From Blunden and Wildgoose (1977).

from the use of the seaweed extract may be due to its cytokinin-like activity (Blunden & Wildgoose 1977). A later trial on potatoes of the variety Kennebec and Russet Burbank by Lang and Langille (1984) also indicated that the effects produced by seaweed extract treatment may be dependent on the cultivar used. A significant increase was achieved in the total yield of Kennebec potatoes, but no effect was recorded for Russet Burbank. Kinetin did not influence the yield of either cultivar when applied during the tuber initiation period.

Close correlation between results obtained in field trials with the use of kinetin and seaweed extracts of equivalent cytokinin activities were also found in the crude protein content of grass (Blunden 1977) and in the reduction in the rate of 'degreening' of limes after post-harvest immersion of the fruit in seaweed extracts and kinetin solutions of equivalent cytokinin activity (Blunden et al. 1978).

Featonby-Smith and Van Staden (1983b) found that the application of Kelpak 66 to Swiss chard produced significant changes in the cytokinin levels of the treated plants; the levels were significantly increased in the roots, but decreased in the leaves. Similar effects were produced with the use of a liquid fertiliser to the soil. However, when the seaweed product and fertiliser were used together as a soil application the cytokinin levels of both roots and shoots were reduced markedly. These plants showed the greatest increase in growth.

Featonby-Smith and Van Staden (1983a) reported that the use of Kelpak 66 on tomato plants both improved root growth and produced a significant reduction in root knot nematode infestation. The authors considered that this reduction could result from the cytokinins demonstrated to be present in the product as it had been shown earlier by Dropkin et al. (1969) that kinetin decreased nematode larval penetration into the roots of tomato plants and also inhibited the development of those which did enter the roots.

The improvement in root growth of tomatoes was studied later by Finnie and Van Staden (1985) who found that Kelpak 66 stimulated the growth of in *vitro* cultured roots. The effects produced could be mimicked by low concentrations of zeatin, although at concentrations of 10^{-6} M and above root growth was inhibited. Other hormones tested, such as indole acetic acid, gibberellic acid (GA_3) and abscissic acid had no stimulating effect on root extension.

Featonby-Smith and Van Staden (1987) reported that the beneficial effects obtained with peanuts after treatment with Kelpak 66 could also be produced by application of the synthetic cytokinin benzyladenine.

Blunden *et al.* (1984) found major discrepancies in the results obtained for the cytokinin contents of seaweed extracts when bioassayed by different methods. For example, in the radish leaf expansion bioassay (Kuraishi & Okumura 1956; Bentley-Mowat & Reid 1968), high levels of cytokinin activity are recorded (Blunden 1977; Williams *et al.* 1981), whereas in others, for example the *Amaranthus* seedling assay (Biddington & Thomas 1973), low levels are found. Similarly, using the soybean-callus assay, cytokinin activities have been reported equivalent to only 1 mg kinetin l^{-1} (Abetz 1980). Briner *et al.* (1979), also using this assay, found that undiluted extract would contain between 2 and 20 mg kinetin eq. l^{-1}. The assays were complicated by the presence of growth inhibitory substances, a problem encountered also by other workers (Blunden 1977; Abetz 1980). The radish leaf expansion bioassay can be affected by substances not normally considered to be cytokinins (Abetz 1980) and so the finding of high levels of activity when this assay is used is not surprising.

More direct proof for the presence of cytokinins in a seaweed product (Kelpak 66) was given by Featonby-Smith and Van Staden (1984), who identified by high-performance liquid chromatography *cis*- and *trans*-zeatin riboside, *trans*-zeatin, dihydrozeatin and $N^6(\Delta^2$-isopentenyl)adenosine. More recently, the six cytokinins, *trans*-zeatin-9-β-D-riboside, *trans*-zeatin, their dihydro derivatives, $N^6(\Delta^2$-isopentenyl)adenine and its 9-β-D-riboside were identified and quantified in Seasol by gas chromatography/mass spectrometry (Fig. 2) (Tay *et al.* 1985). Low concentrations of cytokinins were found and the authors suggested that the levels did not appear to be sufficiently high to be responsible for the reported beneficial effects of the product.

AUXINS

When considering the range of reported effects with the use of seaweed extracts and the levels of cytokinins found in the various products, the presence of other active substances has to be considered. The possible presence of auxins has received the attention of several groups of workers, but a detailed discussion will not be entered into here. Weak auxin activity of one product has been recorded by Mowat (1961), but Williams *et al.* (1981) were unable to detect any significant activity in any of the commercially produced seaweed extracts examined by them. However, Kingman and

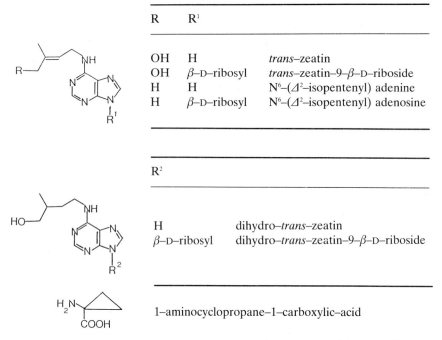

R	R^1	
OH	H	*trans*–zeatin
OH	β–D–ribosyl	*trans*–zeatin–9–β–D–riboside
H	H	N^6–(Δ^2–isopentenyl) adenine
H	β–D–ribosyl	N^6–(Δ^2–isopentenyl) adenosine

R^2	
H	dihydro–*trans*–zeatin
β–D–ribosyl	dihydro–*trans*–zeatin–9–β–D–riboside

1–aminocyclopropane–1–carboxylic–acid

Figure 2. Growth regulatory compounds isolated from commercial seaweed extracts

Moore (1982), using a gas–liquid chromatographic method, reported the presence of indole acetic acid, as well as abscissic acid and adenine, in extracts of *Ascophyllum nodosum*. Unfortunately, the compounds were identified from chromatographic data only. Sumera and Cajipe (1981) studied a hydrolysed extract of *Sargassum polycystum* and found compounds which responded to the *Avena* coleoptile elongation test and to the van Urk colour reagent, but none of the compounds isolated appeared to be indolic in nature.

1-AMINOCYCLOPROPANE-1-CARBOXYLIC ACID

Nelson and Van Staden (1984) found that the use of Kelpak 66 increased markedly the thickness of wheat culms, mainly as a result of an increase in cell size, especially those located in the vascular bundles. As ethylene-releasing chemicals are widely used to prevent lodging in cereals, the authors considered that it was possible that the naturally occurring ethylene-releasing compound, 1-aminocyclopropane-1-carboxylic acid (Fig. 2), could be the active ingredient. Using thin-layer and gas liquid chromatographic techniques, they detected this compound in Kelpak 66 and estimated the concentration of the compound to be 9.29 nmol ml^{-1} (Nelson & Van Staden 1985).

BETAINES

Because of the differences in cytokinin levels recorded for the same seaweed extract using different bioassay procedures, Blunden *et al.* (1984) suggested that the extracts might contain other compounds which behave like cytokinins in certain respects. Betaines were suggested as likely candidates, particularly as it had been shown by Wheeler (1973) that glycinebetaine had activity similar to that of cytokinins in several growth tests. Moreover, certain claims that have been made for the use of seaweed extracts could be explained by the presence of betaines. For example, glycinebetaine has been reported to have a role in frost resistance of plants (Bokarev & Ivanova 1971; Sakai & Yoshida 1968) and, when applied to winter wheat, to enhance both the water utilisation efficiency and the grain yield of the treated plants (Bergmann & Eckert 1984). Glycinebetaine has also been shown to ameliorate salt stress in seedlings and to afford partial protection of some enzymes against salt inhibition (Pollard & Wyn Jones 1979).

Betaines have been reported for most of the species of marine algae used in the manufacture of seaweed extracts. For example, *Ascophyllum nodosum* yields γ-aminobutyric acid betaine, δ-aminovaleric acid betaine and laminine; *Fucus serratus*, γ-aminobutyric acid betaine, glycinebetaine and laminine (Blunden *et al.* 1985); and *Laminaria digitata*, *L. hyperborea* and *L. saccharina*, glycinebetaine, γ-aminobutyric acid betaine, laminine and lysinebetaine (Fig. 3) (Blunden *et al.* 1982). Seaweed extracts prepared from one or more of the algae (SM3, Maxicrop, Seamac, Alginex) were found to contain the compounds expected, although the presence of glycinebetaine in Maxicrop, Seamac and Alginex indicated that the starting material, *Ascophyllum nodosum*, was contaminated with other algae, probably *Fucus* species (Blunden *et al.* 1984, 1986). A proton magnetic resonance spectroscopic assay method for the estimation of betaines in seaweed extracts was

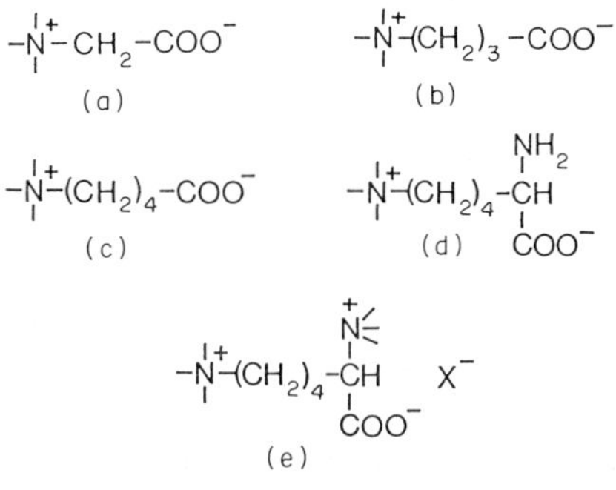

$$-\overset{|+}{\underset{|}{N}}-CH_2-COO^-$$

(a)

$$-\overset{|+}{\underset{|}{N}}-(CH_2)_3-COO^-$$

(b)

$$-\overset{|+}{\underset{|}{N}}-(CH_2)_4-COO^-$$

(c)

$$-\overset{|+}{\underset{|}{N}}-(CH_2)_4-\overset{NH_2}{\underset{|}{CH}}$$

(d) COO^-

$$-\overset{|+}{\underset{|}{N}}-(CH_2)_4-\overset{\overset{+}{N}\lessgtr}{\underset{|}{CH}} \quad X^-$$

(e) COO^-

Figure 3. Betaines isolated from commercial seaweed extracts: a, glycinebetaine; b, γ-aminobutyric acid betaine; c, δ-aminovaleric acid betaine; d, laminine; e, lysinebetaine

developed (Blunden *et al.* 1986); in one product (SM3), concentrations of glycinebetaine varied from 18 to 36 mg l^{-1}, for γ-aminobutyric acid betaine from 19 to 25 mg l^{-1}, and for δ-aminovaleric acid betaine from 9 to 12 mg l^{-1}. A microbiological assay procedure was also developed, based on measuring the growth of the bacterium *Klebsiella pneumoniae* produced by the addition of seaweed extracts to a medium with a growth-inhibitory concentration of sodium chloride (Blunden *et al.* 1986). Using this procedure the betaine content of SM3, calculated as glycinebetaine equivalents, varied from 168 to 355 mg l^{-1}. Whether other components in the extract, in addition to the betaines, play a significant role in overcoming osmotically induced growth inhibition of *K. pneumoniae* is yet to be determined.

Obviously more research is needed on seaweed extracts to elucidate more fully their potential uses and modes of action. Too frequently, results reported with the use of one product are assumed to apply equally to another, even though the two may be manufactured in different ways, from different algae and used at different concentrations. Moreover, separate batches of the same product are likely to vary considerably depending on factors such as the quality of the seaweed used in the preparation of the extracts and the time of year when the seaweed was collected. Standardisation of batches is difficult because it is not known what compounds present in the extract should be evaluated. The radish leaf expansion bioassay was used to determine the cytokinin-like activity of the extracts by Blunden (1977), Blunden and Wild-goose (1977) and Blunden *et al.* (1978), but this proved unreliable because other extracted compounds responded like cytokinins in this test. Also it is doubtful whether standardisation for cytokinins alone is satisfactory.

De Villiers *et al.* (1983) observed that the effects of hormones in plants usually depends on the balance between two or more of these substances and these ratios change continuously from one growth stage to another. Thus, they concluded that if the activity of seaweed extracts is dependent on hormones the effects obtained with their use will depend on the type of crop, its growth stage and the composition and concentration of the seaweed product applied. Furthermore, the hormone content of the seaweed used for the manufacture of the extracts will vary at different times of the year.

Unfortunately, much of the field trial work undertaken with seaweed extracts has not been reported in the scientific literature, but is recorded only in manufacturers' leaflets. Although often of interest, both the experimental design and the degree of replication reported in many of the trials make it difficult to determine the validity of the results. The experimental data have frequently not been analysed statistically, and so it is impossible to determine whether the differences recorded have any significance. It is highly likely that only positive results have been disclosed and the number of trials in which no significant effect was produced is left unrecorded.

Many of the claims made for seaweed extracts have been both overtly commercial and somewhat ridiculous, and this has led to a sometimes hostile attitude to many of the products in academic and governmental circles. Moreover, the unreliability of results obtained with the use of the extracts has detracted from their widespread use. However, there is a sufficient body of information available to show that the use of seaweed extracts is beneficial in certain cases, even though the reasons for the benefits are not fully understood.

REFERENCES

Abetz P. 1980. Seaweed extracts: have they a place in Australian agriculture or horticulture? *J. Aust. Inst. Ag. Sci.* **46**: 23–9.

Abetz P. & Young C.L. 1983. The effect of seaweed extract sprays derived from *Ascophyllum nodosum* on lettuce and cauliflower crops. *Botanica Mar.* **26**: 487–92.

Aldworth S.J. & Van Staden J. 1987. The effect of seaweed concentrate on seedling transplants. *S. Afr. J. Bot.* **53**: 187–9.

Bentley-Mowat J.A. & Reid S.M. 1968. Investigation of the radish leaf bio-assay for kinetins and demonstration of kinetin-like substances in algae. *Ann. Bot. N.S.* **32**: 23–32.

Bergmann H. & Eckert H. 1984. Einfluss von Glycinbetain auf die Wasserausnutzung von Winterweizen *Triticum aestivum* L. *Biologia Plantae* **26**: 384–7.

Biddington N.L. & Thomas T.H. 1973. A modified *Amaranthus* betacyanin bioassay for the rapid determination of cytokinins in plant extracts. *Planta* **111**: 183–6.

Blunden G. 1977. Cytokinin activity of seaweed extracts. In *Marine Natural Products Chemistry*. (Eds. D.J. Faulkner & W.J. Fenical) pp. 337–44. New York: Plenum Press.

Blunden G. & Wildgoose P.B. 1977. The effects of aqueous seaweed extract and kinetin on potato yields. *J. Sci. Food Agric.* **28**: 121–5.

Blunden G., Binns W.W. & Perks F. 1975. Commercial collection and utilisation of maërl. *Econ. Bot.* **29**: 140–5.

Blunden G., Farnham W.F., Jephson N., Fenn R.H. & Plunkett B.A. 1977. The composition of maërl from the Glenan Islands of southern Brittany. *Botanica Mar.* **20**: 121–5.

Blunden G., Jones E.M. & Passam H.C. 1978. Effects of post-harvest treatment of fruit and vegetables with cytokinin-active seaweed extracts and kinetin solutions. *Botanica Mar.* **21**: 237–40.

Blunden G., Wildgoose P.B. & Nicholson F.E. 1979. The effects of aqueous seaweed extract on sugar beet. *Botanica Mar.* **22**: 539–41.

Blunden G., Farnham W.F., Jephson N., Barwell C.J., Fenn R.H. & Plunkett B.A. 1981. The composition of maërl beds of economic interest in northern Brittany, Cornwall and Ireland. In *Proceedings 10th International Seaweed Symposium*. (Ed. T. Levring) pp. 651–6. Berlin: de Gruyter.

Blunden G., Gordon S.M. & Keysell G.R. 1982. Lysine betaine and other quaternary ammonium compounds from British species of the Laminariales. *J. Nat. Prod.* **45**: 449–52.

Blunden G., Rogers D.J. & Barwell C.J. 1984. Biologically-active compounds from British marine algae. In *Natural Products and Drug Development*, Alfred Benzon Symposium 20. (Eds. P. Krogsgaard-Larsen, S. Brøgger Christensen & H. Kofod), pp. 179–90. Copenhagen: Munksgaard.

Blunden G., Gordon S.M., Smith B.E. & Fletcher R.L. 1985. Quaternary ammonium compounds in species of the Fucaceae (Phaeophyceae) from Britain. *Br. Phycol. J.* **20**: 105–8.

Blunden G., Cripps A.L., Gordon S.M., Mason T.G. & Turner C.H. 1986. The characterisation and quantitative estimation of betaines in commercial seaweed extracts. *Botanica Mar.* **29**: 155–60.

Bokarev K.S. & Ivanova R.P. 1971. The effect of certain derivatives and analogs of choline and betaine on content of free amino acids in leaves of two species of potato differing with respect to frost resistance. *Soviet Plant Physiol.* **18**: 302–5.

Booth E. 1965. The manurial value of seaweed. *Botanica Mar.* **8**: 138–43.

Brain K.R., Chalopin M.C., Turner T.D., Blunden G. & Wildgoose P.B. 1973. Cytokinin activity of commercial aqueous seaweed extract. *Plant Sci. Lett.* **1**: 241–5.

Briner G.P., Richards D. & Belcher R.S. 1979. Seaweed products – fertilizer or plant growth regulators. *NZ J. Agric.* **138**: 20.

Chapman V.J. & Chapman D.J. 1980. *Seaweeds and their Uses.* London: Chapman and Hall.

De Villiers J., Kotze W.A.G. & Joubert M. 1983. Effect of seaweed foliar sprays on fruit quality and mineral nutrition. *Deciduous Fruit Grower* March: 97–101.

Dropkin V.H., Helgeson J.P. & Upper C.D. 1969. The hypersensitivity reaction of tomatoes resistant to *Meloidogyne incognita* reversal by cytokinins. *J. Nematol.* **1**: 55–61.

Featonby-Smith B.C. & Van Staden J. 1983a. The effect of seaweed concentrate on the growth of tomatoes in nematode infested soil. *Scientia Horticulturae* **20**: 137–46 .

Featonby-Smith B.C. & Van Staden J. 1983b. The effect of seaweed concentrate and fertilizer on the growth of *Beta vulgaris*. *Z. Pflanzenphysiol.* **112**: 155–62.

Featonby-Smith B.C. & Van Staden J. 1984. Identification and seasonal variation of endogenous cytokinins in *Ecklonia maxima* (Osbeck) Papenf. *Bot. Mar.* **27**: 527–31.

Featonby-Smith B.C. & Van Staden J. 1987. Effects of seaweed concentrate on yield and seed quality of *Arachis hypogaea*. *S. Afr. J. Bot.* **53**: 190–3.

Finnie J.F. & Van Staden J. 1985. Effect of seaweed concentrate and applied hormones on *in vitro* cultured tomato roots. *J. Plant Physiol.* **120**: 215–22.

France R. 1980. Catalytic soil additive. Belgian Patent No. 884 749.

Guiry M.D. 1989. Uses and cultivation of seaweeds. In *Alghe e loro Ultilizzazione Convegno Nazionale* (Ed. Anonymous) pp. 21–56. Lecce: Camera di Commercio.

Ketring D.L. & Schubert A.M. 1981. Reproduction of peanuts treated with a cytokinin-containing preparation. *Agron. J.* **73**: 350–2.

Kingman A.R. & Moore J. 1982. Isolation, purification and quantitation of several growth regulating substances in *Ascophyllum nodosum* (Phaeophyta). *Botanica Mar.* **25**: 149–53.

Kuraishi S. & Okumura F.S. 1956. Effects of kinetin on leaf growth. *Bot. Mag. Tokyo* **69**: 817–18.

Lang D.J. & Langille A.R. 1984. Influence of plant growth stage and concentration of Cytex and kinetin applications on tuber yields of two potato cultivars. *Hort. Sci.* **19**: 582–3.

Mowat J.A. 1961. Auxins and gibberellins in marine algae. In *Proceedings 4th International Seaweed Symposium*. (Eds. A. Davy de Virville & J. Feldmann) pp. 352–9 Oxford: Pergamon.

Nelson W.R. & Van Staden J. 1984. The effect of seaweed concentrate on wheat culms. *J. Plant Physiol.* **115**: 433–7.

Nelson W.R. & Van Staden J. 1985. 1-Aminocyclopropane-1-carboxylic acid in seaweed concentrate. *Bot. Mar.* **28**: 415–17.

Pellegrini M., Pellegrini L., Chabot R., Percehais S. & Yvin J.C. 1987. Effects of a liquid extract derived from *Ascophyllum nodosum* on the ultrastructure of *Vitis vinifera* leaf tissue. *Botanica Mar.* **30**: 437–46.

Pollard A. & Wyn Jones R.G. 1979. Enzyme activities in concentrated solutions of glycinebetaine and other solutes. *Planta* **144**: 291–8.

Primo A.M. 1981. Seaweed extract product and methods of utilising it. Can. CA. Patent No. 1 112 503.

Sakai A. & Yoshida S. 1968. Protective action of various compounds against freezing injury in plant cells. *Teion Kagaku, Seibutsu-Hen* **26**: 13–21 (from *Chem. Abstr.* (1969) **71**: 934y).

Shinkyo Sangyo Co. Ltd. 1982. Soil amendment for curing disorders caused by excessive lime applications. *Chem. Abstr.* **96**: 84632a.

Sumera F.C. & Cajipe G.J.B. 1981. Extraction and partial characterisation of auxin-like substances from *Sargassum polycystum* C.Ag. *Botanica Mar.* **24**: 157–63.

Tay S.A.B., MacLeod J.K., Palni L.M.S. & Letham D.S. 1985. Detection of cytokinins in a seaweed extract. *Phytochemistry* **24**: 2611–14.

Weeks L.E. & Wilson C.L. (to Monsanto Chemical Co.) 1960. Erosion control composition. US Patent No. 2 935 853.

Wheeler A.W. 1973. *Endogenous Growth Substances.* Rep. Rothamsted Exp. Stn. Part 1, pp. 101–2.

Williams D.C., Brain K.R., Blunden G., Wildgoose P.B. & Jewers K. 1981. Plant growth regulatory substances in commercial seaweed extracts. In *Proceedings 8th International Seaweed Symposium.* (Eds. G.E. Fogg & W. Eifion Jones) pp. 760–3. Menai Bridge: The Marine Science Laboratories.

Zavorkhina N.A. & Ben'kovskii V.K. 1958. The mechanism of stabilisation of clay suspensions by an algal extract. *Kolloid Zhur.* **20**: 436–43.

4 Uses of Seaweeds in Cosmetics

Y. DE ROECK-HOLTZHAUER
Centre Atlantique d'Études en Cosmétologie, Nantes, France

With an annual exploitation on a world-wide scale in excess of 3 million t fresh weight, algae and algal products are used mainly as food for humans and animals. Agricultural uses of seaweeds in developed countries have been in decline for some time as chemical fertilizers are more convenient and cheaper, whereas the usage of algae as food and in industry is expanding.

Of the 20 000 species of algae that have been described, only about 60 are used widely in the food, pharmaceutical and cosmetic industries. Four genera are used on a large scale: the red algae *Porphyra* and *Eucheuma*, and the brown algae *Laminaria* and *Undaria*. Other genera with lesser usage include the brown algae *Macrocystis*, *Himanthalia*, *Fucus* and *Ascophyllum*, and the red algae *Gracilaria*, *Gelidium*, *Pterocladia*, *Ahnfeltia*, *Chondrus*, *Mastocarpus*, *Phyllophora* and *Gymnogongrus*.

French legislation recognizes three categories of seaweed:

1. drift or stranded seaweed gathered by the coastal farmers and used as an agricultural fertilizer (*Fucus* and *Ascophyllum*);
2. attached seaweed collected at equinoctial low tides (*Fucus*, *Ascophyllum*, *Chondrus* and *Mastocarpus*);
3. subtidal seaweed, which can only be collected from a boat.

The seaweed collectors are subject to the same rules as marine fishermen and must respect the collection territory and season. In the future, assessment of seaweed resources in France may be carried out by satellite imagery (Belsher 1985a, 1985b), which would allow more rational management of the resource.

Three main categories of seaweed are exploited in Brittany: the Fucales (mainly *Fucus serratus* and *Ascophyllum nodosum*) at a rate of about 3000 t per year; the Gigartinales with about 3000 t of *Chondrus crispus* and *Mastocarpus stellatus*; and the Laminariales with about 65 000 t of *Laminaria digitata* and 2200 t of *L. hyperborea*. The Laminariales and Gigartinales are collected mainly in the summer and the other species during the winter and spring, which gives the seaweed collectors employment throughout most of the year. All of these algae should be collected in non-polluted sites exposed to wave action and oxygenated by strong tidal currents. Species not being

Seaweed Resources in Europe: Uses and Potential. Edited by M. D. Guiry and G. Blunden
© 1991 John Wiley & Sons Ltd

used at present but which are being examined for their potential include *Laminaria saccharina*, *Himanthalia elongata*, species of *Porphyra*, *Palmaria palmata*, *Delesseria sanguinea*, and species of *Enteromorpha* and *Ulva*. The seaweed resources of Brittany are rich in species numbers and biomass and there are many species that should be screened for use in cosmetics.

In cosmetology (the study of cosmetics) the whole alga is now rarely used. It is important to know the biochemical composition and cosmetodynamic potential of extracted material, whether it is a mash, a paste-like mixture of undifferentiated material, or an extract.

EXCIPIENT SUBSTANCES FROM SEAWEEDS

GELLING SUBSTANCES

Since the beginning of the 20th century, it has been possible to extract polysaccharides from the walls of *Laminaria* and *Ascophyllum*. Agar is extracted from various species of *Gelidium*, *Pterocladia* and *Gracilaria*, alginates from *Laminaria*, *Ascophyllum* and *Macrocystis*, and carrageenans from *Chondrus* and *Eucheuma*. The world's annual production in 1984 was 22 000 t of alginates, 13 000 t of carrageenan and 7000 t of agar. The main use of these substances is to increase viscosity and as stabilizers.

Agar

Agar (also known as agar-agar, gelose and agarose) is a polygalactoside extracted from species of *Gelidium* and *Pterocladia* (Gelidiaceae) and *Gracilaria* (Gracilariaceae). Agar-like extracts are also made from *Ahnfeltia* (Ahnfeltiaceae), *Phyllophora* (Phyllophoraceae) and *Gloiopeltis* (Endocladiaceae). Sobigel is at present the only manufacturer of agar in France. One principal use of agar is in bacteriology as a universal culture medium (see Chapter 9), but agar gels are also used in products such as perfumed deodorant sticks, sun creams, and dermatological creams that contain either zinc oxide or penicillin.

Alginates

Alginates were discovered in 1883 by the English chemist E.C. Stanford, who also worked on the extraction of iodine. By a curious reversal of history, it is interesting to note that researchers at the Centre d'Étude et de Valorisation des Algues at Pleubian have shown that iodine may be extracted profitably as a by-product of alginate extraction. Alginates may be extracted from about 300 species of brown algae. In terms of volume, the Laminariales and Fucales are the most important sources, in particular *Laminaria hyperborea*, *L.*

japonica, *Macrocystis pyrifera* and *Ascophyllum nodosum*. The harvesting and sources of supply of the seaweeds used in the European alginates industry are described in Chapter 10.

Only the uses of alginates in cosmetics and pharmacy, which represent about 5% of the market for alginates as compared with 30% in the food market, will be described here. Alginates are used as emulsifiers and emulsion stabilizers in creams and lotions; as excipients absorbable by the epidermis, in preparations such as gels, creams, ointments and pomades; as foam stabilizers; for their gelatinizing and film-producing qualities; and as protective colloids. Alginates are recognized world-wide as products that may be used freely in foodstuffs as emulsifying or stabilizing agents. Accordingly, they are safe for use in skin applications. The alginate-based gels are easier to produce than those based on pectin, as pectin is more sensitive to pH. The alginate gels are easier to spread on the skin and are well tolerated, being both softening and refreshing because of the evaporation of the incorporated water of the gel. Sodium alginate stabilizes the emulsions while playing a softening role. It is, additionally, a very cheap excipient for creams with a low lipid content. Propylene glycol alginate is more viscous than sodium alginate and is recommended in the formulation of hormonal creams in preference to Vaseline® as it facilitates the transepidermal absorption of the hormones. In soaps and shaving creams, sodium alginate acts as a lubricating agent, as a moistening agent to help in softening the hair, and as an activator and stabilizer of foam (thus producing an abundant foam as a softener, absorbable by the epidermis) and finally as a cooling agent that helps in preventing razor burns. Ten litres of 4% Nouralgine® solution (sodium alginate) is thus added to every 100 kg of sodopotassic shaving soap. Alginates are also used to give oiliness to non-foam shaving creams. Similarly, in soap-making, alginates are water-soluble ingredients that are very oily and softening, and are thus preferred to pectins because of their insensitivity to alkalis.

Triethanolamine alginate is film-forming and can be mixed into barrier creams for application to the hands to protect them from machinery, oil and industrial dusts.

In dentifrices, Satiagum® serves as a thickening agent while maintaining a soft and malleable paste, and stabilizes the foam, which is easily rinsed away, and makes the product suitable for the addition of calcium phosphate abrasive agents. It is also inexpensive, giving dentifrices a homogeneous texture, and will not dry up if the cap of the toothpaste tube is left off inadvertently.

Nouralgine® is used in shampoos, creams and liquids, whether they are based on sulphonated fatty acids, oils or eggs. Alginates may replace gum tragacanth in hair creams because of their superior viscosity, which allows the use of less cream and therefore leaves less dry matter on the hair after drying. In hair lotions, the alginate covers the hair and allows easy styling by giving a gliding quality, and also imparting a gloss to the hair. Likewise, an excellent setting lotion may be obtained with Nouralgine®, to which perfume and colour may be added. Application of this lotion to the hair by hand achieves a lasting set; this method is also used in cold straightening of curled hair.

The incorporation of alginates in slimming gels gives a gliding quality during anticellulitic massage. Potassium alginate is also used in making dental impressions, and calcium alginate has been recommended for the treatment of accidental poisoning with radioactive strontium. (Strontium has greater affinity for the alginate than calcium, so it is incorporated into the alginate and then excreted in the faeces.) Calcium alginate also serves as a haemostatic and as a plugging material in dentistry. Bandages woven from calcium alginate fibres are used in the treatment of burns, sores and leg ulcers. After exerting a haemostatic and healing effect, the calcium alginate may be removed by washing with a solution of sodium chloride, the alginate being transformed into sodium alginate, which is soluble in water.

At the market level, Chinese alginate, which has become available recently, is much less expensive than products from other countries, but is also cruder and less purified. Variations in origin of alginates requires rigorous control of their alginic acid content, levels of impurities, aqueous solution pH, optical rotation, and viscosity in aqueous solution. Viscosity is difficult to relate to concentration, but very dependent on pH, the ions present and temperature. Initially, there were problems with the paste being too hard. Recently, poor-quality alginates have been improved by enzymatic modification with C5 epimerases. Producers may find it useful to blend alginates with other gums and celluloses to attain a particular quality.

Carrageenans

The carrageenans were first extracted from several algae such as *Chondrus crispus* (Gigartinaceae) and *Mastocarpus stellatus* (Petrocelidaceae) and subsequently from genera such as *Gigartina* and *Iridaea* (Gigartinaceae), and *Gymnogongrus* and *Phyllophora* (Phyllophoraceae). At present, the underexploitation of *Chondrus* and *Mastocarpus* beds in Brittany and the high cost of collection (see Briand, Chapter 10) has resulted in importation of *Eucheuma* from the Philippines and Indonesia. Cultivation of *Chondrus crispus* is also being attempted in northern France.

Carrageenans of different types are designated kappa, lambda, iota, mu and epsilon, and essentially there is a cline of viscosities depending on the degree of sulphation of the galactan (see Chapter 8). Commercial carrageenans are mainly sold as potassium, sodium and calcium salts. Some 20% of carrageenan production is employed in cosmetology and pharmacy. Certain carrageenans allow very stable jellies to be made. They are used as thickeners and stabilizers of emulsions, particularly of the oil-in-water type, where they thicken the continuous aqueous phase, thus increasing its density and making coalescence more difficult. In pharmacy, carrageenans are invaluable for the manufacture of creams and ointments that are removable by washing after use and thus pleasant to use. In cosmetology, carrageenans are also irreplaceable as viscogenic substances that retain a high proportion of water in dentifrices, as a base for sun screens, as a foam stabilizer in cream shampoos and shaving foams, in soaps, as a fixing agent for hair in lacquers and hair balms, and as an absorbent base in products such as face masks. The carrageenan-based deodorants apply bacteriostatic substances to the skin which are capable of inhibiting growth of the bacteria responsible for the decomposition of sweat and the resulting disagreeable odour.

The water in sun screens applied to the skin in a thin layer evaporates gradually, giving a particularly pleasant sensation of coolness when it is hot and leaving behind a film active against the rays of the sun.

The incorporation of different active elements into algal gels is easy, and a table of the compatibilities and incompatibilities of these easy-to-handle excipients has been published by De Roeck-Holtzhauer (1969). A certain knack is necessary, however, to produce the correct gel; the powdered material must be allowed to fall in a steady stream into water that is agitated constantly until the gel is set. This has to be left to mature and swell for 12–24 h before its incorporation into a preparation like an emulsion.

Recently, new quality requirements have been formulated for carrageenans on the French market, but these have been postponed pending a re-examination of the situation. Gels made with carrageenans are more stable than those made with alginates, and dentifrices and antigingivitis gels have been formulated in my laboratory. The viscogenic capacity of these products has been shown to be a function of carrageenan type, and their stability is a function of pH (Peigné, Centre Atlantique d'Études en Cosmetologie, unpublished data).

Carrageenan powders keep well in the dry state but, on dissolving in water, give viscous solutions that are easily contaminated with airborne organisms, but are easy to protect with antibacterial agents and fungicides. These latter additives must, of course, be water soluble.

France is the fifth largest producer of alginates and the third largest of carrageenans in the world. The market is, however, fragile because of the difficulties of obtaining reliable supplies of raw material to fill the ever-increasing demand, both industrial and cosmetic.

To end this discussion of excipients of algal origin, a very common use of these hydrodispersible powders should be emphasized. The most interesting application is in vanishing creams, which, by rapid evaporation of the aqueous phase of the emulsion on the skin, leave a protective or medicated oily microfilm. Likewise, in hair disentangling creams and conditioners, alginates and carrageenans are often used with quaternary ammonium compounds that are effective against static electricity and also encase the hairs that have been damaged by combing, dying and permanent waving.

The problem of minimum standards of purity of alginates and carrageenans will be posed at the European level. Regulations for agar were proposed recently, but these, in my opinion, were too hasty and premature.

ALGAL FLOUR AND GROUND ALGAE

Algal meals, flours and ground algae are intermediate between the whole alga and the extracts mentioned above. They include mixtures of seaweeds collected by cutting under water or from cast plants. This material may be dried or processed in a number of different ways as outlined below. It is probable that there will be a difference in the chemical composition of a fresh algal paste and that of a poultice prepared from an algal flour dried at 40 °C or higher, even though the same species has been used in each case.

PRODUCTION

In Brittany, some seaweed is harvested using special cutting machines. In future the boats may be equipped exclusively with the 'scoubidou' collection device (see Chapter 10). The seaweeds in a mixed state, are brought by fleets of trucks to treatment factories either near the coast or further inland. The production of algal meal, which was carried out originally at Landerneau, is now being done at CEVA, Pleubian, by passing the algae through a continuously fed oven. Another centre for the production of animal feed has developed at Plougerneau, Brittany, also near the coast.

Cold crushing is carried out on the north coast of Brittany while the more sophisticated process of freeze grinding is employed at St Malo. Algae arriving at the factory are separated from mollusc shells and washed with seawater. The plants are then frozen in rectangular strips which are either treated immediately or stored in a refrigerated shed. These frozen slabs are cut in pieces by a grinder with jaws, then crushed in a system chilled with liquid nitrogen. The green paste thus obtained is then restored to ambient temperature in order to be either packaged immediately or centrifuged to remove the particulate matter, in particular cellulose, and so obtain a clear extract or cytofiltrate of the alga. The liquid, which is an amber yellow to red colour depending on the nature of the original algal material, must be maintained in a sterile vessel or be treated with preservative.

Spray drying is not used very much for algae because of its high cost. This procedure consists of dispersing an algal paste at the top of an atomization chamber transversed by a very rapid current of hot air maintained at 200–400 °C, which dries the droplets of algal liquid.

Freeze drying is carried out in France at only one factory, at Saumur. This procedure requires an early and rapid dispatch of the algae from the collection sites to the treatment factory and the addition of charged substances to obtain a very fine powder.

The technique of microdivision requires an Alpine-type pulverizing grinder that produces particles 10-20 μm in diameter. The use of ultrasonic waves to break open the cells has also been proposed for algae dried at 40–50 °C.

USES

Algal meal is quite granular and this allows it to be placed in fabric sachets for immersion in a bathtub, either in thalassotherapy at a specialized centre or for algal baths at home. These sachets are sometimes marketed with little bottles of essential oils intended to mask partially the strong smell of the alga, which colours the bath with a brown juice by expression of the sachet. These meals are also supplied in metal or plastic bottles and are sometimes tinted with blue or green colouring and herb fragrance in order to transform the bathtub into a 'fragrant, turquoise lagoon'. Bath salts with algae are also marketed; these are sea salts covered with a simple mixture of algal powder allowing the daily bath to be taken with algae and salts. Some of these meals, based on mixed *Fucus*, *Laminaria*, *Ulva* and *Ascophyllum*, are used as poultices, sometimes with the addition of *Lithothamnion* powder (maërl) in order to maintain heat. These sachets are heated to 40–50 °C at marine centres and applied to painful limbs to relieve arthritis or rheumatism.

Algal pastes, obtained by cold grinding or by freeze crushing, are applied to the body in a more or less thick layer in thalassotherapy institutions (as at Biarritz) while placing the patient under infrared rays to reheat the algal paste, which other centres heat first to 35–40 °C before application.

With regard to the principal indications (the relief of rheumatic pain or the removal of cellulite) an intense sweating is induced with the consequent removal of toxins, and it is questionable whether alga/skin cellular exchanges take place. Paste mixtures and creams of algae are also used as massage creams, with or without the addition of a fatty excipient. The hand of the masseur must, in effect, glide without overheating and the cream must not dry to form a peelable film in the course of the treatment.

The same type of product obtained from a mixture of algae is also available in heat-sealed sachets or plastic packs. The material is conditioned during production. For use, the seaweed material is poured into a warm bath, the temperature of which can be selected according to whether a relaxing or an invigorating bath is desired. This algal bath therapy may be achieved, even in bathtubs at home, by programmed jets of water to the foot, ankle, thigh, kidney region, back, nape of the neck, and so on. These baths are reputed to be fat-reducing. The freeze-dried algae must be kept in impermeable, heat-sealed sachets which allow a strongly fragrant, brown-coloured bath to be obtained.

Likewise, application to the breasts with a spray containing the algae in suspension is reputed to give tone. In spas and pools either seawater only or thermal salts are often used, because of the problems caused by the clogging of piping when algal pastes and meals are used.

Given the supposed wealth of the algal constituents, algal powders and pulps could form the basis of numerous cosmetic products, such as thinning creams, treatment creams, paste or gel masks, dentifrices, body lotions, hair setting cream, hair gels with antiseborrhoeic properties, shampoos and conditioners. The big problem in using algal pastes as raw materials in cosmetics is that of the preservation of the end-product. Algal powders and pastes must be supplemented with either one or several antifungal agents as moulds or even filamentous microalgae will flourish in the cream or mask. An antioxidant should also be included so that the cosmetic maintains the light green colour of the algae and does not turn brown.

Vials of cytofiltrate may be packaged in a small box for 18–21 day treatments in an annual or biennial therapeutic course. Pigments, chloroplasts and cellulose are absent from them; the question remains of whether there is any component of value to the skin in this pale yellow or pinkish liquid.

EFFECTIVENESS

The algal content of many of the products, whether an extract, flour or paste, is often very low. The inclusion of 2–5% of most algal extracts just about gives a white and odourless cream, which is only nominally marine; a proportion of 30–40% may be necessary to produce an effect. To determine the efficacy of an alga it would be necessary first to demonstrate a positive effect and then to analyse the material to determine the active compound(s). It would then be essential to establish the optimum collection time(s) for the algae, the best locations for collection and the optimum methods of either extraction or treatment. After this information has been obtained, formulation can proceed. Without such knowledge it is not known whether the incorporation rate of the alga in the final product is too low or at a harmful level.

Microalgae

A particular use may be mentioned in the context of microalgae, in particular those cultured for the purpose of feeding the larvae of young clams or oysters in hatcheries. We have found that the vitamin content, invaluable for the skin, is very high in various strains of *Tetraselmis* (a unicellular, prasinophycean, green alga), but the problem is how to concentrate this material into an active paste and, in particular, how to preserve its richness, given the indispensable addition of chemical preservatives.

Maërl

Maërl is the name given to a mixture of calcareous seaweeds (*Lithothamnion and Phymatolithon*) collected off the coasts of Brittany, the UK and Brazil (see Chapter 3 for agricultural uses; Chapter 10 for harvesting). After being dried and pulverized it is compounded into absorbent beauty masks and face masks; this material has been tested on rabbits and has been found to be harmless. The resulting white powder has a high content of calcium, magnesium, silicon and sulphate ions.

Thalassotherapy

At present, this therapy relies essentially on the therapeutic use of seawater, and the treatment centres store either pulverized algae or algae in mixed pulps. According to the Ministry of Health in France, the application of algal paste in thalassotherapy does not constitute medical treatment. This would be, however, a matter for consideration in a judicious choice between the various powders and pastes proposed in the trade. For practical reasons, some centres maintain the algal pulps all day in a thermostatically controlled tank at 30–40 °C; this procedure is unacceptable given the level of biochemical decomposition and bacterial growth that take place.

Indications for thalassotherapy treatment are many. The range is extensive: functional pathology, rheumatism, osteoporosis, pains of the locomotor apparatus, and the after-effects of orthopaedic surgery and trauma. Doctors, whether they are general practitioners or specialists in rheumatology, sports medicine or functional re-education, are in agreement with the effectivenes of treatments using seawater hydrotherapy, and either local or general application of algae and marine muds.

The mechanism of action of marine muds has not been completely elucidated. Besides the trace elements and mineral salts, microalgae, sulphur bacteria and diatoms have a role to play.

Chemical knowledge of the various algal species used is essential for the future. In this regard, the richness in vitamin D of *Fucus vesiculosus*, in vitamin E of the laminarians, in vitamin K of *Sargassum muticum* and the red alga *Delesseria sanguinea* is of note, as is the interesting balance of vitamins in the phytoplanktonic algae and of vitamins C and K in the unicellular green alga *Chlorella* (Chlorophyta).

Published works identify a certain number of significant components of algae; for example, there is a high concentration of iodine in certain algae, a high concentration of trace elements such as magnesium and zinc in others, and high levels of linoleic acid in *Spirulina platensis*. Similarly, a certain number of original chemical compounds have been demonstrated: terpenes, proteins, pyrrolic substances, phenols, arsenosugars, sterols like fucosterol, amino acids such as chondrine, gigartinine and kainic acid, and colorants such as phycoerythrins from red algae, xanthines from brown algae and cyanin from blue-green algae.

Among species worthy of study are:

1. *Spirulina* and *Ascophyllum nodosum* for their slimming action (Blunden & Gordon 1986);
2. *Delesseria sanguinea* for its anticoagulant sulphated polysaccharides (with heparin-like activity) and its vitamin K content, considered for incorporation into slow anticlotting creams with delesserine as the active principle;
3. *Chondrus crispus* with antigingivitis and antiscarring activity, possibly due to its carrageenan content;
4. *Palmaria palmata* with an antiperspirant activity;
5. *Fucus* species for their heparin-like action, and also for their antiseborrhoeic effect on greasy hair;
6. *Lithothamnion* and *Phymatolithon* for their richness in calcium carbonate and trace elements;
7. cultured *Chlorella*, which is rich in carotenoids, amino acids, antibiotics and antifungal agents;
8. *Porphyra atropurpurea*, which is applied by Hawaiians to wounds and burns;
9. *Hypnea* and *Durvillea* as heparin-like anticoagulants;
10. *Laminaria* species in the manufacture of diet drinks for their richness in iodine, and in massage creams;
11. *Sargassum muticum* for its content of vitamins C and K.

CONCLUSIONS

At this stage, one may hope for a profitable development alga by alga, with an astonishingly rich perspective. There are, however, numerous problems to resolve: choice of algal species, while being assured of a satisfactory potential resource; whether to collect or to culture the alga; harvesting of the alga from a chemically and bacteriologically clean area; culture with the optimum yield of the specific principle being sought; washing of the alga in seawater; choice of treatment or extraction to safeguard the specific principles utilized; determination of the cosmetodynamic efficacy of concentration; establishment of the cosmetic forms with the problems of formulation; solubility of the specific principle; conservation of its effectiveness; conservation of the galenic and microbiological quality of the product; chemical, galenic, microbiological and fungal stability; and development of a judicious cosmetics range as a function of the effectiveness required.

By combining the different efforts at national and European levels, we could expect to develop a Cosmetology based on algae which would be effective and worthwhile. Biomarine Cosmetology should be developed as a matter of urgency, starting with basic and, at present, embryonic ideas.

ACKNOWLEDGEMENTS

The assistance of Mrs Wendy Guiry in translation is gratefully acknowledged.

REFERENCES AND BIBLIOGRAPHY

Arzel P. 1987. *Les Goémoniers*. Edition de l'Estran, Saint-Herblain, 305 pp.

Bezanger-Beauquesne L. 1958. L'utilisation des algues. *Produits Pharmaceutiques* **7**: 339–50.

Belsher T. 1985a. Télédetection et phytobenthos: stratégie pour l'obtention d'informations, par télédetection, sur le phytobenthos marin. *Colloq. Franco-Japonais d'Oceanogr., Marseille*, **3**: 27–32.

Belsher T. 1985b. Télédetection des végétaux marins du phytobenthos du littoral français: l'archipel des Iles Chausey. *Photo Interpretation* **5**: 1–5.

Blunden G. & Gordon S.M. 1986. Medicinal and pharmaceutical uses of algae. *Pharmacy Intern.* **7**: 287–90.

Comyn, J. 1952. Les alginates et leurs utilisations pharmaceutiques. *Bull. Soc. Pharm. Lille* **14**: 22–7.

De Roeck-Holtzhauer Y. 1969. Excipients d'origine algolosique en cosmétologie et en dermopharmacie. Conférence présentée le 26/02 devant la Société Française de Cosmétologie, Paris.

De Roeck-Holtzhauer Y. 1984a. Plantes et algues en cosmétologie. *VII ème Journées Européennes de Cosmétologie*. 292 pp. Nantes: CAEC.

De Roeck-Holtzhauer Y. 1984b. Table ronde sur les algues en Pharmacie et en Cosmétologie. In *Valorisation des Algues et Autres Végétaux Aquatiques*. (Eds. R. Delépine, J. Gaillard & P. Morand) pp. 316. Paris: IFREMER.

De Roeck-Holtzhauer Y. 1984c. Intérêt des algues en cosmétologie et en traitement bucco-dentaire. Exposé présenté au Colloque Assoc. Bucco-Dentaire, Biarritz, June 1984.

De Roeck-Holtzhauer Y. 1984d. La mer et ses bienfaits sur notre peau, biologie marine en cosmétologie. Conférence présentée lors des Ières Journées sur 'Ultimos avances en estetica professional'. Barcelona, 6 October 1984.

De Roeck-Holtzhauer Y. 1986a. Présidence de la table ronde sur 'L'utilisation alimentaire des algues'. *Xèmes Journées Européennes de Cosmétologie*. 39–48. Nantes: CAEC.

De Roeck-Holtzhauer Y. 1986b. *Delesseria sanguinea*: algue à récolter. *Revue Phytothérapie* **7**: 29–32.

De Roeck-Holtzhauer Y. 1987a. Choix des algues spécifiques en cosmétologie. Conférence présentée lors du Colloque International de Phytothérapie, Paris, March 1987.

De Roeck-Holtzhauer Y. 1987b. Produits de la mer: Beauté et Santé. Edition de l'Interligne. 11–18.

Evin L. 1959. Possibilité d'emplois d'alginates et matières pectiques en cosmétologie: vérification et contrôle. *Bull. Soc. Dermopharm.* **3**: 16–21.

Jones A. 1983. L'économie des algues marines. *Biomasse Actualités* **3**: 38–43.

Percehay R. 1984. Techniques de transformation des algues en zône protégée. *VII ème Journées Européennes de Cosmétologie.* pp. 217–20. Nantes: CAEC.

Podesta D., Percehay J. & De Roeck-Holtzhauer Y. pp. 217–20. 1981. Application esthétiques des produits marins. *Colloque Soins Esthétiques en Cosmétologie.* pp. 171–7. Nantes: CAEC.

Vinot C. 1985. *Valorisation d'une algue brune: Undaria pinnatifida.* Rapport pour l'obtention de Diplôme d'Ingénieur en Génie Biologie. Université de compiègne.

5 Bioconversion of Seaweeds

PHILIPPE MORAND[1], BRIGITTE CARPENTIER[2], ROGER H.
CHARLIER[3], JACQUES MAZÉ[4], MIRELLA ORLANDINI[5],
BRIAN A. PLUNKETT[6] and JACOB DE WAART[7]
[1]Centre de Recherche en Ecologie Marine et Aquaculture, CNRS-
IFREMER, L'Houmeau, France, [2]Laboratoire des Sciences et
Technologies Brassicoles, Louvain-la-Neuve, Belgium, [3] HAECON
N.V., Ghent and University of Brussels, Belgium, [4]Centre d'Aide par le Travail de
Quatre-Vaulx, Saint-Cast-Le Guildo, France, [5]Istituto di Chimica Applicata e
Industriale, Universitá di Trieste, Trieste, Italy, [6]Department of Chemistry,
Portsmouth Polytechnic, Portsmouth, UK and [7]CIVO-Instituten TNO, Zeist, The
Netherlands

Seaweeds have numerous uses, but these absorb only a small share of the
annual natural production. Under certain local situations, however, the
exploitation of natural seaweed beds has reached its maximum and, in the
case of some species, cultivation has been introduced. Harvested and cultivated seaweeds have been used principally either as a source of food or as raw
material for industry, resulting in high-cost products. However, manual
harvesting of stranded algae has been carried out for a long time for spreading
on fields as a fertiliser. Historical reports and reviews of the uses of seaweeds
have covered all parts of the world and all types of past and present utilisation
(Sauvageau 1920; Tseng 1944, 1946; Jensen 1979; Chapman & Chapman
1980; Neushul 1987; Delépine et al. 1988).

An idea of seaweed production can only be given for the most widely used
species. In Japan, the largest consumer of seaweed, no less than 21 species of
algae were eaten as early as AD 800. Today, seaweed products include green,
brown and red algae and at least 46 species are in commercial use. In the
Orient, only four genera (Porphyra, Laminaria, Undaria and Eucheuma)
represent the principal seaweeds under exploitation. The 2.4 million t produced yearly have, of course, an important economic impact (Table 1).
During the first 4 years of the 1980s, production in the People's Republic of
China reached close to 1.5 million t from cultivation, Japan approached 0.5
million t (over half of which was harvested from natural strands), Korea
produced about 333 000 t and the Philippines around 116 000 t.

A substantial algal industry exists in Europe. France, the UK and Portugal,
for instance, are major centres, with alginate production the principal activity
(Boude 1983; Kain & Dawes 1987; Charlier 1991). The California-based

Seaweed Resources in Europe: Uses and Potential. Edited by M. D. Guiry and G. Blunden

Table 1. Production of seaweeds in the Orient (t wet weight)

Seaweed species	Country				
	China (1983)	Japan (1981)	Korea (1982)	Philippines (1980)	Total
Porphyra	99 870	340 510	101 559	—	541 939
Laminaria	1 387 776	44 221	—	—	1 431 997
Undaria	—	91 272	231 200	—	322 472
Eucheuma	—	—	—	115 652	115 652
Total	1 487 646	476 003	332 759	115 652	2 412 060

Adapted from Tseng and Fei (1987).

Kelco Co. has built up a huge business on kelp-extracted alginates. Some 136 187 t of kelp are harvested each year in California, about one-seventh the amount of the People's Republic of China (907 800 t). In the USA, a dietary supplement, a seasoning and a laxative were produced from kelp up to the year 1980 by P.R. Park. In Brazil and France, algal-based cosmetics industries have been gaining a strong foothold.

Total world production of seaweed currently amounts to about 3.5×10^6 t, with Asia the leader (84%) (Table 2). These totals fall below actual natural seaweed production for several reasons:

1. Economic motives have led to production decrease; before 1980, about 170 000 t of kelp were harvested in California and this total fell to less than 50 000 t in 1983–1984 (Neushul 1987). Production had been over 1.5×10^6 t

Table 2. Estimated world production of seaweed (t wet weight in 1984)

Continent	Seaweeds		
	Brown	Red	Green
Asia	2 049 337	843 168	8 053
Latin America	71 149	142 019	349
Europe	229 396	26 065	
(EC)[a]	(224 812)	(23 696)	
North America	39 000	19 830	
Others	4 076	4 678	
Total	2 392 958	1 035 760	8 402

After Briand (1988).
[a]Norwegian production is included in the EC data.

between 1913 and 1919, due to wartime requirements, as the USA was then cut off from its overseas sources of potash, a product needed for the manufacture of munitions. In New Zealand, *Pterocladia* tonnage has fallen from 109 t year^{-1} to a mere 20 t year^{-1} over a relatively short period in the second half of this century. Canada has also shown a marked decline in its share.

2. The exploitation of many species would increase the biomass potential considerably. For example, *Macrocystis pyrifera* and *Durvillea* (often spelled *Durvillaea*) *antarctica* alone, harvested once a year over an area of 200 km^2 around the Kerguelen Islands, would yield 0.4×10^6 t of biomass (Delépine 1983). Another significant example is provided by the proliferation in disturbed ecological systems of mostly green (e.g. *Ulva, Enteromorpha* and *Cladophora* species) and red algae (*Gracilaria* and *Porphyra* species) all around the world (Fig. 1). ('Proliferation' is for macroalgae what 'bloom' is for microalgae. The rapid growth of the algae in both cases is caused by the abundant presence of nutrients and favourable meteorological conditions. Proliferation is characterised by the accumulation of seaweeds in confined areas (like bays or lagoons) and/or their stranding along the shore.) The extent of this has been estimated at 1.3×10^6 t (Briand 1988), with the actual tonnage probably being much higher

Figure 1. 'Green tide' in Brittany, France. Cleaning of a beach in Lannion Bay. (photograph courtesy of Jacob de Waart)

98

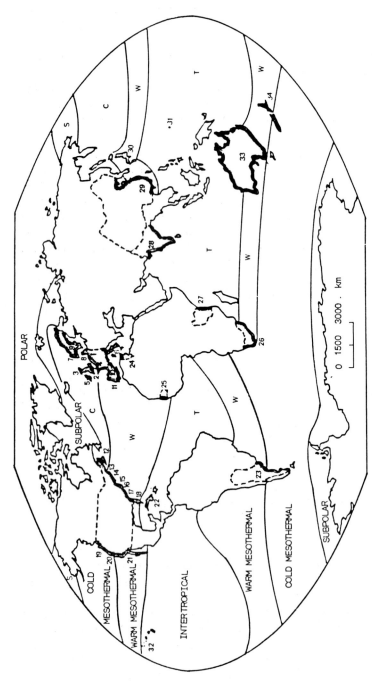

Figure 2. World distribution of algal proliferation (after Briand 1988). Bold indicates the coasts of countries where proliferation is reported. Modified Winkel's 'Tripel' projection. 1, Germany; 2, England and Wales; 3, Scotland; 4, France; 5, Ireland; 6, Italy; 7, Norway; 8, The Netherlands; 9, Sweden; 10, Spain; 11, Portugal; 12–21, USA; 12, Massachusetts; 13, Rhode Island; 14, connecticut; 15, New York; 16, North Carolina; 17, South Carolina; 18, Florida; 19, Washington; 20, Oregon; 21, California; 22, Cuba; 23, Argentina; 24, Tunisia; 25, Senegal; 26, South Africa; 27, Tanzania; 28, India; 29, China; 30, Japan; 31, Guam (USA); 32, Hawaii (USA); 33, Australia; 24, New Zealand.

(Fig. 2). A review of the seaweed-proliferation phenomenon (algal species, location, causes and consequences) may be found in Briand (1989) and in Chapter 10.

3. The possibilities of increased algal biomass production by genetic improvement have not, as yet, been investigated in depth.

4. Finally, the natural productivity of seaweeds is only about 1 t (dry weight) ha^{-1} year^{-1} in nutrient-poor water, the actual productivity depending, of course, on many parameters and on the species (Wise 1981). Productivity may however exceed 40 t (dry weight) ha^{-1} year^{-1} under good cultivation conditions. This is true, for example, of *Laminaria* cultures in nutrient-rich waters or when nutrients are added in controlled algal cultivation systems; 60 t (dry weight) ha^{-1} year^{-1} of *L. japonica* were thus obtained in China (Tseng 1987), a similar yield in small-scale cultivation of *Ulva*, *Chaetomorpha* and *Cladophora* in Sweden (Wachenfeld 1980), and up to 127 t (dry weight) ha^{-1} year^{-1} of *Gracilaria tikvahiae* (of which half was organic matter) in Florida (Hanisak 1987). In the UK, biomass growth rates could reach 20 t (dry weight) ha^{-1} year^{-1} (Morley & Jones 1981). Natural production overall is augmented by increasing the nitrogen and phosphorus content of the coastal waters; this has been a major factor in extending the cultivation area of *L. japonica* geographically, which has increased China's harvest by 33% (Tseng 1987).

Consequently, new uses of seaweeds could be developed at no risk to the existing ones. No body of literature exists, comparable to that available for fish resources, dealing with the major aspects of algal production. A report from the Food and Agriculture Organization (FAO) emphasises a lack of information on rate and timing of harvesting, levels of investment and manpower, ecological impact, and the identification of the economic feasibility of methods of mariculture (FAO 1983).

NEW CONCEPTS OF SEAWEED BIOMASS EXPLOITATION

MARINE FARMING

The concept of marine farms as a source of fuel received a strong impetus in 1968, and was developed afterwards as a result of the energy crisis in the 1970s (Wilcox 1977; North 1980). The Institute of Gas Technology in Chicago initiated the project Methane from Biomass, using *Macrocystis* from the Goleta near-shore farm in California (Chynoweth *et al.* 1987). A breeding programme was launched to establish pedigree lines of high-yielding seaweeds on Long Island Sound in New York State (Brinkhuis *et al.* 1987). Three candidates, *Laminaria saccharina*, *Gracilaria tikvahiae* and *Codium fragile*, were selected which, together, would be able to provide biomass throughout the year; some were grown on small rafts, others in Chinese-type rope farms. Some thought was also given to the growth of *Sargassum* on large retaining structures in the Caribbean and Florida (Flowers & Bird 1984). As natural gas supplies in the USA are adequate until the year 2000, work in this field will proceed at a research level rather than with immediate industrial implementation in mind.

SEAWEED CULTIVATION

The proposed ocean seaweed farms required anchoring support which initially involved extensive engineering (Neushul 1987; North 1987). The only economically viable large structures appear to be the Asiatic systems, made up of rope or net, constructed in shallow water and requiring substantial manpower and little mechanisation (Jensen 1985). Furthermore, in the latter case, seaweeds are used as food and industrial raw material. Other concepts of marine farms are now being tested with the planting of *Macrocystis pyrifera* in shallow water (Neushul & Harger 1985) and other seaweeds in near-shore farms (Neushul & Harger 1987; Brinkhuis *et al.* 1987). Kain and Dawes (1987) reviewed seaweed as a resource in Europe. The most advanced cultivation system (Laminariales) is found in France, a country with a considerable interest in algae; it has an important alginate industry and minerals are still extracted locally from the ash of some *Laminaria* species.

MULTIPURPOSE SCHEMES

As it is difficult to attain economic profitability with energy as the only aim, it appears that the development of seaweed cultures needs an integrated multi-use approach (Jensen 1985; Jackson 1977; Bird 1987). Thus, seaweed biomass can be used as a source of fuel, or of bioconversion products, and simultaneously as a means for pollution abatement, coastal protection and/or fertiliser production, resulting in an integrated system of production for food, raw material, fish and fuel.

Pollution-abatement projects have been attempted along the Brittany coasts and in the Venice Lagoon (Bonalberti & Croatto 1985; Briand & Morand 1987). In the latter case, the construction of a living artificial offshore reef has been investigated. Not only can this reduce the cost of beach maintenance and/or restoration, but it may also generate a cost reduction in the farm operation (Beavis & Charlier 1987; Charlier & Beavis 1991). Novel wave-dampening devices have been studied in connection with the indigenous New York State seaweed programme (Squires & McLay 1982).

Combined production of fertiliser and biogas has been studied in autonomous systems at certain locations, such as along the coast of Senegal, by the Office de la Recherche Scientifique et Technique Outre-mer (ORSTOM), now Institut Français de Recherche Scientifique pour le Développement en Coopération (Biset 1986; Dia 1987).

Finally, a project initiated by Ishikawajima-Harima Heavy Industries should be considered. Here, a system to grow kelp in marine farms and produce from it methane gas, amino acids, alginates, etc., is under study (Anon. 1985). Ingredients extracted from kelp would be supplied to local food, chemical and other manufacturers. Material remaining after the extraction of useful ingredients would be used as either fertiliser or feed. Methane gas produced would be used locally as an energy source. The system's design includes 9 km^2 of kelp-growing rafts installed several kilometers offshore; the kelp is ready for harvest after 8 months. This project is an example of the integration of marine biomass utilisation with a regional development scheme.

Before dealing in greater detail with European developments, the different technical conversion possibilities for novel uses of seaweed will be examined, and results achieved in Europe compared with those obtained world-wide.

BIOMASS TRANSFORMATION METHODS

THERMAL TREATMENT

Thermochemical biomass transformation processes are ancient in origin, and remain in common use in the Third World (wood combustion, carbonisation), or have been employed in particular situations (gas burners during the Second World War). They may benefit from technological progress and lead directly to diverse forms of energy or yield combustibles that may be utilised later. Depending on the process, one may obtain:

1. heat, by combustion of the biomass, gases at a high temperature being utilised directly for a drying process or to generate steam or warm water in a boiler;
2. mechanical energy, as a result of product gasification or of vapour generation and use of the resulting gas or vapour in an engine;
3. a liquid or solid product with a high energy content and in a convenient form for use (for instance charcoal or methanol), which could be used as a combustible to generate heat or electricity, or as a fuel in the engine of a vehicle.

To simplify matters, thermochemical processes that can be applied to biomass have been divided into four categories:

1. *Combustion* is the burning of the biomass, in which it is oxidised, resulting in the production of heat.

Table 3. Processes and target products in pyrolysis

Process designation	Aim
Carbonisation	Charcoal production
Distillation	Gas or pyroligneous liquid production
Gasification	Partial or total transformation into gas

2. *Gasification* is an endothermic process by which the biomass is transformed inside a reactor into simple combustible gases (carbon monoxide and hydrogen) with a more or less large proportion of incombustible gases (carbon dioxide, water, nitrogen). The process is usually carried out at temperatures in the range 800–1000 °C with the necessary heat supplied either externally to the reactor or by partial combustion of the biomass.

3. *Pyrolysis-carbonisation* may be considered as the thermal decomposition of organic materials, in an oxygen-free or oxygen-deficient atmosphere, leading to a breakdown of the molecular structure of the feedstock to yield chemically simpler products, with, by extension, gasification as a particular case. By subjecting the vegetable matter to temperatures above 400 °C, three types of product are obtained: charcoal, gas and pyroligneous liquor. Three commonly used terms are used to describe pyrolysis processes, each placing emphasis on the nature of the final product (Table 3).

4. *Hydroliquefaction* (or hydrogenation) is the transformation of the biomass into liquid fuel, at temperatures around 300 °C and pressures between 7 and 30 MPa (70 and 300 bar), in a reducing atmosphere which can be brought about, for example, by synthesis gas (carbon monoxide and hydrogen).

It is quite evident that boundaries are not always easily drawn between processes that automatically depend on the same thermochemical equilibrium and those that often occur at the same time as, or subsequent to, one another in a given thermal reactor. Pyrolysis, in particular, has received a great deal of attention over the last hundred years and this method has been applied to many organic feedstocks, such as coal, wood and domestic refuse. Many pyrolytic processes have been developed and patents granted for these feedstocks. These processes have been reviewed by Lenihan and Fletcher (1975) and Porteous (1981).

COMPOSTING

Composting is a very old technique involving the aerobic fermentation of degradable substrates leading, through a rapid degradation phase and a maturation phase, to a product usable as humic matter. Composting is a complete process, while aerobic digestion can be any phenomenon of degradation of a substrate in the presence of air by the action of living organisms (e.g. pretreatment in anaerobic fermentation, composting, sawdust degradation during storage).

Numerous substrates have been used for the production of composts, and several books and reviews have examined the composting of different substrates, such as household refuse, agricultural and farm-produce wastes (e.g. De Bertoldi *et al.* 1987), sewage sludges (Goldstein 1985), woody residues (ANRED 1983) and brushwood (Bingelli 1980; Bingelli & Alexandrian 1984). Frequently, these substrates are complemented by one or several natural or artificial fertilisers or mixed with others so that the carbon/nitrogen (C/N) ratio and the structure of the matter to be composted are compatible with the composting process.

Oxidation reactions taking place during composting are caused by living organisms (bacteria, fungi and animals). They are comparable to a slow combustion with release of carbon dioxide, water and heat, the temperature of the composting reaching more than 60 °C during rapid degradation. The thermal output of the reactions is low, however, and the heat is difficult to recover. Generally, methods used for heat recovery lead to a drop in temperature, incompatible with maintenance of the composting process.

The principal interest in composting is to transform refuse or unused biomass into humic matter, which is increasingly in demand. Nevertheless, the value of these products is not very high and, of the two methods used to produce composts, in piles and in vessels, it is mainly the first, less costly, method that has been used most recently. Aeration of the piles has been investigated with both natural and forced aeration, and the time necessary to make a mature compost in piles is now reduced to about 9 months (3 months for the rapid degradation phase and 6 months for the maturation phase), for organic materials with a high lignin content.

Mustin (1987) has recently reviewed current ideas and knowledge on the substrates and techniques of composting and utilisation of composts.

METHANISATION

Methanisation is the result of extremely complex bacterial activity and is generally classified under these headings:

1. hydrolysis and fermentation (or acidogenesis);
2. acetogenesis;
3. methanogenesis.

In practice, hydrolysis and acidogenesis are sometimes separated.

Hydrolytic and fermentative bacteria achieve liquefaction of the biopolymers present in the biomass and transformation of their monomers. The

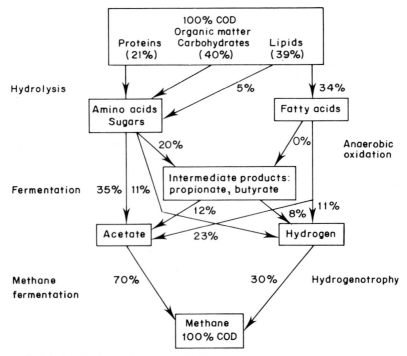

Figure 3. Methanisation: global sketch (according to Kaspar & Wuhrmann 1978). COD, chemical oxygen demand

metabolites produced in these processes (principally volatile fatty acids) are transformed into the direct precursors of methane, acetate and gaseous hydrogen and carbon dioxide, which constitutes acetogenesis. Methanogenesis results either from the decarboxylation of acetate or from the reduction by hydrogen of carbon dioxide (Fig. 3).

Analysis of the product inside the digester for total volatile fatty acids is a useful means of following the behaviour of the fermentation.

The theoretical limits of yield for methane are 415 l kg^{-1} for cellulose, 850 l kg^{-1} for lipids and 370 l kg^{-1} for sugars (Finck & Goma 1983). In practice, biogas contains 5–45% carbon dioxide, depending on the substrate.

Theoretical Considerations

Among the parameters involved in the performance of anaerobic digestion, the process chosen is of prime importance. Indeed, the sophistication of a digester can easily be changed, but microbiological improvement of the process is particularly difficult. However, one can optimise the substrate bioconversion by choosing a process that suits the characteristics of the substrate.

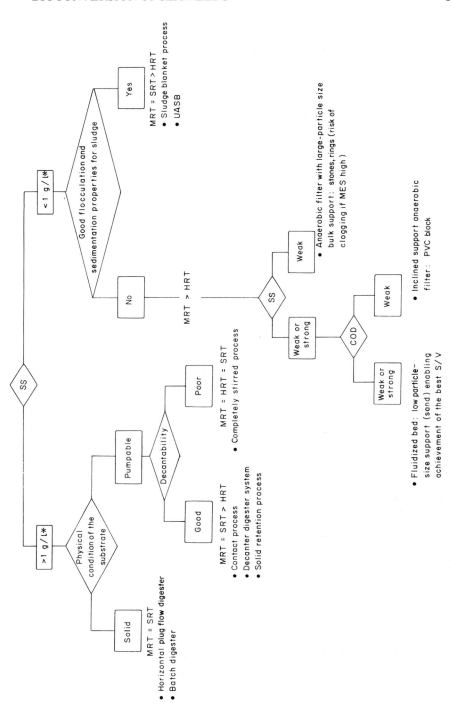

Figure 4. Selection of a process based solely on substrate properties. (*Figure after Bories & Ferrier 1984). MRT, microorganism retention time; SRT, solids retention time; HRT, hydraulic retention time; UASB, upflow anaerobic sludge blanket; PVC, polyvinyl chloride; SS, suspended solids; COD, chemical oxygen demand. (Source: Carpentier 1986)

The procedure followed in the choice of a process consists of promoting the retention time of microorganisms and solids at the expense of the hydraulic retention time (HRT), as far as the characteristics of the substrate will allow (Fig. 4). A substrate pretreatment may be performed so that a fixed bacterial reactor may be used; this is particularly relevant to seaweed. The pretreatment may then be equivalent to the first phase (acidogenesis) of a two-phase process.

The first phase can be accomplished in one or more completely mechanically stirred or gas-stirred reactors, such as a satellite system (Rijkens & Voeteberg 1984), or can be a storage in anaerobic conditions. Methanisable products are, in the latter case, collected by percolation or by simple drain-off. The employment of a number of parallel reactors, as a semi-continuous flow process (Hofenk *et al.* 1985), can improve the system, avoiding large amounts of the liquid at the bottom of each reactor, minimising the inhibition of methanisation by reaction by-products and maximising the use of the reactor volume (an important cost factor). Recently, modelling of the two-phase process, with percolation as the first phase, has been undertaken (Mata-Alvarez 1987).

Utilisation, in the second phase, of a reactor with a theoretical infinite solid retention time (anaerobic vertical or horizontal filter, fluidised bed, upflow anaerobic sludge blanket (UASB) reactor or mixed system) favours the conversion rate of volatile fatty acids (VFA). Recirculation from the methanogenic reactor may be used as a control of the acidogenic phase pH, moisture and temperature, but in seaweed fermentation special attention must be paid to the accumulation of salts and toxic substances, and usually only a partial or intermittent recirculation can be accomplished.

Practical Considerations

The cost of an installation and of its maintenance is a prime factor in the choice of a digester. A compromise must thus be found by balancing laboratory results against those of the technical economic analysis in individual cases. In practice, an anaerobic filter is preferable to a fluidised bed; although the latter is able to absorb substantially higher organic charges, it is very expensive to operate at present. In the same way, a digester of a completely stirred type should be chosen rather than the contact process which necessitates a supplementary installation for recycling and decantation.

The different processes of methanisation are shown diagrammatically in Fig. 5 and examples of applications are given in Table 4; there are numerous variations and a large number of digester types, which have been tested only in the laboratory to date. An example of these digesters is the baffled flow reactor (Fig. 6); some of the latter have been used with aquatic plants.

Stafford *et al.* (1980) provide a general review of all methanisation aspects, except the most modern digester designs.

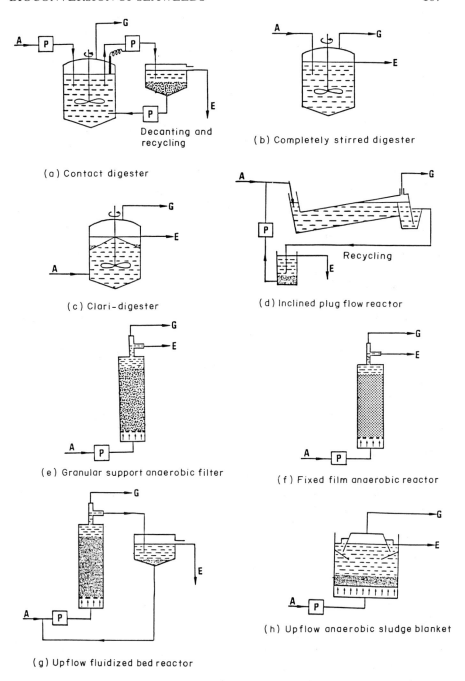

Figure 5. Different processes for anaerobic digestion: A, influent; G, gas output; E, effluent; P, pump. (Source: Carpentier 1986)

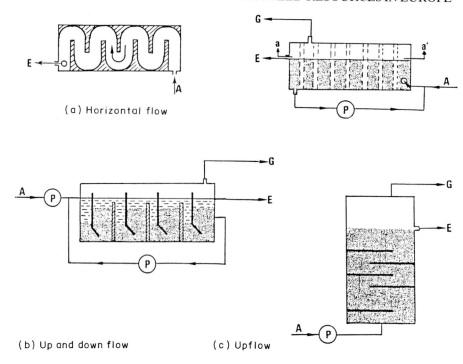

(a) Horizontal flow

(b) Up and down flow   (c) Upflow

Figure 6. Baffled flow reactors. A, influent; G, gas output; E, effluent; P, pump. (a) Horizontal-flow baffled reactor designed for *Laminaria* digestion (vertical view *right* and horizontal a–a' section *left*). Vertical baffles are fixed alternately on the top and base walls of the reactor. Their size increases in the substrate flow direction to reduce accumulation of solid matter in the front part of the reactor. (From Fannin *et al.* 1982.) (b) Up-and-down-flow baffled reactor designed for treatment of wastes with low-to-moderate soluble organic matter content (industrial waste waters). Vertical baffles are positioned to produce an up and down flow. (From Bachmann *et al.* 1985.) (c) Upflow baffled reactor. The baffles are perforated to minimise formation of foam-containing suspended matter. These baffles allow an operating cycle comparable to that of a sludge blanket reactor, where suspended matter settles naturally; here it is artificially trapped. (With a mixture of water hyacinth/waste waters in a ratio of 3 : 1 of suspended matter, a reactor volume of 50 litres, and a volumetric loading rate of 1.6–2.8 kg VSm^{-3} day^{-1}, performances were 20% higher than those obtained by the completely stirred method.) (From Chynoweth *et al.* 1982.) (Source: Carpentier 1986)

COMBINATION OF FERMENTATION WITH CHEMICAL TREATMENT

In 1849, Kolbe observed that a concentrated aqueous solution of the sodium or potassium salt of a fatty acid on electrolysis with platinum electrodes yields alkanes at the anode:

$$2RCOOK \rightarrow R\text{–}R + 2CO_2 + 2K^+ + 2e^-$$

Table 4. Anaerobic digestion processes with examples of their applications

Processes	Substrate	Reactor volume (m³)	Volumetric load (kg m⁻³ day⁻¹)	Purification yield (%)	Source
Completely stirred	Pig manure	200	TS 3.24 VS 2.25	TS 34 VS 39 COD 43	Aubart & Bully (1985)
Contact	Effluent from vegetable preserving plant	2 × 2500	COD ≈4	COD 85–90	Chambarlhac et al. (1982), Albagnac & Verrier (1983)
Fermenter decanter (IRIS process)	Washing waters from sugar plant	2 × 1000	COD 4	COD 90	Lescure et al. (1982)
Inclined plug-flow digester	Cattle manure	680	VS 4	VS 42	Martin & Lichtenberger (1981)
Solid retention reactor (Biomagaz process): laboratory results	Pig manure	6.10⁻³	VS 3.77 COD 6.60	TS 49 VS 57 COD 65–70	Aubart & Bully (1985)
Fixed-support anaerobic filter. Support: modular plastic blocks	Waste waters from a rum distillery	13 000	COD 10	BOD₅ 70–90 COD 65–70	Bolivar (1983)
Fluidized bed. Support: sand (particle diameter 0.1–0.3 mm)	Waste from yeast production plant	0.31	COD 50	COD 70–90	Heijnen (1983)
UASB (Biothane process)	Decanted distillery waters	800	COD 16.25	COD 88	Boulenger et al. (1982)

TS, total solids; VS, volatile solids; COD, chemical oxygen demand, BOD₅, 5-day biochemical oxygen demand.

It has since been shown that yields of 50–90% are obtained for straight-chain acids containing 2–18 carbon atoms and, with minor changes in electrolysis and solution conditions, alcohols, alkenes and esters may be obtained. Modern aspects of Kolbe electrosynthesis have been reviewed by Fleishmann and Pletcher (1971).

Biomass, when fermented, may be a source of high VFA production. This process could provide the raw material for conversion to hydrocarbons by Kolbe electrolysis to obtain a sort of diesel fuel.

SEAWEED CONVERSION

Much attention has been paid over the last few decades to the conversion of seaweed biomass into more useful materials. Most of this work has centred on methanisation, and aerobic digestion for this purpose has been performed on a pilot scale. Mainly fundamental research has been carried out on other biomass-conversion techniques.

THERMAL TREATMENT

Combustion

The combustion of air-dried macroalgae was originally carried out in pits from which a thick mash of grey-black colour was extracted. This, once cooled down and solidified, constituted *varech soda* (Breton), *salin* (French) or *kelp* (middle English *cülp*, now kelp) and was used in the glass industry. After competitive and less expensive products appeared on the market, the wrack (Breton *goëmon*) continued to be incinerated to extract iodine and other minerals. Incineration processes were uneconomic, mainly because of the high temperature necessary and the high heat input required to bring about combustion.

Combustion of algae, at as low a temperature as possible, produces a powdery, friable ash, whereas high temperatures result in a vitreous mass. Carbonisation ovens were thus constructed in an effort to control the process and, as a result, numerous useful products have been obtained.

Pyrolysis

Comparatively little attention has been paid to the study of seaweed pyrolysis. Stanford (1862) was first to record the observation that dry distillation of seaweed produced an oily substance. However, most early work centred around methods for the improvement of potash production rather than specifically for the production of organic chemicals and fuel. Balch (1909) compared the distillation of kelp (*Laminaria* spp.) with that of beech wood

(*Fagus sylvatica*) and observed the formation of acetic acid, methanol and tar in both cases. Green and Johnson (1912) distilled the brown alga *Nereocystis* and expressed the opinion that the distillates were worthless, while Turrentine (1913) distilled *Macrocystis pyrifera* and observed methane, hydrogen and carbon monoxide in the gases that evolved. In neither instance was the chemical nature of the liquid distillate examined. The distillation of *Macrocystis pyrifera* in iron retorts was compared with that of oak and Douglas fir wood by Hoagland (1915). He found that, at temperatures below 530 °C, the distillation yielded, based on dry weight of seaweed, 11.6% water, 5.5% tar, 46% char and 23.5% gas, with an oily liquid remaining. Unlike those from oak or fir, the gases evolved in the early stages of distillation were found to be non-combustible. The char fraction, on leaching with water, yielded charcoal and a liquor containing potassium and iodine.

Turrentine and Shoaff (1919) were commissioned by the United States Department of Agriculture (USDA) to design and operate a plant for the exploitation of that country's seaweed resources. The resulting integrated plant was capable of drying up to 100 t of seaweed a day and pyrolysing it at temperatures up to 980 °C. The products of this process were not described in detail or quantified, but were shown to consist of oil, creosote, pitch, ammonia and char. On extraction, the char yielded activated charcoal, potassium chloride and iodide. These authors concluded that, in this way, a new American chemical industry of considerable size and usefulness could be established.

Spencer (1920) has carried out a detailed study of the distillation of kelp in the temperature ranges 243–305, 400–600 and 800–950 °C. He showed that the nature of the distillation products varied markedly with temperature. In the lowest temperature range the pyrolysate was found to contain 55.0% pitch, 14.9% oil, 0.1% ammonia, 10.8% acids and 9.3% water. At higher temperatures an increased yield of pitch and a decreased yield of oil resulted. Considerable effort was expended to identify the chemical groups present. Phenols, acids, amines, hydrocarbons and alcohols were all mentioned and their percentage formation determined. The exact chemical nature of the products was not established.

Tupholme (1926) investigated the carbonisation of seaweed, for the British Fuel Research Board (BFRB), in an attempt to provide employment for the remote parts of the UK. This study involved the pyrolysis of air-dried mixed *Laminaria* species at 600 °C. The gas liberated initially was found to be very high in carbon dioxide and was allowed to escape, but it was collected as soon as it was capable of combustion (as the temperature of the mass in the furnace climbed towards 600 °C). This gas, which contained 10.6% carbon monoxide, 13% hydrogen, 32.8% hydrocarbons and 38.5% carbon dioxide, had a gross calorific value of 3732 kJ m^{-3}. The distillation also provided a solid residue of some 37% of the original weight of dried seaweed, tar (7.8%), mixed liquor (33.8%) and ammonium sulphate (1.4%).

The BFRB concluded from Tupholme's results that a pyrolysis plant for seaweed would depend for its success on the possibility of making the process thermally self-contained, but this has yet to be achieved.

More recently, Morgan and Smith (1978) have examined the pyrolysis, under nitrogen, of the brown alga *Fucus serratus*. Pyrolysis was carried out at 300, 450 and 800 °C and the yields determined for each temperature. The maximum yield of useful products was obtained at 450 °C. Expressed as a percentage of the weight of the air-dried seaweed, the yields at this temperature were 1.7% hydrocarbon gas, 1.5% carbon monoxide and 12.0% carbon dioxide; total liquid distillate amounted to 42% and solid residue (carbon and inorganic salts) to 32%.

Ingram, Neseyif, Patel & Plunkett (unpublished data) have examined the pyrolysis of the brown algae *Ascophyllum nodosum* and *Sargassum muticum* in a nitrogen atmosphere in the temperature range 300–800 °C and have obtained results similar to those of Morgan and Smith (1978). The distillates obtained from *Sargassum muticum* are undergoing detailed examination at present, using gas chromatography/mass spectrometry and high-pressure liquid chromatography, in an attempt to identify the exact chemical nature of the products (Plunkett 1988).

Simple pyrolysis of seaweed as a source of fuel and organic chemicals suffers from a number of problems that seriously affect the economics of the process. The very high water content of the freshly gathered material means that considerable energy must be consumed to remove it before or during pyrolysis. The bulk density of the material, in both fresh and dried form, is low and leads to high transport and handling costs. The complex mixture of chemicals in the easily condensed fractions may be viewed as both a blessing and a curse. Provided very large quantities of seaweed can be pyrolysed and an efficient means of product separation can be developed, a large number of useful substances may be obtained. However, in general, the separation of complex mixtures of chemicals causes many difficulties and is rarely attempted on a small scale with commercial intent.

COMPOSTING

The high water content of aquatic plants leads to their being considered for composting. This type of conversion has been used with success for the water hyacinth (Parra 1975). As far as marine plants are concerned, compost from the sea-grass *Posidonia oceanica* was obtained in Tunisia and successfully utilised in cultivating tomatoes (Saidane *et al.* 1979; Verlodt *et al.* 1985). Nevertheless, the tradition of directly incorporating plants into the soil explains why composting techniques have not developed for the macroalgae. This situation changed with the proliferation of green algae, as these cannot be spread on the soil in a raw state (Brault *et al.* 1985), and with the composting of ligneous residues, for which seaweed provided a means by which the composition of the substrate to be composted could be improved. Two experiments were performed in Brittany (France), one on the composting of *Ulva* sp. mixed with sawdust and bark (Brault *et al.* 1983) and the other on the composting of different mixtures containing seaweeds, wood, and dung or manure (Potoky 1983).

Similarly, experiments have been carried out in Senegal by the Institut Français de Recherche Scientifique pour le Développement en Coopération (ORSTOM) to utilise stranded algae, notably *Ulva* and *Cladophora*. Composting was studied along with other methods of utilisation and found to be promising (Gningue 1985).

Research in Pleubian (Brittany)

Brault *et al.* (1983, 1985) investigated the uses of *Ulva* sp. and studied methods for the treatment of the algae and conditions necessary to compost them. They concluded that the compost of green algae mixed with wood refuse was rich in organic matter – up to 65% of the dried matter at the end of maturation – in main elements (nitrogen, phosphorus, potassium) and in secondary elements (calcium, magnesium). It was obviously of interest because of its very low content of heavy metals and toxins. Some improvements were still needed where alkalinity and salinity are concerned (CERAA 1983).

Research in Saint-Cast (Brittany)

The experiments carried out by Potoky (1983) and Potoky and Mazé (1988) were based on the work performed on the brushwoods by Pain and Pain (1979). To reduce the C/N ratio of the starting mixture, which was based mainly on wood wastes, thus accelerating composting, the addition of either green or brown seaweed was tested, together with liquid manure and dung.

Agronomic experiments followed the work on composting. These permitted the classification of the new products as either growing media or organic conditioners, and determination of the method of use: doses, frequency of application, and the need for additional fertilisation depending on the end-use.

Composting experiments

In full-scale experiments in the open, approximately 700 m^3 of fresh matter was treated in 39 different mixtures. The volume of the compost heaps constructed ranged from 25 to 50 m^3. The materials used were:

1. wood or bark: oak, elm, poplar, chestnut, maritime pine, cypress, willow, birch, plane and beech;

Figure 7. Seaweed (*Fucus*) component in compost manutacture. (Photograph courtesy of Pierrick Potoky)

2. seaweeds: *Ulva lactuca, Fucus vesiculosus, F. serratus, Laminaria digitata, L. hyperborea, L. saccharina* and *Ascophyllum nodosum* (Fig. 7);
3. manure and dung from poultry and/or rabbits.

The main results of this work were as follows.

Seaweeds allow thermofermentation to proceed more efficiently. The breakdown time is reduced; for example, 18 months were necessary for the breakdown of wood with Jean Pain's method whereas only 8, 10 or 12 months were sufficient when wood/seaweed/dung combinations were used.

More than half of the products obtained had a level of organic matter (with respect to the raw product) equal to or much higher than that of horse manure (15–17% of organic matter/raw product). Over one half had a C/N ratio ≤20, after 6 months composting, indicating a mature compost. The humus conversion coefficients were high (50% minimum).

With several mixtures, nitrogen, phosphorus and potassium contents are comparable with those of a farmyard manure, and calcium, magnesium, sulphur, molybdenum, copper, zinc and manganese contents are higher than those of a farmyard manure. Only the boron content is lower. Except for boron and, possibly, sulphur, the contents analysed are sufficient to satisfy normal agricultural requirements.

The products possessed very low concentrations of organochlorine compounds, non-degradable herbicides and heavy metals.

Composts: agronomic utilisation

As far as their utilisation is concerned, forest composts enriched with sea-weeds and/or animal droppings were competitive, from a technical point of view, as organic improvers, with manures, urban composts and even commercial improvers. If they were composted for several months, they had the advantages of mature composts; they were convenient to spread, they could be applied just before cultivation, and they provided a 'stimulus' effect in making nutrients rapidly available on a relatively long-lasting basis. These points support their use for intensive cultivation both in the field and in the greenhouse.

The addition of algae and/or animal droppings to an organic support must be decided on the basis of a planned fertilisation, namely, an organic enrichment destined to improve the soil's humus content, or the fertiliser effect, with a view to bringing in the major elements of nitrogen, phosphorus and potassium. The algae can thus participate in the making of various organic enriching agents, adapted to different agronomic needs. In this way, a judicious supplementary fertilisation makes it possible to turn mixtures of wood and algae, with lower nitrogen, phosphorus and potassium contents than wood-algae-droppings mixtures, into an economically worthwhile product.

As regards production of compost as a growing medium, a mixture of approximately 25% mature compost and 75% peat was necessary, in the case of moulded blocks, in order to achieve promising agronomic results: sufficient nutrient content, ease of moistening, good moulding ability, pH between 6 and 7, limited conductivity allowing enrichment where needed, and watering convenience. From the trials performed in nurseries, market gardening (truck farming), and flower and vegetable growing, the results seemed very satisfactory when compared with those obtained elsewhere. For other end-uses (e.g. plant potting), the composts could be incorporated in proportions of between 25 and 50%.

METHANISATION

Features of Seaweed as a Methanisation Substrate

Algal biomass can be considered as a semi-solid substrate and thus be compared in its biomethanisation yield to agricultural and urban residues. Unlike terrestrial plants, algae do not possess lignin, a major obstacle to the degradation of cellulose. The composition and structure of algal cell walls show considerable diversity and are greatly different from the cellulose pattern with a crystalline structure found in terrestrial plants. Each taxonomic class of algae possesses particular types of polysaccharides, and when cellulose is present in the seaweeds it is not in a large quantity; in *Macrocystis pyrifera*, for example, it reaches only 8.8% of dry weight (Chynoweth *et al.* 1981).

For this substrate, cellulose degradation is about 75% (Kohler & Hart 1980), but the biodegradable fraction of seaweed mainly consists of carboxy-lated or sulphonated galactose and/or mannose chains, and mannitol. For example, in *Macrocystis pyrifera*, the carbohydrate fraction is about 71% of volatile solids (VS) Chynoweth *et al.* 1981). This high fraction of carbohy-drates leads to a good productivity of volatile fatty acids; 98% of fermentable solids conversion can be obtained in 5 days with continuous removal of acids, although without this removal more time is necessary – about 35 days in the case of the red alga *Chondrus crispus* (Sanderson *et al.* 1978). The microbiol-ogy of seaweed methanisation was recently reviewed (Forro 1987) and, in general, the principal constituents of seaweeds are easily degradable; moreover, mannitol may act as an activator.

The carbon/nitrogen/phosphorus (C/N/P) ratio is another factor the role of which is still not fully understood. Authors refer to quite different ratios such as, for instance, 100/11/52 (Chynoweth *et al.* 1981), 100/3/1 and 100/2/1 (Canovas-Diaz & Howell 1987). It is thus hazardous to link the properties of an alga to its C/N/P ratio and to rely on this ratio for an estimation of the theoretical biogas production. In fact, carbon, nitrogen and phosphorus content is sometimes related to slowly biodegradable compounds unavailable for good development and activity of bacteria. The C/P and C/N ratios can, however, be useful when comparing samples of the same species.

Chynoweth (1980) studied methanisation of *Laminaria*, the C/N ratios of which were 14–24 and concluded that biogas production is higher when C/N ratios are low. However, Habig *et al.* (1984b) observed that biogas production increases with *Ulva* and *Gracilaria* as the C/N ratio increases (from 9 to 31). With *Ulva*, when the algae are low in nitrogen, the soluble carbohydrate concentration is augmented.

As for the content of metals and pH equilibrium, de Waart *et al.* (1987) mention substrates that give rise to unstable digestion and recommend the addition of correcting minerals or mixing different substrates in these cases. These workers suggest that the digestion of *Sargassum muticum* may be accomplished without encountering this type of problem, and, in the litera-ture, no conclusive examples of the inhibition of methanisation of whole seaweeds resulting from an imbalance in mineral content can be found.

Co-digestion

Modification of the C/N/P ratios through the build-up of mixtures and co-digestion of different substrates, for example seaweeds and municipal sludge wastes (MSW), sludges or manure, could, in some cases, improve the process (Ghose & Debabrata 1982). Results from research on this aspect have proved negative. Roustan (1984) studied the fermentation of an '*Ulva*/manure' mixture and found that the biomethane production of the mixture corresponded to the sum of the production of each separate substrate; Carpentier (1986) obtained lower production with an 'alginate extraction residues/manure' mixture than was indicated by the corresponding calculations.

In a similar way, the co-digestion of different seaweeds is often difficult. Because of differences in digestion speeds of algal species, metabolites released by one species during some methanisation phase could inhibit the methanisation of another species, as suggested by the monitoring of the changes in VFA concentration (Jacq, personal communication). Rao et al. (1980) mention, however, that the addition of a small quantity of Ulva to Sargassum tenerrimum (in a ratio of 1:17) accelerates and increases the production of biogas.

Pretreatment

Algae, as semi-solid substrates, need pretreatment; indeed, hydrolysis is the limiting factor in their methanisation.

Mechanical treatment is always used for the digestion of the entire macroalgae. Several types are used from simple chopping to ultrasonic grinding. Operation costs will determine the type of pretreatment to be applied, keeping in mind past improvements in digestion performances and the level of energy required for pumping, feeding and agitation in the digester.

It should be noted that some kinds of pretreatment, e.g. heating, enzymatic treatment and mechanical reduction (to 1–5 mm particle sizes by milling, crushing etc.), increase the accessibility of the biomass and accelerate substrate conversion (Kohler & Hart 1980). Care must be taken in choosing the pretreatment as sometimes chemical, thermochemical and thermal treatments can prove unsuccessful (Schramm & Lehnberg 1984). In fact, each algal substrate must be specifically studied for determination of the optimum treatment to facilitate methanisation.

Specific treatments can be designed either to improve the overall output of methanisation or to diminish the time required for methanisation and minimise the size of the digester. Thus, for Ulva, the separation of a liquid extracted by centrifugation after grinding was investigated in Italy (Camilli et al. 1985). However, it is the spontaneous pretreatments on which attention will be focused. These exploit the natural predegradation of the algae and may be used in different ways.

Percolation, or natural hydrolysis of algae, constitutes a particular case. Simple storage of Ulva at 4 °C for 1 month has been shown to improve the ultimate methanisation, the methane yield being increased by 45% (Carpentier 1986).

Legros et al. (1982), using the freshwater green algae Hydrodictyon reticulatum and Cladophora glomerata, studied a system that takes advantage of natural hydrolysis. The algae were stored in a tank for several days with a water-sprinkling system placed above them, so that the water percolated through to give an effluent that could be methanised in digesters adapted to substrates with a low suspended-matter content. The digestion of these algae proved to be possible at a loading rate greater than the 2.5 g VS l^{-1} day^{-1}, above which the completely mixed digestion undergoes acidification by accumulation of VFA.

For *Hydrodictyon* and *Cladophora*, digestion results (35 °C, pH 7.3, retention time 1.2 days in a 1 litre upflow reactor) were, in terms of chemical oxygen demand (COD), 6.6 g COD l^{-1} day^{-1} loading rate, 0.29 m^3 methane kg^{-1} COD, 71% of methane in the biogas and a 97% COD reduction rate (Legros *et al.* 1982).

After a natural hydrolysis lasting 1–8 months, Brault and Briand (1985a) obtained liquefaction juices that drained off by gravity to the bottom of a container in which the alga, *Ulva* sp., was merely stored. These liquefaction juices could then be methanised in an anaerobic filter (Carpentier 1986). The algae can also be squeezed, resulting in more rapid extraction (1–3 months) of the juices (Briand & Morand 1987).

This type of pretreatment shortens the payback time of investments. Indeed, compared with the digestion of the whole alga in the infinitely mixed process, the reactor size and consumption of biogas for digestate heating will be far less. For *Ulva*, the volume of a fixed bacterial fermenter will be 25 times less than that of an infinitely mixed reactor needed to treat simultaneously an equal quantity of algae; the biogas production will be only three times less in an anaerobic filter (Carpentier 1986). In addition, grinding and dilution of *Ulva*, whose pumping limit is at 6% of dry matter, is rendered unnecessary. Use of the solid by-product of this treatment as a fertiliser is being considered (Brault *et al.* 1985).

Toxicity

Inhibition results from high concentrations of substances such as phenols, heavy metals, sulphides, salts and volatile acids. A very important parameter in the study of the toxicity is the 'acclimatation factor'. When a toxic element is brought into a biological medium progressively, the perturbation produced is markedly weaker than when it is suddenly put into the digester.

When there is a permanent supply of toxic substances, adaptation will be achieved all the more easily because the retention time of the microorganisms will be important. If the supply of toxic substances is transient, the short HRT of the fixed bacteria processes will allow a rapid elution of the toxins. Thus either a short HRT is used or else substantial dilution is employed to minimize the inhibition effect.

Sulphur

One of the general characteristics of marine macroalgae is the presence of at least one sulphated polysaccharide – polymers not found in terrestrial plants

(Percival & McDowell 1967). The sulphur content of seaweeds is high and generally ranges between 0.5 and 1% of dry weight (Show 1985). Some algae contain, under certain conditions, huge quantities of sulphur; for example, *Ulva* (4.4% of dry weight) (Brault & Briand 1985a), *Gracilaria* and *Fucus* (4.6%), and *Iridaea* (8.2%) (Show 1985). Sulphur, an element needed for methanic fermentation, can also be an inhibitor.

If sulphites are omitted, the toxicity of the inorganic sulphur compounds increases as the sulphur oxidation state decreases (Khan & Trottier 1978). Khan and Trottier have shown that the toxicity of sulphur appears only after sulphate reduction to sulphides. Furthermore, sulphur toxicity is a function of the presence of metals (yielding precipitates of metallic sulphides), of the pH and of the temperature (which control the position of chemical equilibria) as well as the biogas circulation, which can entrain hydrogen sulphide.

Parkin and Speece (1983) demonstrated the acclimatisation of anaerobic organisms to concentrations of some toxins of 10–25 times the levels that cause inhibition in unacclimated methanogens. These authors achieved acclimatisation to sulphide on an anaerobic filter fed with an acetate-enriched medium. The maximum concentration of sulphide tolerated with no significant deterioration in process performance was $600 \, \text{mg} \, l^{-1}$. After a progressive addition of this toxin to the digestion of *Ulva* sp. liquefaction juices, Carpentier (1986) observed a 35% decrease in biogas production at $600 \, \text{mg} \, l^{-1}$ sulphide. Without acclimatisation, total inhibition was observed.

Trials have been carried out on the removal of soluble sulphides by precipitation of metallic compounds by adding iron(II) chloride and iron(III) chloride to the digester, and on the inhibition of sulphate reduction activity, in order to avoid methanisation inhibition or to obtain a lower hydrogen sulphide percentage in the biogas. These trials have not been conclusive. With *Ulva* methanisation experiments, Dia (1987) observed a strong improvement in the biogas production by adding iron(II) chloride under initial conditions of slight inhibition; de Waart (1988) introduced iron(III) chloride with *Ulva* into the digester and obtained a reduction in hydrogen sulphide from 5.1 to 1.1% in the biogas, but only at the cost of an appreciable loss in yield (from 303 to $216 \, \text{ml}$ biogas g^{-1} VS). Addition of molybdate, known to inhibit sulphate-reducing activity, had a negative effect on the *Ulva* methanisation by also inhibiting methanogenesis (Dia 1987).

Metals

Other inhibition factors may be considered, for example the presence of heavy metals, which may be a problem where there are not enough soluble sulphides to precipitate them as insoluble products. However, with algae that have a high sulphur content, such as those collected in the Venice Lagoon, the problem does not arise because precipitation in the form of sulphides occurs naturally. On the other hand, a slight concentration of heavy metals can be favourable to anaerobic digestion.

Sodium chloride

Another factor that affects seaweed methanisation is the possible inhibitory effect of salt (sodium chloride). De Baere *et al.* (1984) tested the effect of salt in a fixed bacteria reactor; when introduced suddenly, inhibition at 30 g l^{-1} was observed. On the other hand, the gradual introduction of salt did not cause perturbation until a level of 65 g l^{-1} had been reached. However, in trials involving the desalting of seaweed, Schramm and Lehnberg (1984) noted that methane production decreased and, furthermore, that production was higher in seawater than in freshwater. The partial elimination of salts, by treating the biomass with heat and pressure, leads to a lower biogas production, probably due to the loss of fermentable compounds together with the elimination of the salts (Chynoweth *et al.* 1981; Schramm & Lehnberg 1984). Bioconversion efficiency under marine conditions sometimes appears to be higher with a marine inoculum (Schramm & Lehnberg 1984).

In conclusion, it should be pointed out that it is not possible to generalize particular results because of the many factors involved in the ability of bacteria to tolerate a particular toxic substance. For instance, Carpentier (1986) mentions that the effects of sulphates in sediments and in a digester are not identical. The competitive processes between the bacteria involved in the sulphate reduction and methanisation are well known (Robinson & Tiedje 1984; Dia 1987; Forro 1987), and methane production is strongly reduced in seawater (Sorensen *et al.* 1981) as in freshwater (Winfrey & Zeikus 1977; Lovely & Klug 1983). In a digester, however, methanogenesis is dominant as sulphate reduction diverts only a small part of the substrate's energy potential. Another example of possible toxicity is provided by the difficulties encountered in methanising *Ulva* (which has a high sulphur content) in polyvinyl chloride (PVC) digesters with a high wall-surface/volume ratio (Carpentier 1986).

Inoculum

The inoculum may be an important factor in the methanisation process, especially in its initiation (Schramm & Lehnberg 1984). Some authors are of the opinion that marine and domestic sewage sludge inocula have the same final effect (Chynoweth *et al.* 1981; Schramm & Lehnberg 1984), although marine inocula cause the process to start faster than do traditional ones. This brings to mind the observation of Rao *et al.* (1980) that some marine bacteria, which are able to digest specific phycocolloids, accelerate and increase the biogas production when added to the digester with the inoculum.

Hanisak (1981) shows the poor starting ability of dairy manure and water-hyacinth inocula, and emphasises the fast start (5 days) with a mixture obtained with marine sediments from an area of decaying seaweeds, seawater and untreated algae. Similarly, a rapid start was achieved by using an inoculum extracted from mangrove swamp sludges for seaweed methanisation in Senegal (Leclercq *et al.* 1985).

Fermentative bacterial adaptation poses a problem, and the speed of its completion depends to a large extent on the inoculum source. However, methanisation results are independent of the original source of the inoculum when adaptation is achieved. Bacterial distribution during a 3 month fermentation of *Ulva* pressed juice with retention times of 10 and 6 days showed a very rapid turn over, resulting in a working population completely different from the inoculum population (Bianchi & Randriamahefa 1987).

Temperature

It seems that even inocula from natural areas where methane is being produced at low temperatures have not resulted in profitable fermentation in psychrophylic conditions (Bianchi & Randriamahefa 1987; Schramm & Lehnberg 1984). As for the thermophilic digestion of seaweeds, little or no advantage was found to justify its use (Hansson 1983; Schramm & Lehnberg 1984).

On the other hand, the presence of salts seems to inhibit the thermophilic process, with only a partial adaptation of thermophilic bacteria to this medium and with lower performance of the process as compared with the other substrates under the same conditions (Chynoweth *et al.* 1981).

Finally, the need to maintain a constant temperature during fermentation should be stressed. Several authors mention that production is perturbed by transient shifts in temperature. For instance, low biogas production of *Cladophora* methanisation in Senegal is ascribed to temperature drops at night (Biset 1986).

Methanisation Results

Table 5 summarises the results obtained for seaweed methanisation by numerous research workers (Fig. 8). It should be noted that the modest performances described under certain conditions (such as physiological state of the algae, conditions of storage, pretreatment, type of digester and concentration of soluble sulphides in the digestate) might be improved in others. Nevertheless, it is possible to recognise trends in the overall data by expressing the best biological results of the anaerobic digestion of the various algae in an infinitely mixed process as a function of the volumetric loading rate (Fig. 9), thus giving an overall view of the algal methanisation potential.

In general, brown algae are more easily degraded than green algae which, in turn, are easier to degrade than red algae. There are some exceptions when particular structures or substances are present, such as in the green alga *Enteromorpha* or, frequently, the brown alga *Sargassum*. In the latter case,

Table 5. Characteristics of the anaerobic digestion of seaweeds

Substrate Pretreatment System	Temperature °C	pH	Digester volume[a] (litres)	Retention time (days) RT or HRT	SRT	Loading rate (g l⁻¹ day⁻¹) TS	VS	COD	Biological yield (m³ CH₄/kg) TS	VS	COD	CH₄/biogas (%)	H₂S/biogas (%)	Reduction rate (%) TS	VS	COD	Source
Chlorophyceae																	
Ulva lactuca																	
CM	37		50	26			1.9			0.15			0.95				Wise et al. (1979)
CM	30		1	20		2.5	1.47			0.20		65.3	5.1				de Waart (1988)
Ulva sp.																	
CM	28 ± 3		2	30			1.12			0.15		50.3			41.3		Habig & Ryther (1983)
	28 ± 3		2	40			0.85			0.20		59.0			50.4		
	28 ± 3		2	50			0.68			0.23		60.6			56.1		
CM acidogenesis[b]/CM	37	7.8	2	20		1.25	0.74			0.20		78				52	Brouard (1983)
			10	20						0.27							
Batch	32 ± 3		2	58		0.49[c]	0.34			0.22		53.7			70.1		Habig et al. (1984b)
	32 ± 3		2	58		0.50[c]	0.36			0.23		53.5			77.3		
	32 ± 3		2	58		0.48[c]	0.35			0.33		58.9			86.7		
CM	35		25	11			1.8			0.18–0.20			2		52		Roustan (1984)
acidogenesis[d]/AF	35	7.3						0.66		0.25						73	Petitbon (1985)
CM	37		6	30			1.25			0.19		54	2.7		69		Carpentier (1986)
Ulva rigida (+ *Chaetomorpha aerea*[e] + *Valonia aegagropila*[f])																	
CM	35		3 × 200	20		0.12–0.24						50–65	1				Croatto (1982)
AF	35		5000	8	6.25	0.14[g]							3.5				Nicolini & Viglia (1985)
CM	35		5000	12	5.25	0.18[g]				0.22[g]							Missoni & Mazzagardi (1985)
Centrifugation liquid part/AF			30	0.88	37	37		34	0.05		0.055	60–65	6			40–50	Camilli et al. (1985)
Ulva + *Chaetomorpha* + *Cladophora*																	
CM	35		1.6	11–27			1.1–2.6			0.25–0.35 (inferior)		60			50–55		Hansson (1983)
	55		1.6	11–27			1.1–2.6								50		

Ulva natural hydrolysis juice natural drainage											
UFA	37		1.3	1.4	10		0.36		80	90	Carpentier (1986)
Batch	15	6.3–7	3	80[h]	0.73		0.04	56		68	Bianchi & Randriamahefa (1987)
CM	37	7	1.5	10	7		0.20	87		53	
	37	7	1.5	6	11.5		0.08	85			
pressing UFA	35		12.6	10	6		0.19	80		56	Briand & Morand (1987)
Ulva 60% + sludges 40%											
CM	38			20			0.31		62		Rye (1988)
Enteromorpha intestinalis											
CM	37		2	20	1.36		0.13		65	36	Brouard (1983)
Percursaria percursa + Enteromorpha linza, E. Intestinalis and E. prolifera											
Batch	25		2–3	60[i]	0.12–0.25		0.10		49	39.1	Schramm & Lehnberg (1984)
	30		2–3	60[i]	0.12–0.25		0.17		56	48.7	
	35		2–3	60[i]	0.12–0.25		0.17		57[j]	51.9[j]	
	35		2–3	60[i]	0.12–0.25		0.19		53[j]	58.2[j]	
	35		2–3	60[i]	0.12–0.25		0.19		55[j]	59.1[j]	

Rhodophyceae

Gracilaria confervoides: see *Ulva rigida + Valonia agropila* and note f; see also *Gracilaria verrucosa*

Gracilariaceae											
CM	37		50	26	1.9		0.11				Wise et al. (1979)
Gracilaria tikvahiae											
CM	30 ± 5	5.9	2	10	11[k]	6.4	0.01		30	5.6	Ryther & Hanisak (1981)
	30 ± 5	6.2	2	15	7.3[k]	4.2	0.04		59	9.1	
	30 ± 5	6.4	2	20	5.5[k]	3.2	0.06		59	14.7	
	30 ± 5	6.7	2	30	3.7[k]	2.1	0.13		66	26.2	
	30 ± 5	7.1	2	60	1.8[k]	1.1	0.20		57	47.7	
CM	28 ± 3	6.8	2	20	2.8	1.7	0.05		36.8	18.2	Habig & Ryther (1983)
	28 ± 3	6.9	2	30	1.8	1.1	0.06		39.5	21.2	
	28 ± 3	7.1	2	40	1.3	0.8	0.14		58.4	31.8	
	28 ± 3	7.2	2	50	1.1	0.65	0.19		62.7	39.4	
Batch	32 ± 3		2	58	0.47[l]	0.28	0.22		53.7	75.7	Habig et al. (1984b)
	32 ± 3		2	58	0.45[l]	0.23	0.23		53.5	80.1	
	32 ± 3		2	58	0.57[l]	0.37	0.19		47.5	85.7	

(continued)

Table 5. (continued)

Substrate Pretreatment System	Temperature °C	pH	Digester volume[a] (litres)	Retention time (days) RT or HRT	Retention time (days) SRT	Loading rate (g l⁻¹ day⁻¹) TS	Loading rate VS	Loading rate COD	Biological yield (m³ CH₄/kg) TS	Biological yield VS	Biological yield COD	CH₄/biogas (%)	H₂S/biogas (%)	Reduction rate (%) TS	Reduction rate VS	Reduction rate COD	Source
Gracilaria verrucosa																	
Batch	35		0.125	50			0.14			0.28		60					Archiprêtre (1981)
Phaeophyceae																	
Ascophyllum nodosum																	
CM	35		8	24			1.75			0.11		50		30			Hanssen et al. (1987)
Sargassum muticum																	
Batch	35		0.125	50			0.14			0.01		10					Archiprêtre (1981)
CM	30	7	1	20		2.5	1.7			0.18		64					de Waart (1988)
Sargassum fluitans																	
CM	28 ± 3	6.9	2	20		3.3	2.1			0.08		49.5			20.2		Habig & Ryther (1983)
	28 ± 3	7.0	2	30		2.2	1.4			0.11		58.5			27.4		
	28 ± 3	7.1	2	40		1.6	1.0			0.11		67.5			33.3		
	28 ± 3	7.2	2	50		1.35	0.85			0.14		57.4			40.4		
Macrocystis pyrifera																	
CM	35		1.5	18						0.26		59					Ghosh et al. (1976)
CM	35		1.5	12			1.6			0.24		58					Chynoweth et al. (1978)
	35		1.5	4.8			1.6			0.25		60					
	35		1.5	12			1.6			0.18		54					
	35		1.5	18			1.6			0.26		53					
	26		1.5	18			1.6			0.13		54					
CM	35		1.5	20			3.2			0.18		51					Chynoweth (1979)
CM	35		10	50			1.6			0.35		57					Fannin et al. (1982)
USR	35		6	50	300		1.6			0.37		56					
BFR	35		10	50			1.6			0.38		56					
USR	35		5	27	110		2.4			0.20		47					
CM	35		50	27			2.4			0.16		48					

Laminaria digitata CM	37	1	20	1.8	0.31	63	0.7	52	Fauchille (1984)
Laminaria hyperborea CM	35	8	24	1.65	0.28	53		36	Hanssen *et al.* (1987)
Laminaria saccharina CM	37 37	50 50	25 25	1.09 1.64	0.22 0.20				Troiano *et al.* (1976)
CM	35	2	20	1.0	0.25			72	Asinari *et al.* (1981)
CM	35	8	24	1.65	0.23	51		40	Hanssen *et al.* (1987)
Flotation sludges from the alginic acid extraction on *L. digitata* CM	37 37 37 37	6 6 6 6	20 15 10 7.5	0.91 1.42 1.81 2.55	0.28 0.29 0.29 0.27	62 62 62 62		56 53 49 45	Carpentier *et al.* (1988)

[a] Digester volume is quoted to indicate the scale of the experiment. Sometimes, there may be ambiguities between total and effective volume (indicated preferentially in this table).

[b] Acidogenesis at pH 6.6, with a loading rate of 1.25 TS l^{-1} day^{-1}, in estimating to 15% the dryness of the algae, for a digester volume of 3 litre and a retention time of 6 days. The whole hydrolysate was then introduced in the second reactor.

[c] Volumetric charge of 19.8, 20.7 and 20.2 VS l^{-1} and fermentation duration of 58 days. The methanisation was performed with three lots of algae with different percentages of nitrogen in relation to the dry weight (3.24, 2.15, 0.88, respectively).

[d] Acidogenesis in a 25 litre reactor with enzymes fixed on alumina granules, at pH 5.8 and 35°C, and with a hydraulic retention time of 11 days. The calculation of the biological yield is made from the value of the acidogenic reactor loading rate: 1.03 g VS l^{-1} day^{-1}.

[e] Alga mentioned only by Missoni & Mazzagardi (1985).

[f] Results given with those of *Gracilaria confervoides* (= *Gracilaria verrucosa*), Rhodophyceae. One digester per alga in the first case (Croatto 1982); algae mixed in the three others.

[g] Given numbers: 0.23 and 0.27 m³ biogas kg^{-1} VS, 0.36 m³ biogas kg^{-1} TS, 0.36 m³ biogas ratio of 0.6 in order to compare.

[h] After 90 days of adaptation at 15°C, the reactor was submitted to a thermal shock at 25°C to start the biogas production. The calculations are performed on the mean of the following 80 days.

[i] The experiment was continued for 90 days with a slight increase of the methane production (= 30% at 25°C, 10% at 30°C, 5% at 35°C).

[j] Three experiments performed under different conditions (the first with an inoculum from brackish sediments adapted by use in a previous methanisation experiment, the second with manure inoculum and seawater, the third with manure inoculum and freshwater, but nitrogen-enriched substrate; these three experiments have given the best results of the series.

[k] Charging once a week.

[l] Volumic charge of 16, 13, and 22 g VS l^{-1} and fermentation duration of 58 days. The three experiments were performed with algae of different percentage of nitrogen in relation to the dried weight (respectively 3.65, 2.46 and 1.43).

CM, completely mixed; AF, anaerobic filter; UFA, flow anaerobic filter; USR, upflow sludge reactor; BFR, baffled flow reactor.

Figure 8. Example of laboratory digester: small-scale anaerobic filter in CEVA, Pleubian, Brittany, France. (Photograph courtesy of Jacob de Waart)

methanisation inhibition is probably caused by the presence of phenolic compounds, or oxygen in undamaged aerocysts (Archiprêtre 1981).

Residues of extraction of seaweed polysaccharides can be used. Attempts at double conversion have been undertaken by associating methanisation with the extraction of wall polysaccharides. For red algae, Bird *et al*. (1981) have studied the methanisation of *Gracilaria tikvahiae* followed by agar extraction. The gelling properties of the resulting agar have, however, been shown to be considerably reduced as a consequence of this treatment. King *et al*. (1985) examined the change in properties of carrageenan during the methanisation process of the tropical red alga *Eucheuma cottonii*. Degradation of polymers with a high molecular weight, which have a high added value, is such that their extraction is uneconomic after methanisation.

The reverse procedure – the methanisation of residues from *Gracilaria tikvahiae* after the extraction of agar – has also been abandoned (Bird *et al*. 1981). Indeed, the extraction techniques leave a residue which is largely

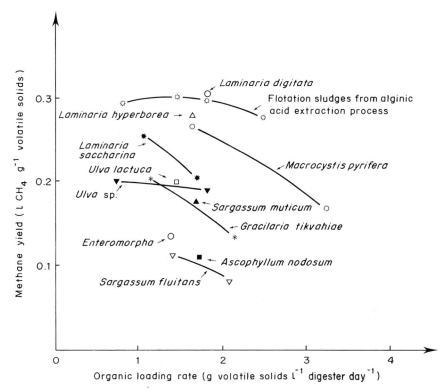

Figure 9. Methane yields *versus* organic loading rate from anaerobic digestion of different algal substrates in completely stirred reactors. Digestion temperatures vary between 35 and 37 °C, except for the experiments with *Gracilaria tikvahiae, Ulva lactuca, Sargassum muticum* and *S. fluitans* ($T = 30$ °C). These results correspond to the best yields reported in the literature (Troiano *et al.* 1976; Chynoweth *et al.* 1978; Asinari *et al.* 1981; Ryther & Hanisak 1981; Brouard 1983; Fauchille 1984; Hanssen *et al.* 1987; Carpentier *et al.* 1988; de Waart 1988). (Adapted from Carpentier *et al.* 1988)

composed of polysaccharides, and poor in proteins and amino acids, and a quite rapid acidification of the digestate has been observed. Nevertheless, Archiprêtre (1981) found that methanisation of extraction residues was comparable with that of the whole alga in *Gracilaria verrucosa*, the agar being very difficult to biodegrade. Similarly, preliminary experiments using extraction residues from *Gelidium* were performed at the Free University of Brussels. Related to the total solids (TS), the results obtained (0.26 m³ methane kg⁻¹ TS, 66% of methane in the biogas) were satisfactory, and a digester of 800 m³ (400 m³ usable volume) has been constructed in Morocco by the Belgian engineering company SA SOPEX NV (Goes 1988).

Using the flotation sludges from alginic acid extraction in an infinitely mixed digester, methanisation results are close to those that can be obtained with the entire algae (Carpentier *et al.* 1988) (Table 5 and Fig. 9). However, the fermentation of residues in the solid retention process proved to be difficult and that of flocculated residues impossible, except when mixed with a synthetic mineral solution or with pig manure, which provided the mineral complement. Thus, although the solid fraction of the residues represents 89% of the total COD, the liquid fraction of the residues contains substances essential for their digestion. Consequently, the results do not conform to the principle of digestion optimization, which is to promote the retention time of solids at the expense of the hydraulic retention time. This phenomenon is similar to that mentioned by de Waart and Motshagen (1982) for the methanisation of spent grain; in this case, addition of pig manure or of a mixture of salts and trace elements was necessary.

Seaweed methanisation results may be classified into three broad categories. In the first, methane yield and methane production rate per unit volume are low. This category is interesting because it illustrates the problems encountered in methane production (bacterial adaptation, overload, inhibition due to sulphur, chemical compounds, oxygen, digester composition, mixing incompatible seaweeds, and either a specific deficiency or a particular difficulty in the methanisation of a species). Some of these problems are scientifically solvable, and can usually be remedied by looking for particular pretreatments or technology. In the second category, the stated characteristics are normally high, showing that seaweeds are methanisation substrates of greater interest than the more traditional substrates. The excellent results obtained in the third category indicate the possibilities offered by treating seaweed so that more efficient reactors can be used.

Methanisation Residues

Many studies have been carried out on the use of methanisation residues from various initial substrates as fertilisers, but few studies have examined seaweeds in this respect.

Early work consisted of recycling the liquid and solid residues of *Gracilaria tikvahiae* digestion for the cultivation of that alga itself (Hanisak 1981). This demonstrated that not only were methanisation residues an excellent source of nutrients for this type of cultivation, but also that the average nitrogen recycling efficiency was 62–83%, depending on the ammonium content, which represented 40–70% of the total nitrogen content (Hanisak 1981; Habig *et al.* 1984a).

Methanisation residues were also tested on terrestrial plants after freeze-drying in Norway and sun-drying in Senegal. The products were water soluble. In Norway, filtration was used and a very low percentage of the dry weight of the residues was removed before freeze-drying was attempted. In the fertilization of lettuce crops, the results were positive with an *Ascophyllum nodosum* methanisation product and negative with *Laminaria hyper-*

borea and *Laminaria saccharina* methanisation products; these latter products may, however, be utilised, but in very small quantities (Hanssen *et al.* 1987). On the other hand, the 'metha-compost' obtained from *Cladophora* methanisation was without immediate effect on groundnuts (a crop which is generally insensitive to fertilisation) but effective on rice. In the latter case, the metha-compost was used to complement other fertilisers because of the sensitivity of rice to salt. It proved an excellent and complete organic improver for millet (Biset 1986).

An original idea for the use of *Laminaria* methanisation residues was in improving the mechanical qualities of peat blocks (Hanssen *et al.* 1987). An incompletely degraded product is able to give mechanical strength to the peat blocks after drying, or to increase it after compression and thus render the peat usable for seed growing.

Biogas Purification

Finally, although the high sulphur level of the seaweed does not generally constitute a toxicity problem, it can limit the direct utilisation of biogas. It seems useful to remove the hydrogen sulphide from the biogas in order to avoid problems in biogas usage.

Preliminary studies of hydrogen sulphide filters have been carried out using washing and biogas recycling for hydrogen sulphide leaching, sulphide precipitation with metals – notably iron (see Perret 1983) – and bacterial action (Kobayashi *et al.* 1983). As far as seaweeds are concerned, de Waart (1988) bound hydrogen sulphide in the liquid of the reactor using $Fe(OH)_3$ slurry from drinking-water purification stations and added it in combination with the daily feeding of the digester. Carpentier (1986) proposed the use of a desulphurising reactor using photosynthetic purple sulphur bacteria, after having tested the functioning of such a reactor, where Thiorodaceae present in the *Ulva* juices colonised glass surfaces.

COMBINATION OF FERMENTATION WITH CHEMICAL TREATMENT

On fermentation, the large amount of carbohydrate in marine biomass can produce a high yield of VFA, if they are continuously removed – 55% of fermentable solids conversion in 5 days (Sanderson *et al.* 1978). Methane production inhibition also favours acid production, and inhibition can be obtained, for instance, by using coenzyme M, 2-bromoethanesulphonic acid (Sanderson *et al.* 1979). The VFA may be separated, either continuously or discontinuously, from the fermentation broth by use of a weak anion-exchange resin, or by solvent extraction followed by extraction with an aqueous base, or preferably by using different kinds of membranes (Sanderson *et al.* 1978).

Fermentation conditions may be controlled to produce either acetic acid or higher acids such as propionic, butyric, valeric and caproic acids. Temperatures at which thermophilic organisms proliferate ($\approx$55 °C) and low conversion rates favour acetic acid production in yielding an acetic acid/total acids ratio in excess of 80% (Sanderson *et al.* 1978). The utilisation of some compounds, such as organochlorines, also inhibits higher acid formation. In the latter case, mesophilic conditions and higher total acid concentrations favour the formation of higher molecular weight fatty acids.

This high VFA product can be used as feedstock for conversion to hydrocarbons by the Kolbe electrosynthesis process. In the case of acetic, valeric and caproic acids, electrolysis at high temperatures, high current density, low voltage and high stirring rate produces alkanes. Isovaleric acid gives equal amounts of alkanes and alkenes. At low current density, low voltage and large electrode area, propionic, butyric and isobutyric acids yield alkenes such as ethylene, propylene and 1-butene (Sanderson *et al.* 1978).

EUROPEAN PROJECTS AND REALISATIONS

Results obtained from research have led to plans for full-scale projects by European organizations and firms. The following may be cited as examples:

1. in Northern Europe, the cultivation of green algae in the waters around Germany, Denmark and Sweden, and biomass transformation into energy;
2. in Belgium, *Laminaria* cultivation on artificial reefs with various uses;
3. in France, composting of seaweeds at Saint-Cast-Le-Guildo; methanisation of *Ulva* from Lannion Bay; methanisation of alginate extraction residues, or treatment by composting of those residues in the factories of the Société Bretonne des Algues et des Colloïdes (SOBALG); methanisation of brown algae on Sein Island;
4. in Italy, methanisation of seaweeds harvested from different lagoons, notably the Venice Lagoon;
5. in Morocco, methanisation of agar extraction residues in a digester built by a Belgian firm;
6. on the coast of Senegal, composting and methanisation of drift seaweeds stranded on beaches, studied by a French organisation.

Only two of these projects have currently reached the implementation stage: the agar extraction residues treatment in Morocco, and the composting at Saint-Cast-Le-Guildo.

SOPEX METHANISATION IN MOROCCO

A reactor of 800 m^3 constructed from flexible material was built in Morocco by the Belgian company SOPEX in order to treat 12 t of daily waste (TS: 11.24%, VS: 9.85%) generated by agar production from *Gelidium*; half of the reactor is devoted to the methanisation process, the upper half acting as a reservoir for the biogas. The biogas production plant includes a boiler of 150 kcal, a hydrogen sulphide filter, and a biogas pressure booster. The total cost of the plant was BFr 6 million (about 140 000 ecu), for an annual production of biogas expected to be of the order of 100 000 m^3 (representing BFr 1 million, about 23 000 ecu) and other benefits in terms of the elimination of environmental pollution (the initial motivation of the Société d'étude et d'exploitation des algues et produits marins (SETEXAM), which ordered the plant) and production of fertiliser, which has yet to be marketed (Goes 1988).

QUATRE-VAULX COMPOSTING IN BRITTANY

In 1980, the Centre de Quatre-Vaulx (Brittany, France) set up a social and economic rehabilitation project involving transformation of biomass (seaweeds, forest waste and poultry dung) into fertilising and humic substances (Fig. 10). The very first year of semi-industrial production from this facility was 1986. Products were:

1. seaweed–woodwaste compost,
2. ready-to-use garden compost (hobby use),
3. compost for professional use,
4. fruit and vegetables grown on a soil fertilised with such compost (Potoky 1988; Potoky & Mazé 1988).

Compared with other commercial organic conditioners, the seaweed/agricultural/forest products obtained, and now marketed, possess a greater organic quality because of the waste resources used (20% seaweed, forest biomass, effluents from livestock farming). It is possible to guarantee minimal contents of organochlorine compounds, non-degradable herbicides and heavy metals, and a high content of secondary elements (magnesium and sulphur), as well as most of the main trace elements (manganese, copper, zinc, molybdenum, iron). Starting from a price level at around FFr 550 (80 ecu) t^{-1} delivered, these products are directed at professionals who operate with high gross profits: vegetable growing, market gardening in the open and under glass, nurseries, provision of open spaces and horticulture.

Establishing such composts as growing media on the non-professional market seems to be the easiest approach initially, both technically and

Figure 10. Piling up of compost made of seaweed, forest waste and dung at Saint-Cast-Le-Guildo, Brittany, France. (Photograph courtesy of Pierrick Potoky)

economically. They could then be placed on the professional market if there is a growing demand for quality and if costs can be held down. In 1986, 20 t of compost were produced and sold. In 1987, 600 t of compost were available for the market. At the end of 1989, a total of 3000 t have been produced and sold (Morand *et al.* 1990). The key problem today is the marketing of these composts. In 1986, the product was sold either directly or through small retailers, but this was not, in the long run, efficient enough. So, in 1987, through large-scale marketing, commercial agreements were signed with 117 supermarkets and hypermarkets in Brittany and in the Loire Valley.

SEAWEED CULTIVATION IN SCANDINAVIAN COUNTRIES

In the Scandinavian countries, it was at first envisaged that cultivation of *Ulva* could be carried out between islets, as yields of about 40–50 t VS ha^{-1} year^{-1} (compared with 60 t dry weight) had been expected after preliminary work (Wachenfeld 1980). This material might then be methanised. So far, studies have been carried out in Ødense Fjord (Denmark), where there is a massive growth of the green alga *Ulva lactuca*. The seaweed was harvested with the purpose of removing the nutrients from the water and utilising the crop for biogas production. The conclusion was that it is possible to remove nutrients by harvesting the seaweeds and to use the biomass for methanisation, but it would not be economically worthwhile at today's energy prices (Rye 1988).

METHANISATION OF ALGINATE EXTRACTION RESIDUES IN FRANCE

A project comparable to that of SOPEX was studied by the Laboratoire de recherche sur les fermentations (LAREF) of the BIOMAGAZ (acronym for Biomasse et Gaz) company for the alginates extraction residues supplied by SOBALG (Carpentier *et al*. 1988). The technical feasibility of the project was demonstrated, but no decision to build a plant was taken by the firm, which also handles treatment of the wastes by composting.

METHANISATION OF LAMINARIACEAE IN FRANCE

A full-scale experiment on *Laminaria digitata* methanisation was carried out in 1984 at Arzano (Brittany) during a summer period using a reactor that normally functioned with manure. This was the basis of a concept of a locally integrated economy on Sein Island, one of the Ponant Islands (Brittany). The experiment is interesting because of the results obtained, and the fact that it is the only experiment of its type carried out on this scale in the world. The results should, however, be treated with caution, as the study was done on little more than two HRT. Generally, conclusions can be drawn about the stability of a process only after four HRT (Show 1985).

The infinitely mixed reactor used had a usable volume of $30\,m^3$; the total seaweed mass was 48 t and 2 t of pebbles were removed before introduction into the digester. Seaweed, and the juice released during stocking on a concrete area, were introduced into the reactor after slight grinding (leaving blades 20 cm long) at the rate of $1\,m^3\,day^{-1}$ between 18 July and 12 August, and $1.5\,m^3\,day^{-1}$ from 13 August to 14 September, at a dry matter content of 6%. There was no bacterial flora adaptation problem during the change from manure to seaweed (or conversely), and there were no hydraulic problems. The average daily results obtained during the last 21 days of the experiment were as follows (Manclière 1985):

1. input substrate: 6.3% TS, 3.9% VS, 58.2 kg VS total;
2. output residues: 4.1% TS, 1.7% VS;
3. methane production: $29.8\,m^3\,day^{-1}$;
4. biogas composition: 61.2% methane, 38.3% carbon dioxide, 0.5% hydrogen.

This means that the methane yield, about $0.5\,m^3\,kg^{-1}$ VS, is approximately equal to the stoichiometric methane yield given by Chynoweth *et al*. (1987) for *Laminaria* sp., and to the theoretical methane yield calculated from the composition of *Laminaria digitata* (cf. Carpentier 1986) and the theoretical yields for the constituents. In spite of the excellent degradability of Laminariaceae (demonstrated here also), it is possible that products with a long degradability time remained from the previous loadings (manure) after two HRT. This experiment ought to be repeated.

In the case of the Sein Island biomass complex, seaweed cultivation, use of stranded algae, methanisation and market gardening are under consideration. The results indicate the feasibility of this operation, if complete integration can be achieved (which is not yet the case) and if the true cost of supplying energy to the island is taken into account.

DEVELOPING COUNTRIES

Another project for local development is proposed by the French ORSTOM for methanisation of drift green algae in Senegal. The proposed digester is of the piston-equipped Transpaille type for fermentation of solids; methane yield has not been optimised, methane production being coupled with the manufacture of organic fertilisers and pollution abatement on beaches; moreover, the need for a hardy and simple-to-use material was a restraint (Leclercq et al. 1985; Biset 1986; Jacq 1986; Dia 1987). Project implementation will depend on local circumstances.

METHANISATION OF PROLIFERATING SEAWEEDS

Pollution abatement is also the principal aim of the two proposals for seaweed fermentation in Brittany and in the Venice Lagoon. These studies are at an advanced stage and economics is the only stumbling block. In France and Italy, the conclusion was reached that it is preferable to methanise a juice derived from *Ulva* in an anaerobic filter digester, rather than to use entire *Ulva* plants in a completely stirred reactor, the respective volume ratio being about 1 : 10 for production of the same effective quantity of methane. The method proposed for juice production is hydrolysis and pressing in Brittany (Brault & Briand 1985a, 1985b; Briand & Morand 1987; Briand 1989) and centrifugation in Italy (Missoni & Mazzagardio 1985).

At present, the treatment of 25 000 m^3 of *Ulva* from Lannion Bay, by the method selected by the Centre d'Etude et de Valorisation des Algues (CEVA), would involve 5000 m^3 for hydrolysis and stocking, and a digester of 150 m^3 useful volume together with its utilities. Both assemblies could be separate, the cost of the first being borne by the public, that of the other by a private company. With the grants generally given for this type of work, the methanisation assembly would allow an investment return in 7 years, but the hydrolysis assembly, financed by the sale of juice and pressed cake, and presuming a latent income for the pollution abatement (at the rate applied at present in France), is redeemable only after 20 years (Lombard, personal communication). The possibility of development of the system thus depends on the importance given to the magnitude of pollution, on the decrease in the cost of hydrolysis and on economies of scale. At this stage, a joint project between France and Italy – over 10^6 t of wet seaweed per year are available in the Venice Lagoon alone (Orlandini 1988) – would perhaps solve the problems and allow the building of an experimental plant.

CULTIVATION OF LAMINARIACEAE AND COASTAL PROTECTION

Finally, it is appropriate to mention the economic appraisal conducted at the HAECON company for onshore cultivation of Laminariaceae in Belgium (Beavis & Charlier 1987). The conclusions of this appraisal are such that a pilot system seems feasible. Here, the principal aim is coastal protection. Hydrological conditions on the Belgian coasts are such as to induce a net sand loss, which has to be replaced so that coastal erosion is reduced, if not avoided. The cost of this replacement may reach US\$ 222 m^{-1} $year^{-1}$ (195 ecu). A cumbersome structure could support the growth of *Laminaria* which, in turn, would favour sand sedimentation and avoid the need for periodic replacement of sand by artificial means. The cost of this structure (anchoring and cages) is evidently substantial, the annual amortised investment being US\$ 2704 (2400 ecu) for an 81 m length pilot farm, protecting a 100 m linear zone, as compared with the revenue from the sale of products, US\$ 35.2 (31 ecu) representing US\$ 24 (21 ecu) for alginates and US\$ 11.2 (10 ecu) for fermentation products. The benefit appears to lie in the savings achieved in coastal maintenance (US\$ 22 200 or 19 500 ecu). All included, the internal rate of return would then be of the order of 19%.

CONCLUSIONS

Seaweeds have a potential productivity superior to that of agricultural plants. They are not subject to water stress, and several further possibilities exist for cultivation improvement, as this aspect of their study has been neglected compared with that of terrestrial plants. In the future, their role may expand in, among other things, pollution abatement and local energy generation.

In assessing seaweed biomass production and its energy use, it is essential to consider the kind of seaweed, its calorific content per unit dry weight, its solar conversion efficiency and subsequent maximum yield. For example, calorific values (in terms of litres methane kg^{-1} TS) are, for seaweeds found in North Brittany: 316 for *Enteromorpha* sp., 305 for *Laminaria digitata*, 295 for *Ulva* sp. and 253 for *Porphyra umbilicalis* (Briand 1989). The higher production (kg dry weight m^{-2} $year^{-1}$) obtained from brown algae such as *Laminaria*, *Macrocystis* and *Fucus* gives the highest total calorific content (kcal m^{-2} $year^{-1}$) to a cultivation of these seaweeds. They are followed by red algae such as *Chondrus*, *Gracilaria*, *Porphyra*, *Gigartina* and *Hypnea*, and by green algae such as *Enteromorpha* (Show 1985).

These considerations indicate the main species that should be investigated for the production of biogas and other energetic compounds without overlooking seaweed production as it relates to local pollution problems. Technical solutions exist, even if they require appropriate adaptation in each case, and sometimes specific studies.

CONVERSION BY DIFFERENT PROCEDURES

Thermal Treatment

Thermal treatment of seaweed biomass, by either pyrolysis or incineration, holds great promise as it may lead to a feedstock of useful chemicals. Incineration has provided inorganic chemicals such as iodine and potassium for many years, but pyrolysis offers potential for the production of basic organic chemicals, which may be in short supply when liquid fossil fuels are exhausted. The low dry-matter content of seaweed is a major barrier to economic thermal exploitation at present, although catalytic oxidation, reduction and conversion may overcome this eventually.

Composting

Composting is a technique that is now well developed, and seaweeds can be used with advantage to improve processing and the quality of the final product. The technique is doubly useful in that it removes polluting biomass and provides material that can be used to improve soil and minimise the use of artificial nutrients. Algal consumption for compost making (about 20% of the compost pile's composition) is likely to remain on a local scale for some time into the future.

Methanisation

There is no doubt that the biomass potential of fast-growing and proliferating algae, or the availability of residues from the algal extraction industry, make methanisation a reasonable choice under certain conditions. The economic viability of methanisation, however, depends very strongly on local criteria, e.g. the geographical location (Laminariaceae methanisation project on Sein Island), the possibility of multipurpose utilisation (Japanese project), the scale effect (American Marine Farm Project), and the existence of an environmental problem (*Ulva* methanisation projects in Brittany and the Venice Lagoon). Previous experience clearly indicates that, when such a project is envisaged, a preliminary study should always be conducted to define the optimum choice for seaweed utilisation and to reduce the possibility of unforeseeable setbacks (such as the inhibition of *Sargassum* fermentation by polyphenols and oxygen, and the inhibition of *Ulva* juices fermentation by sulphide).

Combination of Fermentation with Chemical Treatment

Numerous products could be obtained by combining fermentation with chemical methods, for instance, the use of hydrolytic juices to synthesise volatile fatty acids, which are in turn converted electrochemically into fuels or high-cost compounds. So far, there is too little published work in this field to reach a reliable conclusion regarding its future.

SOCIAL AND ECONOMIC CONSIDERATIONS FOR SEAWEED CONVERSION

The social and economic aspects have principally been considered for wet techniques. As regards the future, many different possibilities exist for the utilisation of seaweed, from the most basic to the most sophisticated. It must also be emphasised that, as far as research on seaweed as a source of energy is concerned, the energy balance of the methods of conversion is not always positive and must be improved for materials with a longer life and for different savings, or offset by looking for processes to manufacture valuable by-products.

Brittany

Brittany is particularly significant, as numerous studies have been undertaken there. When the aspect of energy production alone is taken into account, the total cost (1984) of a therm from seaweed would range between FFr 0.73 and 1.15 (0.10 and 0.18 ecu) depending on the origin of the material (stranded or harvested from the sea) and the methanisation technique. This may be compared with the cost of a therm from gas-oil (FFr 0.31, 0.05 ecu), coke (FFr 0.27, 0.05 ecu), propane (FFr 0.44, 0.07 ecu) and wood (FFr 0.19, 0.03 ecu) for domestic use (Dersoir 1985). Dersoir has also pointed out the importance of decentralised production for a local population, and some shortcomings of the cost evaluation; for example, electricity on Ouessant Island (one of the Ponant Islands) sold at FFr 0.6 per kW h (0.1 ecu) although its real cost was FFr 2.2 per kW h (0.35 ecu). A fair evaluation is difficult to make; electricity price dumping and failure to capitalise negative costs seriously skew any assessment. Furthermore, cost evaluation should consider the problem of wastes, pollution, soil impoverishment and erosion. If these factors were taken into account as indirect revenues, reducing the cost per therm, methanisation could be economically viable, with local settlements possibly using several substrates; composting could also be competitive, with

Figure 11. Seaweed harvesting in Orbetello Lagoon, Italy. (Photograph, courtesy of Philippe Morand)

a market for the products obtained from seaweed/(agriculture/)forest mixtures at FFr 400 t^{-1} (56 ecu).

Italy

In Italy, proliferation of algae, mainly *Chaetomorpha*, *Gracilaria* and *Ulva*, poses serious eutrophication problems (Lenzi & Bombelli 1985; Sfriso *et al.* 1988). *Gracilaria* is collected by hand in the Venice Lagoon and transported to Parma, where agar is extracted in the B&V (Buzzonetti & Vicentti) factory. The firm is transferring operations to a new facility near Venice, with the intention of reducing production costs. However, algal beds (*Cladophora*, *Chaetomorpha*) in Orbetello (Grossetto, north of Rome on the Tyrrhenian Sea), which must be continuously reduced, are merely an economic burden; the harvest is transported to a dump and remains unused (Fig. 11). It is, for the moment, a first step required for ecological, economic and social reasons (survival of fisheries). However, one must concede that the algal resources remain under-used and, sometimes, unwanted.

GAS PRODUCTION COSTS IN DIFFERENT CULTIVATION SYSTEMS

Similar conclusions concerning the necessity of multipurpose use of algal material have been reached by different authors. The costs of gas production from several seaweed cultivation systems have been reviewed recently (Bird 1987). The economic aim is considered to be US\$ 6 GJ^{-1} (5.3 ecu, i.e. 0.023 ecu per therm). The costs have been split under two headings: seaweed cultivation and harvesting, and gas production and purification. Variations in costs of gas production and purification are relatively low, from US\$ 2.50 GJ^{-1} (2.2 ecu) for very advanced techniques to US\$ 5.50 GJ^{-1} (4.8 ecu) as a baseline, the methane yield generally hypothesised to be 0.43 m^3 kg^{-1} VS. On the other hand, feedstock costs vary considerably: US\$ 2.30 GJ^{-1} (2 ecu) for a tidal-flat farm (*Gracilaria, Ulva*) with a production of 23 t VS ha^{-1} year^{-1}, but US\$ 3.60 (3.2 ecu) at 11 t VS ha^{-1} year^{-1}; US\$ 3–6 (2.6–5.3 ecu) for floating seaweed cultivation (*Sargassum*) with 22–45 t VS ha^{-1} year^{-1} produced; between US\$ 3.50 and 5.50 (3.1–4.8 ecu) for *Macrocystis* near-shore farms with seaweed yields of 50 and 34 t VS ha^{-1} year^{-1}, respectively; and US\$ 12–44 (10.5–39 ecu) for a rope system (*Gracilaria, Laminaria*) depending on technology and productivity (11–45 t VS ha^{-1} year^{-1}). Bird concludes that:

1. If conditions are favourable, some systems are close to being competitive.
2. The co-production of methane with other products would decrease the cost of methane, for example, from US\$ 12 GJ^{-1} (10.5 ecu) to US\$ 1.3 GJ^{-1} (1.1 ecu), which is only an academic hypothesis, the energy demand being without possible comparison with the demand for these products.
3. More realistically, such a co-production would be possible on a local scale, the estimated methane cost being then US\$ 5 GJ^{-1} (4.4 ecu).
4. Methane production in a pollution abatement plant would be possible, the analysis giving a cost of US\$ 2.5 GJ^{-1} (2.2 ecu) for a water hyacinth-based operation.

The approach to the problem is different on each side of the Atlantic. For instance, in Europe, emphasis has not been placed on productivity and costly systems of nutrient provision. It has been viewed as important mainly at the local level, because of seaweed proliferation, or because of the need for pollution abatement, and it has been kept in mind that solar, and *a fortiori* biomass, energy is naturally decentralised. To say the least, there remain many unanswered questions in all aspects of this area, and small-scale and demonstration operations are necessary. The determination to carry on the research will only come about, and the financial means will only be provided, if there is a major change in the ecological and economic climate.

ACKNOWLEDGEMENTS

The authors express their sincere appreciation to Serge Maestrini, Director of CREMA-L'Houmeau, for providing logistical support, to Évelyne Richard for her bibliographical help, and to Karine Mounier and Régine Voig for the care with which they have typed the first draft of this manuscript. We thank all those who generously furnished additional information and illustrative materials. We are particularly grateful to Michael Guiry for critically reading the manuscript and to the EC for grants under the aegis of COST48, which have allowed us to meet for the fruitful discussions that culminated in the completion of this chapter.

REFERENCES

Albagnac G. & Verrier D. 1983. Méthanisation des effluents d'industries agro-alimentaires. In *Le Biogaz. Biomasse Actualités* **9**(Suppl. 2): 17–21.

Anon. 1985. Japon: utilisation de la biomasse marine. *Tech. Res. Océan.* **5**: 7.

ANRED. 1983. Valorisation des résidus ligneux. *Compost Inf.* **12**: 1–44.

Archiprêtre M. 1981. *Culture et utlisation d'algues marines: étude de méthanisation d'algues marines.* Mémoire de Diplôme d'Études Approfondies: Amélioration et transformation des productions végétales et microbiennes. Univ. Sci. Techn. Lille I, France. vii + 52 pp.

Asinari C.-M., Legros A., Piron C., Sironval C., Nyns E.-J. & Naveau H.P. 1981. Methane production by anaerobic digestion of algae. In *Energy from Biomass.* Series E, Vol. 1. Proceedings of the EC Contractors' Meeting, Copenhagen, June 1981. (Ed. P. Chartier & W. Palz) pp. 113–20. Dordrecht: Reidel.

Aubart C. & Bully F. 1985. Anaerobic digestion of pig manure: results on farm scale and new process. In *Energy from Biomass.* 3rd EC Conference, Venice 25–29 March 1985. (Ed. W. Palz, J. Coombs & D.O. Hall) pp. 489–92. London: Elsevier Applied Science.

Bachmann A., Beard V.L. & McCarty P.L. 1985. Performance characteristics of the anaerobic baffled reactor. *Water Res.* **19**: 99–106.

Balch D.M. 1909. On the chemistry of certain algae of the Pacific Coast. *J. Ind. Eng. Chem.* **1**: 777–9.

Beavis A. & Charlier R.H. 1987. An economic appraisal for the on-shore cultivation of *Laminaria* spp. *Hydrobiologia* **151/152**: 387–98.

Bianchi A. & Randriamahefa H. 1987. *Méthanisation de macro-algues marines à 37 et à 15 °C.* Agence Française pour la Maîtrise de l'Énergie. Rapport de contrat no 5-01-1017. Marseille: Univ. Provence. 53 pp.

Bingelli F. 1980. Utilisation agronomique de broussailles compostées. *Rev. Hortic. Suisse* **53**: 5–51.

Bingelli F. & Alexandrian D. 1984. *L'écologie prend le maquis.* pp. 55–90. Aix-en-Provence: Edisud.

Bird K.T. 1987. Cost analyses of energy from marine biomass. In *Seaweed Cultivation for Renewable Resources.* (Eds. K.T. Bird & P.H. Benson) pp. 327–50. Amsterdam: Elsevier.

Bird K.T., Hanisak M.D. & Ryther J.H. 1981. Changes in agar and other chemical constituents of the seaweed *Gracilaria tikvahiae* when used as a substrate in methane digestion. *Res. Conserv.* **6**: 321–7.

Biset C. 1986. Mesure de l'efficacité sur trois cultures tropicales des apports de compost issu de la méthanisation d'une algue échouée au Sénégal (*Cladophora* sp.). Mémoire de fin d'études de l'École Supérieure d'Ingénieurs et de Techniciens Pour l'Agriculture, Val de Reuil, France. ii + 22 pp.

Bolivar J.A. 1983. The Bacardi Corporation digestion process for stablizing rum distillery wastes and producing methane. *MBAA Tech. Q.* **20**: 119–28.

Bonalberti E. & Croatto U. 1985. Use of algal systems as a source of fuel and chemicals. In *Energy from Biomass*. 3rd EC Conference, Venice, 25–29 March 1985. (Eds. W. Palz, J. Coombs & D.O. Hall) pp. 158–62. London: Elsevier Applied Science.

Bories A. & Verrier D. 1984. Les perspectives d'évolution des fermenteurs de deuxième génération pour le traitement anaérobie des effluents. *Ind. Aliment. Agric.* **101**: 493–7.

Boude J.-P. 1983. L'économie des algues marines. In *Les végétaux aquatiques. Biomasse actualités* **12** (Suppl. 3): 38–41.

Boulenger P., Versprille B., Pette K.C. & Zoetmeyer R.J. 1982. Digestion méthanique des effluents: application du procédé Biothane UASB en sucreries-distilleries. *Ind. Aliment. Agric.* **99**: 565–9.

Brault D. & Briand X. 1985a. *Les marées vertes: mise au point d'une technique de stockage de l'algue Ulva sp. faisant office de prétraitement pour sa méthanisation.* Agence Française pour la Maîtrise de l'Énergie. Rapport de contrat no 3-320-1847. 106 pp. Pleubian, France: Centre d'Expérimentation et de Recherche Appliquée en Algologie.

Brault D. & Briand X. 1985b. *Les marées vertes: Étude des phases acidogène et méthanogène* d'Ulva *sp.* Agence Française pour la Maîtrise de l'Énergie. Rapport de contrat no 4-320-2278. 103 pp. Pleubian, France: Centre d'Expérimentation et de Recherche Appliquée en Algologie.

Brault D., Golven P. & Briand X. 1983. Compostage d'algues vertes. Étude expérimentale. *Les végétaux aquatiques. Biomasse actualités* **12** (Suppl. 3): 31–4.

Brault D., Briand X. & Golven P. 1985. 'Les Marées Vertse'. Premier bilan concernant les essais de valorisation. In *Bases Biologiques de l'Aquaculture*. Montpellier, France, 12–16 Décember 1983. *Institut Français de Recherche pour l'Exploitation de la MER, Actes de colloques* **1**: 33–42.

Briand X. 1988. Exploitation of seaweeds in Europe. In *Aquatic Primary Biomass (Marine Macroalgae): Biomass Conversion, Removal and Use of Nutrients. I.* Proceedings of the 1st Workshop of the COST 48 Sub-Group 3. L'Houmeau, France. 12–14 February 1987. (Eds. P. Morand & E.H. Schulte) pp. 53–65. Brussels: CEC.

Briand X. 1989. *Prolifération de l'algue verte Ulva sp. en baie de Lannion (France): étude d'une nuisance et de son traitement par fermentation anaérobie.* Thèse de 3ème cycle: Biologie et Physiologie Végétale. Lille I, France: vii + 210 pp.

Briand X. & Morand P. 1987. *Ulva*, stranded algae: a way of depollution through methanisation. In *Biomass for Energy and Industry*. 4th EC Conference, Orléans, France, 11–15 May 1987. (Eds. G. Grazi, B. Delmon, J.-F. Molle & H. Zibetta) pp. 834–9. London: Elsevier Applied Science.

Brinkhuis B.H., Levine H.G., Schlenk C.G. & Tobin S. 1987. *Laminaria* cultivation in the Far East and North America. In *Seaweed Cultivation for Renewable Resources.* (Eds. K.T. Bird & P.H. Benson) pp. 107–46. Amsterdam: Elsevier.

Brouard F. 1983. *Digestion anaérobie de la biomasse végétale* aquatique. Thèse de Docteur-Ingénieur. Institut National des Sciences Appliquées, Univ. Toulouse, France. 120 pp.

Camilli M., Sanna P., Gulinelli S. & Minosso M. 1985. Anaerobic digestion of algae in fixed bed reactors. In *Third EC Conference, Energy from Biomass*. Venice, 25–29 March 1985. *Abstracts*. PII/092.

Canovas-Diaz M. & Howell J.A. 1987. Stratified ecology techniques in the start-up of an anaerobic downflow fixed film percolating reactor. *Biotech. Bioeng.* **30**: 289–96.

Carpentier B. 1986. *Digestion anaérobie de la biomasse algale: Les résidus de l'extraction de l'acide alginique. Les ulves de marée verte.* Thèse de 3ème cycle: Algologie. Paris VI, France. 101 pp.

Carpentier B., Festino C. & Aubart C. 1988. Anaerobic digestion of flotation sludges from the alginic acid extraction process. *Biol. Wastes* **23**: 269–78.

CERAA. 1983. Compostage de l'algue verte *Ulva lactuca.* In *Le compostage de déchets en mélange. Compost Inf.* **14**: 30–8.

Chambarlhac B., Bebin J. & Albagnac G. 1982. Stabilization and methane production by commercial scale digestion of green vegetable cannery wastes. In *Symposium papers. Energy from Biomass and Wastes. VI.* Lake Buena Vista, Florida, 25–29 January 1982. pp. 483–507. Chicago: Institute of Gas Technology.

Chapman V.J. & Chapman D.J. 1980. *Seaweeds and their Uses.* 3rd edn. 334 pp. London: Chapman & Hall.

Charlier R.H. 1991. Economic and environmental aspects of seaweed utilization. Part II: Algae: Resource or Sewage? *Int. J. Environ. Studies* (in press).

Charlier R.H. & Beavis A. 1991. Development of the near-shore weed screen. *Int. J. Environ. Studies* (in press).

Chynoweth D.P. 1979. Anaerobic digestion of marine biomass. *Biogas and Alcohol Seminar*, Chicago, 25–26 October 1979. Argonne, IL: Argonne National Laboratories.

Chynoweth D.P. 1980. Gasification process development. In *Proceedings of Bio-Energy '80 World Congress.* Atlanta, Georgia, 21–24 April 1980. pp. 476–8. Washington, DC: Environmental Protection Agency.

Chynoweth D.P., Klass D.L. & Ghosh S. 1978. Biomethanation of giant brown kelp *Macrocystis pyrifera.* In *Symposium papers. Energy from Biomass and Wastes. II.* pp. 229–51. Chicago: Institute of Gas Technology.

Chynoweth D.P., Ghosh S. & Klass D.L. 1981. Anaerobic digestion of kelp. In *Biomass Conversion Processes for Energy and Fuels.* (Eds. S.S. Sofer & O.R. Zaborsky) pp. 315–38. New York: Plenum Press.

Chynoweth D.P., Dolenc D.A., Ghosh S., Henry M.P., Jerger D.E. & Srivastava V.J. 1982. Kinetics and advanced digester design for anaerobic digestion of water hyacinth and primary sludge. *Biotech. Bioeng. Symp.* **12**: 381–98.

Chynoweth D.P., Fannin K.F. & Srivastava V.J. 1987. Biological gasification of marine algae. In *Seaweed Cultivation for Renewable Resources* (Eds. K.T. Bird & P.H. Benson) pp. 285–303. Amsterdam: Elsevier.

Croatto U. 1982. Energy from macroalgae of the Venice Lagoon. In *Energy from Biomass.* 2nd EC Conference, Berlin, 20–23 September 1982. (Eds. A. Strub, P. Chartier & G. Schlesser) pp. 329–33. London: Elsevier Applied Science.

De Baere L.A., Devocht M., Van Assche P. & Verstraete W. 1984. Influence of high NaCl and NH_4Cl salt levels on methanogenic associations. *Water Res.* **18**: 543–8.

De Bertoldi M., Ferranti M.P., L'Hermite P. & Zucconi F., Eds. 1987. *Compost: Production, Quality and Use.* Proceedings of Symposium, Udine, Italy, 17–19 April 1986. London: Elsevier Applied Science.

Delépine R. 1983. Les grandes algues aux îles Kerguelen. In *Les végétaux aquatiques. Biomasse Actualités* **12** (Suppl.3): 16–17.

Delépine R., Gaillard J. & Morand P., Eds. 1988. *Valorisation des algues et autres végétaux aquatiques.* ii + 350 pp. Brest: Institut Français de Recherche pour l'Exploitation de la Mer; Paris: Centre National de la Recherche Scientifique.

Dersoir M.-C. 1985. *Les filières de la méthanisation. Aspects énergétiques, environnementaux, agronomiques. Étude de cas appliquée à la Bretagne.* Thèse de 3ème cycle: Économie de la production. Rennes I, France. 484 pp.

Dia D. 1987. *Étude de la fermentation méthanique d'une algue marine verte du Sénégal.*

Mémoire de Diplôme d'Études Approfondies. Univ. Cheikh Antadiop. Dakar, Senegal. 107 pp.

Fannin K.F., Srivastava V.J. & Chynoweth D.P. 1982. Unconventional anaerobic digester designs for improving methane yields from sea kelp. In *Symposium papers. Energy from Biomass and Wastes. VI.* Lake Buena Vista, Florida, 25–29 January 1982. pp. 373–96. Chicago: Institute of Gas Technology.

FAO, Ed. 1983. The world seaweeds industry and trade. Serie Infofish. *Market Report* 6.

Fauchille S. 1984. *Digestion anaérobie de végétaux aquatiques.* Thèse de Docteur-Ingénieur. Institut National Polytechnique de Lorraine, Univ. Nancy, France. 120 pp.

Finck J.D. & Goma G. 1983. Les principes fondamentaux des mécanismes. In *Le biogaz. Biomasse actualités* 9(Suppl.2): 5–11.

Fleishmann M. & Pletcher D. 1971. In *Reactions of Molecules at Electrodes.* (Ed. N.S. Hush). London: Wiley Interscience.

Flowers A. & Bird K. 1984. Marine biomass: a long-term methane supply option. *Hydrobiologia* 116/117: 272–5.

Forro J. 1987. Microbial degradation of marine biomass. In *Seaweed Cultivation for Renewable Resources.* (Eds. K.T. Bird & P.H. Benson) pp. 305–25. Amsterdam: Elsevier.

Ghose T.K. & Debabrata das. 1982. Maximization of energy recovery in biomethanisation process. Part 2. Use of mixed residue in batch system. *Process Biochem.* 17: 39–42.

Ghosh S., Conrad J., Sedzielarz F., Griswold K., Henry M., Bortz S. & Klass D. 1976. *Research Study to Determine the Feasibility of Producing Methane Gas from Sea Kelp.* Report for US Navy, contract no N00123-76-L-0271.

Gningue I. 1985. *Les algues marines du Sénégal: Étude de leur action fertilisante en cultures maraîchères.* Thèse de Docteur-Ingénieur en Chimie. Univ. Cheikh Antadiop. Dakar, Senegal. 105 pp.

Goes J. 1988. Methanization of algal residues after extraction of agar-agar from *Gelidium.* In *Aquatic Primary Biomass (Marine Macroalgae): Biomass Conversion, Removal and Use of Nutrients.* I. Proceedings of the 1st Workshop of the COST 48 Sub-Group 3, L'Houmeau, France, 12–14 February 1987. (Eds. P. Morand & E.H. Schulte) pp. 111–13. Brussels: CEC.

Goldstein N. 1985. Sewage sludge composting facilites on the rise. *Biocycle* 26: 19–24.

Green A. & Johnson J. 1912. The distillation of *Nereocystis. Chem. Eng.* 15: 55–6.

Habig C. & Ryther J.H. 1983. Methane production from the anaerobic digestion of some marine macrophytes. *Res. Conserv.* 8: 271–9.

Habig C., Andrews D.A. & Ryther J.H. 1984a. Nitrogen recycling and methane production using *Gracilaria tikvahiae*: a closed system approach. *Res. Conserv.* 10: 303–13.

Habig C., DeBusk T.A. & Ryther J.H. 1984b. The effect of nitrogen content on methane production by the marine algae *Gracilaria tikvahiae* and *Ulva* sp. *Biomass* 4: 239–51.

Hanisak M.D. 1981. Recycling the residues from anaerobic digesters as a nutrient source for seaweed growth. *Bot. Mar.* 24: 57–61.

Hanisak M.D. 1987. Cultivation of *Gracilaria* and other macroalgae in Florida for energy production. In *Seaweed Cultivation for Renewable Resources.* (Eds. K.T. Bird & P.H. Benson) pp. 191–218. Amsterdam: Elsevier.

Hanssen J.F., Indergaard M., Ostgaard K., Bævre O.A., Pedersen T.A. & Jensen A. 1987. Anaerobic digestion of *Laminaria* spp. and *Ascophyllum nodosum* and application of end products. *Biomass* 14: 1–13.

Hansson G. 1983. Methane production from marine, green macroalgae. *Res. Conserv.* **8**: 185–94.

Heijnen J.J. 1983. Development of a high-rate fluidized bed biogas reactor. In *Proceedings, Anaerobic Waste Water Treatment Symposium*, Noordwijkerhout, The Netherlands. pp. 283–91.

Hoagland D.R. 1915. The destructive distillation of Pacific Coast kelps. *J. Ind. Eng. Chem.* **7**: 673–4.

Hofenk G., Lips S.J.J., Rijkens B.A. & Voeteberg J.W. 1985. *Two-Phase Anaerobic Digestion of Solid Organic Wastes Yielding Biogas and Compost*. EC Energy Program Project E: Energy from Biomass. EUR 9942 En Report. Report of contract no ESE-E-R-040-NL. 57 pp. Luxembourg: CEC.

Jackson G.A. 1977. Biological constraints of seaweeds culture. In *Biological Solar Energy Conversion*. (Eds. A. Mitsui, S, Miyachi, A., San Pietro & S. Tomura) pp. 437–48. New York: Academic Press.

Jacq V.A. 1986. La fermentation méthanique au service de la dépollution: trois exemples d'applications au Sénégal. In *Les Comptes-rendus de la Conférence-Atelier sur l'Importance des Technologies propres pous un Développement économique durable*, 12–15 February 1986, Dakar, Sénégal. pp. 28–54. Dakar, Sénégal: Ministère de la Protection de la Nature; Paris: Ministère de l'Environnement.

Jensen A. 1979. Industrial utilization of seaweeds in the past, present and future. In *Proc. 9th Int. Seaweed Symp.*, Santa Barbara, CA., 20–27 August 1977. (Eds. A. Jensen & J.R. Stein) pp. 17–34. Princeton: Science Press.

Jensen A. 1985. Possibilities and problems of energy production from macroalgae. In *Bioenergy 84*. (Eds. H. Egnéus & A. Ellegård) pp. 143–53. London: Elsevier Applied Science.

Kain J.M. & Dawes C.P. 1987. Useful European seaweeds: past hopes and present cultivation. *Hydrobiologia* **151/152**: 173–81.

Kaspar H.F. & Wuhrmann K. 1978. Product inhibition in sludge digestion. *Microb. Ecol.* **4**: 241–8.

Khan A.W. & Trottier T.M. 1978. Effect of sulfur containing compounds on anaerobic degradation of cellulose to methane by mixed cultures obtained from sewage sludge. *Appl. Env. Microbiol.* **35**: 1027–34.

King G.M., Guist G.G. & Lauterbach G.E. 1985. Anaerobic degradation of carrageenan from the red macroalga *Eucheuma cottonii*. *Appl. Env. Microbiol.* **49**: 588–92.

Kobayashi H.A., Stenstrom M. & Mah R.A. 1983. Use of photosynthetic bacteria for hydrogen sulfide removal from anaerobic waste treatment effluent. *Water Res.* **17**: 579–87.

Kohler G.O. & Hart M.R. 1980. Pretreatment–post treatment processes. In *Proceedings of Bio-Energy '80 World Congress*. Atlanta, Georgia, 21–24 April 1980. pp. 478–9. Washington, DC: Environmental Protection Agency.

Leclercq S., Tine E. & Suisse de Sainte Claire E. 1985. *Fermentations méthaniques de macrophytes marins*. Document scientifique no 102. Centre de Recherches Océanographiques de Dakar-Thiaroye/Institut Sénégalais de Recherches Agricoles. Dakar, Sénégal. 22 pp.

Legros A., Asinari di San Marzano C.M., Naveau H.P., Nyns E.J. 1982. Improved methane production from algae using 2nd generation digesters. In *Energy from Biomass*. 2nd EC Conference, Berlin, 20–23 September 1982. (Eds. A. Strub, P. Chartier & G. Schlesser) pp. 609–14. London: Elsevier Applied Science.

Lenihan J. & Fletcher W.W. 1975. *Energy Resources and the Environment*. Glasgow: Blackie.

Lenzi M. & Bombelli V. 1985. Prime valutazioni della biomassa macrofitica nella laguna di Orbetello (GR) in considerazione di uno sfruttamento industriale. *Nova Thalassia* **7**(Suppl. 3): 355–60.

Lescure J.P., Chanderis J. & Oger P. 1982. Applications de la digestion anaérobie dans les industries agro-alimentaires. *Ind. Aliment .Agric*, **99**: 123–30.

Lovely D.R. & Klug M.J. 1983. Sulfate reducers can outcompete methanogens at freshwaters sulfate concentration. *Appl. Env. Microbiol.* **45**: 187–92.

Manclière P. 1985. Méthanisation des algues: de l'énergie à revendre? *Équinoxe* **3**: 7–12.

Martin J.H. & Lichtenberger P.P. 1981. Operation of a commercial farm scale plug flow manure digester plant. In *Symposium Papers. Energy from Biomass and Wastes. V.* Lake Buena Vista, Florida, 26–30 January 1981. pp. 439–62. Chicago: Institute of Gas Technology.

Mata-Alvarez J. 1987. A dynamic simulation of a two-phase anaerobic digestion system for solid waste. *Biotech. Bioeng.* **30**: 844–51.

Missoni G. & Mazzagardi M. 1985. Production of algal biomass in Venice Lagoon, environmental and energetic aspects. In *Energy from Biomass.* 3rd EC Conference, Venice, 25–29 March 1985. (Eds. W. Palz, J. Coombs & D.O. Hall) pp. 384–6. London: Elsevier Applied Science.

Morand P., Charlier R.H. & Mazi J. 1990. European bioconversion projects and realizations for macroalgal biomass: Saint-Cast-Le-Guilds (France) experiment. *Hydrobiologia* **204/205**: 301–8.

Morgan, P.J. & Smith K. 1978. Potentiality of seaweed as a resource: analysis of the pyrolysis products of *Fucus serratus. Analyst* **103**: 1053–9.

Morley J.C. & Jones J.M. 1981. Growth of marine biomass on artificial structures as a renewable source of energy. In *Energy from Biomass.* 1st EC Conference, Brighton, 4–7 November 1980. (Eds. W. Palz, P. Chartier & D.O. Hall) pp. 681–4. London: Elsevier Applied Science.

Mustin M. 1987. *Le compost. Gestion de la matière organique.* 954 pp. Paris: François Dubusc.

Neushul M. & Harger B.W.W. 1985. Studies of biomass yield from a near-shore macroalgal test farm. *J. Solar Energy Eng.* **107**: 93–6.

Neushul M. & Harger B.W.W. 1987. Nearshore kelp cultivation, yield and genetics. In *Seaweed Cultivation for Renewable Resources.* (Eds. K.T. Bird & P.H. Benson) pp. 69–93. Amsterdam: Elsevier.

Neushul P. 1987. Energy from marine biomass: the historical record. In *Seaweed Cultivation for Renewable Resources.* (Eds. K.T. Bird & P.H. Benson) pp. 1–38. Amsterdam: Elsevier.

Nicolini S. & Viglia A. 1985. Anaerobic digestion of macroalgae in the Lagoon of Venice: experience with a 5 m³ capacity pilot reactor. *In Energy from Biomass.* 3rd EC Conference, Venice, 25–29 March 1985. (Eds. W. Palz, J. Coombs & D.O. Hall) pp. 614–16. London: Elsevier Applied Science.

North W.J. 1980. Biomass from marine macroscopic plants. *Solar Energy* **25**: 387–95.

North W.J. 1987. Oceanic farming of *Macrocystis*, the problems and non-problems. In *Seaweed Cultivation for Renewable Resources.* (Eds. K.T. Bird & P.H. Benson) pp. 39–67. Amsterdam: Elsevier.

Orlandini M. 1988. Harvesting of algae in polluted lagoons of Venice and Orbetello and their effective and potential utilization. In *Aquatic Primary Biomass (Marine Macroalgae): Biomass Conversion, Removal and Use of Nutrients. II.* Proceedings of the 2nd Workshop of the COST 48 Sub-Group 3, Zeist and Yerseke, The Netherlands, 25–27 October 1988. (Eds. J. de Waart & P.H. Nienhuis) pp. 20–3. Brussels: CEC.

Pain I. & Pain J. 1979. *Les méthodes de Jean Pain ou un autre jardin*. 6th edn. 52 pp. Villecroze, France: Ed. Pain.

Parkin G.E. & Speece R.E. 1983. Attached *versus* suspended growth anaerobic reactors: response to toxic substances. *Water Sci. Tech.* **15**: 261–89.

Parra J.V. 1975. The use of water-hyacinth (*Eichhornia crassipes*) as a soil amendment and source of plant nutrients. *Diss. Abstr. Int. B Sci. Eng.* **36**: 1016–17.

Percival E. & McDowell H.R. 1967. *Chemistry and Enzymology of Marine Algal Polysaccharides*. 219 pp. London: Academic Press.

Perret J.P. 1983. *Mise en oeuvre et utilisation du biogaz*. pp. 27–55. Paris: Agence Française pour la Maîtrise de l'Énergie.

Petitbon A. 1985. *Fixation d'enzymes et de microorganismes sur céramiques microporeuses. Application à la valorisation énergétique de biomasse végétale aquatique.* Agence Française pour la Maîtrise de l'Énergie. Rapport de contrat no 4-320-2286. 25 pp. Marcoussis, France: Compagnie Générale d'Électricité.

Plunkett B. 1988. The pyrolysis of *Sargassum muticum*. In *Aquatic Primary Biomass (Marine Macroalgae): Biomass Conversion, Removal and Use of Nutrients. II.* Proceedings of the 2nd Workshop of the COST 48 Sub-Group 3, Zeist and Yerseke. The Netherlands, 25–27 October 1988. (Eds. J. de Waart & P.H. Nienhuis) pp. 27–33. Brussels: CEC.

Porteous A. 1981. *Refuse Derived Fuels*. London: Elsevier Aplied Science.

Potoky P. 1983. Compostage d'algues mélangées. La méthanisation des algues: un pilote en vraie grandeur. In *Les végétaux aquatiques. Biomasse Actualités* **12** (Suppl. 3): 35.

Potoky P. 1988. Seaweeds for making fertilizing substances in France. In *Aquatic Primary Biomass (Marine Macroalgae): Biomass Conversion, Removal and Use of Nutrients. I.* Proceedings of the 1st Workshop of the COST 48 Sub-Group 3, L'Houmeau, France, 12–14 February 1987. (Eds. P. Morand & E.H. Schulte) pp. 17–18. Brussels: CEC.

Potoky P. & Mazé J. 1988. Effect of seaweed inclusion in compost preparation on the quality of the composts obtained. In *Aquatic Primary Biomass (Marine Macroalgae): Biomass Conversion, Removal and Use of Nutrients. I.* Proceedings of the 1st Workshop of the COST 48 Sub-Group 3, L'Houmeau, France, 12–14 February 1987. (Eds. P. Morand & E.H. Schulte) pp. 67–86. Brussels: CEC.

Rao P.S., Tarwade S.J. & Sarma K.S.R. 1980. Seaweed as source of energy. I: Effect of a specific bacterial strain on biogas production. *Bot. Mar.* **23**: 599–602.

Rijkens B.A. & Voeteberg J.W. 1984. Two-step anaerobic digestion of solid wastes. In *Anaerobic Digestion and Carbohydrate Hydrolysis of Waste*. (Eds. G.L. Ferrero, M.P. Ferranti & H. Naveau) pp. 479–81. London: Elsevier Applied Science.

Robinson J.A. & Tiedje J.M. 1984. Competition between sulfate-reducing and methanogenic bacteria for H_2 under resting and growing conditions. *Arch. Microbiol.* **137**: 26–32.

Roustan J.L. 1984. Fermentation des algues en comparaison avec le lisier de bovin et en mélange. In *Comité technique de méthanisation des végétaux marins. Bulletin no. 2.* 7 pp. Pleubian, France: Centre d'Expérimentation et de Recherche Appliquée en Algologie.

Rye C. 1988. The use of algae for nutrient removal and as raw material for the industry with examples from Danish activities. In *Aquatic Primary Biomass (Marine Macroalgae): Biomass Conversion, Removal and Use of Nutrients. II.* Proceedings of the 2nd Workshop of the COST 48 Sub-Group 3, Zeist and Yerseke. The Netherlands, 25–27 October 1988. (Eds. J. de Waart and P.H. Nienhuis) pp. 8–11. Brussels: CEC.

Ryther, J.H. & Hanisak M.D. 1981. Anaerobic digestion and nutrient recycling of small benthic or floating seaweeds. In *Symposium Papers. Energy from Biomass and*

Wastes V. Lake Buena Vista, Florida, 26–30 January 1981. pp. 383–412. Chicago: Institute of Gas Technology.

Saidane A., De Waele N. & Van de Velde R. 1979. Contribution à l'étude du compostage de plantes marines en vue de la préparation d'un amendement organique et d'un substrat horticole. *Bull. Inst. Océanogr. Pêche, Salammbô* **6**: 133–50.

Sanderson J.E., Wise D.L. & Augenstein D.C. 1978. Organic chemical and liquid fuels from algal biomass. *Biotech. Bioeng. Symp.* **8**: 131–51.

Sanderson J.E., Wise D.L., Levy P.F. & Molyneux M.S. 1979. *Liquid Fuels Production from Biomass.* Progress report no 8 for US Dept. of Energy, contract no AC-02-77-ET-20050. July 1–September 30. 33 pp. Cambridge, Mass.: Dynatech Research and Development Co.

Sauvageau C. 1920. *Utilisation des algues marines.* 394 pp. Paris, France: Gaston Doin et Cie.

Schramm W. & Lehnberg W. 1984. Mass culture of brackish-water-adapted seaweeds in sewage-enriched seawater. II: Fermentation for biogas production. *Hydrobiologia* **116/117**: 282–7.

Sfriso A., Pavoni B., Marcomini A. & Orio A.A. 1988. Annual variations of nutrients in the Lagoon of Venice. *Mar. Pollut. Bull.* **19**: 54–60.

Show Jr I.T. 1985. Marine biomass. In *Biomass Conversion Processes for Energy and Fuels.* (Eds. S.S. Sofer & O.R. Zaborsky) pp. 57–77. New York: Plenum Press.

Sorensen J., Christensen D. & Jorgensen B.B. 1981. Volatile fatty acids and hydrogen as substrates for sulfate-reducing bacteria in anaerobic marine sediment. *Appl. Env. Microbiol.* **42**: 5–11.

Spencer G.C. 1920. Potash from kelp, the preliminary examination of kelp distillates. *J. Ind. Eng. Chem.* **12**: 786–92.

Squires D.F. & McLay L. 1982. *Marine Biomass: New York State Species and Site Studies.* Annual report GRI 81/0023. Chicago, IL: Gas Research Institute.

Stafford D.A., Hawkes D.L. & Horton R. 1980. *Methane Production from Waste Organic Matter.* viii + 268 pp. Boca Raton, Florida: CRC Press.

Stanford E.C.C. 1862. Distillation of seaweed. *Chem. News (Lond.)* **5**: 167–9.

Troiano R.A., Wise D.L., Augenstein D.C., Kispert R.G. & Kooney C.L. 1976. Fuel gas production by anaerobic digestion of kelp. *Res. Recovery Conserv.* **2**: 171–6.

Tseng C.K. 1944. Utilization of seaweeds. *Sci. Monthly* **119**: 37–46.

Tseng C.K. 1946. Seaweeds products and their uses in America. *J. N. Y Bot. Gard.* **47**: 1–9.

Tseng C.K. 1987. Some remarks on the kelp cultivation industry of China. In *Seaweed Cultivation for Renewable Resources.* (Eds. K.T. Bird & P.H. Benson) pp. 147–53. Amsterdam: Elsevier.

Tseng C.K. & Fei X.G. 1987. Macroalgal commercialization in the Orient. *Hydrobiologia* **151/152**: 167–72.

Tupholme C.H.S. 1926. Carbonization of seaweed. *Chem. Met. Eng.* **32**: 81–2.

Turrentine J.W. 1913. Notes on the distillation of kelp. *Proc. 8th Int. Congr. Applied Chem.* **15**: 313.

Turrentine J.W. & Shoaff P.S. 1919. Potassium from kelp: the experimental plant of the United States Department of Agriculture. *J. Ind. Eng. Chem.* **11**: 864–74.

Verlodt H., Zouaoui M. & Harbaoui Y. 1985. Relationship between physical and chemical properties of the substrate and foliar analysis with growth and yield results of a tomato crop cultivated in reutilized *Posidonia oceanica* L. seagrass substrates. *Acta Hortic. (The Hague)* **172**: 231–44.

Waart J. de 1988. Biogas from seaweeds. In *Aquatic Primary Biomass (Marine Macroalgae): Biomass Conversion, Removal and Use of Nutrients. I.* Proceedings of the 1st Workshop of the COST 48 Sub-Group 3, L'Houmeau, France, 12–14 February 1987. (Eds. P. Morand & E.H. Schulte) pp. 109–10. Brussels: CEC.

Waart J. de & Motshagen M.E. 1982. Effect of additives on biogas production from a substrate. In *Energy from Biomass*. 2nd EC Conference, Berlin, 20–23 September 1982. (Eds. A. Strub, P. Chartier & G. Schleser) pp. 559–64. London: Elsevier Applied Science.

Waart J. de, van der Most M.M. & Motshagen M.E. 1987. Production of biogas from organic waste material available in developing countries. In *Biomass for Energy and Industry*. 4th EC Conference, Orléans, France, 11–15 May 1987. (Eds. G. Grazi, B. Delmon, J.-F. Molle & H. Zibetta) pp. 814–17. London: Elsevier Applied Science.

Wachenfeld T. von 1980. The Swedish marine biomass programme. In *Proceedings of Bio-Energy '80 World Congress*. Atlanta, Georgia, 21–24 April 1980. pp. 340–1. Washington, DC: Environmental Protection Agency.

Wilcox H.A. 1977. The ocean food and energy farm project. In *Technology Assessment and the Oceans*. Proc. Int. Conf. Technol. Assessment, Monaco, 26 October 1975. (Eds. P.D. Wilmot & A. Slingerland) pp. 67–76. Guildford, UK: IPC.

Winfrey M.R. & Zeikus J.G. 1977. Effect of sulfate on carbon and electron flow during microbial methanogenesis in freshwater sediments. *Appl. Env. Microbiol.* **33**: 275–81.

Wise D.L. 1981. Probing the feasibility of large-scale aquatic biomass energy farms. *Solar Energy* **26**: 455–7.

Wise D.L., Augenstein D.C. & Ryther, J.H. 1979. Methane fermentaion of aquatic biomass. *Res. Recovery Conserv.* **4**: 217–37.

6 Seaweeds for Waste Water Treatment and Recycling of Nutrients

WINFRID SCHRAMM
Institut für Meereskunde, Universität Kiel, Germany

Waste waters such as domestic or municipal sewage, and agricultural or industrial effluents usually carry large amounts of the nutrient elements nitrogen and phosphorus, even when treated in the conventional way by removal of suspended solids and bacterial remineralisation of dissolved organic compounds (see Goldman *et al.* 1974; Giaccone *et al.* 1976).

As a typical example of northern European standards at the beginning of the 1980s, the effluents from the urban sewage treatment plant of the city of Kiel, Germany, contained an average of 41 mg dm^{-3} inorganic nitrogen and 6.5 mg dm^{-3} total phosphorus during the period 1980–1984 (Table 1).

Similarly, agricultural waste effluents contain high concentrations of nutrients, as for example liquid pig manure (Table 2).

Although in recent years increasing efforts have been made to protect terrestrial and freshwater environments, along the coasts of most European countries and world-wide, nutrient-rich waste waters, either treated or untreated, are still discharged directly into the sea. Together with anthropogenic river input and atmospheric fallout, direct discharge of waste water nutrients may add significantly to the nutrient budget locally and considerably alter the natural nutrient and productivity pattern of the recipient coastal ecosystems. Recently, alarming signs of change have been reported for many European coastal areas. In most cases, these have been related to increasing man-made eutrophication and pollution. Only a few examples will be mentioned here, such as increasing phytoplankton production (Aertebjerg-Nielsen *et al.* 1981; Radach & Berg 1986) and mass development of algae, such as the exceptional phytoplankton blooms in the North Sea (Gillbricht 1983) and 'green tides' along the French Atlantic coasts (Briand 1988) and in Mediterranean lagoons (Orlandini & Favretto 1988). Oxygen depletion has become more frequent in the Baltic (Gerlach 1984) and in the North Sea (Westernhagen *et al.* 1986). Significant changes in the benthic vegetation have been observed in areas such as the Baltic (Wennberg 1987; Breuer & Schramm 1988). As the nutrients in waste water effluents are a considerable burden and nuisance to

Seaweed Resources in Europe: Uses and Potential. Edited by M. D. Guiry and G. Blunden
© 1991 John Wiley & Sons Ltd

Table 1. Nutrient loads (μg dm^{-3}) of secondary effluents discharged daily into the Baltic from the municipal sewage treatment plant of the city of Kiel (northern Germany)

1980–1984	Nitrite	Nitrate	Ammonia	Total nitrogen	Phosphate
Annual mean	236	106	40 544	40 891	6 775
Maximum	2562	1680	62 405	62 450	14 558
Minimum	0	0	15 750	15 810	1 394

Average N/P ratio (by atoms) is 13 : 1.

the recipient terrestrial and aquatic environments, legislation has been enacted in some European countries to reduce nitrogen as well as phosphorus concentrations of the treated waste water effluents.

At present, three main types of treatment are used: chemical precipitation of phosphorus, microbial denitrification, and biological removal of nitrogen and phosphorus through aquatic primary producers. Although an extensive literature exists on the use of freshwater plants, either unicellular algae or macrophytes, for waste water treatment, recycling of nutrients or utilisation of the resulting biomass (e.g. Reddy & DeBusk 1987), comparatively little information is available on the usage of marine plants for this purpose. A number of arguments and considerations, however, support the use of marine macrophytes, in particular seaweeds and marine phanerogams, for the treatment of waste water or the recovery of nutrients, especially in coastal regions. One important argument is that marine areas are usually more readily available than limited and valuable land and freshwater areas. For example, shallow bays, fjords and lagoons with natural macrophyte vegetation can be used as natural recipients for controlled waste-water discharge. Additionally, marine macrophytes are comparatively easy to harvest; this is particularly true of seaweeds, which can be cultivated free-floating. These plants can then be utilized in many different ways, such as for manure, fodder or bioenergy production, and to provide valuable raw material for specific chemical com-

Table 2. Nutrient concentrations (μmol dm^{-3}) of liquid pig manure

	Nitrite	Nitrate	Ammonia	Total nitrogen	Phosphate
Mean	1 400	990	44 000	48 000	1020
Maximum	32 000	5600	124 300	127 700	9400
Minimum	0	0	5 500	5 900	60
Sample number	76	76	67	70	78

The average N/P ratio (by atoms) is 13 : 1.
After De Pauw et al. 1980.

pounds such as phycocolloids, vitamins and antibiotics. Last but not least, numerous physiological and ecophysiological investigations have shown that seaweeds in particular have the ability to take up and accumulate considerable amounts of nutrient elements, particularly phosphorus. Furthermore, many seaweeds have comparatively low nitrogen: phosphorus (N/P) ratios for nutrient uptake, and show a preference for ammonia as a nitrogen source. They may also be more suitable for growth in sewage-enriched seawater with typically lower N/P ratios and high ammonia concentrations compared with unenriched seawater. The ability of seaweeds to accumulate certain substances, for example heavy metals, by several orders of magnitude, may be important in this connection.

The suitability of a particular seaweed species for waste-water treatment and recycling of nutrients depends to a great extent on specific ecophysiological, biological and chemical characteristics and requirements. These include:

1. the ability to utilise specific nutrients and combinations of nutrients as well as to tolerate the nutrient concentrations or other possibly deleterious properties of the waste waters;
2. the response and tolerance to the varying environmental conditions (such as extremes of temperature, light and salinity), which may occur in the treatment systems;
3. the periodicity of reproduction and vegetative growth;
4. the productivity potential;
5. the usability of the biomass produced as manure, fodder or food, or for the production of specific chemical compounds or bioenergy. In this connection the possible contamination with toxic substances from the waste waters must be closely monitored.

The ability and preference of many seaweeds to take up ammonium, which is the prevalent nitrogen compound in most domestic and agricultural waste waters, has been demonstrated in numerous investigations (e.g. Yamada 1961; D'Elia & DeBoer 1978; Haines & Wheeler 1978; Wallentinus 1984; De Busk *et al.* 1986). Typically, the uptake of other types of nitrogen compounds is suppressed in the presence of ammonium ions, although some seaweeds show different reaction patterns (see Prince 1974; Bird 1976; Topinka 1978).

Nutrient concentrations for saturated uptake or growth vary considerably depending on external environmental conditions such as temperature, light and salinity, as well as on 'internal' factors such as species-specific physiological properties, internal nutrient status, state of development and age (see DeBoer *et al.* 1978; Birch *et al.* 1981; Wallentinus 1984; Lehnberg & Schramm 1984; Schramm *et al.* 1988). Half saturation constants (k_m) for nutrient uptake and growth are usually high in monostromatic green algae and filamentous, finely branched forms from the intertidal zone, or in actively growing parts of the plants, e.g. *Fucus* 'tips' (Gordon *et al.* 1981; Wallentinus

1984). Similarly, the capacity for nitrogen incorporation varies with external factors and from species to species. For example, in the red alga *Gracilaria tikvahiae* grown in seawater enriched with 0–1500 μmol nitrogen dm^{-3}, tissue nitrogen content varied between 1.3 and 5.3% (Bird *et al.* 1981). In general, red algae show higher tissue nitrogen concentrations in comparison with other seaweeds (Niell 1976; Birch *et al.* 1981; Kornfeldt 1982).

Similarly, phosphorus uptake is influenced by external and internal factors. An important feature of many seaweeds, however, is the ability to take up and accumulate phosphorus in excess of limiting internal concentrations required for maximal growth (see Kuhl 1974; Lin 1977; Schramm & Booth 1981). Consequently, the N/P ratios in seaweeds may vary considerably depending on external conditions, and may be much lower than is usually found either in marine phytoplankton or in aquatic phanerogams. This may be advantageous because N/P ratios in sewage effluents are usually high compared with natural seawater. For example, N/P ratios by atoms varied from 7 to 28 in *Porphyra tenera* (Iwasaki & Matsudaira 1954; and 8 to 66 in *Cladophora glomerata* (Wallentinus 1976). N/P uptake ratios were 3–69 in *Enteromorpha compressa* (Kautsky 1982). Prince (1974) determined N/P ratios between 30 : 1 and 39 : 1 for *Fucus vesiculosus*, *Chondrus crispus* and *Enteromorpha linza* cultivated in artificially enriched seawater or sewage-enriched seawater. In *Enteromorpha prolifera* grown in 10–30% sewage-enriched seawater, the N/P ratio varied from 16 to 10 (Lehnberg & Schramm 1984). Optimal growth was found at a ratio of 5 for *Ectocarpus* (Boalch 1961), and at 13–20 for *Cladophora* aff. *albida* (Gordon *et al.* 1981). Production of *Enteromorpha compressa* decreased with increasing ratios of N/P concentrations in the culture media or N/P uptake ratios. Productivity was highest at media concentration ratios between 0.9 and 5.5 (Kautsky 1982).

Admixture of sewage is limited not only because of the negative effects of decreased salinity on marine plants, but also because of potential detrimental effects of extreme nutrient concentrations, which can be higher by orders of magnitude compared with the natural nutrient concentrations in the sea. Detrimental effects of ammonium have been observed for *Ulva lactuca* at concentrations above 60 μmol dm^{-1} (Waite & Mitchell 1972) and for *Fucus vesiculosus* at 200 μmol dm^{-1} (Prince 1974), whereas in other experiments the optimal nitrogen concentration for cultivation of *Ulva*, *Ectocarpus*, *Porphyra* and some other red algae was in the range 120–2000 μmol dm^{-3} (Boalch 1961; Fries 1963; Steffensen 1976). *Percursaria percursa* and *Enteromorpha* species from the Baltic tolerated ammonium or nitrate concentrations as high as 1000–2000 μmol l^{-1} for several weeks (Schramm & Lehnberg 1985). These varying observations may be the result of species-specific differences in ammonium tolerance of the seaweeds in question. Possibly also the degree of formation of unionised, toxic ammonia may play a role, which may vary considerably depending on temperature, salinity and pH (Turner *et al.* 1986). Pronounced seasonal fluctuations of the key environmental factors light and temperature are typical of the temperate climates found in higher latitudes in Europe, which limit the application of primary producers for continuous waste-water treatment in different ways. During the winter, low temperature and low irradiance may drastically reduce the ability of aquatic plants to grow and to take up nutrients.

In sewage-treatment experiments with green algae from the Baltic Sea adapted to brackish water, growth almost ceased at temperatures below 6 °C during the winter months. Attempts were made to use waste heat from the sewage, which even during the coldest months was never below 10 °C, to avoid freezing of the seaweed cultures (Schramm & Lehnberg 1985). Another possibility would be the use of cooling seawater from power plants to heat the seaweed cultures during the winter months (see, for example, Friedlander & Zelikovitch 1984). Irradiance would still be a limiting factor, however. Ryther *et al.* (1979) report, for example, that growth of *Gracilaria tikvahiae* and *Agardhiella subulata* declined rapidly in autumn and ceased or fell to very low levels during winter, although the culture medium was heated and its temperature never fell below 13 °C.

In summer, on the other hand, temperature and irradiance in shallow coastal waters, particularly in artificial land-based systems, may be above optimum and tolerance levels of marine macrophytes. Addition of waste water, which is basically freshwater, decreases the salinity of the seawater. This salinity reduction must not only be tolerated by the plants, but also influences nutrient uptake and the effect of other factors, such as temperature or light, on productivity and reproduction (Gessner & Schramm 1971). In general, intertidal or estuarine forms, notably green algae, show the widest osmotic tolerance range. Species of *Enteromorpha*, *Monostroma* and *Cladophora* from the Baltic are adapted to brackish water and thrive at salinities from full marine conditions down to 1–3‰. Also, most *Gracilaria* species, which are among the most promising candidates for waste-water treatment and recycling of nutrients, generally show a wide range of osmotic tolerance. It is particularly interesting that some seaweeds at high nutrient concentrations show enhanced nutrient uptake with decreasing salinity (e.g. Neish *et al.* 1977; Lehnberg & Schramm 1984).

Another important aspect is the seasonal dependence and control of reproduction and vegetative growth periods of plants. The necessity for continuous operation of waste treatment systems throughout the seasons excludes or at least limits the application of monospecies cultures, particularly of short-lived annual forms, although these usually show the highest production as well as the highest nutrient uptake rates. A possible solution is the application of multispecies systems with successive cultures of entities with different growth and reproduction periods as suggested by Edler *et al.* (1980) (Fig. 1). Furthermore, reproductive and vegetative growth periods can be manipulated, to a certain extent, for the provision of seed material over longer periods of the year to be used as inoculum for treatment systems.

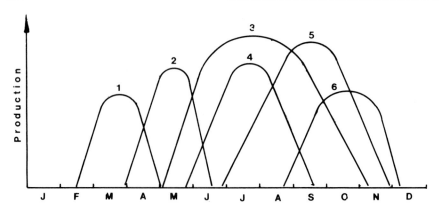

Figure 1. Hypothetical succession of production periods of seaweeds from the Western Baltic (southern Sweden). 1, *Monostroma grevillei*; 2, *Cladophora glomerata*; 3, *Ulvaria oxysperma*; 4, *Ulva lactuca*; 5, *Chaetomorpha linum*; 6, *Cladophora glomerata*. After Edler *et al.* 1980, modified

Development of spores, growth of sporelings as well as of juvenile plants of *Enteromorpha*, for example, could be retarded by several months and induced within days by the use of particular combinations of temperature, irradiance, day-length and nutrient levels (Schramm & Lehnberg 1985). Another practicable method is to use seaweeds capable of proliferating vegetatively; cultures of *Gracilaria tikvahiae*, for example, have been maintained in this way for several years (Hanisak 1984).

The biomass produced in waste-water treatment systems or in sewage-enriched cultures can be utilised in various ways, although with some reservations. For aesthetic as well as sanitary reasons they have not been used as human food to date. Utilisation as animal fodder or manure depends to a great extent on possible contamination of the plants with toxic substances taken from the waste water. It is known that marine plants tend to concentrate some trace metals many times above the levels of the surrounding medium (see Morris & Bale 1975; Phillips 1977). In particular, heavy metals frequently present at high concentrations in urban or industrial waste water should be monitored. In our investigations, the heavy metal content (mercury, arsenic, cadmium, copper, lead, zinc) of mixed cultures of *Enteromorpha prolifera*, *E. linza* and *Percursaria percursa* from 0–49% sewage-enriched flow cultures in a four-step cascade system was determined. During experiments of 2 months' duration, significant increases of metal content were found only for cadmium and mercury. Some data for mercury content are given in Table 3.

Altogether some 50–60 species of marine macrophytes, mainly seaweeds, have been screened or tested for their suitability for waste-water treatment, recycling of waste nutrients, or biomass production in sewage-enriched cul-

Table 3. Mercury content (ng per g wet weight) in mixed green algal populations (*Enteromorpha prolifera, E. linza, Percursaria percursa*) cultivated in 20% seawater enriched with sewage (20% secondary effluent from the municipal sewage-treatment plant in Kiel, northern Germany) in a four-step cascade system

Day	Cascade step			
	1	2	3	4
0	34	34	34	34
33	255	283	94	62
40	201	155	112	72
53	147	159	69	45

tures (Table 4). In general, intertidal and estuarine green algae have proved to be most suitable. Of the red and brown algae, which are of interest because of their commercial value, tropical or subtropical forms have been successfully used, while cold–temperate species were usually too sensitive to the seasonally changing environmental conditions in treatment systems. No investigations have been made on the use of marine phanerogams for waste-water treatment and recycling of nutrients. Investigations on nutrient kinetics and fertilising experiments suggest that they would be useful in waste-water treatment applications (see Feldner 1977; Orth 1977).

In most investigations, secondary effluents from domestic or municipal treatment plants have been used in the laboratory or in small- to medium-sized outdoor tank cultures, either in batch or in flow-through mode. In short-term laboratory culture experiments in seawater media enriched with 5–25% secondary domestic sewage effluents, growth of *Ulva lactuca* was stimulated by 5–15% sewage additions. At higher concentrations (20 and 25%) growth and nutrient uptake were less than in controls (Guist & Humm 1976). In laboratory and field experiments, Feldner (1976) found positive effects of municipal secondary sewage effluents on growth and photosynthesis in seaweeds from the Western Baltic. In the course of investigations into the mariculture potential of *Sargassum muticum*, additional nutrients in the form of secondary sewage effluents had only minimal effects on productivity (Gellenbek 1984). For germlings of *Sargassum johnstonii*, on the other hand, 0.1–1% additions of secondary sewage to the culture medium significantly increased the length and width of the pseudophylls, but 20% sewage inhibited the development of the plants (Tewari & Rao 1982). In southern France (the Mediterranean), the influence of various factors on growth of *Ulva lactuca* and *Enteromorpha intestinalis* in sewage-enriched seawater has been investi-

Table 4. Seaweeds tested or used for waste-water treatment or recycling nutrients from waste waters

Species	Modes of cultivation	Source
Ulva lactuca	Secondary sewage, laboratory, batch, short-term	Guist & Humm (1976)
Fucus vesiculosus *Enteromorpha linza* *Chondrus crispus*	Secondary sewage, laboratory, batch, growth	Prince (1974)
Chondrus crispus *Palmaria palmata* *Hypnea musciformis* *Gracilariopsis sjoestedtii* *Agardhiella subulata* (=*Neoagardhiella baileyi*) *Gracilaria tikvahiae* *Enteromorpha clathrata* *Ulva lactuca* *Chaetomorpha linum*	Secondary sewage, maricultural effluents, flow culture, outdoor, tanks, ponds, race ways, short- and long-term; altogether 24 species screened	Goldman *et al.* (1974) Ryther *et al.* (1979)
Enteromorpha intestinalis *E. flexuosa* *E. prolifera* *E. jugoslavica* *Ulva rigida* *U. rotunda* *Ulothrix flacca* *Bryopsis hypnoides* *Bangia atropurpurea* *Audouinella secundata* *Gracilaria verrucosa* *Ectocarpus siliculosus* *Scytosiphon lomentaria*	Secondary sewage, laboratory, batch, growth reproduction, plastid structure (partly metabolism)	Giaccone *et al.* (1976)
Hypnea musciformis	Oil-refinery effluents, laboratory, batch	Haines & Monahan (1977)
Hypnea musciformis	Secondary sewage, maricultural effluents, flow culture, laboratory	Langton *et al.* (1977)
Gracilaria verrucosa	Urban waste waters, laboratory bioassay	Giaccone *et al.* (1979)
Ulva lactuca *Gracilaria* species	Maricultural effluents, recirculating laboratory system	Harlin *et al.* (1979)
Bossiella orbigniana *Lithothrix aspergillum*	Untreated primary and secondary sewage,	Kindig & Littler (1980)

Table 4. (*continued*)

Species	Modes of cultivation	Source
Amphiroa zonata *Corallina officinalis* var. *chilensis*	Chlorinated secondary sewage, laboratory growth, metabolism	
Gracilaria verrucosa *Valonia aegagropila*	Industrial waste effluents, laboratory, batch	Rizzi-Longo *et al.* (1982)
Sargassum johnstonii	Secondary sewage, laboratory, batch, morphological development	Tewari & Rao (1982)
Ulva lactuca *Enteromorpha* sp.	Secondary sewage, agricultural waste effluents, laboratory, outdoor, growth	Houvenaghel & Mathot (1983)
Laminaria digitata *L. saccharina* *Alaria esculenta*	Mariculture effluents, *in situ* growth	Indergaard & Jensen (1983)
Sargassum muticum	Secondary sewage, flow culture, growth	Gellenbek (1984)
Furcellaria lumbricalis *Fucus vesiculosus* *Enteromorpha linza* *E. prolifera* *E. intestinalis* *Percursaria percursa* *Monostroma grevillei* *Chaetomorpha linum* *Cladophora glomerata*	Secondary urban sewage, laboratory, outdoor, batch and flowthrough	Lehnberg & Schramm (1984) Schramm & Lehnberg (1985)
Eucheuma spinosum *E. striatum* *Gracilaria coronipifolia*	Secondary domestic sewage, batch and outdoor	Schramm unpublished data
Porphyra yezoensis	Secondary municipal sewage, growth, laboratory	Maruyana *et al.* (1985)
Ulva rotunda *U. pseudocurvata* *Enteromorpha compressa* *E. intestinalis* *E. usneoides* *E. species* *Gracilaria multipartita* *G. verrucosa*	Freshwater purification concentrates, laboratory, growth	Dion (1988)

gated (Sauze 1983). *Enteromorpha intestinalis* adapted to brackish water was grown outdoors in basins or in semi-artificial environments receiving waste water for water purification and biomass production (Chassany de Casabianca 1980, 1982). In laboratory experiments with *Porphyra yezoensis*, growth and numbers of living cells decreased rapidly when municipal secondary sewage effluents were added above 5% by volume (Maruyana *et al.* 1985).

On a large scale, the use of seaweeds for treatment of secondary municipal sewage effluents, recycling of nutrients and marine biomass production was investigated in the USA at Woods Hole, Massachusetts and in Fort Pierce, Florida (Harbor Branch Laboratory) in the 1970s (Ryther *et al.* 1972, 1979). Basically, the concept of this system was to grow marine phytoplankton in sewage-enriched seawater to remove the major nutrients and to feed the algae to filter-feeding molluscs. As a considerable proportion of the nutrients assimilated by the phytoplankton was regenerated by the cultivated animals, a third polishing step was introduced in later experiments, using seaweeds to remove the nutrients before discharging the effluents from the bivalve mollusc cultures into the sea (Goldman *et al.* 1974). Subsequently, seaweeds were cultivated in sewage-enriched seawater as a one-step waste recycling/ mariculture system. A total of 24 seaweed species was screened, and partly used in sewage treatment experiments. In preliminary experiments, growth of *Fucus vesiculosus*, *Enteromorpha linza* and *Chondrus crispus* was determined over several weeks of flow cultivation in seawater enriched with 10% secondary sewage effluent and added nutrient chemicals in concentrations equivalent to a 10–15% sewage admixture (Prince 1974).

The removal efficiency of a total system with phytoplankton as a first step, oysters as a second, and *Chondrus crispus* as a third seaweed polishing step was as follows (Goldman *et al.* 1974). Of the nutrients added in the form of 25% secondary sewage admixture, 86.9% of total nitrogen and 47.3% of phosphorus (in the form of phosphate) were removed under batch-feed conditions, and 96.2% of total nitrogen and 60.6% of phosphorus (phosphate) in the continuous-flow system. Nitrogen removal in the seaweed system alone was 94.1%. Further studies were carried out in outdoor flow cultivation systems varying from 50 dm^3 to several m^3 in volume, or in 12 m raceways. The seaweeds were grown either in the effluents from the mariculture system or in seawater mixed with 10–15% secondary sewage effluents. The yields obtained in the experiments in Massachusetts were remarkably high, with a maximum 43 g dry weight m^{-2} day^{-1} for *Gracilaria tikvahiae* and 41 g dry weight m^{-2} day^{-1} for *Agardhiella subulata* during the summer. Although the seaweed cultures received heated effluents from the mariculture systems during the colder 6 months of the year such that water temperatures never fell below 13 °C, yields of both species declined rapidly in autumn and early winter, and were zero in *Gracilaria* by mid-December, whereas *Agardhiella* remained viable at a production rate of 6 g dry weight m^{-2} day^{-1}. The mean annual production rate under these temperature conditions was estimated as 17.3 g dry weight m^{-1} day^{-1} or 63.2 t ha^{-1} $year^{-1}$ for *Agardhiella* and 8.9 g dry weight m^{-2} d^{-1} or 32.9 t ha^{-1} $year^{-1}$ for *Gracilaria* (De Boer & Ryther 1976; Ryther *et al.* 1979). For unheated cultivation, assuming a 5–6 month growing season, annual production was estimated as 41.6 and 25.8 t ha^{-1} $year^{-1}$ for *Agardhiella* and *Gracilaria*, respectively. Under more favourable winter conditions, higher annual yields may be expected. Based on 6 month experiments (July to February) with *Gracilaria tikvahiae* in Florida, where an average yield of 30.7 g dry weight m^{-2} day^{-1} was obtained (Lapointe *et al.* 1976), an annual yield of 112 t ha^{-1} $year^{-1}$ was calculated. Taking these production values and assuming that the seaweed contains 5% nitrogen on a dry weight basis, Ryther *et al.* (1979) extrapolate that under the above experimental conditions the seaweeds would be capable of removing 7.9 and 15.4 kg N ha^{-1} day^{-1} in Massachusetts and Florida, respectively. Assuming a per capita production of 10 g waste nitrogen per day, the nitrogen from the sewage effluents of a municipality of 10 000 could theoretically be removed for half the year in New England in a 13 ha culture area, and throughout the year in Florida in a similar 6 ha facility.

In Europe, a concept similar to that described above was used for a marine polyculture system developed in Kiel, northern Germany, where the end consumers were fish larvae and oyster spat. As addition of sewage reduces the salinity of the medium, predominantly brackish water-adapted seaweeds were used in these experiments (Lehnberg & Schramm 1984; Schramm & Lehnberg 1984, 1985). In all, nine different littoral seaweeds from the western Baltic were tested in laboratory experiments (Table 2), of which the green algae *Enteromorpha prolifera*, *E. linza*, *E. intestinalis*, *Percursaria percursa* and *Monostroma grevillei* gave the most promising results.

In further ecophysiological experiments, growth, photosynthesis and nutrient uptake at varying combinations of nutrient concentration (0–2000 μmol inorganic nitrogen dm^{-3}, 0–200 μmol phosphorus dm^{-3}), salinity (7–33%) and temperature (5–20% °C) were investigated. Sewage treatment and biomass production were studied in outdoor batch cultures as well as continuous flow systems from 400 to 5000 dm^3 volume. During the winter, sewage was utilised as a heat source so that culture temperatures could be maintained at 6–8 °C. During extremely cold periods the temperature dropped to 1–2 °C and productivity and nutrient uptake decreasing almost to zero. Sewage admixture ranged from 0 to 49%, and salinity varied accordingly from 15 to 8%.

In flow-through mode, over an experimental period of several months, an average of 55% of inorganic nitrogen and 60% of phosphorus were removed from a 14% sewage admixture, and 30% of nitrogen and phosphorus from a 38% admixture. Under these conditions, maximal tissue nutrient contents on a dry weight basis were 6.5% nitrogen and 0.8% phosphorus. Yields ranged from 88 g wet weight m^{-2} day^{-1} in summer to zero during the coldest and darkest periods of the year.

Combined mariculture and recycling of nutrients employing seaweeds, the original aim of the projects described above, has also been tested on a small scale in combination with an artificial upwelling system on St Croix, US Virgin Islands (Haines 1976; Langton et al. 1977). Effluents from four different cultured populations of the bivalve mollusc Tapes japonica containing up to 13 μmol ammonia nitrogen dm^{-3} were utilised to grow the red seaweed Hypnea musciformis in 4.6 dm^3 tanks at a water-exchange rate of 37.6 volumes per day. The removal of nitrogen was a function of the ammonium concentration of the incoming shellfish culture effluents. Maximal removal of about 70% of the available nitrogen was attained when the inflowing concentration was above 4 μmol ammonia nitrogen dm^{-3}. Fragmentation of Hypnea occurred at higher concentrations, which was thought to be related to lack of trace elements or high temperature and light levels.

In closed animal mariculture systems, accumulation of ammonia, nitrite, urea and even nitrate to toxic levels may become a serious problem. In laboratory experiments, Harlin et al. (1979) have therefore used the seaweeds Ulva lactuca and Gracilaria sp. to remove excess nutrients and to produce valuable biomass at the same time. In closed recirculating 60 dm^3 aquaria systems each with 250 g fish (Fundulus heteroclitus) and seaweeds, Ulva removed 62.4% at 15 °C and 32% at 20 °C of the nitrogen produced by the fish, and Gracilaria 83.3 and 112%, respectively.

Another combination of mariculture, and recycling of waste nutrients with at least the partial help of seaweeds has been examined in South Africa (Turner et al. 1986). In this case, chlorinated secondary domestic sewage effluents have been utilised to increase primary production of phytoplankton and Enteromorpha sp. in Tilapia (milkfish) culture ponds. The chlorinated sewage was added as a sewage-seawater mixture at a 1 : 3 v/v ratio to provide 2–3 kg nitrogen (ammonia plus nitrate) ha^{-1} day^{-1}. No negative effects of the residual chlorine in the effluents were observed.

An interesting approach may be the use of seaweeds for in situ treatment and recycling of wastes from marine animal farms to reduce the frequently observed self-contamination. In Norway, Indergaard and Jensen (1983) attempted the cultivation of the brown algae Laminaria saccharina, L. digitata and Alaria esculenta in the eutrophicated neighbourhood of fish farms to utilise the nutrients originating from excretion and waste fodder from the farming enclosures. Preliminary experiments carried out in the Philippines to examine in situ polyculture of molluscs, sea urchins and sea cucumbers in combination with Eucheuma and Gracilaria for the purpose of recycling the nutrients from the animal cultures have shown promising results (Schramm unpublished data).

In northern Italy (Trieste), attempts to grow Gracilaria verrucosa in combination with mussel cultures also showed promising results, as the quality of the agar produced improved significantly. At present, experiments are being carried out to utilise the waste products of cage-cultured bass for cultivation of *Gracilaria dura* (M. Orlandini, personal communication). Similarly, effluents from eel farms were successfully used in Sweden to fertilise seaweeds (Pedersen, personal communication).

Wastes other than domestic or municipal secondary sewage and mariculture effluents have also been treated or utilised. In short-term metabolic studies and long-term culture experiments, Kindig and Littler (1980) examined the effects of untreated primary and secondary as well as chlorinated secondary sewage effluents on various southern Californian coralline algae. Chlorination was found to have only short-term negative effects. Houvenaghel and Mathot (1983) used urban sewage, rural run-off and liquid pig manure as fertiliser in outdoor tank cultivation experiments with *Ulva lactuca* from the coast of Brittany, France.

The suitability of solid animal wastes as nutrient sources for seaweed culture has been demonstrated in short-term laboratory experiments with *Gracilaria tikvahiae* and *Agardhiella subulata* (Asare 1980). Filtrates of seawater extracts from dried rabbit and sheep faeces were added as an enrichment medium in amounts equivalent to 0.008–0.08% dry weight. The extracts from 20 g dry weight dm^{-3} of rabbit and sheep waste contained 96 and 53 μmol nitrate nitrogen and 101 and 173 μmol ammonia nitrogen, respectively. Both stimulated growth significantly. In *Agardhiella*, addition of 0.04% rabbit faeces increased the yield by 4.5 times over the unfertilised control.

The effects of several urban and industrial waste effluents from the city of Trieste, Italy, on growth, reproduction, plastidial apparatus, and in some cases on nutrient uptake and photosynthesis has been tested in laboratory experiments for 14 different seaweeds (Giaccone *et al.* 1976). To assess the influence of specific pollutants in the waste waters, bioassays were performed on *Gracilaria verrucosa* and other agarophytes (Giaccone *et al.* 1979). Industrial waste effluents have also been used in laboratory experiments with *Gracilaria verrucosa* and *Valonia aegagropila* (Rizzi-Longo *et al.* 1982). Whereas slaughterhouse waste effluents rich in nitrate stimulated metabolic activity, and waste water from mechanical industries was toxic for both species, other waste effluents such as from food, paper and tobacco industries had varying effects. The effluents from two oil refineries were also toxic. Growth of the carrageenanophyte *Hypnea musciformis* decreased with increasing admixture of the effluents to the seawater medium. At 5% admixture of the two types of effluent, growth dropped to 49 and 76% of controls, and growth ceased completely at concentrations of 40 and 80%, respectively (Haines & Monahan 1977).

In the context of seaweed culture for bioenergy production, a special application of seaweeds for the recycling of nutrients has been suggested by Hanisak (1981) who used the nutrient-rich solid or liquid residues from anaerobic digestion of *Gracilaria tikvahiae* to methane as fertiliser for further *Gracilaria* cultivation (see Chapter 5). In this way, an overall recycling efficiency of 73% of the nitrogen was attained. Hanisak calculated that even with a recycling efficiency of only 45% it was possible to maintain intensive cultures of *Gracilaria* at a productivity rate of 20 g dry weight m^{-2} day^{-1} without any additional external nutrient source.

Seaweeds for waste treatment and nutrient recycling are presently being tested for a special type of waste water in France (Brittany), where freshwater containing excessive levels of nitrate must be purified to obtain drinking-water quality according to EC directives (< 50 mg nitrate dm^{-3}; Dion 1988). In a denitrification step employing reverse osmosis, concentrates are produced containing about 4.4 g dm^{-3} nitrate, 5.3 g dm^{-3} chloride and 3.5 g dm^{-3} sulphate. The aim is to discharge the effluents (45–120 m^3 day^{-1}) into a coastal lagoon, and to remove the excess nitrogen with the aid of seaweeds. In short-term laboratory experiments, growth of various *Ulva*, *Enteromorpha* and *Gracilaria* species (Table 3) was determined in the diluted or undiluted concentrate conditions (14–23 °C, 30 μmol photons m^{-2} s^{-1}). It was concluded from preliminary experiments that of the seaweeds tested the green algae, particularly *Enteromorpha usneoides*, would be most suitable. Based on the growth experiments, and assuming an average tissue nitrogen content of 4%, it was estimated that a sea area of 8–10 ha would be necessary to remove the average of 210 kg day^{-1} nitrate discharged.

In coastal areas, particularly in closed and sheltered areas such as fjords and lagoons, where eutrophication frequently causes mass development of primary producers (mostly green seaweeds) harvesting and utilisation of the plant biomass suggests itself as a possible means of removing excess nutrients from the system. In Europe, various attempts in this direction have been made. In Italy, for example, the 50 000 ha lagoon of Venice receives urban and industrial waste waters from the city of Venice and the town of Chioggia together with agricultural run-off from approximately 200 000 ha of farmland. Additionally, 60 m^3 s^{-1} of the heated seawater from power and steam plants are discharged into the lagoon. Effects on algal production are evident. The annual harvest of *Gracilaria* increased from about 120 t dry weight in 1946 to 1700 t dry weight in 1985. The present production potential is estimated as approximately 110 000 t dry weight $year^{-1}$ or 800 t of agar. Experiments have also been carried out to utilise the increasing biomass of green algae, mainly *Ulva rigida*, for biogas production (Missoni & Mazzagardi 1985; Chapter 5). Similarly, in the lagoon of Lesina (Foggia) which receives the urban sewage effluents from two municipalities, *Gracilaria* has been harvested since 1974 (Trotta 1981). In the small bay of Goro, which is influenced by the nutrient- and sediment-rich waters of the river Po, almost monospecific natural populations of *Gracilaria* are periodically exploited for agar extraction (Lenzi & Angelini 1984; Lenzi 1985). In the vicinity of Palermo, Sicily and Ponto Torres, Sardinia, the use of the seagrass *Posidonia* and *Gracilaria* for pollution abatement is under investigation (Orlandini & Favretto 1988).

Another example of systematic utilisation of natural sea areas for waste-water treatment, recycling of nutrient and biomass production is the Odense Fjord in Denmark (Frederiksen 1987). Since the 1970s, increasing eutrophication of this fjord-like inlet from the Kattegatt resulting from municipal sewage discharge and nutrient input from the surrounding farm lands caused mass development or green algae, mainly *Ulva lactuca*. In 1981, the municipality of Odense initiated a project to remove excess nutrient from the fjord by harvesting of the mostly free-floating seaweeds. The average annual production was estimated as 9 t dry weight ha^{-1} or approximately 10 000 t dry weight for the total harvesting area. The average nutrient content of the dried algae was 3.6% nitrogen and 0.5% phosphorus. For the year 1985, removal of 450 t nitrogen and 55 t phosphorus was estimated, which is 56% of the 800 t nitrogen and 39% of the 140 t phosphorus annually discharged into the fjord. In 1984, the project was continued by two private companies, which investigated the usability and profitability of the seaweed harvest for fodder, fertiliser, compost and energy production (see Chapter 5). On the basis of anaerobic digestion experiments, which yielded nearly 0.5 m^3 methane per kg volatile solids, and assuming an annual harvest of 9000 t dry weight, energy production of 63 000 GJ $year^{-1}$ was expected.

CONCLUDING REMARKS FROM A EUROPEAN PERSPECTIVE

Although numerous investigations demonstrated the high nutrient uptake capability of seaweeds, their utility in waste water treatment and recycling of nutrients from waste waters has not been widely recognised up to now. In the mid-1970s interest was triggered by the shortage of fossil fuels. The rapid growth of seaweeds in waste water recycling systems made them attractive candidates for production of renewable bioenergy. Today, the urgent need to protect marine ecosystems from further eutrophication and pollution may again attract attention to marine macrophytes as candidates for tertiary waste-water treatment. Existing information suggests that seaweeds are particularly suited for the purification of nitrogen-rich domestic and urban sewage, and also agricultural and some industrial waste effluents. The observed high removal efficiency for nitrogen could certainly be further improved by choosing adequate retention times and optimising other factors, such as carbon supply, stocking density and harvesting frequency.

Domestic or urban secondary sewage effluents usually contain higher concentrations of phosphorus, mostly originating from detergent phosphates, than of nitrogen relative to the needs of seaweeds and their incorporation capabilities. In extreme cases, N/P ratios of 2 : 1 have been observed (e.g. Turner *et al.* 1986). Therefore, nitrogen may become depleted before phosphorus, and thus be growth-limiting.

With the introduction of chemical precipitation steps from the 1970s on, and the reduced use of detergent phosphates, phosphorus loads have decreased drastically; in fact, these are sometimes below the requirements for optimal growth of seaweeds, as we have found in our own investigations.

For maximal nutrient removal using seaweeds in a tertiary biological polishing step, the adjustment of N/P ratios for optimal seaweed growth through fractional chemical precipitation of phosphates would be a necessary and technically feasible solution.

As will be discussed in Chapter 12, the continuous cultivation of seaweeds in northern Europe throughout the year would be largely limited by climatic conditions. Whereas it may be possible to raise low winter temperatures through the utilisation of waste heat (for example, from sewage or cooling water from power plants) the low irradiance levels during the winter months in the higher latitudes would greatly reduce the applicability of primary producers for continuous waste-water treatment. Along the Atlantic and Mediterranean coasts of southern parts of Europe, however, where winter irradiance levels and temperature conditions are more favourable, the use of seaweeds for waste-water treatment and nutrient recycling certainly shows promise in the prevention of further destruction of the coastal waters.

REFERENCES

Aertebjerg-Nielsen G., Jacobsen T.S., Gargas E. & Buch E. 1982. *Evaluation of the Physical, Chemical and Biological Measurements. The Belt Project*. National Agency of Environmental Protection, Denmark. pp. 122.

Asare S.O. 1980. Animal waste as nitrogen source for *Gracilaria tikvahiae* and *Neoargardhiellia baileyi* in culture. *Aquaculture* 21: 87–91.

Birch P.B., Gordon D.M. & McComb A.J. 1981. Nitrogen and phosphorus nutrition of *Cladophora* in the Peel–Harvey system. *Botanica Mar.* 24: 381–7.

Bird K.T. 1976. Simultaneous assimilation of ammonium and nitrate by *Gelidium nudifrons* (Gelidiales, Rhodophyta). *J. Phycol.* 12: 238–41.

Bird K.T. & DeBusk T. 1982. Nitrogen allocation and storage patterns in *Gracilaria tikvahiae* (Rhodophyta). *J. Phycol.* 18: 344–8.

Bird K.T., Hanisak M.D. & Ryther J.H. 1981. Chemical quality and production of agars extracted from *Gracilaria tikvahiae* grown in different nitrogen enrichment conditions. *Botanica Mar.* 24: 441–4.

Boalch G.T. 1961. Studies on *Ectocarpus* in culture. II. Growth and nutrition of bacteria-free culture. *J. Mar. Biol. Ass. UK* 41: 287–304.

Breuer G. & Schramm W. 1988. Changes in macroalgal vegetation of Kiel Bight (Western Baltic) during the past 20 years. *Kieler Meeresforsch.* 6: (Suppl.) 241–55.

Briand X. 1988. Stranded algae and disposable biomass. In *Proc. Ist Workshop COST 48, subgroup 3*. L'Houmeau, France, 1987. (Eds. P. Morand & E.H. Schulte) pp. 53–66. Brussels: European Commission.

Chassany de Casabianca M.L. 1980. Données et problèmes écologique concernant l'aquaculture de la biomasse végétale en milieu saumâtre. *La Technique de l'Eau et de l'Assainissement* 398: 28–31.

Chassany de Casabianca M.L. 1982. Systèmes de production à macrophytes saumâtres sur eaux résiduaires urbaines. *La Technique de l'Eau et de l'Assainissement* **422**: 17–22.

De Pauw N., Verlet H. & De Leenheer Jr. L. 1980. Heated and unheated outdoor cultures of marine algae with animal manure. In: *Algae Biomass*. (Eds. G. Shelef & C.J. Soeder) pp. 315–41. London: Elsevier.

DeBoer J.A. & Ryther J.H. 1976. Potential yields from a waste recycling algal mariculture system. In: *The Marine Plant Biomass of the Pacific Northwest Coast*. (Ed. R.W. Krauss) pp. 231–24. Corvallis: Oregon State University Press.

DeBoer J.A., Guigli H.J., Israel T.L. & D'Elia C.F. 1978. Nutritional studies of two red algae. 1. Growth rate as a function of nitrogen source and concentration. *J. Phycol.* **14**: 261–6.

DeBusk T.A., Blakeslee M. & Ryther J.H. 1986. Studies on the outdoor cultivation of *Ulva lactuca* L. *Botanica Mar.* **29**: 381–6.

D'Elia C.F. & DeBoer J.A. 1978. Nutritional studies of two red algae. II. Kinetics of ammonium and nitrate uptake. *J. Phycol.* **14**: 266–72.

Dion P. 1988. *Étude préliminaire des possibilites de traitment par culture d'algues de l'eluat de régeneration qui sera produit par l'usine de denitration de Kernilis*. Rapport. Centre d'Étude et de Valorisation des Algues, Pleubian, France, no. 34, pp. 1–21.

Dreno J.P. Perez R. & Barbaroux O. 1984. L'algue rouge *Eucheuma spinosum*: un essai de culture intensive en milieu enrichi. *Sci. Pêche* **348**: 10–20.

Edler L., Emmelin L. & von Wachenfeldt T. 1980. Marin biomassa: alger som energikälla. *Techn. Rep. Nämden för energiproduktions forskning*, Stockholm. 100 pp.

Feldner R. 1976. Untersuchungen über die eutrophierende Wirkung einiger Nährstoffkomponenten häuslicher Abwässer auf Benthosalgen der Kieler Bucht. Unpublished dissertation, University of Kiel, 134 pp.

Feldner J. 1977. Ökologische und produktionsbiologische Untersuchungen am Seegras *Zostera marina* L. in der Kieler Bucht (Westliche Östsee). *Rep. Sonderforschungsbereich 95, Univ. Kiel*, **30**: 1–170.

Frederiksen O.T. 1987. The fight against eutrophication in the inlet of 'Odense fjord' by reaping of sea lettuce (*Ulva lactuca*). *Water Sci. Technol.* **19**: 81–7.

Friedlander M. & Zelikovitch N. 1984. Growth rates, phycocolloid yield and quality of the red seaweeds, *Gracilaria* sp., *Pterocladia capillacea*, *Hypnea musciformis* and *Hypnea cornuta*, in field studies in Israel. *Aquaculture* **40**: 57–66.

Fries L. 1963. On the cultivation of axenic red algae. *Physiol. Plant.* **16**: 695–708.

Gellenbek K. 1984. Growth characteristics, nutrient uptake and reproduction of *Sargassum muticum* (Phaeophyta) in free-floating culture. *J. Phycol* **4**: (Suppl.): 4 (abstract).

Gerlach S.A. 1984. Oxygen depletion 1980–1983 in coastal waters of the Federal Republic of Germany. *Ber. Inst. Meeresk. Univ. Kiel* **130**: 1–87.

Gessner F. & Schramm W. 1971. Salinity – plants. In: *Marine ecology*. (Ed. O. Kinne) 1(2), pp. 706–820. London: Wiley Interscience.

Giaccone G., Princi M. & Rizzi-Longo L. 1976. Riposte morfologiche e fisiologiche di alghe marine in coltura all'inquinamento di liquami urbani e industriali. *Ingegneria Ambientale* **5**: 572–82.

Giaccone G., Princi M., Feoli E., Locar Coassini L, Rizzi Longo L. & Tortul V. 1979. Valutazione delle risorse vegetali lagunari del basso Tirreno e sperimentazione die coltivazione controllata dell'alga rossa *Gracilaria verrucosa* e di altre agarofite in Sicilia. *Atti Conv. Scient. Nazion. Oceanografia e Fondi Marini, Roma* **1**: 423–35.

Gillbricht M. 1983. Eine 'red tide' in der südlichen Nordsee und ihre Beziehungen zur Umwelt. *Helgol. Wiss. Meeresunters.* **36**: 393–426.

Goldman J.C., Tenore K.R., Ryther J.H. & Corwin N. 1974. Inorganic nitrogen removal in a combined tertiary treatment–marine aquaculture system. I. Removal efficiencies. *Water Res.* **8**: 45–54.

Gordon D.M., Birch P.B. & McComb A.J. 1981. Effects of inorganic phosphorus on the growth of an estuarine *Cladophora* in culture. *Botanica Mar.* **24**: 93–106.

Guist G.G. & Humm H.J. 1976. Effects of sewage effluent on growth of *Ulva lactuca*. *Florida Scientist* **39**: 267–71.

Haines K.C. 1976. Growth of the carrageenan-producing tropical red seaweed *Hypnea musciformis* in surface water, 870 m deep water, effluent from a clam mariculture system and in deep water enriched with artificial fertilizers or domestic sewage. In: *Proc. 10th Eur. Mar. Biol. Symp.*, Ostend (Eds. G. Persoone & E. Jaspers) pp. 207–20. Wettern: University Press.

Haines K.C. & Monahan R.K. 1977. Use of the seaweed *Hypnea musciformis* (Rhodophyta) in treating oil refinery wastes. *Proc. Ass. Isl. Mar. Lab. Caribb.* **12**: 1–12.

Haines K.C. & Wheeler P.A. 1978. Ammonium and nitrate uptake by the marine macrophytes *Hypnea musciformis* (Rhodophyta) and *Macrocystis pyrifera* (Phaeophyta). *J. Phycol.* **14**: 319–24.

Hanisak M.D. 1981. Recycling the residues from anaerobic digesters as a nutrient source for seaweed growth. *Botanica Mar.* **24**: 57–61.

Harlin M.M., Thorn-Miller B. & Thusby G.B. 1979. Ammonium uptake by *Gracilaria* spec. (Florideophyceae) and *Ulva lactuca* (Chlorophyceae) in closed system fish culture. In: *Proceedings of the IXth International Seaweed Symposium..* (Eds. A. Jensen & J.R. Stein) pp. 285–92. Princeton: Science Press.

Houvenaghel G.T. & Mathot J.F. 1983. The production of marine green algae in coastal waters and their culture in ponds enriched with waste waters. In: *Energy from Biomass* (Eds. A. Strub, A. Chartier, P. Schleser & G. Schleser) pp. 308–12A. London: Elsevier Applied Science.

Indergaard M. & Jensen A. 1983. Seaweed biomass production and fish farming. In: *Energy from Biomass* (Eds. A. Strub, A. Chartier, P. Schleser & G. Schleser) pp. 313–18. London: Elsevier Applied Science.

Iwasaki H. & Matsudaira C. 1954. Studies on cultural grounds of laver, *Porphyra tenera* Kjellmann in Matsukawa-Ura Inlet. I. Environmental characteristics affecting nitrogen and phosphorus contents of laver. *Bull. Jap. Soc. Sci. Fish.* **20**: 112–19.

Kautsky L. 1982. Primary production and uptake kinetics of ammonium and phosphate by *Enteromorpha compressa* (L.) Grev. *Aquat. Bot.* **12**: 23–40.

Kindig A.C. & Littler M.M. 1980. Growth and primary productivity of marine macrophytes exposed to domestic sewage effluents. *Mar. Environ. Res.* **3**: 81–100.

Kornfeldt R.A. 1982. Relation between nitrogen and phosphorus content of macroalgae and the waters of Northern Öresund. *Botanica Mar.* **24**: 197–201.

Kuhl A. 1974. Phosphorus. In: *Algal Physiology and Biochemistry* (Ed. W.D.P. Stewart) pp. 636–54. *Botanical Monographs* Vol. 10. London: Blackwell Scientific.

Langton R.W., Haines K.C. & Lyon R.E. 1977. Ammonia-nitrogen production by the bivalve molluscs *Tapes japonica* and its recovery by the red seaweed *Hypnea musciformis* in a tropical mariculture system. *Helgoländer Wiss. Meeresunters.* **30**: 217–29.

Lapointe B.E., Williams L.D., Goldman J.C. & Ryther J.H. 1976. The mass outdoor culture of macroscopic marine algae. *Aquaculture* **8**: 9–21.

Lehnberg W. & Schramm W. 1984. Mass culture of brackish-water-adapted seaweeds in sewage-enriched seawater. I. Productivity and nutrient accumulation. *Hydrobiologia* **116/117**: 276–81.

Lenzi M. 1985. Valutazioni sulla possibilita di realizzaare raccolte e coltivazioni della rodoficea *Gracilaria confervoides* Grev. nella laguna di Orbetello. *Atti Mus. Civ. Stor. Nat. Grosseto* **6**: 17–22.

Lenzi M. & Angelini M. 1984. Indagine sulle condizioni ambientali della laguna di Orbetello: chimico-fisica e carico microfitico. *Atti. Mus. Civ. Stor. Nat. Grosseto* **3**: 18–30.

Lin C.K. 1977. Accumulation of water soluble phosphorus and hydrolysis of polyphosphates by *Cladophora glomerata* (Chlorophyceae). *J. Phycol.* **13**: 46–51.

Maruyana T., Miura A. & Yoshida T. 1985. The effect of effluent of municipal wastewater on the growth of *Porphyra yezoensis* in case of static culture (in Japan). *Bull. Jap. Soc. Sci. Fish.* **51**: 315–20.

Missoni G. & Mazzagardi M. 1985. Production of algal biomass in Venice Lagoon: environmental and energetic aspects. In: *Proc. 3rd. EC Conference,* Venice 1985: *Energy from Biomass* (Eds. W. Paslz, J. Coombs & D.O. Hall) pp. 384–6. London: Elsevier Applied Science.

Morris A.W. & Bale A.J. 1975. The accumulation of cadmium, copper, manganese, and zinc by *Fucus vesiculosus* in the Bristol Channel. *Estuar. Coast. Mar. Sci.* **3**: 153–63.

Neish I.C., Shacklock P.F., Fox C.H. & Simpson F.J. 1977. The cultivation of *Chondrus crispus*: factors affecting growth under greenhouse conditions. *Can. J. Bot.* **55**: 2263–71.

Niell F.X. 1976. C : N ratio in some marine macrophytes and its possible ecological significance. *Botanica Mar.* **19**: 347–50.

Orlandini M. & Favretto L. 1988. Utilization of macroalgae in Italy for pollution abatement and as source of energy and chemicals. In *Proc. 1st Workshop COST 48 (subgroup 3)*, L'Houmeau, France, 1987. (Eds. P. Morand & E.H. Schulte) pp. 25–8. Brussels: European Commission.

Orth R.J. 1977. Effect of nutrient enrichment on growth of the eelgrass *Zostera marina* in the Chesapeake Bay, Virginia, USA. *Mar. Biol., Berl.* **44**: 187–94.

Phillips D.J.H. 1977. The use of biological indicator organisms to monitor trace metal pollution in marine and estuarine environments: a review. *Environ. Poll.* **13**: 281–317.

Prince J.S. 1974. Nutrient assimilation and growth of some seaweeds in mixtures of sea water and secondary sewage treatment effluents. *Aquaculture* **4**: 69–79.

Radach G. & Berg J. 1986. Trends in den Konzentrationen der Nährstoffe und des Phytoplanktons in der Helgoländer Bucht (Helgoländer Reede Daten). *Ber. Biol. Anstalt Helgoland* **2**: 1–63.

Reddy K.R. & de Busk T.A. 1987. State-of-the-art utilization of aquatic plants in water pollution control. *Water Sci. Technol.* **19**: 61–79.

Rizzi-Longo L., Giaccone G., Princi M. & Tortul V. 1982. Variazioni dell'attivita metabolica die alghe marine bentoniche in cultura in presenza die liquami industriali. *Naturalista Sicil.* Ser. 4, 6 (Suppl.) **2**: 61–9.

Ryther J.H., Dunstan W.M., Tenore K.R. & Huguenin J.E. 1972. Controlled eutrophication: increasing food production from the sea by recycling human wastes. *AIBS J.* **22**: 144–52.

Ryther J.H., DeBoer J.A. & Lapointe B.E. 1979. Cultivation of seaweeds for hydrocolloids, waste treatment and biomass for energy conversion. *Proceedings of the IXth International Seaweed Symposium.* (Eds. A. Jensen & J.R. Stein) pp. 1–16. Princeton: Science Press.

Ryther J.H., Corwin N., DeBusk T.A. & Williams L.D. 1981. Nitrogen uptake and storage by the red alga *Gracilaria tikvahiae* (McLachlan 1979). *Aquaculture* **26**: 107–15.

Sauze F. 1983. Increasing the productivity of macroalgae by the action of a variety of factors. In: *Energy from Biomass* (Eds. A. Strub, A. Chartier, P. Schleser & G. Schleser) pp. 324–8. London: Elsevier Applied Science.

Schramm W. & Booth W. 1981. Mass bloom of the alga *Cladophora prolifera* in

Bermuda. Productivity and phosphorus accumulation. *Botanica Mar.* **24**: 419–26.
Schramm W. & Lehnberg W. 1984. Mass cultivation of brackish-water adapted seaweeds in sewage-enriched seawater. II. Fermentation for biogas production. In: *Proceedings of the XIth International Seaweed Symposium.* (Eds. C.J. Bird & M.A. Ragan) pp. 282–7. Dordrecht: Junk.
Schramm W. & Lehnberg W. 1985. 1. Aufnahme und Akkumulation anorganischer Nährstoffe durch benthische Größalgen aus Abwässern. 2. Untersuchungen zur Produktion und Fermentation mariner Primärbiomasse unter Verwendung von Kulturen benthischer Größalgen in abswasserangereichertem Meerwasser. pp. 26. Schulßbericht MFE 0501-BMFT. Bonn: Ministry for Research and Technology.
Schramm W., Abele D. & Breuer G. 1988. Nitrogen and phosphorus nutrition of two community forming seaweeds (*Fucus vesiculosus*, *Phycodrys rubens*) from the Western Baltic (Kiel Bight) in the light of eutrophication processes. *Kieler Meeresforsch.* **6**: (Suppl.) 221–40.
Steffensen D.A. 1976. The effect of nutrient enrichment and temperature on the growth in culture of *Ulva lactuca* L. *Aquat. Bot.* **2**: 337–51.
Tewari A. & Rao P.S. 1982. Effect of domestic sewage on the vegetative growth of juvenile plants of *Sargassum johnstonii* in laboratory culture. *Mahasagar* **15**: 157–62.
Topinka J.A. 1978. Nitrogen uptake by *Fucus spiralis* (Phaeophyceae). *J. Phycol.* **14**: 241–7.
Trotta P. 1981. On the rhodophyte *Gracilaria confervoides* Grev. in Lesina lagoon: field survey and *in vitro* culture. In: *Proc. Convegno Int. Fitodepurazione e Impieghi delle Biomasse prodotte*, Parma, 1981. pp. 15–16.
Turner J.W.D., Sibbald R.R. & Hemens J. 1986. Chlorinated secondary domestic sewage effluent as a fertilizer for marine aquaculture. I. *Tilapia* culture. II. Protein supplemented prawn culture. *Aquaculture* **53**: 133–55.
Waite T. & Mitchell R. 1972. The effect of nutrient fertilisation on the benthic alga *Ulva lactuca*. *Botanica Mar.* **15**: 151–6.
Wallentinns I. 1976. Environmental influences on benthic macrovegetation in the Trosa–Askö area, northern Baltic proper. I. Hydrographical and chemical parameters, and the macrophytic communities. *Contrib. Askö Lab., Univ. Stockholm* **15**: 1–138.
Wallentinus I. 1984. Comparison of nutrient uptake rates for Baltic macroalgae with different thallus morphologies. *Mar. Biol.* **80**: 215–25.
Wennberg T. 1987. Long-term changes in the composition and distribution of the macroalgal vegetation in the southern part of Laholm Bay, south-west Sweden, during the last thirty years (in Swedish). *Naturvardsverket Papp.* 3290. pp. 47.
Westernhagen H. von, Hickel W., Bauerfeind E., Niermann U. & Kröncke I. 1986. Sources and effects of oxygen deficiencies in the south-eastern North Sea. *Ophelia* **26**: 457–73.
Yamada N. 1961. Studies on the manure for seaweeds. I. On the change of nitrogenous component of *Gelidium amansii* Lmx. cultured with different nitrogen sources. *Bull. Jap. Soc. Sci. Fish.* **27**: 953–7.

7 Polysaccharides for Food and Pharmaceutical Uses

MENTZ INDERGAARD and KJETILL ØSTGAARD
The Norwegian Institute of Technology, Trondheim, Norway

The whole seaweed plant as a foodstuff was discussed in Chapter 2. The phycocolloids extracted from seaweeds are, however, far more common in modern food, but this is not because of their nutritional value. Seaweed phycocolloids, which are polysaccharides, have the ability to give viscosity, gel strength and stability to aqueous mixtures, solutions and emulsions. They include the alginates from brown algae and the more or less sulphated galactans such as agar and carrageenans from red algae. How molecular structure determines their macroscopic physical properties is treated in Chapter 8, and by Walker (1984) and Kennedy *et al.* (1984). As the literature on this subject is fairly recent and abundant, the present chapter will only touch on the various topics involved, ranging from marine botany to applied biopolymer chemistry and chemical engineering. Levring *et al.* (1969), International Trade Center (1981), Glicksman (1983), Sandford and Baird (1983), Sandford (1985, 1988a), Yalpani and Sandford (1987), and papers in McHugh (1987a), Mitchell and Ledward (1986) and Phillips *et al.* (1986) have reviewed the phycocolloid resources and types at present in industrial use, including food and pharmacy. The usage of phycocolloids in pharmacy is described by Hoppe *et al.* (1979), Hoppe and Levring (1982), Colwell (1985), Shimizu *et al.* (1985) and Vreeland and Laetsch (1985), and the employment of phycocolloids in food is reviewed by Glicksman (1987).

Phycocolloids are used in the modern food and pharmaceutical industries world-wide. It is, therefore, pointless to separate the European applications. The phycocolloids are all officially accepted as additives for human foodstuffs. In addition they have a range of properties that fulfill the requirements of the food industry. The combination of non-toxicity and unique rheological properties give the phycocolloids some advantages over other industrial gums. In many cases, however, low cost is preferred to high quality, especially in times of economic recession. Cheaper substitutes from other sources may then replace phycocolloids in certain uses and regions. Booth (1975, 1977, 1979) gave a vivid description of the history of the uses of phycocolloids and their manufacture.

Seaweed Resources in Europe: Uses and Potential. Edited by M. D. Guiry and G. Blunden
© 1991 John Wiley & Sons Ltd

SOURCES AND PRODUCTION

The total world market value of phycocolloids is now estimated to be about US$ 550 million (Moss & Doty 1987; McHugh 1987a). An estimate of the amounts produced globally and used in the food and pharmaceutical industries is given in Table 1. The production of phycocolloids in Europe is shown in Table 2. There is no direct correlation between a country's harvest of seaweeds and its phycocolloid production, as some phycocolloid-producing countries rely on large amounts of imported raw material.

The total European output of algal products is probably of the order of 200 million ecu annually (wholesale value). (The ecu is the European Community

Table 1. Phycocolloids: global production, retail price, gross value and percentage used in food and pharmacy

Product	Global production (t year^{-1})	Retail price (US$ kg^{-1})	Approximate gross market value (US$ year^{-1} = 10^6)	Amount used Food (%)	Pharmacy (%)
Agar	6 000[a]	15–40	125	80	ca.10[a]
Alginate	27 000[b]	5–15	230	30	5
Carrageenans	15 500[c]	5–10	100	80	10

[a]Mostly bacteriological grade agar.
[b]Including 3000 MT technical grade alginate (see Table 2).
[c]Including 2500 MT technical grade carrageenan (alkali-modified).
Based on Yalpani and Sandford (1987), Armisen and Galatas (1987), Stanley (1987) and Moss and Doty (1987).

Table 2. Estimated European production of phycocolloids for all kinds of end-uses

Country	Alginate[a] (t year^{-1})	Agar (t year^{-1})	Carrageenans (t year^{-1})
Norway	6000		
France	1300	65	1000
UK	5000		
Denmark			1000
Spain		890	
Portugal		320	
Italy		100	
European USSR	?	?	?

[a]Technical grade (seaweed meal treated with alkali to exchange calcium with sodium) not included, estimated as 3000 t in 1987.
Based on Armisen and Galatas (1987), Stanley (1987), Moss and Doty (1987) and Orlandini (1988).

Currency Unit, currently about US$ 1.3.) Of this, some 2–5 million ecu is from seaweed meal, seaweed extracts and seaweed composts, the remainder being from the production of phycocolloids.

The sulphated galactans from red algae principally serve the same industrial purposes as the alginates. They may be separated into two important groups: agars, which have a relatively low sulphate content and are good gelling agents with water, and the carrageenans which do not form gels with water but need the addition of salts to do so.

AGAR

The manufacture of a relatively pure agar started in the Far East in the latter half of the 17th century (Booth 1979). The preferred genera for extraction of agar and agarose are *Gelidium*, *Gelidiella*, *Gracilaria*, *Acanthopeltis* and *Pterocladia*, and *Ahnfeltia plicata* in the USSR. European production is summarized in Table 2. The neutral fraction of agar, lacking sulphate and other charged groups, is called agarose (Chapter 8). Currently, there is a shortage of both agar and agarose on the world market, resulting in increasing prices. Standard food agar was priced at US$ 13 kg^{-1} in 1985, and the retail price of bacteriological agar was about US$ 25 kg^{-1} (Moss & Doty 1987), although agarose may fetch US$ 500 kg^{-1} or more.

CARRAGEENANS

Contrary to popular belief, Mitchell and Guiry (1983) found no evidence that the name carrageen (from which carrageenan was derived) came from a particular placename in Ireland. The first mention of its use in an industrial context was as a fining agent in a Bavarian brewery in 1842 (Booth 1979). The main sources of carrageenans are species of *Eucheuma* cultivated in the Philippines, a mixture of *Chondrus crispus* and *Furcellaria lumbricalis* harvested in Canada, and *Chondrus crispus*, *Mastocarpus stellatus* and *Gigartina* spp. harvested in France, Spain and Portugal (Stanley 1987; Moss & Doty 1987; Chapter 1). Furcellaran, a carrageenan extracted from *F. lumbricalis*, of which 4000 t are harvested off Denmark (Rye 1985), resembles $\varkappa$-carrageenan, but has a lower sulphate content. Because of their price, availability and improved properties, carrageenans from alkali-modified extracts of *Eucheuma* and *Chondrus* have largely taken over the canned-food market earlier dominated by agar (Booth 1975; Witt 1985). Prices of carrageenans are currently in the range US$ 5–10 kg^{-1} (Moss & Doty 1987).

ALGINATE

In 1881, E.C.C. Stanford was issued a British patent for the manufacture of alginates, and he also proposed many applications for this most recent of the phycocolloids to be put to industrial use. The large-scale industrial manufacture of alginates started in California in 1927, after an abortive attempt in the mid-1920s in the Orkney Islands (Booth 1975). Today, alginate production is based mainly on harvested *Macrocystis pyrifera* in the USA, *Durvillea* spp. and *Lessonia* sp. in Chile, and small amounts of *Ecklonia* spp., *Eisenia* sp. and to some extent *Laminaria japonica* (mostly for polypropylene glycol alginate; PGA) in the Far East. In Europe, the raw materials are *Laminaria digitata* in France and *L. hyperborea* and *Ascophyllum nodosum* in the UK and Norway. In the mid-1980s Protan Biopolymers of Norway produced *ca.* 6000 t of alginate per year, of which about 30% was used in the food industry and 15% in pharmaceutical applications. Depending on properties and usage, the price range of alginates is US$ 5–20 kg^{-1}.

LAMINARAN

This is a phycocolloid extracted from brown algae (*Laminaria* sp.), which has found no commercial uses on an industrial scale. Hoppe (1979) points to a future market for potential applications of sodium laminaran sulphate in pharmacy.

HEALTH SAFETY

There is a continuous debate concerning the safety of all additives in food. To date, the phycocolloids are generally considered to be quite harmless. All are accepted as food additives: as GRAS ('Generally Recognized As Safe') by the US Food and Drug Administration (1978, 1979); listed in the Food and Agriculture Organization (FAO)/World Health Organization (WHO) of the United Nations *Codex Alimentarius*; and accepted by the European Community (Overeem 1984).

Food-grade carrageenan was accepted by the US Food and Nutrition Board (1981) as being safe, but there has been some concern about various physiological effects, possibly connected with some degraded forms of the polymer (Booth 1975; Martin 1984; Stanley 1987). Grasso *et al.* (1973) found that native or degraded carrageenan produced ulceration in the large intestine of guinea-pigs and rabbits, whereas no effects were observed in rats, hamsters, squirrels, monkeys and ferrets. They also stated, however, that carrageenan was unlikely to be involved in the aetiology of human ulcerative colitis. Conning *et al.* (1984), using rats in their studies, found that carrageenan within the tissues did not elicit a specific anticarrageenan antibody response. Tveter-Gallagher *et al.* (1982) and Tveter-Gallagher and Mathieson (1985) pointed to the importance of working with well defined samples of carrageenan, with respect to type, molecular weight and dosage. The purity of the product being tested is of course crucial. The inclusion of carrageenan in various popular accounts of food additives as a 'suspect' substance is therefore largely without scientific foundation.

Work on the enormous number of various oligomers that can be produced from the phycocolloids and their immunological responses is, however, only in its infancy (Yalpani & Sandford 1987; Casu 1987).

APPLICATIONS IN FOOD

The human body does not digest phycocolloids (Mori *et al.* 1981). It should be noted that 'food' in this section includes not only products for human consumption, but also for animals. Petfood, mainly for dogs and cats, is one important field of application of phycocolloids. Fodder for fur-producing mammals and fish fodder in aquaculture should also be mentioned. In Norway, some 3000 t of technical grade 'alginate' (seaweed meal treated with alkali to replace calcium with sodium) is used as a binder in moist fish feeds, made from fresh wildfish offal mixed with various dry components (not included in Table 2).

Practical approaches to the use of phycocolloids in various foodstuffs have been treated by Walker (1984), Morley (1984), Glicksman (1984, 1987) and Rizzotti *et al.* (1984), and by the papers in McHugh (1987a). It should be noted that food additives are often complex systems, where polysaccharides from various sources, structural proteins and salts are mixed to solve various rheological problems (Morley 1984; Dea 1987; Sandford 1988b). It is, therefore, not always easy to describe precisely the actual physical and chemical role of an individual phycocolloid additive. Moreover, new food products are often developed on a purely empirical basis, to optimize organoleptic factors such as body, texture, flavour-enhancement, mouth feel, chewiness, smell and taste. An attempt is made to summarize the main functions of phycocolloids as food additives and illustrate the diversity of products in Table 3.

The viscosity of a solution of macromolecules depends primarily on the effective volume occupied by the macromolecules. In aqueous systems, this is a property that is closely related to their ability to bind water. Phycocolloids are therefore used in a huge number of food products to give the proper thickening. Both price and chemical properties are important considerations when selecting the algal polysaccharide to be applied in each case.

The stabilizing properties of phycocolloids are intimately related to their viscosity, and are often also called water-holding properties. Many food products are not homogeneous. Water-soluble phycocolloids act as stabilizers in complex systems to keep particles or small droplets evenly distributed in the water phase, mainly by increasing the viscosity of the water phase. This will prevent both precipitation and separation. Furthermore, the addition of charged polymers such as alginate may produce charged films at the interface, so that individual particles or droplets will repel each other (see also Table 3).

Gel formation is important in some products. Since the main mechanism of gel formation is widely different for agar (heating/cooling), alginate (addition of divalent cations) and carrageenan (addition of monovalent ions), each phycocolloid has found its application in different types of products. In many cases, such as in petfoods, pieces and particles of edible foodstuffs are embedded by the gel phase. The gel former is therefore often referred to as a binding agent (see also Table 3).

Table 3. Main functions of phycocolloids in various foods listed according to products

Phycocolloid	Product	Viscosifier (thickening)	Stabilizer/ emulsifier	Gel former/ binder
Agar	Pie-fillings and icings		★	
	Canned foods			★
	Confectionery products			★
Carrageenan	Canned foods		★	★
	Ice-cream		★	
	Instant milk puddings		★	
	Chocolate milk		★	
	Dessert gels			★
	Low-calorie jellies			★
	Canned pet foods		★	
	Syrups		★	
	Imitation coffee creams		★	
	Puddings		★	
	Artificial whipped toppings		★	
Alginate	Ice-cream	★		
	Ready-made soups	★		
	Sauces	★	★	
	Dressings	★	★	
	Ketchup	★		
	Mayonnaise	★		
	Margarine	★		
	Milkshakes	★		
	Fruit juices	★		
	Liquors	★		
	Frozen foods		★	
	Desserts and dessert gels		★	★
	Syrups		★	
	Dry mixes		★	
	Pastry fillings		★	
	Bakery icings		★	
	Jams			★
	Puddings			★
	Baking whipped cream			★
	Pie fillings			★
	Mashed potatoes			★
	Restructured food (see text)			★

The stabilizing and binding functions described above may also be important for the retention of food structure during processing, such as in the heat sterilization of canned food. In such cases, the phycocolloids are commonly referred to as protective or preservative agents.

AGAR

Booth (1979) attributed the discovery of the freeze–thaw extraction of agar to Japan around 1658. It has been eaten for more than 300 years, giving it a reliable safety record in the human food industry. From the beginning, it has been used as a gelling agent for fruit and vegetable jellies. Over 65% of the agar production in Japan and China is sold directly for human consumption.

Heat is necessary to dissolve agar in water. Solutions with 1–1.5% agar stiffen to a firm gel by cooling to 36–42 °C and the gel will not melt below 85–90 °C. A large market for agar in the western world is in canned foods, especially canned petfoods. Agar is capable of withstanding the sterilization process; the neutral gel is also much more stable in acidic conditions than either carrageenans or gelatin. It is therefore considered to be a preservative. One special application is as a gelling agent in confectionery, marshmallows and candies, and also in the prevention of dehydration of confectionery bakery products. The relative gel strength of agar is four to five times that of any other phycocolloid (Armisen & Galatas 1987). Agar is also used as a protective and stabilizing agent in some other applications (Table 3).

CARRAGEENANS

The first mention of the use of carrageenan in the food industry is from the mid-19th century as a fining agent in beer brewing (Booth 1979). Before this it had been used in making a pudding by boiling carrageenophytes such as *Chondrus* for some hours and then cooling the liquid and mixing it with milk; sulphated galactans are very reactive with milk proteins. The industry's ability to produce carrageenans standardized to certain specifications, allied with competitive and relatively stable prices, has led to a rapid expansion in their use over the last two decades, playing a large part in the replacement of agar as a low-cost hydrocolloid, particularly as a preservative in canned foods (Bixler 1979). Thickening, suspension and fat stabilization are also often considered as important effects in such products.

Among the phycocolloids, the carrageenans have by far the widest application in the food industry. Their particular reactivity with milk proteins such as casein finds use in a wide range of dairy products. The concentrations added range from 0.06% for stabilizers to 2% for air-freshener gels (Stanley 1987). The ability to interact with and stabilize milk proteins is used in instant milk puddings to produce gelling when added to cold milk and for stabilizing cocoa in chocolate milk. This type of protein interaction will probably also be useful with new protein sources and will increase with the expansion of the convenience food market.

Carrageenans act as secondary stabilizers in ice-cream, adding creaminess and preventing syneresis and crystal formation under freeze–thaw conditions. Beverages and bakery products, dietetic food, dressings and sauces, and frozen food are also among the products into which carrageenans find their way, acting as thickeners, stabilizers and emulsifiers (Table 3). The resulting effects are often referred to as 'bodying' of syrups, sauces or imitation milk. A semi-refined carrageenan is used almost exclusively for the large petfood market.

ALGINATE

The first uses of alginate in food were described in the early patents of Kelco (a US alginate manufacturer) in the 1930s. Special attention was given to a gradual improvement in the ability of the product to suspend cocoa in chocolate milk drinks, a use for which carrageenans have now replaced alginate (Booth 1975). Subsequently, it was used as an ice-cream stabilizer, and the extension into the general food market was a natural consequence.

Alginates are now used as low-price viscosifiers or thickeners in a wide range of products (Table 3). They are also employed as stabilizers and emulsifiers, for instance to prevent water leakage from frozen fish during thawing, or to prevent the degradation of starch. Furthermore, alginates will stabilize oil-and-water emulsions, such as mayonnaise and ketchup, and suspensions of finely distributed solid material in water, such as some salad dressings. Its action as an emulsifier is utilized in salad dressings, and meat and flavour sauces. New applications appear regularly.

The next landmark in the development of outlets for alginates was the introduction of polypropylene glycol alginate (PGA) patented by Steiner (1947, cited in Booth 1975). This patent gave Kelco a monopoly on a new product which was stable under acidic conditions. It was soon widely used to suspend the pulp in fruit drinks, with a dramatic improvement in their appearance. In acid emulsions, such as French dressings, PGA is especially effective, as ordinary alginate will precipitate in acidic conditions. Another new use for this product was to stabilize beer foam; the addition of 50–100 ppm PGA stabilizes the froth by reacting with the protein without haze formation. The method was first suggested by Stanford in the 1880s (Booth 1975); recent uses in the brewing industry were described by Simpson (1973).

Gel formation or binding constitutes another important application of alginates. A solution of 1–2% sodium alginate will stiffen to a gel by addition of calcium ions (50 mM) or other divalent ions (Ba^{2+}, Pb^{2+}, Sr^{2+}, etc.; see Chapters 8 and 9). The divalent ions work in a similar manner to the lock of a zipper, binding the alginate chains together into the three-dimensional gel network. Alginate gels have various strengths, largely dependent on their content of polyguluronic acid blocks (Smidsrød 1973, McHugh 1987b, Chapter 8). By choosing the right type of alginate one can determine the properties of the gel: brittle, elastic or soft. The gel stability is not temperature dependent. A developing field of application is in restructured food, such as crabsticks and onion rings, and the pimiento stuffing of olives (Table 3).

Present uses of alginates in food are also described by Sime (1984), Imeson (1984) and Eklund (1985).

APPLICATIONS IN PHARMACY

Pharmaceuticals are medicines used in the prevention or cure of illness. The current most important uses of phycocolloids are closely related to their physical properties, as described for alginates by Skaugrud and Westre (1988). The role of phycocolloids in pharmaceuticals as thickening or binding agents is similar to that in food. However, this role must be separated from their biochemical action (Witczak & Whistler 1987), particularly as oligosaccharides (Casu 1987). Only in a few instances may the phycocolloid component be considered as the active therapeutic agent. Some products might also be better classified as cosmetics (see Chapter 4).

AGAR

The oldest use is perhaps in emulsions with liquid paraffin for the treatment of constipation, but it is also used in lubricating jellies, emulsions and ointments (Booth 1975). Agar acts as a suspending agent in the radiological uses of barium sulphate. It is used as a disintegrating agent and excipient in tablets and in the compounding of slow-release capsules. It is also employed as an antirheumatic agent for prolonged treatments, and in the stabilization of cholesterol solutions (Armisen & Galatas 1987).

CARRAGEENANS

A traditional use is in cough medicines, and this use still persists (Booth 1975). Combinations of λ-, $\varkappa$- and ι-carrageenans enhance the texture of toothpastes. ι-Carrageenan gives either stable emulsions or suspensions of insoluble drug preparations and gives body to lotions (Stanley 1987).

ALGINATE

A combination of water-soluble and water-insoluble alginates acts as a binder in dry tablets and promotes tablet disintegration in water by the water absorption properties of the alginate. Alginate is also applied as an antirefluxant, a suspension agent and tablet binder, for sustained release, as an X-ray contrast medium thickener, as an adjuvant for haemodialysis, and in haemostasis and wound healing (Fujihara *et al.* 1984; McHugh 1987b; Skaugrud & Westre 1988). In the latter case, calcium/sodium alginate is deployed as thread to make a woven fabric. Medical dressings made from woven alginate were suggested many years ago (Miller & Caldwell 1971; cited in Booth 1975), but they have been commercially available only in recent years (Dixon 1986). The dressings are woven as calcium alginate and then modified to give a mixture of sodium and calcium alginates, resulting in a product that gels on contact with the wound and one that has good haemostatic qualities. This type of fabric is available as first-aid dressings and is particularly useful in the treatment of burns.

The selective ion-binding properties of alginate have made it an interesting agent for the blocking of poisoning by ingestion of certain heavy metals and radionucleides. Alginate binding increases with the valency of the cations; affinity series are given in Chapters 8 and 9. The selective binding capacity for multivalent ions is closely related to the polyguluronic acid block content. As expected, alginate will accumulate radionuclides such as ^{90}Sr and ^{144}Ce, but not ^{137}Cs, ^{65}Zn or ^{144}Tl (Tsytsugina *et al.* 1976). The effects on uptake of strontium isotopes when alginate is included in food has been extensively studied in animals and humans (Borght *et al.* 1971, Tanaka *et al.* 1972). A strongly reduced uptake of strontium has been obtained without severe reduction of calcium levels when sodium alginate is used. Similar effects have been observed for the uptake of ^{226}Ra (Borght *et al.* 1971). The therapeutic value of the alginate treatment depends primarily on the time elapsed since contamination occurred, as binding only affects ions still present in (or excreted into) the gastrointestinal system.

Further uses at the interface between pharmacy and biotechnology are mentioned in Chapter 9.

FUTURE TRENDS

The traditional market for polysaccharides used in food will probably continue to increase at the rate of the market demand for such food (Sandford 1988a). Phycocolloids are mainly used in convenience food and in food of non-essential nutritional value. It is likely that this market will develop steadily, largely due to increasing product diversity. Restructured food, which makes use of raw material that would otherwise be useless, will remain an expanding field of application.

New markets for polysaccharides will mainly be found in pharmaceutical applications such as vaccines, drug delivery, anticancer, antithrombogenic and antiadhesive drugs, and diagnostics (Sandford 1988a). The volume of phycocolloids needed for such purposes will be relatively small, but chemical purity and precisely identified structural composition will definitely be reflected in increased prices. The production of such phycocolloids will be challenging but economically rewarding.

The wild resources of brown algae for alginate are thought to be able to tolerate a five- to ten-fold expansion in harvesting (Jensen 1978). Carrageenan supply has been stabilized and can easily grow to satisfy increased demands, mainly through the development of *Eucheuma* farming in southeast Asia. The problem is that wild resources of agarophytes are being heavily harvested, and that at present no cultivation is envisaged to ensure a steady and increased supply at stable prices.

It should be noted that the market for phycocolloids largely depends on their low price. Increasing agar costs have led to the carrageenan takeover in canned food. However, the phycocolloids must also compete, at least in some cases, with gums from flowering plants, such as guar gum and locust bean gum, and cheaper cellulose derivatives (carboxymethyl cellulose (CMC) and others). A similar development is apparent for gel media in microbiology, where a variety of agar substitutes have been developed. This includes both alginate (Draget *et al.* 1989) and polysaccharides of non-algal origin such as Plantgar and gellan. Competition is also different in different uses and regions of the world based on price and availability. In some markets and for some uses one phycocolloid may compete with another; in others there is only one choice.

It is unlikely that the increasing food market can lead to dramatically improved phycocolloid prices. The market for alginate, for instance, has been steady at 20 000–24 000 t per annum for the last decade (International Trade Centre 1981; McHugh 1987b); it is also thought that the international organization of phycocolloid producers called Marinalg (International Trade Centre 1981) prevents devastating price wars to some extent. Price is not always decisive; quality, regular supply and reproducibility from one batch to another may often be more important (Bixler 1979). The low concentration levels employed are also important; the use of a 1% solution of the colloid means that a 20% price difference has little impact on the total cost of the product. However, several products (e.g. petfoods) are in an extremely competitive situation, operating on very narrow price margins.

REFERENCES

Armisen R. & Galatas F. 1987. Production, properties and uses of agar. In *Food and Agriculture Organization of the United Nations (FAO) Fisheries Technical Paper no. 288.* (Ed. D.J. McHugh) pp. 1–57. Rome: Food and Agriculture Organization of the United Nations (FAO).

Bixler H.J. 1979. Manufacturing and marketing carrageenan. In *Actas Primer Symposium sobre Algas Marinas Chilenas.* (Ed. B. Santelices) pp. 259–74. Santiago de Chile: Subsecretaria de Pesca, Ministeriode Economia Fomento y Reconstruccion.

Booth E. 1975. Seaweeds in industry. In *Chemical Oceanography*. Vol. 4. (Eds. J.P. Riley & G. Skirrow) pp. 219–68. London: Academic Press.

Booth E. 1977. The history of the seaweed industry. Part 1. The alginate industry. *Chem. Ind.* 528–34.

Booth E. 1979. The history of the seaweed industry. Part 4. A miscellany of industries. *Chem. Ind.* 378–83.

Borght O. van der, van Puymbroek S. & Colard J. 1971. Intestinal absorption and body retention of 226Ra and 47Ca in mice. *Health Phys.* **21**: 181–96.

Casu B. 1987. Trends in the development of oligo- and polysaccharides of medical interest. In *Industrial Polysaccharides*. (Eds. S.S. Stivala, V. Crescenzi & I.C.M. Dea) pp. 189–94. London: Gordon & Breach Science.

Colwell R.R. 1985. Marine polysaccharides for pharmaceutical and microbiological applications. In *Biotechnology of Marine Polysaccharides*. (Eds. R.R. Colwell, E.R. Pariser & J . Sinskey) pp. 363–76. London: McGraw-Hill.

Conning D.M., Mallett A.K. & Nicklin S. 1984. Novel toxicological aspects of gums and stabilisers. In *Gums and Stabilisers for the Food Industry*. Vol. 2. (Eds. G.O. Phillips, D.J. Wedlock & P.A. Williams) pp. 389–404. Oxford: Pergamon Press.

Dea I.C.M. 1987. Mixed polysaccharide systems. In *Industrial Polysaccharides*. (Eds. S.S. Stivala, V. Crescenzi & I.C.M. Dea) pp. 367–86. London: Gordon & Breach Science.

Dixon B. 1986. Seaweed for wound dressing. *Bio-Technology* **4**: 604.

Draget K.I., Østgaard K. & Smidsrød O. 1989. Alginate-based solid media for plant tissue culture. *Appl. Microbiol. Biotechnol.* **31**: 79–83.

Eklund T. 1985. Alginate in der Lebensmittelindustrie: Herstellung, Eigenschaften, Anwendungen. *Int. Z. Lebensmittel-Technol. Verfahrenstechnik* **36**: 143–5.

Fujihara M., Komiyama K., Umezawa I. & Nagumo T. 1984. Antitumor activity and action-mechanisms of sodium alginate isolated from the brown seaweed *Sargassum fulvellum*. *Chemotherapy* **32**: 1004–9.

Glicksman M. 1983. Red seaweed extracts (agar, carrageenan, furcellaran). *Food Hydrocoll.* **2**: 73–113.

Glicksman M. 1984. The role of hydrocolloids in food processing: cause and effect. In *Gums and Stabilisers for the Food Industry*. Vol. 2. (Eds. G.O. Phillips, D.J. Wedlock & P.A. Williams) pp. 297–320. Oxford: Pergamon Press.

Glicksman M. 1987. Utilization of seaweed hydrocolloids in the food industry. In *Proceedings of the Twelfth International Seaweed Symposium*. (Eds. M.A. Ragan & C.J. Bird) pp. 31–49. Dordrecht: W. Junk.

Grasso P., Sharratt M., Carpanini F.M.B. & Gangolli S.D. 1973. Studies on carrageenan and large-bowel ulceration in mammals. *Food Cosmet. Toxicol.* **11**: 555–64.

Hoppe H.A. 1979. Marine algae and their products and constituents in pharmacy. In *Marine Algae in Pharmaceutical Science*. (Eds. H.A. Hoppe, T. Levring & Y. Tanaka) pp. 25–121. Berlin: de Gruyter.

Hoppe H.A. & Levring T. 1982. *Marine Algae in Pharmaceutical Science*. Vol. 2. Berlin: de Gruyter.

Hoppe H.A., Levring T. & Tanaka Y. 1979. *Marine Algae in Pharmaceutical Science*. Vol. 1. Berlin: de Gruyter.

Imeson A.P. 1984. Recovery and utilisation of proteins using alginates. In *Gums and Stabilisers for the Food Industry*. Vol. 2. (Eds. G.O. Phillips, D.J. Wedlock & P.A. Williams) pp. 189–99. Oxford: Pergamon Press.

International Trade Centre 1981. *Pilot Survey of the World Seaweed Industry and Trade*. Geneva: International Trade Centre.

Jensen A. 1978. Industrial utilization of seaweeds in the past, present and future. In *Proceedings of the Ninth International Seaweed Symposium*. (Eds. A. Jensen & J.R. Stein) pp. 17–34. Princeton: Science Press.

Kennedy J.F., Griffiths A.J. & Atkins D.P. 1984. The application of hydrocolloids: recent developments, future trends. In *Gums and Stabilisers for the Food Industry*. Vol. 2. (Eds. G.O. Phillips, D.J. Wedlock & P.A. Williams) pp. 417–55. Oxford: Pergamon Press.

Levring T., Hoppe H.A. & Schmid O.J. 1969. *Marine Algae – A Survey of Research and Utilization*. Hamburg: Cram, de Gruyter.

Martin G. 1984. Toxicological evaluation of carrageenans. 2. Definition, structure, manufacture, properties and applications. *Sci. Aliments* **4**: 335–46.

McHugh D.J. 1987a. Production and utilization of products from commercial seaweeds. *Food and Agriculture Organization of the United Nations (FAO) Fisheries Technical Paper no. 288*. iii + 189 pp.

McHugh D.J. 1987b. Production, properties and uses of alginates. In *Food and Agriculture Organization of the United Nations (FAO) Fisheries Technical Paper no. 288*. (Ed. D.J. McHugh) pp. 58–115. Rome: Food and Agriculture Organization of the United Nations (FAO).

Miller J.H.H. & Caldwell R. 1971. British Patent No. 1 231 596. (Cited by Booth 1975).

Mitchell M.E. & Guiry M.D. 1983. Carrageen: a local habitation or a name? *J. Ethnopharmacol.* **9**: 347–51.

Mitchell J.R. & Ledward D.A. 1986. *Functional Properties of Food Macromolecules*. London: Elsevier.

Mori B., Kusima K., Iwasaki T. & Okiya H. 1981. Dietary fiber content of seaweed. *Nippon Nōgeikagaku Kaishi* **55**: 787–91.

Morley R.G. 1984. Utilisation of hydrocolloids in formulated foods. In *Gums and Stabilisers for the Food Industry*. Vol. 2. (Eds. G.O. Phillips, D.J. Wedlock & P.A. Williams) pp. 211–39. Oxford: Pergamon Press.

Moss J.R. & Doty M.S. 1987. *Establishing a Seaweed Industry in Hawaii: an Initial Assessment*. Honolulu: Hawaii State Department of Land and Natural Resources.

Orlandini M. 1988. Harvesting of algae in polluted lagoons of Venice and Orbetello and their effective and potential utilization. In *Proceedings of the Second Workshop of the COST 48 Subgroup 3: Biomass Conversion, Removal and Use of Nutrients*. (Eds. J. de Waart & P.H. Nienhuis) pp. 20–23. Brussels: COST 48, CEC Directorate Biology, Division Biotechnology.

Overeem A. 1984. Legislation and toxicology and food hydrocolloids. In *Gums and Stabilisers for the Food Industry*. Vol. 2. (Eds. G.O. Phillips, D.J. Wedlock & P.A. Williams) pp. 369–77. Oxford: Pergamon Press.

Phillips G.O., Wedlock D.J. & Williams P.A. 1986. *Gums and Stabilisers for the Food Industry*. Vol. 3. London: Elsevier.

Rizzotti R., Tilly G. & Patterson R.A. 1984. The use of hydrocolloids in the dairy industry. In *Gums and Stabilisers for the Food Industry*. Vol. 2. (Eds. G.O. Phillips, D.J. Wedlock & P.A. Williams) pp. 285–93. Oxford: Pergamon Press.

Rye C. 1985. Tang – dyrkning, høstning og anvendelser I. *Norsk Fiskeoppdrett* **3**: 22–3, 53. [In Danish].

Sandford P.A. 1985. Applications of marine polysaccharides in the chemical industries. In *Biotechnology of Marine Polysaccharides*. (Eds. R.R. Colwell, E.R. Pariser & J. Sinskey) pp. 454–516. London: McGraw-Hill.

Sandford P.A. 1988a. Phycocolloids *versus* microbial polysaccharides: production and application perspectives. In *Proceedings of a Workshop on Phycocolloids and Fine Chemicals*. (Eds. S. Paoletti & G. Blunden) pp. 44–60. Brussels: COST 48, CEC Directorate Biology, Division Biotechnology.

Sandford P.A. 1988b. Mixed polysaccharide systems for biotechnology. In *Proceedings of a Workshop on Phycocolloids and Fine Chemicals*. (Eds. S. Paoletti & G.

Blunden) pp. 44–60. Brussels: COST 48, CEC Directorate Biology, Division Biotechnology.

Sandford P.A. & Baird J. 1983. Industrial utilization of polysaccharides. In *The Polysaccharides*. Vol. 2. (Ed. G.O. Aspinall) pp. 411–90. London: Academic Press.

Shimizu Y., Tanaka M. & Hayashi T. 1985. Antitumor marine biopolymers. In *Biotechnology of Marine Polysaccharides*. (Eds. R.R. Colwell, E.R. Pariser & J. Sinskey) pp. 377–88. London: McGraw-Hill.

Sime W.J. 1984. The practical utilisation of alginates in food gelling systems. In *Gums and Stabilisers for the Food Industry*. Vol. 2. (Eds. G.O. Phillips, D.J. Wedlock & P.A. Williams) pp. 177–88. Oxford: Pergamon Press.

Simpson F.J. 1973. Seaweed and brewing. *Tech. Q. Master Brewers Ass. America* **10**: 199–202.

Skaugrud Ø. & Westre G. 1988. Pharmaceutical applications of alginate. In *Proceedings of a Workshop on Phycocolloids and Fine Chemicals*. (Eds. S. Paoletti & G. Blunden) pp. 166–79. Brussels: COST 48, CEC Directorate Biology, Division Biotechnology.

Smidsrød O. 1973. *Some Physical Properties of Alginates in Solution and the Gel State*. D.Sc. thesis, University of Trondheim, Trondheim: NTNF's Institutt for Marin Biokjemi.

Stanley N. 1987. Production, properties and uses of carageenan. In *Food and Agriculture Organization of the United Nations (FAO) Fisheries Technical Paper no. 288*. (Ed. D.J. McHugh) pp. 116–46. Rome: Food and Agriculture Organization of the United Nations (FAO).

Steiner A.B. 1947. United States Patent no. 2 426 125. (Cited by Booth 1975.)

Tanaka Y., Hurlburt A.J., Angeloff L., Skoryna S.C. & Stara J.F. 1972. Application of algal polysaccharides as *in vivo* binders of metal pollutants. In *Proceedings of the Seventh International Seaweed Symposium*. (Ed. K. Nisizawa) pp. 620–7. Tokyo: University of Tokyo Press.

Tsytsugina V.G., Risik N.S. & Lazorenko G.E. 1975. Extraction of radionuclides by alginic acid from seawater. In *Artificial and Natural Radionuclides in Marine Life*. (Ed. G.G. Polikarpov) pp. 68–77. Jerusalem: Keter Publ. House. [Translated from Russian.]

Tveter-Gallagher E. & Mathieson A.C. 1985. Biological properties of carrageenans. In *Biotechnology of Marine Polysaccharides*. (Eds. R.R. Colwell, E.R. Pariser & J. Sinskey) pp. 414–28. London: McGraw-Hill.

Tveter-Gallagher E., Wight T.N. & Mathieson A.C. 1982. Effects of various types of carrageenans on human fibroblasts *in vitro*. In *Marine Algae in Pharmaceutical Science*. Vol. 2. (Eds. H.A. Hoppe & T. Levring) pp. 51–64. Berlin: de Gruyter.

US Food and Drug Administration. 1978. Certain brown and red algae and their extractives. Proposed affirmation of GRAS status of a brown alga, with specific limitations as a direct human food ingredient. *Fed. Reg.* **43**: 34500–3.

US Food and Drug Administration. 1979. Carrageenan, salts of carrageenan, and *Chondrus* extract (carrageenin); withdrawal of proposal and termination of rule-making procedure. *Fed. Reg.* **44**: 40343–5.

US Food and Nutrition Board.1981. Committee on Codex Specification, Carrageenan. In *Food Chemicals Codex*. 3rd edn. pp. 74–5. Washington DC: National Academy Press.

Vreeland V. & Laetsch W.M. 1985. Monoclonal antibodies to seaweed carbohydrates. In *Biotechnology of Marine Polysaccharides* (Eds. R.R. Colwell, E.R. Pariser & J. Sinskey) pp. 399–412. London: McGraw-Hill.

Walker B. 1984. Gums and stabilisers in food formulations. In *Gums and Stabilisers for the Food Industry*. Vol. 2. (Eds. G.O. Phillips, D.J. Wedlock & P.A. Williams) pp. 137–61. Oxford: Pergamon Press.

Witczak Z.J. & Whistler R.L. 1987. Structure and antitumor activity of polysaccharides. In *Industrial Polysaccharides*. (Eds. S.S. Stivala, V. Crescenzi & I.C.M. Dea) pp. 157–74. London: Gordon & Breach Science.

Witt, H.J. 1985. Carrageenan, Nature's most versatile hydrocolloid. In *Biotechnology of Marine Polysaccharides*. (Eds. R.R. Colwell, E.R. Pariser & J. Sinskey) pp. 346–60. London: McGraw-Hill.

Yalpani M. & Sandford P.A. 1987. Commercial polysaccharides: recent trends and developments. In *Industrial Polysaccharides*. Progress in Biotechnology Vol. 3. (Ed. M. Yalpani) pp. 311–36. Amsterdam: Elsevier.

8 Molecular Structure and Physical Behaviour of Seaweed Colloids as Compared with Microbial Polysaccharides

OLAV SMIDSRØD and BJØRN E. CHRISTENSEN
Norwegian Institute of Technology, Trondheim, Norway

Phycocolloids are polysaccharides derived from algae. Strictly speaking, this term should include polysaccharides from both the benthic macroalgae and the planktonic microalgae. In practice, the name is used exclusively for polysaccharides from macroalgae, and in this chapter we will use it in this sense. Polysaccharides from microalgae might also be classified as microbial polysaccharides, as the microalgae certainly are microorganisms. However, because of the lack of industrial use of microalgae as producers of polysaccharides, they will not be considered further here and the term microbial polysaccharides will be used for polysaccharides derived from bacteria and microscopic fungi.

Many different polysaccharides from both algae and microorganisms have been isolated and described. This review will focus mainly on the polysaccharides that are used commercially. It should also be noted that a large group of polysaccharides, namely the industrially important ones from higher plants (e.g. cellulose, starches, guar gum, locust bean gum), is not included in this review. However, their industrial applications may overlap those of phycocolloids and microbial gums.

LOCATION AND EXTRACTION

Phycocolloids are parts of the cell walls or intercellular matrix of algae and must first be extracted from the plants. The methods for isolating various phycocolloids will not be described here. However, the purity and heterogeneity of such extracts may vary, and their physical properties will depend on both purity and modifications occurring in the course of extraction. The intrinsic properties of the different macromolecular components of a given phycocolloid may differ more or less from those determined from the crude

Seaweed Resources in Europe: Uses and Potential. Edited by M. D. Guiry and G. Blunden

phycocolloid itself and thus a comparison with other gums and polysaccharides may not always be totally justified. For instance, agar contains both agarose and agaropectin, which differ only slightly in structure but have very different physical properties. Nevertheless, it is the physical properties of agar that are often described and compared with other polysaccharides, which may have the same industrial applications.

Bacteria and fungi also contain polysaccharides as integral parts of their cell walls. These cell wall constituents must be extracted, and problems, such as varying purity and structural modifications similar to those found in phycocolloid extracts, must be considered. In addition, many bacteria produce extracellular polysaccharides, either as a cell-bound capsule or as a soluble slime. Such polysaccharides are easily produced by fermentation in high yields. Culture supernatants may contain large amounts of the product in a very pure form. In other cases the product may contain, in addition to the polysaccharide in question, contaminating proteins, nucleic acids, other polysaccharides, and cell debris.

CHEMICAL STRUCTURE

GENERAL FEATURES

The number and diversity of algal and bacterial polysaccharides are very large (Painter 1983; Kenne & Lindberg 1983). Despite this the polysaccharides can be classified according to their source, biosynthesis, structure, and physical or biological properties.

Many microbial polysaccharides seem to consist of oligosaccharide repeating units, either linear or branched, usually with two to eight sugars in each unit. Such polymers are synthesised via lipid-linked intermediates, where the complete oligosaccharide is transferred to the growing chain (Sutherland 1985). This gives rise to a very regular structure, especially along the backbone of the chain. Structural heterogeneity in single chains does often occur, however, owing to the lack of complete assembly of oligosaccharide units at the lipid level. For instance, in the biosynthesis of xanthan gum, an oligosaccharide may be transferred to a growing chain even if the glucuronic acid and the terminal β-mannose residue are missing (Betlach *et al.* 1987).

Certain red algae (Rhodophyta) produce polysaccharides with repeating disaccharide units in the backbone. However, in contrast to their bacterial counterparts, such repeating units are the result of successive transfer of single sugars (from sugar nucleotides) to the growing chain (Nikaido & Hassid 1971). Furthermore, several modifications of the polysaccharide may occur at the polymer level, for instance the addition of sulphate half-esters or formation of anhydrosugars by enzymatic elimination of sulphate (James *et al.* 1985).

Pure homopolymers, namely polysaccharides with only one type of sugar as a building block, are commonly produced by both macroalgae and microorganisms. These may be strictly linear or have a more or less complicated pattern of branches.

The third group includes heteropolysaccharides with a more or less irregular structure. Such polysaccharides include block copolymers and polysaccharides where the component sugars are randomly or near randomly assembled within the molecule.

PHYCOCOLLOIDS

The macroscopic algae produce a large number of complex polysaccharides (Painter 1983), but only a few of these are produced industrially in a pure form. The major phycocolloids which will be described here include alginate, carrageenans, agar and laminaran.

Alginate

Alginate occurs both in brown algae and in certain bacteria, and could be considered both as a phycocolloid and as a microbial polysaccharide. It is a family of linear copolymers containing 1,4-linked β-D-mannuronic acid (M) and its 5-epimer α-L-guluronic acid (G) (Fig. 1). The conversion (epimerisation) of M into G occurs at the polymer level, in other words on polymannuronic acid chains (Haug & Larsen 1974), a mechanism which is also known for certain mammalian proteoglycans containing D-glucuronic acid and L-iduronic acid (Höök *et al.* 1974).

The distribution of M and G in alginate chains gives rise to three different block types, namely blocks of poly-M, blocks of poly-G and alternating blocks of the type M–G–M–G. The most successful way of describing the composition of alginate is to determine the frequencies of diads and triads (Tables 1 and 2), obtained by nuclear magnetic resonance (NMR) techniques (Grasdalen *et al.* 1979). The use of 400–500 MHz ^{1}H-NMR or 100–125 MHz ^{13}C-NMR is generally necessary to obtain triad frequencies (Grasdalen 1983).

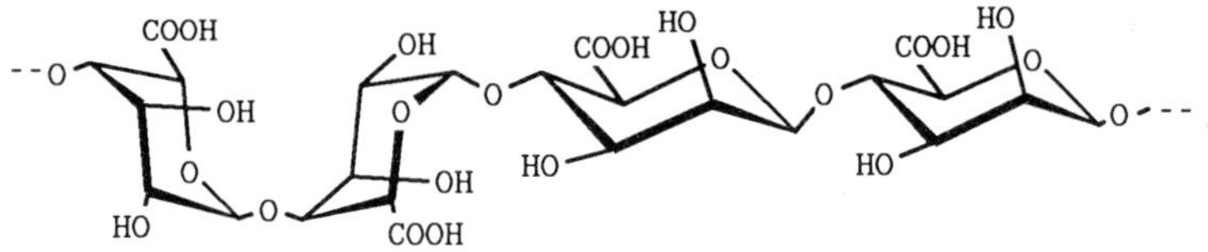

L-GulA-α-1,4-L-GulA-α-1,4-D-ManA-β-1,4-D-ManA

Figure 1. Partial structure of an alginate chain. GulA, L-guluronic acid; ManA, D-mannuronic acid

Table 1. Comparison between algal and bacterial alginates

Source	Composition								
	F_G	F_M	F_{GG}	F_{MG}	F_{MM}	F_{GGG}	F_{MGM}	F_{GGM}	$\bar{N}_{G>1}$
Ascophyllum nodosum	0.36	0.64	0.16	0.20	0.44	0.12	0.15	0.06	3.9
Macrocystis pyrifera	0.39	0.61	0.16	0.23	0.38	0.12	0.20	0.03	6.3
Laminaria digitata	0.41	0.59	0.25	0.16	0.43	0.20	0.11	0.05	6.0
Dictyosiphon foeniculaceus	0.67	0.33	0.61	0.06	0.27	0.57	0.02	0.04	16.2
Laminaria hyperborea	0.79	0.21	0.70	0.09	0.12	0.66	0.05	0.04	18.5
Pseudomonas aeruginosa DE27	0.00	1.00	0.00	0.00	1.00				
Pseudomonas mendocina 10541	0.26	0.74	0.00	0.26[a]	0.48	0.00	0.26		
Pseudomonas putida 1007	0.37	0.63	0.00	0.37[a]	0.26	0.00	0.40		
Pseudomonas fluorescens 10255	0.40	0.60	0.00	0.40[a]	0.20	0.00	0.40		
Azotobacter vinelandii TL	0.45	0.55	0.42	0.03[a]	0.52	0.41	0.02		
Azotobacter vinelandii IV	0.94	0.06	0.93	0.01	0.04				

F_M, F_G, etc., are frequencies of monads, diads and triads as shown in Table 2. $\bar{N}_{G>1}$ is the average length of G-blocks.
[a] $F_{MG} + F_{GM}$.
From Skjåk-Bræk *et al.* 1986a, b.

Table 2. Calculation of the composition of alginates based on observed frequencies of monads, diads and triads

Frequencies are denoted F with the corresponding structure

Two possible monads: G and M
$$F_G + F_M = 1$$

Four possible diads: GG, MM, MG and GM
$$F_G = F_{GG} + F_{GM}$$
$$F_M = F_{MM} + F_{MG}$$
$$F_{GM} = F_{MG} \text{ (for long chains)}$$

Eight possible triads: GGG, GGM, GMM, GMG, MMM, MMG, MGG and MGM
$$F_{GG} = F_{GGG} + F_{GGM}$$
$$F_{GM} = F_{GMG} + F_{GMM}$$
etc.

Table 3. Relationships between diad and triad frequences and the average length of G-blocks ($\bar{N}_G$) and M-blocks ($\bar{N}_M$)

$$\bar{N}_G = \frac{F_G}{F_{GM}} \qquad\qquad \bar{N}_{G>1} = \frac{F_G - F_{MGM}}{F_{GGM}}$$

$$\bar{N}_M = \frac{F_M}{F_{MG}} \qquad\qquad \bar{N}_{M>1} = \frac{F_M - F_{GMG}}{F_{MMG}}$$

The expressions $\bar{N}_{G>1}$ and $\bar{N}_{M>1}$ do not include single G (M\underline{G}M) and M (G\underline{M}G), which are not regarded as true blocks.

From such data further information, for instance the average block length, can be extracted as shown in Tables 2 and 3.

The composition and quality of commercial alginates vary considerably. This is mainly due to the variation found in different species of brown algae, and also to large variations in different parts of the same plant. For example, the fronds of *Laminaria* species contain alginate with a relatively low content of G, but the more rigid stipes contain alginate rich in poly-G blocks (Painter 1983). Some data on the composition of alginate from various algae are given in Table 1.

The α-L-guluronic acid residues have a $^1C_4$ conformation which results in the linkage between two such units being diaxial. This, and the block-like distribution of L-guluronic acid residues, are important considerations for an understanding of the gelling of alginates with divalent cations. The mechanism of gelling is discussed later in this chapter.

Carrageenan

The carrageenans include another large family of polysaccharides found in many red algae. The main structural features of the most important groups of these linear D-galactans are shown in Fig. 2. Several other structures have also been found, but it is outside the scope of this chapter to discuss them in detail. Different carrageenans have varying amounts of 3,6-anhydro-D-galactose and variations in the amount and position of sulphate half-esters. The designations $\varkappa$-, ι- and λ-carrageenan refer to certain idealised structures with quite different physical properties. The preparation of a carrageenan fraction containing, for example, a 100% $\varkappa$-structure has not yet been achieved. On the contrary, there is much evidence that the carrageenans are hybrids or copolymers in the sense that different structural features may be present in a single polysaccharide chain, sometimes in a block-wise arrangement. The development of techniques for analysing not only the

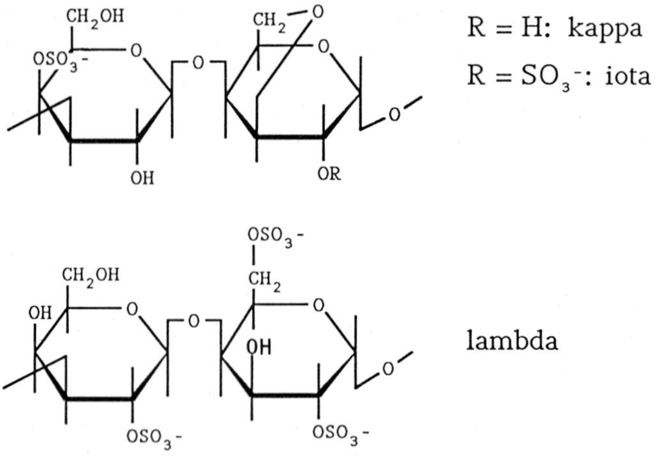

R = H: kappa

R = SO$_3^-$: iota

lambda

Figure 2. The repeating units of $\varkappa$-, ι- and λ-carrageenan

amount and position of the sulphate groups, but also their *distribution* along the chains is a challenging task which has engendered much of the current research activity in Europe.

Agar

The agar family differs from the carrageenans by having 4-linked L-galactose instead of D-galactose (Fig. 3). In addition, sulphate ester, O-methyl and pyruvate occur as structural modifications, and the presence of carboxyl groups has also been implicated (Renn 1984). It should be mentioned that certain red algae contain sulphated galactans with agar-type (D–L) and carrageenan-type (D–D) structures most probably present in the same chain (Hirase *et al.* 1967; Nunn *et al.* 1971). The study of such hybrids represents a large area of research among the 4300 species of red algae.

   High content of 3,6-anhydro-L-galactose and low degrees of substitution favour gelation of agar. Fractionation into a good gelling fraction (agarose; Fig. 3) and a residual fraction with poor gelling properties (agaropectin), as

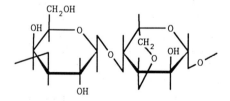

Figure 3. Idealised structure of the repeating unit in agarose

demonstrated in classical Japanese work (Araki 1965), is also well established commercially. Challenging research areas include the determination of minute amounts of substituents influencing the physical and technological properties of agarose, and the detailed chemical and physical characterisation of the agaropectins contained in many red algae.

Laminaran

Laminaran, which is now commercially available, is a family of β-glucans produced by both brown algae (Phaeophyta) and diatoms (Bacillariophyta) (Painter 1983). The backbone consists of β-1,3-linked glucose and may contain one residue of mannitol at the reducing end. Branching occurs mainly in the 6-position. The average degree of polymerisation (DP_n) is 20–25. The low molecular weight as compared with structurally similar β-glucans such as curdlan and scleroglucan (see below) precludes the use of laminaran as a typical viscosifier.

MICROBIAL POLYSACCHARIDES

Microbial polysaccharides containing oligosaccharide repeating units may contain many different sugars (Kenne & Lindberg 1983). Sugars like D-glucose, D-galactose, D-mannose, L-fucose, L-rhamnose, D-glucuronic acid, D-galacturonic acid, N-acetyl-D-glucosamine and others are commonly found. Additionally, many unusual and exotic sugars are often found, especially among the bacteria. Despite this diversity, sugars with amines (positively charged sugars) are yet to be found. Instead, amino sugars, which are common, appear as N-acetyl derivatives. Furthermore, non-carbohydrate substituents, such as O-acetate and pyruvate diketal, but apparently not the sulphate half-ester, are common. Again, the variable presence of such substituents along a chain gives rise to heterogeneity, partly due to incomplete biosynthesis and partly resulting from hydrolysis during processing of the polysaccharide.

Several microbial polysaccharides with oligosaccharide repeat units other than those described below have been isolated and described (Kenne & Lindberg 1983). The reason for this is their biological properties, such as their roles in parasite–host interactions, and in particular their roles as immunological determinants. Many of these polysaccharides have apparently not been studied for their physical properties. Such data would be valuable not only for scientific reasons – for example in an examination of the relationship between primary structure, chain conformation and physical properties – but also in the assessment of their potential use as industrial gums.

A second class of microbial polysaccharides includes those lacking oligosaccharide repeat units. They are usually homopolymers or, at least in one instance (bacterial alginate), block copolymers (Skjåk-Bræk et al. 1986a).

Xanthan

Xanthan gum, the extracellular polysaccharide produced by several *Xanthomonas* strains, may serve as a typical example of a microbial polysaccharide with oligosaccharide repeating units (Fig. 4). The unit contains five sugars with two $\beta(1 \rightarrow 4)$ linked D-glucose residues in the backbone and a trisaccharide side-chain linked to position 3 of every second glucose residue in the main chain (Jansson *et al.* 1975). The structure of the side chain is:

$$\beta\text{-D-Man-}(1 \rightarrow 4)\text{-}\beta\text{-D-GlcA-}(1 \rightarrow 2)\text{-}\alpha\text{-D-Man-}(1 \rightarrow 3)\text{-backbone}$$

where the α-mannose is linked to the glucan backbone. The α-mannose usually contains an acetyl group in the 6 position and the β-mannose may contain pyruvate diketal linked to positions 4 and 6. Commercial xanthan contains variable amounts of acetate and pyruvate; the cause of this may be either varying bacterial strains or different fermentation conditions. Furthermore, *O*-acetate groups hydrolyse relatively rapidly in alkaline solutions and pyruvate is easily lost in acidic conditions, especially if heated. Even at moderate pH values a substantial loss of pyruvate and acetate is experienced on heating (Foss *et al.* 1987), especially under oilfield conditions (Ash *et al.* 1983). The glucuronic acid and the pyruvate in the side-chain may contribute a maximum of two negative changes per repeat unit. The content of *O*-acetyl may vary from less than 0.5 to 2 groups per repeating unit. The counterions may be exchanged freely, but in commercial preparations are the result of equilibrium ion binding with the cations in the fermentation broth.

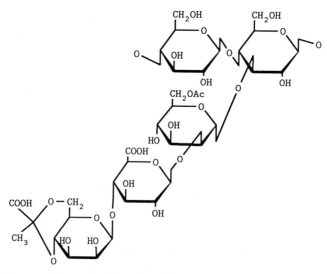

Figure 4. The repeating unit of the microbial polysaccharide xanthan. Ac, acetate

The backbone of xanthan is identical to that of cellulose, but the physical properties of xanthan are very different. Recently, xanthan with only α-mannose in the side-chains has been obtained by inducing genetic changes in the producing strain of *Xanthomonas* (Betlach *et al.* 1987).

Gellan Gum and Related Polysaccharides

Six bacterial polysaccharides with essentially the same tetrasaccharide backbone in the repeat unit, but with different side-chains, have recently been described and partly commercialised. The polysaccharide from *Pseudomonas elodea*, S-60 or gellan gum, has no side-chains. The repeat unit of the polysaccharide is (Jansson *et al.* 1983; O'Neill *et al.* 1983):

-3)-β-D-Glc-(1 $\rightarrow$ 4)-β-D-GlcA-(1 $\rightarrow$ 4)-β-D-Glc-(1 $\rightarrow$ 4)-α-L-Rha-(1 $\rightarrow$

All sugars are in the pyranose form. Except for the 1,3-linkages of α-L-rhamnose units, the other linkages are β-1,4 with sugars in the configuration of D-glucose as in cellulose or in the backbone of xanthan.

Another polysaccharide from strains of *Alcaligenes*, S-130 (welan), can be regarded as a derivative of gellan, containing either a single α-L-mannose or a α-L-rhamnose attached to the 3-position of the second glucose in the backbone. The structure of welan is thus (Jansson *et al.* 1985):

-3)-β-D-Glc-(1 $\rightarrow$ 4)-β-D-GlcA-(1 $\rightarrow$ 4)-β-D-Glc-(1 $\rightarrow$ 4)–α-L-Rha-(1 $\rightarrow$
$\qquad\qquad\qquad\qquad\qquad\qquad\qquad\qquad$ | (1 $\rightarrow$ 3)
$\qquad\qquad\qquad\qquad\qquad\qquad\qquad$ α-L-Man or α-L-Rha

The third polysaccharide in this series, S-194 (rhamsan), is also produced by strains of *Alcaligenes*. The side-chain of rhamsan is gentiobiose instead of either L-mannose or L-rhamnose, and is attached to the 'first' glucose residue in the repeating unit. The structure of rhamsan is thus (Jansson *et al.* 1986b):

-3)-β-D-Glc-(1 $\rightarrow$ 4)-β-D-GlcA-(1 $\rightarrow$ 4)-β-D-Glc-(1 $\rightarrow$ 4)-α-L-Rha-(1 $\rightarrow$
$\qquad$ | (1 $\rightarrow$ 6)
α-D-Glc
$\qquad$ | (1 $\rightarrow$ 6)
β-D-Glc

The polysaccharide S-88, which is obtained from *Pseudomonas* ATCC 31554, differs slightly from welan (S-130) in that the side-chain can only be α-L-rhamnose, but the L-sugar in the main chain is either α-L-rhamnose or α-L-mannose (Jansson *et al.* 1986a). The structure of S-88 is thus:

-3)-β-D-Glc-(1$\rightarrow$4)-β-D-GlcA-(1$\rightarrow$4)-β-D-Glc-(1$\rightarrow$4)-α-L(Rha/Man)(1$\rightarrow$
$\qquad\qquad\qquad\qquad\qquad\qquad\qquad\qquad$ | (1 $\rightarrow$ 3)
$\qquad\qquad\qquad\qquad\qquad\qquad$ α-L-Rha

A polysaccharide produced by *Alcaligenes* ATCC 31853, S-198, has the same structure as S-88 except that the side-chain is linked to the 4-position of the first glucose residue (Chowdury *et al.* 1987a). The structure of S-198 is:

-3)-β-D-Glc-(1→4)-β-D-GlcA-(1→4)-β-D-Glc-(1→4)-α-L-(Rha/Man)-(1→
    | (1 → 4)
α-L-Rha

Xanthomonas ATCC 53159 produces a polysaccharide S-657. The backbone has the gellan (S-60) structure, and the disaccharide side-chain consisting of two α-L-rhamnose units is linked to the 3-position of the second glucose residue in the backbone (Chowdury *et al.* 1987b). The structure of S-657 is:

-3)-β-D-Glc-(1 → 4)-β-D-GlcA-(1 → 4)-β-D-Glc-(1 → 4)-α-L-Rha-(1 →
                                        | (1 → 3)
                                     α-L-Rha
                                        | (1 → 4)
                                     α-L-Rha

In addition to the special physical properties of gellan, welan and rhamsan, the polysaccharides in this series are useful probes for studying the influence of side-chains on the conformational properties of polysaccharides (Crescenzi *et al.* 1987).

Dextran

Dextran is a family of α-1,6-linked glucans (Fig. 5) produced from sucrose by the bacterium *Leuconostoc mesenteroides*. Dextran contains branches in varying amounts and lengths. The commercial dextrans contain more than 95% 1,6-linkages. The branches are very short and the molecule can be regarded essentially as a linear macromolecule (Sandford & Baird 1983).

Pullulan

The structure of pullulan (Gorin & Barreto-Bergter 1983) is shown in Fig. 6. This polysaccharide is commercially available from Japan. It is a linear polymer containing maltotriose repeating units linked by α-1,6-linkages as in dextran. Small amounts of maltotetraose units also seem to be present. Pullulan is produced from starch by the bacterium *Aureobasidium pullulans*.

Curdlan and Scleroglucan

Curdlan (Fig. 7) and scleroglucan (Fig. 8) both contain β-1,3-linkages in the main chain (Sandford & Baird 1983). Curdlan is unbranched whereas sclero-glucan has a single glucose unit attached in the 6-position to every third residue

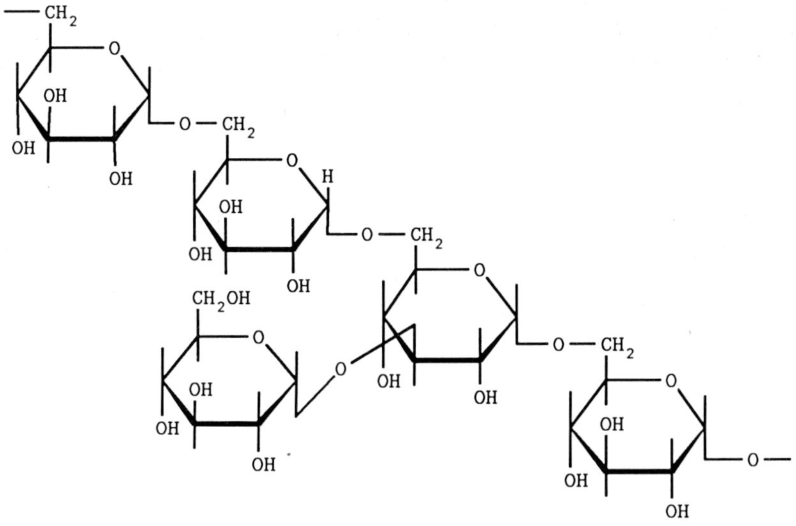

Figure 5. The chemical structure of dextran, a linear β-1,6 linked glucan with short branches

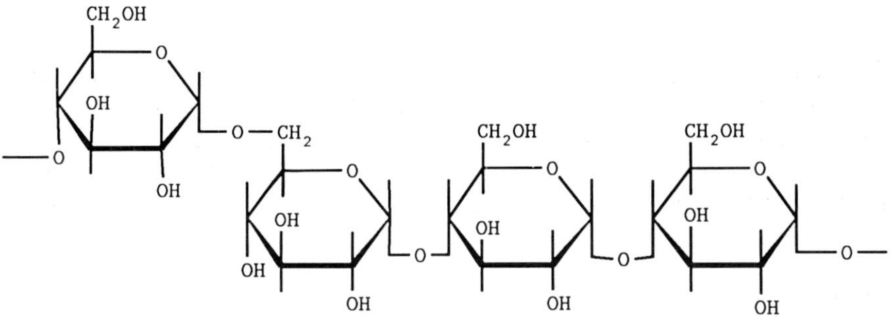

Figure 6. The chemical structure of pullulan

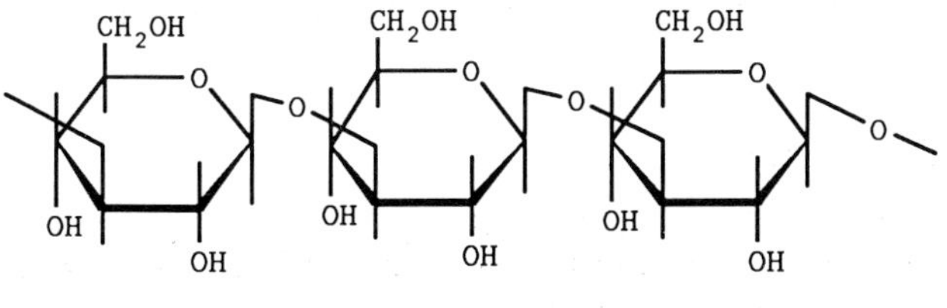

Figure 7. The chemical structure of curdlan

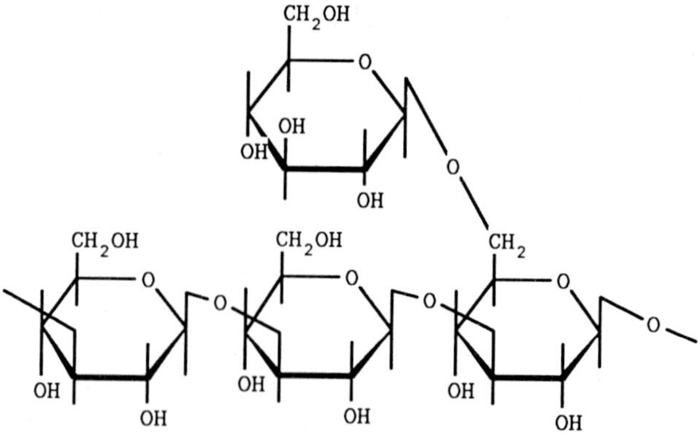

Figure 8. The chemical structure of scleroglucan

in the chain backbone. Curdlan is produced by a mutant of the bacterium *Alcaligenes faecalis* and some strains of *Agrobacterium*. Scleroglucan is produced by fungi belonging to the genus *Sclerotium*.

Bacterial Alginates

Bacterial alginates represent a special class of polysaccharides. Like algal alginates they are copolymers of D-mannuronic acid (M) and its 5-epimer L-guluronic acid (G). However, the distribution of M and G along the chain differs from most preparations of algal alginates. A comparison between algal and bacterial alginates in terms of frequencies of various block elements is shown in Table 1 (p.188). Alginate produced by *Pseudomonas* sp. lacks homopolymeric blocks of α-L-guluronic acid, which are essential for gel formation (see below). Furthermore, bacterial alginates contain O-acetate groups in varying amounts, which are absent in algal alginates. Acetate is only found on mannuronic acid residues linked at either O–2 or O–3, or possibly both (Skjåk-Bræk *et al.* 1986a; Gacesa 1988).

Alginate from *Azotobacter vinelandii* seems to be a possible commercial contender to algal alginate, as it may contain a high proportion of poly-G blocks and its viscosity is reported to be superior to that of algal alginate (Chen *et al.* 1985). However, this organism has some limitations in fermentation processes (Gacesa 1988).

CONCLUSIONS

Is it possible to make some generalisations regarding the chemical structure of phycocolloids and microbial polysaccharides? Based on the few examples of polysaccharides discussed here the following generalisations are possible:

1. Microbial polysaccharides generally have more regular repeating units than typical phycocolloids.
2. Microbial polysaccharides have a variable distribution of branches and non-carbohydrate substituents.
3. Sulphate half-esters are common in phycocolloids and rare in microbial polysaccharides.

Because alginate is both a phycocolloid and a microbial polysaccharide, interesting comparisons of chemical composition are possible (Table 1). Some bacterial alginates are outside the range found in alginates from common seaweeds, with respect to both chemical composition (acetylation) and sequence (block structure). From a commercial point of view, this means that new types of alginates may be produced. However, it is absolutely essential to perform a detailed investigation of the chemical composition and the resultant physical properties of the alginate in question before choosing a bacterial strain for industrial production.

PHYSICAL BEHAVIOUR

CONFORMATION OF POLYSACCHARIDE CHAINS IN SOLUTION

The properties of dilute polymer solutions are intimately related to the conformations or shapes of the polymers. The three basic shapes of polymers are a solid sphere, a stiff rod and a random coil. These and their intermediate forms are conveniently represented by a triangle (Fig. 9). Much work on the properties of polymers in solution is aimed at studying conformations and conformational transitions along the lines of the triangle.

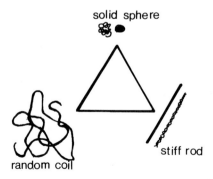

Figure 9. Schematic representation of the basic shapes of polymers and their intermediate forms

One of the most important properties is the performance of the polymers as viscosifying agents according to the Mark–Houwink equation, which links the intrinsic viscosity, $[\eta]$ (defined as $\lim(\eta_{sp}/c)$, $c \to \infty$), to the molecular weight (M) and a shape-dependent parameter (a):

$$[\eta] = KM^a$$

The exponent (a) is zero for compact spheres and ranges from 0.5 to 1.8 when going from random coils to stiff rods with intermediate values for chains with different stiffnesses.

Another property closely related to chain conformation is the so-called salt tolerance, which is of critical importance for the use of polymers in offshore enhanced oil recovery, where seawater is used as solvent. For polyelectrolytes, the reduction in intrinsic viscosity induced on the addition of salts (normalised to a certain intrinsic viscosity at an ionic strength of 0.1 mol l^{-1}) (Smidsrød & Haug 1971) is directly correlated to the stiffness of the chains as measured by the Kuhn statistical segment length (Fig. 10). An important exception is polymers that undergo conformational transitions following changes in the ionic strength. It is obvious from Fig. 10 that only very stiff

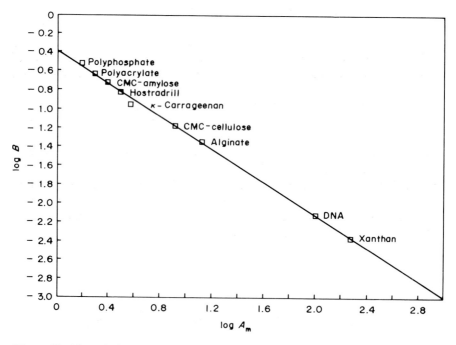

Figure 10. The relationship between the stiffness parameter, B, for polyelectrolytes (obtained by measuring the intrinsic viscosity at different ionic strengths) and the Kuhn length, A_m. CMC, carboxymethyl cellulose

polyelectrolytes have good viscosifying effects at the high ionic strength of seawater (approx. 0.5 mol l^{-1}).

Dilute solutions of polymer molecules in certain solvents (θ-solvents) are some of the best understood two-component systems in chemistry. This is because of the conformational calculations introduced by Flory (1953), and carried further for polysaccharides most vigorously by D. Brant and co-workers (Burton & Brant 1983; Talashek & Brant 1987). In θ-solvents, weak and attractive forces between sugar residues (both intermolecular and intra-molecular) cancel out excluded volume effects. The expansion of the chain is then determined, to a first approximation, by the chemistry of the chain, giving a set of geometrical and conformational restrictions, and may thus be calculated. A convenient and important parameter for such chain expansion, or stiffness, is the characteristic ratio (C_∞). The characteristic ratio is a dimensionless quantity related to the relative extension of random polymers defined as:

$$C_\infty = \frac{\langle r^2 \rangle}{n l^2} \quad n \to \infty$$

where $\langle r^2 \rangle$ is the mean square of the end-to-end distance of an indefinitely long chain with n bonds of length l. C_∞ may be calculated by statistical methods based on the following assumptions:

1. The sugar rings are fixed in one of the preferred conformations.
2. The torsion around the two single bonds (three bonds in 1,6-linkages) of the glycosidic linkage (Fig. 11) is distributed according to the Boltzmann principle.
3. The torsion-dependent energies are calculated by potential functions for the non-bonded interaction between adjacent rings.

The characteristic ratios calculated for some typical linkage types in homo-polymers (Burton & Brant 1983) and for some microbial heteropolymers (Talashek & Brant 1987) are given in Table 4. The calculations demonstrate that the extension of the polysaccharides may be altered by two orders of magnitude just by changing the type of glycosidic linkage. The 1,6-linkage, as in the main chain of dextran, is by far the most flexible, and the diaxial 1,4-

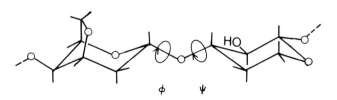

Figure 11. Torsional angles around a glycosidic bond

Table 4. Calculated characteristic ratios (C_∞) for homopoly-saccharides with a given glycosidic linkage and some microbial polysaccharides

Polymer/linkage	Configuration	C_∞	Example
α1,4-D-Glc-p	Axial–equatorial	5	Amylose
β1,4-D-Glc-p	Equitorial–equatorial	100	Cellulose
α-1,4-D-Gal-p	Axial–axial	193	Pectin
β-1,3-D-Glc-p	Equatorial–equatorial	3	Curdlan
α-1,6-D-Glc-p	—	1.5	Dextran
Pullulan		2.4	
Gellan		17.9	
Welan		18.5	
Rhamsan		23.2	

From Burton and Brant (1983) and Talashek and Brant (1987).

linkage (as in blocks of L-guluronic acid and in pectin) gives the stiffest chains. Such differences in chain extension have an enormous effect on the viscosity of polysaccharide solutions, as may be seen from the Flory equation for the intrinsic viscosity:

$$[\eta] = \Phi \langle r^2 \rangle^{3/2} M^{-1}$$

where Φ is the Flory parameter, $\langle r^2 \rangle$ is the mean square of the end-to-end distance (i.e. extension) and M is the molecular weight.

Some viscosity data for different phycocolloids and microbial polysaccharides are given in Table 5. Although these data are somewhat scattered, with

Table 5. Viscosity parameters of polysaccharides

Polymer	Solvent	Molecular weight range	K^{a}	a^{a}	Max. $[\eta]$ (ml g^{-1})
Alginate	0.1 M NaCl	10^4 to 10^6	2×10^{-3}	1.0	3 000
$\varkappa$-Carrageenan	0.1 M NaCl	4×10^3 to 7×10^5	8.8×10^{-3}	0.86	900
ι-Carrageenan	0.1 M LiI	5×10^5			1 000
Curdlan	Water/dimethyl sulphoxide				(5)
Dextran	0.1 M NaCl	5×10^4 to 2×10^6	2.5×10^{-1}	0.42	50
Pullulan	Water	5×10^3 to 1.2×10^6	2.4×10^{-1}	0.66	240
Xanthan	0.75 M NaCl	4×10^6 to 1.5×10^7		0.96	12 000
Scleroglucan	0.01 M NaCl	6×10^5 to 6×10^6		1.1–1.8	17 000
Gellan (S-60)	0.1 M TMACl	5×10^5			2 000
Welan (S-130)	0.15 M NaCl				14 000
Rhamsan (S-194)	0.15 M NaCl				1 100

[a] Mark–Houwink equation: $[\eta] = KM^a$.

respect to both the range of molecular weights and solvent conditions, there is a clear tendency for the maximum observed viscosities to be related to the different C_∞-values given in Table 4. There are some exceptions, however. Xanthan with a β-1,4-linkage in the main chain, and in particular scleroglucan with β-1,3-linkages, yield intermediate and low values of $C\infty$, respectively, when calculated as single-stranded chains. However, both have much higher intrinsic viscosities than the other polysaccharides. For these polysaccharides the statistical mechanical calculations of the type presented in Table 4 do not reflect the solution properties. The most probable explanation for this discrepancy is that both xanthan and scleroglucan may exist in solution as multistranded, stiff, ordered structures.

Order–disorder transitions, usually induced by changes in temperature or solvent conditions, have been detected and discussed in many polysaccharide systems, as shown in Table 6. The strandedness of the ordered structure has been debated vigorously in the last decade. Many polysaccharides, including dextran and alginate, are undoubtedly single-stranded in unaggregated solutions. There seems to be agreement that a triple-stranded helix represents the ordered conformation for the β-1,3-type of polymers curdlan (Saito 1981) and scleroglucan (Yanaki et al. 1981). The status of the carrageenans (especially $\varkappa$- and ι-) has been studied by several groups, and differing views have been expressed (Smidsrød 1980; Rees et al. 1982). Although one of the present authors (Smidsrød 1980) has proposed a single-stranded ordered structure in $\varkappa$- and ι-carrageenan, it is presently our impression that the evidence in favour of the double helix structure outweighs that for the single helix. The existence of folded chains, which could reconcile some of the experimental data, should not be excluded.

For xanthan, both single-stranded (Norton et al. 1984a; Lambert et al. 1985; Milas & Rinaudo 1986; Jones et al. 1987) and double-stranded (Sato et al. 1985; Stokke et al. 1986; Liu et al. 1987), ordered conformations have been proposed. Electron microscopic studies of xanthan indicate that the perfectly

Table 6. Ordered and disordered polysaccharides

Source	Disordered polysaccharides	Polymers with order–disorder transitions
Algal	λ-Carrageenan Alginate Laminaran	$\varkappa$-Carrageenan ι-Carrageenan Agarose
Microbial	Dextran Pullulan Rhamsan (?)	Curdlan Scleroglucan Gellan Xanthan

matched double-stranded chain can be regarded as the lowest free-energy conformation in aqueous solutions well below the transition temperature (Stokke *et al.* 1986). Chains folding back on themselves, forming hairpin-shaped structures with antiparallel chains have also been observed (Stokke *et al.* 1989). When xanthan is partly disordered, the thick and stiff double-stranded chains may separate partly into thinner and more flexible single-stranded chains (Stokke *et al.* 1986), as shown in Fig. 12.

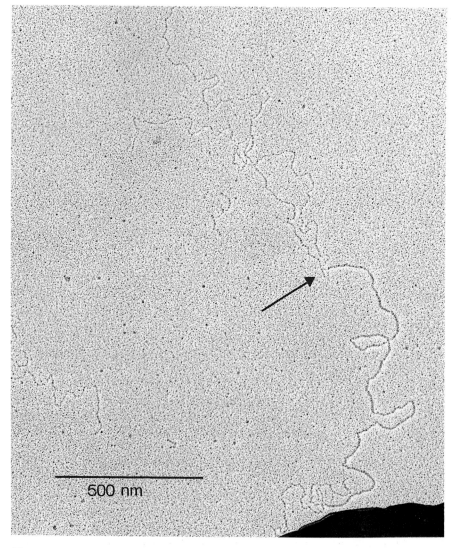

Figure 12. Electron micrograph of the bacterial polysaccharide xanthan. Note the thicker chain splitting into two thinner and more flexible chains (arrow)

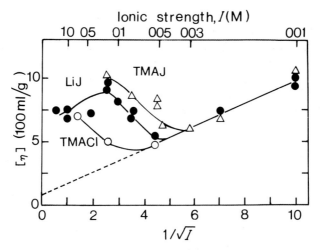

Figure 13. $\varkappa$-Carrageenan: the transition from a disordered to an ordered conformation revealed as an increase in the intrinsic viscosity $[\eta]$, when the ionic strength, I, increases above approx. 0.05 M. TMA, tetramethylammonium

Two examples of the salt-induced formation of ordered structures with concomitant increase in intrinsic viscosity are given for the phycocolloid $\varkappa$-carrageenan and the microbial polysaccharide gellan in Figs. 13 and 14, respectively. Viscosity increase is directly correlated to a change in optical rotation both for $\varkappa$-carrageenan (optical rotation not shown in Fig. 13) and for gellan (Fig. 14).

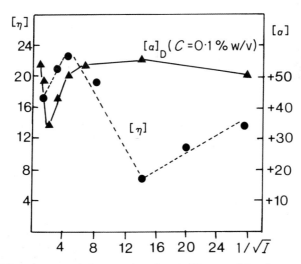

Figure 14. Gellan (tetramethylammonium form). The transition from a disordered to an ordered conformation revealed as an increase in the intrinsic viscosity $[\eta]$, and a decrease in the optical rotation, α, when the ionic strength, I, increases

A detailed understanding of conformational properties including order–disorder transitions is of prime importance as a basis for both physical behaviour and technological properties of polysaccharide solutions, and continued research in this area is urgently needed. It is clear that among both the phycocolloids and the microbial polysaccharides one may find all types of conformational behaviours, from nearly random coils to extremely stiff extended molecules with high viscosifying power. However, the most extreme cases are found in microbial polysaccharides such as xanthan and scleroglucan.

SOLUBILITY

Polysaccharides used in the solid state in the form of either amorphous or crystalline films and fibres are not the subject of this review, but this usage is an area of continuing industrial growth.

Solubility may be understood qualitatively by considering:

1. Melting of crystalline or semicrystalline regions in the solid state
2. Mixing of the amorphous polymers with water.

As a first step, the general effect of polymer structure may be understood by considering the melting temperature, T_m, which equals $\Delta H_m / \Delta S_m$, where ΔH_m and ΔS_m are the differences in enthalpy and entropy between the crystalline and the dissolved states, respectively. Solubility is generally favoured by lowering T_m. Any regularity in the sequence of monomers and substituents that leads to stronger interactions between chains (increasing ΔH_m will increase T_m and hence reduce solubility. A low value of ΔS_m, which will be the case for stiff polymers, will lead to the same effect.

Some structural features that influence solubility are listed in Table 7, which is self-explanatory except for the feature 'block size'. Heteropolymers with long homopolymeric blocks tend to be less soluble than heteropolymers with either short blocks or a more random distribution of monomer residues. Within the alginates, a good example is the general insolubility at low pH values, except for alginates with very short blocks (certain fractions from *Ascophyllum nodosum*), which are soluble at all pH values (Smidsrød 1970).

In general, most polysaccharides, both algal and microbial, are either soluble or gel-like in their native state. The only well-known insoluble, extracellular polysaccharide of industrial importance is curdlan (Saito 1981).

In the mixing step (step 2 above) the ordering of water molecules around the chains may be critically dependent on the type and concentration of inorganic salt. Such effects are poorly understood. They act in addition to the general effect of salts in influencing the solubility of polyelectrolytes. The salt lithium iodide seems to increase solubility in many polysaccharide systems, probably by reducing the loss of entropy for water molecules interacting with

Table 7. Structural features of polysaccharides influencing their solubility

Feature	Polymers with related compositions	Solubility
Fixed charges	Alginate (Na^+ form)	Soluble
	Alginate (H^+ form)	Insoluble
Chain flexibility	Dextran and pullulan (flexible glucans)	Soluble
	Cellulose (stiff glucan)	Insoluble
Side-chains	Scleroglucan (glucan with side-chains)	Soluble
	Curdlan (linear glucan)	Insoluble
Substituents (non-sugar)	Native gellan (Ca^{2+} or Mg^{2+} form)	Soluble
	Deacetylated gellan (Ca^{2+} or Mg^{2+} form)	Forms gels
Block size	Alginates with long homopolymeric blocks (poly-M or poly-G)	Insoluble
	Alginates with alternating sequences or random distribution of M and G	Soluble

the polymer chains. There appear to be few thorough studies on the solubility of polysaccharides.

ION-EXCHANGE PROPERTIES

A very characteristic feature of alginate and carrageenan is the selectivity for the alkaline earth metal and the alkaline metal ions, respectively. In alginate this is due to its content of homopolymeric blocks of L-guluronic acid (Smidsrød & Haug 1972; Smidsrød et al. 1972) as seen in Figs. 15 and 16, and in carrageenans it is due to the $\varkappa$-type of chemical structure (Smidsrød 1980) as shown in Fig. 17. Relatively few studies have been made on cation selectivities among the microbial polyelectrolytes. Gellan (Figs. 18 and 19) seems to lack both types of selectivities mentioned above (Grasdalen & Smidsrød 1987). The affinity for cations in the order:

$$Pb^{2+} > Cu^{2+} > Zn^{2+} > Sr^{2+} > Ca^{2+}, Mg^{2+}$$

is typical for an isolated carboxyl group with no possibility for the chelate type of binding that exists in alginate (Haug & Smidsrød 1970).

POLYSACCHARIDE GELS

The gel state is of the utmost importance for many technical uses of polysaccharides, but the state is considerably more difficult to describe and understand at a molecular level than in dilute solutions. Many gels are far from any thermodynamic equilibrium, and they can be regarded as phase

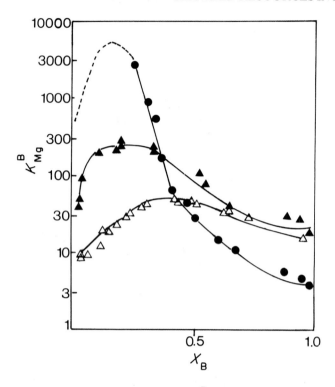

Figure 15. Alginate: the selectivity coefficient K_{Mg}^B as a function of the fraction, X_B, of different alkaline earth metal ions, B, for an alginate fragment with 90% guluronic acid. $\triangle$, B = Ca^{2+}; $\blacktriangle$, B = Sr^{2+}; $\bullet$, B = Ba^{2+}

separations or precipitations where the second phase has not separated out for kinetic reasons. The slow molecular reorganisation in the gels is most probably due to kinetically stable *inter*-chain contact zones (junctions) between long sequences of ordered chain segments.

For polyelectrolytes like alginate and $\varkappa$-carrageenan the strength of the contact zone is critically dependent on the type of ions present. A correlation between cation binding and strength of junctions is observed both in alginate (Smidsrød 1974) (Cf. Figs. 15, 16 and 23) and in $\varkappa$-carrageenan (Smidsrød & Grasdalen 1984), suggesting an active role of the cations at the junction zones.

The gelation of alginate involves blocks of polyguluronic acid (Fig. 20), and gel strength increases with increasing content of guluronic acid (F_G) (Fig. 21). However, alginates containing guluronic acid only in alternating sequences, even if the total content is close to 40%, do not form gels. A better correlation exists between the gel strength and the fraction of GGG-blocks

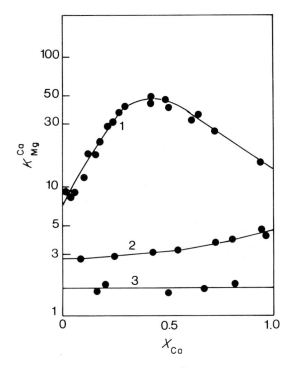

Figure 16. Alginate: the selectivity coefficient K_{Mg}^{Ca} as a function of the fraction, $X_{Ca^{2+}}$, of bound calcium for blocks of polyguluronic acid (curve 1), polymannuronic acid (curve 2) and an alternating sequence (curve 3)

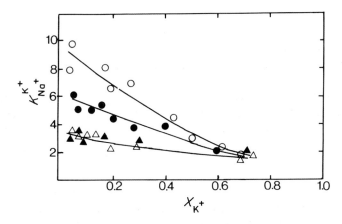

Figure 17. Carrageenan: the selectivity coefficient K_{Na}^{K} as a function of the fraction $X_{K^{+}}$ of bound potassium carrageenans from *Eucheuma cottoni* ($\circ$) ($\varkappa$-type), *Chondrus crispus* ($\bullet$), *Eucheuma spinosum* ($\blacktriangle$) (ι-type) and *Gigartina acicularis* ($\triangle$) (λ-type)

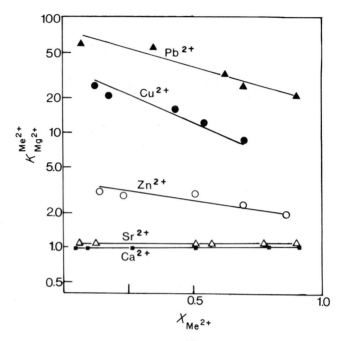

Figure 18. Gellan: the selectivity coefficient K_{Mg}^{Me} as a function of the fraction, $X_{Me^{2+}}$, of bound cations (Me)

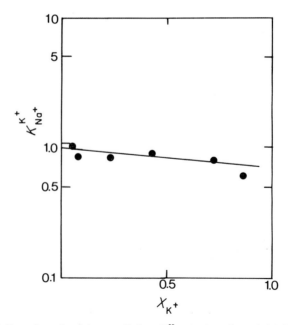

Figure 19. Gellan: the selectivity coefficient K_{Na}^{K} as a function of the fraction, X_{K^+}, of bound potassium ions

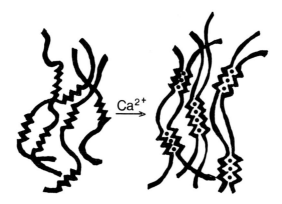

Figure 20. The egg-box model for the gelation of alginate by calcium ions. The sawtooth structures represent homopolymeric blocks of α-L-guluronic acid

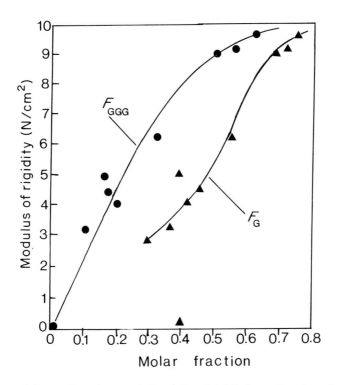

Figure 21. Alginate: the gel strength (modulus of rigidity) as a function of the fraction of guluronic acid (F_G) and the fraction of GGG (F_{GGG})

(F_{GGG}), as demonstrated in Fig. 21, or between the gel strength and the average length of G-blocks (Fig. 22). These data confirm many earlier observations which have led to the generally recognised theory for the gelation of alginate, sometimes referred to as the egg-box model (Rees et al. 1982). The G-blocks, because of the diaxial linkage between residues of α-L-guluronic acid ($^1C_4$-conformation), form cavities into which divalent gel-inducing cations like calcium fit perfectly and bind adjacent G-blocks strongly as shown schematically in Fig. 20.

The gelling of carrageenans is favoured by a high content of 3,6-anhydro-D-galactose and a low content of sulphate. The gelling occurs in two steps: a conformational ordering of the chains followed by cation-mediated association of chains to form junction zones (Smidsrød 1980). There is some debate as to the nature of the chain-ordering step, but the evidence to date seems to favour a double-stranded ordered conformation.

In carrageenan gel systems there are also considerable anion effects. It is a matter of debate whether they are due to binding of anions to the chains or to perturbations of the water structure (Grasdalen & Smidsrød 1981; Norton et al. 1984b).

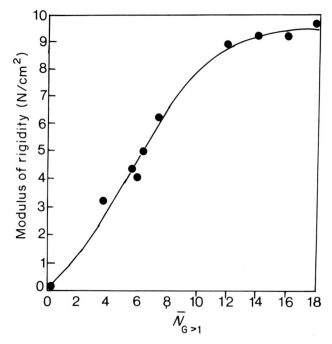

Figure 22. Alginate: gel strength as a function of the average length of polyguluronic acid. Note the low gel strength for the sample with no blocks of guluronic acid. This sample contains close to 50% guluronic acid, but only in alternating sequences

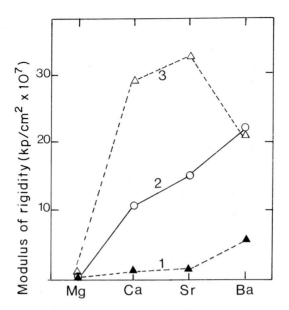

Figure 23. Alginate: modulus of rigidity for different alkaline earth polyuronate gels: 1, alginate with 10% guluronic acid; 2, alginate with 38% guluronic acid; 3, pectate (polygalacturonic acid) from Fluka. Polymer concentration: 3%

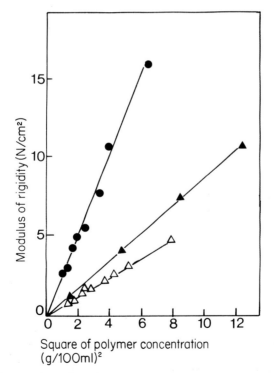

Figure 24. Gel strength as a function of polysaccharide concentration. ●, agarose; ▲, alginate with 38% guluronic acid; △, carrageenan from *Chondrus crispus*

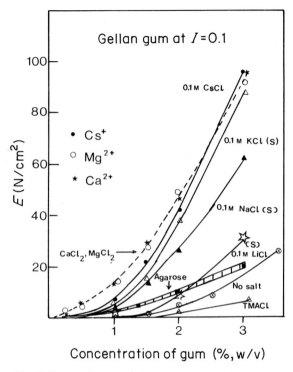

Figure 25. Gellan: gel strength in the presence of monovalent cations

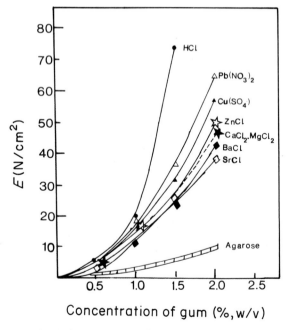

Figure 26. Gellan: gel strength in the presence of divalent cations

The maximum gel strengths obtained with the phycocolloids agarose, alginates rich in L-guluronic acid, and carrageenans rich in $\varkappa$-carrageenan are almost the same (Fig. 24), provided that the gels are made with an excess of calcium and potassium chlorides for alginate and carrageenan, respectively. The correlation between ion binding and gel strength is not observed in gellan gum for monovalent cations (Grasdalen & Smidsrød 1987). The alkaline metal ions induce widely different gel strengths (Fig. 25) although no selectivities in ion binding are observed. The different degrees of hydration of the alkaline metal ions of different sizes may be a controlling factor in this type of gelation. Among the divalent metal ions a correlation between ion binding and gel strength is again evident, as may be seen by comparing Fig. 18 and Fig. 26.

One very important result in Fig. 25 and Fig. 26 is that gellan gum in the presence of divalent ions and certain monovalent ions is a far better gelling agent than the phycocolloids, as represented by agarose. There are no solid experimental data available to suggest any molecular reasons for this difference.

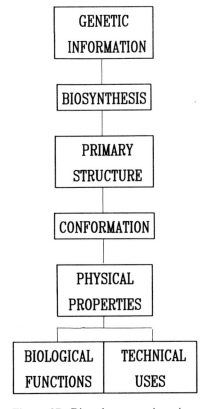

Figure 27. Biopolymer engineering

FUTURE TRENDS

A diagram describing a developing field in biotechnology, which we have named biopolymer engineering, is shown in Fig. 27. When we learn the relationship between genetic information, primary structures, and physical and technical behaviour, we may be able to tailor polysaccharides with the desired technical properties. Cloning of genes from *Acetobacter xylinum* controlling the biosynthesis of cellulose has already been achieved in our laboratory (Valla 1989; Valla *et al.* 1989). The cloning of the genes for the production of C-5-mannurono-epimerase is under way. Additionally, protoplasts of certain brown and red algae are now routinely produced in our laboratory (unpublished data). Such developments suggest that biopolymer engineering may be used in the not too distant future in order to synthesise polysaccharides with predetermined and highly specialised physical behaviours.

ACKNOWLEDGEMENTS

We are grateful to Bjørn T. Stokke, of the University of Trondheim, who provided the electron micrograph of xanthan.

REFERENCES

Araki C. 1965. Some recent studies on the polysaccharides of agarophytes. *Proc. Int. Seaweed Symp.* **5**: 3–17.
Ash S.G., Clarke-Sturman A.J., Calvert R. & Nisbet T.M. 1983. Chemical stability of biopolymer solutions. *SPE-preprint* 12085, presented at the 58th Annual SPE Technical Conference, San Francisco, 5–8 October 1983.
Betlach M.R., Capage M.A., Doherty D.H., Hassler R.A., Henderson N.M. & Vanderslice R.W. 1987. Genetically engineered polymers: manipulation of xanthan biosynthesis. Polytrimer production by *Xanthomonas campestris* mutant. *Abstr. Pap. Am. Chem. Soc.* 193 Meet., CARB65.
Burton B.A. & Brant D.A. 1983. Comparative flexibility, extension, and conformation of some simple polysaccharide chains. *Biopolymers* **22**: 1769–92.
Chen W.P., Chen J.Y., Chang S.C. & Su C.L. 1985. Bacterial alginate produced by a mutant of *Azotobacter vinelandii*. *Appl. Environ. Microbiol.* **49**: 543–6.
Chowdury T.A., Lindberg B., Lindquist U. & Baird J. 1987a. Structural studies of an extracellular polysaccharide (S-198) elaborated by *Alciligenes* ATCC 31853. *Carbohydr. Res.* **161**: 127–32.
Chowdury T.A., Lindberg B., Lindquist U. & Baird J. 1987b. Structural studies of an extracellular polysaccharide, S-657, elaborated by *Xanthomonas* ATCC 53159. *Carbohydr. Res.* **164**: 117–22.
Crescenzi V., Dentini M. & Dea I.C.M. 1987. The influence of side-chains on the dilute-solution properties of three structurally related, bacterial anionic polysaccharides. *Carbohydr. Res.* **160**: 283–302.
Flory P.J. 1953. *Principles of Polymer Chemistry*. Ithaca: Cornell University Press.

Foss P., Stokke B.T. & Smidsrød O. 1987. Thermal stability and chain conformational studies of xanthan at different ionic strengths. *Carbohydr. Polymers* **7**: 421–33.

Gacesa P. 1988. Alginates. *Carbohydr. Polymers* **8**: 1–22.

Gorin P.A.J. & Barreto-Bergter E. 1983. The chemistry of polysaccharides of fungi and lichens. In *The Polysaccharides*. Vol. 2. (Ed. G.O. Aspinall) pp. 365–409. London: Academic Press.

Grasdalen H. 1983. High-field ^{1}H-n.m.r. spectroscopy of alginate: sequential structure and linkage conformations. *Carbohydr. Res.* **118**: 255–60.

Grasdalen H. & Smidsrød O. 1981. Iodide specific formation of $\varkappa$-carrageenan single helices. ^{127}I-n.m.r. spectroscopic evidence for selective site binding of iodide anions in the ordered conformation. *Macromolecules* **14**: 1842–5.

Grasdalen H. & Smidsrød O. 1987. Gelation of gellan gum. *Carbohydr. Polymers* **7**: 371–93.

Grasdalen H., Larsen B. & Smidsrød O. 1979. A p.m.r. study of the composition and sequence of uronate residues in alginates. *Carbohydr. Res.* **68**: 23–31.

Haug A. & Larsen B. 1974. Biosynthesis of algal polysaccharides. In *Plant Carbohydrate Biochemistry*. (Ed. J.B. Pridham) pp. 207–18. London: Academic Press.

Haug A. & Smidsrød O. 1970. Selectivity of some anionic polymers for divalent metal ions. *Acta Chem. Scand.* **24**: 843–54.

Hirase S., Araki C. & Watanabe K. 1967. Component sugars of the polysaccharide of the red seaweed *Grateloupia elliptica*. *Bull. Chem. Soc. Jap.* **40**: 1445–8.

Höök M., Lindahl U., Bäckström G., Malmström A. & Fransson L.Å. 1974. Biosynthesis of heparin. III. Formation of iduronic acid residues. *J. Biol. Chem.* **249**: 3908–15.

James D.W., Preiss J. & Elbein A.D. 1985. Biosynthesis of polysaccharides. In *The Polysaccharides*. Vol. 3. (Ed. G.O. Aspinall) pp. 107–207. London: Academic Press.

Jansson P.E., Kenne L. & Lindberg B. 1975. Structure of the extracellular polysaccharide from *Xanthomonas campestris*. *Carbohydr. Res.* **45**: 275–82.

Jansson P.E., Lindberg B. & Sandford P.A. 1983. Structural studies of gellan gum, an extracellular polysaccharide elaborated by *Pseudomonas elodea*. *Carbohydr. Res.* **124**: 135–9.

Jansson P.E., Lindberg B., Widmalm G. & Sandford P.A. 1985. Structural studies of an extracellular polysaccharide (S-130) elaborated by *Alcaligenes* ATCC 31555. *Carbohydr. Res.* **139**: 217–23.

Jansson P.E., Kumar N.S. & Lindberg B. 1986a. Structural studies of a polysaccharide (S-88) elaborated by *Pseudomonas* ATCC 31554. *Carbohydr. Res.* **156**: 165–72.

Jansson P.E., Lindberg B., Lindberg J., Maekawa E. & Sandford P.A. 1986b. Structural studies of a polysaccharide (S-194) elaborated by *Alcaligenes* ATCC 31961. *Carbohydr. Res.* **156**: 157–63.

Jones S.A., Goodall D.M., Cutler A.N. & Norton I.T. 1987. Applicaiton of conductivity studies and polyelectrolytic theory to the conformation and order–disorder transition of xanthan polysaccharide. *Eur. Biophys. J.* **15**: 185–91.

Kenne L. & Lindberg B. 1983. Bacterial polysaccharides. In *The Polysaccharides*. Vol. 2. (Ed. G.O. Aspinall) pp. 287–363. London: Academic Press.

Lambert F., Milas M. & Rinaudo M. 1985. Sodium and calcium counterion activity in the presence of xanthan polysaccharide. *Int. J. Biol. Macromol.* **7**: 49–52.

Liu W., Sato T., Norisuye T. & Fujita H. 1987. Thermally induced conformational change of xanthan in 0.01 M aqueous sodium chloride. *Carbohydr. Res.* **160**: 267–81.

Milas M. & Rinaudo M. 1986. Properties of xanthan gum in aqueous solutions: role of the conformational transition. *Carbohydr. Res.* **158**: 191–204.

Nikaido H. & Hassid W.Z. 1971. Biosynthesis of saccharides from glycopyranosyl esters of nucleoside pyrophosphates ('sugar nucleotides'). *Adv. Carbohydr. Chem. Biochem.* **26**: 351–483.

Norton I.T., Goodall D.M., Frangou S.A., Morris E.R. & Rees D.A. 1984a. Mechanism and dynamics of conformational ordering in xanthan polysaccharide. *J. Mol. Biol.* **175**: 371–94.

Norton I.T., Morris E.R. & Rees D.A. 1984b. Lyotropic effects of simple anions on the conformation and interactions of $\varkappa$-carrageenan. *Carbohydr. Res.* **134**: 89–101.

Nunn J.R., Parolis H. & Russell I. 1971. Sulphated polysaccharides of the Solieriaceae family. Part I. Polysaccharide from *Anatheca dentata*. *Carbohydr. Res.* **20**: 205–15.

O'Neill M.A., Selvendran R.R. & Morris V.J. 1983. Structure of the acidic extracellular gelling polysaccharide produced by *Pseudomonas elodea*. *Carbohydr. Res.* **124**: 123–33.

Painter T.J. 1983. Algal polysaccharides. In *The Polysaccharides*. Vol. 2. (Ed. G.O. Aspinall) pp. 195–285. London: Academic Press.

Rees D.A., Morris E.R., Thom D. & Madden J.K. 1982. Shapes and interactions of carbohydrate chains. In *The Polysaccharides*. Vol. 1. (Ed. G.O. Aspinall) pp. 195–290. London: Academic Press.

Renn D.W. 1984. Agar and agarose: indispensable partners in biotechnology. *Ind. Eng. Chem. Prod. Res.* **23**: 17–21.

Saito H. 1981. Conformation, dynamics, and gelation mechanism of gel-state $(1 \rightarrow 3)$-β-D-glucans revealed by C-13 NMR. In *Solution Properties of Polysaccharides*. (Ed. D.A. Brant). American Chemical Society Symp. Series 150 pp. 125–47. Washington, DC: American Chemical Society.

Sandford P. & Baird J. 1983. Industrial utilization of polysaccharides. In *The Polysaccharides*. Vol. 2. (Ed. G.O. Aspinall) pp. 411–90. London: Academic Press.

Sato T., Norisuye T. & Fujita H. 1985. Double-stranded helix of xanthan: dissociation behavior in mixtures of water and cadoxen. *Polymer J.* **17**: 729–35.

Skjåk-Bræk G., Grasdalen H. & Larsen B. 1986a. Monomer sequence and acetylation pattern in some bacterial alginates. *Carbohydr. Res.* **154**: 239–50.

Skjåk-Bræk G., Smidsrød O. & Larsen B. 1986b. Tailoring of alginates by enzymatic modification *in vitro*. *Int. J. Biol. Macromol.* **8**: 330–6.

Smidsrød O. 1970. Solution properties of alginate. *Carbohydr. Res.* **13**: 359–72.

Smidsrød O. 1974. Molecular basis for some physical properties of alginates in the gel state. *Faraday Disc. Chem. Soc.* **57**: 263–74.

Smidsrød O. 1980. Structure and properties of charged polysaccharides. In *27th International Congress of Pure and Applied Chemistry*. (Ed. A. Varmavuori) pp. 315–27. Oxford: Pergamon Press.

Smidsrød O. & Grasdalen H. 1984. Polyelectrolytes from seaweeds. *Hydrobiologia* **116/117**: 19–28.

Smidsrød O. & Haug A. 1971. Estimation of the relative stiffness of the molecular chain in polyelectrolytes from measurements of viscosity at different ionic strengths. *Biopolymers* **10**: 1213–27.

Smidsrød O. & Haug A. 1972. Dependence upon the gel–sol state of the ion-exchange properties of alginates. *Acta Chem. Scand.* **26**: 2063–74.

Smidsrød O., Haug A. & Whittington S.G. 1972. The molecular basis for some physical properties of polyuronides. *Acta. Chem. Scand.* **26**: 2563–6.

Stokke B.T., Elgsæter A. & Smidsrød O. 1986. Electron microscopic study of single- and double-stranded xanthan. *Int. J. Biol. Macromol.*. **8**: 217–25.

Stokke B.T., Smidsrød O. & Elgsæter A. 1989. Electron microscopy of native xanthan and xanthan exposed to low ionic strength. *Biopolymers*. **28**: 617–37.

Sutherland I.W. 1985. Biosynthesis and composition of gram-negative bacterial extracellular and wall polysaccharides. *Ann. Rev. Microbiol.* **39**: 243–70.

Talashek T.A. & Brant D.A. 1987. The influence of sidechains on the calculated dimensions of three related bacterial polysaccharides. *Carbohydr. Res*. **160**: 303–16.

Valla S. 1989. *Acetobacter xylinum* as a model system for cloning of genes involved in the synthesis of cellulose. In *Cellulose and Wood-Chemistry and Technology*. (Ed. C. Schuerch) pp. 559–71. New York: John Wiley & Sons.

Valla S., Coucheron, D.H., Fjærvik E., Kjosbakken J ., Weinhouse H., Ross P., Amikam D. & Benziman M. 1989. Cloning of a gene involved in cellulose biosynthesis in *Acetobacter xylinum*; complementation of cellulose-negative mutants by the UDPG pyrophosphorylase structural gene. *Mol. Gen. Genet*. (In press).

Yanaki T., Kojima T. & Norisuye T. 1981. Triple helix of scleroglucan in dilute aqueous sodium hydroxide. *Polymer J*. **13**: 1135–43.

9 Applications of some Algal Polysaccharides in Biotechnology

GUDMUND SKJÅK-BRÆK and ANITA MARTINSEN
Norwegian Institute of Technology, Trondheim, Norway

Polysaccharides encompass an almost infinite variety of chemical structures, differing in monomeric composition, anomeric configuration, sequence, position of linkages, charge density and molecular size, and as such they exhibit a wide range of physical properties. It is this diversity in functional properties that has made polysaccharides useful industrially. The most widely used polysaccharides are still derived from terrestrial plant materials such as cellulose and starch or from marine algae yielding polymers such as agar, alginate and carrageenan. The latter group, which have the common characteristic of forming gels, have found many technical applications. These form the economic basis for the exploitation of seaweeds in the West, and have a world market value in excess of US$ 250 million per year.

Recently algal polysaccharides have found new uses in the field of biotechnology, mainly as materials for immobilization of biocatalysts, and in the present chapter we will discuss some of these new applications. Emphasis will be put on the structure–function relationships of alginate as an immobilization material.

IMMOBILIZATION

One of the greatest prospects in modern biotechnology is the use of biocatalysts in industrial processes. Biocatalysts have some remarkable features which are lacking in most non-biological catalysts:

1. They have extremely high catalytic activity.
2. They have unique specificity both for substrate and product.
3. Virtually all organic and many inorganic reactions can be catalysed.
4. Reactions can be carried out under mild conditions (normal pressure, ambient temperature and in aqueous solution.

Despite such desirable characteristics, except for a few successful applications, most chemical processes in industry are still based on traditional chemical catalysts.

Seaweed Resources in Europe: Uses and Potential. Edited by M. D. Guiry and G. Blunden
© 1991 John Wiley & Sons Ltd

This is because of some serious disadvantages in the use of enzymes, which limit their practical application:

1. They have low stability under the unfavourable operational conditions outside the cellular environment.
2. Since the catalyst is water soluble, it is difficult to handle; enzymes are lost in the process, and consequently they cannot be used in a continuous system.
3. Troublesome contamination of the product may also occur.

To circumvent these problems a major breakthrough was made two decades ago with the successful immobilization of enzymes (Zaborsky 1973).

Immobilization means that an enzyme in its soluble (mobile) state is transferred into an insoluble (immobile) state without losing its catalytic activity. This can be achieved either by cross-linking the protein molecules (making protein particles) or by binding the protein molecules to an inert insoluble material. A great number of coupling techniques and materials have been used (Zaborsky 1973; Mosbach 1976). In many cases, although the immobilized enzyme loses some of its activity, its stability under operational conditions may be greatly enhanced (Klibanov 1983).

IMMOBILIZED CELLS

Immobilized enzymes are normally used for catalysing single reactions like hydrolyses, hydroxylations, isomerizations and epimerizations, and are generally limited to reactions that do not require cofactors. Immobilized enzymes can be replaced by immobilized whole cells, which offer some advantages compared with single enzymes; isolation and purification of the enzyme can be omitted and the enzymes will in many cases be more stable inside the cell. By taking advantage of the large array of enzyme systems that are organized in living cells, and their ability to regenerate their cofactors, multi-step reactions can be performed and complex compounds like amino acids, peptides, hormones and even proteins and polysaccharides can be produced (Mattiasson 1983; Rosevear et al. 1987; Scott 1987).

Cells can be immobilized by techniques similar to those used for single enzymes to obtain some of the same advantages. Even though cells are not water soluble, they become very much easier to handle on an industrial scale after they have been immobilized. As has been found with enzymes, some cells are reported to have enhanced stability, viability and productivity in an immobilized state (Cheetham et al. 1985).

However, immobilization of living cells normally precludes the use of chemical coupling or covalent cross-linking, organic solvents, high temperature, etc. For very fragile cells, such as animal cells (Nilsson & Mosbach 1980) and plant protoplasts (Linse & Brodelius 1984), only very mild procedures, such as gel entrapment or microencapsulation in ionic hydrogels, can be used. In recent years, entrapment within spheres of calcium alginate gel and, to a lesser extent, potassium ϰ-carrageenan and agarose has become the most widely used technique for immobilizing living cells (Mattiasson 1983; Scott 1987). This kind of immobilization can be carried out in a single step under very mild conditions, and is therefore compatible with most living cells. It has been applied to a large number of different cells such as bacteria (Kierstan & Bucke 1977), cyanobacteria (Musgrave *et al.* 1982), algae (Robinson *et al.* 1986), fungi (Kopp & Rehm 1983), yeasts (Kierstan & Bucke 1977), plant protoplasts (Linse & Brodelius 1984), plant cells (Brodelius *et al.* 1979) and animal cells (Nilsson & Mosbach 1980). Such gel-entrapped cells are used as biocatalysts in several commercial processes ranging from ethanol production by yeast cells (Oda *et al.* 1983) to production of monoclonal antibodies from hybridoma cells (Jarvis & Grdima 1983). Since gel beads are easier to handle than free cells, this technique has also found many new uses in connection with handling and manipulation of cells.

Immobilization of cells by entrapping them in a hydrogel is generally carried out by mixing the cells with a water-soluble polymer, and subsequent gelling of the polymer by adding cross-linking agents (Fig. 1). For alginate and carrageenan, gelling is induced by adding cations such as calcium (Smidsrød 1974) and potassium (Tosa *et al.* 1979), respectively. With agarose, gelling is induced by cooling the preheated polymer–cell mixture (Matsunaga *et al.* 1980).

Numerous studies of cells in phycocolloid gels have been carried out. However, with a few exceptions (Klein *et al.* 1979, 1983; Cheetham 1979; Tanaka *et al.* 1984b; Martinsen *et al.* 1989), relatively little has so far been reported on the immobilization material itself. In the following account, we

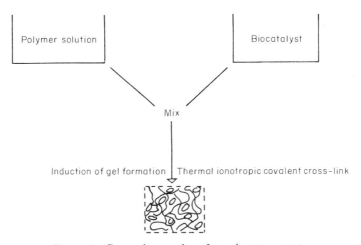

Figure 1. General procedure for gel entrapment

will discuss some properties of gels relevant to their use as immobilization materials. Since alginate gels are currently most prominent as immobilization matrices and at the same time represent the most heterogeneous group of polymers with respect to structure and properties, emphasis will be placed on this group of marine polymers.

IMMOBILIZATION MATERIALS

Agar/Agarose

For more than a century agars have been used as solid media for the growth, identification and propagation of all types of microorganisms, and of plant and animal cells. They are derived mainly from species of the red algal genera *Gelidium*, *Pterocladia* and *Gracilaria* as a heterogeneous group of variously substituted galactans with a range in functional properties depending on the source and extraction procedures. Substituents occur in naturally derived polymers as sulphate half-esters, pyruvic acid ketals or *O*-methyl groups (Painter 1983).

Agarose is the gelling component in agar. Chemically, it is a binary linear copolymer of alternating 1,3-linked β-D-galactose and 1,4-linked 3,6-anhydro-α-L-galactose containing less than 0.5% sulphate esters (see Fig. 3 in Chapter 8). Agar and agarose form strong, transparent, thermoreversible gels at concentrations of polymer greater than 0.2%. Unmodified agarose has setting and melting temperatures of about 40 and 90 °C, respectively. The melting and setting temperatures of agarose can be reduced, at the expense of the mechanical gel strength, by chemical substitution with methyl, hydroxyethyl or hydroxypropyl groups.

Carrageenan

'Carrageenans' is a collective term for partly sulphated linear polymers of β-D-galactose and 3,6-anhydro-α-D-galactose with alternating 1,4- and 1,3-linkages, as in agar. They are found in red seaweeds belonging to the families Gigartinaceae, Solieriaceae, Phyllophoraceae and Hypneaceae (see Fig. 2 in Chapter 8). The $\varkappa$-form, containing sulphate at position 4 on the D-galactose unit, gives strong thermoreversible gels in the presence of an excess of potassium ions, comparable in mechanical rigidity to agarose and alginate gels (see Fig. 24 in Chapter 8).

Alginate

Alginates, which are widely used to prepare viscous solutions and to produce gels with multivalent cations such as Ca^{2+}, can be regarded as a family of

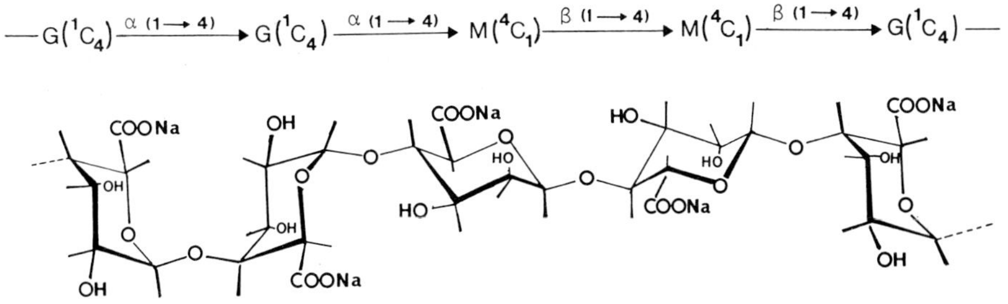

$$-G(^1C_4) \xrightarrow{\alpha\ (1\rightarrow 4)} G(^1C_4) \xrightarrow{\alpha\ (1\rightarrow 4)} M(^4C_1) \xrightarrow{\beta\ (1\rightarrow 4)} M(^4C_1) \xrightarrow{\beta\ (1\rightarrow 4)} G(^1C_4)-$$

Figure 2. Structure of sodium alginate. Alginate is a linear binary block-copolymer of D-mannuronic acid (M) and L-guluronic acid (G)

linear binary copolymers of 1,4-linked β-D-mannuronic acid (M) and its C-5 epimer α-L-guluronic acid (G) in various proportions (see Fig. 2). Its occurrence in nature is limited mainly to the marine brown algae (Painter 1983), although exocellular polymeric material resembling alginates from brown algae is also produced by soil bacteria such as *Azotobacter vinelandii* (Gorin & Spencer 1966) and several species of *Pseudomonas* (Linker & Jones 1966; Govan *et al.* 1981). The algal polymers and the deacetylated product from *A. vinelandii* form ionotrophic gels with divalent cations such as calcium.

Agar, carrageenan and alginate must be regarded as groups of polymers with a wide range of chemical composition, molecular size and, hence, of functional properties vital to their use as immobilization matrices. It is therefore important to work with well-characterized samples to obtain reproducible results.

IMMOBILIZATION PROCEDURES

Agar/Agarose

Entrapment of living cells in agarose is normally performed (Matsunaga *et al.* 1980) by mixing the cells with a warm ($\approx$40 °C) 1–3% aqueous solution of agarose and allowing the gel to set by cooling. For preparation of agarose beads, an emulsion of the polymer cell suspension is formed before cooling. Both paraffin oil and various non-toxic seed oils have been used successfully (Nilsson *et al.* 1983). To avoid high temperatures, agars with low setting and melting temperatures are best.

$\varkappa$-Carrageenan

Gel-entrapment in $\varkappa$-carrageenan is generally carried out (Kierstan & Coughlan 1985) by mixing a cell suspension with a 1–3% solution of $\varkappa$-

carrageenan (normally as the potassium salt) at 40 °C, and allowing droplets
of the mixture to fall into an aqueous solution containing potassium chloride
(0.3 M). If a low gelling temperature is essential, the cold-water-soluble
sodium or tetramethylammonium form must be used.

Alginate

Three main immobilization procedures utilize alginate as the gel matrix.

Gel entrapment

Entrapment of cells in alginate gels was initially described by Hackel *et al.*
(1975), who used aluminium ions, and by Kierstan and Bucke (1977), who used
calcium ions. This technique had, in principle, been applied for many years by
the food industry for making such products as artificial berries (Cottrell &

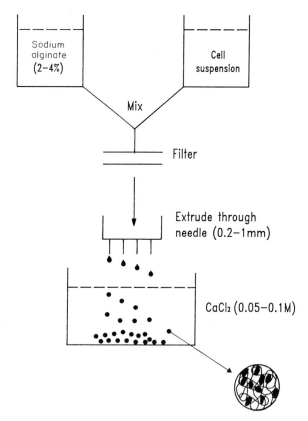

Figure 3. Gel-entrapment in calcium alginate

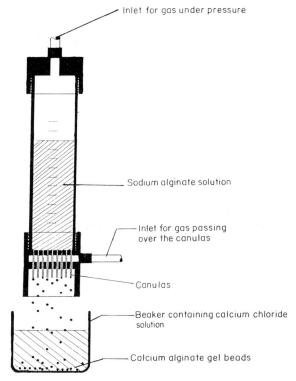

Figure 4. Preparation of calcium alginate gel beads

Kovacs 1980), and a description of the structure of calcium alginate gel beads
was published by Baardseth as early as 1965.

   Entrapment is carried out by mixing aqueous sodium alginate with cells
(see Fig. 3 and Table 1) and dripping the mixture into a solution containing
multivalent cations such as Ca^{2+}, Sr^{2+}, Ba^{2+} or Al^{3+}. The droplets will
instantaneously form gel spheres by ionotropic gelation, entrapping the cells
within the three-dimensional lattice of an ionically cross-linked polymer. The
size of the beads depends on factors such as the viscosity of the (sodium)
alginate solution, and the type and concentration of alginate. The size can be
controlled easily by applying a coaxial air stream (Klein *et al.* 1979) as shown
in Fig. 4, to blow off the droplets, and beads ranging from 200 to 5000 μm in
diameter can be made. Smaller beads (10–200 μm) require more sophisticated equipment (Klein *et al.* 1979).

Encapsulation in alginate polycation microcapsules

Another technique reported by Lim and Sun (1980), and patented as the
Encapsel technique (Lim 1981) is illustrated in Fig. 5. Cells are initially

Table 1. Procedure for immobilization of cells in calcium alginate beads

---

1. *Preparation of polymer solution* A 1.5–4% w/v aqueous solution of sodium alginate is prepared by suspending the polymer in either distilled water or a buffer. The suspension should be stirred by a magnetic stirrer for 6 h, or left overnight at room temperature on a rotary shaker.
2. *Sterilization* Alginate can be sterilized either by autoclaving or by sterile filtration. Since high temperatures will cause some depolymerization, sterile filtration is recommended. (If autoclaving is chosen, the alginate solution should be buffered to pH 5–6 before raising the temperature, and if possible an alginate with a high molecular weight and low phenolic content should be used.) The polymer solution should then be passed successively through 1.2, 0.8 and 0.45 μm membrane filters to remove particles, and finally through a 0.22 μm filter.
3. *Mixing with cells* The sterile alginate solution should be mixed with a more or less equal volume of suspended cells (10–30 g dry weight 100 ml^{-1}) to give a final polymer concentration not lower than 1% w/v. Phosphate should be avoided and multivalent cations kept at the lowest possible level in the cell suspension.
4. *Immobilization* Preparation of the gel beads is carried out by dripping the alginate cell suspension through a syringe (0.12 mm in diameter) from a height of 20 cm into a sterile aqueous solution containing 10–100 mM calcium ions. The beads should be kept in the calcium solution for at least 20 min to allow the beads to harden before they are transferred to the desired media. (Substances with high affinity for calcium ions will destabilize the gel. This precludes use of buffers containing phosphate or citrate. Destabilization will also occur by exchange with sodium, potassium and magnesium ions. It is therefore recommended that 3 mM calcium ions be included in the medium and the sodium/calcium ratio should be less than 25 : 1.)

---

entrapped in calcium alginate beads as described above. The beads are then transferred to a solution containing a polycation such as polylysine or polyornithine. The polycation forms a membrane-like complex with the polyanionic alginate on the surface of the beads, which enforces them and makes a denser network than in the alginate gel itself.

By treating the beads with citrate (0.05 M, pH 7.4) the calcium ions in the gel are sequestered, and the gel dissolved, leaving a capsule with a semipermeable polyanion–polycation membrane around a liquid core containing cells. This technique is applied by Damon Biotech Corporation, Boston, for production of monoclonal antibodies from hybridoma cells (Duff 1985), and has also been suggested for encapsulation of islets of Langerhans for the purpose of transplanting insulin-producing tissue into diabetics (Lim & Sun 1980; Tze & Tai 1982).

Similar capsules can be formed by replacing the polypeptide with either partly quaternized polyethyleneimine (Tanaka *et al.* 1984a) or chitosan (Hwang *et al.* 1986). The latter type of capsules can be made either by direct gelling of a sodium alginate droplet in a solution containing chitosan and calcium, or by mixing the cells in chitosan and calcium and allowing the suspension to drip into an alginate solution (Rha 1984). These techniques can

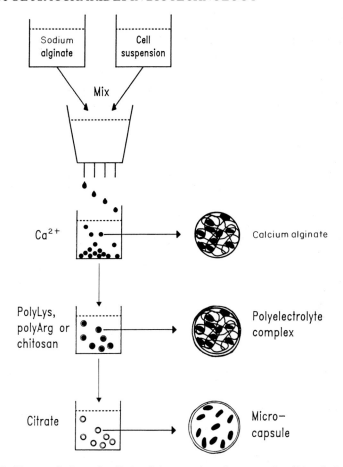

Figure 5. Encapsulation of cells in alginate polycation capsules (Lim & Sun 1980)

also be used to form hollow fibres by extruding the cell polymer mixture as a continuous stream into the gel-inducing solution (Vorlop *et al.* 1986).

Encapsulation in calcium alginate

Recently, another very simple technique has been described by Spiekerman *et al.* (1987) for making calcium alginate capsules in a one-step process. By allowing a viscous drop containing calcium ions and cells to fall into a solution of alginate, a calcium alginate gel is formed around the droplets when the calcium ions diffuse out into the alginate solution. The viscosifier has to be a non-gelling polysaccharide. Of the many different polysaccharides tested, methyl cellulose was reported to give the best results when the capsules were used for growing mouse hybridoma cells. Another possible technique for

Table 2. Advantages of gel entrapment in calcium alginate

---

1. *Gentle for the cells* Immobilization is carried out under very mild conditions resulting in little loss of viability for most cells. No chemical coupling is required, and the cells are not exposed to any harmful chemicals. The process can be performed in an isotonic buffered medium at neutral pH and at a range of temperatures from 0 to 100 °C.
2. *Rapid to produce* Reaction time varies from 2 to 30 min including hardening of the gel beads in the calcium chloride solution.
3. *Easy to sterilize* Gel entrapment can be performed easily under sterile conditions by either autoclaving or sterile filtration of the sodium alginate solution before it is mixed with the cells. Once immobilized, the cells are protected from contaminating cells.
4. *Lasting viability* Calcium alginate gels seem to be compatible with most living cells. In several cases the viability and/or enzyme activity are stabilized over considerable periods of time.

---

making calcium alginate capsules without using polymers other than alginate is described below. Further details of the gel-entrapment procedure and some characteristics of the immobilization methods and of the calcium alginate beads are summarized in Tables 1–3.

The success of the alginate gel-entrapment and encapsulation techniques is mainly due to their mildness. However, if alginate-immobilized cells are to be applied as biocatalysts in a fermenter, in a continuous system, or as carriers for transplantation of cells into a living organism, certain demands as to chemical and mechanical stability, diffusion characteristics and biocompatability have to be met.

Gel entrapment in alginate, as the technique is known today, has some major disadvantages:

1. *Low stability* Substances with high affinity for calcium ions such as phosphate or citrate will sequester the cross-linking calcium ions and consequently destabilize the gel. Since the calcium ions can be exchanged

Table 3. Characteristics of calcium alginate beads

---

1. *Easy to produce* The gel beads are easy to mass produce without any sophisticated equipment.
2. *Wide range of size* The diameter can be varied from 200 to 5000 μm, with a narrow size distribution ($\approx 10\%$).
3. *Thermostability* Calcium alginate gels are, in contrast to other phycocolloid gels, such as agar and carrageenan, stable over a temperature range of 0–100 °C.
4. *Open structure* The beads are transparent and have an open pore structure with pore sizes ranging from 50 to 2000 Å.
5. *Easy to dissolve* The beads can be dissolved under mild conditions and cells recovered without being harmed.

Table 4. Polyphenolic and protein content in some commercial alginates

Source	Proteins (%)	Polyphenols (%)[a]
Laminaria hyperborea	0.5–1.50	0.10–0.13
L. digitata	0.40–0.50	0.10
Macrocystis pyrifera	0.30–0.40	0.07
Ascophyllum nodosum	1.5	3.5–1.0
L. hyperborea	0.15	0.006[b]

[a]Determined by fluorescence spectroscopy (Skjåk-Bræk *et al.* 1989c).
[b]Sample purified by a combination of extraction procedures and chromatography on polyphenol-absorbing materials.

with other cations, the gel will also be destabilized by high concentrations of ions that do not produce gels, such as sodium and magnesium ions.

2. *High porosity* The lattice is quite open, resulting in a leakage of the biocatalyst, and the pore size distribution is wide, which makes controlled release difficult.
3. *Lack of homogeneity* Alginate cells exhibit various degrees of inhomogeneity, depending on how the gel-inducing ion is added (Skjåk-Bræk *et al.* 1986b, 1989b).
4. *Toxicity* Although alginate meets the legal requirements for additives in food and pharmaceuticals, some alginates contain small amounts of polyphenols (Skjåk-Bræk *et al.* 1989c), which might be harmful to sensitive cells. For transplantation purposes, the alginate must also be free from pyrogens (Tze & Tai 1982) and immunogenic materials such as proteins and complex carbohydrates. Table 4 gives the content of proteins and polyphenolic compounds in a range of commercial and laboratory-made alginates.

Choice of alginate type

There is of course no such thing as an ideal alginate bead to meet the requirements of all immobilized cell systems. However, alginate gel beads should ideally have high mechanical and chemical stability, controllable swelling properties, a low content of toxic, pyrogenic and immunogenic contaminants, a defined pore size, and a narrow pore-size distribution.

These criteria may be met by:

1. Selection and purification of alginates from either seaweeds or bacteria, and further refinement by chemical fractionation and modification, or by enzymatic modification.
2. Control of the gelling process.
3. Combination with other biopolymers.

Structure Selection of alginates requires some knowledge of alginate chemistry and the relationship between structure and functional properties. The monomers are arranged in a blockwise pattern along the polymeric chain, in which homopolymeric regions are interspaced with sequences containing both monomers. The proportions and sequential arrangement of the uronic acids depend on the species of alga and the kind of algal tissue from which it is prepared (Haug 1964; Smidsrød 1974). Although viscosity depends mainly on the molecular size only, the affinity for divalent ions essential for the gelforming properties is related to the content of, and sequential arrangement of, guluronic acid (G) residues (Smidsrød & Haug 1972; Smidsrød 1974).

Two consecutive diaxially linked G-residues form binding sites for calcium ions, and long sequences of such sites form cross-links with similar sequences in other alginate molecules, giving rise to junctions in the gel network (Smidsrød *et al.* 1972a, 1972b; Smidsrød 1974) (Fig. 6). This mechanism is also referred to as the egg-box model (Rees 1981). Hence, the proportion and the length of G-blocks are the main structural features contributing to gel formation (Smidsrød & Haug 1972; Skjåk-Bræk *et al.* 1986b).

Since the uronic acid residues in alginate are not randomly distributed along the chain, the sequential arrangement cannot be calculated from compositional data alone, but by measurements of diad, triad and higher-order frequencies. The four diad (nearest neighbour) frequencies, F_{GG}, F_{GM}, F_{MG} and F_{MM}, and the eight possible triad frequencies, F_{GGG}, F_{GGM}, F_{MGG}, F_{MGM}, F_{MMM}, F_{MMG}, F_{GMM} and F_{GMG} can be measured by nuclear magnetic resonance (NMR) techniques (Grasdalen *et al.* 1979, 1981; Grasdalen 1983). The relationship between the monad and the diad frequencies is given by:

$$F_{GG} + F_{MM} + F_{GM} + F_{MG} = 1 \tag{1}$$
$$F_{GG} + F_{MG} = F_G, \; F_{MM} + F_{MG} = F_M \tag{2}$$

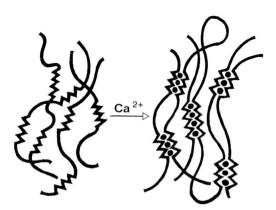

Figure 6. Egg-box model for alginate gel formation. The buckled part of the polymer represents the diaxially linked G-blocks

For long chains, where the contribution from the end-groups can be neglected, $F_{MG} = F_{GM}$. For the triad frequencies the following relationships are valid for long chains:

$$F_G = F_{GGG} + F_{MGG} + F_{GGM} + F_{MGM} \tag{3}$$
$$F_{MG} = F_{GM} = F_{GGM} + F_{MGM} \tag{4}$$
$$F_{MGG} = F_{GGM} \tag{5}$$

Knowledge of the diad and triad frequencies also allows calculation of average block length:

$$\bar{N}_G = F_G/F_{MG} \quad \text{and} \quad \bar{N}_M = F_M/F_{MG}$$

For blocks consisting of at least two contiguous units:

$$\bar{N}_{G>1} = F_G - F_{MGM}/F_{MGG} \quad \text{and} \quad \bar{N}_{M>1} = F_M - F_{GMG}/F_{MMG}$$

Commercial alginates are produced mainly from *Laminaria hyperborea*, *Macrocystis pyrifera* and *Ascophyllum nodosum*, and to a lesser extent from *L. digitata*, *L. japonica*, *Ecklonia maxima*, *Lessonia nigrescens* and species of *Sargassum*. Tables 5 and 6 give some sequential parameters (determined by high field NMR spectroscopy) for samples of these alginates. The composition and sequential structure may, however, vary seasonally and with growing conditions (Haug 1964; Indergaard & Skjåk-Bræk 1987). The highest content of α-L-guluronic acid residues is usually found in alginate prepared from stipes of old *L. hyperborea* plants. Alginates from *A. nodosum* and *L. japonica* are characterized by a low content of G-blocks and low gel strength. The alginate from *M. pyrifera*, which is most frequently used for immobilization (generally because it is the only alginate type in the Sigma Chemical Corporation catalogue), gives gels with lower strength and stability than those made from *L. hyperborea* alginates, but it is better than other alginates with the same guluronic acid content. This is because of the unusual sequential arrangements of the monomers in *Macrocystis* alginate, which is characterized by a high content of alternating structure and some very long G-blocks (Grasdalen 1983; Skjåk-Bræk *et al.* 1986b). The correlation between the average length of G-blocks and the modulus of compression is given in Fig. 7 in Chapter 8.

Alginates with more extreme compositions can be isolated from bacteria. *Azotobacter vinelandii* produces *O*-acetylated alginate with a content of L-guluronic acid ranging from 15 to 90% (Skjåk-Bræk *et al.* 1986a). *Pseudomonas aeruginosa* produces polymannuronic acid under certain conditions, but none of the alginate-producing pseudomonads is able to produce polymers containing G-blocks, and consequently these alginates are of little interest as gel-formers (Skjåk-Bræk *et al.* 1986a).

Table 5. Monad and diad frequencies in alginates

Source	F_G	F_M	F_{GG}	F_{MM}	$F_{GM,MG}$
Laminaria longicruris[a]	0.33	0.67	0.23	0.57	0.10
L. japonica	0.35	0.65	0.18	0.48	0.17
L. digitata	0.41	0.59	0.25	0.43	0.16
L. saccharina[b]					
New blade	0.35	0.65	0.25	0.55	0.10
Old blade	0.46	0.54	0.32	0.40	0.14
L. brasiliensis					
Blade	0.53	0.47	0.33	0.27	0.20
Stipe	0.54	0.46	0.31	0.23	0.23
L. hyperborea					
Blade	0.55	0.45	0.38	0.28	0.17
Stipe	0.68	0.32	0.56	0.20	0.12
Outer cortex	0.75	0.25	0.66	0.16	0.09
Saccorhiza polyschides[b]					
Blade	0.58	0.42	0.46	0.30	0.12
Stipe	0.49	0.51	0.34	0.36	0.15
Lessonia nigrescens[a]	0.38	0.62	0.19	0.43	0.19
Ecklonia maxima	0.45	0.55	0.22	0.32	0.23
Macrocystis pyrifera	0.39	0.61	0.16	0.38	0.23
Egregia laevigata[a]	0.43	0.57	0.26	0.40	0.17
Eisenia bicyclis[a]	0.38	0.62	0.25	0.49	0.13
Durvillea antarctica	0.29	0.71	0.15	0.57	0.14
Ascophyllum nodosum					
Fruiting body	0.10	0.90	0.04	0.84	0.06
Old tissue	0.36	0.64	0.16	0.44	0.20
Hormosira banksii[b]	0.39	0.61	0.35	0.57	0.04
Himanthalia elongata	0.39	0.61	0.21	0.43	0.18
Dictyosiphon foeniculaceus	0.67	0.33	0.61	0.27	0.06
Elachista fucicola	0.78	0.22	0.68	0.12	0.10
Scytosiphon lomentaria[a]	0.50	0.50	0.41	0.41	0.09

[a]Data provided by Bjørn Larsen.
[b]Data provided by Mentz Indergaard.

Alginate with a high content of guluronic acid can also be prepared from specific algal tissues such as the outer cortex of old stipes of *L. hyperborea* (see Table 5), by chemical fractionation (Rivera Carro 1985), or by enzymatic modification *in vitro* using mannuronan C-5 epimerase from *A. vinelandii* (Skjåk-Bræk *et al.* 1986b). This enzyme is able to introduce G-blocks into an existing alginate polymer, producing polymers with very good gel-forming properties.

In a recent study (Martinsen *et al.* 1989) of the correlation between structure and functional properties of alginate gel beads, it was demonstrated that the mechanical and swelling properties were strongly dependent on the monomeric composition, block structure and molecular size of the alginate molecules. Calcium alginate gels shrink during gel formation, leading to loss

Table 6. Composition and sequence parameters for some alginates

Source	F_G	F_{GG}	F_{GGG}	$\bar{N}_{G>1}$
Ascophyllum nodosum				
Old tissue	0.36	0.16	0.115	3.9
Macrocystis pyrifera	0.39	0.16	0.12	5.0
Ecklonia maxima	0.45	0.22	0.17	5.4
Laminaria digitata	0.41	0.25	0.20	6.0
L. hyperborea				
Blade	0.55	0.38	0.32	7.3
Stipe	0.68	0.56	0.50	10.3
Outer cortex	0.75	0.66	0.62	17.5

of water and an increase in the polymer concentration in the gel relative to that in the alginate solution. This is illustrated in Fig. 7, where the largest shrinkage was found in beads made from 'low-G' alginates. When alginate gel beads are used for immobilization, the shrinkage also results in an increase in the concentration of cells, a phenomenon which may explain some of the increase in catalytic activity reported for alginate gel-entrapped cells.

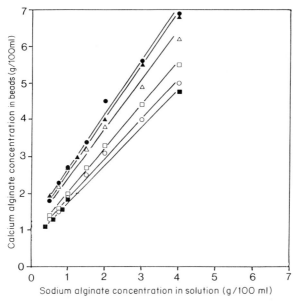

Figure 7. Calcium alginate concentration in the gel beads *versus* sodium alginate in the solution for six different types of alginate (Martinsen *et al.* 1989): ■, *Laminaria hyperborea* (outer cortex), $F_G = 0.75$; ○, *L. hyperborea* (stipe), $F_G = 0.70$; □, *L. hyperborea* (blade), $F_G = 0.55$; △, *Durvillea antarctica*, $F_G = 0.34$; ▲, *Macrocystis pyrifera*, $F_G = 0.43$; ●, *L. digitata*, $F_G = 0.41$

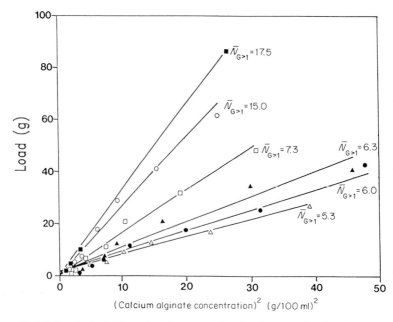

Figure 8. Mechanical rigidity of alginate gel beads given as the load necessary to compress the beads 1 mm *versus* the square of the polymer concentration for the six alginates in Fig. 7 (Martinsen *et al.* 1989)

Mechanical properties   The mechanical strength of calcium gel beads made from various types of well characterized alginates is shown in Fig. 8, and the stability towards sodium ions of two types of beads in Fig. 9. The results demonstrate that the properties of the beads vary very much with the composition of the alginate and that beads with the highest mechanical strength, the lowest shrinkage and the highest stability towards monovalent cations were made from alginate with a content of α-L-guluronic acid higher than 70% and an average of G-block length ($\bar{N}_{G>1}$) of about 15. Additionally, the turbidity of calcium gels depends on the composition, as demonstrated in Fig. 10 (Smidsrød & Haug 1972).

   As mentioned previously, the mechanical strength of alginate gels is determined mainly by the chemical composition and block structure and is independent of the molecular weight of the polymers. This is not the case, however, for low-molecular-weight alginates, and as low-viscosity alginates are preferred, because they are easier to sterilize by membrane filtration, it should be noted that below a certain critical molecular weight the gel-forming properties of alginates change rapidly.

   The effect of molecular weight on gel strength (Fig. 11) is such that, when approaching the critical overlap intrinsic viscosity given by the equation $[\eta]^* = 2.5/c$, gel strength is strongly dependent on molecular weight.

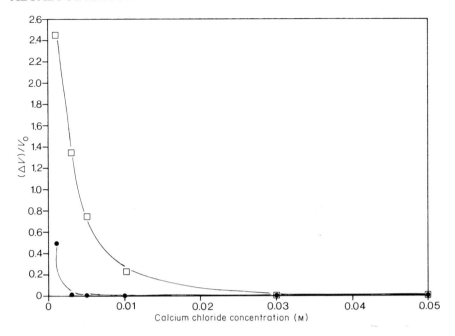

Figure 9. Swelling of calcium alginate beads in 0.9% sodium chloride solution in the presence of calcium ions. ΔV, increase in volume after swelling for 3 days; V_0, initial volume of the calcium alginate beads. ●, *Laminaria hyperborea*, $F_G = 0.70$; □, *L. digitata*, $F_G = 0.41$

Chemical stability   The major limitation of the use of calcium alginate as a cell immobilization matrix is its sensitivity towards chelating compounds, such as phosphate and lactate, or non-gelling cations such as sodium and magnesium. Various ways to overcome this have been suggested, the simplest being to keep the gel beads in a medium containing several millimoles per litre of free calcium ions. However, alginate gels can also be stabilized by replacing calcium ions with other divalent cations having a higher affinity for alginate. The affinity series for various divalent cations is (Haug 1964):

$$Pb > Cu > Cd > Ba > Sr > Ca > Co \, , \, Ni \, , \, Zn > Mn$$

In a study of the correlation between mechanical gel strength and affinity for cations (Smidsrød & Haug 1972), it was shown that the rigidity of alginate gels generally increased with affinity except in the case of cadmium and nickel:

$$Pb > Cu, \, Ba > Sr > Ni > Cd > Ca > Zn > Co > Mn$$

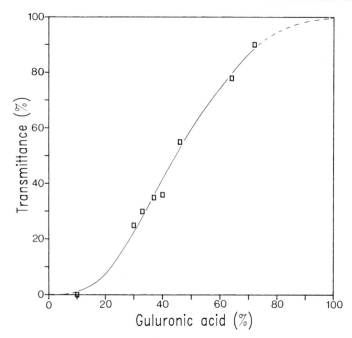

Figure 10. Light transmittance in calcium alginate gels as a function of the chemical composition of the alginates (Smidsrød & Haug 1972)

Because of their high toxicity, the use of lead, copper and cadmium is strictly limited and only stabilization with strontium and barium (Hiemstra *et al.* 1983) can be used for entrapment of living cells. Stabilization of calcium alginate gels by adding other multivalent ions such as Ti^{3+} (Burns *et al.* 1985) and Al^{3+} (Rochefort *et al.* 1986) have been reported.

Alginate forms strong complexes with polycations such as chitosan (Rha 1984), polypeptides (Lim & Sun 1980), and synthetic polymers such as polyethylenimine (Veliky & Williams 1981; Tanaka *et al.* 1984a). These complexes do not dissolve in the presence of calcium chelators or non-gelling cations, and can thus be used both for stabilization of the gel and in reducing porosity.

A common approach to the stabilization of alginate gels is covalent cross-linking. Various techniques have been used, including direct cross-linking of the carboxyl groups with glutaraldehyde. A two-step method consists of activating the polymer by either carbon diimide or periodate oxidation before gel formation, followed by cross-linking the beads with polyethyleneimine (Birnbaum *et al.* 1981). Covalent grafting of alginate with polyacrylamide has been described (Rosevear 1981; Kuu & Polack 1983), which results in gels with improved stability and mechanical strength. However, all these techni-

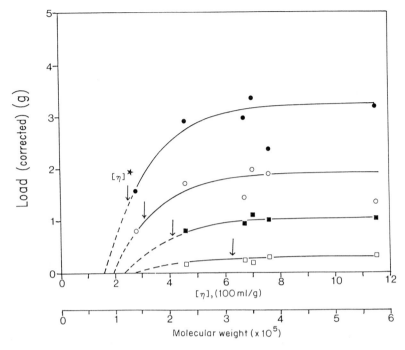

Figure 11. Mechanical rigidity of calcium alginate beads from *Laminaria hyperborea* (outer cortex) alginate ($F_G = 0.75$; $N_{G>1} = 17.5$) at different concentrations as a function of molecular weight. Arrows indicate the critical overlap intrinsic viscosity, $[\eta]^*$ (Martinsen *et al.* 1989). ●, 1%; ○, 0.8%; ■, 0.6%; □, 0.4% (w/v)

ques involve reactive chemicals and their applications are mainly limited to immobilization of either enzymes or dead cells.

Porosity   Diffusion characteristics are essential for the use of alginate gels. It is therefore important to know the pore sizes and the pore size distribution. Diffusion of smaller molecules seems to be little affected by the alginate gel matrix (Tanaka *et al.* 1984b), whereas transport of molecules by convection is restricted by the gel network. The self-diffusion of small molecules like glucose and ethanol has been reported to be as high as 90% of the diffusion rate in water (Tanaka *et al.* 1984b; Axelson & Persson 1987). The diffusion rate depends, however, on the cell load of the beads. For larger molecules, such as proteins, diffusional resistance occurs, although even large proteins with molecular weights in excess of 3×10^5 Da will leak out of the gel beads at a rate dependent on their molecular size (Tanaka *et al.* 1984b; Martinsen *et al.* 1989). The highest diffusion rates of proteins, indicating the most open pore structure, are found in beads made from high-G alginates (Klein *et al.* 1983;

Martinsen *et al.* 1989). This might be related to the lower shrinkage of these types of gels.

The porosity of alginate gels has been studied by various techniques (Andresen *et al.* 1977; Klein *et al.* 1983; Tanaka *et al.* 1984b; Axelson & Persson 1987; Casson & Emery 1987). An electron micrograph of a 2% calcium alginate gel (Fig. 12) shows pores ranging from 5 to 200 nm. The pore size distribution in a lead alginate gel determined from an electron micrograph is shown in Fig. 13. Using another approach, Klein *et al.* (1983) determined porosity by packing alginate gel beads in columns and recording the exclusion volumes for standard macromolecules. Their results indicated a cut-off value of the order of 12–16 nm, suggesting a more narrow network on the bead surface than in the gel core. Such 'skin formation' has also been reported by Cheetham *et al.* (1982), who found that gel beads made from guluronic acid-rich alginates were characterized by the occurrence of a dense, highly polymerized skin around a looser core.

The gelling process   Anisotropy of alginate gels of the type mentioned above is probably determined by the kinetics of the gel formation rather than the composition of the alginate molecules. Calcium alginate gels made in the laboratory are very different from the native gels found in *Laminaria hyperborea* stipes (Andresen *et al.* 1977). The native gel is not only 50 times stronger (against compression), but has smaller pores and a more uniform pore size distribution than artificial gels containing the same type and the same concentration of polymer. Of course, the formation of calcium alginate

Figure 12. Electron micrograph of a calcium alginate gel (Skjåk-Braek *et al.* 1989a)

gels *in vivo* is a very complex process. It involves the enzymatic introduction of G-blocks by a C-5 epimerase in the presence of calcium ions, and it is possible that the enzyme modifies two alginate chains simultaneously and literally 'sews' them together. The simulation of such natural processes is a very difficult task. However, alginate gels are non-equilibrium gels, and consequently their properties will depend on how they are made. Because gel formation *in vivo* is taking place in the presence of a mixture of several gelling and non-gelling ions (Ca^{2+}, Sr^{2+}, Ba^{2+}, Na^+ and Mg^{2+}), we have recently studied gel formation by allowing the gel-inducing ion to diffuse into the polymer solution in the presence of non-gelling cations (Skjåk-Bræk *et al.* 1989b). Calcium gels of alginate or pectate (but not *ϰ*-carrageenan) exhibited various degrees of inhomogeneity. Depending on how the calcium ions were added, a high polymer concentration at the polymer/calcium solution interface and decreasing concentration towards the centre of the gel was sometimes observed. This heterogeneity is probably a result of an irreversible gelling mechanism characterized by strong site binding of cross-linking ions. When the gel was formed in the presence of a non-gelling cation, homogeneous calcium alginate gels were formed. This might explain some of the differences in strength and structure between natural and laboratory-made gels.

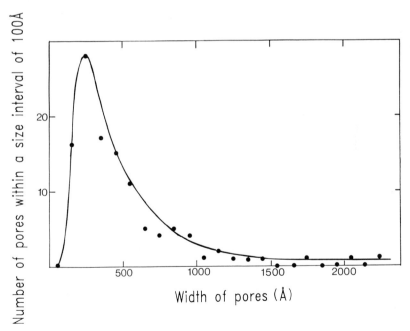

Figure 13. Pore size distribution in a 2% lead alginate gel as revealed by electron microscopy (Andresen *et al.* 1977)

The inhomogeneity of alginate gels formed by diffusion seemed to be further governed by the rate of diffusion of calcium ions into the gel relative to the rate of self-diffusion of the polymer molecules inside the beads. This implies that it is determined in part by the dimensions of the gel, because the smaller these are the steeper are the polymer concentration gradients.

By varying these factors, the distribution of polymer in the gel can be controlled, and alginate beads with a capsular structure (i.e. with a polymer concentration of about 10% on the surface and less than 0.2% in the core, as shown in Fig. 14) have been made without adding polycations or any other non-gelling polymer.

Homogeneous alginate gels can also be made by internal release of calcium from calcium EDTA (Toft 1982; Skjåk-Bræk *et al.* 1986b) or from calcium citrate (Pelaez & Karel 1981) in the presence of a slow acidifier like glucono-δ-lactone (GDL). The alginate molecules are then 'locked' in a mixed H^+-Ca^{2+} gel, which can be converted into the complete calcium form by dialysis against a calcium chloride solution (Skjåk-Bræk *et al.* 1986b). By applying this technique for immobilizing cells, alginate gels with various shapes can be made (Flink & Johansen 1985). However, because of the acidifier and the low

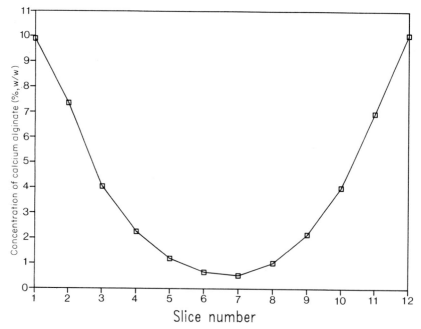

Figure 14. Concentration profile of calcium alginate in a gel cylinder formed by dialysing a 4% (w/v) aqueous solution of low molecular weight ($[\eta] = 3(100 \, \text{ml g}^{-1})$) sodium alginate from *Laminaria hyperborea* (outer cortex) against 0.01 M calcium chloride (Skjåk-Bræk *et al.* 1989b)

pK values of the calcium complexing agents, the pH in the gel would have to be between 3 and 4 to obtain gel formation, which is too low for many living cells.

Combination with other polymers   Several of the procedures mentioned above for stabilizing alginate gels will also have some influence on the porosity. Polyethylenimine (Tanaka *et al.* 1984a) and acrylate/methacrylate (Hartmeier & Heinrichs 1986) have been used to retain soluble enzymes in the beads. Likewise, formation of polyanion–polycation membranes with polypeptides or chitosan has been used to prevent diffusion of antibodies through the capsular membrane. The Encapsel techniques (Lim 1981) have been used for generating certain cut-off values for proteins. By controlling the molecular weight of the polycations (Goosen *et al.* 1984) pore sizes below certain cut-off values have been obtained. The influence of the polycation on the pore size distribution is, however, not clear. Treatment of calcium alginate beads with Zn^{2+} ions (Gray & Dowsett 1988) has been reported to prevent leakage of insulin out of the gel. Similar results were obtained with glycoamylase immobilized in ferric alginate (Klein *et al.* 1983). This is most probably due to some interaction between the multivalent ions and the proteins rather than an effect on gel porosity.

Finally, the porosity of calcium alginate gel may easily be reduced by partially drying the beads (Klein *et al.* 1979; Burns *et al.* 1985). Provided the beads are made out of an alginate rich in guluronic acid, the beads will not re-swell significantly in water (Skjåk-Bræk *et al.* 1989d).

Comparison of alginate, ×-carrageenan and agar/agarose as immobilization matrices

The gel made from either a good ×-carrageenan or high-quality agarose can be compared mechanically with a calcium alginate gel formed from *L. hyperborea* stipe alginate (see Fig. 24 in Chapter 8). Agarose gels are the most brittle. Due to strong site-binding of the cross-linking cations, alginate forms a gel very rapidly, independently of temperature, and perfectly spheri-cal, transparent beads are thus produced. By varying the gelling conditions (including the presence of non-gelling ions), the distribution of the polymer in the gel beads can be controlled (Skjåk-Bræk *et al.* 1989a).

In contrast, the formation of a ×-carrageenan gel with potassium ions is a slower process induced by an increase in ionic strength; hence, carrageenan beads are rarely spherical, but are homogeneous. Spherical agarose/agar gel beads are normally formed either by emulsion techniques or by cooling melted drops of agarose in an oil bath, but agarose beads can also be formed either by a moulding technique or by mechanical disintegration of an agarose gel block (Brodelius 1983).

Alginate gels have the most open structure, and x-carrageenan and agarose form denser networks, but none of these is well suited for immobilization of soluble enzymes without additional treatment.

With regard to chemical stability, x-carrageenan and agarose gels are superior to alginate gels in the presence of phosphate or other metabolites with an affinity for calcium ions. However, if recovery of cells from the beads is required, an alginate gel would be preferable.

As ionic gels, calcium alginate and potassium x-carrageenan will be destabilized in the presence of high concentrations of non-gelling salts, including Mg^{2+}, K^+ and Na^+ for alginate and Na^+ for x-carrageenan. Because of the highly selective binding of multivalent cations, alginate gels might also deplete nutritive media of essential trace metals. However, the charge on the polymer network in anionic gels appears to stabilize biological activity rather than harming living cells (Brodelius 1983).

In contrast to alginate and carrageenan, agarose gels have a very low charge and as such will not be affected by or interact with cations. These properties, which have made agarose gels so attractive as a separation medium in electrophoresis and chromatography of charged species, can also be an advantage for immobilization purposes, as binding of charged nutrients or products to the gel can be minimized. The use of agarose as an immobilization material is limited, however, mainly by its high price.

APPLICATIONS

ALGINATES

Chemical Production

Cells immobilized with alginate have been investigated for many different applications, some of which are listed in Table 7. The most popular appears to be production of ethanol from various carbohydrates. The organism of choice is the well characterized *Saccharomyces cerevisiae*, which is now used for commercial production of ethanol from glucose in Japan. Other microorganisms have been evaluated, and a yeast, *Kluyveromyces* sp. (Marwaha & Kennedy 1984b), and a bacterium, *Zymomonas mobilis* (Klein & Kressdorf 1984), have some potential.

Carbohydrates other than glucose have also been investigated. This includes D-xylose (Linko *et al.* 1986) and more complex (and cheaper) carbohydrates such as cellobiose (Jain & Ghose 1984), lactose (Marwaha & Kennedy 1984a) and starch (Tanaka *et al.* 1986). In these latter cases, mixed cell cultures are needed to convert the substrate into ethanol, and co-immobilization of two cell types or of a cell and a single enzyme in alginate gel beads has been shown to be effective. These systems consist of one type of

Table 7. Examples of alginate immobilized cells

Cells	Product	References
Bacteria		
Alcaligenes sp.	Degrading of 4-chlorophenol	Westmeier & Rehm (1985)
Arthrobacter simplex	Prednisolone	Kloosterman & Lilly (1986)
Clostridium acetobutylicum	Acetone/butanol	Schoutens *et al.* (1984)
Erwinia rhapontici	Isomaltulose	Cheetham *et al.* (1985)
Gluconobacter oxydans	Dihydroxyacetone	Holst *et al.*(1982)
Lactobacillus bulgaricus	Lactic acid	Steenroos *et al.* (1981)
Leuconostoc oenos	Wine	Spettoli *et al.* (1984)
Methanosarcina barkeri	Methane	Scherer *et al.* (1981)
Mycobacterium sp.	Ethylene oxide	Bont *et al.* (1983)
Klebsiella pneumonia	2,3-butanediol cellobiose	Lee & Maddox (1986)
Pseudomonas sp.	L-thyrosine	Stöcklein *et al.* (1983)
P. denitrificans	Drinking water	Nilsson *et al.* (1979)
Zymomonas mobilis	Ethanol	Klein & Kressdorfer (1984)
Blue-green algae		
Anabaena sp.	Ammonia	Musgrave *et al.* (1982)
Synechococcus sp.	Glutamate	Matsunaga *et al.* (1988)
Fungi		
Aspergillus niger	Citric acid	Eikmeier & Rehm (1987)
Aureobasidium pullulans	Glucoamylase	Federici *et al.* (1987)
Claviceps purpurea	Alkaloids and ergotoxins	Kopp & Rehm (1983)
Kluyveromyces bulgaricus	Hydrolysis of whey	Decleire *et al.* (1985)
K. marxianus	Ethanol	Marwaha & Kennedy (1984)
Penicillium chrysogenum	Penicillin	Abdel-Halim *et al.* (1986)
Pichia etchellsii	Hydrolysis of whey	Jain & Ghose (1984)
Streptomyces parvullus	Actinomycin	Dalili & Chau (1986)
S. tendae	Nikkomycin	Veelken & Pape (1984)
Fusarum sp.	Gibberellic acid	Kahlon & Malhotra (1986)
Saccharomyces cerevisiae	Ethanol	Oda *et al.* (1983)
	Glycerol	Bisping & Rehm (1984)
Algae		
Dunaliella tertiolecta	Glycerol	Grizeau & Navarro (1986)
Botryococcus braunii	Hydrocarbons	Bailliez *et al.* (1985)
Chlorella sp.	Oxygen	Adlercreutz & Mattiasson (1982)
Plant cells		
Catharanthus roseus	Alkaloids	Brodelius (1983)
Daucus carota	Alkaloids	
Digitalis lanata	Digitoxins	Alferman *et al.* (1980)
Mammalian cells		
Hybridoma	Monoclonal antibodies	Duff (1985)
Islets of Langerhans	Insulin	Lim & Sun (1980)
Fibroblasts	Interferon β	Jarvis & Grdima (1983)
Lymphoma cells	Interferon α	Jarvis & Grdima (1983)
Rat hepatocytes	Detoxification of blood	Tompkins *et al.* (1988)

Table 8. Examples of co-immobilized systems in phycocolloid gels

Organisms	Organism/enzyme	Product	Material	References
Gluconobacter suboxidans	*Chlorella sorokiniana*	Sodium gluconate	Alginate	Callegari *et al.* (1987)
Aspergillus awamori	*Streptococcus lactis*	L-Lactic acid	Alginate	Kurosawa *et al.* (1988)
A. awamori	*Zymomonas mobilis*	Ethanol	Alginate	Tanaka *et al.* (1986)
Zymomonas mobilis	β-Galactosidase	Ethanol	Alginate	Lee & Woodward (1983)
Saccharomyces cerevisiae	β-Glucosidase	Ethanol	Alginate	Hahn-Hägerdal (1984)
Parococcus denitrificans	*Corynobacterium* sp.	L-Phenylalanine	ϰ-carrageenan	Nishida *et al.* (1987)

organism with a capacity to degrade polysaccharides or oligosaccharides into monosaccharides which can then serve as substrates for an ethanol-producing organism. Using starch as a feedstock, Tanaka et al. (1986) have described a system based on an aerobic amyolytic mould, *Aspergillus awamori*, co-immobilized in calcium alginate beads with an anaerobic bacterium, *Zymomonas mobilis*, serving as an ethanol producer. The aerobic mould mycelium grows on the outside or in the outer part of the gel beads, leaving the bacteria in the anaerobic core. By replacing the bacteria with a lactic acid-producing bacterium, *Streptococcus cerevisiae*, lactic acid could be produced from starch (Kurosawa et al. 1988).

Waste material such as cheese whey has also been considered as a feed-stock for producing ethanol and other chemicals by *Kluyveromyces* sp. (Marwaha & Kennedy 1984b; Hahn-Hägerdal 1985), or by co-immobilization of a β-galactosidase, either as a free enzyme or in a cell with *Saccharomyces cerevisiae* (Hartmeier et al. 1984) or Z. *mobilis*. Other examples of mixed cell systems successfully co-immobilized in hydrocolloid gel are listed in Table 8.

Cells immobilized in alginate are also used for production of other chemicals such as ethylene oxide, butanediol and isomaltulose (see Table 7).

Food and Beverage Production

Cells immobilized in alginate have also been evaluated for production of various alcohol-containing beverages. A continuous process for the brewing of beer using alginate-immobilized yeast has been described by Onaka et al. (1985). It offers some advantages over traditional batch fermentation and a significant reduction in production time has been reported in Japan (Onaka et al. 1985).

In the wine industry, immobilized *Lactobacillus* has been evaluated for enhancement of malolactic fermentation (Gestrelius 1981; Spettoli et al. 1984). However, of more interest is the use of immobilized yeast in the production of sparkling wine (Durand et al. 1985). The best sparkling wines are produced by the *méthode champenoise*, which entails a secondary fermentation in the bottle after the addition of sugar to the fermented wine. This produces enough carbon dioxide for a sparkling effect, but also forms sediments of yeast cells and cellular debris, which must be removed completely before the wine can be offered for sale. The process consists of continually giving the bottles a sharp twist which slides the lees towards the cork of the bottle before it is removed by a special freezing technique. Such a time-consuming and expensive process can be reduced by carrying out the secondary fermentation with alginate-immobilized yeast cells, which are much easier to remove from the bottles than free cells. This technique is at present being evaluated by several producers.

Biomedical Applications

The biotechnology industry has focused considerable interest on potential biomedical applications of immobilized systems. The main areas of interest have been the production of pharmaceuticals such as antibiotics, and assessment of mammalian cell culture systems for production of monoclonal antibodies and proteins such as interferons. Cells entrapped in alginate gels have been used for the production of a range of pharmaceuticals, including antibiotics, alkaloids and steroids, although not on a commercial scale. Some examples are listed in Table 7.

In the field of mammalian cell cultures, however, commercial production is taking place in the USA of monoclonal antibodies from alginate-encapsulated hybridoma cells (Duff 1985). In a process originally described by Lim and Sun (1980), hybridomas are immobilized in capsules made from calcium alginate and polylysine, as described previously. This technique has been adopted by Damon Biotech in Boston, USA, for production of monoclonal antibodies on a large scale. These are produced for diagnostic purposes, for use in large-scale separation of other high-cost mammalian cell products, and in cancer therapy. The cells are protected against shear forces and mechanical stress inside the capsules, and cell densities much higher than conventional suspension cultures can be achieved. Cell densities larger than 10^8 cells ml^{-1} and concentrations of monoclonal antibodies as high as 0.5–3 mg ml^{-1} have been reported (Duff 1985). By controlling the porosity of the polyanion–polycation membrane the antibodies are retained inside the capsules, separate from any contaminating antibodies in the growth medium. This greatly facilitates downstream processing and purification after the capsules have been harvested.

The original idea (Lim & Sun 1980) of using encapsulated insulin-producing cells as a bioartificial pancreas is being investigated by Damon Biotech in the USA and the Connought Group in Canada. Islets of Langerhans are being encapsulated within a semipermeable membrane, which allows transport of insulin out of the capsules. The idea is to implant such capsules into the body of a patient suffering from *diabetes mellitus* and thus provide the recipient with a constant supply of insulin. The capsule membrane must have a defined pore size or a narrow pore size distribution, preventing immunogenic attack from the body immunoglobulins, and at the same time open enough to release insulin. Transplants of encapsulated islets have already been successfully achieved in rats and dogs, but implantation in humans has not yet been reported. Whether this technique, or the alternative approach of using direct transplants of immunogenically clean islets, are potential alternatives to the present treatment with insulin injections remains to be seen.

Other Applications

Immobilized cells are not only used for the production of metabolites. Gel beads are easier to handle than free cells, and at the same time the gel matrix provides the cells with a protective barrier to infection, mechanical stress and desiccation. Thus gel immobilization has found many new uses in the mass handling of cells.

A good example is the handling of fragile cells such as plant protoplasts (Linse & Brodelius 1984; Linsefors & Brodelius 1985), which are very sensitive to mechanical stress. The gel gives the protoplasts mechanical support to balance turgor pressure and to withstand external pressure. In addition, it protects against fluctuations in pH, temperature and ionic strength, thus improving cell survival. Protoplasts that have been entrapped in alginate and agarose gels include those of *Daucus carota*, *Vicia fabia* (Linse & Brodelius 1984), *Brassica napus*, *Nicotiana sandrea*, *Solanum juzepszukii* and *Panax ginseng* (Draget *et al.* 1988b). Alginate immobilization has also been described as a simple method for preparation of transmission electron micrographs of protoplasts (Draget *et al.* 1988a).

Some very promising potentially large-scale applications of gels are found in the field of agriculture. The application of gels for synthetic seed technology is especially interesting. Alginate gel-entrapment techniques, marketed by the California-based company Plant Genetics under the trade name Gelcoat®, have been adapted to a wide range of agricultural uses such as encapsulation of somatic embryos and pregerminated seeds (Fujii *et al.* 1987). An additional benefit is the possibility for co-immobilization of the seeds with nutrients, herbicides or fungicides. The possibility of co-immobilization can also be extended to symbiotic organisms such as the nitrogen-fixing bacterium *Rhizobium* with soya beans (Jung & Mugnier 1983) or other legumes, or to higher plant fungi such as Mycorrhiza with various trees.

Alginate beads have also been applied directly for encapsulation of herbicides as a controlled-release approach to weed control (Duncan & Rawson 1984). Both chemical and biological herbicides have been investigated, including mycoherbicides from the fungi *Alternaria cassiae* and *Phyllosticta sorghicola*. Filaments of these fungi are entrapped in calcium alginate beads, where they grow and develop infectious spores. Such beads may be applied directly to the soil, or the spores may be recovered from the beads and distributed in a foliar spray. Another potential use of alginate gel beads is in biological insect control. Kaya and Nelsen (1985), in a very interesting study, showed how alginate-immobilized entomogeneous nematodes could be used for infecting some host insects. Steinernematid and Heterorhabditid nematodes were entrapped in calcium alginate gel beads and fed to host insects, which became infected.

CARRAGEENAN

Only $\varkappa$-carrageenan has found uses in biotechnology as an immobilization matrix for microorganisms. Several commercial processes for production of ethanol and organic acids by microorganisms entrapped in $\varkappa$-carrageenan have been developed by Chibata and co-workers in Osaka, Japan. Examples include a continuous process for the bioconversion of fumaric acid into L-malic acid, exploiting a single enzyme activity, fumarase, in cells of *Brevibacterium flavum* (Takata *et al.* 1982; Chibata *et al.* 1983, 1987). L-Malic acid is applied in the food industry as an acidulant and is produced exclusively by enzymes in industry. Single-enzyme activities of entrapped microbial cells are also used for the production of amino acids (Chibata *et al.* 1986).

Aspartic acid is made from fumaric acid and ammonia by the action of aspartase from immobilized *Escherichia coli* cells (Chibata *et al.* 1986). A continuous process for the bioconversion of L-aspartic acid into L-alanine by the action of aspartate β-decarboxylase from carrageenan-entrapped cells of *Pseudomonas dacunhae* has been developed by the same group (Takamatsu *et*

Table 9. Examples of $\varkappa$-carrageenan immobilized cells

Cells	Product	References
Bacteria		
Acetobacter aceti	Vinegar	Tezuka (1983)
Bacillus subtilis	α-Amylase	Chevalier & De la Noue (1987)
B. polymyxa	Butane-2,3-diol	Willets (1988)
Brevibacterium flavum	L-Malic acid	Chibata *et al.* (1983)
		Chibata *et al.* (1987)
	L-Glutamate	Karube *et al.* (1987)
Clostridium acetobutylicum	Acetone/butanol	Frick & Schuegerl (1986)
Escherichia coli	L-Aspartic acid	Chibata *et al.* (1986)
Lactobacillus sp.	Wine	Crapisi *et al.* (1987)
Pseudomonas dacunhae	L-Alanine	Takamatsu *et al.* (1983)
P. putida	L-Aspartic acid	Michelet *et al.* (1984)
Zymomonas mobilis	Ethanol	Klein & Kressdorft (1984)
Fungi		
Candida tropicalis	Citric acid	Potvin *et al.* (1988)
Conidiobolus sp.	Proteases	Sutar *et al.* (1986)
Saccharomyces cerevisiae	Ethanol	Wada *et al.* (1979)
Penicillium chrysogenum	Penicillin-G	Deo & Gaucher (1984)
Pichia farinosa	Glycerol	Vijaikishore & Karanth (1986)
Algae		
Scenedesmus sp.	Drinking water	Chevalier & De la Noue (1985)
Plant cells		
Daucus carota		Linse & Brodelius (1984)

al. 1983). Other applications of carrageenan-entrapped cells are listed in Table 9.

AGAR/AGAROSE

In addition to its use as a medium support, applications of agar and agarose in biotechnology include electrophoresis, gene mapping, and the separation and isolation of DNA fragments. Beaded agarose is also one of the main chromatography materials used in separation of biological macromolecules. This includes gel-permeation chromatography, ion-exchange and affinity chromatography. Cross-linked agarose beads are also used widely as a matrix for immobilization of free enzymes. These aspects of agarose are treated extensively elsewhere (Meer 1980; Anonymous 1988) and will not be discussed further in this chapter.

Table 10. Examples of agar/agarose immobilized cells

Cells	Product	References
Bacillus megaterium	L-Aspartic acid	Cannon (1984)
Saccharomyces cerevisiae	Ethanol	Okawa T. (1986)
Yeast	Beer	Li & Ye (1986)
Kluyveromyces marxianus	Ethanol	Bajpai & Margaritis (1985)
Pichia stipitis	Ethanol	Linko *et al.* (1986)
Tagetes minuta	Secondary metabolites	Ketel *et al.* (1987)
Islets of Langerhans	Insulin	Gin *et al.* (1987)
Hybridomas	Monoclonal antibodies	Nilsson *et al.* (1983)
Lymphoblastoids	Interleukins	Nilsson *et al.* (1983)

However, agar and agarose are also used for gel-entrapment and encapsulation of a wide range of cells, either for the production of metabolites or, as with alginate and ϰ-carrageenan, as an easier way of handling cells. For incorporation and recovery of heat-labile material, low setting and melting temperatures are essential, and a range of low-melting agars is commercially available. Some examples of agar/agarose-entrapped cells are listed in Table 10.

CONCLUSIONS

Cells entrapped in phycocolloid gels have many potential applications in biotechnology, ranging from biocatalysts in fermentation to artificial seeds in agriculture and carrier materials for transplantation of living tissue. However, since the gelling material is a heterogeneous group of polymers, with a wide range of functional properties, their success as immobilization matrices will depend on a proper choice of material and methodology for each application. This must be based on knowledge of the chemical composition, correlations between structure and functional properties, and a deeper understanding of the behaviour of polysaccharide solutions and gels on the macroscopic as well as at the molecular level. As they are quite difficult to characterize chemically, manufacturers should give more detailed information about their products, including, for example, sources, chemical composition, molecular weights, filterability and gel-forming characteristics. For work with living cells, especially in the biomedical area, the polymers should have a low content of contaminating materials such as metal ions, polyphenols, proteins and complex carbohydrates.

ACKNOWLEDGEMENTS

We are grateful to our colleagues in Trondheim: to Professor Bjørn Larsen and Dr Mentz Indergaard for providing us with NMR data of various alginates, and to Professors T. J. Painter and O. Smidsrød, and Technician W. Strand for valuable help with this manuscript.

REFERENCES

Abdel-Halim M., El-Sayed M. & Rehm H.J. 1986. Morphology of *Penicillium chrysogenum* strains immobilized in calcium alginate beads and used in penicillin fermentation. *Appl. Microbiol. Biotechnol.* **24**: 89–94.

Adlercreutz P. & Mattiasson B. 1982. Oxygen supply to immobilized cells. I. Oxygen production by immobilized *Chlorella pyrenoidosa*. *Enzyme Microb. Technol.* **4**: 332–6.

Alfermann A.W., Schuller I. & Reinhardt E. 1980. Biotransformation of cardiac glycosides by immobilized cells of *Digitalis lanata*. *Planta Medica* **40**: 218–23.

Andresen I.L., Skipnes O., Smidsrød O., Østgaard K. & Hemmer P.C. 1977. Some biological functions of matrix components in benthic algae in relation to their chemistry and the composition of seawater. *Am. Chem. Soc. Symp.* **48**: 361–81.

Anon. 1988. Agarose monograph. In *FMC Bio-Products Source Book*. pp. 51–106. Rockland, Maine: Food Manufacturing Corp.

Axelson A. & Persson B. 1987. Determination of effective diffusion coefficients in calcium alginate gel plates with varying cell content. In *Proceedings of the Fourth European Congress on Biotechnology*. Vol. 1. (Eds. O.M. Neijssel, R.R. van der Meer & K.C.A.M. Luyben). Amsterdam: Elsevier.

Baardseth E. 1965. Localization and structure of alginate gels. In *Proceedings of the Fifth International Seaweed Symposium*. (Eds. E.G. Young & J.L. McLachlan) pp. 19–28. Oxford: Pergamon Press.

Bailliez C., Largeau C. & Casadevall E. 1985. Growth and hydrocarbon production of *Botryococcus braunii* immobilized in calcium alginate gel. *Appl. Microbiol. Biotechnol.* **23**: 99–105.

Bajpai P. & Margaritis A. 1985. Immobilization of *Kluyveromyces marxianus* cells with inulinase in agar. *J. Gen. Appl. Microbiol.* **31**: 297–303.

Birnbaum S., Pendelton R., Larsson P.O. & Mosbach K. 1981. Covalent stabilization of alginate gel for the entrapment of living whole cells. *Biotechnol. Lett.* **3**: 393–400.

Bisping B. & Rehm H.J. 1984. Production of glycerol by immobilized yeast cells. *Third Eur. Congr. Biotechnol.* **2**: 125–31.

Bont J.A.M. de, van Ginkel C.G., Tramper J. & Luyben K.C.A.M. 1983. Ethylene oxide production by immobilized *Mycobacterium* Py1 in a gas–solid bioreactor. *Enzyme Microb. Technol.* **5**: 55–9.

Brodelius P. 1983. Immobilized plant cells. In *Immobilized Cells and Organelles.* Vol. I. (Ed. B. Mattiasson) pp. 27–55. Boca Raton, Florida: CRC Press.

Brodelius P., Deus B., Mosbach K. & Zenk M.H. 1979. Immobilized plant cells for the production and transformation of natural products. *FEBS Lett.* **103**: 93–7.

Burns M.A., Kvesitadze G.I. & Graves D.J. 1985. Dried calcium alginate/magnetite spheres: a new support for chromatographic separations and enzyme immobilization. *Biotechnol. Bioeng.* **27**: 137–45.

Callegari J.P., Van den Broeck L., Simkens E., De Wannenmaeker B. & Simon J.P. 1987. Growth kinetics and photosynthetic oxygen evolution by *Chlorella* immobilized in calcium alginate. In *Proceedings of the Seventh International Congress on Photosynthesis.* (Ed. J. Biggins) pp. 399–402. Dordrecht: Nijhoff.

Cannon J.J. 1984. *Immobilization of Active Microorganisms in Agar Gel Fibers.* European Patent Application No. EP 125105 A2.

Casson D. & Emery A.N. 1987. On the elimination of artefactual effects in assessing the structure of calcium alginate cell immobilization gels. *Enzyme Microb. Technol.* **9**: 102–6.

Cheetham P.S.J. 1979. Physical studies on the mechanical stability of columns of calcium alginate gel pellets containing entrapped microbial cells. *Enzyme Microb. Technol.* **1**: 183–8.

Cheetham P.S.J., Imber C.E. & Isherwood J. 1982. The formation of isomaltulose by immobilized *Erwinia rhapontici. Nature Lond.* **299**: 628–31.

Cheetham P.S.J., Garrett C. & Clark J. 1985. Isomaltulose production using immobilized cells. *Biotechnol. Bioeng.* **27**: 471–80.

Chevalier P. & De la Noue J. 1985. Wastewater nutrient removal with microalgae immobilized in carrageenan. *Enzyme Microb. Technol.* **7**: 621–4.

Chevalier P. & De la Noue J. 1987. Enhancement of α-amylase production by immobilized *Bacillus subtilis* in an airlift fermenter. *Enzyme Microb. Technol.* **9**: 53–6.

Chibata I., Tosa T. & Takata I. 1983. Continuous production of L-malic acid by immobilized cells. *Trends Biotechnol.* **1**: 9–11.

Chibata I., Tosa T. & Sato T. 1986. Continuous production of L-aspartic acid: improvement of productivity by both development of immobilization method and construction of a new *Escherichia coli* strain. *Appl. Biochem. Biotechnol.* **13**: 231–40.

Chibata I., Tosa T., Yamamoto K. & Takata I. 1987. Production of L-malic acid by immobilized microbial cells. *Methods Enzymol.* (Immobilized Enzymes Cells Pt. C) **136**: 455–63.

Cottrell I.W. & Kovacs P. 1980. Alginates. In *Handbook of Water Soluble Gums and Resins.* (Ed. R.L. Davidson) pp. (2) 1–43. New York: McGraw-Hill.

Crapisi A., Nuti M.P., Zamorani A. & Spettoli P. 1987. Improved stability of immobilized *Lactobacillus* sp. cells for the control of malolactic fermentation in wine. *Am. J. Enol. Vitic.* **38**: 310–12.

Dalili M. & Chau P.C. 1988. Production of actinomycin D with immobilized *Strep-*

tomyces parvullus under nitrogen and carbon starvation condition. *Biotechnol. Lett.* **10**: 331–6.

Decleire M., van Huynh N., Motte J.C. & De Cat W. 1985. Hydrolysis of whey by whole cells of *Kluyveromyces bulgaricus* immobilized in calcium alginate gels and in hen egg white. *Appl. Microbiol. Biotechnol.* **22**: 438–41.

Deo Y. & Gaucher G.M. 1984. Semicontinuous and continuous production of penicillin-G by *Penicillium chrysogenum* cells immobilized in *x*-carrageenan beads. *Biotechnol. Bioeng.* **26**: 285–95.

Draget K., Myhre S., Evjen K. & Østgaard K. 1988a. Plant protoplasts immobilized in alginate: a simple method of preparing fragile cells for transmission electron microscopy. *Stain Technol.* **63**: 159–64.

Draget K., Myhre S., Skjåk-Bræk G. & Østgaard K. 1988b. Regeneration, cultivation and differentiation of plant protoplasts immobilized in Ca-alginate beads. *J. Plant Physiol.* **132**: 552–6.

Duff R.G. 1985. Microencapsulation technology: a novel method for monoclonal antibody production. *Trends Biotechnol.* **3**: 167–70.

Duncan N. & Rawson J. 1984. Encapsulation with seaweed-based gels: a new process. *Agricultural Res.* **June**: 8–9.

Durand M., Lahmani P. & Durand S. 1985. Encapsulated living cells and their biotechnological applications particularly in the wine industry. *Fr. Demande* 258625 CL:C12N11/10 1987.

Eikmeier H. & Rehm H.J. 1987. Semicontinuous and continuous production of citric acid with immobilized cells of *Aspergillus niger*. *Naturforsch. Sect. C. Biosc.* **42**: 408–13.

Federici F., Miller M.W. & Petruccioli M. 1987. Glucoamylase production by immobilized *Aureobasidium pullulans* in sequential batch processes. *Ann. Microbiol.* **37**: 17–24.

Flink J.M. & Johansen A. 1985. A novel method for immobilization of yeast cells in alginate gels of various shapes by internal liberation of Ca-ions. *Biotechnol. Lett.* **7**: 765–8.

Frick C. & Schuegerl K. 1986. Continuous acetone-butanol production with free and immobilized *Clostridium acetobutylicum*. *Appl. Microbiol. Biotechnol,.* **25**: 186–93.

Fujii J.A.A., Slade D.T., Redenbaugh K. & Walker K.A. 1987. Artificial seeds for plant propagation. *Tibtech* **5**: 335–9.

Gestrelius S.A. 1981. A potential application of immobilized viable cells in industry: malolactic fermentation of wine. In *Sixth Enzyme Engineering Conf.* Japan: Kashi-kojima.

Gin H., Dupuy B., Baquey C., Ducassou D. & Aubertin J. 1987. Agarose encapsulation of islets of Langerhans: reduced toxicity *in vitro*. *J. Microencapsulation* **4**: 239–42.

Goosen M.F.A., O'Shea G.M., Gharapetian H.M., Chou S. & Sun A.M. 1984. Optimization of microencapsulation parameters: semipermeable microcapsules as a bioartificial pancreas. *Biotechnol. Bioeng.* **27**: 146–50.

Gorin P.A.J. & Spencer J.F.T. 1966. Exocellular alginic acid from *Azotobacter vinelandii*. *Can. J. Chem.* **44**: 993–8.

Govan J.R.W., Fyfe J.A.M & Jarman T.R. 1981. Isolation of alginate-producing mutants of *Pseudomonas fluorescens*, *Pseudomonas putida* and *Pseudomonas mendocina*. *J. Gen. Microbiol.* **125**: 217–20.

Grasdalen H. 1983. High-field ¹H-nmr spectroscopy of alginate: sequential structure and linkage conformation. *Carbohydr. Res.* **118**: 255–60.

Grasdalen H., Larsen B. & Smidsrød O. 1979. A pmr study of the composition and sequence of uronate residues in alginate. *Carbohydr. Res.* **68**: 23–31.

Grasdalen H., Larsen B. & Smidsrød O. 1981. ^{13}C-nmr studies of monomeric composition and sequence in alginate. *Carbohydr. Res.* **89**: 179–91.
Gray C.J. & Dowsett J. 1988. Retention of insulin in alginate gel beads. *Biotechnol. Bioeng.* **31**: 607–12.
Grizeau D. & Navarro J.M. 1986. Glycerol production by *Dunaliella tertiolecta* immobilized within calcium alginate beads. *Biotechnol. Lett.* **8**: 261–4.
Hackel U., Klein J., Megenet R. & Wagner F. 1975. Immobilization of microbial cells in polymeric matrices. *Eur. J. Appl. Microbiol. Biotechnol.* **1**: 291–3.
Hahn-Hägerdal B. 1984. An enzyme co-immobilized with a microorganism: the conversion of cellobiose to ethanol using β-glucosidase and *Saccharomyces cerevisiae* in calcium alginate gels. *Biotechnol. Bioeng.* **26**: 771–4.
Hahn-Hägerdal B. 1985. Comparison between immobilized *Kluyveromyces fragilis* and *Saccharomyces cerevisiae* coimmobilized with β-galactosidase, with respect to continuous ethanol production from concentrated whey permeate. *Biotechnol. Bioeng.* **27**: 914–16.
Hartmeier W. & Heinrichs A. 1986. Membrane enclosed alginate beads containing *Gluconobacter* cells and molecular dispersed catalase. Biotechnol. Lett. **8**: 567–72.
Hartmeier W., Jankovic E.D., Forster U. & Tramm-Werner S. 1984. Ethanol formation from lactose using yeast and bacterial cells coimmobilized with β-galactosidase. *Proc. Biotech. Europe* **1984**: 415–26.
Haug A. 1964. *Composition and Properties of Alginates.* Rep. Norw. Inst. Seaweed Res. No. **30**. pp. 25–45.
Hiemstra H., Dijkhuizen L. & Harder W. 1983. Diffusion of oxygen in alginate gels related to the kinetics of methanol oxidation by immobilized *Hansenula polymorpha* cells. *Eur. J. Appl. Microbiol. Biotechnol.* **18**: 189–96.
Holst O., Enfors S.O. & Mattiasson B. 1982. Oxygenation of immobilized cells using hydrogen peroxide: a model study of *Gluconobacter oxydans* converting glycerol to dihydroxyacetone. *Eur. J. Appl. Microbiol. Biotechnol.* **14**: 64–8.
Hwang C., Rha C. & Sinskey A.J. 1986. Encapsulation with chitosan: trans-membrane diffusion of proteins in capsules. In *Chitin in Nature and Technology*. (Eds. R. Muzzarelli, C. Jeuneaux & G.W. Gooday) pp. 389–96. New York: Plenum Press.
Indergaard M. & Skjåk-Bræk G. 1987. Characteristics of alginate from *Laminaria digitata* cultivated in a high-phosphate environment. In *Proceedings of the Twelfth International Seaweed Symposium*. (Eds. M.A. Ragan & C.J. Bird) pp. 541–9. Dordrecht: Junk.
Jain D. & Ghose T.K. 1984. Cellobiose hydrolysis using *Pichia etchellsii* cells immobilized in calcium alginate. *Biotechnol. Bioeng.* **26**: 340–6.
Jarvis A.P. & Grdima T.A. 1983. Production of biologicals (interferon) from microencapsulated living cells. *BioTechniques* **1**: 24–7.
Jung G. & Mugnier J. 1983. *Inoculum having a Low Water Activity and Resistance to Temperature and Dehydration*. European Patent Application EP 83267.
Kahlon S.S. & Malhotra S. 1986. Production of gibberellic acid by fungal mycelium immobilized in sodium alginate. *Enzyme Microb. Technol.* **8**: 613–16.
Karube I., Wang Y., Tamiya E. & Kawarai M. 1987. L-Glutamate production by protoplast immobilized in carrageenan gel. *J. Biotechnol.* **6**: 1–7.
Kaya H.K. & Nelsen C.E. 1985. Encapsulation of Steinernematid and Heterorhabditid nematodes with calcium alginate: a new approach for insect control and other applications. *Environ. Entomol.* **14**: 572–4.
Ketel D.H., Hulst A.C., Gruppen H., Breteler H. & Tramper J. 1987. Effects of immobilization and environmental stress on growth and production of non-polar metabolites of *Tagetes minuta* cells. *Enzyme Microb. Technol.* **9**: 303–7.

Kierstan M. & Bucke C. 1977. The immobilization of microbial cells, subcellular organelles, and enzymes in calcium alginate gels. *Biotechnol. Bioeng.* **19**: 387–97.

Kierstan M.P.J. & Coughlan M.P. 1985. Immobilisation of cells and enzymes by gel entrapment. In *Immobilized Cells and Enzymes – A Practical Approach*. (Ed. J. Woodward) pp. 39–54. Oxford: IRL Press.

Klein J. & Kressdorf B. 1984. Production of ethanol with immobilized *Zymomonas mobilis* cells. *Third European Congress on Biotechnology* **2**: 375–9.

Klein J., Vorlop K.D., Eng H., Kluge H.M. & Washausen P. 1979. Procedures for polymer entrapment of whole cells. *Deutsche Gesellschaft für chemisches Apparatewesen Monographien* **84**: 274–6.

Klein J., Stock J. & Vorlop K.D. 1983. Pore size and properties of spherical Ca-alginate biocatalysts. *Eur. J. Microbiol. Biotechnol.* **18**: 86–91.

Klibanov A.M. 1983. Immobilized enzymes and cells as practical catalysts. *Science* **219**: 722–7.

Kloosterman J. & Lilly M.D. 1986. Pilot-plant production of prednisolone using calcium alginate immobilized *Arthrobacter simplex*. *Biotechnol. Bioeng.* **28**: 1390–5.

Kopp B. & Rehm H.J. 1983. Alkaloid production by immobilized mycelia of *Claviceps purpurea*. *Eur. J. Appl. Microbiol. Biotechnol.* **18**: 257–63.

Kurosawa H., Ishikawa H. & Tanaka H. 1988. L-Lactic acid production from starch by coimmobilized mixed culture system of *Aspergillus awamori* and *Streptococcus lactis*. *Biotechnol. Bioeng.* **31**: 183–7.

Kuu W.Y. & Polack J.A. 1983. Improving immobilized biocatalysts by gel phase polymerization. *Biotechnol. Bioeng.* **25**: 1995–2006.

Lee H.K. & Maddox I.S. 1986. Continuous production of 2,3-butanediol from whey permeate using *Klebsiella pneumoniae* immobilized in calcium alginate. *Enzyme Microb. Technol.* **8**: 409–11.

Lee J.M. & Woodward J. 1983. Properties and applications of immobilized β-D-glucosidase coentrapped with *Zymomonas mobilis* in calcium alginate. *Biotechnol. Bioeng.* **25**: 2441–51.

Li Y. & Ye L. 1986. *Immobilized Growing Yeast Cells for Producing Beer*. Patent Application Faming Zhuanli Shenqing Gongkai Shuomingshu CN 85100466 A.

Lim F. 1981. *Encapsulation and Release of Core Material*. UK Patent GB 2 094 750 A.

Lim F. & Sun A.M. 1980. Microencapsulated islets as bioartificial endocrine pancreas. *Science* **210**: 908–10.

Linker A. & Jones R.S. 1966. A new polysaccharide resembling alginic acid isolated from *Pseudomonas*. *J. Biol. Chem.* **241**: 3845–51.

Linko Y.Y., Kautola H., Uotila S. & Linko P. 1986. Alcoholic fermentation of D-xylose by immobilized *Pichia stipitis* yeast. *Biotechnol. Lett.* **8**: 47–52.

Linse L. & Brodelius P. 1984. Immobilization of plant protoplasts. *Ann. NY Acad. Sci.* **434**: 487–90.

Linsefors L. & Brodelius P. 1985. Immobilization of plant protoplasts: viability studies. *Plant Cell Rep.* **4**: 23–7.

Martinsen A., Skjåk-Bræk G. & Smidsrød O. 1989. Alginate as immobilization material. I. Correlation between chemical and physical properties of alginate gel beads. *Biotechnol. Bioeng.* **33**: 79–89.

Marwaha S.S. & Kennedy J.F. 1984a. Ethanol production from whey permeate by immobilized yeast cells. *Enzyme Microb. Technol.* **6**: 18–22.

Marwaha S.S. & Kennedy J.F. 1984b. Alcohol production from whey permeate by immobilized and free cells of *Kluyveromyces marxianus*. **19**: 79–80.

Matsunaga T., Karube I. & Suzuki S. 1980. Some observations on immobilized hydrogen-producing bacteria: behavior of hydrogen in gel membranes. *Biotechnol. Bioeng.* **22**: 2607–15.

Matsunaga T., Nakamura N., Tsuzaki N. & Takeda H. 1988. Selective production of glutamate by an immobilized marine blue green alga, *Synechococcus* sp. *Appl. Microbiol. Biotechnol.* **28**: 373–6.

Mattiasson B. 1983. Immobilization methods. In *Immobilized Cells and Organelles.* Vol. I. (Ed. B. Mattiasson) pp. 3–35. Boca Raton, Florida: CRC Press.

Meer W. 1980. Gum Arabic. In *Handbook of Water-Soluble Gums and Resins* (Ed. R.L. Davidson). pp. (8) 1–24. New York: McGraw-Hill.

Michelet J., Deschamps A. & Lebeault J.M. 1984. Production of L-aspartic acid from fumaric acid by bioconversion. *Third European Congress on Biotechnology* **2**: 133–8.

Mosbach K. 1976. Immobilized enzymes. *Methods in Enzymology.* Vol. 44. (Ed. K. Mosbach). New York: Academic Press.

Musgrave S.C., Kerby N.W., Codd G.A. & Stewart W.D.P. 1982. Sustained ammonia production by immobilized filaments of the nitrogen-fixing cyanobacterium *Anabaena* 27893. *Biotechnol. Lett.,* **4**: 647–52.

Nilsson K. & Mosbach K. 1980. Preparation of immobilized animal cells. *FEBS Lett.* **118**: 145–50.

Nilsson K., Ohlson S., Häggström L. Molin N. & Mosbach K. 1979. Denitrification of water using immobilized *Pseudomonas denitrificans* cells. *Eur. J. Appl. Microbiol. Biotechnol.* **10**: 261–74.

Nilsson K., Scheirer W., Merten O.W., Østberg L., Liehl E., Katinger H.W.S. & Mosbach K. 1983. Entrapment of animal cells for production of monoclonal antibodies and other biomolecules. *Nature Lond.* **302**: 629–30.

Nishida Y., Nakamichi K., Nabe K. & Tosa T. 1987. Continuous production of L-phenylalanine from acetamidocinnamic acid using co-immobilized cells of *Corynebacterium* sp. and *Paracoccus denitrificans. Enzyme Microb. Technol.* **9**: 479–3.

Oda G., Sameyiuna H. & Yameda T. 1983. Continuous alcohol fermentation technologies using immobilized yeast cells. In *Proc. Biotech. London* **1983**: 597–611.

Okawa T. 1986. *Yeast Cells Immobilized in Agar for Continuous Ethanol Manufacture.* Patent Jap. Kokai Tokkyo Koho JP 61/260883 A2.

Onaka T., Nakanishi K., Inoue T. & Kubo S. 1985. Beer brewing with immobilized yeast. *Biotechnology* **3**: 467–70.

Painter T.J. 1983. Algal polysaccharides. In *The Polysaccharides. Vol. 2.* (Ed. G.O. Aspinal) pp. 196–286. London: Academic Press.

Pelaez C. & Karel M. 1981. Improved method for preparation of fruit-simulating alginate gels. *J. Food Processing Preservation* **5**: 63–81.

Potvin J., Desrochers M. & Archand Y. 1988. Fermentation of kraft black liquor for the production of citric acid by *Candida tropicalis. Appl. Microbiol. Biotechnol.* **28**: 350–5.

Rees D.A. 1981. Polysaccharide shapes and their interactions: some recent advances. *Pure Appl. Chem.* **53**: 1–14.

Rha C.K. 1984. Chitosan as a biomaterial. In *Biotechnology in the Marine Sciences.* (Eds. R.R. Colwell, E.R. Pariser & A.J. Sinskey) pp. 177–89. New York: Wiley.

Rivera Carro H. 1985. *Block Structure and Sequence in Alginates.* Unpublished Ph.D. thesis, Division of Biotechnology, Norwegian Institute of Technology, Trondheim.

Robinson P.K., Mak A.L. & Trevan M.D. 1986. Immobilized algae: a review. *Process Biochem.* **21**: 122–7.

Rochefort W.E., Rehg T. & Chau P.C. 1986. Trivalent cation stabilization of alginate gel for cell immobilization. *Biotechnol. Lett.* **8**: 115–20.

Rosevear A. 1981. *Improvements in Composite Materials.* European Patent 048109 A2.

Rosevear A., Kennedy J.F. & Cabral J.M.S. 1987. *Immobilized Enzymes and Cells.* Bristol: Adam Hilger.

Scherer P., Kluge M. & Klein J. 1981. Immobilization of the methanogenic bacterium *Methanosarcina barkeri. Biotechnol. Bioeng.* **23**: 1057–65.

Schoutens G.H., Nieuwenhuizen M.C.H. & Kossen N.W. 1984. Butanol production by immobilized *Clostridia*: achievable on a large scale? *Third European Congress on Biotechnology* **2**: 139–43.

Scott C.D. 1987. Immobilized cells: a review of recent literature. *Enzyme Microb. Technol.* **9**: 66–73.

Skjåk-Bræk G., Grasdalen H. & Larsen B. 1986a. Monomer sequence and acetylation pattern in some bacterial alginates. *Carbohydr. Res.* **154**: 239–50.

Skjåk-Bræk G., Smidsrød O. & Larsen B. 1986b. Tailoring of alginates by enzymatic modification in vitro. *Int. J. Biol. Macromol.* **8**: 330–6.

Skjåk-Bræk G. Grasdalen H., Draget K. & Smidsrød O. 1989a. Inhomogeneous calcium alginate beads. In *Recent Development in Industrial Polysaccharides.* (Eds. V. Crescenzi, I.C.M. Dea & S.S. Stivala). pp. 345–63. New York: Gordon & Breach.

Skjåk-Bræk G., Grasdalen H. & Smidsrød O. 1986b. Inhomogeneous polysaccharide ionic gels. *Carbohydr. Polymers* **10**: 31–54.

Skjåk-Bræk G., Murano E. & Paoletti S. 1989c. Alginate as immobilization material. II. Determination of polyphenol contaminants by fluorescence spectroscopy, and evaluation of methods for their removal. *Biotechnol. Bioeng.* **33**: 90–4.

Skjåk-Bræk G., Zanetti F. & Paoletti S. 1989d. Effect of acetylation on some solution and gelling properties of alginates. *Carbohydr. Res.* **185**: 131–8.

Smidsrød O. 1974. Molecular basis for some physical properties of alginates in the gel state. *Chem. Soc. Faraday Disc.* **57**: 263–74.

Smidsrød O. & Haug A. 1972. Properties of poly(1,4-hexuronates) in the gel state. II. Comparison of gels of different chemical composition. *Acta Chem. Scand.* **26**: 79–88.

Smidsrød O., Haug A. & Lian B. 1972a. Properties of poly(1,4-hexuronates) in the gel state. I. Evaluation of a method for the determination of stiffness. *Acta Chem. Scand.* **26**: 71–8.

Smidsrød O., Haug A. & Whittington S. 1972b. The molecular bases for some physical properties of polyuronides. *Acta Chem. Scand.* **26**: 2563–9.

Spettoli P., Nuti M.P., Dal A., Peruffo B. & Zamorani A. 1984. Malolactic fermentation and secondary product fermentation in wine by *Leuconostoc oenos* cells immobilized in a continuous-flow reactor. In *Enzyme Engineering.* Vol. 7. (Eds. A.L. Laskin, G.T. Tsao & L.B. Wingard Jr.) pp. 461–4. New York: New York Academy of Sciences.

Spiekerman P., Vorlop K.D. & Klein J. 1987. Animal cells encapsulated in Ca-alginate hollow spheres. *Proceedings of the Fourth European Congress on Biotechnology* **1987**: 590–3.

Steenroos S.L., Linko Y.Y. & Linko P. 1981. Lactic acid fermentation with immobilized *Lactobacillus* sp. In *Sixth Enzyme Engineering Conference* Japan: Kashikojima.

Stöcklein W., Eisgruber A. & Schmidt H.L. 1983. Conversion of L-phenylalanine to L-tyrosine by immobilized bacteria. *Biotechnol. Lett.* **5**: 703–8.

Sutar I.I., Vartak H.G., Srinivasan M.C. & Raman H.S. 1986. Production of alkaline protease by immobilized mycelium of *Conidiobolus. Enzyme Microb. Technol.* **8**: 632–4.

Takamatsu S., Tosa T. & Chibata I. 1983. Continuous production of L-alanine using *Pseudomonas dacunhae* immobilized with ×-carrageenan. *Nippon Kagaku Kaishi* **9**: 1369–76.

Takata I., Kayashima K., Tosa T. & Chibata I. 1982. Improvement of stability of fumarase activity of *Brevibacterium flavum* by immobilization with ϰ-carrageenan and polyethyleneimine. *J. Ferment. Technol.* **60**: 431–7.

Tanaka H., Kurosawa H., Kokufuta E. & Veliky I.A. 1984a. Preparation of immobilized glucoamylase using Ca-alginate gel coated with partially quaternized poly(ethyleneimine). *Biotechnol. Bioeng.* **26**: 1393–4.

Tanaka H., Matsumura M. & Veliky I.A. 1984b. Diffusion characteristics of substrates in Ca-alginate gel beads. *Biotechnol. Bioeng.* **26**: 53–8.

Tanaka H., Kurosawa H. & Murakami H. 1986. Ethanol production from starch by a coimmobilized mixed culture system of *Aspergillus awamori* and *Zymomonas mobilis*. *Biotechnol. Bioeng.* **28**: 1761–8.

Tezuka Y., 1983. Production of vinegar by immobilized acetic acid bacteria. *Yamanashi-ken Shokuhin Kogyo Shidosho Kenkyu Kokoku* **15**: 72–5.

Toft K. 1982. Interactions between pectins and alginates. In *Progress in Food and Nutritional Science*. (Eds. G.O. Phillips, D.J. Wedlock & P.A. Williams) pp. 89–96 Oxford: Pergamon Press.

Tompkins R.G., Carter E.A., Carlson J.D. & Yarmush M.L. 1988. Enzymatic function of alginate immobilized rat hepatocytes. *Biotechnol. Bioeng.* **31**: 11–18.

Tosa T., Sato T., Mori T., Yamamoto K., Takata I., Nishida Y. & Chibata I. 1979. Immobilization of enzymes and microbial cells using carrageenan as matrix. *Biotechnol. Bioeng.* **21**: 1697–709.

Tze W.J. & Tai J. 1982. Biocompatibility and immunological studies of microencapsulation with cross-linked alginate capsules. *Transplantation* **33**: 563–4.

Veelken M. & Pape H. 1984. Production of nokkomycin by immobilized *Streptomyces* cells: physiological properties. *Appl. Microbiol. Biotechnol.* **19**: 146–52.

Veliky I.A. & Williams R.E. 1981. The production of ethanol by *Saccharomyces cerevisiae* immobilized in polycation-stabilized calcium alginate gels. *Biotechnol. Lett.* **33**: 275–80.

Vijaikishore P. & Karanth N.G. 1986. Glycerol production by immobilized cells of *Pichia farinosa*. *Biotechnol. Lett.* **8**: 257–60.

Vorlop K.D., Steinert J. & Klein J. 1987. Cell immobilization within coated alginate beads or hollow fibers formed by ionotropic gelation. In *Enzyme Engineering*. Vol. 8. (Eds. A.L. Laskin, K. Mosbach, D. Thomas & L.B. Wingard Jr.) pp. 339–42. New York: New York Academy of Sciences.

Wada M., Kato J. & Chibata I. 1979. A new immobilization of microbial cells: immobilized growing cells using carrageenan gel and their properties. *Eur. J. Appl. Microbiol. Biotechnol.* **8**: 241–7.

Westmeier F. & Rehm H.J. 1985. Biodegradation of 4-chlorophenol by entrapped *Alcaligenes* sp. A 7-2. *Appl. Microbiol. Biotechnol.* **22**: 301–5.

Willetts A. 1988. Use of immobilized microbial cells for accelerated maturation of beer. *Biotechnol. Lett.* **10**: 473–8.

Zaborsky O.R. 1973. *Immobilized Enzymes*. Boca Raton, Florida: CRC Press.

10 Seaweed Harvesting in Europe

XAVIER BRIAND
*Société des Englais Composés Minéraux et Amendements (SECMA),
Pontrieux, France* and Centre d'Étude et de Valorisation des Alques,
Pleubian, France*

The seaweed resources of Europe are variable. Two regions can be distinguished: an area where mostly brown seaweed is gathered along the northern coasts (Norway, Atlantic France, Iceland, Ireland and the UK), and an area where the collection of red seaweeds predominates along the southern coasts (Mediterranean France, Spain, Portugal and Italy).

Of the native European marine algae, 15 genera are exploited by the seaweed industry: *Laminaria, Ascophyllum, Fucus* (Phaeophyta); *Chondrus, Mastocarpus, Gracilaria, Gelidium, Pterocladia, Furcellaria, Palmaria, Porphyra, Lithothamnion, Phymatolithon* (Rhodophyta); *Ulva* and *Enteromorpha* (Chlorophyta) (Figs 1–3). Use of *Palmaria* and *Porphyra* involves hand collection on a small scale and these seaweeds are treated in Chapter 2 and will not be discussed here.

According to the Food and Agriculture Organization (FAO) statistics for 1985, seaweed production in the European Community was 27 630 wet t of red algae and 229 173 wet t of brown algae, but these data are incomplete. In the international context, these quantities are trivial, representing only 2.7 and 9% of world production, respectively (Fig. 4). This disparity is due to the importance of seaweed as a food in Asia, where Japan alone produces more than 700 000 t (Pryet 1986). However, the market share of production is much larger for colloid-producing seaweeds (McHugh & Lanier 1983), representing 34% of alginate-producing, 21% of carrageenan-producing, and nearly 18% of agar-producing seaweeds.

Although the use of seaweed as food is much older, industrial usage in Europe dates back to the end of the last century with the extraction of saltwort, iodine and, later, phycocolloids (Booth 1964; Jensen 1978). Seaweed gathering remained traditional for a long time, the seaweeds being collected largely as drift, either by hand or using rudimentary tools. Changes in this activity are very recent. In 1913, the Pacific Mulch Co., and later Kelco in 1937, initiated mechanical harvesting of *Macrocystis pyrifera* in California

---

*Present address.

Seaweed Resources in Europe: Uses and Potential. Edited by M. D. Guiry and G. Blunden
© 1991 John Wiley & Sons Ltd

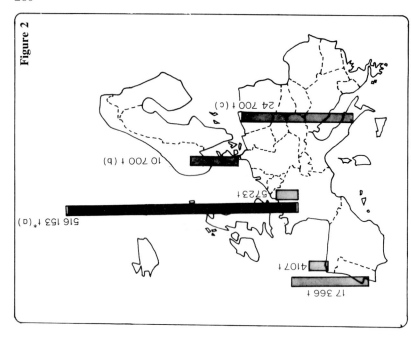

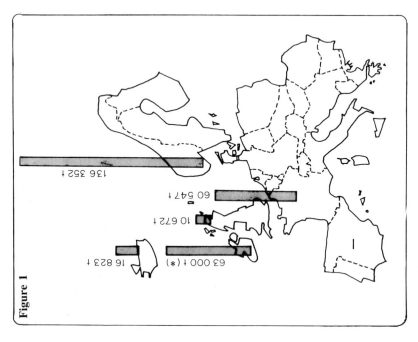

Figure 1. Harvesting of brown seaweed (wet weight) in Europe. (Data from FAO statistics, except *Guiry & Blunden 1981)
Figure 2. Harvesting of red seaweed on Europe (except *Lithothamnion and Phymatolithon). (Data from: a, Syndicate National des Armateurs extracteurs de Matériaux Marins 1985; b, Naylor 1977; c, Orlandini & Fravetto 1987)

Figure 3. Harvesting of green seaweed in Europe (Briand 1988)

(Whitney 1987) for alginate production. The development of seaweed harvesting remains closely linked to the colloid industry. Large companies monopolize the production of colloids and the demand for raw material is steadily increasing. Since 1975, the collection of brown and red seaweeds has doubled in Europe, but a different strategy has been chosen from that used in Japan, where more than 80% of production is by cultivation. Europe has opted for the utilization of its natural resources by the development of new collection techniques and mechanical harvesting. It has thus been possible to reverse the falling trend of European seaweed harvest, and to improve the production of brown seaweed (Figs 5 and 6).

In the present chapter, seaweed harvesting techniques in Europe will be described together with brief mention, where appropriate, of their use elsewhere in the world. Particular attention will be paid to the following aspects: development of harvesting techniques, areas of production, regulations, impact of harvesting and resource management.

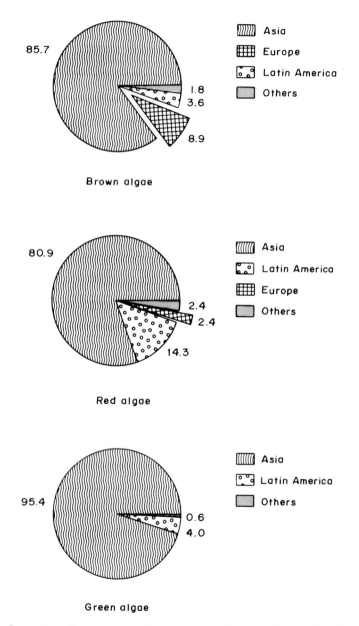

Figure 4. Percentage European contribution to world seaweed harvesting (Data from FAO 1984; Briand 1988)

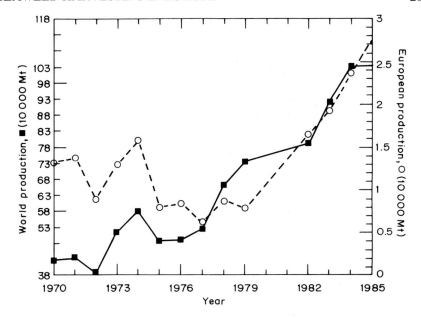

Figure 5. Recent trends in red seaweed production (World, ■ and Europe, ○)

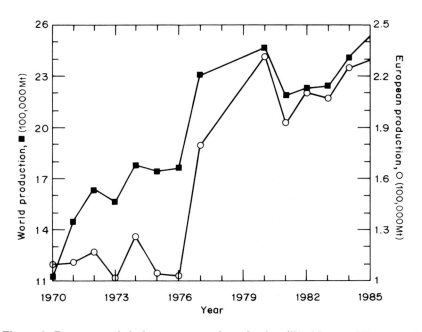

Figure 6. Recent trends in brown seaweed production (World, ■ and Europe, ○)

Figure 7. Collection of *Ascophyllum* with sickle in Brittany (unpublished photograph)

ASCOPHYLLUM NODOSUM

DISTRIBUTION AND ECOLOGY

Ascophyllum nodosum, like *Fucus vesiculosus* and *F. serratus*, is usually found growing in the intertidal. It is perennial, growing on large stones and rocks at the same level as *F. vesiculosus*, and may reach 1.5 m in length (Munda 1972). In Europe, *A. nodosum* is found largely at latitudes from 40 to 77 °N, and is very common along the west coast of Norway, around Iceland, the UK and Ireland, and the coasts of northern France (Munda 1964; Gayral 1966; Baardseth 1968). It is absent from the west coast of Denmark and the Belgian, Dutch and Basque coasts. The species is eurythermic and euryhaline, and populations are under threat from pollution in the sheltered inlets in which it thrives (Gayral 1966; Lobban *et al.* 1985; Seip *et al.* 1979).

HARVESTING IN EUROPE

Harvesting of *Ascophyllum nodosum* was only carried out by hand until 1960. The seaweed was cut with a sickle or knife, just above the holdfasts (Fig. 7). This very simple technique is still used, especially in France, Scotland and Ireland. *F. serratus* and *F. vesiculosus* are also harvested in this way.

France

The harvesting areas are easy to reach from the coast, which makes it possible to load the cut seaweed directly onto tractors. In some places, the sea

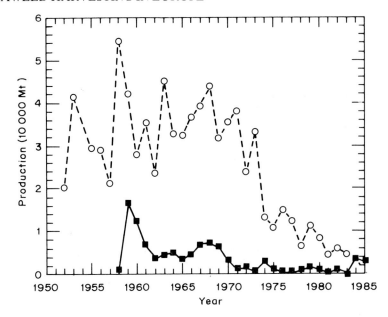

Figure 8. Trends in *Ascophyllum* (■) and *Fucus* (○) production in France 1952–1985

penetrates far inland, and because of the strong amplitudes of the tides (10–12 m) large populations of *Ascophyllum* occur. Harvesting takes place mainly around Pleubian in north-western France; the company SETALG uses nearly 90% of the harvest. The seaweed is dried in a rotary-drum drier and then ground. The material is used for the production of agricultural products, animal fodder and, recently, cosmetics (see Chapter 4). This company also processes large quantities of *Fucus serratus* in the same way. In the 1970s, market losses, especially in the cattle-feed industry, led to a fall in the production of *A. nodosum* and *Fucus* (Fig. 8), which is linked to the introduction of mechanical harvesting of *Laminaria digitata*. Another French company, Agrimer, offers the same products, but they are dried using a different technique. The seaweed is placed in ventilated drying-cupboards identical to those used for tobacco drying. The costs are reduced by preliminary drying out of doors. The *goëmoniers* (Breton: seaweed collectors) carry out this dehydration (to 30% moisture) before delivering the seaweed to the factories, and the process lasts 2–3 weeks, depending on weather conditions, and takes place between May and September.

Other companies include Goëmar and Phytomer in Saint-Malo, both of whom use wet seaweed without any preliminary drying. The former company produces seaweed creams by grinding frozen plants, and liquid extracts by ultrafiltration. These expensive products are used in the preparation of fertilizers and cosmetics (Chapter 4). Phytomer prepares freeze-dried products for dietetic and cosmetic uses.

Scotland and Ireland

In these areas, the topography does not always make it possible to reach the harvesting sites directly, and small boats are often used for access. The bladders of *Ascophyllum nodosum* allow the cut seaweed to float, and it may be enclosed by either nets or ropes, and the rafts so formed towed to the coast for transport by road (Anon. 1969). Each net can enclose about 1 t of seaweed, and the daily output is 7–8 t per person.

In Scotland, harvesting is carried out along the east coasts of the Hebrides around Loch Duich and Sunart. This activity provides jobs for about 60–70 people: 40 on North Uist, where the largest amounts of *A. nodosum* are found, and 10–15 in Loch Duich and Sunart (Searle personal communication). Since the closing of the Orosay factory on South Uist in 1978 and the Spanish-owned factory on North Uist in 1986, *A. nodosum* is no longer dried on the Island but is sent directly by cargo-boat to the main factory (Alginate Industries) at Girvan. The drying and grinding unit at Keose (Lewis Island) is still operational, producing a powder made from *A. nodosum* for the production of alginates (90%) and agricultural products (10%). This powder is obtained by dehydration on a drying belt (Searle personal communication).

In Ireland, exploitation of seaweed is centered mostly on *A. nodosum* (Guiry & Blunden 1981). The main areas of collection are: Connemara (Co. Galway), Co. Mayo, Co. Donegal and the Shannon estuary (especially Co. Clare) (Guiry & Blunden 1980). Yearly production increased markedly between 1973 and 1979 from 39 000 to 62 000 t (wet weight). According to Cullinane (1984), this constitutes about 40% of the available biomass. Smaller quantities are also harvested in Co. Cork, Co. Kerry and Co. Sligo. The seaweed is taken by road to factories at Kilkieran, Co. Galway and Meenmore Quay, Co. Donegal, which dry and grind the seaweed for export to Scotland for alginate production by Alginate Industries. No commercial alginate extraction has ever been carried out in Ireland, although it has been contemplated on several occasions (Guiry personal communication). Another factory, situated in Kilrush, Co. Clare, produces seaweed meal for animal fodder and the preparation of liquid extracts for use in agriculture and horticulture (see Chapter 3). These meals are mainly exported (Guiry & Blunden 1981). A factory at Newport, Co. Mayo, mentioned by Guiry and Blunden (1981), has recently ceased operations and a new drying plant is planned for this area (Guiry personal communication).

Iceland and Norway

The growth in demand for *A. nodosum* since the 1960s caused Alginate Industries and Aquamarine Corporation to test equipment used for the harvesting of seaweeds in Canada. The equipment, altered and adapted for the harvest of *A. nodosum*, has been very satisfactory and has led to

Figure 9. The Aquamarine aquatic weed harvester as modified for *Ascophyllum* harvesting in south-western Nova Scotia: A, stainless steel mesh conveyor belt for unloading; B, reciprocating cutter blade; C, paddlewheel; D, unloading conveyor; E, air-cooled diesel engines. (After Sharp 1987, with permission)

mechanical harvesting supplanting harvesting by hand. By 1971, Canada was obtaining more than 80% of *A. nodosum* production by means of the 'Aquamarine' (Fig. 9), a low-draughted barge (10.5 m long, 4.9 m wide and 2.9 m high) propelled by two paddle wheels on either side, and supplied with hydraulic engines. At the front of the barge, a sawtooth blade that moves back and forth cuts the seaweed on to a steel conveyor belt, which transfers it to a storage container. The height of the cut is regulated by pulling the conveyor belt either up or down. The average height of the cut is about 13 cm, and the material left behind represents 10–20% of the original biomass. Once the cutting barge is full (about 1.4 t), the seaweed is transferred into a collecting barge. The main drawbacks of this machine are the low efficiency of its propulsion and the fact that it is too open to the wind, which makes it difficult to operate in winds in excess of 30 km h^{-1}; its use is therefore limited to sheltered areas. This machine is also used in Iceland (International Trade Centre 1981) and in the Lofoten Islands, Norway, by the Nordtang company, which produces seaweed powders (Indergaard personal communication).

In Iceland, *Ascophyllum* is harvested mainly in the west (Breidafjördur) and south (especially around Eyrarbakki and Stokkseyri). In the south the average biomass is estimated at 6.2 kg m^{-2} with a maximum of 12 kg m^2 (Munda 1964, 1987). The seaweed is dried using geothermal energy and then ground

Figure 10. Rear view of Norwegian suction cutter used for harvesting *Ascophyllum*: A, propulsion jet; B, collection bag; C, released bag. (After Sharp 1987, with permission)

(Hallson 1964). A powder is exported for alginate extraction, for animal fodder and for the production of cosmetics.

In Norway, a 'suction cutter' (5 m long, 2.2 m wide and 2.3 m high) with a smaller surface area (8 m^2) is in use (Figs 10 and 11), but it cannot operate in waves more than 70 cm in height. Propulsion is by means of nozzles, on each side at the bow and at the stern, through which water is pumped under pressure. The seaweed is cut with a wing-blade situated at the extremity of a steel suction pipe (25 cm in diameter), through which the cut weed is drawn and deposited in a net on the quarter-deck. Once the net is full, it is ejected and replaced; nets are either towed behind the barge or left for collection by another boat. The distances between the collection areas and the drying factories often necessitate storage of the nets in the sea for about a week until a cargo-boat is able to collect them. This vessel has a capacity of about 300 t of *A. nodosum* (International Trade Centre 1981).

Another seaweed-harvesting machine (Fig. 12), which is not a boat as such, has been designed for use at the mouth of Trondheimsfjord; this uses a reciprocating cutter kept afloat by two outriggers (Indergaard personal communication).

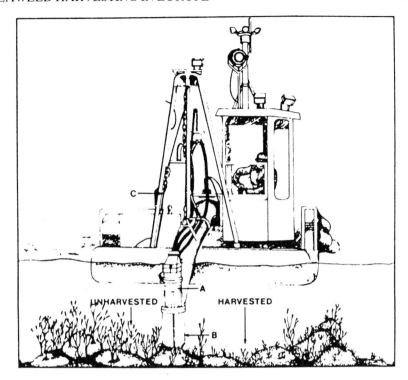

Figure 11. Front view of a Norwegian suction cutter used for harvesting *Ascophyllum*: A, hydraulic motor drive for impeller; B, cutter/suction head; C, intake pipe and elevation mechanism. (After Sharp 1987, with permission)

RESOURCE MANAGEMENT AND REGULATION

For economic purposes, only vegetative regeneration from the base of *Ascophyllum* is effective. Seip (1980) and others have found that when an area is cleared completely of *Ascophyllum*, *Fucus vesiculosus* or *F. spiralis* rapidly dominates the cleared area and it takes from 3 to 8 years for mature populations of *Ascophyllum* to re-establish.

In France, seaweed harvesting from the shore is controlled by the following regulations issued by the office of the Secretary of State for Transport: order no. 2606 P4 (7 August 1975) and order no. 34 (7 April 1976), which forbid the hand-collection of seaweed, and the turning over of pebbles and shingle to which seaweeds are attached. Two cuts may be permitted each year, the dates of which are set at the beginning of each year in an order issued by the Head of Maritime Affairs, after consultation with the Institut Français de Recherche pour l'Exploitation de la mer (IFREMER) and the Mayors of the

Figure 12. *Ascophyllum* cutter. (Unpublished photograph, courtesy of M. Inder-gaard)

Communes concerned. The length of each period, which must include a
spring tide, cannot be less than 30 days. Bills, posted at least 10 days in
advance by the Town Councils, report the date of opening and the length of
each period of harvest. When circumstances justify it, the Heads of Maritime
Affairs, with advice from IFREMER, can grant extra harvesting periods
between 1 July and 30 October. Around Pleubian, the period of harvesting is
between April and October.

In Ireland, *Ascophyllum* is harvested all year around. Cutting is carried out
15 cm from the base of the plant in order to protect the algal population
(Baardseth 1955; Guiry & Blunden 1980), but no regulations exist to enforce
this practice. Rotation of harvesting is in 3–4 year cycles. *Ascophyllum*
collection sites in Ireland are 'commonage'; in other words, when a portion of
agricultural land near the sea is purchased, rights to a section of shore for the
collection of seaweed may be included. No government regulation of cutting
times or sites exist at present (Guiry personal communication).

In Scotland, the harvest is not subject to any regulations, but Alginate
Industries, which has a near-monopoly of the exploitation of seaweed in the
area, asks the collectors to rotate the harvesting areas over 2–3 years.

In Norway, the impact of cutting *Ascophyllum* on its regrowth has been
particularly well studied. Seip (1980) has shown that the quantity of holdfasts
and the biomass left after the harvest are important factors, which determine
the extent of regrowth. For example, when the residual biomass was 0.5 and

12% of the original, at the conclusion of the third year after harvesting, the regenerated biomass represented, respectively, 23 and 70% of the initial stock. In reality, the quantity of biomass usually left after cutting is about 2%, which corresponds to a cut 10 cm above the holdfasts. Consequently, harvesting strategies need to take into account both short- and long-term production. Seip (1980) condemns the traditional procedures of cutting, which are detrimental to long-term output; 40–70% improvement in production can be achieved by leaving a greater quantity of biomass for regrowth. However, *Ascophyllum* must be harvested every 2 years in order to take full advantage of this process. New mechanical harvesting techniques offer a better means of exploiting this resource since they leave behind a greater proportion of intact young plants. An optimum for the degree of cut can be defined according to the periodicity of the harvest: 20–30% should be cut on a 2 year rotation; 8–10% for a 3 year rotation; and 3–4% for a 4 year rotation.

LAMINARIA DIGITATA

DISTRIBUTION AND ECOLOGY

Laminaria digitata is one of the largest seaweeds found along the European littoral, mature plants being 1–2 m in length. The seaweed is composed of a smooth and pliable stipe and a blade of jagged ribbons. The plants are attached to boulders by holdfasts in the lower intertidal and shallow subtidal down to a depth of 10 m (Gayral 1966). The species flourishes in fairly exposed areas or in areas with strong currents, and is very common over much of northern Europe. However, *L. digitata* is absent in the Baltic Sea because of its sensitivity to low salinities (Gayral & Cosson 1973). The southern boundary is thought to be the île Noirmoutier, France.

HARVESTING IN EUROPE

Ireland

Laminaria production is not very large. Cast *L. digitata* is harvested at Inishiar (Aran Islands) and Quilty, Co. Clare. The seaweed is dried partially in the open air before being oven-dried in a factory at Kilrush. The products are used in food and agriculture (Guiry & Blunden 1981).

France

Until relatively recently, *Laminaria digitata* was harvested by hand with special tools. Arzel (1987) gives a full description of the evolution of the seaweed harvester; the 'guillotine', a kind of long-shafted sickle, made it possible to cut the stipes on the sea bottom and to lift the blades onto a boat. It was necessary to see the plants in order to cut them, which forced the *goëmoniers* to work near the shore. In 1961, the 'scoubidou' succeeded the guillotine (Didou 1983); this has a small hook at one extremity, while at the other end of the long shaft is a crank which is activated by the collector. The seaweed is pulled up in this way from the sea bottom along a steel shaft.

The increasing demands of the alginate industry made it necessary to mechanize the harvest (Fig. 13). The first prototype of a seaweed harvesting boat was built in 1963. This was a trawler 15 m long by 4 m wide, which had an iron grating open to the sea in the hold. The seaweed was cut on the sea bottom by a Scuba diver with a sickle. The cut weed was pumped up through a large pipe and deposited in the hold of the boat, the storage capacity of which made it capable of holding 7 t of wet seaweed, the iron grating allowing the draining of surplus water. In spite of improvements carried out up to 1965, some hydraulic difficulties remained. Many other constraints also hampered the development of this new technique. The necessity for using a scuba diver constituted the main obstacle because of the age of the *goëmoniers* (65% were more than 40 years old) and the high cost of professional scuba divers. The long and painstaking unloading required nearly 6 h. However, the development of scuba diving put an end to the use of the guillotine and scoubidou.

A different design was proposed in 1967 (Arzel 1984, 1987), inspired by the principle of the scoubidou. After a few years of improvement, this technique was adopted by the seaweed harvesters. From 1971 (Didou 1983), the mechanical scoubidou was used to equip the seaweed-collecting fleet. It consists of a round hook (30 mm in diameter, 3.5 m long) made of iron, mounted on a jointed crane (Figs 14 and 15). During collection it turns like a gimlet within a radius of about 50 cm. The seaweed is rolled up along it before being pulled from the rock and it can be used to a depth of 5 or 6 m. After making sure of the density of the *Laminaria*, the boat is anchored and, while easing off the anchor cable, it circles about extracting the weed for 5–6 min before weighing anchor and moving. A single scoubidou extraction lasts 30 s, on average, and yields about 10 kg of *Laminaria*. When the scoubidou is hoisted on board the screw is reversed and the seaweed falls into the hold. A pump is used to drain water out of the hold. Sorting of unwanted seaweed and stones is carried out by hand, knife or sickle. Daily harvests vary between 10 and 30 t, depending on the kind of boat (8–12 m). The larger boats are equipped with two scoubidous, one on either side of the boat. In the small harbours, the *goëmoniers* unload the seaweed with the aid of tractors. At the extremity of the jointed handle, the hydraulic engine of the scoubidou is replaced with a fork. It takes 2.5 h to load 20 t of *Laminaria* onto trucks. In the bigger harbours, the unloading is managed by the alginate industry, which uses trucks equipped with grabs. At the rate of 500–600 kg of seaweed

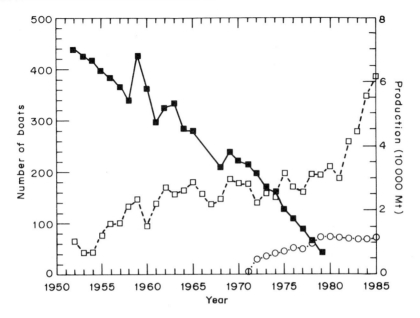

Figure 13. Trends in *Laminaria digitata* production (□) and fishing fleet (■, mechanized boats; ○, non-mechanized boats) in France 1950–85

Figure 14. Collection of *Laminaria digitata* in Brittany, France. (Unpublished photograph, courtesy of P. Arzel)

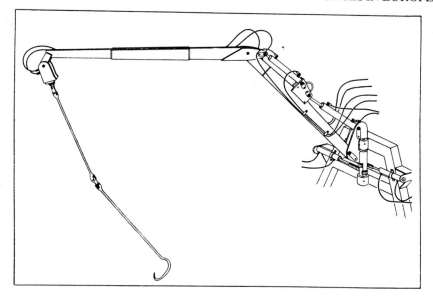

Figure 15. Scoubidou apparatus. (After Arzel 1987, with permission)

collected with each grab, it takes less than 40 min to unload 35 t of *Laminaria*. The seaweed is purchased wet by alginate industry brokers who supervise the weighing and give out delivery slips. The areas of Molène and Plouguerneau in northern Finistère alone supply 80% of French production.

The mechanization of collection has made it possible to improve the output of seaweed considerably. From 1970 to 1985, production doubled from 30 900 to 61 580 t (Fig. 13), but opportunities for expansion are now limited in the areas exploited. As a result, the Interprofessional Committee for Maritime Seaweed has instituted a system of licences which limits the fishing fleet to 70 boats in order to guarantee the average income of *goëmoniers*, and replacements are allowed only on the retirement of a seaweed harvester. In 1984, the average investment for the purchase of a 10 m boat was FFr 600 000 and of a 12 m boat, FFr 1 250 000, which was then about 2 years' turnover. The season lasts about 5 months, from May to September. The remainder of the collectors' income is achieved by fishing activities (scallops, shellfish and fish).

LAMINARIA HYPERBOREA

DISTRIBUTION AND ECOLOGY

Together with the previous two species, *Laminaria hyperborea* is one of the most exploited seaweeds in Europe. The distribution of this species is limited to the northern and eastern Atlantic and adjacent seas (Chapman 1948; Lüning 1969; Kain 1971). It is found along the west coasts of Sweden and Norway, around Iceland (except for the east coast), the UK and Ireland, the north coast of France, and the north coast of Spain and northern Portugal, which is its southern boundary (Ardré 1970). *L. hyperborea* is a subtidal species which exclusively colonizes rocky substrata. Its upper limit is just below the level of low water at the lowest tides, but its depth penetration is more variable and is dependent mainly on water turbidity. In clear water, populations of *L. hyperborea* can reach depths of 30 m or more. The stiffness of the stipe and its effect of leverage on the holdfast make *L. hyperborea* more sensitive to wave action than *L. digitata* (Kain 1971). As a result, large concentrations of drift seaweed are found in some places.

HARVESTING IN EUROPE

Portugal

Exploitation of *Laminaria* (*L. ochroleuca*, *L. hyperborea* and *L. saccharina*) began in 1978 (Oliveira personal communication). Yearly production is about 1000 t (200 t dry weight), exported mainly to France.

Ireland

Drift *L. hyperborea* is harvested (Guiry & Blunden 1981) after spring storms on the coast of Co. Clare (mainly around Kilkee and Quilty). Annual production is about 7000 t of stipes (1200 t dry weight) and 2500 t of blades (500 t dry weight). The stipes are oven-dried at a factory in Kilkieran before being exported to Scotland (Alginate Industries) for alginate production. The blades are oven-dried in a factory at Kilrush and then powdered before export for use in animal feeds and for the preparation of liquid seaweed extracts (see Chapter 3).

France

L. hyperborea stipes are also harvested after spring storms along the coasts of Finistère. The annual production is low: 490 t in 1987 (Arzel personal communication). The seaweed is treated at the Satia factory in Lannilis for the production of gelling alginates. Exploitation of the *L. hyperborea* beds has also been considered by the alginate industry since the beginning of the 1980s. The exploitable stock is considerable (about 1 000 000 t; Le Grill personal communication). Trials made in 1983–84 have made it possible to develop a dredge which only harvests the mature stipes (Braud 1984). Divers were able to confirm that 50% of the plants, including the youngest, remained, which is very important for the renewal of the stock. A device has been developed that separates the blade from the stipe during collection; the latter is subsequently chopped to reduce its size so that it can be loaded economically into the hold of the boat. However, further improvements were considered necessary with regard to the filling of the dredge. This programme has currently been suspended for two reasons. On the one hand, exploitation of *L. hyperborea* is meeting with strong opposition from fishermen, who are concerned about fish and shellfish depletion in the collection areas. On the other hand, predicted increases in the market for gelling alginates have not materialized.

Scotland

Trials on the harvesting of *L. hyperborea* began in the late 1940s. MacKenzie (1947) described a prototype that used a reciprocating cutter placed in a cage covered with an iron grating, at the top of which was fixed a pliable rubber tube linked to a boat. The device was towed on the sea bottom; the minced seaweed was pulled up to the surface by suction provided by a centrifugal pump (MacKenzie 1947).

A major drawback of this technique is the necessity of harvesting the whole plant. Unlike *L. digitata*, the part used by industry is the stipe and not the blade. The requirement for rapid processing of ground seaweed after harvesting because of the ready hydrolysis of the organic compounds constitutes an additional handicap. In 1952, the Institute of Seaweed Research in Scotland (now defunct) considered two new processes. The first technique used a grapnel, which made it possible to pull up the seaweed away from the

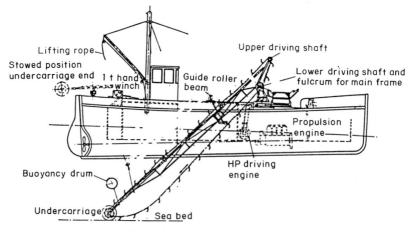

Figure 16. Belt harvester. (After Jackson & Wolff 1985, with permission)

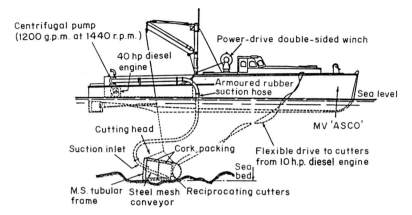

Figure 17. Suction harvester. (After Jackson 1957, with permission)

substratum (Jackson 1952a, 1952b). This method was refined in a second phase in order to obtain non-stop harvesting (J. M. May 1952), which was achieved by attaching hooks to a conveyor belt (Fig. 16). One end of the belt was dragged along the sea bottom on two pneumatic tyres, the steel mesh of the belt flattening down the seaweed and converting it into a dense mass before the 'cakes' of seven hooks picked them up (Jackson & Wolff 1955; Jackson 1957) (Fig. 16). The belt was then rotated in the opposite direction to that of the boat to avoid jamming the belt and to protect the hooks. The maximum output achieved with this system was $12\,t\,h^{-1}$, but the depth of harvesting seemed to be limited to about 6 m.

The second technique consisted of a dredge fitted with blades with back and forth movements (Jackson & McIver 1952). In this the seaweed was not collected mechanically, but by using a hydraulic system (Jackson 1952a, 1952b, 1957) (Fig. 17). The dredge was dragged along the sea bottom, and the seaweed was cut and sucked up by a collecting pipe (Fig. 18). Despite many trials, severe difficulties were encountered with the hydraulic system and this

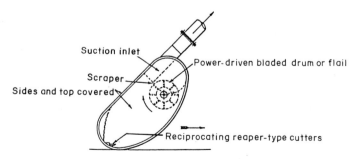

Figure 18. Diagrammatic arrangement of shortened cutting head. (After Jackson 1957, with permission)

method is no longer used. Today, the production of *L. hyperborea* is dependent on drift seaweed, mainly along the western coasts of the Hebrides Islands (South Uist and Bara) (Aberdein 1968), and around Tiree, and the Orkney Islands (Searle personal communication). The biggest quantities of drift seaweed are found on Ronaldsay Island. The collection of stipes of *L. hyperborea* constitutes a major activity for the crofters. Thirty people harvest from October to March on the Hebrides and on Tiree, and 120–150 harvest on the Orkney Islands. The best collectors gather up to 200 t of wet seaweed (40 t dry weight) each year. The seaweed is dried on iron gratings to allow for air circulation. In May–June the dried plants are sent to Alginate Industries in Oban for alginate production.

Norway

Mechanization of the harvest began in 1964 (Svendsen 1972). The seaweed-harvesting machine has a cutting dredge and a trawl net (Figs 19 and 20). The dredge, which is towed by a crane, cuts the stipes with a blade 5–20 cm above the holdfasts, a series of skis protecting the blades from damage by stones. The bottom of the dredge is solid sheet metal, but the sides and top are covered by an iron grating; the sack at the stern is protected, as are the bottoms of the trawl. The machine is usable on ground composed of stones, or even of rocks. The quantity of seaweed lost during the trawling is low. On

Figure 19. Specially designed vessel for *L. hyperborea* harvesting in Norway. (Unpublished photograph, courtesy of Protan, Norway)

the other hand, results are not so satisfactory from areas where the rocks are more scattered; both rocks and seaweed can be turned over and gathered in the dredge.

Two different sizes of dredge are in use: 7–8 m long and 12–21 m long, the capacities of which are 300 kg and 1000 kg, respectively. Most seaweed-collection vessels use dredges 14–17 m long, and a 100-horsepower engine (Arzel, personal communication). The boats dredge at a depth of 1–20 m, the daily load being about 6 t for the smallest boats and 20–25 t for the larger ones. The crew is composed of two men: one surveys the density of the *Laminaria* beds with an echo-sounder from a bridge situated near the prow of the boat, while the other manipulates the crane and winch. This method of harvesting has developed along the west coast of Norway in an area from the south to the Lofoten Islands (59 °N and 63 °N). The harvested seaweed is unloaded by cranes into hoppers at pretreatment centres, where it is finely ground, placed on a conveyor belt and transported to big silos, where it is treated with formaldehyde for storage. Six pretreatment centres are spread out along the coast of Norway, whence the treated *Laminaria* is taken by cargo-boat to the main alginate extraction factory in Drammen. The industrial group Protan and Fagertun supervises all factories (Arzel, personal communication).

A different harvesting machine, still undergoing trials, is used in the White Sea near Solvetski Ostrova (Anon. 1978). This machine, made in the USSR

Figure 20. Dredge with *L. hyperborea* stipes, Norway. (Unpublished photograph, courtesy of M. Indergaard)

and built in Murmansk and Archangel, has a blade that can operate at depths of 4–12 m, and a conveyor belt which brings the cut seaweed to the surface. The boat is crewed by three people.

RESOURCE MANAGEMENT

The development and maintenance of *Laminaria* collection in Norway requires constant consideration to be given to the resource. The influence of dredging on beds of *L. hyperborea* situated at depths of 4–10 m was studied by Svendsen (1972). The regrowth of the dredged areas was carefully observed for 3 years and it was found that the harvested areas were quickly overgrown with new plants of *L. hyperborea*. After a year the population was already dense and well developed. Sampling carried out 18 months after collection showed a density of about 150 plants m^{-2}, which is equivalent to 6 kg m^{-2} in the densest areas. The rate of growth increased during the second and third year after harvest. Stipes reached about 40 cm in length after 2 years and 95 cm after 3 years. The beds had completely regenerated after 3–4 years. At that time, the small size of the plants in comparison with the size reached at maturity (2 m after 4 years) is compensated for by a greater number of plants per square metre and a better quality of stipe (fewer epiphytes).

CHONDRUS CRISPUS AND *MASTOCARPUS STELLATUS*

DISTRIBUTION AND ECOLOGY

Chondrus crispus and *Mastocarpus stellatus* are bushy red seaweeds, 6–15 cm in length, which grow largely in the intertidal. Although *C. crispus* may occur in considerable quantities to a depth of 12 m in the subtidal of the Maritime Provinces of Canada (McLachlan personal communication), in Europe it is found mainly in intertidal rock pools and from just above low water to just below low water, and sporadically to a depth of about 6–7 m (Naylor 1977; Guiry, personal communication), subtidal populations never reaching the densities found in Canada. *M. stellatus* is also found in rock pools, but also occurs in considerable quantities in the mid-intertidal of semi-exposed shores and is very rare in the subtidal. Both species are found from northern Norway south to Portugal and *Mastocarpus* reaches its southern limit in Morocco.

HARVESTING IN EUROPE

C. crispus and *M. stellatus* are collected by hand-picking and hand-raking.

Ireland

C. crispus and *M. stellatus* are gathered interchangeably and sold as Carrageen Moss (see Mitchell & Guiry (1984) for an account of the origin of the name 'carrageen') or Irish Moss; the former is collected from more sheltered coasts and the latter from semi-exposed coasts (Guiry personal communication). Collection carried out from June to September on the coasts of Co. Clare (Castlegregory, Quilty, Kilkee, and the Burren), Co. Kerry (Fenit, Dingle Peninsula), Co. Sligo and Co. Galway supplies more than 1000 t of *Chondrus* wet weight per annum (165 t dry weight) (Guiry & Blunden 1981). The seaweed is dried and bleached in the open and sold to factories in Kilrush, Maam Cross, Moycullen and Newport, and then exported as a health food and as finings for brewing. Only one factory, situated in Moycullen, Co. Galway, markets whole and ground *Chondrus* for food. No carrageenan extraction is currently carried out in Ireland, although an extraction plant is planned.

France

Again, both *C. crispus* and *M. stellatus*, known collectively as 'lichen', are harvested along the coast between Cherbourg and île Noirmoutier. The collectors deliver the plants either in a wet state or dried and bleached to brokers who work for a carrageenan factory (SATIA, Baupte). This harvesting (3387 wet t in 1987; Fig. 21) was sufficient for French industrial needs until 1970; today, it fills no more than 10% of the requirement of this factory. The other 90% of the raw material for carrageenan production comes from Indonesia and the Philippines, where *Eucheuma*, another carrageenophyte, is

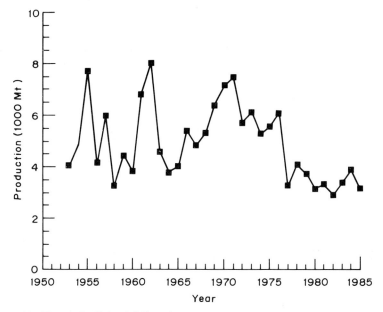

Figure 21. Trends in 'lichen' (*Chondrus crispus* and *Mastocarpus stellatus*) production in France, 1953–85

cultivated in the open sea (Bodeau-Bellion 1987). In France, prices are fixed every year, as is the case for the other commercially harvested seaweeds, by the Interprofessional Committee for Maritime Seaweed. This Committee represents the seaweed collectors and the industry.

Although the price of lichen is 2.5 times that of Indonesian and Philippine seaweed, its collection is no longer considered sufficiently economic and has tended to decline since the late 1970s. Concerned about supplies of raw material, SATIA has examined the possibility of cultivating *C. crispus* in the sea. However, the cost of cultivation was found to be so high that industrial development is not planned at present. On a smaller scale, the Violets Company in Brest treats about 550 t of lichen for the production of dietetic and food products.

Portugal

Chondrus crispus and *Mastocarpus stellatus* have been exploited, especially in the north (Minho, Douro, Beira) (Palminha 1971), for about 30 years. The seaweed is hand-raked and then sun-dried on litters before being bagged (de Oliveira personal communication) (Figs 22–24). Production is low, however (250 t in 1987; de Oliveira personal communication), and 80–90% is exported, the rest being used by a local carrageenan industry.

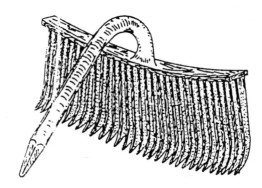

Figure 22. Hand-rake for the collection of *Chondrus crispus* and *Mastocarpus stellatus*. (Unpublished drawing, courtesy of De Oliveira)

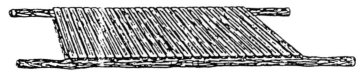

Figure 23. Stretcher for drying red algae. (Unpublished drawing, courtesy of De Oliveira)

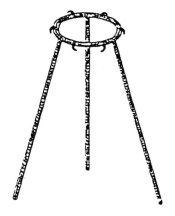

Figure 24. Device for putting seaweed into sacks. (Unpublished drawing, courtesy of De Oliveira)

Spain

C. crispus, *M. stellatus*, *Gigartina teedii* and *G. acicularis* are collected interchangeably as Irish Moss. Harvesting is also carried out with rakes. The total harvest ranges from 310 to 1333 t dry weight year^{-1}, with an average crop of 689 ± 300 t dry weight year^{-1} (Gallardo *et al.* 1990). This material is processed by two carrageenan companies (capacity of 580 t dry weight year^{-1} each) at Vigo and Burgos.

RESOURCE MANAGEMENT

In France, regulations similar to those described above for *Ascophyllum nodosum* cover the collection of lichen. In Portugal, collection is also controlled by regulations, which first date from 1909, that specify periods of harvest (from July to November), require the issuing of licences for each area of the coastline, and control prices (De Oliveira personal communication). No regulations exist in Ireland.

Largely because of the limited size and distribution of *C. crispus* and *M. stellatus* in Europe, the methods of harvesting plants of these species in Canada (Figs 25 and 26) are not used.

FURCELLARIA LUMBRICALIS

DISTRIBUTION AND ECOLOGY

Furcellaria lumbricalis is a perennial red seaweed that grows on rocky substrata (Czapke 1964). It is found along the northern coasts of the Atlantic,

Figure 25. *C. crispus* harvesters using handrakes in south-western Nova Scotia. (After Sharpe & Roddick 1982, with permission)

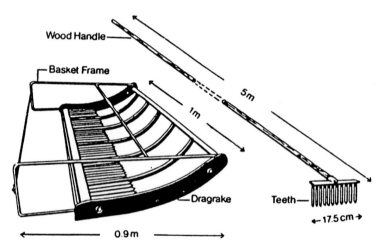

Figure 26. Types of rakes employed in the harvesting of *C. crispus* in eastern Canada. (After Pringle, 1978, with permission)

in the English Channel, the Baltic, the Mediterranean and the Black Sea (Gayral 1966).

HARVESTING IN EUROPE

Commercial beds of *F. lumbricalis* are found in Denmark, whereas in the rest of Europe the biomass is not sufficient for harvesting. Exploitation began in 1943 and the species was collected exclusively in Denmark until 1964 (Bjerre-

Petersen *et al.* 1973). Today, storm-cast *F. lumbricalis* is also collected in Canada along the coasts of the lower Gulf of St Lawrence (McLachlan personal communication). Attached and unattached plants (known as f. *aegagropila*) are harvested in Denmark, whereas the plants collected in Canada are of *F. lumbricalis*. In Europe, *F. lumbricalis* reproduces by gametes and spores, whereas f. *aegagropila* remains sterile.

Denmark

Harvesting requires a specific trawl, the net of which is attached to a movable mast and dragged along the side of the boat at a depth of 4–16 m. Seines, with nets similar to those used for fishing, are also used. The net is cast in a circle and, once the bottom is closed, the net is hoisted on board the vessel (International Trade Centre 1981). Harvesting is confined mainly to the area of the Kattegat (Tangen) near the coast of Jutland, but other sites have also been exploited since 1979.

F. lumbricalis grows at depths of 2–30 m, but the maximum biomass is found at 2–4 m, with a density in excess of 4 kg wet weight m^{-2} (Holmsgaard *et al.* 1981). At this depth, *Furcellaria* constitutes 80% of the plant cover. Biomass generally ranges from 2 to 10 kg m^{-2} and represents, at these levels, nearly 60% of the cover. Associated species are *Fucus serratus*, *Phyllophora* sp. and *Delesseria sanguinea*. Attached plants dislodged by wave action and

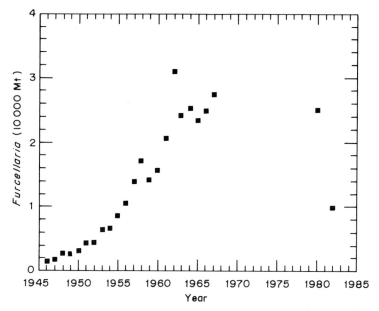

Figure 27. Trends in *F. lumbricalis* harvesting in Denmark, 1946–82

detached plants gather in areas with particular conditions of current and sea bottom. The seaweed can be harvested throughout the year, except during harsh winters, when ice prevents collection. Since the 1960s, large quantities of *F. lumbricalis* have been washed up on the coasts and harvested. On the beach the weed is contaminated with other seaweeds, animals, sand and gravel, and these impurities can represent 15–20% of the total material collected. In 1967, drift material constituted 20–27% of total production (Lund & Christensen 1969).

Material used by local industry is treated directly in the wet state, whereas that for export is dried and either tied up in bundles or bagged. Harvesting of *F. lumbricalis*, used for the production of furcellaran (a type of carrageenan), rose continually between 1946 and 1958 and reached its highest level of 31 000 t in 1962 (Lund & Bjerre-Petersen 1964; Lund & Christensen 1969). Over-exploitation of stocks has led to a fall in production (Fig. 27) and annual collection is currently about 10 000 t (International Trade Centre 1981).

GRACILARIA VERRUCOSA

DISTRIBUTION AND ECOLOGY

The red seaweed *Gracilaria* is now the most important raw material for the agar industry and yields 60–70% of the world's agar (Nelson *et al.* 1983; McLachlan 1985). Close to 5000 t of agar are being produced annually from 25 000–30 000 t of *Gracilaria* harvested mainly from the wild in Argentina, Brazil, Chile and South Africa and from fishpond culture in Taiwan, Hainan Island, China, and mainland China (Santelices & Doty 1989). In excess of 160 species of the genus are known, but only a few of them are used by the agar industry. Among these species, *Gracilaria verrucosa* is regarded as being widespread and common, but there is considerable doubt now that a single biological entity is involved (see Chapter 11). In northern Europe, *G. verrucosa* and *Gracilariopsis lemaneiformis* (see Fredericq & Hommersand 1989) are perennial plants (15–40 cm in length on average) which grow in intertidal pools and in channels in the lower intertidal and shallow subtidal. They usually grow attached by holdfasts and rhizoids to rock, pebbles, shells and gravel. Sandy bays and lagoons are favoured places for the growth of these plants. In certain areas, sterile unattached forms accumulate (Causey *et al.* 1946) in a similar manner to *Furcellaria lumbricalis* f. *aegagropila*. Virstein and Carbonara (1985) point out that high densities of *Gracilaria* are associated with nutrient inputs from human populations, which is the case particularly in the lagoons of Orbetello, Lessina and Venice in Italy (Lenzi & Bombelli 1985). Croatto (1982) recorded densities of 15 kg m^{-2} in areas where the water is heavily polluted by domestic, agricultural and industrial effluents in the Venice Lagoon.

HARVESTING IN EUROPE

Methods for harvesting *Gracilaria* have, until relatively recently, been rudimentary in spite of intensive exploitation. In Chile, grapnels or long rakes were used initially for harvesting natural populations (Kim 1970; Cable 1974), but an out-planting system that takes advantage of the plants' ability to form rhizoids is now used (Santelices & Doty 1989).

Italy

Since 1974, collection of *Gracilaria* in the lagoon of Lessina has been undertaken from May to July, using forks from small motorized flat-bottomed boats 6–7 m in length (Trotta 1981) operated by one or two people (Fig. 28). The bed, composed mainly of *Gracilaria*, covers more than 100 ha (Trotta 1981). The seaweed is spread out for sun-drying at the edges of the lagoons (Trotta personal communication), and turned over from time to time with a fork to speed the rate of drying. The dry weed is then either tied up in bundles or loaded by cranes into a truck for transportation to an agar-extraction factory at Parme. This manual process will probably be discontinued shortly because of the high costs of manpower, even though the collection method has the advantage of selecting mature plants, especially in the areas where the density is less than 4 kg wet weight m^{-2}. Yearly production is estimated at

Figure 28. Collection of *Gracilaria* by pitchfork in Italy. (Photograph courtesy of P. Trotta)

Figure 29. Collection of *Gracilaria* by net in Italy. (Photograph courtesy of M. Lenzi)

6400 t in the Orbettello Lagoon, 1000 t in the Lessina Lagoon, and 10 000 t in the Venice Lagoon. In 1985, the price was fixed at 50 000 lire t^{-1} of seaweed (Orlandini & Favretto 1987).

Since 1984, Ittiogenica S. Liberata has been studying methods of improving the methods of collection, while reducing the costs (Lenzi 1985). The Orbettello Lagoon, where unattached *Gracilaria* is harvested at a depth of about 1 m, has been chosen for this study. The shallow depth and the soft muddy bottom require the use of mechanical harvesting. Two things have to be taken into account in the design of the equipment: minimal disturbance of the soft mud and the use of a boat with a shallow draught, even when fully laden. Initial experiments were carried out in 1984–86 with a barge 22 m long and 9 m in width. During harvesting, the boat pulled a fixed net on a rectangular frame (Fig. 29); once full, the net was hoisted to make the seaweed fall into the hold of the barge. In 1987, a modified procedure was tested, in which the net was replaced by a conveyor belt, which strained off the water and

Figure 30. Collection of *Gracilaria* by conveyor belt in Italy. (Photograph courtesy of M. Lenzi)

transported the seaweed to the hold (Fig. 30). The control room occupied a strategic position between the conveyor belt and the container. Two people were required for navigation, supervision of harvesting, and loading. Handling was possible only if the boat was steadied by two jacks. Propulsion of the 83 h.p. boat was ensured by two hydraulic wheels 1.5 m in diameter, which made it possible to reach a speed of 2.5 knots. The storage capacity of the boat was 20 m³, and it was unloaded by a hydraulic crane, 6 m long, placed at the stern. The maximum load of the vessel was 1.5 t. This prototype, created by Nettuno Metalmeccanica in collaboration with Ittiogenica S. Liberata, made it possible to harvest 437 t (wet weight) in 116 h during July and August 1987 (Lenzi personal communication). In 1988, the harvest was estimated at 5000 t, which was about 10% of the macroalgal biomass of the lagoon, although the green alga *Chaetomorpha* sp. forms the major proportion of the standing biomass.

A type of sledge used in New Zealand (Fig. 31) may be suitable for harvesting *Gracilaria* in European intertidal areas, but this would not be suitable in the Mediterranean as tides are essentially absent.

Spain

Along the coasts of Spain, harvesting of cast *Gracilaria* is carried out with nets (International Trade Centre 1981).

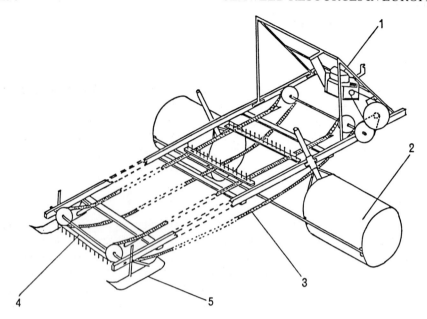

Figure 31. Sketch of prototype *Gracilaria* harvester used in New Zealand: 1, petrol engine; 2, buoyancy outrigger; 3, elevator chain; 4, rake; 5, ski. (After Luxton 1977)

Portugal

Limited quantities of *G. verrucosa* are harvested for the extraction of agar (de Oliveira personal communication).

GELIDIUM AND *PTEROCLADIA*

DISTRIBUTION AND ECOLOGY

Geldium sesquipedale, *G. latifolium* and *Pterocladia capillacea* contain a higher proportion of agarose than species of *Gracilaria* and are thus in demand for particular applications. These algae are found along the coasts of the English Channel, the Atlantic and Mediterranean, but the south-west of France and the western coasts of Spain and Portugal are the only areas where economically harvestable quantities occur. All three species are perennial and form small bunches; *G. sesquipedale* is 25–35 cm in length, *G. latifolium* 5–6 cm, and *P. capillacea* 10–20 cm (Gayral 1966). All grow attached to rocky substrata; *G. latifolium* grows in calm water in the mid-intertidal, and *G. sesquipedale* and *P. capillacea* grow in semi-exposed to exposed locations in the lower intertidal and shallow subtidal.

HARVESTING IN EUROPE

France

Cast *G. sesquipedale* is collected in south-west France near Hendaye, St Jean-De-Luz, Bidart and Biarritz. Collection is from mid-August to February. The seaweed is gathered with a fork fixed on a tractor and taken for treatment to the agar extraction factory (Sobigel at Hendaye). The yearly harvest of *G. sesquipedale* varies from 1500 to 35 000 t wet weight.

Portugal

In Portugal, as in Japan (Silverthorne 1977; Cuyvers 1978), divers are used for 90% of the harvesting of *Gelidium*. They dive either with a snorkel in shallow waters or in deeper waters (15–20 m) with a *marghileh* connected to an air compressor in the boat (De Oliveira personal communication). The divers pull the seaweed from rocks and load it into sacks fixed around their waists; once the sacks are full, they are hoisted to the surface with a boom (Fig. 32). The remainder of the harvest is collected from cast material between July and November. Other harvesting techniques involving either

Figure 32. Boat equipped for scuba diving for the collection of *Gelidium*. (From Correia da Costa & Paes da Franca 1984, with permission)

manual cutting (scissors, sickle) or mechanical cutting (a small reaping machine, which sucks up seaweed) were introduced, but these did not find favour with the collectors; the low output from manual cutting and the choking of the mechanical cutter were the main difficulties encountered.

Of the yearly production of *Pterocladia capillacea*, 80% is obtained by diving; the other 20% is from storm-cast weed in the spring (Fralick & Andrade 1981). The drift seaweed is either hand-picked or gathered with different kinds of net.

Pterocladia capillacea is harvested around the whole archipelago of the Azores. The largest biomass is found in the vicinity of Flores, Graciosa, Terceira and S. Miguel (Palminha 1971). The harvesting fleet is composed of 52 motor boats and a few sailing vessels, located in the centre and south of the archipelago, each with about four or five divers (Correia da Costa & Paes da Franca 1984). After collection, the seaweed is air dried before packing and delivery to agarextraction factories based in Porto, Figueira da Foz, Alverca and Coina (Palminha 1971; Oliveira personal communication).

Exploitation of *G. sesquipedale* and *G. latifolium* in Portugal began in 1942. The areas of Minho, Dourou, Estremadura, Boixo, Alentejo and Algarve are the main centres of collection (Palminha 1971).

Spain

The main areas for the harvesting of agarophytes are located on the north-west coast, mainly in the regions of Santander and Asturias. Storm-cast *Gelidium* is collected from the shoreline with forks or similar implements. Divers have been used since 1958 for the collection of *Gelidium* at depths of 2–10 m (Gallardo *et al.* 1990). A hand-held cutting tool (CASM-G) has been developed by Travocean (France) for use by the divers. This tool, which both cuts and lifts the algae, enables about 3 t of *Gelidium* to be cut per diver each day. This new tool does not damage the basal parts of the plants, so regeneration can take place. Experience has shown that the use of this collection method has led to an increase in biomass of from 50 to 100% after 1 year of exploitation. In 1989, ten CASM-Gs operated on the north-west coast of Spain.

Gelidium sesquipedale is the most collected species in Spain, the highest standing crops being found from north-eastern Asturias to the border with France. Total *Gelidium* biomass in northern Spain is about 150 000 t fresh weight and the harvest in 1973–88 ranged from 3603 to 10 754 t dry weight per year (Gallardo *et al.* 1990).

RESOURCE MANAGEMENT

Sexual and spore reproduction in *Gelidium* and *Pterocladia* species is thought to be low. Consequently, preservation of the rhizoids, which make regeneration possible, is essential for continuing harvests (Carter & Anderson 1985). However, *Gelidium* is less of a problem in this respect than *Pterocladia*; most of the plant is readily collected but the rhizoid structure remains, because of its greater resistance to being uprooted.

In Spain, the advent of collecting by divers has led to concerns about over-harvesting. The use of the cutting tool mentioned above has allowed regeneration, but it has been suggested that the beds be divided into plots that would be harvested sequentially over a 3 year period (Gallardo *et al.* 1990).

In Portugal, risks are linked to the over-exploitation of the resource. The harvesting of *Gelidium* is covered by the same regulations as those for *Chondrus crispus* (p. 283). In June and July, the biomass of the known beds of *Gelidium* is estimated to be about 9000 t (wet weight). Quotas for production are fixed for each area, and in 1987 production was 4800 t, about half of the biomass. Investigations of the extent of the *Gelidium* beds and of the biomass before and after harvesting show a near steady state of the resource. Even if present production remains under the proposed quotas, the fishing effort (licences for boats and divers), the production, and the state of the resource will be supervised closely.

Fralick and Andrade (1981) discuss problems with the regeneration of *P. capillacea* in the Azores. These are connected with an increasing number of scuba divers who want high output rather than the preservation of the rhizoidal bases. These abuses have led the authorities to take measures for

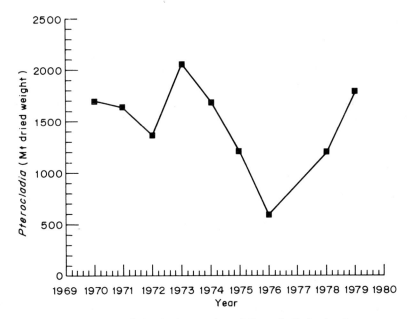

Figure 33. Trends in the harvesting of *Pterocladia* in the Azores

the control of collection and to avoid excessive damage to the rhizoids. According to Fralick and Andrade (1981), the maximum limit of the exploitable stock (6000 t wet weight; 2000 t dry weight) has almost been reached, which limits the capacity for future expansion of the colloid industry in the Azores (Fig. 33). In 1979, about 5400 t of *P. capillacea* (1800 t dry weight) was processed by two local factories to produce 325 t of high-grade agar.

In Spain, holdfast damage and over-exploitation of the *Gelidium* beds has resulted in the depletion of the sites. Since 1987, divers' licences have been cancelled and only operators who own a tool capable of cutting *Gelidium* without damaging the rhizoidal bases may obtain a licence.

MAËRL

DISTRIBUTION AND ECOLOGY

The Breton term *maërl* or *Lithothamnion* refers to marine sediments composed almost entirely of small coralline algae (2–10 mm in diameter). The commonest species are *Phymatolithon corallioides* and *Lithothamnion calcareum*, which can be found in varying proportions depending on location. Live *P. corallioides* plants are generally reddish or pink whereas *L. calcareum* is more of a steel-blue colour. During drying, maërl turns blue-grey.

In Europe, maërl beds are found from Norway to the Mediterranean basin (Jacquotte 1962). Exploitation is confined, however, to the Cornish coast of England (Falmouth Harbour), and to the coast of Brittany (Baie de Paimpol, Saint-Brieuc, Iles de Glénan, Plateau de Molène) (Blunden *et al.* 1981). Maërl has been harvested in Cornwall since the 18th century, but in France its exploitation is more recent, dating back only to the 19th century. Maërl, which takes the form of a solid and compact sediment, is found in banks, the depths of which vary with water turbidity, and requires low irradiance levels for growth. The plants are found in areas exposed to strong currents on sandy bottoms at 9–28 m in Norway, 10–18 m in the UK, 0–32 m in Ireland (deepest population was dredged east of the Aran Islands, Galway Bay) and 0–20 m on the coast of Brittany, with an optimum of 10 m, and 30–66 m on the Mediterranean coasts (Blunden *et al.* 1977; Guiry personal communication). Maërl grows unattached on the seabed, but the plants are initially attached and, as they grow and develop branches, these become detached by the action of waves and currents. The fragments thus formed continue to grow and are transported by currents to form the maërl banks. The rate of growth is extremely slow, about 1 mm per year, but the formation of branches lasts up to ten years. The live plants grow in shallow water, whereas the dead ones accumulate in deeper waters. In the Baie de Paimpol (France), maërl deposits extend for over 3 km^2 and are up to 15 m thick. Accessible deposits of maërl in Galway Bay and Connemara (Ireland) are estimated to exceed 8×10^6 t

(Guiry personal communication). Details of commercial harvesting in Cornwall are given by Blunden *et al.* (1981).

HARVESTING IN EUROPE

France

At the beginning of the present century, harvesting was carried out from
small boats which were beached on the maërl banks at low tide, and filled
using a shovel and wheelbarrow. In the 1920s, these boats were motorized,
but harvesting was still time-consuming and difficult. In 1930, a *gabare* was
fitted out with an engine-driven winch and a bucket, which completely
changed the working conditions. The fact that the *goëmoniers* did not have to
beach the boats on the maërl banks allowed more time for collection and for
delimiting the harvesting areas. The boats collect the maërl in groups and
derricks are used to transfer material from one boat to another.

Nowadays, two methods for maërl collection are employed in northern
France. The grab method (Fig. 34), is used by 17 boats, each 200–400 t
(Syndicat National des Armateurs extracteurs de Matériaux Marins 1985);
but, more recently (1974), pump-dredgers (Fig. 35) have been introduced,
the maërl being sucked up and loaded onto 500–1800 t boats, of which there
are 16. Three people man a grab-boat and five a pump-dredger. After a few

Figure 34. Collection of maërl in northern France by grab. (Unpublished photograph)

Figure 35. Collection of maërl by pump dredger in northern France. (Unpublished photograph)

days storage, the maërl is processed by factories in Pontrieux (SECMA) and Saint-Malo (TIMAC). After grinding, it is dehydrated in rotary drum driers (Blunden *et al.* 1981).

The industrial exploitation of maërl has increased considerably over the last 20 years. However, because of the very slow growth rate of this seaweed, stocks are being reduced and, in the long run, regrowth will not make up the deficit caused by intense exploitation (Cabioch 1987). In 1984, harvested maërl represented less than 50% of the agricultural calcium requirements of Brittany (1 300 000 t). In spite of the potential market, the quantity of maërl collected has fallen to 520 000 t per annum compared with the 650 000 t gleaned in 1977 (Fig. 36). Quotas and the difficulties raised by the low profitability of the product explain this falling trend. Also the fall in production is associated with a reduction of 50% in the number of small naval dockyards from 30 in 1979 to 15 in 1985. Only industrial naval dockyards keep vessel production steady. As a result, boats equipped with grabs have become old and have had to be laid up gradually (21 boats since 1979), but these have not been replaced with boats equipped with sucking dredges (Fig. 37). Despite some penetration into the cosmetic and pharmaceutical markets, maërl remains essentially a cheap product used as a calcium/magnesium soil additive in agriculture, and as a mineral complement in animal fodder; it is also used for the treatment of acidic drinking waters.

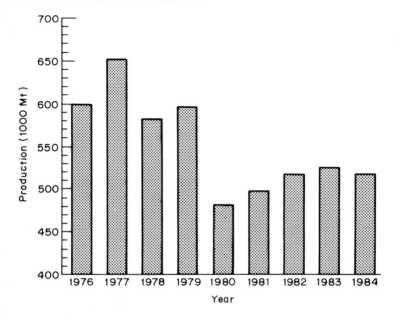

Figure 36. Trends in maërl production in France, 1976–84

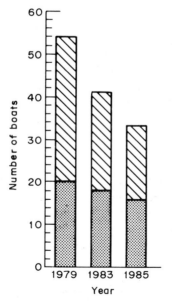

Figure 37. Structure of the maërl fishing fleet in France 1979, 1983, 1985: ▦, pump dredger; ◪, grab

ULVA AND *ENTEROMORPHA*

DISTRIBUTION AND ECOLOGY

In recent years, some of the industrialized countries of Europe have been confronted with macroalgal blooms, particularly green seaweeds such as *Ulva* and *Enteromorpha*. These blooms are linked to problems of pollution and the consequent eutrophication of coastal ecosystems. In Europe, the phenomenon has been particularly prevalent in the UK, Italy ad France (Briand 1989). The biomass produced decomposes either *in situ* or in large drifts. These substantial quantities of drift weed are not collected for industrial use, but need to be removed because they are a nuisance. In some areas the density of green algae is between 10 and 90 kg m^{-2}. This is the case along the Breton coasts, where, every year, more than 50 000 m^3 of *Ulva* plants are collected.

HARVESTING IN EUROPE

Bulldozers, raking machines, sifting machines and *goëmoniers* are all used for cleaning the beaches at the present time. The use of bulldozers is necessary (Fig. 38) in areas where the deposits are considerable, for example in the Baie de Lannion, where these deposits can reach 1 m in thickness. The hourly

Figure 38. Collection of *Ulva* by bulldozer in Lannion Bay, France. (Unpublished photograph)

collection rate is between 300 and 700 m³, but this process is not selective enough as large quantities of sand are also collected. Another machine, pulled by a tractor, and called a *goëmonier*, is very simple and is based on the principle of agricultural harrows. Other equipment has also been tested, including an ensilage machine (Fig. 39) and a baler (Fig. 40) (Golven personal communication). The principle on which the raking machine works (Fig. 41) has been inspired by various agricultural machines. A swivel belt fitted with supple sawteeth rakes the sand and pulls up the seaweed into a container (1–2 m³), the low volume of which, however, necessitates frequent emptying; this takes 30 s, on average, to unload (Golven personal communication). An hydraulic handle makes it possible to lift the bucket 2.45 m and the contents are tipped into a truck (Raking machine RP200-Rolba). The hourly output is 70–80 m³ (thickness of the deposit 5 cm), and the cleaned beach surface is

Figure 39. Ensilage machine in France. (Unpublished photograph, courtesy of CEVA)

Figure 40. Baler (hay-press) in France. (Unpublished photograph, courtesy of CEVA)

Figure 41. Raking machine in France. (Unpublished photograph, courtesy of CEVA)

Figure 42. Sifting machine. (Unpublished photograph, courtesy of CEVA)

about $6000-6500\ m^{-2}\ h^{-1}$, with a tractor which moves at $3\ km\ h^{-1}$. This machine is used particularly when the deposits are not very thick (Golven personal communication).

The sifting machine (Fig. 42) ensures cleaning of the beach by sifting the sand (using a sifter and a conveyor belt made of supple steel mesh) and by collecting the seaweed in a container placed at the back of the machine. The output is between 30 and $50\ m^{-3}\ h^{-1}$. The surface cleaned is smaller than the preceding one (between 2400 and 3200 m^2, deposits less than 5 cm, and its use is limited to small deposits (Golven personal communication).

The scraping machine (marketed by EGMO) has a scraper, developed originally for collecting hydrocarbons (Golven personal communication). The vehicle moves along the shore at the water's edge (Fig. 43) and a rolling belt, fitted with blades, collects seaweed from the top few centimetres of water. This gathering-head sweeps continuously.

Caustier also manufacture a boat (Salabre: $7.2 \times 2.51.1 \times 1.8$ m; draught of 35 cm) for the cleaning of coastal waters, which is equipped with a conveyor of jointed sheets, 2.2 m in width, of wire netting (Fig. 44). The vessel has a bucket of 3.5 m^3 where the seaweed is stocked (Golven personal communication).

The cost of collection of 1 t of *Ulva* varies from FFr 50 to 800, depending on the type of machine used and the area. Specialized companies carry out beach cleaning at the expense of the taxpayer. The harvested seaweed is afterwards

Figure 43. Scraping machine in France. (Unpublished photograph, courtesy of CEVA)

Figure 44. Boat with conveyor belt–collector in France. (Unpublished photograph, courtesy of CEVA)

spread on fields as a soil additive, stocked in dumps, or dehydrated for use in premixed poultry feeds (Brault *et al.* 1983).

CONCLUSIONS

In Europe, expansion of the colloid market has made it necessary to increase the exploitation of natural seaweed stocks. The development of harvesting techniques, which used to be a matter for the individual, is now carried out by industry. This technological revolution has developed in two stages. First, boats were motorized and collection machinery was improved, and this has completely changed seaweed harvesting. Mechanical cutting and lifting are now common practices in benthic seaweed harvesting. In Norway, *Ascophyllum nodosum* is harvested and loaded on boats, either by a conveyor belt or by being sucked up. In France, *Laminaria digitata* is harvested by a mechanical scoubidou, whereas in Norway a rake dredge is used to pick up the stipes of *L. hyperborea*. The exploitation of maërl is an exception because of the nature of the seaweed itself. Gradually, boats with a sucking device are replacing boats with grabs. The equipment used for harvesting unattached seaweeds is less sophisticated: harvesting of *Furcellaria* is carried out in Denmark using dredges; harvesting of *Gracilaria* is carried out using conveyor belts fitted with filters in Italy. In France, several harvesting machines are used for cleaning some resort beaches of considerable deposits of *Ulva*; sifting machines, raking machines, bulldozers, and barges fitted with a collection belt are all used.

The following parameters have to be taken into account in the development and adjustment of harvesting equipment: the efficiency and selectivity of the equipment; its robustness; its seaworthiness; its storage capacity, the cost of investment and operation; the adequacy of its draught; the method of propulsion and the depth of the populations being harvested; and, where appropriate, the use of techniques which allow for regrowth (Bombelli 1986).

With the mechanization of harvesting and an increase in collection effort, the danger of over-exploitation emerges (Caddy & Fisher 1985). At this stage, good management of the resource becomes essential, which implies that action has to be taken to determine the extent of available biomass, to estimate stocks and the production of the plants in the harvesting areas, to monitor the collection of plants in sensitive areas, and to control the rapid development of harvesting devices. The use of satellite imaging, developed by IFREMER, in addition to traditional techniques, might make it possible to obtain reliable information concerning the state and development of algal stocks (Belsher 1985a, 1985b).

In the case of some seaweeds, for example *Chondrus crispus* and *Mastocarpus stellatus*, exploitation comes up against another kind of difficulty, that of under-exploitation. No mechanization of the harvest has occurred, because of the small size and topographical features of the collection areas. Harvesting these species requires a considerable amount of professional labour as fishermen have concluded that this activity is not financially rewarding and have tended to give it up. The paradox is now that the value of the seaweed is too low for people to collect it, but is too high for the industry, especially because of competition from material grown in the Philippines and Indonesia. Expansion of new seaweed markets for human food and cosmetics is restricted by the lack of raw material, and this would need to be overcome by the development of algal cultivation.

The European share of the market will need to be maintained by improving methods of mechanization and strict resource management. Improvements in quality brought about by algal cultivation will also need attention.

ACKNOWLEDGEMENTS

The author would like to express his grateful thanks to: Drs P. Arzel, T. Belsher, G. Blunden, V. Bombelli, D. Brault, J. Christensen, F. Correia da Costa, E.C. De Oliveira, P. Golven, M.D. Guiry, M. Indergaard, J. Kain, M. Lanzi, J. McLachlan, F. Malecot, I.K. Munda, M. Orlandini, J.L. Sanderson, K. Searle and P. Trotta for information that helped in the writing of this chapter, and to L. Le Cam Hernandez and M.G. Houriez for translating it into English.

REFERENCES

Aberdein C. 1968. Scope for expansion and new techniques. *Fish. News Int.* **2**: 24–8.
Anon. 1969. Alginates. *CIBA Rev.*, **2**: 3–11.
Anon. 1978. Seaweed scooper. *Fish. News Int.* **17**: 15.
Ardré F. 1970. Contribution à l'étude des algues marines du Portugal. I. La flore. *Port. Acta Biol: Sér B* **10**: 137–555.
Arzel P. 1984. *Traditional Management of Seaweeds in the District of Léon.* Fish. Tech. Pap. FAO no. 249. pp. 1–49.
Arzel P. 1987. *Les Goëmoniers.* pp. 294. St-Herblain: Éditions de l'Estran.
Baardseth E. 1955. *Regrowth of* Ascophyllum nodosum *after Harvesting.* pp. iv + 67. Dublin: Institute for Industrial Research and Standards.
Baardseth E. 1968. Synopsis of biological data on *Ascophyllum nodosum* (Linnaeus) Le Jolis. *Fish. Synopsis FAO* no. 38: ii, 1–36.
Belsher T. 1985a. Télédétection et phytobenthos: stratégie pour l'obtention d'informations, par télédétection, sur le phytobenthos marin. *Colloq. Fr.-Japon Oceanogr. Marseille* **3**: 27–32.
Belsher T. 1985b. Télédétection des végétaux marins du phytobenthos du littoral français: l'archipel des Iles Chausey. *photo. Interprétation* **5**: 1–5.
Bjerre-Petersen E., Christensen J. & Hemmingsen P. 1973. Furcellaran. In *Industrial Gums: Polysaccharides and their Derivatives.* 2nd edn. (Ed. R.L. Whistler) pp. 123–36. New York: Academic Press.

Blunden G., Farnham W.F., Jephson N., Fenn R.H. & Plunkett B.A. 1977. The composition of maërl from the Glenán Islands of southern Brittany. *Botanica Mar.* **20**: 121–5.

Blunden G., Farnham W.F., Jephson N., Barwell C.J., Fenn R.H. & Plunkett B.A. 1981. The composition of maërl beds of economic interest in Northern Brittany. Cornwall and Ireland. *Proc. Int. Seaweed Symp.* **10**: 651–74.

Bodeau-Bellion C. 1987. Les carraghénanes. In *Symposium sur les Algues Marines*. (Ed. J.Y.-Floc'h) pp. 18–20. Brest: Université de Bretagne Occidentale et Chambre de Commerce et d'Industrie de Breas.

Bombelli V. 1986. Aquatic crops: problems and perspectives concerning harvesting technologies. In *Energy Biomass from Harvesting to Storage*. pp. 1–8. Rome: EEC-ITABIP.

Booth E. 1964. The seaweed industry in Great Britain. *Fish. News Int.* **3**: 229–33.

Braud J.P. 1984. Essai de dragage de *Laminaria hyperborea*. In *Symposium sur les Algues Marines*. (Ed. J.Y.-Floc'h) pp. 1–19. Brest: Université de Bretagne Occidentale et Chambre de Commerce et d'Industrie de Breas.

Brault D., Briand X. & Golven P. 1983. 'Les marées vertes': premier bilan concernant les essais de valorisation. In: *Bases Biologiques de l'Aquaculture*. pp. 33–42. Montpellier: IFREMER.

Briand X. 1988. Exploitation of seaweed in Europe. In *Aquatic Primary Biomass (Marine Macroalgae): Biomass Conversion, Removal and Use of Nutrients. 1. Proceedings of the First Workshop of the COST 48 Sub-group*. (Ed. P. Morand & E.H. Schulte) pp. 53–65. Brussels: COST 48.

Briand X. 1989. *Proliferation de l'Algue Verte* Ulva sp. *en Baie de Lannion (France): Étude d'une Nuisance et de son Traitement par Fermentation Anaérobie*. Thèse de Doctorat en Biologie et Physiologie Végétale. pp. 209. Lille: Université de Lille.

Cabioch J. 1987. Biologie du maërl et des concrétionnements calcaires à algues rouges. In *Symposium sur les algues Marines*. (Ed. J.Y.-Floc'h) pp. 38–41. Brest: Université de Bretangne Occidentale et Chambre de Commerce et d'Industrie de Breas.

Cable W.D. 1974. A description of the activities of the Maullin (Chile) fishing cooperative in the extraction of the marine alga *Gracilaria* sp. *Botanica Mar.* **27**: 60–2.

Caddy J.F. & Fisher W.A. 1985. FAO interests in promoting understanding of world seaweed resources, their optimal harvesting and fishery and ecological interactions. *Hydrobiologia* **124**: 111–21.

Carter A.R. & Anderson R.J. 1985. Regrowth after experimental harvesting of the agarophyte *Gelidium pristoides* in the eastern Cape Province. *S. Afr. J. Mar. Sci.* **3**: 111–18.

Causey N.B., Pryterch J.P., McCaskill J., Humm H.J. & Wolf F.A. 1946. Influence of environmental factors upon the growth of *Gracilaria confervoides*. *Bull. Duke. Univ. Mar. Stat.* **3**: 19–24.

Chapman V.J. 1948. Seaweed resources along the shores of Great Britain. *Econ. Bot.* **2**: 363–78.

Correia da Costa F. & Paes da Franca M.L. 1984. *Pesca Artesanal na Zona Centro da Costa Ocidental Portuguesa No. 4*. pp. 4. Lisbon: Instituto Nacional de Invetigaçao das Pescas.

Croatto U. 1982. Energy from macroalgae of the Venice Lagoon. *International Conference on the Biomass. Second EEC Conference*, Berlin, 20–23 September 1982. (Eds. A. Strub, P. Chartier & G. Schlesser) pp. 329–33. London: Elsevier Applied Science.

Cullinane J.P. 1984. A quantitative survey of the harvestable intertidal seaweed on the west coast of Ireland. *Hydrobiologia* **116/117**: 338–41.

Cuyvers L. 1978. Harvesting red seaweeds in Japan. *Tengusa* **9/10**: 285–94.

Czapke K. 1964. L'agar-agar, produit du *Furcellaria fastigiata* de la mér baltique *Proc. Int. Seaweed Symp.* **4**: 393–7.

Didou H. 1983. Techniques de récolte des algues rouges et algues brunes. *Biomasse Actaulités Spécial* **3**: 24–5.

Fralick R.A. & Andrade F. 1981. The growth, reproduction, harvesting and management of *Pterocladia pinnata* in the Azores, Portugal. *Proc. Int. Seaweed Symp.* **10**: 289–95.

Fredericq S. & Hommersand M.H. 1989. Comparative morphology and taxonomic status of *Gracilariopisis* (Gracilariales, Rhodophyta). *J. Phycol.* **25**: 228–41.

Gallardo T., Alvarez Cobelas M. & Alvarez de Meneses A. 1990. Current state of seaweed resources in Spain. *Proc. Int. Seaweed Symp.* **14**: 287–92.

Gayral P. 1966. *Les Algues des Côtes Françaises.* pp. 632. Paris: Éditions Doin.

Gayral P. & Cosson J. 1973. Exposé synoptique des données biologiques sur la laminaire digitée *Laminaria. Fish. Synop. FAO* **89**: 1–61.

Guiry M.D. & Blunden G. 1980. What hope for Irish seaweed? *Technology Ireland* **9**: 38–43.

Guiry M.D. & Blunden G. 1981. The commercial collection and utilisation of seaweeds in Ireland. *Proc. Int. Seaweed Symp.* **10**: 675–80.

Hallson S.V. 1964. The uses of seaweed in Iceland. *Proc. Int. Seaweed Symp.* **4**: 398–405.

Holmsgaard J.E., Greenwell M. & McLachlan J. 1981. Biomass and vertical distribution of *Furcellaria lumbricalis* and associated algae. *Proc. Int. Seaweed Symp.* **10**: 309–14.

International Trade Centre. 1981. *Pilot Survey of the World Seaweed Industry and Trade.* pp. 110. Geneva: International Trade Centre UNCTAD/GATT.

Jackson P. 1952a. Harvesting of brown sublittoral seaweeds. *The Engineer* no. 193. 718–20.

Jackson P. 1952b. Harvesting of brown sublittoral seaweeds. *The Engineer* no. 193. 750–751.

Jackson P. 1957. Harvesting machinery for brown sublittoral seaweed II. *Engineer* no. 203. 439–41.

Jackson P. & McIver R.F. 1952. Harvesting of brown sublittoral seaweeds III. *Engineer* no. 194. 2–5.

Jackson P. & Wolff R. 1955. Sublittoral seaweed harvester. *Research* **8**: 435–44.

Jacquotte R. 1962. Étude des fonds de maërl de Méditerranée. *Rec. Trav. St Mar. Endoume* **26**: 141–215.

Jensen A. 1978. Industrial utilization of seaweeds in the past, present and future. *Proc. Int. Seaweed Symp.* **9**: 17–34.

Kain J.M. 1971. Synopsis of biological data on *Laminaria hyperborea. Fish. Synopsis FAO* **87**: 1–68.

Kim D.H. 1970. Economically important seaweed in Chile. I. *Gracilaria. Botanica Mar.* **13**: 140–62.

Lenzi M. 1985. Valutazioni sulla possibilita di realizzare raccolte e coltivazioni della rodoficea *Gracilaria confervoides* nella laguna di Orbettelo *Atti. Mus. Civ. Stor. Nat. Grosseta* **6**: 17–22.

Lenzi M. & Bombelli V. 1985. Prime valutazioni della biomassa macrofitica nella laguna di Orbetello in considerazione di uno sfruttamento industriale. *Nova Thalassia* **7**: 355–60.

Lobban C.S., Harrison P.J. & Duncan M.J. 1985. *The Physiological Ecology of Seaweeds.* 237 pp. Cambridge: Cambridge University Press.

Lund S. & Bjerre-Petersen E. 1964. Collection and utilization of Danish *Furcellaria*, 1946–1960 *Proc. Int. Seaweed Symp.* **4**: 410–11.

Lund S. & Christensen J. 1969. On the collection of *Furcellaria* in Denmark during the years 1961–1967. *Proc. Int. Seaweed Symp.* **6**: 699–701.

Lüning K. 1969. Standing crop and leaf area index of the sublittoral *Laminaria* species near Helgoland. *Mar. Biol.* **3**: 282–6.

Luxton D.M. 1981. Experimental harvesting of *Gracilaria* in New Zealand. *Proc. Int. Seaweed Symp.* **10**: 693–8.

MacKenzie W. 1947. Seaweed harvesting methods. *Engineer* no. 184. 337–87.

May J.M. 1952. Harvesting of brown sublittoral seaweed. II. The continuous grapnel method. *Engineer* no. 193. 814–17.

McHugh D.G. & Lanier B.V. 1983. *The World Seaweed Industry and Trade: Developing Asian Producers and Prospects for Greater Participation.* Kuala Lumpur: ADB/FAO INFOFISH Market Report. Vol. 6.

McLachlan J. 1985. Macroalgae (seaweeds): industrial resources and their utilization. *Pl. Soil* **89**: 137–57.

Mitchell M.E. & Guiry M.D. 1984. Carrageen: a local habitation or a name? *J. Ethnopharmacol.* **9**: 347–51.

Munda I. 1964. The quantity and chemical composition of *Ascophyllum nodosum* along the coast between the rivers Olfusa and Thjorsa (southern Iceland). *Botanica Mar.* **7**: 76–88.

Munda I. 1972. On the chemical composition, distribution and ecology of some common benthic marine algae from Iceland. *Botanica Mar.* **25**: 1–45.

Munda I. 1987. Distribution and use of economically important seaweeds in Iceland. *Hydrobiologia* **151/152**: 257–60.

Naylor J. 1977. *Production, commerce et utilisation des algues marines et produits dérivés.* Fish Tech. Pap. FAO no. 159, p. 76.

Nelson S.G., Yang S.S., Wang C.Y. & Chiang Y.M. 1983. Yield and quality of agar from species of *Gracilaria* collected from Taïwan and Micronesia. *Botanica Mar.* **26**: 361–6.

Orlandini M. & Favretto L. 1987. Utilization of macroalgae in Italy for pollution abatement and as source of energy and chemicals. In *Aquatic Primary Biomass (Marine Macroalgae): Biomass Conversion, Removal and Use of Nutrients. 1. Proceedings of the First Workshop of the COST 48 Sub-group.* (Ed. P. Morand & E.H. Schulte; pp. 25–8. Brussels: COST 48.

Palminha F. 1971. Exploraçao e utilizaçao de algas marinhas na plataforma continental portuguesa e na ilhas do Arquipelago dos Açores. *Boletim Junta Nac. Fomento Pescas* **7**: 25–36.

Pringle J.D. 1978. Aspects of the ecological impact of *Chondrus crispus* harvesting in eastern Canada. *Proc. Int. Seaweed Symp.* **9**: 225–32.

Pryet M. 1986. *L'exemple de la Filère des Algues Alimentaires au Japon.* 198 pp. Toulouse: Ecole Supérieure d'Agriculture (ESAP).

Santelices B. & Doty M.S. 1989. A review of *Gracilaria* farming. *Aquaculture* **78**: 95–133.

Seip K.L. 1980. A computational model for growth and harvesting of the marine alga *Ascophyllum nodosum. Ecol. Modelling* **8**: 189–99.

Seip K.L., Lunde G., Melson S., Mehlum E., Melhuss A. & Seip H.M. 1979. A mathematical model for the distribution and abundance of benthic algae in a Norwegian fjord. *Ecol. Modelling* **6**: 133–66.

Sharp G. 1987. *Ascophyllum nodosum* and its harvesting in eastern Canada. In *Case Studies of Seven Commercial Seaweed Resources.* (Eds. M.S. Doty, J.F. Caddy & B. Santelices) pp. 3–38. Rome: FAO.

Sharp G.J. & Roddick D.L. 1982. *Catch and Effort Trends of the Irish Moss Fishery in Southwestern Nova Scotia.* Tech. Rep. Can. Fish. Aquat. Sci. no. 1118. pp. 1–43.

Silverthorne W. 1977. Optimal production from a seaweed resource *Botanica Mar.* **20**: 75–98.

Syndicat National des Armateurs extracteurs de Matériaux Marins (SNAM). 1985. *Armements Français de Navires Sabliers*. 7 pp. Nantes: Éditions Syndicat National des Armateurs extracteurs de Matériaux Marins.

Svensen P. 1972. Some observations on commercial harvesting and regrowth of *Laminaria hyperborea*. *Soestsykk Av. Fiskets Gang.* **22**: 448–60.

Trotta P. 1981. On the rhodophyta *Gracilaria confervoides* in Lesina lagoon: field survey and *in vitro* culture. In *Convegno Internazzionale Fitodepurazione e Impieghi delle Biomass Prodotte* (Ed. Anon). pp. 91–6. Parme.

Virstein R.W. & Carbonara P.A. 1985. Seasonal abundance and distribution of drift algae and seagrasses in the mid-Indian River lagoon. *Aquat. Bot.* **23**: 67–82.

Whitney L.L. 1987. Macroalgal commercialization in the United States. *Hydrobiologia* **151/152**: 183–8.

11 Cultivation of Attached Seaweeds

JOANNA M. KAIN (JONES)
Port Erin Marine Laboratory, Isle of Man, UK

The technology allowing the cultivation of seaweeds attached to structures in the sea is well advanced in Asia, where large quantities of some species are now produced on the coasts of several nations. In contrast, the farming of marine algae in Europe is in its infancy and the sale of material produced in this way has taken place only during the last few years, in relatively small quantities. One reason for this has been that the coasts of Europe bear considerable natural algal resources (Levring 1977), which were adequate for its own needs until about the middle of this century. Since then, however, imports of phycocolloid algae have been necessary for economic reasons and now probably exceed the tonnage of seaweeds harvested from natural populations (Kain & Dawes 1987). Another reason has been that westerners have eschewed seaweed as food and it is for this purpose that most of the cultivation in Asia takes place. The western attitude is, however, changing, partly as a result of immigration but also because of a more cosmopolitan outlook by indigenous Europeans. The result is a considerable importation of seaweed for human consumption into Europe. This chapter aims to show that so much importation may not be necessary; many parts of the extensive European coastline are suitable for seaweed farming.

If Europe has extensive natural populations of seaweeds why advocate cultivation? There are a number of reasons why it may be superior to harvesting existing beds:

1. Harvesting itself may be difficult, particularly of subtidal beds on uneven rock and on exposed coasts vulnerable to unpredictable storms.
2. There is poor quality control of the harvested material; it is likely to be a mixture both of species and of ages.
3. Improvement of the quality through genetic selection is only feasible with cultivated stocks.

Most of the economically important algal genera occur in European waters, particularly those which are cultivated for food in Asia. There is therefore no compelling reason to introduce alien genera or species; one of the endemic

Seaweed Resources in Europe: *Uses and Potential.* Edited by M. D. Guiry and G. Blunden
© 1991 John Wiley & Sons Ltd

ones may well be just as suitable. Introductions should be avoided because of the possible foreseen and unforeseen consequences to marine ecosystems. It is pertinent therefore to look only at native genera.

Seaweed cultivation has been comprehensively reviewed by Mathieson (1982, 1986).

THE ENVIRONMENT

Just as types of successful agricultural crops vary with climate, the seaweeds that could be farmed in any one place must depend on the environmental conditions. It is therefore pertinent to look at how the principal factors affecting marine macroalgae vary around the coasts of Europe, in order to assess which sea areas might be suitable for farming species of possible economic interest. It is also pertinent to compare these attributes of the environment with those prevailing in the parts of Asia where related species are successfully farmed.

Temperature is an important factor in determining which algal species is favoured. It is partly, but not wholly, dependent on latitude; in the sea, water circulation patterns modify the direct effect of the amount of energy received from the sun. In the northern hemisphere the sea temperature minimum is in February and the maximum in August. Some idea of the temperature range to which different parts of the European and Pacific Asian coasts are exposed can be obtained from Fig. 1. The February temperature range is identical for the two regions, 2–15 °C, but throughout the range a given temperature is found at a higher latitude in Europe than in Asia. Looked at in another way, where there is overlap in latitude the European shore has water 8–10 °C warmer than the Asian shore (Fig. 1). Although the identical temperature range might seem to indicate that winter-grown species could be grown in Europe if they can in Asia, the difference in latitude in February could mean that light would be limiting. In winter, reduction in day length and in irradiance act in concert with latitude; there is thus a marked reduction in total light received further north in the northern hemisphere. In December the daily photon exposure at 50 °N is about a third of that at 30 °N (Kain & Norton 1990, Fig. 1). This does not mean that algae could not be grown in Europe in winter beyond 46 °N (the northern limit of Japan), because in Asia the northern limit is probably determined by temperature; it merely means that in midwinter light is the likely limiting factor in Europe.

In summer, day length and irradiance counteract each other with change in latitude, and the total daily photon exposure varies little in June (Kain & Norton 1990, Fig. 1). On the other hand, the August temperature range on the coast of Europe is lower than that in Asia, although where there is overlap it is at the same latitude (Fig. 1). Thus, as light is unlikely to be limiting in

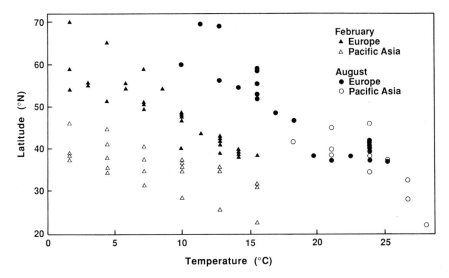

Figure 1. The relationship between latitude and mean sea surface temperature on coasts of Pacific Asia where seaweeds are cultivated and Europe for the coldest and warmest months of the year. Each point is derived from where an isotherm (in degrees Fahrenheit) meets the coast (Department of the Navy 1973)

summer, some European waters may not be warm enough for seaweed crops normally grown at this time of year in Asia.

For convenience of discussion the shores of Europe have been divided into 11 parts, based on the areas referred to by South and Tittley (1986). They are shown, together with mean sea surface temperatures for February and August and tidal ranges, in Table 1. The most extreme temperatures occur in the south-eastern North Sea and the Baltic, both of which have favourable growth temperatures in the summer, although clearly the highest tempera- tures are to be found in the Azores and the Mediterranean. It should be stressed that these temperatures apply only to the open coast; in inlets waters will be colder in winter and warmer in summer.

Most macroalgae are tolerant of some fluctuation in salinity, optimum growth often occurring over a range of at least 10‰, although high salinity may be less well tolerated than low (Kain & Norton 1990). The North Sea and the Atlantic coast have a salinity range of 30–36‰ (Directorate of Fisheries Research 1981), likely to be favourable to all the species considered. Most of the Mediterranean, however, is above this and parts reach 39‰, which could be unfavourable. The Baltic proper has surface salinities of 6–8‰ (Bock 1971) and these may be lower still in inner parts of archipelagos in spring (Wallentinus personal communication), precluding most of the species of

Table 1. Parts of the European coasts referred to in later tables, showing the open coast mean sea surface temperature ranges for the months of the winter minimum, the summer maximum and extreme tidal ranges (lowest to highest astronomical tide) calculated from data for standard and secondary ports within the areas

Code	South & Tittley (1986) areas	Shores of land areas or seas	February[a] (°C)	August[a] (°C)	Tide range[b] (m)
E1	14,15	Spitzbergen, Bear Island and Jan Mayen	Ice	1–4	1.0–2.0
E2	8	Norway north of 68 °N	1–4	8–13	2.6–3.8
E3	16	Iceland	2–5	8–11	3.3–5.0
E4	7,13	Norway south of 68 °N, Faeroe Islands	2–6	10–17	0.3–3.8
E5	6	Baltic Sea	Ice–2	15–18	0
E6	4,5	West Sweden, Denmark, Germany, Netherlands, Belgium	1–5	16–18	0.5–7.2
E7	9–12	British Isles	5–9	12–16	1.6–10.5
E8	3	France (Atlantic)	5–11	17–19	5.0–13.8
E9	1,2	Spain (Atlantic) and Portugal	11–15	19–22	3.7–5.1
E10	0	Azores	16	23	~ 1
E11	—	Mediterranean Sea	7–15	22–25	0–1.2

[a]Lenz 1971; Department of the Navy 1973; Directorate of Fisheries Research 1981.
[b]Admiralty 1983.

interest for cultivation. There is obviously a graded salinity transition between the North Sea and the Baltic. There may also be a reduction in salinity, particularly at the surface, on entering fjords, lochs and certainly estuaries. Such sites would have to be assessed separately for the cultivation of any individual species.

Growing algae need a supply of nutrients, most of which are plentiful in seawater, although nitrogen can become limiting (Dring 1982). In temperate waters this usually happens in spring after the phytoplankton bloom, particularly when a thermocline develops, trapping nutrients below. From this point of view, winter is therefore a good time to cultivate macroalgae, but there are other considerations. Whether there is enough nitrogen for successful cultivation depends on a number of local factors, such as the stability of the water column, tidal streaming, influx from rivers or sewage, and the sea area. If an area is suitable in other ways but nitrogen is limiting, it is possible to fertilize artificially (Tseng 1981a).

Currents, at moderate speeds, usually favour algal growth because of increased provision of nutrients. The extent of tidal streaming depends on both the tidal range and topography, which may create a funnelling effect. The range of extreme differences in tidal heights for European coasts are shown in Table 1. Tidal ranges are greatest in the Channel between the

French and British coasts and the least in the Baltic and Mediterranean. Even in the latter, however, strong currents can be found where the topography is favourable, as in the Straits of Messina, Italy.

RED SEAWEEDS

PORPHYRA

Porphyra, known variously as laver, nori, zakai, kim, karengo, sloke or slukos, is a popular foodstuff in Asia and is eaten in other parts of the world. In 1984, Japan exported 4 dry t to European countries (Nisizawa 1987). Historically, it was the first seaweed to be cultivated, starting in Tokyo Bay around either 1640 (Miura 1975) or 1736 (Okazaki 1971) and about 200 years ago in China (Tseng 1981a). The early methods consisted merely of providing suitable substrata for the settlement of spores from natural populations; in Japan these were brushwood bundles set in shallow water (Okazaki 1971) and in China shallow rocks were mechanically cleaned at the appropriate season (Tseng 1981a). The last few decades have witnessed extensive sophistication of the cultivation methods, necessarily based on a thorough understanding of the life history and biology of the alga.

Some of the current knowledge of the life history of *Porphyra* is summarized by West and Hommersand (1981) but a brief outline is given here (Fig. 2) as a prerequisite for an understanding of the cultivation systems being employed. The genus contains many species with consequent variations in detail, both in life history and in the effects of environmental factors. The following is therefore a generalization drawn from the more important or better known species.

Laver itself (i.e. that which is eaten) has been variously called leafy, foliose, phylloid and thalloid, but perhaps a blade is the most appropriate term, as it is flat (membranous) but not morphologically analogous to higher plant leaves. Blades are haploid and can produce haploid monospores which germinate into further blades. Under different environmental conditions blades become sexual, producing non-motile male gametes which fertilize females *in situ* on blades; the resulting zygote then divides into a variable number of diploid spores (carpospores) which are liberated. These spores do not develop into blades but into filaments, known as the conchocelis phase, which normally live within the material of dead mollusc shells. Under certain environmental conditions this diploid conchocelis phase produces diploid monospores, which produce more conchocelis plants, but under different conditions distinctive conchosporangia are produced in rows. The conchospores (referred to as monospores or fertile cell rows in some of the literature) released from these germinate into the haploid blade. The reduction division necessary for this change in ploidy may not take place until the conchospore

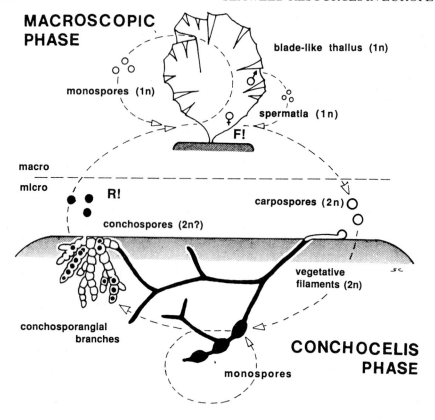

Figure 2. The life history of *Porphyra*, adapted from Campbell (1980) courtesy of Blackwell Scientific Publications. Monospores do not occur in all species. The site of reduction division (R!) may vary (see text)

germinates (Ma & Miura 1984; Burzycki & Waaland 1987; Tseng & Sun 1989). The blade may thus be a chimaera of two separate sets of cells, differing genetically from each other.

The pattern of this life history is usually related to seasons (Iwasaki 1961). In the species cultivated in Asia the haploid blade is favoured by winter conditions: large blades grow well at low temperature (Zeng 1984), conchospore production is stimulated by short days (Kurogi & Sato 1962a; Dring 1967) and conchospore liberation by reduced temperature (Kurogi & Akiyama 1966). The diploid filamentous conchocelis phase of these species, however, seems to be well adapted to summer conditions; it grows well at higher temperatures (Miura 1975; Tseng 1981a) and carpospores (which germinate into the conchocelis phase) may be produced only in long days (Iwasaki 1961; Suto 1972).

In 1983, the world's cultivated *Porphyra* amounted to 542×10^3 wet t, 60% of which was produced by Japan, with China and Korea each producing about 20% (Tseng & Fei 1987).

Cultivation Techniques in Asia

The cultivation technique is an annual cycle based on the seasonal require-ments of the alga. In early spring the adult blades produce carpospores, the release of which is induced by previous drying (Miura 1975), squeezing (Korringa 1976) or pulverization of the blades (Chiang 1984). The spore suspension in seawater is then poured into tanks containing mollusc shells. The shells used are those most easily available locally, usually oyster or scallop, and they are spread on the bottom of the tank with the inner smooth surface facing upwards. Carpospores settle on the shells and germinate, and the filaments, being negatively phototropic (Tussenbroek 1984), bore into the shell material. In Japan, the shells are suspended by string in deep tanks (Miura 1975; Korringa 1976), but in China the shells are left on the floor of shallow tanks. The tanks contain stirred seawater enriched with 0.1 mM nitrate and 0.01 mM phosphate (Tseng 1981a). The temperature of the seawater is not controlled but the tanks are situated in glasshouses, allowing a favourable rise in temperature and irradiance in the summer. Under these conditions the conchocelis filaments grow well within the shells, forming extensive patches, possibly increased in number through the production of diploid monospores perpetuating the conchocelis phase. The fact that the filaments reside within the shell material is of great help in controlling contaminants such as diatoms and other algae. These settle only on the surface of the shells and can be brushed off. If this is done at intervals of a few weeks, algal contaminants are controlled and the conchocelis filaments are heavily favoured. After this summer growth the amount of light is reduced with adjustable shading cloths beneath the roofs before the natural daylight reduction in autumn (Tseng 1981a). The lowered temperature and shortened day length favour the formation of conchosporangia on the tips of filaments at the shell surface. In September or October (Miura 1975), the conchospores are seeded onto nets suitable for the growth of the blade phase in the sea.

There are a number of different methods of seeding, all depending on a massive output of conchospores from the shells (up to 20 million spores from a shell of 7 cm diameter; Tseng (1981a)), triggered by environmental condi-tions. Day lengths of less than 12 h stimulate release (Miura 1975; Waaland *et al.* 1987), which is concentrated around dawn (Miura 1975; Chihara 1981). The shells may be placed in a great net pocket supported horizontally in the sea, the cultivation nets placed over them and the whole wrapped in vinyl sheets to prevent spore loss (Kiura 1975; Chihara 1981). In Japan, four different techniques have been employed for seeding on land (Bardach *et al.* 1972; Korringa 1976). The two main methods (Chihara 1981) consist of laying the conchocelis-bearing shells on the floor of tanks and exposing the cultivation nets above them. In the first, long tanks are used, the nets are suspended horizontally and the conchospores are suspended and thrown against the net meshes by vigorous aeration. In the second, a batch of 10–20 nets is wound around a large drum which dips into a smaller tank. As the drum rotates, stirring the water, the conchospores are suspended and caught by the nets. The short-term exposure to the air of those parts of the nets on the drum which are out of the water is tolerated. In China, the first tank method is used but the agitation is created with a water pump (Tseng 1981a). A high irradiance is said to be necessary for attachment and germination of conchospores (Tseng 1981a). In Korea, the shells are placed on top of 30 short (>4 m) lengths of net, wrapped in polyethylene sheets and placed in the sea for 10–14 days (Sohn & Kain 1989a).

It is possible to bypass the blade phase and seed nets from free-living conchocelis continuously maintained indoors; this is already practised in Korea (Sohn & Kain 1989a) and by some farmers in Taiwan (Chiang 1982, 1984). It would also be possible, in species such as *P. yezoensis*, which easily produce vegetative monospores from the blade phase, to bypass the conchocelis phase and seed nets directly from blade-produced spores, after cold storage of the blades (Ying 1984).

In Japan, the cultivation nets are 1.2–1.8 m wide (Miura 1975) and 18–45 m long (Bardach *et al.* 1972), while in China they are 1.8×60 m (Tseng 1981b) and in Korea 1.6×18 or 1.2×24 m (Sohn & Kain 1989a). After seeding, the nets are deployed in the sea in such a way that, for at least the first few weeks, they are exposed to the air for some hours each day (Miura 1975; Zeng 1984). This has two favourable consequences. Firstly, the opportunistic fast-growing algae that are competitive colonizers of the net when it is in the sea are less tolerant of drying out than are *Porphyra* blades (Miura 1975); desiccation is thus being used as a selective weedkiller. Secondly, blades are more likely to produce haploid self-perpetuating monospores if they are sometimes exposed to air (Chihara 1981). This can be exploited by exposing unseeded nets in close proximity to the seeded ones; these collect enough monospores for satisfactory blade production (Bardach *et al.* 1972; Miura 1975). An intertidal position for nets for the whole growing period was included in earlier methods of cultivation in both Japan (Okazaki 1971) and China (Tseng 1981b; Zeng 1984) and is still practised where possible. However, the available area of sufficiently shallow sea had become inadequate by 1965 so many nets are now also deployed on floating structures for most of the growing period (Oohusa 1984). An example of the type of net and rope structure used in Japan is shown in Fig. 3. Nets destined for deep-water floating structures may be temporarily exposed in groups of 5–20 between posts or on frames in shallow water (Korringa 1976). Alternatively, the nets may be floated in deep water and manually raised and lowered (Tseng 1981a). This is the practice in Korea (Sohn & Kain 1989a).

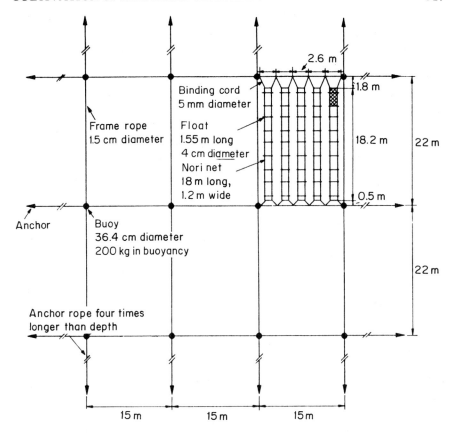

Figure 3. Development of nori nets in Japan. (From Miura (1975), courtesy of Dr W. Junk, publishers)

A useful property of the young *Porphyra* blades is their ability to withstand freezing (Migita 1966), which means that seeded cultivation nets may be stored at −20 °C and used to replace failed nets at a later date. Newly seeded nets may be frozen and stored (Korringa 1976) or it may be more advantageous to allow blades to grow to a length of 2–3 cm before freezing (Chihara 1981). The growing period for the blades on nets in the sea is from October to April, May or June (Miura 1975). Harvesting can start in November, taking parts of the plants off the nets with a special harvesting apparatus (Korringa 1976).

Earlier this century the main species under cultivation was *Porphyra tenera* but for some time now production has been mainly of *P. yezoensis* in Japan (Miura 1975), Korea (Kang 1972) and northern China, while *P. haitanensis* is used in southern China (Tseng 1981a). Selection by farmers has resulted in longer-bladed and more productive forms (Miura & Merrill 1982).

The most well established and widely used (in Asia) *Porphyra* cultivation technique employs the natural cycle between haploid and diploid phases, including meiosis and sexual fusion, presumably resulting in a wide variation in genetic constitution. Efficient farming techniques must eventually involve genetic improvement of crops, before which techniques allowing controlled breeding and gene transmission must be developed. Stocks of *P. tenera* have already been improved in Japan (Chihara 1981) and those of *P. yezoensis* in China (Zhang *et al.* 1985). Fortunately both the blade and the conchocelis phases grow quite well unattached in glass vessels of seawater medium (Imada *et al.* 1972) so that stocks of known strains can be maintained easily in the laboratory. Before breeding experiments on any particular species are carried out it is necessary to know whether conchospores are haploid or diploid. If they are the former, inbreeding from a single monoecious blade must produce a completely homozygous conchocelis phase, with the resulting progeny being effectively clonal. If, however, meiosis occurs after conchospore germination, which seems likely to be the case in many species (p. 314), inbreeding from a single blade with potentially genetically different vegetative cells could result in conchocelis filaments of differing genotypes.

Another method of using clonal material is the propagation of protoplasts and of tissue, which is already successful in work on this genus (Polne-Fuller *et al.* 1984; Chen 1986, 1987; Liu & Gordon 1987).

Choice of Species for Europe

There are 60–70 reported species of *Porphyra* worldwide (Mumford & Cole 1977), the greatest number being in the north Pacific (Table 2). Each plant of the blade phase consists of a thin membrane of cells of great flexibility; in life there is no rigidity, the thallus being conformed by water movement or gravity. Between species there is considerable variation in the shape of the blade, from funnel-shaped to linear (Kurogi 1972). The blade is usually monostromatic, though there are some distromatic species. Most species are monoecious but some have separately sexed plants. The chromosome number is generally low, $n = 3–4$ usually, although $n = 7$ (Yabu 1975) and even $n = 12$ (Conway & Wylie 1972) have been recorded. Although the alternation of haploid and diploid phases may appear to be the norm, some of the species investigated cytologically have the haploid number throughout the life history (Kapraun & Freshwater 1987). Most species are intertidal but some are subtidal.

Eleven species have been reported from European coasts (Table 2). Of these *P. thulaea* is known only from Iceland and Greenland (Munda & Pedersen 1978), *P. abyssicola* is confined to north Norway (Jaasund 1965), *P. amethystea* requires taxonomic reinvestigation (Parke & Dixon 1976), *P. amplissima* has been said to be synonymous with *P. miniata* (Hollenberg 1972), *P. drachii* has not yet been recorded outside northern France (South &

Table 2. Occurrence of species of *Porphyra* on the coasts of various land areas

Species	Area code																
	E1	E2	E3	E4	E5	E6	E7	E8	E9	E10	E11	ANA	SA	ASA	PNA	PA	Aus
P. miniata	+	+	+	+	−	+	+	+	−	−	−	+	−	−	+	−	−
P. purpurea	−	+	+	+	?	+	+	+	+	−	−	−	−	−	−	+	−
P. umbilicalis	−	+	+	+	−	+	+	+	+	−	+	−	−	−	−	−	−
P. linearis	−	−	+	+	−	+	+	+	+	−	+	+	−	−	−	−	−
P. leucosticta	−	−	+	+	−	+	+	+	+	+	+	+	−	+	−	−	−
P. thulaea	−	−	+	−	−	−	−	−	−	−	−	−	−	−	−	−	−
P. abyssicola	−	+	+	+	−	?	−	−	−	−	−	−	−	−	−	−	−
P. amethystea	−	−	−	+	−	−	+	−	−	−	−	−	−	−	−	−	−
P. amplissima	+	+	−	?	−	−	−	−	−	−	−	−	−	−	−	+	−
P. drachii	−	−	−	−	−	−	−	+	−	−	−	−	−	−	−	−	−
P. yezoensis	−	−	−	−	−	+	−	−	−	−	−	−	−	−	−	+	−
P. tenera	−	−	−	−	−	−	−	−	−	−	−	−	−	−	−	+	−
Total species	2	5	7	6	0	5	6	6	4	1	3	5	1	1	19	30	6

E1–11, areas of Europe designated in Table 1. E1–10, South & Tittley (1986); E11, Giaccone *et al.* (1985); ANA, Atlantic North America, Coll & Cox (1977), South & Tittley (1986); SA, South Africa, Isaac (1957); ASA, Atlantic South America, Taylor (1960), Oliveira Filho & Coll (1975), Coll & Oliveira Filho (1976); PNA, Pacific North America, Dawson (1953), Abbott & Hollenberg (1976), Conway *et al.* (1975), Conway & Cole (1977); PA, Pacific Asia, Lee & Kang (1986), Yoshida *et al.* (1985a); Aus, Australasia, Chapman (1969), Levring (1953).

Tittley 1986), and *P. yezoensis* is probably a recent immigrant to Helgoland (Kornmann 1986). The remaining five species are widely distributed (Table 2) and are potential candidates for cultivation.

Some of the known attributes of these five species, together with those of the two species commonly cultivated in Asia, are shown in Table 3. Only *P. miniata* is not intertidal; if exposure to air is used in cultivation to discourage competitors, subtidal species may not be suitable. Also a subtidal species may be more prone to photoinhibition when grown on shallow nets (Herbert & Waaland 1988) although this might not be a problem in winter. The cultivated Japanese species flourish in the winter (Kurogi 1972); this is so for only one of the European species, *P. linearis*. Perhaps the most important attribute in species of *Porphyra* destined for the human food market is taste. In Wales, according to Newton (1951), the laver eaten was *P. laciniata*, now known as *P. purpurea* (Kornmann 1961). In North America 'experienced nori eaters', tasting the flavour of the species of the Atlantic coast, have favoured *P. linearis* (McLachlan *et al.* 1972).

The ease of the transfer of cultivation technology from Asia to Europe may depend on how similar are the environmental requirements of the species involved. Some reported optimal temperatures for the different steps in the life history of *Porphyra* species are shown in Table 4. Perhaps the conchocelis phase of the European species is favoured by lower temperatures than that of the Japanese species, but indoor culture conditions for this part of the operation can be controlled. Less is known about the requirements of the blade phase. Clearly if a species grows naturally in an area it must be able to tolerate local temperatures, but algae may grow fastest at temperatures higher than those encountered in their natural habitat. A good indication of the temperature tolerance of blades of *Porphyra* could be their geographical distribution. *P. miniata* is a northern species, absent from Spain, Portugal and the Mediterranean (Table 2). *P. purpurea* and *P. umbilicalis* occur throughout Atlantic Europe, the latter also in the Mediterranean. *P. leucosticta* and *P. linearis* are absent from northern Norway; in the latter case this is likely to be because the blades normally flourish in winter. This would be more likely to be related to lack of irradiance at the high latitude in winter than to temperature because *P. linearis* certainly tolerates low temperatures and even icing in Nova Scotia (Bird 1973).

If the seasonal cycle of the Asian cultivation method is to be used in Europe, the likely choice of species would seem to be *P. yezoensis* or *P. linearis* because these are the only ones that flourish during winter in the blade phase. They are also apparently the most palatable. However, *P. yezoensis* is not native to Europe; it has so far been recorded only in Helgoland, and it would be unwise to introduce it to other coasts. Although *P. linearis* does not produce monospores perpetuating the blade phase in Nova Scotia (Bird 1973), this form of reproduction is common on Scottish coasts (Cole & Conway 1980). Satisfactory densities can also be achieved with only conchospores in *P. pseudolinearis* (Yoshida 1972).

Table 3. Some characteristics of European species of *Porphyra*, compared with the two Asian crop species (lower)

Species	Blade	Sexuality	Chromosome number (blade/conchocelis)	Habitat	Season	Authors
P. miniata	Distromatic	Androdioecious	3/6	Subtidal	Spring	Conway (1964a); Hollenberg (1972); Kito et al. (1971); Conway & Cole (1977)
P. purpurea	Monostromatic		5/10	Intertidal	Spring/summer	Conway (1964a); Kito et al. (1971); Conway & Cole (1977)
P. umbilicalis	Monostromatic	Monoecious	4/8	Intertidal	Spring/summer	Conway (1964a,b); Conway & Cole (1977); Kapraun & Freshwater (1987)
P. linearis	Monostromatic	Monoecious		Intertidal	Winter	Conway (1964a); Bird et al. (1972); Conway & Cole (1977)
P. leucosticta	Monostromatic	Monoecious	4/4	Intertidal	Summer	Conway (1964a); Conway & Cole (1977); Kapraun & Freshwater (1987)
P. tenera	Monostromatic	Androdioecious	3/6–4/8	Intertidal	Winter	Kurogi (1972); Yabu (1975)
P. yezoensis	Monostromatic	Monoecious	3/6	Intertidal	Winter	Kurogi (1972)

322

Table 4. Optimal temperatures for the development of different stages in the life history of some species of *Porphyra*

Species	Carpospores	Vegetative conchocelis	Conchospores	Blades Experimental	Blades Ambient sea	References
P. tenera				15–25		Ohno (1969)
		20–25	15–20			Kurogi & Akiyama (1966)
		17–19	25–28	13–28		Imada et al. (1972)
P. yezoensis		15–25	10–20			Kurogi & Akiyama (1966)
	10–15	< 28	21–22		14–22	Miura (1975)
	10–15	> 23	< 22			Korringa (1976)
		22–27	23		20–23	Tseng (1981a)
		20–25				Zeng (1984)
P. pseudolinearis		15–20	15–20			Kurogi & Akiyama (1966)
P. kuniedai		15–20	15–25			Kurogi & Akiyama (1966)
P. angusta		20–25	20–25			Kurogi & Akiyama (1966)
P. suborbiculata		20–25	12–20			Kurogi & Akiyama (1966)
		20	25			Iwasaki & Sasaki (1972)
P. haitanensis		25–31	10–15		14–24	Tseng (1981a)
P. torta		10–15				Waaland et al. (1987)
P. carolinensis			10		7–18	Freshwater & Kapraun (1986)
P. leucosticta	15–25	15–25	25	10–25		Edwards (1969)
P. umbilicalis		5–7				Conway (1964b)
P. linearis	5–15	5–15	13		0–11	Bird et al. (1972); Bird (1973)

If a summer species is cultivated there are two options: manipulate its phenology and grow the blades in winter, or radically change the cultivation system and grow them in the summer. Both have obvious hazards but either might succeed. In most of the species that have been tested the development of conchosporangia is stimulated by short days and conchospore liberation is often linked to photoperiod (Table 5). This is associated with the fact that, in most of the species tested, the blade form predominates in the winter. Recent work has demonstrated long-day triggering in several summer species, but another, *P. leucosticta*, forms conchosporangia only in short days, which is rather puzzling (Table 5). Nothing is known of the day-length responses of the other European species. Although perhaps not essential to the cultivation technique, there is no doubt that the manipulation of day length is a very convenient method of producing, in the first place, massive vegetative growth of conchocelis filaments and, in the second, vast quantities of conchospores. The same control may be possible through the manipulation of temperature, but as the same temperature may be favourable for both processes it may not be feasible to trigger conchospore release suddenly.

Much could be learnt about the transference of the *Porphyra*-growing technology from those workers involved in the development in Puget Sound, Washington, USA (Mumford & Melvin 1983; Melvin *et al.* 1986; Cheney & Mumford 1986; Mumford 1987; Merrill 1989). Over a period of years the techniques in use in Japan and Korea were adapted for use under somewhat different conditions. Although six native species were tested, half of which are favoured by spring/summer conditions, *P. yezoensis* was imported from Japan and tested as well, but only as certified pathogen-free cultures. Farming became a commercial success in Washington in 1987 (Merrill 1988).

Choice of Sites in Europe

Clearly several environmental factors have to be considered when evaluating potential sites for *Porphyra* cultivation. One of these is salinity. Early cultivation of nori in Japan was carried out in estuarine bays. The success of this may have been associated with increased nutrients rather than decreased salinity, but clearly the cultivated species tolerated the latter. In the laboratory the European species *P. umbilicalis* is very tolerant of reduced salinity (Ogata & Schramm 1971), but in Iceland it penetrates in three fjords only to where the low tide salinity is 18‰, whereas *P. purpurea* and *P. leucosticta* apparently tolerate 3–5‰ (Munda 1978). The last species also flourishes at the head of Limski Kanal in Yugoslavia where salinity can drop to zero (Zavodnik 1987). On the other hand, no species of *Porphyra* occurs in the Baltic proper (Table 2) and none penetrates beyond the outer area of the Hardangerfjord, where the minimum surface salinity is about 27‰ (Jorde & Klavestad 1963). All the four intertidal native European species shown in Table 3 occur in the Kattegat (South & Tittley 1986) and must therefore

Table 5. Main season of blade abundance and the response of the conchocelis phase of species *Porphyra* from different regions

Species	Site	Latitude	Blade abundance season	Photoperiod affects		Authors
				Concho-sporangia	Concho-spores	
P. tenera	Honshu, Japan	~ 38 °N	Winter	SD	SD	Kurogi (1959)
				—	SD	Kurogi et al. (1962)
				SD	SD	Kurogi & Sato (1962a)
				SD	SD	Iwasaki & Matsudaira (1963)
				SD		Dring (1967)
P. yezoensis	Honshu, Japan	~ 38 °N	Winter	SD	SD	Kurogi & Sato (1962b)
P. pseudolinearis	Honshu, Japan	~ 38 °N	Winter	SD	SD	Kurogi & Sato (1962b)
P. kuniedai	Honshu, Japan	~ 38 °N	Winter	SD	SD	Kurogi & Sato (1962b)
P. angusta	Honshu, Japan	~ 38 °N	Winter	SD	SD	Kurogi & Sato (1962b)
P. suborbiculata f. *latifolia*	Kyushu, Japan	33 °N	Winter		SD	Iwasaki & Sasaki (1972)
P. angustata	Taiwan	25 °N		—		Chiang & Wang (1980)
P. torta	Washington, USA	48 °N	Winter	—	SD	Waaland et al. (1987)
P. fallax[a]	Washington, USA	48 °N	Summer	—	—	Mumford (1973)
				SD	LD	Waaland & Duffield unpublished data
P. nereocystis	Washington, USA	48 °N	Summer	—	—	Mumford (1980)
				SD	SD/LD[b]	Dickson & Waaland (1985)
P. pseudolanceolata	Washington, USA	48 °N	Winter	SD	SD[c]	Waaland et al. unpublished data
P. abbottae	Washington, USA	48 °N	Summer	LD	LD	Waaland et al. unpublished data
P. miniata	Nova Scotia, Canada	45 °N	Spring		SD	Chen et al. (1970)
P. rosengurtii	N. Carolina, USA	34 °N		SD	SD	Kapraun & Luster (1980)
P. carolinensis	N. Carolina, USA	34 °N	Winter		SD	Freshwater & Kapraun (1986)
P. leucosticta	Texas, USA	28 °N	Summer	SD	SD	Edwards (1969)
P. spiralis var. *amphipholia*	Venezuela	12 °N		SD	SD	Kapraun & Lemus (1987)

—, day length neutral; SD, short days; LD, long days, stimulate conchosporangia production or conchospore release.
[a]Previously *P. perforata* (Lindstrom unpublished data).
[b]Short days followed by long days.
[c]12 h day optimal.

tolerate surface salinities of less than 30‰ (Bock 1971). This somewhat conflicting evidence emphasizes our lack of knowledge of the tolerances of the two phases of the European species. If the conchocelis phase is more salinity sensitive and limits the distribution of the blade phase, cultivation could be feasible in sites such as the Baltic and Norwegian fjords where the blade phase does not grow naturally. Research on the effect of salinity on the growth rate of the blade phase of endemic species would be necessary before these areas could be utilized. From the point of view of salinity it is likely that most open coasts of Europe would be suitable.

In temperate coastal waters the nutrients necessary for algal growth fluctuate seasonally, being high in winter. The timing of the traditional *Porphyra* cultivation period thus reduces the likelihood of nutrient shortage. However, the plant can require quite high nitrogen levels for optimum development; *P. haitanensis* suffered from the 'green disease', due to inadequate nitrogen supply, at $1.4\,\mu$mol l^{-1} nitrogen (Dahua & Yashui 1984). In the Adriatic Sea *P. leucosticta* was four times as productive in brackish water with about 30 μmol l^{-1} nitrogen than in full salinity seawater with about 2 μmol l^{-1} nitrogen (Zavodnik 1987). Furthermore, high-quality (as human food) laver has a high protein content and this is dependent on ambient inorganic nitrogen (Kudoh 1987). Nitrogen influx from a river can raise the protein content of farmed *Porphyra* (Kim & Kang 1986). Therefore, unless there is local eutrophication or artificial fertilization, it would seem unlikely that *Porphyra* could be cultivated satisfactorily in summer on European coasts.

GRACILARIA

The interest in *Gracilaria* as a crop is relatively recent. The genus is a useful source of agar used by the food industry (Armisen & Galatas 1987). It has been cultivated successfully since 1967 in shallow ponds in Taiwan (Chiang 1981; Tseng 1981a), but as the plants are unattached the technique is inappropriate to this chapter.

The life history of *Gracilaria* is of the type which is most common in the red algae (Fig. 4). There is an apparent alternation between haploid and diploid generations, the tetrasporophyte and separate male and female gametophytes, all of which have an identical appearance. However, although the non-motile male gametes are liberated from the parent plants, the female gamete is retained and is fertilized *in situ*. The resulting zygote and its products are effectively another diploid phase, the carposporophyte, which is borne by the female gametophyte. This phase does nothing but produce a considerable number of replicates of the zygote (carpospores), each of which can develop into a tetrasporophyte. Thus a single act of fertilization can result in a great many (effectively genetically indentical) individuals.

There have been a number of experimental approaches, in widely separated parts of the world, to the cultivation of attached *Gracilaria* (Santelices

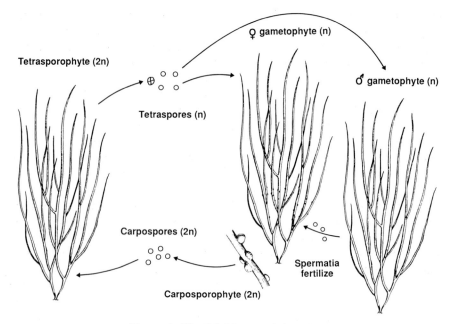

Figure 4. The life history of *Gracilaria*

& Doty 1989). In India, pieces of the alga were inserted into the lay of rope which was held horizontally, attached to stakes in the sand of a protected shore (Raju & Thomas 1971). A harvest of 3 kg fresh weight per m of rope was achieved. In China, nets were used initially (Tseng 1981a) but later rafts bearing horizontal or vertical ropes with attached *Gracilaria* seemed effective (Ren *et al.* 1984; Li *et al.* 1984). On the Atlantic coast of Canada, the plants were attached to lines tied to frames (Edelstein *et al.* 1981), and in the West Indies rope or lines were attached to stakes and *Gracilaria* was grown on the lines (Smith *et al.* 1984). In Brazil, various methods of planting out pieces of the alga on ropes and nets have been tried, some quite successful with good yields (Câmara Neto 1987). Lines, particularly polyamide monofilament, are preferable to nets (Santelices & Doty 1989).

On the Pacific coast of South America there has been distinct economic success for *Gracilaria* cultivation using vegetative propagation. In Chile, a completely different approach has been made, not involving ropes, nets or rafts. It was found that if short pieces of *G. lemaneiformis* are pushed into a sandy bottom, they rapidly become established and produce erect thalli (Santelices *et al.* 1984). It was then shown that if pieces of the alga are held on the bottom by being trapped under sand-filled tubes of soft polyethylene the plants also grow well (Pizarro & Barrales 1986). The plastic eventually disintegrates but by that time an underground thallus system has developed

(Santelices & Ugarte 1987). By 1985 there were 60 farms in Chile and 410 dry t of *Gracilaria* were produced by cultivation, partly because of over-exploitation of natural harvestable beds (Santelices & Ugarte 1987). Similar pinning of *Gracilaria* fragments to a sandy bottom has also been successful off the coast of Namibia (Anderson *et al.* 1989).

Propagation by spores has also had some success, particularly in Malaysia (Santelices & Doty 1989). Nursery tanks containing suitable substrata of coral gravel or shells, with fertile *Gracilaria* plants held above them by netting, are placed in the sea for spore release and settlement. The substrata are later outplanted in suitable farm areas. In a similar way, spores have been seeded onto lines, later being deployed on stakes in shallow water (Santelices & Doty 1989).

Gracilaria is an even larger genus than *Porphyra* and its taxonomy has been conservatively described as problematic (Bird & McLachlan 1982). Over 150 species have been named (Bird *et al.* 1982). In one case recent research has shown that one variable species existed where two or more had been iden-tified (Chapman *et al.* 1977), but at least two species thought to be widespread have been shown to consist of more than one entity in different areas (Bird *et al.* 1982; Guiry & Freamhainn 1986). *G. verrucosa* is one of these and was once thought to have world-wide occurrence, but its apparent distribution has been gradually eroded as careful examination has shown that plants in various places differ from those of Atlantic Europe (McLachlan 1979; Bird *et al.* 1982; Zhang & Xia 1984; Abbott 1985a; Gargiulo *et al.* 1985). Cultivation of *G. verrucosa* in Europe should be based on local material as there is no guarantee that material of '*G. verrucosa*' from elsewhere is the same species. The greatest concentration of species is probably in the tropical Pacific (Table 6); in the Atlantic there are more species in the Caribbean (Norris 1985a) than in the northern USA and Canada (Chapman *et al.* 1977) and on the Iberian peninsula than further north (Table 6). The Mediterranean is rela-tively rich in species of *Gracilaria* (Table 6).

It is thus clear that *Gracilaria* is mainly a warm-water genus. In the western Atlantic there are 15 species at the equator but there are only single species at the northern and southern limits of about 46 ° latitude (Oliveira 1984). In the Eastern Atlantic, in northern Europe, *G. verrucosa* is the only species (Table 6), with a limit at about 60 °N (South & Tittley 1986). Experimental cultiva-tion of this species near its geographical limit, although in the relatively warm summer water of Oslofjord, was not very successful, epiphyte biomass exceeding that of the crop (Rueness *et al.* 1987). The optimum growth temperature of 15 isolates of *Gracilaria* from widely different latitudes lay between 15 and 32 °C, with three European species being favoured by 20 °C (McLachlan & Bird 1984). *G. tikvahiae*, a native of Atlantic North America, has the fastest recorded relative growth rate in a red alga (Kain 1987). It achieved this at 30 °C (Lapointe *et al.* 1984), a fact of some relevance. The fastest growth rates in the field have been recorded when the ambient

Table 6. Occurrence of species of *Gracilaria* on the coasts of various land areas

Species	E1	E2	E3	E4	E5	E6	E7	E8	E9	E10	E11	ANA	ASA	PNA	PSA	PA	Ind	PI	Aus
G. verrucosa	−	−	−	+	−	+	+	+	+	−	−[a]	−[b]	?	−[c]	?	+	+?	+?	+?
G. bursa-pastoris	−	−	−	−	−	−	+	+	+	−	+	−	−	−	−	−	−	−	−
G. multipartita	−	−	−	−	−	−	+	+	+	−	+	−	+	−	−	−	−	−	−
G. cervicornis	−	−	−	−	−	−	−	−	+	−	−	+	+	−	−	−	−	−	−
G. vieirae	−	−	−	−	−	−	−	+	+	−	−	−	−	−	−	−	−	−	−
G. conferta	−	−	−	−	−	−	−	−	+	−	+	−	−	−	−	−	−	−	−
G. dura	−	−	−	−	−	−	−	−	+	−	+	−	−	−	−	−	−	−	−
G. arcuata	−	−	−	−	−	−	−	−	−	−	+	−	−	−	−	+	+	+	+
G. armata	−	−	−	−	−	−	−	−	−	−	+	−	−	−	−	+	+	−	−
G. corallicola	−	−	−	−	−	−	−	−	−	−	+	−	−	−	−	−	−	−	−
G. dendroides	−	−	−	−	−	−	−	−	−	−	+	−	−	−	−	−	−	−	−
G. divergens	−	−	−	−	−	−	−	−	−	−	+	−	−	−	−	−	−	−	−
G. heteroclada	−	−	−	−	−	−	−	−	−	−	+	−	−	−	−	−	−	−	−
Total species	0	0	0	1	0	1	3	3	7	0	10	20	19	22	5	26	16	23	10?

E1–11, areas of Europe designated in Table 1. E1–10, South & Tittley (1986); E11, Feldmann (1937), Gargiulo *et al.* (1985), Giaccone *et al.* (1985); ANA, Atlantic North America and Caribbean, Bird & McLachlan (1982), Oliveira (1984), Norris (1985a); ASA, Atlantic South America, Oliveira (1984); PNA, Pacific North America, Dawson (1961), Abbott & Hollenberg (1976), Bird & McLachlan (1982), Abbott & McLachlan (1982), Norris (1985b); PSA, Pacific South America, Norris (1985b); PA, Pacific Asia, Bird & McLachlan (1982), Yamamoto (1984), Bangmei (1985), Chiang (1985), Yoshida *et al.* (1985a), Xia (1986), Abbott (1988), Zhang & Xia (1988a); Ind, India, Umamaheswara Rao (1972); PI, Pacific Islands (Hawaii, Micronesia, Philippines), Hoyle (1984), Abbott (1985b), Tsuda (1985), Abbott (1985c), Bird & Rice (1990); Aus, Australasia, Chapman (1979), Cribb (1983).

Previous records not substantiated: [a]Gargiulo *et al.* (1985); [b]McLachlan (1979); [c]Bird *et al.* (1982), Abbott (1985a).

temperatures have been at their highest (Jones 1959; Penniman *et al.* 1986; Rueness *et al.* 1987). In experimental raft cultivation it has been clear that better growth is achieved if the *Gracilaria* is not planted out in the sea until the water temperature has risen high enough for the cultivar to outgrow the epiphytes (Ren *et al.* 1984; Li *et al.* 1984).

Some species of *Gracilaria* are tolerant of brackish water, but not isolates of three species from the south coast of Britain or one from Italy (Bird & McLachlan 1986). None of these tolerated salinities less than 15‰, although one species, *G. verrucosa*, maintained its growth in Oslofjord during the summer when the salinity dropped to 10.4‰ (Rueness *et al.* 1987). Reduced salinity can result in lower agar gel strength (Daugherty & Bird 1988). The absence of the genus from the Baltic (South & Tittley 1986) could be associated with salinity, temperature or both; it is an unlikely venue for successful *Gracilaria* cultivation.

Fast algal growth must be supported by a rapid nutrient flux, a problem in European waters in summer when the ambient levels are low in many places. During summer in Florida the supply of phosphorus restricts the growth of *G. tikvahiae* more than that of nitrogen, but both are too low to support maximum growth (Lapointe 1987). Similarly, off New York, *G. tikvahiae* hung from a raft designed primarily for *Laminaria* cultivation (p. 345) grew poorly unless fertilized (Brinkhuis *et al.* 1987). When nitrogen-starved, the species can rapidly take up inorganic nitrogen (Ryther *et al.* 1981), so pulse fertilization is effective (Lapointe 1985).

In some species most plants become fertile when they are large enough, e.g. *G. verrucosa* in Britain (Jones 1959) and *G. tikvahiae* in New Hampshire, USA (Penniman *et al.* 1986). In Chile, however, most plants remain sterile and reproduce through vegetative fragments (Black & Fonck 1981). There is no doubt that species of *Gracilaria* regenerate easily when cut into pieces (Goldstein 1973; Edelstein 1977; Bird *et al.* 1977; Hurtado-Ponce & Umezaki 1987). Farming does not therefore need to involve the whole life history: spores can be bypassed. This allows the use of clonal material, which is of advantage if genetic selection has been practised; this is already well advanced with two north American species (Patwary & van der Meer 1983; van der Meer & Patwary 1983; Hansen 1984) and could presumably be applied to European species. On the other hand cultures are not always stable; eight morphologically different strains resulted from a single plant of *G. secundata* (Lignell & Pedersén 1989). Protoplast isolation and culture has also been successful in this genus (Cheney *et al.* 1986), which may allow genetic modification, resulting in improved agar quality (Cheney 1984).

Another attribute of the genus that could be useful in cultivation is the fact that it can be preserved at low temperature and retain its vitality. Provided that a cryoprotectant is used, *G. tikvahiae* can be stored at $-25\,°C$ (van der Meer & Simpson 1984).

The Mediterranean seems a likely venue for successful cultivation of this genus. The water temperatures are relatively high, the salinity is suitable and there are a number of species to choose from. Whether one of these has all the attributes required of a crop is unknown. It should have a fast growth rate for high production within the season and for success in competition. It should regenerate readily from small vegetative pieces. If it is to be cultivated by the Chilean method it should have a rhizome-like system from which erect thalli arise. If it is necessary to supply nutrients artificially the species should be able to absorb them rapidly and store them. This may not be necessary where there is eutrophication, such as in parts of the Adriatic. Finally, it should have as high a quality of agar as can be expected from *Gracilaria*.

PALMARIA

Dulse, *Palmaria palmata* (*Rhodymenia palmata*) has long been eaten as a sea vegetable (Newton 1951) and is of high value nutritionally (Morgan *et al.* 1980). It could become popular on the human food market. As a tank crop it has been the subject of considerable experimental effort in North America (see Chapter 12), but it is feasible that it could be grown attached to ropes or nets.

Only one species of *Palmaria* is known in Europe and its distribution includes both sides of the North Atlantic. Many Pacific records of this species have recently been shown to belong to other species of the genus (Guiry 1975; van der Meer & Bird 1985; Hawkes 1985), which may or may not be as palatable. No conclusion can therefore be drawn from the fact that the genus is not important in the Asian diet.

Palmaria has an unusual life history (Fig. 5) in which the female plants are reduced to almost microscopic size and no carpospores are produced, the macroscopic thalli consisting of either males or tetrasporophytes (van der Meer & Todd 1980). Although there are usually more tetrasporophytes in a population (Guiry 1974), half the spores produced, being female, cannot develop further under culture conditions. In the wild, the females would be fertilized by spermatia from mature males of a previous generation and tetrasporangial thalli would develop. In isolated culture, however, only males can develop to macroscopic size from spores. In addition, in culture, *Palmaria* spores often die before germinating and, although the spores can attach to rope, the survival of the sporelings is poor (Omar, unpublished data). It is clearly possible to maintain stocks in tanks on land (Morgan *et al.* 1980.) and the conditions could be manipulated to stimulate tetraspore production (Omar, unpublished data) so obtaining 'seed' would not be as much of a problem as its survival.

Palmaria is perennial and when regrowth occurs in winter new blades emerge from the edge of the previous season's blade (Rosenvinge 1931); similar regeneration can also take place from cut surfaces. It seems probable

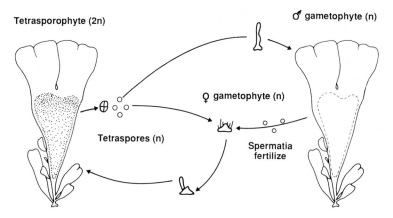

Figure 5. The life history of *Palmaria*

that harnessing this attribute would be more likely to lead to successful cultivation than attempting to seed nets or ropes with spores. Rope laid in a twist (not plaited) can be opened, material pushed in and the rope allowed to close, holding the material quite firmly (Fig. 6). In China, young *Laminaria* sporophytes are trapped in this way and a device has been developed to perform the process mechanically. The same method has been suggested for vegetative propagation of red algae (Waaland 1983). This has recently been

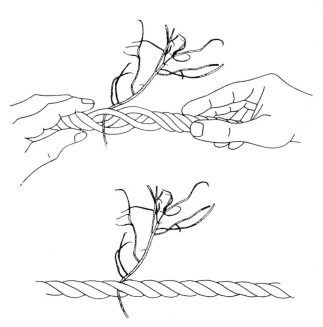

Figure 6. How to trap an alga in the lay of a rope

quite successful with *P. palmata* off the Isle of Man, in the Irish Sea (Omar 1989).

CHONDRUS

Chondrus crispus contains carrageenan in useful quantities and has been extensively harvested on the Atlantic coast of Canada for many years. There has been considerable interest in tank culture (see Chapter 9) but at present there is a plentiful supply of carrageenan from the cultivation of the faster-growing *Eucheuma* in the tropical Pacific. For the cultivation of *Chondrus* to be considered in Europe there would have to be a marked change in the world's requirement, for example, a particular need for λ-carrageenan because the main *Eucheuma* species in cultivation contain either ι- or $\varkappa$-carrageenan (Stanley 1987).

A closely related genus, *Gigartina*, has been grown successfully on ropes on a variety of frame structures on the Pacific coast of North America (Waaland 1973; Mumford & Waaland 1980; Waaland 1981).

GELIDIUM AND PTEROCLADIA

Plants of these two genera contain agar of bacteriological quality (with a high gel strength), which is sometimes in short supply (Moss 1977). It is almost exclusively harvested from natural stocks (Armisen & Galatas 1987), although tank cultivation may be on the verge of economic success.

The life history in the two genera is probably usually of the same type as described for *Gracilaria* (Fig. 4) (West & Hommersand 1981). Not only are species difficult to distinguish but it is virtually impossible to tell the two genera apart in the absence of carposporophytes (Santelices & Stewart 1985), although in this respect it has been suggested that apical structure could be used (Rodríguez & Santelices 1987).

About seven species of *Gelidium* and just one of *Pterocladia* are currently recognized on European coasts, mainly in the southern parts (Table 7) because the genera are favoured by warm water. There are many more species in Pacific Asia, where *G. amansii* is commercially important, particularly in Japan (Segi 1966). Populations of *Pterocladia* on the shores of the British Isles are never fertile and appear to reproduce vegetatively (Dixon 1958). Perennation rather than recruitment also occurs in Australia (Jernakoff 1986) and may be the basis for the remarkable ability of these plants to recover after harvesting in South Africa (Carter & Simons 1987). Although a capacity for regeneration is an asset in tank cultivation, the lack of spores could cause difficulties in seeding ropes or nets.

Both genera are slow growing; it takes at least 4 weeks for the biomass to double (Santelices 1976; Hansen 1980; Oliger & Santelices 1981). Coupled with this is a fairly low light requirement (Oliger & Santelices 1981; Correa *et*

Table 7. Occurrence of species of *Gelidium* and *Pterocladia* on the coast of various land areas

Species	E1	E2	E3	E4	E5	E6	E7	E8	E9	E10	E11	ANA	ASA	PNA	PSA	PA	Aus
Gelidium																	
G. pusillum	–	–	–	+	–	+	+	+	+	+	+	+	+	+	+	+	+
G. latifolium	–	–	–	+	–	–	+	+	+	+	+	–	–	–	–	–	–
G. sesquipedale	–	–	–	–	–	–	+	+	+	+	+	+	+	–	–	–	–
G. cantabricum	–	–	–	–	–	–	–	–	+	–	–	–	–	–	–	–	–
G. microdon	–	–	–	–	–	–	–	–	+	+	–	–	–	–	–	–	–
G. melanoideum	–	–	–	–	–	–	–	–	+	–	+	–	–	–	–	–	–
G. pectinatum	–	–	–	–	–	–	–	–	+	–	+	–	–	–	–	–	–
Total species	0	0	0	2	0	1	3	3	7	4	5	4	3	11	4?	26	8
Pterocladia																	
P. capillacea	–	–	–	–	–	?	+	+	+	+	+	+	+	+	–	+	+
Total species												3	1	3	?	4	3

E1–11, areas of Europe designated in Table 1. E1–10, South & Tittley (1986); E11, Giaccone *et al.* (1985); ANA, Atlantic North America and Caribbean, Taylor (1960); South & Tittley (1986); ASA, Atlantic South America, Taylor (1960); PNA, Pacific North America, Dawson (1953), Abbott & Hollenberg (1976), Stewart (1968), Stewart & Norris (1981); PSA, Pacific South America, Oliger & Santelices (1981); PA, Pacific Asia, Lee & Kang (1986), Yoshida *et al.* (1985a), Zhang & Xia (1988b); Aus, Australasia, Chapman (1969).

al. 1985; Macler & West 1987) and inhibition by high (Macler & West 1987) or continuous light (Oliger & Santelices 1981).

In Japan, the first stage of field cultivation has been practised; new substrata suitable for colonization have been provided and better growth obtained when the areas were fertilized with inorganic nitrogen (Yamada 1972). Although said to be too labour intensive to be profitable (Suto 1974), attempts at more advanced cultivation of *G. amansii* have been made; portions of plants of at least 5 mm in length were entrapped in the lay of rope placed in the sea in a calm bay where during the spring they grew at a rate of about 6% in weight per day (Akatsuka 1986). The plants were well established after 2 months and could be harvested, leaving the basal portions, at intervals of 2 months. Seeded ropes would probably be best placed in the sea in autumn, as *G. amansii* starts growing in December when competitors would not be greatly favoured (Akatsuka 1986). In contrast, two American west-coast species (*G. nudifrons* and *G. robustum*), on pieces of rope attached to subtidal frames in the sea off California, grew faster during the summer than between October and March (Wheeler *et al.* 1981). A similar system has been used with *G. rex* in central Chile and growth rates of up to 3% per day have been achieved (Santelices 1987).

Cultivation of the European species *G. sesquipedale* on cylinders of concrete conglomerate or suitable natural rock, hung from buoys and ropes in the sea, has been proposed for the Atlantic coast of Spain (Seoane-Camba 1989). This species grows relatively rapidly (Oliveira 1989).

BROWN SEAWEEDS

LAMINARIALES

A number of genera of kelps are important commercially, being sold both as human food (Nisizawa 1987) and for the extraction of alginates (McHugh 1987). The largest is the giant kelp, *Macrocystis*, and before going on to the success stories of *Laminaria* and *Undaria* cultivation an explanation is due as to why the cultivation of the largest seaweed in the world should not be advocated for Europe.

Macrocystis pyrifera is an often long-lived perennial plant with a variable number of unbranched stipes bearing a series of blades, each with a gas bladder at its base. These fronds, as they are called, are thus buoyant and whether the plant is attached to very shallow rock or in 30 m of water much of the frond length is on the surface and most of the blades are in a good position to absorb light (North 1971). This is clearly of great competitive advantage to the plant, which must always form the forest canopy wherever it can grow. The habit is also of commercial advantage because it makes harvesting simple; the fronds are chopped off just below the surface and are easily removed from the sea. Juvenile fronds, at most times growing continuously from the branched base of the plant, soon reach the surface and replace the canopy. The kelp beds off the Californian coast have been harvested for most of this century and between 1950 and 1980 the mean annual wet weight yield was 123 000 t (North 1987a). This material was used for alginate extraction but during the oil crisis of the 1970s the large potential biomass of *Macrocystis* became attractive as an alternative energy source. However, the existing kelp beds already needed to be managed carefully for their yield to be maintained (North 1976), so this resource was limited. Cultivation seemed an appropriate alternative to harvesting natural beds, particularly if sea areas without competing interests, but with available nutrients, could be used. Thus a large complex culture structure, which included a pump which artificially upwelled nutrient-rich oceanic water, was deployed some distance off the Californian coast (Leone 1980). The structure proved unsuitable for the survival of mature kelp plants because of differential movement, by wave action, of the buoyant fronds and the wire ropes on the structure, resulting in abrasion of the fronds (North *et al.* 1982). Less ambitious but more suitable farms have been designed (Neushul 1982; Harger & Neushul 1983; Neushul & Harger 1985, 1987; North 1987b), but commercial production seems unlikely in the near future.

Before cultivation was attempted in the USA, importation was considered in Europe (Pérez 1972). *M. pyrifera* is native to the eastern Pacific and the Southern Ocean but has not crossed the warm-water barrier into the North Atlantic (Womersley 1954). For the European alginate industry the temptation to introduce it was great; endemic kelps grow mainly below low water and are not buoyant, so most are difficult to harvest. On the other hand, the massive size and canopy-forming habit of *Macrocystis* would have a devastating effect on European subtidal ecosystems, as well as creating a navigational nuisance (Boalch 1981). A much safer alternative to the importation of such a plant, with its uncertain consequences, is to solve the harvesting problem by cultivating native species. High-quality crops can be grown on ropes and harvested at least as easily as *Macrocystis*, and the farms can be placed in agreed positions without fear of the escape of unwelcome plants. It has now been shown that endemic kelp cultivation is feasible in Europe (Kain & Dawes 1987).

There are over 27 genera in the order Laminariales (Wynne & Kraft 1981) and they are mostly fairly large plants to which the name kelp is somewhat loosely applied. In general, it is a colder water group, inhabiting the arctic and temperate seas; the species at low latitudes inhabit deep water below the summer thermocline. Although quite a few genera are harvested from natural populations in various parts of the world, only those that have been cultivated somewhere will be considered here. Three of these genera are native to Europe and one has been introduced (Table 8). The largest is *Laminaria*, currently with about 30 species. Some have divided and some have simple blades. The European species are listed in order of their distribution in Table 8. *L. solidungula* occurs only within the Arctic Circle. In the western Atlantic, *L. longicruris* may be conspecific with *L. saccharina* (Chapman 1973, 1974, 1975), and western Atlantic *L. longicruris* is interfertile with eastern Atlantic *L. saccharina* (Lüning *et al.* 1978). The inclusion of *L. longicruris* in Table 8 may therefore seem unjustified, but there are genetic differences between these interfertile populations; the stipe of *L. longicruris* is hollow in sheltered sites in the western Atlantic and the Faeroe and Shetland Islands only (Kain 1976). Also there are bullate and smooth genotypes of *L. saccharina* (Lüning *et al.* 1978). This species also occurs on the Pacific coast of North America, and material from there is interfertile with Atlantic material (Bolton *et al.* 1983). *L. saccharina* is the closest, morphologically, to the Asian species that is cultivated extensively, *L. japonica*. This species and *L. digitata* extend from the Arctic to north Spain and Brittany, respectively, while *L. hyperborea* occurs from northern Norway to Portugal. These three therefore have a similar distribution, but *L. ochroleuca*, morphologically rather similar to *L. hyperborea*, does not occur north of the Bristol Channel off south-western England (Norton 1985), although it is also present in the Mediterranean. *L. rodriguezii* occurs only in deep water in the Mediterranean.

There are 14 currently recognized species of *Alaria* (Widdowson 1971), all occurring in high northern latitudes, but only one on European coasts (Table 8). *A. esculenta* is absent from the southern North Sea and Kattegat and the Iberian peninsula (South & Tittley 1986).

There are only two species of *Saccorhiza* (Norton 1970), both confined to the Atlantic (Table 8). It is *S. polyschides* that is of interest in cultivation; it extends relatively far south and into the Mediterranean.

Undaria does not occur naturally outside Pacific Asia (Fritsch 1945) and there are just three species in Japan (Yoshida *et al.* 1985b).

The members of the Laminariales share an almost identical life history (Fig. 7). The kelp plant itself is diploid and in every case a flat blade is included in the morphology. When the plant is mature, reproductive patches, consisting of sporangia packed between paraphyses, appear on the surface of the thallus. Within each sporangium a series of cell divisions, including meiosis, results in 32 (or a further power of 2) haploid zoospores. The spores are so small and the sporangia packed so tightly that of the order of 50 million spores are produced per square centimetre of blade (Kain 1975). Such great fecundity is very useful to the cultivator; once sporophytes are fertile there is no shortage of spores. Each spore, after settling, grows into a microscopic gametophyte, which may consist of very few cells or may become a branched mass of filaments depending on environmental conditions (Kain 1964). In most species, half the spores develop into female gametophytes and half into male. After one to a few weeks of the right environmental conditions the gametophytes become mature and produce gametes; eggs are released mainly

Table 8. Occurrence of three genera of Laminariales on the coasts of various land areas

Species	D/S[a]	E1	E2	E3	E4	E5	E6	E7	E8	E9	E10	E11	ANA	SA	ASA	PNA	PSA	PA
Laminaria																		
L. solidungula		+	–	–	–	–	–	–	–	–	–	–	+	–	–	–	–	–
L. longicruris	S	+	–	–	+	–	–	–	–	–	–	–	+	–	–	–	–	–
L. digitata	D	+	+	+	+	–	+	+	+	–	–	–	+	–	–	–	–	–
L. saccharina	S	+	+	+	+	–	+	+	+	+	–	–	+	–	–	+	–	+
L. hyperborea	D	–	+	+	+	–	+	+	+	+	+	+	–	–	–	–	–	–
L. ochroleuca	D	–	–	–	–	–	–	+	+	+	+	–	–	–	–	–	–	–
L. rodriguezii	S	–	–	–	–	–	–	–	–	–	–	+	–	–	–	–	–	–
L. japonica	S	–	–	–	–	–	–	–	–	–	–	+[b]	–	–	–	–	–	+
Total species		4	3	3	4	0	3	4	4	3	1	3	4	2	2	10	0	15
Alaria																		
A. esculenta		+	+	+	+	–	–	–	+	+	–	–	–	–	–	–	–	–
Total species													2	0	0	7	0	5
Saccorhiza																		
S. dermatodea		+	+	–	+	–	–	–	+	–	+	–	+	–	–	–	–	–
S. polyschides		–	–	–	+	–	–	+	+	+	+	–	–	–	–	–	–	–
Undaria																		
U. pinnatifida		–	–	–	–	–	–	–	+[b]	–	–	+[b]	–	–	–	–	–	+
Total species		0	0	0	0	0	0	0	0	0	0	0	0	0	0	0	0	2

E1–11, European sites designated in Table 1. *Laminaria*: Atlantic Europe, South & Tittley (1986); Mediterranean, Giaccone *et al.* (1985); ANA, Atlantic North America, South & Tittley (1986); SA, South Africa, Simons (personal communication); ASA, Atlantic South America, Joly & Oliveira Filho (1967); PNA, Pacific North America, Abbott & Hollenberg (1976), Druehl (1968, 1979); PSA, Pacific South America; PA, Pacific Asia, Tokida *et al.* (1980), Druehl & Kaneko (1973). *Alaria*: Widdowson (1971), South & Tittley (1986). *Saccorhiza*: Norton (1970). *Undaria*: Yoshida *et al.* (1985b), Floc'h *et al.* (1988).
a D, divided blade; S, simple blade.
b Exotic.

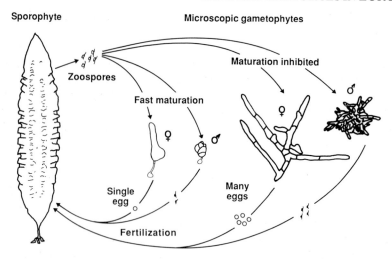

Figure 7. The life history of *Laminaria*

during the first half hour of darkness (Lüning 1981) and then emit a pheromonal substance that both stimulates the release of antherozoids and attracts them (Lüning & Müller 1978). After fertilization the young sporophyte grows rapidly and soon becomes attached by a rhizoid.

This last sequence can be delayed, however, by a different set of environmental conditions that prevent maturation of the gametophytes. Vegetative growth can then continue indefinitely, resulting in many-celled gametophytes or, if these are broken up, in many more gametophytes. If conditions are subsequently changed to those favouring maturity then, as any cell can produce a gamete, the reproductive potential is greatly increased. One important condition controlling maturity is light wavelength. Under red light most gametophytes remain vegetative, particularly at higher temperatures (although still less than 20 °C), while in white or blue light they rapidly produce gametes (Lüning & Dring 1975). In one species, *Saccorhiza dermatodea*, fertility is controlled by day length; gametes are produced only in short days (Henry 1987). This is not the case with most of the European species of *Laminaria*, the gametophytes of which can become fertile in continuous light (Kain 1969).

The influence of temperature on gametophyte fertility is different from its influence on growth. In three European species of *Laminaria*, 15 °C allows optimal growth but not optimal fertility; the latter is favoured by a lower temperature (Lüning 1980). The gametophytes of *L. japonica* respond in a similar way (Tseng *et al.* 1962; Nakahara 1984). In neither case, however, would the difference allow complete separation of vegetative growth from development to maturity without some other influence. There are clearly also chemical factors inhibiting gamete production in culture (Kain 1979); for example vitamin C (Fang & Kiang 1974) or the lack of available iron (Motomura & Sakai 1981, 1984a,b). These alternative routes for gametophyte development allow some manipulation of the life history of kelps, which is of use to the cultivator, for example when wild sporophytes are not fertile at the best seeding season (Druehl & Boal 1981). Another use would be in breeding experiments where a bank of haploid clones could be established (Fang *et al.* 1978; Fang 1984). Another technique useful for this is tissue culture (Fries 1980; Yan 1984; Butler & Evans 1987; Polne-Fuller & Gibor 1987).

The temperate nature of *Laminaria* has been demonstrated in growth experiments where sporophytes of five of the European species showed optimal elongation rates at 10–15 °C and a reduced rate at 20 °C; they died at 23 °C (Bolton & Lüning 1982). Eastern Atlantic species from different latitudes showed no genotypic adaptation (Bolton & Lüning 1982), but western Atlantic *L. saccharina*, at its southern limit, showed greater tolerance to raised temperature than near the middle of its range (Gerard & Du Bois 1988). At that southern limit the species is as productive as further north (Brady-Campbell *et al.* 1984) and juveniles show a higher growth rate (Gerard *et al.* 1987). Japanese species of *Laminaria* react similarly to temperature, which has also been shown to influence the blade shape; this is broader at higher temperatures (Okada *et al.* 1985).

The growth pattern of European *Laminaria* species is distinctly seasonal, with fast growth during the first half of the year and slower growth during the second, although the degree of difference between the rates varies with the species (Kain 1979, Fig. 4). The drop in growth rate takes place later in first-year plants (Lüning 1979), a fact of considerable importance to cultivators. In one site in the western Atlantic it was shown experimentally that the sharp drop in the growth rate of *L. longicruris* was due to the depletion of ambient nitrate (Chapman & Craigie 1977) and this was confirmed by the observation of differing growth strategies at sites with differing nitrogen levels in the summer (Anderson *et al.* 1981; Gagné & Mann 1981; Gagné *et al.* 1982). On the other hand, one difference in growth pattern between sites remained unexplained by nitrogen levels (Gerard & Mann 1979) and adaptation to low ambient levels has been demonstrated in a natural population (Espinoza & Chapman 1983). Off Scotland, the growth pattern of *L. digitata* seems to be correlated with nitrate concentration (Davison *et al.* 1984) and the plants may continue fast growth until later if the water is enriched (Conolly & Drew 1985). On the other hand, nitrogen does not seem to control periods of fast growth in *L. saccharina*, *L. hyperborea* (Kain 1989) and *Alaria esculenta* (Buggeln 1978).

The development of reproductive tissue on the blades of sporophytes of European species is to a greater or lesser extent a seasonal occurrence. In *L. saccharina* it can occur at any time of year but is most common in the winter

(Parke 1948). The same is true in Nova Scotia (Chapman 1973); at its southern limit in the western Atlantic the zoospores are not viable in early winter (Lee & Brinkhuis 1986). *L. digitata* can also be fertile throughout the year, although the peak period is between June and October on the coast of France (Cosson 1976) and fertility is confined to between May and December off Helgoland (Lüning 1982). *L. hyperborea* has a precise sporing period during the winter from October to March inclusive (Kain 1975).

Cultivation Techniques in Asia

The basic cultivation technique consists of inducing zoospore release from fertile adult sporophyte blades, settling these onto string, providing the gametophytes developing on the string with adequate conditions in tanks and eventually transferring the sporophyte-bearing string to the sea. The development of the system in China will be described first.

Until this century there were no *Laminaria* species on the coast of China, but it had been eaten by the Chinese people for perhaps two millennia, being imported from Korea and Japan at various times (Tseng 1981a). *L. japonica* was accidently introduced into Dalian in the north in 1927 (Tseng 1981a) and was later harvested from subtidal rocks (Tseng 1987a). These beds were inadequate to satisfy the need for kelp in China and in order to become self-sufficient in *haidai* (the Chinese name for *Laminaria*) it was essential to cultivate it. The southern limit of the genus in Japan is at 30 °N (Okazaki 1971), similar to the latitude of Dalian. Most of the coast of China thus seemed unsuitable for the growth of *Laminaria*, which meant that the cultivation technique had to embrace a sea-temperature problem; *L. japonica* will not grow at temperatures higher than 20 °C (Tseng *et al.* 1957). This could be overcome by exposing the plants in the sea only after the sea temperature had dropped to below 20 °C in late October, but if they were very young at that time, as was the case if October-fertile sporophytes were used for seeding, competitors arising from the spores of other algae choked the tiny sporelings. This problem was solved by seeding in early summer and maintaining the gametophytes and early sporophytes in tanks of temperature-controlled seawater in glasshouses on land until the autumn (Tseng *et al.* 1955a; Tseng 1981a). At the same time, plant breeding techniques produced a strain of *L. japonica* that was more tolerant of increased temperature (Fang *et al.* 1963). This was done by exposing gametophytes to 20–22 °C and using those surviving for further cultivation.

Early cultivation of *Laminaria* in China took place in sewage-polluted bays as farms on the open coast produced unsaleable plants of very poor quality. It was realized that this was due to another major problem with the coast of China; most of the open sea is very low in nutrients. This problem was initially solved by filling unglazed pottery jars, which are slightly porous, with inorganic nitrogen and phosphorus (Tseng *et al.* 1955b; Tseng 1981a). These jars were encased in baskets to which the young sporophytes were attached by hand (Tseng *et al.* 1955b; Cheng 1969) and the leaching out of the fertilizer allowed the growth of high-quality plants. This was a costly technique, however, and later plastic bags with tiny holes in them were hung among the ropes bearing the growing sporophytes (Tseng 1981b, 1987a). Later still, after experimental evidence had shown that nitrogen-starved kelps take up nutrients rapidly to a level higher than required for their immediate needs, fertilizer was applied intermittently by spraying (Tseng 1987a).

By these means the apparently unsuitable Chinese coast has been rendered hospitable to cultivated *Laminaria*, the farms eventually reaching 23 °N, a surprising 15° of latitude further south and at a summer sea temperature 6 °C higher than natural beds of the genus in Asia (Zeng 1984).

The modern *Laminaria* cultivation method used in China has been clearly described by Tseng (1987a) and is as follows. String, usually made of palm fibre, is wound around frames which are then placed in shallow concrete tanks containing cooled seawater in a glasshouse. In early summer, fertile blades of mature sporophytes are slightly dried out and plunged into the seawater. This stimulates the release of the zoospores which settle and attach to the string. The frames are then held in circulating nutrient-enriched seawater, supported by ropes in tanks. The temperature is held at 8–10 °C and natural light is received through the glass roof. Designs vary but one particular set-up (Tseng 1987a) consists of paired tanks 12 m long by 2.4 m wide and 0.2–0.3 m deep placed in a longitudinal series differing in height by 0.2–0.3 m so that seawater can flow from one to another before cooling and pumping. Each tank has four ropes bearing pairs of frames measuring 1.2 × 0.5 m, placed in pairs across the tank. The gametophytes develop on the string, become mature, release gametes which fuse and numerous sporophytes are formed. The quality of the circulating seawater must be carefully controlled, both to avoid algal contamination and to prevent damage from toxins. There was a problem with sulphate-reducing bacteria which flourished in necrotic tissue of mature blades and in the circulating system, producing, under anaerobic conditions, highly toxic hydrogen sulphide (Wu *et al.* 1979). This was solved by separating the water used for holding mature sporophytes from that used for seeding strings and by sterilizing the circulation system with hypochlorite before the seeding season.

At the end of the summer, strings crowded with sporophytes a few mm long are placed in the sea, having been loosened from the frames (Tseng 1987a). Here the plants grow to a length of 10–15 cm in 1–2 months. At this size, each sporophyte is individually placed into the lay of rope, usually by hand although a mechanical device has been developed for this (Wu, personal communication). The ropes are deployed in the sea on long lines in one of two designs (Tseng 1987a). The first consists of a rope, about 60 m long, held at the surface by buoys (usually glass spheres held in netting) at 2–3 m intervals and anchored at each end with a diagonal rope attached to a post

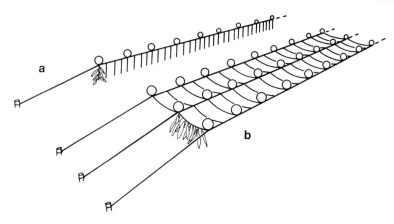

Figure 8. Two methods of deploying *Laminaria*-bearing ropes in China. (After Tseng 1987a)

driven into the bottom (Fig. 8a). The long lines are placed 8 m apart. The ropes bearing the sporophytes are tied onto the horizontal long line at intervals of about 0.5 m and these hang vertically in the water, each weighted with a mesh bag of stones. The length of the vertical rope is varied with the water transparency (Zeng 1984), being 2 m in the Qingdao region, with about 30 plants on the rope (Tseng 1987a). When ropes are longer than this, it is necessary to invert them once or twice during the growing season so that lower plants get enough light (Zeng 1984). The second, less common, method (Fig. 8b) deploys long lines in threes, buoyed in a similar manner to the first method, with the plant-bearing ropes attached at each end across the long lines instead of hanging down from them (Cheng 1969; Tseng 1987a). Recently, rope grids have been used near Dalian, 60 m wide and over 200 m long and containing rectangles of 1 × 8 m with a buoy at each corner. The plant-bearing ropes are slung from each buoy, attached at both ends as in the second method above (Moller, personal communication).

Fertilization with nutrients is effected by spraying the areas of rope structures, which are in rectangles with room for boats to pass between them, with a nitrate solution held in a tank in a motor-boat, using a powerful pump. This is done in rotation so that each receives an intermittent dose adequate for growth, with little wastage (Tseng 1987a). No fertilizer is applied during the last month before harvest in July (Tseng 1981a).

The blade of *Laminaria* grows at its base, so the tissue at the tip is the oldest. When it is a certain age this may decay and be lost. It was found that if the distal third of the blade was cut off the plant in early April there was an increase in plant weight at harvest because of reduced shading and/or drag (Wu *et al.* 1981), amounting to an increase in overall production, including the cut tips, of 15% (Zeng 1984). Production per plant has also been increased by plant breeding, which has resulted in a strain of *L. japonica* with a longer growing period, each mature plant then being longer, broader and heavier and almost unrecognizable as the original species (Fang 1983; Fang *et al.* 1963). There have been some problems with diseases but these seem to have been overcome (Wu *et al.* 1983).

The development of the *Laminaria* cultivation system in China has been so successful that by 1983 1.4 million wet t were produced (Tseng & Fei 1987), amounting to over half the total tonnage of cultivated seaweed in Asia (Tseng & Fei 1987). The annual production of 15 dry t ha^{-1} in the Yellow Sea compares favourably with production of land plants (Tseng 1987b).

Hokkaido, the northern island of Japan, is blessed with a high diversity of endemic species of *Laminaria* growing in profusion (Okazaki 1971). For this reason, although the demand for kombu (the Japanese name for *Laminaria*) for food is high, it has only recently become necessary to embark on cultivation. At first, this consisted of creating new areas suitable for growth by the deployment of concrete blocks or stones, or by blasting reefs (Hasegawa 1976). During the 1970s the annual harvest of natural populations fluctuated between 110 000 and 160 000 wet t, while the cultivated crop rose from nil in 1970 to 44 000 wet t in 1981 (Kawashima 1984).

Although various species of *Laminaria* are harvested commercially in Japan, it is *L. japonica* that is the most valuable (Kawashima 1984); however, it has the disadvantage that in natural beds it does not reach full size or maturity until its second year of growth (Hasegawa 1972). A cultivation technique that requires a rope system and space for nearly 2 years to achieve one crop would be too costly to be economical. The first problem that was tackled, therefore, was that of compressing the phenology of the species in Japan. The technique, which became known as 'forced cultivation', involved culturing the early stages on land in tanks, using artificial light, and placing young sporophytes of about 1 mm in length on rope in the sea in November. Recruits in the natural population do not reach this size until the following February (Hasegawa 1972). This head-start of 3 months allows the plants to mature within a year.

The overall cultivation technique, clearly described by Kawashima (1984), differs somewhat from that used in China partly because of the different latitude. In August, spores are obtained from mature blades of plants in the natural beds and settled onto 3 mm diameter string, wound around prism-shaped or rectangular frames which are then held in relatively small tanks of sterilized seawater. The seawater is enriched with nitrogen, phosphorus and iodine and does not circulate, although it is changed every 10–15 days. The culture tanks are immersed in concrete baths, the temperature of which is controlled. At first it is 15 °C but later it is dropped slightly to induce fertility. White fluorescent lamps provide 50–100 μmol photons m^{-2} s^{-1} at day lengths of 12–16 h. In November, the strings are unwound from the frames and tied loosely to vertical ropes in the sea for 7–10 days while healthy

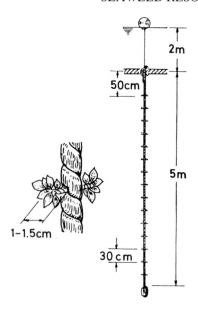

Figure 9. The method by which sporophyte-bearing string is attached to rope and this is hung in the sea in Japan. (From Kawashima (1984) courtesy of the *Japanese Journal of Phycology*)

sporophytes become more firmly attached. The strings are then cut into 5 cm lengths and inserted at 30 cm intervals into the lay of 5 m pieces of rope (Fig. 9) which are hung from submerged horizontal long lines in a grid (Fig. 10). During the winter the groups of plants arising from the short lengths of string are thinned so that only 4–5 remain in each group and weak-looking holdfasts are reinforced by binding with soft tape. The necessity for this process to be carried out at the coldest time of year precludes farming on the northernmost coasts of Japan. Further farming care involves the removal of epiphytes by hand. In spring the lower end of each hanging rope is tied to the adjacent horizontal rope, similar to one of the configurations used in China (Fig. 8b). The horizontal ropes are raised gradually until they are 0.5 m below the surface in May. Harvesting takes place in July–August. A different rope system has been used experimentally; the plant-bearing ropes are deployed in V-shapes, each suspended from two buoys with a single sinker at the base of the V (Bird 1987).

It seems that it is not necessary to apply nitrogen fertilizer to the *Laminaria* farms in Japanese waters, although there is no detectable nitrate in the waters of the main farming area off south Hokkaido between May and October (Sanbonsuga 1984). The maximum level in March of 14 μmol nitrogen l^{-1} is presumably sufficient to allow growth to the maximum plant size by June (Sanbonsuga 1984), by which time internal nitrate reserves have dropped to

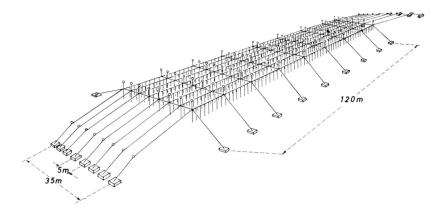

Figure 10. The grid rope structure in use in Japan for *Laminaria* cultivation. (From Kawashima (1984) courtesy of the *Japanese Journal of Phycology*)

nil (Yokoyama & Sanbonsuga 1979). After this there is a period of continued increase in dry matter, mainly mannitol, which is termed the 'substantialization phase' by Sanbonsuga (1984). Another major difference from the Chinese method is that the crop's parents come from wild plants and are not selected strains.

Undaria pinnatifida is a highly prized foodstuff (called *wakame*) in Japan and occurs around most of the coast except the cold north and southeast sides of Hokkaido (Saito 1975). It is therefore favoured by warmer waters than are species of *Laminaria*. In the 1960s the harvest from natural beds was around 60 000 wet t year^{-1} and inadequate for demand. Cultivation of this genus therefore took place earlier than that of *Laminaria* and equalled the natural harvest in 1966 (Saito 1975; Akiyama & Kurogi 1982). The annual cultivated production was 91 000 wet t in Japan in 1981 but 231 000 wet t in Korea in 1982 (Tseng & Fei 1987).

In principle the Japanese cultivation system, described by Saito (1975), is the same as with *Laminaria*, the life history being identical. Square frames with sides of 50 cm are used and synthetic string, treated with resin to prevent unravelling, wound round them. Seeding the string with spores takes place between April and July and the frames are hung in tanks of nutrient-enriched seawater in greenhouses. The water temperature is controlled so that it does not exceed 28 °C and shading may be necessary to prevent photoinhibition. This tank-culture phase may be partly or wholly replaced by *in situ* cultivation in which the frames are hung in the sea. When the ambient temperature drops to below 20 °C between September and November, the string is unwound from the frames and either wound around the culture rope or cut into short lengths and inserted into the lay. The ropes are deployed either horizontally or as vertical lines, in a similar configuration to those of *Laminaria* farms.

Harvesting takes place in March–May in southern Japan but May–July in Hokkaido. When plant density is high there may be a preliminary harvest of thinnings.

In Korea the technique is slightly different (Sohn & Kain 1989b). Strings are seeded with spores in April and the frames maintained in tanks of seawater, replaced monthly but not usually nutrient-enriched. In September or October the string is wound around a combination of rope and rubber/ fabric thong: the main function of the latter is tensioning but also its square section keeps the turns of the string in place. All these ropes are maintained at 1–2 m below the sea surface by small buoys and vertical lines. A common type of farm consists of a grid with ropes 10–20 m apart, buoyed at 2 m intervals, the kelp bearing ropes being slung between. Harvesting is initially by thinning, the last plants being removed in April.

Experimental Cultivation Elsewhere

In British Columbia, Canada, at a latitude of 49 °N, a series of experimental farms were set up (Druehl et al. 1988). String seeded with spores was maintained in a greenhouse and outplanted in January by inserting short lengths into the rope at 30 cm intervals. The rope was held horizontally at 2 m below the sea surface at several different sites. L. groenlandica grew quite well but did not reach full size during the first season. When harvested in July of the next year, however, the yield was 20 kg wet weight per metre of rope at the best site. A crop of this species could be obtained in 1 year, although this had to include a full winter, if a departure was made from the natural seasonal sequence by using cloned gametophytes. This technique follows from the fact that gametophytes can be prevented from maturing, for example by providing only red light, when they can grow vegetatively indefinitely (p. 338). Such gametophytes can be used to produce sporophytes at any time of year by stimulating fertility. L. saccharina, however, did not require two seasons for adequate development. After outplanting in February, a harvest of 8 kg per metre of rope was obtained in September (Druehl et al. 1988).

Further north on the same coast, at 58 °N in Alaska, ropes were laid down on subtidal sand and weighted with rocks (Ellis & Calvin 1981). The ropes were naturally colonized by L. groenlandica during the winter but again plants did not grow to a harvestable size until the second year.

In the western Atlantic L. saccharina has been the focus of attention, starting with tank cultivation in a glasshouse and then deploying measured plants in the field on rafts (Brinkhuis et al. 1983a, 1983b). Initially a considerable variety of raft type was considered, some quite complex and with rigid sections (Brinkhuis et al. 1983a), which caused trouble by abrading the plants (Brinkhuis et al. 1983b). The growth rate in length of the plants was followed for 18 months and was found to be faster during the first growing season (November to June) than the second (Brinkhuis et al. 1984). A later development was the design of rope structure based on those in Asia but using wire rope (Brinkhuis *et al.* 1987). Six 37 m long wire ropes were held parallel 3 m apart by wire rope across the ends and the grid was held at 2 m below the sea surface by 54 buoys and four anchors. Culture ropes were hung from this grid, using three different seeding methods, and growth rates were measured (Brinkhuis *et al.* 1987).

In the eastern Atlantic, in a Norwegian fjord, the growth of *L. saccharina*, *L. digitata* and *Alaria esculenta* was monitored on ropes adjacent to a fish farm (Indergaard & Jensen 1983). No enhancement of growth from the potential eutrophication was detected.

Finally, there was a proposal to combine the prevention of coastal erosion with cultivating *Laminaria* for biomass as an energy source (Jacques *et al.* 1980; Beavis *et al.* 1986; Beavis & Charlier 1987). The proposal, for complex underwater structures, took no account of the known biology and ecology of the plant species intended as crops.

Cultivation in Europe

European species of Laminariales have been grown on ropes off the Isle of Man in the Irish Sea since 1981 (Holt & Kain 1983; Holt 1984; Jones & Holt 1985; Kain & Holt 1985; Dawes 1987; Kain & Dawes 1987). The initial techniques were based on those used in Asia but the species cultivated were *Laminaria saccharina*, *Alaria esculenta* and *Saccorhiza polyschides*. Spores were settled onto string and the gametophytes were cultured in shallow trays in the laboratory for 20–30 days before outplanting onto horizontal ropes in the sea (Holt 1984; Kain & Holt 1984). It was found that more plants were produced when the gametophytes were cultured in a 12 : 12 h light : dark cycle than in continuous light (Dawes 1987; Kain & Dawes 1987), presumably because of the increased likelihood of egg fertilization after synchronized release (Lüning 1981). When the string was twisted around the rope, water movement pushed all the twists to one end of the rope and left the remainder of the string in a loop separated from the rope (Jones & Holt 1981; Holt 1984). Thus, instead, the string was cut into short lengths and inserted into the lay of the rope at various distances (Kain & Holt 1982). Groups of plants developed on the string and adjacent rope. Seeding between December and February was most satisfactory; if it was delayed until April many of the young plants were smothered by diatoms unless the rope was at more than 2 m below the sea surface or at 7–10 m for the first 6 weeks and then raised to 2–3 m (Kain & Dawes 1987). *A. esculenta* seeded in November–February ceased growing at the end of May, while plants seeded in April continued growing for a further month. Similarly seeded *L. saccharina* grew until July and August, respectively. These facts cast doubt on any assumption that the cessation of fast growth is linked to nutrient depletion in the sea. Surface nitrate is reduced to about 1 μmol l^{-1} (Slinn & Eastham 1984) but the exposure of farmed plants to strong tidal streams may offset this. The biomass produced in each group of plants was only adversely affected by adjacent groups when the strings were placed less than 25 cm apart (Holt 1984; Jones & Holt 1985). While *A. esculenta* and *L. saccharina* adhered to the ropes well in a fairly exposed site, *S. polyschides* was often lost under the influence of wave action and was not considered further as a crop (Jones & Holt 1985).

In a subsequent attempt to reduce the labour necessary for successful seeding, the string stage was abandoned and an intermediate-sized 'cord' of 6 mm diameter was both seeded and used as the cultivation substratum (Kain & Dawes 1987). The cord was wound around buoyant frames, seeded with spores while lying horizontal in a seawater tank and then held vertically in a temperature-controlled tank of circulating enriched seawater in daylight under a green filter (Kain & Dawes 1987, Fig. 4). When deployed in the sea, the cord was cut into 8 m lengths, tied at the top to a buoyed horizontal rope and weighted at the bottom with a 1 kg concrete sinker. The cords were 1 m apart and the lower ends were raised by the tidal current prevalent at the site so that most of each cord received enough light for the production of at least 1 kg fresh weight per metre (Kain & Dawes 1987). Recently, the system has been modified further and a grid, similar to that in use in Japan (Fig. 10), anchored with concrete blocks (Holt & Dawes 1989). Cords are still seeded directly but these are tied at each end to adjacent ropes, thus being slung between the ropes rather than hanging down from them (Fig. 11). This system is expected to increase production per unit area.

The choice of a site suitable for a kelp farm is important and not obvious. An apparently suitable site may prove unfavourable; testing is important (Dawes 1988).

Concurrently with this development, *Undaria pinnatifida* was being culti- vated off the west coast of Brittany, France (Pérez *et al.* 1984). This exotic species was introduced accidentally to the Étang de Thau, connected to the Mediterranean, and now seems to be established in this lagoon where it grows well and has a similar phenology to that in Asia, reproducing in May and June (Pérez *et al.* 1981). For the cultivation system, an entirely new seeding technique has been developed using 'free-living' gametophytes (Pérez *et al.* 1984). These are gametophytes whose sexual development has been pre- vented while vegetative growth has continued (see p. 338); in addition, they have remained planktonic in the culture medium. The last is achieved by introducing the original spores into a mixture of Miquel's and Provasoli's type 6 medium (Provasoli *et al.* 1957), in which a precipitate forms and the spores become attached to the precipitate, which is later broken up by aeration (Pérez *et al.* 1984). The gametophytes are prevented from maturing by maintaining them at 22 °C, a relatively high temperature allowing rapid vegetative growth. The temperature is gradually raised to 27 °C and when seeding material is required it is gradually dropped to 17 °C, which stimulates gamete production. The culture is sprayed onto string attached to frames and

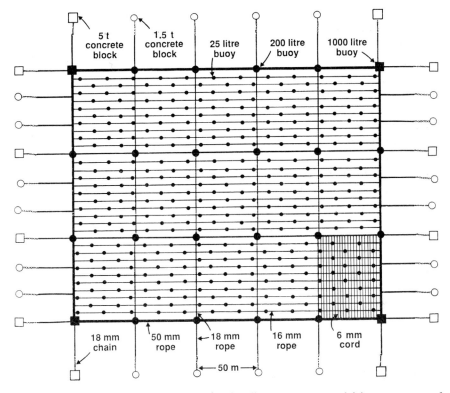

Figure 11. Diagram of the rope system (anchor lines are not to scale) in current use of the Isle of Man, UK. (Unpublished, courtesy of T.J. Holt and C.P. Dawes)

the gametophytes and gametes adhere to the string. The frames are then hung in enriched seawater in reduced daylight before deployment in the sea. In this instance winding the string around rope in the sea has been successful; it is tied to the rope at intervals. The first sea structure was a buoyed and weighted horizontal rope (Pérez *et al*. 1984), similar to that used off the Isle of Man, but more recently a grid has been used, with the cultivation ropes being held at 2 m below the sea surface (M. Moigne, personal communication via C.P. Dawes). In 1987, the cultivation of *Undaria* off France was suspended pending the outcome of an enquiry into the advisability of growing this exotic alga in the open sea (R. Pajot, personal communication via C.P. Dawes). It was already too late; cultivated *Undaria* plants had reproduced *in situ* and numerous sporophytes have colonized the bay of Lampaul in Ouessant, Brittany (Floc'h *et al*. 1988). The estimated potential range for this species extends northwards to Scotland and Norway (Floc'h *et al*. 1988) and its competitive ability in European waters is unknown.

Perhaps this case should serve as a warning to would-be species importers. When *Undaria* was originally transferred to Brittany it was claimed that local summer sea temperatures were too low to allow reproduction (International Council for the Exploration of the Sea 1984). It was already known, however, that gametophytes could grow and sporophytes could be formed at temperatures well within the range of the sea off Britanny (Akiyama 1965). Any introduction of an exotic species should be preceded by thorough investigation, both of the literature and of the biology of the species.

More recently French workers have been developing cultivation techniques with native species of Laminariales. After laboratory seeding on string, *Saccorhiza polyschides* grew rapidly on experimental horizontal ropes off the north coast of Brittany (Dion & Golven 1989). Hybrids of *L. digitata*, *L. saccharina* and *Saccorhiza* also grew quite well on ropes, the *L. digitata* crosses faster than wild plants (Cosson 1989).

SARGASSUM

Although *Sargassum* contains alginates, these have a poor viscosity (McHugh 1987). There is, however, current interest in some species as an energy crop in the USA, but the farms would consist of floating unattached plants (Hanisak 1987), not pertinent to this chapter. The genus does, however, have potential as an attached crop.

Sargassum is a warm-water genus; in Europe there were no species north of the south-east shores of the North Sea and most of the species are confined to the Mediterranean, Iberia and the Azores (Table 9). *S. muticum* is present as an unwelcome immigrant (Farnham *et al.* 1973) that has spread from the English Channel as far as Denmark (Christensen 1984), Norway and Sweden (Rueness 1989) and has been found in the Mediterranean (Critchley 1983a). Besides being an invasive species (Norton 1981a; Critchley 1983b, 1983c; Critchley et al. 1987) it shows a fast growth rate (Kane & Chamberlain 1979), regenerates easily (Fletcher & Fletcher 1975a), and has other features that would make a good crop (Fletcher & Hales 1989). It would be wrong, however, to grow this species outside its present range and thereby encourage its spread.

Sargassum belongs to the Fucales, a group of brown algae without alternating phases in their life history. The plant is diploid and produces gametes that fuse to form a new plant. In *S. muticum* this often occurs on the surface of the thallus and the zygote, still attached to the parent plant, develops to form a propagule which is relatively advanced when it is released (Fletcher 1980; Norton 1981b). Expulsion of eggs is rhythmic, influenced by the lunar (tidal) cycle (Fletcher 1980; Norton 1981b; Mooney & Van Staden 1984). Fecundity is high; tissues involved with reproduction can form half the plant's biomass (Norton & Deysher 1989). Reproduction is controlled mainly by temperature and occurs in summer in Europe (Fletcher & Fletcher 1975b; Deysher 1984).

In Japan, blocks have been artificially seeded with *Sargassum* and then placed in the sea (Yoshikawa 1986). Two years were necessary for the plants

Table 9. Occurrence of species of *Sargassum* on the coast of various land areas

Species	E1	E2	E3	E4	E5	E6	E7	E8	E9	E10	E11	ANA	ASA	PNA	PA	PI	Aus
S. natans	—	—	—	—	—	+	+	+	+	+	—	+	+	—	—	—	—
S. muticum	—	—	—	+a	—	+a	+a	+a	—	—	+a	—	—	+a	+a	—	—
S. flavifolium	—	—	—	—	—	—	—	+	+	—	+	+	—	—	—	—	—
S. vulgare	—	—	—	—	—	—	—	—	+	+	+	+	+	—	—	—	—
S. cymosum	—	—	—	—	—	—	—	—	—	+	—	—	—	—	—	—	—
S. desfontaisii	—	—	—	—	—	—	—	—	—	+	—	—	—	—	—	—	—
S. acinarium	—	—	—	—	—	—	—	—	—	—	+	+	+	—	—	—	—
S. linifolium	—	—	—	—	—	—	—	—	—	—	+	—	—	—	—	—	—
S. salicifolium	—	—	—	—	—	—	—	—	—	—	+	—	—	—	—	—	—
S. hornschuchii	—	—	—	—	—	—	—	—	—	—	+	—	—	—	—	—	—
S. trichocarpum	—	—	—	—	—	—	—	—	—	—	+	—	—	—	—	—	—
Total species	0	0	0	1	0	2	2	3	3	4	9	15	12	3	61	8	18

E1–11, area of Europe designated in Table 1. E1–10, South & Tittley (1986); E11, Feldmann (1937), Giaccone et al. (1985), Rueness (1989); ANA, Atlantic North America, Taylor (1960), South & Tittley (1986); ASA, Atlantic South America, Taylor (1960); PNA, Pacific North America, Abbott & Hollenberg (1976); PA, Pacific Asia, Lee & Kang (1986), Yoshida et al. (1985b), Yoshida (1988); PI, Pacific islands (Hawaii, Micronesia), Magruder (1988), Tsuda (1988); Aus, Australasia, Lindauer et al. (1961), Womersley (1987).
[a] Exotic.

to reach a useful size. More recently, experiments were made on cultivating three species on nets (Y. Ishikawa, personal communication). Fertile plants were shaken in a tank of seawater, depositing fertilized eggs on the bottom. After decanting, the concentrated zygote suspension was poured into a large shallow tank containing several layers of the nets used for *Porphyra* cultivation. The nets were later deployed in the sea, suspended below the surface. The growth period was during the winter and, although few of the plants survived, those that did grew to a large size.

GREEN SEAWEEDS

Green algae in the form of membranes or flat tubes are eaten extensively in Asia (Okazaki 1971; Nisizawa 1987), and occasionally in the past in Scotland (Chapman 1970); these algae could be cultivated in Europe. Three main genera are involved: *Enteromorpha*, which is tubular; *Ulva*, which is flat with two layers of cells; and *Monostroma*, which is also flat but, as its name implies, consists of a single layer of cells. *Monostroma* is now considered to include several genera because of differences in the life history (Tanner 1981). There is considerable taxonomic uncertainty about many of the species in each of these genera so only the commonest are shown in Table 10. There are about 26 species of *Enteromorpha* in Europe, even excluding some uncertain ones (South & Tittley 1986), though there are fewer at high latitudes. The number of species of *Ulva* in Europe is twelve while a total of seven European species have been placed in *Monostroma sensu lato*.

Enteromorpha and *Ulva* have the same basic life history (illustrated by Tanner 1981), consisting of an alternation of morphologically identical haploid and diploid generations. The gametes produced by the haploid gametophytes have two flagella and look the same although each has a potential sex (or mating type), while the spores produced after meiosis by the sporophytes have four flagella. This basic alternation is modified in some species by complications such as parthenogenesis and in others by simplification to an asexual non-alternating life history (Tanner 1981). Some species, which have until recently been placed in *Monostroma*, have a similar life history but others, including *M. grevillei* (Kornmann 1973) and the Japanese *M. nitidum* (Hirose & Yoshida 1964), have a heteromorphic (with dissimilar phases) alternation of generations (Tanner 1981). The blade is the haploid gametophyte and, after fusion of its gametes, a thick-walled cyst is formed, now regarded as a sporophyte (Tatewaki 1972). This sometimes penetrates and lives in mollusc shells.

Some species of *Enteromorpha* are remarkably euryhaline; *E. intestinalis* can grow in freshwater, although there is evidence for the existence of genetic strains adapted to high and low salinities (Reed & Russell 1979). Although other species are less tolerant (Koeman & Hoek 1982) seven of them do

Table 10. Occurrence of species of *Enteromorpha*, *Ulva* and taxa placed in *Monostroma* on the coasts of various land areas

Species	E1	E2	E3	E4	E5	E6	E7	E8	E9	E10	E11	E	ANA	ASA	PNA	PA	Aus
Enteromorpha																	
E. intestinalis	–	+	+	+	+	+	+	+	+	+	+	+	+	+	+	+	+
Other European	1	5	5	10	6	18	11	18	14	4	12	25	13	6	5	6	7
Non-European													6	4	0	4	0
Total species	1	6	6	11	7	19	12	19	15	5	13	26	20	11	6	11	8
Ulva																	
U. lactuca	+	+	+	+	–	+	+	+	+	+	+	+	+	+	+	+	+
Other European	0	1	1	2	0	4	1	8	9	0	6	11	3	1	2	2	2
Non-European													1	1	7	10	3
Total species	1	2	2	3	0	5	2	9	10	1	7	12	5	3	10	13	6
Monostroma etc.																	
M. grevillei	–	+	+	+	+	+	+	+	+	?	–	+	+	–	+	+	–
Other European	2	3	4	4	1	4	3	2	2	0	1	6	7	1	1	3	1
Non-European													0	0	1	11	1
Total species	2	4	5	5	2	5	4	3	3	0	1	7	8	1	3	15	2

E1–11, areas of Europe designated in Table 1; E, total for Europe; E1–10, South & Tittley (1986); E6, Wallentinus (1979); E11, Feldmann (1937), Giaccone *et al.* (1985); ANA, Atlantic North America, South & Tittley (1986); ASA, Atlantic South America, Taylor (1960); PNA, Pacific North America, Abbott & Hollenberg (1976); PA, Pacific Asia, Lee & Kang (1986), Yoshida *et al.* (1985b); Aus, Australasia, Womersley (1984).

inhabit the Baltic (Table 10) with *E. intestinalis* being the most abundant (Wallentinus 1979). On the other hand *Ulva*, although containing some fairly tolerant species, is generally more stenohaline (Koeman & Hoek 1981) and there are no species in the Baltic (Table 10). Some species placed in *Monostroma* are regarded as brackish and *M. grevillei* thrives in the Baltic.

Enteromorpha and *Ulva* can show remarkably high growth rates; in 1 day *U. lactuca* can double its area (Parker 1981) and *E. prolifera* can nearly double its length (Soe-Htun *et al.* 1986), while *E. compressa* can be the first apparent colonizer on disturbed temperate shores (Jones 1948). Coupled to fast growth is a high light requirement (King & Schramm 1976; FitzGerald 1978; Ramus 1978; Duke *et al.* 1986) and an ability to absorb nutrients rapidly (Ramus & Venable 1987). These species may show their greatest biomass in summer when there is most light (Munda & Markham 1982), but *U. lactuca* can adapt to low light and grow in winter in Denmark (Vermaat & Sand-Jensen 1987) and both are present on the shore all through the year, although individual plants are not perennial (Knight & Parke 1931; Mathieson & Hehre 1983). *M. grevillei*, however, grows in very early spring in the Baltic, using the nutrients before the phytoplankton bloom (Wallentinus 1979) and is absent from New Hampshire shores during the summer (Mathieson & Hehre 1983). *Enteromorpha* often appears to be favoured by pollution but it cannot be taken as an indicator of such because it also thrives in clean, moving water (Wallentinus 1979); its fast growth must require a good nutrient supply, which either sewage can provide or water movement can enhance. *E. intestinalis* and many other species of the genus are normally free of epiphytes because the plants continuously shed a layer from the surface of the thallus (McArthur & Moss 1977), a feature that could be of considerable importance to cultivators because epiphytes can be difficult to control and clearly damage the purity of a crop.

Enteromorpha and *Ulva* can be reproductive at any time of year (Blackler 1956) but reproduction is maximal in the summer (Knight & Parke 1931); this is probably a reflection of the pseudoperennial habit, with short-lived plants becoming fertile at a developmental stage rather than through an environmental trigger. Swarmer release in *E. intestinalis* is controlled by such a trigger, however; this can occur in a lunar periodicity such that release takes place before or during spring tides (Christie & Evans 1962; Pandey & Ohno 1985), but this may be modified by other environmental factors such as degree of emersion (Pringle 1986). A similar periodicity has been reported for a Pacific species of *Ulva*, gametes and zoospores being released only at spring tides (Smith 1947). *M. grevillei* reproduces in the spring in the British Isles (Blackler 1956) and in the western Atlantic (Coleman & Mathieson 1975). The Japanese *M. nitidum*, which produces gametes rhythmically at neap tides (Ohno 1972), is reported to require blue light for gamete release (Ohno & Nozawa 1972).

Monostroma (mainly *M. nitidum*) has been cultivated for food in Japan for some years and 15 000 wet t were produced in 1970 (Suto 1974). Nets, similar to those used for *Porphyra*, are held in the intertidal by bamboo poles (Ohno 1977) or floated below the sea surface, and the plants grow during the winter (Ohno 1972) with a biomass peak in March (Pandey & Ohno 1985). The seeding of the nets is from zoospores from natural populations (Segi & Kida 1961). *Enteromorpha* is also prized as a food in Japan and natural populations of the alga have recently become inadequate for demand and cultivation has been started (Ohno & Miyanoue 1980). In Korea, *Enteromorpha* is grown on parallel ropes, ~20 cm apart, supported by 1.5 m lengths of bamboo. They are seeded by being exposed at certain sites in the summer and then moved to the culture ground in September. Several crops are taken (Sohn & Kain 1989b).

Enteromorpha cultivation was also successful on the coast of northern India, where *Porphyra*-type nets were fixed with iron bars in tide pools (Ohno *et al.* 1981). Mature fertile plants of *E. flexuosa*, collected at dawn from the shore at the appropriate lunar period, dried slightly with blotting paper, plunged into seawater and exposed to bright light, liberally released swarmers (Oza *et al.* 1985). The swarmer suspension was applied to the nets in seawater in tanks and kept in the dark for attachment to take place. The growing period was during the winter in these tropical waters (Oza *et al.* 1985).

LEGAL ASPECTS

Before setting up a seaweed farm in the sea it is necessary to obtain the right to use the particular area (sometimes called 'water rights'). The legal position and the required procedure varies considerably and can only be outlined for some countries here. It is assumed that the area that would be required is seawards of extreme low tide but within territorial waters and clear of busy shipping lanes.

In Norway, it is necessary to apply through the local harbour master, if such exists for the area, to the Ministry of Fisheries. At present it should not be difficult to get permission, as there is still plenty of available coast in spite of numerous fish farms. The laws are fairly diffuse but will be clarified in a few years' time.

In Sweden, permission should be sought from the county administration (Länsstyrelsen) who would be responsible for establishing site suitability and the absence of conflicting activities, including the preservation of wildlife (there are a number of reserves). Some areas close inshore are in private hands and permission would need to be sought from these owners. At present it would probably not be too difficult to obtain water rights for a small seaweed farm in Sweden.

In Denmark, it is also the Ministry of Fisheries to whom application should be made, but they have to consult the Ministry of Environment, the Forest and Nature Department, and the local county authority. This all takes time and it may be 1–2 years before permission is granted. Permission for fish and mussel farms are at present blocked because of problems caused by eutrophication.

In Germany, several bodies have to be consulted: the central government Water and Shipping Authority (Wasse- und Schiffahrtsbehörde), the Local Government Protection Board (Umweltamt) and the Ministry for Agriculture and Forestry. It would be difficult to get permission because the coastline is limited in extent and much of it is already committed to wildlife reserves, military activities and tourism.

In the UK, application has to be made to the Crown Estate Commissioners, who will then consult a number of possibly interested parties, prolonging the procedure to over a year at best.

In Ireland, a licence is required from the government Department of the Marine.

In the Netherlands, permission should be sought from the North Sea Directorate, Ministry of Transport and Public Works (Rijkswaterstaat).

In France, application should be made to the local Administrateur des Affaires Maritimes for permission from the Direction des Affaires Maritimes, under the Secretariat d'Etat à la Mer within the Ministère des Transports.

In Spain, only estuaries, bays and lagoons are controlled by local governments and inshore waters can be used by anyone. It is important to obtain the friendly agreement of the local fishermen, but this applies to any country.

In Portugal, application should be made to the Direção-Geral das Pescas in Lisbon.

In Italy, exact details of the proposer, the proposed farm, the proposed site and the intended product would have to be furnished to the Port Authority, who would need to obtain the agreement of the Public Works Ministry and the Ministry for Financial Affairs. This could take 6 months even if the proposal were very carefully prepared.

In Yugoslavia, permission would have to be sought from the local authority, the national harbour authority and the army. It would be necessary to establish that the farmer was qualified to grow seaweed and was financially dependent on it. Permission would be difficult to obtain.

In Greece, the responsible authority would be the new Aquaculture branch of the Ministry of Agriculture.

CONCLUSIONS

Clearly, economic considerations will determine both whether attached seaweeds will be cultivated in Europe and which species are chosen. Cultivation is most likely to be profitable when a superior crop is required (e.g. human food, particular phycocolloids or pharmacological products). As a biomass source, seaweed will need to wait until the next energy crisis.

There are no serious technological barriers; the way has already been demonstrated spectacularly in Asia. Care must be taken to suit the alga to the conditions, learning as much as possible about the requirements of the proposed crop and about the environment during the season that growth is expected to take place. The occurrence of a species at a particular site should be encouraging, but if it is absent it may still be possible to cultivate it, as has been shown repeatedly elsewhere. There is also scope for crop improvement by genetic selection.

Any attempt to cultivate an alga must be based on a thorough knowledge of the biology of the plant: growth rate, reproduction, morphology, life history and the effects of environmental factors on these, including what triggers phase changes. It is therefore very important that biologists should take part in the planning and operation of a farm. With rope structures, fishermen with practical experience of ropes in the sea are also useful. No complex mechanical structure has been economically successful in growing attached seaweeds, so engineers need not be involved.

ACKNOWLEDGEMENTS

Professor Inger Wallentinus kindly collected information about the Baltic Sea and the following people went to some trouble looking into the legal position in their countries: Cand. real. Menz Indergaard (Norway), Professor Inger Wallentinus (Sweden), Aase Kristiansen (Denmark), Dr Winfrid Schramm (Germany), Dr M.D. Guiry (Ireland), Dr S.J. de Groot (Netherlands), Dr Xavier Niell (Spain), Dr J.C.F. Oliveira (Portugal), Professor G. Tripodi (Italy), Dr Ivka Munda and Dr Mitja Grosman (Yugoslavia) and Professor S. Haritonidis (Greece). Drs T.J. Holt and C.P. Dawes allowed me to use their unpublished diagram in Fig. 11. I am extremely grateful to them all.

REFERENCES

Abbott I.A. 1985a. *Gracilaria* from California: key, list and distribution of the species. In *Taxonomy of Economic Seaweeds with Reference to Some Pacific and Caribbean Species*. (Eds. I.A. Abbott & J.N. Norris) pp. 97–9. La Jolla: California Sea Grant College Program.

Abbott I.A. 1985b. *Gracilaria* from Hawaii: key, list and distribution of the species. In *Taxonomy of Economic Seaweeds with Reference to Some Pacific and Caribbean Species*. (Eds. I.A. Abbott & J.N. Norris) pp. 85–7. La Jolla: California Sea Grant College Program.

Abbott I.A. 1985c. *Gracilaria* from the Philippines: list and distribution of the species. In *Taxonomy of Economic Seaweeds with Reference to Some Pacific and Caribbean*

Species. (Eds. I.A. Abbot & J.N. Norris) pp. 89–90. La Jolla: California Sea Grant College Program.

Abbott I.A. 1988. Some species of *Gracilaria* and *Polycavernosa* from Thailand. In *Taxonomy of Economic Seaweeds with Reference to Some Pacific and Caribbean Species*. Vol. II. (Eds. I.A. Abbott) pp. 137–50. La Jolla: California Sea Grant College Program.

Abbott I.A. & Hollenberg G.J. 1976. *Marine Algae of California*. Stanford: Stanford University Press.

Admiralty 1983. *Admiralty Tide Tables. Vol. 1. 1984. European Waters Including Mediterranean Sea*. Hydrographer of the Navy.

Akatsuka I. 1986. Japanese Gelidiales (Rhodophyta), especially *Gelidium*. *Oceanogr. Mar. Biol. Ann. Rev.* **24**: 171–263.

Akiyama K. 1965. Studies of ecology and culture of *Undaria pinnatifida* (Harv.) Sur. II. Environmental factors affecting the growth and maturation of gametophyte. *Bull. Tohoku Reg. Fish. Res. Lab.* **25**: 143–70.

Akiyama K. & Kurogi M. 1982. Cultivation of *Undaria pinnatifida* (Harvey) Suringar, the decrease in crops from natural plants following crop increase from cultivation. *Bull. Tohoku Reg. Fish. Res. Lab.* **44**: 91–100.

Anderson M.R., Cardinal A. & Larochelle J. 1981. An alternative growth pattern for *Laminaria longicruris*. *J. Phycol.* **17**: 405–11.

Anderson R.J., Simons R.H. & Jarman N.G. 1989. Commercial seaweeds in southern Africa: a review of utilization and research. *S. Afr. J. Mar. Sci.* **8**: 277–99.

Armisen R. & Galatas F. 1987. Production, properties and uses of agar. In *Production and Utilization of Products from Commercial Seaweeds*. (Ed. D.J. McHugh) pp. 1–57. Rome: FAO Fisheries Technical Paper 288.

Bangmei X. 1985. *Gracilaria* from China: key, list and distribution of the species. In *Taxonomy of Economic Seaweeds with Reference to Some Pacific and Caribbean Species*. (Eds. I.A. Abbott & J.N. Norris) pp. 71–6. La Jolla: California Sea Grant College Program.

Bardach J.E., Ryther J.H. & McLarney W.O. 1972. *Aquaculture. The Farming and Husbandry of Freshwater and Marine Organisms*. New York: Wiley-Interscience.

Beavis A. & Charlier R.H. 1987. An economic appraisal for the onshore cultivation of *Laminaria spp. In Proceedings of the Twelfth International Seaweed Symposium*. (Eds. M.A. Ragan & C.J. Bird) pp. 387–98. Dordrecht: Junk.

Beavis A., Charlier R.H. & De Meyer C. 1986. *Laminaria* spp. as energy source. In *Oceans '86 Conference Record: Science-Engineering-Adventure*. Vol. 2. pp. 621–6. New York: IEEE Publishing.

Bird C.J. 1973. Aspects of the life history and ecology of *Porphyra linearis* (Bangiales, Rhodophyceae) in nature. *Can. J. Bot.* **51**: 2371–9.

Bird K.T. 1987. Cost analysis of energy from marine biomass. In *Seaweed Cultivation for Renewable Resources*. (Eds. K.T. Bird & P.H. Benson) pp. 327–50. Amsterdam: Elsevier.

Bird C.J. & McLachlan J. 1982. Some underutilized taxonomic criteria in *Gracilaria* (Rhodophyta, Gigartinales). *Botanica Mar.* **25**: 557–62.

Bird C.J. & McLachlan J. 1986. The effect of salinity on distribution of species of *Gracilaria* Grev. (Rhodophyta, Gigartinales): an experimental assessment. *Botanica Mar.* **29**: 231–8.

Bird C.J. & Rice E.L. 1990. Recent approaches to the taxonomy of the Gracilariaceae (Gracilariales, Rhodophyta) and the *Gracilaria verrucosa* problem. In *Proceedings of the Thirteenth International Seaweed Symposium*. (Eds. S.C. Lindstrom & P.W. Gabrielson) pp. 111–8. Dordrecht: Kluwer.

Bird C.J., Chen L.C.-M. & McLachlan J. 1972. The culture of *Porphyra linearis* (Bangiales, Rhodophyceae). *Can. J. Bot.* **50**: 1859–63.

Bird N., McLachlan J. & Grund D. 1977. Studies on *Gracilaria*. 5. *In vitro* life history of *Gracilaria* sp. from the Maritime Provinces. *Can. J. Bot.* **55**: 1282–90.

Bird C.J., Van der Meer J.P. & McLachlan J. 1982. A comment on *Gracilaria verrucosa* (Huds.) Papenf. (Rhodophyta: Gigartinales). *J. Mar. Biol. Ass. UK* **62**: 453–9.

Black H.J. & Fonck E. 1981. On the vegetation dynamics of *Gracilaria* sp. in Playa Changa, Coquimbo, Chile. In *Proceedings of the Tenth International Seaweed Symposium*. (Ed. T. Levring) pp. 223–8. Berlin: de Gruyter.

Blackler H. 1956. The phenology of certain algae at St Andrews, Fife. *Trans. Proc. Bot. Soc. Edinb.* **37**: 61–78.

Boalch G. 1981. Do we really need to grow *Macrocystis* in Europe? In *Proceedings of the Tenth International Seaweed Symposium*. (Ed. T. Levring) pp. 657–67. Berlin: de Gruyter.

Bock K.H. 1971. Monatskarten des Salzgehaltes der Ostsee dargestellt für verschiedene Tiefenhorizonte. *Ergänz. Dt. Hydrograph. Z. Reihe B* **4**: (12) 1–147.

Bolton J.J., & Lüning K. 1982. Optimal growth and maximal survival temperatures of Atlantic *Laminaria* species (Phaeophyta) in culture. *Mar. Biol. Berlin* **66**: 89–94.

Bolton J.J., Germann I. & Lüning K. 1983. Hybridization between Atlantic and Pacific representatives of the Simplices section of *Laminaria* (Phaeophyta). *Phycologia* **22**: 133–40.

Brady-Campbell M.M., Campbell D.B. & Harlin M.M. 1984. Productivity of kelp (*Laminaria* spp.) near the southern limit in the northwestern Atlantic Ocean. *Mar. Ecol. Prog. Ser.* **18**: 79–88.

Brinkhuis B.H., Breda V.A., Tobin S. & Macler B.A. 1983a. New York marine biomass program–culture of *Laminaria saccharina*. *J. World Maricult. Soc.* **14**: 360–79.

Brinkhuis B.H., Macler B.A., Hanisak M.D., Zatorski R., Liu P. & Tsay T.K. 1983b. In *Seaweed Raft and Farm Design in the United States and China*. (Ed. L.B. McKay) pp. 6.1–6.19. New York: New York Sea Grant Publication.

Brinkhuis B.H., Mariani E.C., Breda V.A. & Brady-Campbell M.M. 1984. Cultivation of *Laminaria saccharina* in the New York marine biomass program. In *Proceedings of the Eleventh International Seaweed Symposium*. (Eds. C.J. Bird & M.A. Ragan) pp. 266–71. Dordrecht: Junk.

Brinkhuis B.H., Levine H.G., Schlenk C.G. & Tobin S. 1987. *Laminaria* cultivation in the far east and North America. In *Seaweed Cultivation for Renewable Resources*. (Eds. K.T. Bird & P.H. Benson) pp. 107–46. Amsterdam: Elsevier.

Buggeln R.G. 1978. Physiological investigations on *Alaria esculenta* (Laminariales, Phaeophyceae). IV. Inorganic and organic nitrogen in the blade. *J. Phycol.* **14**: 156–60.

Burzycki G.M. & Waaland J.R. 1987. On the position of meiosis in the life history of *Porphyra torta* (Rhodophyta). *Botanica Mar.* **30**: 5–10.

Butler D.M. & Evans L.V. 1987. Tissue culture and protoplast formation in *Laminaria saccharina*. In *Seaweed Protoplast and Tissue Culture*. (Eds. M. Indergaard, K. Østgaard & M.D. Guiry) pp. 12. Brussels: COST 48.

Câmara Neto C. 1987. Seaweed culture in Rio Grande do Norte, Brazil. In *Proceedings of the Twelfth International Seaweed Symposium*. (Eds. M.A. Ragan & C.J. Bird) pp. 363–7. Dordrecht: Junk.

Campbell S.E. 1980. *Palaeoconchocelis starmachii*, a carbonate boring microfossil from the Upper Silurian of Poland (425 million years old): implications for the evolution of the Bangiaceae (Rhodophyta). *Phycologia* **19**: 25–36.

Carter A.R. & Simons R.H. 1987. Regrowth and production capacity of *Gelidium pristoides* (Gelidiales, Rhodophyta) under various harvesting regimes at Port Alfred. *Botanica Mar.* **30**: 227–31.

Chapman A.R.O. 1973. Phenetic variability of stipe morphology in relation to season, exposure, and depth in the non-digitate complex of *Laminaria* Lamour. (Phaeophyta, Laminariales) in Nova Scotia. *Phycologia* **12**: 53–7.

Chapman A.R.O. 1974. The genetic basis of morphological differentiation in some *Laminaria* populations. *Mar. Biol. Berlin* **24**: 85–91.

Chapman A.R.O. 1975. Inheritance of mucilage canals in *Laminaria* (section Simplices) in eastern Canada. *Br. Phycol. J.* **10**: 219–223.

Chapman A.R.O. & Craigie J.S. 1977. Seasonal growth in *Laminaria longicruris*: relations with dissolved inorganic nutrients and internal reserves of nitrogen. *Mar. Biol. Berlin* **40**: 197–205.

Chapman A.R.O., Edelstein T. & Power P.J. 1977. Studies on *Gracilaria*. I. Morphological and anatomical variation in samples from the lower Gulf of St Lawrence and New England. *Botanica Mar.* **20**: 149–53.

Chapman V.J. 1969. *The Marine Algae of New Zealand, Part III: Rhodophyceae, Issue 1: Bangiophycidae and Florideophycidae (Nemalionales, Bonnemaisoniales, Gelidiales)*. Lehre: J. Cramer.

Chapman V.J. 1970. *Seaweeds and their Uses*. London: Methuen.

Chapman V.J. 1979. *The Marine Algae of New Zealand, Part III: Rhodophyceae, Issue 4: Gigartinales*. Lehre: J. Cramer.

Chapman V.J. & Chapman D.J. 1980. *Seaweeds and their Uses*. London: Chapman & Hall.

Chen L.C.-M. 1986. Cell development of *Porphyra miniata* (Rhodophyceae) under axenic culture. *Botanica Mar.* **29**: 435–9.

Chen L.C.-M. 1987. Protoplast morphogenesis of *Porphyra leucosticta* in culture. *Botanica Mar.* **30**: 399–403.

Chen L.C.-M. 1989. Cell suspension culture from *Porphyra linearis* (Rhodophyta), a multicellular red alga. *J. Appl. Phycol.* **1**: 153–9.

Chen L.C.-M., Edelstein T., Ogata E. & McLachlan J. 1970. The life history of *Porphyra miniata. Can. J. Bot.* **48**: 385–9.

Cheney D.P. 1984. Genetic modification in seaweeds: applications to commercial utilization and cultivation. In *Biotechnology in the Marine Sciences*. (Eds. R.R. Colwell, E.R. Pariser & A.J. Sinskey) pp. 161–75. New York: Wiley.

Cheney D.P. & Mumford T.F. 1986. *Shellfish & Seaweed Harvests of Puget Sound*. Seattle: Washington Sea Grant.

Cheney D.P., Mar E., Saga N. & van der Meer J. 1986. Protoplast isolation and cell division in the agar-producing seaweed *Gracilaria* (Rhodophyta). *J. Phycol.* **22**: 238–43.

Cheng T.H. 1969. Production of kelp—a major aspect of China's exploitation of the sea. *Econ. Bot.* **23**: 215–36.

Chiang Y.-M. 1981. Cultivation of *Gracilaria* (Rhodophycophyta, Gigartinales) in Taiwan. In *Proceedings of the Tenth International Seaweed Symposium*. (Ed. T. Levring) pp. 570–4. Berlin: de Gruyter.

Chiang Y.-M. 1982. Cultivation of *Porphyra* in Taiwan. In *Proceedings of Republic of China—United States Cooperative Science Seminar on Cultivation and Utilization of Economic Algae*. (Eds. R.T. Tsuda & T.M. Chiang) pp. 105–7. Mangilao, Guam: University of Guam Marine Laboratory.

Chiang Y.-M. 1984. Seaweed aquaculture and its associated problems in the Republic of China. In *Proceedings of ROC-Japan Symposium on Mariculture*. (Eds. I.C. Liao & R. Hirano) pp. 99–190. Pintung, Taiwan: Tungkang Marine Laboratory.

Chiang Y.-M. 1985. *Gracilaria* from Taiwan: key, list and distribution of the species. In *Taxonomy of Economic Seaweeds with Reference to Some Pacific and Caribbean Species*. (Eds. I.A. Abbott & J.N. Norris) pp. 81–3. La Jolla: California Sea Grant College Program.

Chiang Y.-M. & Wang J.-C. 1980. A study on the production of conchosporangia in the conchocelis phase of *Porphyra angusta* Okamura et Ueda. *Phycologia* **19**: 20–4.

Chihara M. 1981. Recent advances in the cultivation of macro-algae in Japan. In *Proceedings of the Eighth International Seaweed Symposium.* (Eds. G.E. Fogg & W.E. Jones) pp. 36–45. Menai Bridge: The Marine Science Laboratories.

Christensen T. 1984. Sargassotang, en ny algeslægt i Danmark. *Urt* 1984: 99–104.

Christie A.O. & Evans L.V. 1962. Periodicity in the liberation of gametes and zoospores of *Enteromorpha intestinalis* Link. *Nature, Lond.* **193**: 193–4.

Cole K. & Conway E. 1980. Studies in the Bangiaceae: reproductive modes. *Botanica Mar.* **23**: 545–53.

Coleman D.C. & Mathieson A.C. 1975. Investigations of New England marine algae VII: seasonal occurrence and reproduction of marine algae near Cape Cod, Massachusetts. *Rhodora* **77**: 76–104.

Coll J. & Cox J. 1977. The genus *Porphyra* C. Ag. (Rhodophyta, Bangiales) in the American North Atlantic. 1. New species from Carolina. *Botanica Mar.* **20**: 155–9.

Coll J. & Oliveira Filho E.C. de. 1976. The genus *Porphyra* C. Ag. (Rhodophyta-Bangiales) in the American South Atlantic. II Uruguayan species. *Botanica Mar.* **19**: 191–6.

Conolly N.J. & Drew E.A. 1985. Physiology of *Laminaria*. III. Effect of a coastal eutrophication gradient on seasonal patterns of growth and tissue composition in *L. digitata* Lamour. and *L. saccharina* (L.) Lamour. *Pubbl. Staz. Zool. Napoli. I. Mar. Ecol.* **6**: 181–95.

Conway E. 1964a. Autecological studies of the genus *Porphyra*: I. The species found in Britain. *Br. Phycol. Bull.* **2**: 342–8.

Conway E. 1964b. Autecological studies of the genus *Porphyra*: II. *Porphyra umbilicalis* (L.) J. Ag. *Br. Phycol. Bull.* **2**: 349–63.

Conway E. & Cole K. 1977. Studies in the Bangiaceae: structure and reproduction of the conchocelis of *Porphyra* and *Bangia* in culture (Bangiales, Rhodophyceae). *Phycologia* **16**: 205–16.

Conway E. & Wylie A.P. 1972. Spore organization and reproductive modes in two species of *Porphyra* from New Zealand. In *Proceedings of the Seventh International Seaweed Symposium.* (Ed. K. Nisizawa) pp., 105–110. Tokyo: University of Tokyo Press.

Conway E., Mumford T.F. & Scagel R.F. 1975. The genus *Porphyra* in British Columbia and Washington. *Syesis* **8**: 185–244.

Correa J., Avila M. & Santelices B. 1985. Effects of some environmental factors on growth of sporelings in two species of *Gelidium* (Rhodophyta). *Aquaculture* **44**: 221–7.

Cosson J. 1976. Evolution de la fertilité des populations de *Laminaria digitata* (L.) Lamouroux (Phéophycée, Laminariale) au cours de l'année. *Bull. Soc. Phycol. Fr.* **21**: 28–34.

Cosson J. 1989. Selection and hybridization of Laminariales. In *Outdoor Seaweed Cultivation, Proceedings of the Second Workshop of COST 48 Subgroup 1.* (Eds. J.M. Kain, J.W. Andrews & B.J. McGregor) pp. 15–18. Brussels: Commission of the European Communities.

Cribb A.B. 1983. *Marine Algae of the Southern Great Barrier Reef. Part I Rhodophyta.* Brisbane: Australian Coral Reef Society.

Critchley A.T. 1983a. *Sargassum muticum*: a taxonomic history including world-wide and western Pacific distributions. *J. Mar. Biol. Ass. UK* **63**: 617–25.

Critchley A.T. 1983b. The establishment and increase of *Sargassum muticum* (Yendo) Fensholt populations within the Solent area of southern Britain. I. An investigation of the increase in number of population individuals. *Botanica Mar.* **26**: 539–45.

Critchley A.T. 1983c. The establishment and increase of *Sargassum muticum* (Yendo) Fensholt populations within the Solent area of southern Britain. II. An investigation of the increase in canopy cover of the alga at low water. *Botanica Mar.* **26**: 547–52.

Critchley A.T., Nienhuis P.H. & Verschuure K. 1987. Presence and development of populations of the introduced brown alga *Sargassum muticum* in the southwest Netherlands. In *Proceedings of the Twelfth International Seaweed Symposium*. (Eds. M.A. Ragan & C.J. Bird) pp. 245–55. Dordrecht: Junk.

Dahua L. & Yushui L. 1984. Studies on the green disease of *Porphyra haitanensis* Chang & Zheng caused by nitrogen deficiency. In *Proceedings of the Eleventh International Seaweed Symposium*. (Eds. C.J. Bird & M.A. Ragan) pp. 453–5. Dordrecht: Junk.

Davison I.R., Andrews M. & Stewart W.D.P. 1984. Regulation of growth in *Laminaria digitata*: use of in-vivo nitrate reductase activities as an indicator of nitrogen limitation in field populations of *Laminaria* spp. *Mar. Biol. Berlin* **84**: 207–17.

Dawes C.P. 1987. *The cultivation and alginate content of Laminariales in the Irish Sea*. Unpublished Ph.D. thesis, University of Liverpool.

Dawes C.P. 1988. Seaweed culture technology. In *Feasibility Study on the Technology of Mariculture. Vol. II: Review of Technologies and Services*. (Eds. Aberdeen University Marine Studies, Mackay Consultants & A. Munro) pp. 107–16. Aberdeen: University Marine Studies.

Dawson E.Y. 1953. Marine red algae of Pacific Mexico. Part I. Bangiales to Corallinaceae Subf. Corallinoideae. *Allan Hancock Pacif. Exped.* **17**: 1–239.

Dawson E.Y. 1961. Marine red algae of Pacific Mexico. Part 4. Gigartinales. *Pacif. Nat.* **2**: 191–343.

Department of the Navy. 1973. *World Atlas of Sea Surface Temperatures*. Washington: US Naval Oceanographic Office.

Deysher L.E. 1984. Reproductive phenology of newly introduced populations of the brown alga, *Sargassum muticum* (Yendo) Fensholt. In *Proceedings of the Eleventh International Seaweed Symposium*. (Eds. C.J. Bird & M.A. Ragan) pp. 403–7. Dordrecht: Junk.

Dickson L.G. & Waaland J.R. 1985. *Porphyra nereocystis*: a dual-daylength seaweed. *Planta* **165**: 548–553.

Dion P. & Golven P. 1989. The nearshore cultivation of *Laminaria hyperborea* and *Saccorhiza polyschides*. In *Outdoor Seaweed Cultivation, Proceedings of the Second Workshop of COST 48 Subgroup 1*. (Eds. J.M. Kain, J.W. Andrews & B.J. McGregor) pp. 38–41. Brussels: Commission of the European Communities.

Directorate of Fisheries Research. 1981. *Atlas of the Sea Around the British Isles*. Ministry of Agriculture, Fisheries and Food.

Dixon P.S. 1958. The structure and development of the thallus in the British species of *Gelidium* and *Pterocladia*. *Ann. Bot.* **22**: 353–68.

Dring M.J. 1967. Effects of daylength on growth and reproduction of the conchocelis-phase of *Porphyra tenera*. *J. Mar. Biol. Ass. UK* **47**: 501–10.

Dring M.J. 1982. *The Biology of Marine Plants*. London: Edward Arnold.

Druehl L.D. 1968. Taxonomy and distribution of northeast Pacific species of *Laminaria*. *Can. J. Bot.* **46**: 539–47.

Druehl L.D. 1979. On the taxonomy of California *Laminaria* (Phaeophyta). *J. Phycol.* **15**: 337–8.

Druehl L.D. & Boal R. 1981. Manipulation of the laminarialean life-cycle and its consequences for kombu mariculture. In *Proceedings of the Tenth International Seaweed Symposium*. (Ed. T. Levring) pp. 575–80. Berlin: de Gruyter.

Druehl L.D. & Kaneko T. 1973. On *Laminaria saccharina* from Hokkaido. *Bot. Mag. Tokyo* **86**: 323–7.

Druehl L.D., Baird R., Lingwall A., Lloyd K.E. & Pakula S. 1988. Longline cultivation of some Laminariaceae in British Columbia, Canada. *Aquacult. Fish. Manag.* **19**: 253–63.

Duke C.S., Lapointe B.E. & Ramus J. 1986. Effects of light on growth, RuBPCase activity and chemical composition of *Ulva* species (Chlorophyta). *J. Phycol.* **22**: 362–70.

Edelstein T. 1977. Studies on *Gracilaria* sp.: experiments on inocula incubated under greenhouse conditions. *J. Exp. Mar. Biol. Ecol.* **30**: 249–59.

Edelstein T., Bird C. & McLachlan J. 1981. Preliminary field studies on *Gracilaria* sp. from the lower Gulf of St Lawrence, Canada. In *Proceedings of the Eighth International Seaweed Symposium*. (Eds. G.E. Fogg & W.E. Jones) pp. 320–2. Menai Bridge: The Marine Science Laboratories.

Edwards P. 1969. Field and cultural studies on the seasonal periodicity of growth and reproduction of selected Texas benthic marine algae. *Contr. Mar. Sci.* **14**: 59–114.

Ellis R.J. & Calvin N.I. 1981. Rope culture of the kelp *Laminaria groenlandica* in Alaska. *Mar. Fish. Rev.* **43**: 19–21.

Espinoza J. & Chapman A.R.O. 1983. Ecotypic differentiation of *Laminaria longicruris* in relation to seawater nitrate concentration. *Mar. Biol. Berlin* **74**: 213–8.

Fang T.C. 1983. A summary of the genetic studies of *Laminaria japonica* in China. In *Proceedings of the Joint China-U.S. Phycology Symposium*. pp. 123–36. Beijing, China: Science Press.

Fang T.C. 1984. Some genetic features revealed from culturing the haploid cells of kelps. In *Proceedings of the Eleventh International Seaweed Symposium*. (Eds. C.J. Bird & M.A. Ragan) pp. 317–8. Dordrecht: Junk.

Fang T.C. & Kiang N.N. 1974. Responses to vitamin C of the female gametophytes of *Laminaria japonica*. *Acta Bot. Sin.* **16**: 333–41.

Fang T.C., Wu C.Y., Jiang B.Y., Li J.J. & Ren K.Z. 1963. The breeding of a new variety of haidai (*Laminaria japonica* Aresch.). *Scientia Sin.* **12**: 1011–8.

Fang T.C., Tai C.H., Oü Y.L., Tsuei C.C. & Chen T.C. 1978. Some genetic observations on the monoploid breeding of *Laminaria japonica*. *Scientia Sin.* **11**: 401–8.

Farnham W.F., Fletcher R.L. & Irvine L.M. 1973. Attached *Sargassum* found in Britain. *Nature, Lond.* **243**: 231–2.

Feldmann J. 1937. Les algues marines de la côte des Albères. I–III. Cyanophycées, Chlorophycées, Phéophycées. *Rev. Algol.* **9**: 141–335.

FitzGerald W.J. 1978. Environmental parameters influencing the growth of *Enteromorpha clathrata* (Roth.) J. Ag. in the intertidal zone on Guam. *Botanica Mar.* **21**: 207–20.

Fletcher R.L. 1980. Studies on the recently introduced brown alga *Sargassum muticum* (Yendo) Fensholt. III. Periodicity in gamete release and 'incubation' of early germling stages. *Botanica Mar.* **23**: 425–32.

Fletcher R.L. & Fletcher S.M. 1975a. Studies on the recently introduced brown alga *Sargassum muticum* (Yendo) Fensholt. II. Regenerative ability. *Botanica Mar.* **18**: 157–62.

Fletcher R.L. & Fletcher S.M. 1975b. Studies on the recently introduced brown alga *Sargassum muticum* (Yendo) Fensholt. I. Ecology and reproduction. *Botanica Mar.* **18**: 149–56.

Fletcher R.L. & Hales J.M. 1989. Ecological and life history studies of *Sargassum muticum* pertinent to its cultivation. In *Outdoor Seaweed Cultivation, Proceedings of the Second Workshop of COST 48 Subgroup 1*. (Eds. J.M. Kain, J.W. Andrews & B.J. McGregor) pp. 23–30. Brussels: Commission of the European Communities.

Floc'h J.Y., Pajot R. & Wallentinus I. 1988. The Japanese brown alga *Undaria pinnatifida* on the coasts of France and the possibilities of its establishment in European waters. *ICES C.M. 1988/Mini No 2.*

Freshwater D.W. & Kapraun D.F. 1986. Field, culture and cytological studies of *Porphyra carolinensis* Coll et Cox (Bangiales, Rhodophyta) from North Carolina. *Jap. J. Phycol.* **34**: 251–62.

Fries L. 1980. Axenic tissue cultures for the sporophytes of *Laminaria digitata* and *Laminaria hyperborea* (Phaeophyta). *J. Phycol.* **16**: 475–7.

Fritsch F.E. 1945. *The Structure and Reproduction of the Algae. Vol. II. Foreword, Phaeophyceae, Rhodophyceae, Myxophyceae.* Cambridge: University Press.

Gagné J.A., & Mann K.H. 1981. Comparison of growth strategy in *Laminaria* populations living under differing seasonal patterns of nutrient availability. In *Proceedings of the Tenth International Seaweed Symposium.* (Ed. T. Levring) pp. 297–312. Berlin: de Gruyter.

Gagné J.A., Mann K.H. & Chapman A.R.O. 1982. Seasonal patterns of growth and storage in *Laminaria longicruris* in relation to differing patterns of availability of nitrogen in the water. *Mar. Biol. Berlin* **69**: 91–101.

Gargiulo G.M., De Masi F. & Tripodi G. 1985. A study on *Gracilaria dendroides* sp. nov. (Gigartinales, Rhodophyta) from the Bay of Naples. *Br. Phycol. J.* **20**: 357–64.

Gerard V.A. & Du Bois K.R. 1988. Temperature ecotypes near the southern boundary of the kelp *Laminaria saccharina*. *Mar. Biol. Berlin* **97**: 575–80.

Gerard V.A. & Mann K.A. 1979. Growth and production of *Laminaria longicruris* (Phaeophyta) populations exposed to different intensities of water movement. *J. Phycol.* **15**: 33–41.

Gerard V.A., DuBois K. & Greene R. 1987. Growth responses of two *Laminaria saccharina* populations to environmental variation. In *Proceedings of the Twelfth International Seaweed Symposium.* (Eds. M.A. Ragan & C.J. Bird) pp. 229–32. Dordrecht: Junk.

Giaccone G., Collonna P., Graziano C., Mannino A.M. , Tornatore E., Cormaci M., Furnari G. & Scammacca B. 1985. Revisione della flora marina di Sicilia e isole minori. *Boll. Accad. Gioenia Sci. Nat.* **18**: 537–781.

Goldstein M.E. 1973. Regeneration and vegetative propagation of the agarophyte *Gracilaria debilis* (Forsskål) Børgesen (Rhodophyceae). *Botanica Mar.* **16**: 226–8.

Guiry M.D. 1974. A preliminary consideration of the taxonomic position of *Palmaria palmata* (Linnaeus) Stackhouse = *Rhodymenia palmata* (Linnaeus) Greville. *J. Mar. Biol. Ass. UK* **54**: 509–28.

Guiry M.D. 1975. An assessment of *Palmaria palmata* forma *mollis* (S. et G.) comb. nov. (= *Rhodymenia palmata* forma *mollis* S. et G.) in the eastern North Pacific. *Syesis* **8**: 245–61.

Guiry M.D. & Freamhainn M.T. 1986. Biosystematics of *Gracilaria foliifera* (Gigartinales, Rhodophyta). *Nord. J. Bot.* **5**: 629–37.

Hanisak M.D. 1987. Cultivation of *Gracilaria* and other macroalgae in Florida for energy production. In *Seaweed Cultivation for Renewable Resources.* (Eds. K.T. Bird & P.H. Benson) pp. 191–218. Amsterdam: Elsevier.

Hansen J.E. 1980. Physiological considerations in the mariculture of red algae. In *Pacific Seaweed Aquaculture.* (Eds. I.A. Abbott, M.S. Foster & L.F. Eklund) pp. 80–91. La Jolla, California: California Sea Grant College Program.

Hansen J.E. 1984. Strain selection and physiology in the development of *Gracilaria* mariculture. In *Proceedings of the Eleventh International Seaweed Symposium.* (Eds. C.J. Bird & M.A. Ragan); pp. 89–94. Dordrecht: Junk.

Harger B.W.W. & Neushul M. 1983. Test farming of the giant kelp, *Macrocystis*, as a marine biomass producer. *J. World Maricul. Soc.* **14**: 392–403.

Hasegawa Y. 1972. Forced cultivation of *Laminaria*. In *Proceedings of the Seventh*

International Seaweed Symposium. (Ed. K. Nisizawa) pp. 391–3. Tokyo: University of Tokyo Press.

Hasegawa Y. 1976. Progress of *Laminaria* cultivation in Japan. *J. Fish Res. Bd Can.* **33**: 1002–6.

Hawkes M.W. 1985. *Palmaria hecatensis* sp. nov. (Rhodophyta, Palmariales) from British Columbia and Alaska with a survey of other *Palmaria* species. *Can. J. Bot.* **63**: 474–82.

Henry E.C. 1987. Primitive reproductive characters and a photoperiodic response in *Saccorhiza dermatodea* (Laminariales, Phaeophyta). *Br. Phycol. J.* **22**: 23–31.

Herbert S.K. & Waaland J.R. 1988. Photoinhibition of photosynthesis in a sun and shade species of the red algal genus *Porphyra*. *Mar. Biol. Berlin* **97**: 1–7.

Hirose H. & Yoshida K. 1964. A review of the life history of the genus *Monostroma*. *Bull. Jap. Soc. Phycol.* **12**: 19–31.

Hollenberg G.J. 1972. Phycological notes. VII. Concerning three Pacific coast species, especially *Porphyra miniata* (C.Ag.) C.Ag. (Rhodophyceae, Bangiales). *Phycologia* **11**: 43–6.

Holt T.J. 1984. *The development of techniques for the cultivation of Laminariales in the Irish Sea.* Unpublished Ph.D. thesis, University of Liverpool.

Holt T.J. & Dawes C.P. 1989. Cultivation of Laminariales in the Irish Sea. In *Outdoor Seaweed Cultivation, Proceedings of the Second Workshop of COST 48 Subgroup 1.* (Eds. J.M. Kain, J.W. Andrews & B.J. McGregor; pp. 34–37. Brussels: Commission of the European Communities.

Holt T.J. & Kain J.M. 1983. The cultivation of large brown algae as an energy crop. In *Energy from Biomass, 2nd E.C. Conference.* (Eds. A. Strub, P. Chartier & G. Schleser) pp. 319–23. London: Applied Science Publishers.

Hoyle M.D. 1984. Taxonomic features used in discriminating some central and eastern Pacific species of *Gracilaria*. In *Proceedings of the Eleventh International Seaweed Symposium.* (Eds. C.J. Bird & M.A. Ragan) pp. 47–50. Dordrecht: Junk.

Hurtado-Ponce A.Q. & Umezaki I. 1987. Growth rate studies of *Gracilaria verrucosa* (Gigartinales, Rhodophyta). *Botanica Mar.* **30**: 223–6.

Imada O., Saito Y. & Teramoto K. 1972. Artificial culture of laver. In *Proceedings of the Seventh International Seaweed Symposium.* (Ed. K. Nisizawa) pp. 358–63. Tokyo: University of Tokyo Press.

Indergaard M. & Jensen A. 1983. Seaweed biomass production and fish farming. In *Energy from Biomass, 2nd EC. Conference.* (Eds. A. Strub, P. Chartier & G. Schleser) pp. 313–8. London: Applied Science Publishers.

International Council for the Exploration of the Sea. 1984. Report of the Working Group on Introductions and Transfers of Marine Organisms. *ICES C.M. 1984/F:35.*

Isaac W.E. 1957. The distribution, ecology and taxonomy of *Porphyra* on South African coasts. *Proc. Linn. Soc. Lond.* **168**: 61–5.

Iwasaki H. 1961. The life cycle of *Porphyra tenera* in vitro. *Biol. Bull. Mar. Biol. Lab., Woods Hole* **121**: 173–87.

Iwasaki H. & Matsudaira C. 1963. Observations on the ecology and reproduction of free-living conchocelis of *Porphyra tenera*. *Biol. Bull. Mar. Biol. Lab., Woods Hole* **124**: 268–76.

Iwasaki H. & Sasaki N. 1972. The *Conchocelis*-phase of *Porphyra suborbiculata* forma *latifolia*. In *Proceedings of the Seventh International Seaweed Symposium.* (Ed. K. Nisizawa) pp. 364–67. Tokyo: University of Tokyo Press.

Jaasund E. 1965. Aspects of the marine algal vegetation of North Norway. *Botanica Gothoburg.* **4**: 1–174.

Jacques J.M., Beavis A. & Delmotte A. 1980. The present day uses and industrial potential of seaweeds: the development of a new technology. *Bull. Soc. Chim. Belg.* **89**: 1093–9.

Jernakoff P. 1986. Experimental investigations of interactions between the perennial red alga *Gelidium pusillum* and barnacles on a New South Wales rocky shore. *Mar. Ecol. Prog Ser.* **28**: 259–63.

Joly A.B. & Oliveira Filho E.C. 1967. Two Brazilian Laminariales. *Publ. Inst. Pesq. Mar.* **4**: 1–13.

Jones N.S. 1948. Observations and experiments on the biology of *Patella vulgata* at Port St Mary, Isle of Man. *Proc. Trans. Liverpool Biol. Soc.* **56**: 60–77.

Jones W.E. 1959. The growth and fruiting of *Gracilaria verrucosa* (Hudson) Papenfuss. *J. Mar. Biol. Ass. UK* **38**: 47–56.

Jones J.M. & Holt T.J. 1981. Biomass from offshore sea areas. In *Solar Energy R & D in the European Community, Series E: Energy from Biomass*, Vol. 1. (Eds. P. Chartier & W. Palz) pp. 85–9. Dordrecht, Holland: D. Reidel.

Jones J.M. & Holt T.J. 1985. The cultivation of large brown algae as an energy crop. *Comm. Eur. Commun., Dir.Gen. Sci. Res. Devel. Rep., EUR 9990 EN.* 78 pp.

Jorde I. & Klavestad N. 1963. The natural history of the Hardangerfjord. 4. The benthonic algal vegetation. *Sarsia* **9**: 1–99.

Kain J.M. 1964. Aspects of the biology of *Laminaria hyperborea*. III. Survival and growth of gametophytes. *J. Mar. Biol. Ass. UK* **44**: 415–33.

Kain J.M. 1969. The biology of *Laminaria hyperborea*. V. Comparison with early stages of competitors. *J. Mar. Biol. Ass. UK* **49**: 455–73.

Kain J.M. 1975. The biology of *Laminaria hyperborea*. VII. Reproduction of the sporophyte. *J. Mar. Biol. Ass. UK* **55**: 567–82.

Kain J.M. 1976. New and interesting marine algae from the Shetland Islands II. Hollow and solid stiped *Laminaria* (Simplices). *Br. Phycol. J.* **11**: 1–11.

Kain J.M. 1979. A view of the genus *Laminaria*. *Oceanogr. Mar. Biol. Ann. Rev.* **17**: 101–61.

Kain J.M. 1987. Seasonal growth and photoinhibition in *Plocamium cartilagineum* (Rhodophyta) off the Isle of Man. *Phycologia* **26**: 88–99.

Kain J.M. 1989. The seasons in the subtidal. *Br. Phycol. J.* **24**: 203–215.

Kain J.M. & Dawes C.P. 1987. Useful European seaweeds: past hopes and present cultivation. In *Proceedings of the Twelfth International Seaweed Symposium*. (Eds. M.A. Ragan & C.J. Bird) pp. 173–81. Dordrecht: Junk.

Kain J.M. & Holt T.J. 1982. Biomass from offshore sea areas. In *Solar Energy R & D in the European Community, Series E: Energy from Biomass*, Vol. 3. (Eds. G. Grassi & W. Palz) pp. 120–5. Dordrecht, Holland: D. Reidel.

Kain J.M. & Holt T.J. 1984. Biomass from offshore sea areas. In *Solar Energy R & D in the European Community, Series E: Energy from Biomass*, Vol. 5. (Eds. W. Palz & D. Pirrwitz) pp. 168–76. Dordrecht, Holland: D. Reidel.

Kain J.M. & Holt T.J. 1985. Biomass from offshore sea areas. In *Bioenergy. European Research and Development*. (Ed. W. Palz) pp. 68–9. Luxembourg: Commission of the European Communities.

Kain J.M. & Norton T.A. 1990. Marine ecology. In *The Biology of the Red Algae*. (Eds. K.M. Cole & R.G. Sheath) pp. 377–422. New York: Cambridge University Press.

Kane D.F. & Chamberlain A.H.L. 1979. Laboratory growth studies on *Sargassum muticum* (Yendo) Fensholt. I. Seasonal growth of whole plants and lateral sections. *Botanica Mar.* **22**: 1–9.

Kang J.W. 1972. Species of cultivated *Porphyra* in Korea. In *Proceedings of the Seventh International Seaweed Symposium*. (Ed. K. Nisizawa) pp. 108–10. Tokyo: University of Tokyo Press.

Kapraun D.F. & Freshwater D.W. 1987. Karyological studies of five species of *Porphyra* (Bangiales, Rhodophyta) from the North Atlantic and Mediterranean. *Phycologia* **26**: 82–7.

Kapraun D.F. & Lemus A.J. 1987. Field and culture studies of *Porphyra spiralis* var. *amplifolia* Oliveira Filho et Coll (Bangiales, Rhodophyta) from Isla de Margarita, Venezuela. *Botanica Mar.* **30**: 483–7.

Kapraun D.F. & Luster D.G. 1980. Field and culture studies of *Porphyra rosengurtii* Coll et Cox (Rhodophyta, Bangiales). *Botanica Mar.* **23**: 449–57.

Kawashima S. 1984. Kombu cultivation in Japan for human foodstuff. *Jap. J. Phycol.* **32**: 379–94.

Kim D.H. 1970. Economically important seaweeds in Chile I *Gracilaria*. *Botanica Mar.* **13**: 140–62.

Kim N.G. & Kang J.W. 1986. Effect of inflowing river-water on the farming of laver in Chonsu Bay. *Korean J. Phycol.* **1**: 259–79.

King R.J. & Schramm W. 1976. Photosynthetic rates of benthic marine algae in relation to light intensity and seasonal variations. *Mar. Biol. Berlin* **37**: 215–22.

Kito H., Ogata E. & McLachlan J. 1971. Cytological observations on three species of *Porphyra* from the Atlantic. *Bot. Mag. Tokyo* **84**: 141–8.

Knight M. & Parke M.W. 1931. *Manx Algae*. Liverpool: The University Press.

Koeman R.P.T. & Hoek C. van den 1981. The taxonomy of *Ulva* (Chlorophyceae) in the Netherlands. *Br. Phycol. J.* **16**: 9–53.

Koeman R.P.T. and Hoek C. van den 1982. The taxonomy of *Enteromorpha* Link, 1920, (Chlorophyceae) in the Netherlands. I. The section *Enteromorpha*. *Arch. Hydrobiol. Suppl.* **63.3**: 279–330.

Kornmann P. 1961. Kenntnis der *Porphyra*-Arten von Helgoland. *Helgoländer wiss. Meeresunters.* **8**: 176–92.

Kornmann P. 1973. Codiolophyceae, a new class of Chlorophyta. *Helgol. Wiss. Meeresunters.* **25**: 1–13.

Kornmann P. 1986. *Porphyra yezoensis* bei Helgoland—eine entwicklungsgeschichtliche Studie. *Helgoländer Meeresunters.* **40**: 327–42.

Korringa P. 1976. *Farming Marine Organisms Low in the Food Chain*. Amsterdam: Elsevier Scientific Publishing Co.

Kudoh S. 1987. The efficacy of dissolved inorganic nitrogen for quality in cultivated laver. In *Proceedings of the Twelfth International Seaweed Symposium*. (Eds. M.A Ragan & C.J. Bird) pp. 443–6. Dordrecht: Junk.

Kurogi M. 1959. Influence of light on the growth and maturation of *Conchocelis*-thallus of *Porphyra*. I. Effect of photoperiod on the formation of monosporangia and liberation of monospores. *Bull. Tohoku Reg. Fish. Res. Lab.* **15**: 33–42.

Kurogi M. 1972. Systematics of *Porphyra* in Japan. In *Contributions to the Systematics of Benthic Marine Algae of the North Pacific*. (Eds. I.A. Abbott & M. Kurogi) pp. 167–91. Kobe, Japan: Japanese Society of Phycology.

Kurogi M. & Akiyama K. 1966. Effects of water temperature on the growth and maturation of *Conchocelis*-thalli in several species of *Porphyra*. *Bull. Tohoku Reg. Fish. Res. Lab.* **26**: 77–85.

Kurogi M. & Sato S. 1962a. Influences of light on the growth and maturation of *Conchocelis*-thallus of *Porphyra*. II. Effect of different photoperiods on the growth and maturation of *Conchocelis*-thallus of *P. tenera*. *Bull. Tohoku Reg. Fish. Res. Lab.* **20**: 127–37.

Kurogi M. & Sato S. 1962b. Influences of light on the growth and maturation of *Conchocelis*-thallus of *Porphyra*. III. Effect of photoperiod on the different species. *Bull. Tohoku Reg. Fish. Res. Lab.* **20**: 138–56.

Kurogi M., Akiyama K. & Sato S. 1962. Influences of light on the growth and maturation of *Conchocelis*-thallus of *Porphyra*. I. Effect of photoperiod on the formation of monosporangia and liberation of monospores. *Bull. Tohoku Reg. Fish. Res. Lab.* **20**: 121–6.

Lapointe B.E. 1985. Strategies for pulsed nutrient supply to *Gracilaria* cultures in the Florida Keys: interactions between concentration and frequency of nutrient pulses. *J. Exp. Mar. Biol. Ecol.* **93**: 211–22.

Lapointe B.E. 1987. Phosphorus- and nitrogen-limited photosynthesis and growth of *Gracilaria tikvahiae* (Rhodophyceae) in the Florida Keys: an experimental study. *Mar. Biol. Berlin* **93**: 561–8.

Lapointe B.E., Tenore K.R. & Dawes C.J. (1984). Interactions between light and temperature on the physiological ecology of *Gracilaria tikvahiae* (Gigartinales: Rhodophyta). *Mar. Biol. Berlin* **80**: 161–70.

Lee J.E. & Brinkhuis B.H. 1986. Reproductive phenology of *Laminaria saccharina* (L.) Lamour. (Phaeophyta) at the southern limit of its distribution in the northwestern Atlantic Ocean. *J. Phycol.* **22**: 276–85.

Lee I.K. & Kang J.W. 1986. A check list of marine algae in Korea. *Korean J. Phycol.* **1**: 311–25.

Lenz W. 1971. Monatskarten der Temperatur der Ostsee dargestellt für verschiedene Tiefenhorizonte. *Ergänz. Dt. Hydrograph. Z. Reihe B* **4**: (11) 1–148.

Leone J.E. 1980. Marine biomass energy project. *Mar. Technol. Soc. J.* **14**: 12–30.

Levring T. 1953. The marine algae of Australia. I. Rhodophyta: Goniotrichales, Bangiales and Nemalionales. *Ark. Bot.* **2**: 457–530.

Levring T. 1977. Potential yields of marine algae—with emphasis on European species. In *The Marine Plant Biomass of the Pacific Northwest Coast.* (Ed. R.W. Krauss) pp. 251–70. Corvallis: Oregon State University Press.

Li R.Z., Chong R.T. & Meng Z.C. 1984. A preliminary study of raft cultivation of *Gracilaria verrucosa* and *Gracilaria sjoestedtii*. In *Proceedings of the Eleventh International Seaweed Symposium.* (Eds. C.J. Bird & M.A. Ragan) pp. 252–8. Dordrecht: Junk.

Lignell Å. & Pedersén M. 1989. Agar composition as a function of morphology and growth rate. Studies on some morphological strains of *Gracilaria secundata* and *Gracilaria verrucosa* (Rhodophyta). *Botanica mar.* **32**: 219–27.

Lindauer V.W., Chapman V.J. & Aiken M. 1961. The marine algae of New Zealand. II. Phaeophyceae. *Nova Hedwigia* **3**: 129–350.

Liu X.W. & Gordon M.E. 1987. Tissue and cell culture of New Zealand *Pterocladia* and *Porphyra* species. In *Proceedings of the Twelfth International Seaweed Symposium.* (Eds. M.A. Ragan & C.J. Bird) pp. 147–54. Dordrecht: Junk.

Lüning K. 1979. Growth strategies of three *Laminaria* species (Phaeophyceae) inhabiting different depth zones in the sublittoral region of Helgoland (North Sea). *Mar. Ecol. Prog. Ser.* **1**: 195–207.

Lüning K. 1980. Critical levels of light and temperature regulating the gametogenesis of three *Laminaria* species (Phaeophyceae). *J. Phycol.* **16**: 1–15.

Lüning K. 1981. Egg release in gametophytes of *Laminaria saccharina*: Induction by darkness and inhibition by blue light and U.V. *Br. J. Phycol.* **16**: 579–93.

Lüning K. 1982. Seasonality in larger brown algae and its possible regulation by the environment. In *Synthetic and Degradative Processes in Marine Macrophtyes.* (Ed. L. Srivastava) pp. 47–67. Berlin: de Gruyter.

Lüning K. & Dring M.J. 1975. Reproduction, growth and photosynthesis of gametophytes of *Laminaria saccharina* grown in blue and red light. *Mar. Biol. Berlin* **29**: 195–200.

Lüning K. & Müller D.G. 1978. Chemical interaction in sexual reproduction of several Laminariales (Phaeophyceae): release and attraction of spermatozoids. *Z. Pfl. Physiol.* **89**: 333–41.

Lüning K., Chapman A.R.O. & Mann K.H. 1978. Crossing experiments in the non-digitate complex of *Laminaria* from both sides of the Atlantic. *Phycologia* **17**: 293–8.

Ma J. & Miura A. 1984. Observations on the nuclear division in conchospores and their germlings in *Porphyra yezoensis*. *Jap. J. Phycol.* **32**: 373–8.

Macler B.A. & West J.A. 1987. Life history and physiology of the red alga, *Gelidium coulteri*, in unialgal culture. *Aquaculture* **61**: 281–93.

Magruder W.H. 1988. *Sargassum* (Phaeophyta, Fucales, Sargassaceae) in the Hawaiian Islands. In *Taxonomy of Economic Seaweeds with Reference to Some Pacific and Caribbean Species. Vol. II.* (Ed. I.A. Abbott) pp. 65–87. La Jolla: California Sea Grant College Program.

Mathieson A.C. 1982. Seaweed cultivation: a review. In *Proceedings of the Sixth U.S.–Japan Meeting on Aquaculture, Santa Barbara, California.* (Ed. C.J. Sindermann) pp. 25–66. U.S. Dep. Commer., Rep. NMFS Circ. 442.

Mathieson A.C. 1986. A comparison of seaweed mariculture programs–activities. In *Realism in Aquaculture: Achievements, Constraints, Perspectives.* (Eds. M. Bilio, H. Rosenthal & C.J. Sindermann) pp. 107–40. Bredene, Belgium: European Aquaculture Society.

Mathieson A.C. & Hehre E. 1983. The composition and seasonal periodicity of the marine-estuarine Chlorophyceae in New Hampshire. *Rhodora* **85**: 275–99.

McArthur D.M. & Moss B.L. 1977. The ultrastructure of cell walls in *Enteromorpha intestinalis* (L.) Link. *Br. Phycol. J.* **12**: 359–68.

McHugh D.J. 1987. Production, properties and uses of alginates. In *Production and Utilization of Products from Commercial Seaweeds.* (Ed. D.J. McHugh) pp. 58–115. Rome: FAO Fisheries Technical Paper 288.

McLachlan J. 1979. *Gracilaria tikvahiae* sp. nov. (Rhodophyta, Gigartinales, Gracilariaceae), from the northwestern Atlantic. *Phycologia* **18**: 19–23.

McLachlan J. & Bird C.J. 1984. Geographical and experimental assessment of the distribution of *Gracilaria* species (Rhodophyta: Gigartinales) in relation to temperature. *Helgoländer Meeresunters.* **38**: 319–34.

McLachlan J., Craigie J.S. & Chen C.-M. 1972. *Porphyra linearis* Grev.—an edible species of nori from Nova Scotia. In *Proceedings of the Seventh International Seaweed Symposium.* (Ed. K. Nisizawa) pp. 473–6. Tokyo: University of Tokyo Press.

Melvin D.J., Mumford T.F., Byce W.J., Inayoshi M. & Bryant V.M. 1986. *Equipment and Techniques for Nori Farming in Washington State. Volume 1. Conchocelis Culture.* Washington State: Department of Natural Resources.

Merrill J.E. 1988. Commercial developments—American Sea Vegetable Company. *Appl. Phycol. Forum* **5**: 7.

Merrill, J.E. 1989. Commercial nori (*Porphyra*) sea farming in Washington State. In *Outdoor Seaweed Cultivation, Proceedings of the Second Workshop of COST 48 Subgroup 1.* (Eds. J.M. Kain, J.W. Andrews & B.J. McGregor) pp. 90–105. Brussels: Commission of the European Communities.

Migita S. 1966. Freeze-preservation of *Porphyra* thalli in viable state. II. Effect of cooling velocity and water content of thalli on the frost-resistance. *Bull. Fac. Fish. Nagasaki Univ.* **21**: 131–8.

Miura A. 1975. *Porphyra* cultivation in Japan. In *Advance of Phycology in Japan.* (Eds. J. Tokida & H. Hirose) pp. 273–304. The Hague: Junk.

Miura A. & Merrill J.E. 1982. Genetic studies and crop improvement of *Porphyra* in Japan. *First Int. Phycol. Congr. St John's, Newfoundland, Abstr.* p. a33.

Mooney P.A. & Van Staden J. 1984. Lunar periodicity of the levels of endogenous cytokinins in *Sargassum heterophyllum* (Phaeophyceae). *Botanica Mar.* **27**: 467–72.

Morgan K.C., Shacklock P.F. & Simpson F.J. 1980a. Some aspects of the culture of *Palmaria palmata* in greenhouse tanks. *Botanica Mar.* **23**: 765–70.

Morgan K.C., Wright J.L.C. & Simpson F.J. 1980b. Review of chemical constituents of the red alga *Palmaria palmata*. *Econ. Bot.* **34**: 27–50.

Moss J.R. 1977. Essential considerations for establishing seaweed extraction factories. In *The Marine Plant Biomass of the Pacific Northwest Coast*. (Ed. R.W. Kauss) pp. 301–14. Corvallis: Oregon State University Press.

Motomura T. & Sakai Y. 1981. Effect of chelated iron in culture media on oogenesis in *Laminaria angustata*. *Bull. Jap. Soc. Sci. Fish.* **47**: 1535–40.

Motomura T. & Sakai Y. 1984a. Ultrastructural studies of gametogenesis in *Laminaria angustata* (Laminariales, Phaeophyta) regulated by iron concentration in the medium. *Phycologia* **23**: 331–43.

Motomura T. & Sakai Y. 1984b. Regulation of gametogenesis of *Laminaria* and *Desmarestia* (Phaeophyta) by iron and boron. *Jap. J. Phycol.* **32**: 209–15.

Mumford T.F. 1973. *Observations on the taxonomy and ecology of some species of Porphyra from Washington and Vancouver Island, British Columbia*. Unpublished Ph.D. thesis, University of Washington.

Mumford T.F. 1980. The reproductive biology *in vitro* of nine species of *Porphyra* (Bangiales, Rhodophyta) from Washington. *J. Phycol.* **16** (Suppl.): 29.

Mumford T.F. 1987. Commercialization strategy for nori culture in Puget Sound, Washington. In *Seaweed Cultivation for Renewable Resources*. (Eds. K.T. Bird & P.H. Benson) pp. 351–68. Amsterdam: Elsevier.

Mumford T.F. & Cole K. 1977. Chromosome numbers for fifteen species in the genus *Porhyra* (Bangiales, Rhodophyta) from the west coast of North America. *Phycologia* **16**: 373–7.

Mumford T.F. & Melvin D.J. 1983. Pilot-scale mariculture of seaweeds in Washington. In *Seaweed Raft and Farm Design in the United States and China*. (Ed. L.B. McKay) pp. 1.1–1.18. New York: New York Sea Grant Publication.

Mumford T.S. & Miura M. 1988. *Porphyra* as food: cultivation and economics. In *Algae and Human Affairs*. (Eds. C.A. Lembi & J.R. Waaland) pp. 87–117. Cambridge: University Press.

Mumford T.F. & Waaland J.R. 1980. Progress and prospects for field cultivation of *Iridaea cordata* and *Gigartina exasperata*. In *Pacific Seaweed Aquaculture*. (Eds I.A. Abbott, M.S. Foster & L.F. Eklund) pp. 92–105. La Jolla, California: California Sea Grant College Program.

Munda I.M. 1978. Salinity dependent distribution of benthic algae in estuarine areas of Icelandic fjords. *Botanica Mar.* **21**: 451–68.

Munda I.M. & Markham J.W. 1982. Seasonal variations of vegetation patterns and biomass constituents in the rocky eulittoral of Helgoland. *Helgoländer Meeresunters.* **35**: 131–51.

Munda I.M. & Pedersen P.M. 1978. *Porphyra thulaea* sp. nov. (Rhodophyceae, Bangiales) from east Iceland and west Greenland. *Botanica Mar.* **21**: 283–8.

Nakahara H. 1984. Alternation of generations of some brown algae in unialgal and axenic cultures. *Sci. Pap. Inst. Algol. Res., Fac. Sci. Hokkaido Univ.* **7**: 77–194.

Neushul M. 1982. Propagation, cultivation and harvest of the giant kelp, *Macrocystis*. In *Proceedings of Republic of China–United States Cooperative Science Seminar on Cultivation and Utilization of Economic Algae*. pp. 95–103. Mangilao, Guam: University of Guam Marine Laboratory.

Neushul M. & Harger B.W.W. 1985. Studies of biomass yield from a near-shore macroalgal test farm. *J. Solar Energy Eng.* **107**: 93–6.

Neushul M. & Harger B.W.W. 1987. Nearshore kelp cultivation, yield and genetics. In *Seaweed Cultivation for Renewable Resources*. (Eds. K.T. Bird & P.H. Benson) pp. 69–93. Amsterdam: Elsevier.

Newton L. 1951. *Seaweed Utilisation*. London: Sampson Low.

Nisizawa K. 1987. Preparation and marketing of seaweeds as foods. In *Production and Utilization of Products from Commercial Seaweeds*. (Ed. D.J. McHugh) pp. 147–89. Rome; FAO Fisheries Technical Paper 288.

Norris J.N. 1985a. *Gracilaria* and *Polycavernosa* from the Caribbean and Florida: key and list of the species of economic potential. In *Taxonomy of Economic Seaweeds with Reference to Some Pacific and Caribbean Species*. (Eds. I.A. Abbott & J.N. Norris) pp. 101–13. La Jolla: California Sea Grant College Program.

Norris J.N. 1985b. *Gracilaria* from the Gulf of California: key, list and distribution of the common species. In *Taxonomy of Economic Seaweeds with Reference to Some Pacific and Caribbean Species*. (Eds. I.A. Abbott & J.N. Norris) pp. 93–6. La Jolla; California Sea Grant College Program.

North W.J. 1971. Introduction and background. In *The Biology of Giant Kelp Beds (Macrocystis) in California*. (Ed. W.J. North) pp. 1–97. Lehre, FRG: Cramer.

North W.J. 1976. Aquacultural techniques for creating and restoring beds of giant kelp, *Macrocystis* spp. *J. Fish. Res. Bd Can.* **33**: 1015–23.

North W.J. 1987a. Biology of the *Macrocystis* resource in North America. In *Case Studies of Seven Commercial Seaweed Resources*. (Eds M.S. Doty, J.F. Caddy & B. Santelices) pp. 265–311. Rome: FAO Fisheries Technical Paper 281.

North W.J. 1987b. Oceanic farming of *Macrocystis*, the problems and non-problems. In *Seaweed Cultivation for Renewable Resources*. (Eds. K.T. Bird & P.H. Benson) pp. 39–67. Amsterdam: Elsevier.

North W.J., Gerard V. & Kuwabara J. 1982. Farming *Macrocystis* at coastal and oceanic sites. In *Synthetic and Degradative Processes in Marine Macrophytes*. (Ed. S. Srivastava) pp. 247–64. Berlin: de Gruyter.

Norton T.A. 1970. Synopsis of biological data on *Saccorhiza polyschides*. *Fish. Synops. FAO* **83**: pag. var.

Norton T.A. 1981a. *Sargassum muticum* on the Pacific coast of North America. In *Proceedings of the Eighth International Seaweed Symposium*. (Eds. G.E. Fogg & W.E. Jones) pp. 449–56. Menai Bridge: The Marine Science Laboratories.

Norton T.A. 1981b. Gamete expulsion and release in *Sargassum muticum*. *Botanica Mar.* **24**: 465–70.

Norton T.A. 1985. *Provisional Atlas of the Marine Algae of Britain & Ireland*. Huntingdon: Institute of Terrestrial Ecology.

Norton T.A. & Deysher L.E. 1989. The reproductive ecology of *Sargassum muticum* at different latitudes. In *Reproduction, Genetics and Distribution of Marine Organisms*. (Eds. J.S. Ryland & P.A. Tyler) pp. 147–52. Fredensborg: Olsen & Olsen.

Ogata E. & Schramm W. 1971. Some observations on the influence of salinity on growth and photosynthesis in *Porphyra umbilicalis*. *Mar. Biol. Berlin* **10**: 79–6.

Ohno M. 1969. A physiological ecology of the early stage of some marine algae. *Rep. Usa Mar. Biol. Stn Kochi Univ.* **16**: 1–46.

Ohno M. 1972. The periodicity of gamete liberation in *Monostroma*. In *Proceedings of the Seventh International Seaweed Symposium*. (Ed. K. Nisizawa) pp. 405–9. Tokyo: University of Tokyo Press.

Ohno M. 1977. On the height of the cultivated net in *Monostroma* cultivation. *Rep. Usa Mar. Biol. Stn Kochi Univ.* **24**: 45–51.

Ohno M. & Miyanoue K. 1980. The ecology of the food alga *Enteromorpha prolifera*. *Rep. Usa Mar. Biol. Inst.* **2**: 11–17.

Ohno M. & Nozawa K. 1972. Observations of spore formation and photosynthetic activities on *Monostroma nitidum*. *Bull. Jap. Soc. Phycol.* **20**: 30–5.

Ohno M., Mairh O.P., Chauhan V.D., Tewari A., Oza R.M., Joshi H.V., Pandy R.S. & Rao P.S. 1981. Mass cultivation of green algae *Enteromorpha* on the coast of Okha, India. *Rep. Usa Mar. Biol. Inst.* **3**: 51–9.

Okada Y., Sanbonsuga Y. & Machiguchi Y. 1985. The effects of temperature on the growth and shape of the early sporophytes of *Laminaria japonica, L. diabolica, L. religiosa* and *L. angustata* var. *longissima* in culture. *Bull. Hokkaido Reg. Fish. Res. Lab.* **50**: 27–44.

Okazaki A. 1971. *Seaweeds and Their Uses in Japan.* Tokai, Japan: Tokai University Press.

Oliger P. & Santelices B. 1981. Physiological ecology studies on Chilean Gelidiales. *J. Exp. Mar. Biol. Ecol.* **53**: 65–75.

Oliveira E.C. de 1984. Taxonomic criteria in the genus *Gracilaria* Grev. (Rhodophyta): an experience with the western Atlantic species. In *Proceedings of the Eleventh International Seaweed Symposium.* (Eds. C.J. Bird & M.A. Ragan) pp. 55–88. Dordrecht: Junk.

Oliveira Filho E.C. de & Coll J. 1975. The genus *Porphyra* C. Ag. (Rhodophyta-Bangiales) in the American South Atlantic. I. Brazilian species. *Botanica Mar.* **18**: 191–7.

Oliveira J.C. 1989. A note on the elongation rate of *Gelidium sesquipedale* in *in situ* cages in Portugal. In *Outdoor Seaweed Cultivation, Proceedings of the Second Workshop of COST 48 Subgroup 1.* (Eds. J.M. Kain, J.W. Andrews & B.J. McGregor) pp. 69–75. Brussels: Commission of the European Communities.

Omar H. 1989. An assessment of potential of red seaweed *Palmaria palmata* for mariculture in the Irish Sea. Unpublished Ph.D. thesis, University of Liverpool.

Oohusa T. 1984. Technical aspects of nori (*Porphyra*) cultivation and quality preservation of nori products in Japan today. In *Proceedings of the Eleventh International Seaweed Symposium.* (Eds. C.J. Bird & M.A. Ragan) pp. 95–101. Dordrecht: Junk.

Oza R.M., Tewari A., Joshi H.V., Mairh O.P. & Taqui Khan M.M. 1985. Further experiments on the field cultivation of *Enteromorpha* on the coast of Okha, Gujarat. In *Marine Plants* (Eds. V. Krishnamurthy & A.G. Untawale) pp. 153–66. Madras: Seaweed Research and Utilization Association.

Pandey R.S. & Ohno M. 1985. An ecological study of cultivated *Enteromorpha. Rep. Usa Mar. Biol. Inst.* **7**: 21–31.

Parke, M. 1948. Studies on British Laminariaceae. I. Growth in *Laminaria saccharina* (L.) Lamour. *J. Mar. Biol. Ass. UK* **27**: 651–709.

Parke M. & Dixon P.S. 1976. Check-list of British marine algae—third revision. *J. Mar. Biol. Ass. UK* **56**: 627–94.

Parker H.S. 1981. Influence of relative water motion on the growth, ammonium uptake and carbon and nitrogen composition of *Ulva lactuca* (Chlorophyceae). *Mar. Biol. Berlin* **63**: 309–18.

Patwary M.U. & van der Meer J.P. 1983. Improvement of *Gracilaria tikvahiae* (Rhodophyceae) by genetic modification of thallus morphology. *Aquaculture* **33**: 207–14.

Penniman C.A., Mathieson A.C. & Penniman C.E. 1986. Reproductive phenology and growth of *Gracilaria tikvahiae* McLachlan (Gigartinales, Rhodophyta) in the Great Bay Estuary, New Hampshire. *Bot. Mar. Berlin* **24**: 147–54.

Pérez R. 1972. Opportunité de l'implantation de l'algue *Macrocystis pyrifera* sur les côte bretonnes. *Sci. Pêche* **135**: 1–9.

Pérez R., Lee J.Y. & Juge C. 1981. Observations sur l'algue japonaise *Undaria pinnatifida* (Harvey) Suringar introduite accidentellement dans l'étang de Thau. *Sci. Pêche* **315**: 1–12.

Pérez R., Kaas R. & Barbaroux O. 1984. Culture expérimentale de l'algue *Undaria pinnatifida* sur les côtes de France. *Sci. Pêche* **343**: 1–15.

Pizarro A. & Barrales H. 1986. Field assessment of two methods for planting the agar-containing seaweed, *Gracilaria*, in northern Chile. *Aquaculture* **59**: 31–43.

Polne-Fuller M. & Gibor A. 1987. Calluses and callus-like growth in seaweeds: induction and culture. In *Proceedings of the Twelfth International Seaweed Symposium*. (Eds. M.A. Ragan & C.J. Bird) pp. 131–8. Dordrecht: Junk.

Polne-Fuller M., Biniaminov M. & Gibor A. 1984. Vegetative propagation of *Porphyra perforata*. In *Proceedings of the Eleventh International Seaweed Symposium*. (Eds. C.J. Bird & M.A. Ragan) pp. 308–13. Dordrecht: Junk.

Pringle J.D. 1986. Swarmer release and distribution of life-cycle phases of *Enteromorpha intestinalis* (L.) (Chlorophyta) in relation to environmental factors. *J. Exp. Mar. Biol. Ecol.* **100**: 97–111.

Provasoli L., McLaughlin J.J.A. & Droop M.R. 1957. The development of artificial media for marine algae. *Arc. Mikrobiol.* **25**: 392–428.

Raju P.V. & Thomas P.C. 1971. Experimental field cultivation of *Gracilaria edulis* (Gmel.) Silva. *Botanica Mar.* **14**: 71–5.

Ramus J. 1978. Seaweed anatomy and photosynthetic performance: the ecological significance of light guides, heterogeneous absorption and multiple scatter. *J. Phycol.* **14**: 352–62.

Ramus J. & Venable M. 1987. Temporal ammonium patchiness and growth rate in *Codium* and *Ulva* (Ulvophyceae). *J. Phycol.* **23**: 518–23.

Reed R.H. & Russell G. 1979. Adaptation to salinity stress in populations of *Enteromorpha intestinalis* (L.) Link. *Estuar. cstl. mar. Sci.* **8**: 251–8.

Ren G.-Z., Wang J.-C. & Chen M.-Q. 1984. Cultivation of *Gracilaria* by means of low rafts. In *Proceedings of the Eleventh International Seaweed Symposium*. (Eds C.J. Bird & M.A. Ragan) pp. 72–6. Dordrecht: Junk.

Rodríguez D. & Santelices B. 1987. Patterns of apical structure in the genera *Gelidium* and *Pterocladia* (Gelidiaceae, Rhodophyta). In *Proceedings of the Twelfth International Seaweed Symposium*. (Eds. M.A. Ragan & C.J. Bird) pp. 199–203. Dordrecht: Junk.

Rosenvinge L.K. 1931. The marine algae of Denmark. Contributions to their natural history. Part IV. Rhodophyceae IV. (Gigartinales, Rhodymeniales, Nemastomatales). *K. Danske Vidensk. Selsk. Skr.*, 7 Raekke, **7**: 491–630.

Rueness J. 1989. *Sargassum muticum* and other introduced Japanese macroalgae: biological pollution of European coasts. *Mar. Pollut. Bull.* **20**: 173–6.

Rueness J., Mathisen H.A. & Tananger T. 1987. Culture and field observations on *Gracilaria verrucosa* (Huds.) Papenf. (Rhodophyta) from Norway. *Botanica Mar.* **30**: 267–76.

Ryther J.H., Corwin N., DeBusk T.A. & Williams L.D. 1981. Nitrogen uptake and storage by the red alga *Gracilaria tikvahiae* (McLachlan, 1979). *Aquaculture* **26**: 107–15.

Saito Y. 1975. *Undaria*. In *Advance of Phycology in Japan* (Eds. J. Tokida & H. Hirose) pp. 304–20. The Hague: Dr W. Junk b.v. Publishers.

Sanbonsuga Y. 1984. Studies of the growth of forced *Laminaria*. *Bull. Hokkaido Reg. Fish. Res. Lab.* **49**: 1–82.

Santelices B. 1976. Nota sobre cultivo masivo de algunas especies de Gelidiales (Rhodophyta). *Revta. Biol. Mar. Dep. Oceanol. Univ. Chile* **16**: 27–33.

Santelices B. 1987. The wild harvest and culture of the economically important species of *Gelidium* in Chile. In *Case Studies of Seven Commercial Seaweed Resources*. (Eds. M.S. Doty, J.F. Caddy & B. Santelices) pp. 165–92. Rome: FAO Fisheries Technical Paper 281.

Santelices B. & Doty M.S. 1989. A review of *Gracilaria* farming. *Aquaculture* **78**: 95–133.

Santelices B. & Stewart J.G. 1985. Pacific species of *Gelidium* Lamouroux and other Gelidiales (Rhodophyta), with keys and descriptions to the common or economically important species. In *Taxonomy of Economic Seaweeds with Reference to*

Some Pacific and Caribbean Species. (Eds. I.A. Abbott & J.N. Norris) pp. 17–27. La Jolla: California Sea Grant College Program.

Santelices B. & Ugarte R. 1987. Production of Chilean *Gracilaria*: problems and perspectives. In *Proceedings of the Twelfth International Seaweed Symposium*. (Eds. M.A. Ragan & C.J. Bird) pp. 295–9. Dordrecht: Junk.

Santelices B., Vázsquez J., Ohme U. & Fonck E. 1984. Managing wild crops of *Gracilaria* in central Chile. In *Proceedings of the Eleventh International Seaweed Symposium*. (Eds. C.J. Bird & M.A. Ragan) pp. 77–89. Dordrecht: Junk.

Segi T. 1966. On the species and distribution of *Gelidium* in Japan. In *Proceedings of the Fifth International Seaweed Symposium*. (Eds. E.G. Young & J.L. McLachlan) pp. 205. Oxford: Pergamon Press.

Segi T. & Kida W. 1961. On the relation between distribution of early germlings of *Monostroma* and tidal current in the culture ground. *Botanica Mar.* **2**: 223–30.

Seoane-Camba J.A. 1989. On the possibility of culturing *Gelidium sesquipedale* by vegetative propagation. In *Outdoor Seaweed Cultivation, Proceedings of the Second Workshop of COST 48 Subgroup 1*. (Eds. J.M. Kain, J.W. Andrews & B.J. McGregor) pp. 59–68. Brussels: Commission of the European Communities.

Slinn D.J. & Eastham J.F. 1984. Routine hydrographic observations in the Irish Sea off Port Erin, Isle of Man, during 1972–1981 inclusive. *Ann. Biol. Copenh.* **38**: 42–4.

Smith G.M. 1947. On the reproduction of some Pacific coast species of *Ulva*. *Am. J. Bot.* **34**: 80–7.

Smith A.H., Nichols K. & McLachlan J. 1984. Cultivation of seamoss (*Gracilaria*) in St Lucia, West Indies. In *Proceedings of the Tenth International Seaweed Symposium*. (Ed. T. Levring) pp. 249–51. Berlin: de Gruyter.

Soe-Htun U., Ohno M. & Mizuta S. 1986. Effects of salinity and temperature on the growth of the green alga *Enteromorpha prolifera*. *Rep. Usa Mar. Biol. Inst. Kochi Univ.* **8**: 9–13.

Sohn C.H. & Kain J.M. 1989a. *Porphyra* cultivation in Korea. In *Outdoor Seaweed Cultivation, Proceedings of the Second Workshop of COST 48 Subgroup 1*. (Eds. J.M Kain, J.W. Andrews & B.J. McGregor) pp. 106–9. Brussels: Commission of the European Communities.

Sohn C.H. & Kain J.M. 1989b. *Undaria, Laminaria* and *Enteromorpha* cultivation in Korea. In *Outdoor Seaweed Cultivation, Proceedings of the Second Workshop of COST 48 Subgroup 1*. (Eds. J.M. Kain, J.W. Andrews & B.J. McGregor) pp. 42–5. Brussels: Commission of the European Communities.

South G.R. & Tittley I. 1986. *A Checklist and Distributional Index of the Benthic Marine Algae of the North Atlantic Ocean*. Newfoundland: Huntsman Marine Laboratory and the British Museum (Natural History).

South G.R. & Whittick A. 1987. *Introduction to Phycology*. Oxford: Blackwell Scientific Publications.

Stanley N. 1987. Production, properties and uses of carrageenan. In *Production and Utilization of Products from Commercial Seaweeds*. (Ed. D.J. McHugh) pp. 116–46. Rome: FAO Fisheries Technical Paper 288.

Stewart J.G. 1968. Morphological variation in *Pterocladia pyramidale*. *J. Phycol.* **4**: 76–84.

Stewart J.G. & Norris J.N. 1981. Gelidiaceae (Rhodophyta) from the northern Gulf of California, Mexico. *Phycologia* **20**: 273–84.

Suto S. 1972. Variation in species characters of *Porphyra* under culture conditions. In *Contributions to the Systematics of Benthic Marine Algae of the North Pacific*. (Eds. I.A. Abbott & M. Kurogi) pp. 193–201. Kobe, Japan: Japanese Society of Phycology.

Suto S. 1974. Mariculture of seaweeds and its problems in Japan. *Proceedings of the*

First U.S.–Japan Meeting on Aquaculture. pp. 7–16. Seattle, Washington: National Marine Fisheries Service.

Tanner C.E. 1981. Chlorophyta: life histories. In *The Biology of Seaweeds.* (Eds. C.S. Lobban & M.J. Wynne) pp. 218–47. Oxford: Blackwell.

Tatewaki M. 1972. Life history and systematics in *Monostroma.* In *Contributions to the Systematics of Benthic Marine Algae of the North Pacific.* (Eds. I.A. Abbott & M. Kurogi) pp. 1–15. Kobe, Japan: Japanese Society of Phycology.

Taylor W.R. 1960. *Marine Algae of the Eastern Tropical and Subtropical Coasts of the Americas.* Ann Arbor: University of Michigan Press.

Tokida J., Nakamura Y. & Druehl L.D. 1980. Typification of species of *Laminaria* (Phaeophyta, Laminariales) described by Miyabe, and taxonomic notes on the genus in Japan. *Phycologia* **19**: 317–28.

Tseng C.K. 1981a. Marine phycoculture in China. In *Proceedings of the Tenth International Seaweed Symposium.* (Ed. T. Levring) pp. 123–52. Berlin: de Gruyter.

Tseng C.K. 1981b. Commercial cultivation. In *The Biology of Seaweeds.* (Eds. C.S. Lobban & M.J. Wynne) pp. 680–741. Oxford: Blackwell.

Tseng C.K. 1987a. *Laminaria* mariculture in China. In *Case Studies of Seven Commercial Seaweed Resources.* (Eds. M.S. Doty, J.F. Caddy & B. Santelices) pp. 239–63. Rome: FAO Fisheries Technical Paper 281.

Tseng C.K. 1987b. Some remarks on the kelp cultivation industry of China. In *Seaweed Cultivation for Renewable Resources.* (Eds. K.T. Bird & P.H. Benson) pp. 147–53. Amsterdam: Elsevier.

Tseng C.K. & Fei X.G. 1987. Macroalgal commercialization in the Orient. In *Proceedings of the Twelfth International Seaweed Symposium.* (Eds. M.A. Ragan & C.J. Bird) pp. 167–72. Dordrecht: Junk.

Tseng C.K. & Sun A. 1989. Studies on the alternation of the nuclear phases and chromosome numbers in the life history of some species of *Porphyra* from China. *Botanica Mar.* **32**: 1–8.

Tseng C.K., Sun K.Y. & Wu C.Y. 1955a. On the cultivation of haitai (*Laminaria japonica* Aresch.) by summering young sporophytes at low temperature. *Acta Bot. Sin.* **4**: 255–64.

Tseng C.K., Sun K.Y. & Wu C.Y. 1955b. Studies on fertilizer application in the cultivation of haitai (*Laminaria japonica* Aresch.). *Acta Bot. Sin.* **4**: 375–92.

Tseng C.K., Wu C.Y. & Sun K.Y. 1957. The effect of temperature on the growth and development of haitai (*Laminaria japonica* Aresch.). *Acta bot. Sin.* **6**: 103–30.

Tseng C.K., Wu C.Y. & Ren K.Z. 1962. The influence of temperature on the growth and development of the haidai (*Laminaria japonica*) gametophytes. *Oceanol. Limnol. Sin.,* **4**: 22–8.

Tsuda R.T. 1985. *Gracilaria* from Micronesia: key, list and distribution of the species. In *Taxonomy of Economic Seaweeds with Reference to Some Pacific and Caribbean Species.* (Eds. I.A. Abbott & J.N. Norris) pp. 91–2. La Jolla: California Sea Grant College Program.

Tsuda, R.T. 1988. *Sargassum* from Micronesia. In *Taxonomy of Economic Seaweeds with Reference to Some Pacific and Caribbean Species* Vol. II. (Ed. I.A. Abbott) pp. 59–63. La Jolla: California Sea Grant College Program.

Tussenbroek B.I. van 1984. Effect of continuous unilateral irradiation on the conchocelis of *Porphyra umbilicalis* (L.) J.Ag. and some other red algae. *J. Exp. Mar. Biol. Ecol.* **83**: 263–74.

Umamaheswara Rao M. 1972. On the Gracilariaceae of the seas around India. *J. Mar. Biol. Ass. India* **14**: 671–96.

van der Meer J.P. & Bird C.J. 1985. *Palmaria mollis* stat. nov.: a newly recognised species of *Palmaria* (Rhodophyceae) from the northeast Pacific Ocean. *Can. J. Bot.* **63**: 398–403.

van der Meer J.P. & Patwary M.U. 1983. Genetic modification of *Gracilaria tikvahiae* (Rhodophyceae). The production and evaluation of polyploids. *Aquaculture* **33**: 311–6.

van der Meer J.P. & Simpson F.J. 1984. Cryopreservation of *Gracilaria tikvahiae* (Rhodophyceae) and other macrophytic marine algae. *Phycologia* **23**: 195–202.

van der Meer J.P. & Todd E.R. 1980. The life history of *Palmaria palmata* in culture. A new type for the Rhodophyta. *Can. J. Bot.* **58**: 1250–6.

Vermaat J.E. & Sand-Jensen K. 1987. Survival, metabolism and growth of *Ulva lactuca* under winter conditions: a laboratory study of bottlenecks in the life cycle. *Mar. Biol. Berlin* **95**: 55–61.

Waaland J.R. 1973. Experimental studies on the marine algae *Iridaea* and *Gigartina*. *J. Exp. Mar. Biol. Ecol.* **11**: 71–80.

Waaland J.R. 1981. Colonization and growth of populations of *Iridaea* and *Gigartina* on artificial substrates. In *Proceedings of the Eighth International Seaweed Symposium*. (Eds. G.E. Fogg & W.E. Jones) pp. 507–12. Menai Bridge: The Marine Science Laboratories.

Waaland J.R. 1983. Cloning marine algae for mariculture. *J. World Maricult. Soc.* **14**: 404–14.

Waaland J.R., Dickson L.G. & Carrier J.E. 1987. Conchocelis growth and photoperiodic control of conchospore release in *Porphyra torta* (Rhodophyta). *J. Phycol.* **23**: 399–406.

Wallentinus I. 1979. Environmental influences on benthic macrovegetation in the Trosa-Askö area, northern Baltic proper II. The ecology of macroalgae and submersed phanerograms. *Contrib. Askö Lab. Univ. Stockholm* **25**: 210 pp.

West J.A. & Hommersand M.H. 1981. Rhodophyta: life histories. In *The Biology of Seaweeds*. (Eds. C.S. Lobban & M.J. Wynne) pp. 133–93. Oxford: Blackwell.

Wheeler W.N., Neushul M. & Harger B.W.W. 1981. Development of a coastal marine farm and its associated problems. In *Proceedings of the Tenth International Seaweed Symposium*. (Ed. T. Levring) pp. 631–6. Berlin: de Gruyter.

Widdowson T.B. 1971. A taxonomic revision of the genus *Alaria* Greville. *Syesis* **4**: 11–49.

Womersley H.B.S. 1954. The species of *Macrocystis* with special reference to those on southern Australian coasts. *Univ. Calif. Publs Bot.* **27**: 109–122.

Womersley H.B.S. 1984. *The Marine Benthic Flora of Southern Australia. Part I.* South Australia: Government Printer.

Womersley H.B.S. 1987. *The Marine Benthic Flora of Southern Australia. Part II.* South Australia: Government Printer.

Wu C.Y., Gao N., Chen D., Chou B., Cai P., Dong S., Wen Z. & Cong R. 1979. On the malformation disease of *Laminaria* sporelings. *Oceanol. Limnol. Sin.* **10**: 238–50.

Wu C.Y., Zheng S.Q. & Tseng C.K. 1981. Tip-cutting as a means of increasing production in *Laminaria* aquaculture. In *Proceedings of the Tenth International Seaweed Symposium*. (Ed. T. Levring) pp. 637–42. Berlin: de Gruyter.

Wu C.Y., Chen D. & Li J. 1983. On the diseases of cultivated *Laminaria japonica*. In *Proceedings of the Joint China-U.S. Phycology Symposium*. pp. 211–20. Beijing, China: Science Press.

Wynne M.J. & Kraft G.T. 1981. Classification summary. In *The Biology of Seaweeds*. (Eds. C.S. Lobban & M.J. Wynne) pp. 743–50. Oxford: Blackwell.

Xia B. 1986. On *Gracilaria salicornia* (C. Agardh) Dawson. *Chin. J. Oceanol. Limnol.* **4**: 100–6.

Yabu H. 1975. Cytological studies of the Rhodophyta and Chlorophyta. In *Advance of*

Phycology in Japan. (Eds. J. Tokida & H. Hirose) pp. 125–35. The Hague: Junk.

Yamada N. 1972. Manuring for *Gelidium*. In *Proceedings of the Seventh International Seaweed Symposium*. (Ed. K. Nisizawa) pp. 385–90. Tokyo: University of Tokyo Press.

Yamamoto H. 1984. An evaluation of some vegetative features and some interesting problems in Japanese populations of *Gracilaria*. In *Proceedings of the Eleventh International Seaweed Symposium*. (Eds. C.J. Bird & M.A. Ragan) pp. 51–4. Dordrecht: Junk.

Yan Z.M. 1984. Studies on tissue culture of *Laminaria japonica* and *Undaria pinnatifida*. In *Proceedings of the Eleventh International Seaweed Symposium*. (Eds. C.J. Bird & M.A. Ragan) pp. 314–6. Dordrecht: Junk.

Ying L.S. 1984. The ecological characteristics of monospores of *Porphyra yezoensis* Ueda and their use in cultivation. In *Proceedings of the Eleventh International Seaweed Symposium*. (Eds. C.J. Bird & M.A. Ragan) pp. 255–8. Dordrecht: Junk.

Yokoyama M. & Sanbonsuga Y. 1979. On a seasonal variation in nitrate-N content of *Laminaria* during forced cultivation. *Bull. Hokkaido Reg. Fish. Res. Lab.* **44**: 67–72.

Yoshida T. 1972. Growth patterns and behaviour of two species of *Porphyra* under conditions of cultivation. In *Contributions to the Systematics of Benthic Marine Algae of the North Pacific*. (Eds. I.A. Abbott & M. Kurogi) pp. 203–11. Kobe, Japan: Japanese Society of Phycology.

Yoshida T. 1988. Japanese and Taiwanese species of *Sargassum* subgenus *Sargassum*. In *Taxonomy of Economic Seaweeds with Reference to Some Pacific and Caribbean Species* Vol. II. (Ed. I.A. Abbott) pp. 5–21. La Jolla: California Sea Grant College Program.

Yoshida T., Nakahima Y. & Nakata Y. 1985a. Preliminary check-list of marine benthic algae of Japan-II. Rhodophyceae. *Jap. J. Phycol.* **33**: 249–75.

Yoshida T., Nakajima Y. & Nakata Y. 1985b. Preliminary check-list of marine benthic algae of Japan-I. Chlorophyceae and Phaeophyceae. *Jap. J. Phycol.* **33**: 249–75.

Yoshikawa Y. 1986. Studies on the formation of *Sargassum* beds. II. The growth of three Sargassaceae by placed blocks on the bottom with artificial seedlings and transplanted by matured plants. *Bull. Nansei Reg. Fish. Res. Lab.* **20**: 137–46.

Zavodnik N. 1987. Seasonal variations in the rate of photosynthetic activity and chemical composition of the littoral seaweeds *Ulva lactuca* and *Porphyra leucosticta* from the north Adriatic. *Botanica Mar.* **30**: 71–82.

Zeng C. (Tseng C.K.) 1984. Phycological research in the development of the Chinese seaweed industry. In *Proceedings of the Eleventh International Seaweed Symposium*. (Eds. C.J. Bird & M.A. Ragan) pp. 7–18. Dordrecht: Junk.

Zhang J. (Chang C.F.) & Xia B. 1984. Some problems in the taxonomy of Chinese species of *Gracilaria* (Rhodophyta). In *Proceedings of the Eleventh International Seaweed Symposium*. (Eds. C.J. Bird & M.A. Ragan) pp. 59–62. Dordrecht: Junk.

Zhang J. (Chang C.F.) & Xia B. 1988a. On two new *Gracilaria* (Gigartinales, Rhodophyta) from south China. In *Taxonomy of Economic Seaweeds with Reference to Some Pacific and Caribbean Species* Vol. II. (Ed. I.A. Abbott) pp. 131–6. La Jolla: California Sea Grant College Program.

Zhang J. (Chang C.F.) & Xia B. 1988b. Chinese species of *Gelidium* Lamouroux and other Gelidiales (Rhodophyta), with key, list, and distribution of the common species. In *Taxonomy of Economic Seaweeds with Reference to Some Pacific and Caribbean Species* Vol. II. (Ed. I.A. Abbott) pp. 109–13. La Jolla: California Sea Grant College Program.

Zhang Y.-J., Yang Y.-X., Wang Q.-Y. & Wang S.-R. 1985. Studies on the breeding and genetics of *Porphyra yezoensis* Ueda. *Trans. Oceanol. Limnol.* **4**: 44–52.

12 Cultivation of Unattached Seaweeds

WINFRID SCHRAMM

Mass cultivation of seaweeds in the sea usually requires attachment of the plants to natural or artificial hard substrata. The management of these so-called 'attached cultures' (see Chapter 11) on the first hand involves the improvement of substratum conditions. The control or manipulation of other factors, such as water dynamics, temperature, light, chemical composition of the medium (in particular nutrients, salinity), of grazers or epiphytes, etc., which may be of great importance for the quality as well as for the quantity of the seaweed harvest, is usually difficult, if not impossible, in natural habitats. Improvement is thus limited to the selection of culture sites with appropriate conditions. Exceptions are artificial fertilizing of attached cultures as frequently applied in Asian countries, and, to a certain extent, the control of competing organisms by labour-intensive weeding. Another, possibly more promising approach is, therefore, the cultivation of seaweeds in more controllable water bodies, such as land-based tanks, raceways, ponds or land-locked sea areas, which is 'mariculture' in the strict sense of Chapman and Chapman (1980).

This approach includes the possibility of growing the seaweeds free-floating, in other words, not attached to any substratum, which may be advantageous for several reasons. Planting and harvesting is comparatively easy and less labour and capital intensive. The density of the cultures can easily be controlled and maintained at desired optimal levels by continuous intermediate removal of biomass. Additionally, the density of the cultures and therefore yield per unit area can be considerably higher, particularly if a sufficient supply of radiant energy, carbon and nutrients can be provided, and if metabolic waste products are removed.

Whereas cultivation of attached seaweeds under natural conditions is quite an old and established technique—for example, the growth of *Ulva* and *Porphyra* on either bamboo poles or mangrove stakes in Asian countries is many centuries old—attempts to mass produce unattached seaweeds in natural or artificial environments is comparatively new.

Major research programmes on the mariculture of free-floating seaweeds were initiated notably by research groups in Canada (Atlantic Research

Seaweed Resources in Europe: *Uses and Potential*. Edited by M. D. Guiry and G. Blunden
© 1991 John Wiley & Sons Ltd

Laboratory, Halifax) and in the USA (Woods Hole Oceanographic Institution) in the early seventies (Neish *et al.* 1977; Ryther *et al.* 1978). Comparatively little work has been carried out or at least published in Europe.

In this chapter various aspects of cultivation of unattached seaweeds will be considered from a European point of view, but other general information from outside Europe will be included. Likewise, the list of references has been extended to a more general bibliography of related literature.

SEAWEEDS FOR UNATTACHED CULTIVATION

In principle, most seaweeds can be grown unattached, at least in laboratory cultures. In this context, we shall therefore mainly consider species used or at least tested for mass cultivation. The list of such seaweeds compiled in Table 1 cannot be considered as complete.

One could conclude that seaweeds which grow permanently or temporarily unattached under natural conditions are particularly suitable for free-floating cultivation (e.g. *Sargassum*, *Fucus*, *Ascophyllum*, *Gracilaria*, *Furcellaria*, *Enteromorpha*, *Monostroma*, *Ulva*, *Cladophora*), but many other forms seem to be equally suited. An important feature is the ability of many seaweeds to propagate vegetatively (Norton & Mathieson 1983). Unlike sexual or asexual reproduction, where cultivation from the microscopic reproductive stages to harvestable biomass is time-consuming, vegetative propagation allows for a rapid build up and the maintenance of optimal crop levels and continuous harvesting. Vegetative propagation in free-floating cultures has been successfully achieved with a number of species (e.g. *Gracilaria tikvahiae*, Hanisak & Ryther 1984; *Gigartina exasperata*, Waaland 1977; *Chondrus crispus*, Shacklock *et al.* 1975), while others failed to propagate vegetatively (e.g. *Palmaria palmata*, Neish 1976; *Iridaea* (also spelled *Iridea* by some authors) *cordata*, Waaland 1976; *Porphyra tenera*, Mencher *et al.* 1983).

Another promising aspect of vegetative propagation is its application to the selection of certain strains which enables mass cultures of clones with special structural or metabolic properties to be built up. Cloning for unattached mass cultivation has been investigated or practised, for example, in *Gigartina exasperata* (Waaland 1983), *Chondrus crispus* (Neish & Shacklock 1971; Cheney *et al.* 1981), *Ulva lactuca* (DeBusk *et al.* 1986), *Gracilaria tikvahiae* (Hanisak and Ryther 1984) and *Gracilaria sjoestedtii* (Hansen 1984).

CULTIVATION OF UNATTACHED SEAWEEDS: BIOMASS PRODUCTION AND CRITICAL VARIABLES

In principle, four technical approaches to the mariculture of unattached seaweeds can be distinguished. These include:

Table 1. Seaweeds used or tested for free floating (unattached) mass cultivation

Species	Source	Remarks
Iridaea cordata	Waaland (1976)	USA, Washington, tank, outdoor
Chondrus crispus	Neish *et al.* (1977)	Canada, tank, outdoor
Porphyra tenera	Mencher *et al.* (1983)	Hawaii, tank, OTEC deep water
Ascophyllum nodosum	Rheault & Ryther (1983)	USA, Florida, spray culture
Gelidium coulteri	Hansen (1983)	USA, Florida, tank
Eucheuma spinosum	Dreno *et al.* (1984)	French Antilles, tank
Pterocladia capillacea	Friedlander & Zelikovitch (1984)	Israel, pond
Hypnea musciformis		
H. cornuta		
Enteromorpha linza	Schramm & Lehnberg (1984, 1985)	Germany, tank, outdoor, laboratory
E. prolifera	Lehnberg & Schramm (1984)	
E. intestinalis		
Monostroma grevillei		
Percursaria percursa		
Furcellaria lumbricalis		
Sargassum muticum	Gellenbek (1984)	USA, California, tank, outdoor
Eucheuma isiforme	Guist *et al.* (1985)	USA, Florida, tank, outdoor
Sargassum fluitans	Lapointe & Hanisak (1985)	USA, Florida, cage, *in situ*
S. natans		
Laminaria saccharina	Levine & Brinkhuis (1985)	USA, Florida, tank, greenhouse
Ulva lactuca	DeBusk *et al.* (1986)	USA, Florida, tank, outdoor
Ascophyllum nodosum	Indergaard *et al.* (1986)	Norway, spray culture, greenhouse
Furcellaria lumbricalis		
Ahnfeltia plicata		
Porphyra yezoensis	Zhang *et al.* (1985)	China, tank, laboratory
Gracilaria tikvahiae	Ryther *et al.* (1979)	USA, Massachusetts, Florida, outdoor
Hypnea musciformis		tanks, raceways, ponds, sprays
Chaetomorpha linum	Goldman & Ryther (1977)	

(continued)

Table 1. (*continued*)

Species	Source	Remarks
Gracilariopsis sjoestedtii		
Neoagardhiella baileyi		
Chondrus crispus		
Enteromorpha clathrata		
Gracilaria verrucosa	Giaccone *et al.* (1979)	Italy, lagoon
Gracilaria tikvahiae	Lapointe & Ryther (1978)	USA, Massachusetts, tank, outdoor
Chondrus crispus	Braud & Delépine (1980)	France, tank
Palmaria palmata	Morgan *et al.* (1980)	Canada, tank, greenhouse
Iridaea cordata	Mumford & Waaland (1980)	USA, Washington, tank
Gigartina exasperata		
Ulva fasciata	Lapointe & Tenore (1981)	USA, Georgia, tank
Gracilaria edulis	Raju & Thomas (1971)	
Gelidium filicinum	Santelices *et al.* (1981)	Chile, laboratory
G. lingulatum		
G. spinulosum		
Gracilaria confervoides	Trotta (1981); Lenzi (1985)	Italy, lagoon
Entermorpha intestinalis	Chassany de Casabianca (1982)	France, tank
Ascophyllum nodosum	Moeller *et al.* (1982)	Spray culture
Ulva lactuca	Houvenaghel & Mathot (1983)	France, tank, outdoor
Ascophyllum nodosum	Lignell & Pedersen (1986)	Sweden, spray culture, greenhouse
Furcellaria lumbricalis		
Chondrus crispus		
Polyides rotundus		

Species	Reference	Location
Rhodomela confervoides		
Polysiphonia sp.		
Fucus serratus		
Fucus vesiculosus		
Halidrys siliquosa		
Laminaria saccharina		
Sargassum cymosum	Hanisak (1987)	USA, Florida, tank
S. filipendula		
S. polyceratium		
S. pteropleuron		
S. fluitans		
S. natans		
Gracilaria secundata	Lignell *et al.* (1987)	Sweden, tank, spray culture
Ectocarpus siliculosus		
Ceramium rubrum		
Enteromorpha intestinalis		
Furcellaria lumbricalis	Haglund & Pedersen (1988)	Sweden, spray culture
Chondrus crispus		
Ahnfeltia plicata		
Gracilaria secundata		
Pterocladia capillacea		
Gelidium sp.		
Ascophyllum nodosum		
Fucus vesiculosus		
Ulva lactuca		
Grateloupia filicina	Zablakis (1987)	USA, Hawaii, tank

1. Management of natural populations or cultivation of seaweeds in land-locked sea areas, such as lagoons, fjords and embayments.
2. Cage culture and floating marine farms.
3. Onshore cultivation in land-based tanks, ponds or raceways.
4. Spray culture.

The utilization of naturally or artificially closed-off sea areas for cultivation of unattached seaweeds (e.g., Simonetti *et al.* 1970; Shang 1976; Doty 1979) has been directed mostly towards increasing the production of temporarily free-floating seaweeds (e.g. *Enteromorpha, Monostroma, Ulva, Gracilaria*) from existing natural populations by controlled or uncontrolled additional nutrient supply (e.g. in the form of domestic or industrial waste water).

In Italy, for example, various lagoonal systems that receive municipal or agricultural waste effluents produce considerable and increasing amounts of *Gracilaria* or green algae. Orlandini and Favretto (1988) found that the annual harvest of *Gracilaria verrucosa* from the Venice Lagoon has increased considerably in recent years, possibly as a result of increasing eutrophication, and was approximately 1700 t dry weight in 1985. The present potential yield of the lagoon is estimated to be around 11 000 t dry weight year^{-1}, yielding about 800 t of agar. Similarly, urban sewage favours the growth of *Gracilaria* in the lagoons of Orbetello or Lesina in Italy where harvesting of *Gracilaria* has been carried out since 1974 (Trotta 1981). In the Odense Fjord (Denmark), which is about 54 km^2 in extent, mass development of free-floating green algae (species of *Ulva, Monostroma* and *Enteromorpha*), clearly the result of eutrophication from discharge of municipal sewage plant effluents and land run-off (2850 t nitrogen year^{-1}, 290 t phosphorus year^{-1}), are harvested and used commercially either as fertilizer or for biogas production (Toft-Frederiksen 1987).

Attempts to cultivate unattached floating seaweeds in cages in the sea have been made, for example, with *Sargassum fluitans*, *S. natans*, and *Gracilaria tikvahiae* in Florida (Lapointe & Hanisak 1985, Hanisak 1987) and with *Gracilaria coronipifolia* in the Philippines (Schramm, unpublished data). The major problem in these experiments was heavy epiphyte growth and fouling, so that sustainable yields were not obtained for longer than 1–2 months, although short-term yields were relatively high (Table 2).

The most common approach to mass production of unattached seaweeds is cultivation in land-based systems, such as tanks, ponds and raceways. Major impetuses in this work have come from various research projects in North America, particularly the research teams organized by Ryther in Woods Hole, Massachusetts and Neish in Halifax. Land-based culture techniques have been employed on different scales elsewhere, ranging from smaller laboratory test systems up to commercial levels. The efficiency of land-based systems depends to a great extent on the intput of energy. Yields obtained from high-intensive cultures supplied with vigorous agitation and rapid exchange of nutrient-enriched and heated seawater are among the most productive systems known. Annual average growth rates of *Gracilaria tikvahiae* in smaller (55 litres) intensive tank cultivation systems with the seaweeds kept in suspension by vigorous aeration and rapid exchange (20–30 volumes day^{-1}) of nutrient-enriched seawater were 35 g dry weight m^{-2} day^{-1} (ranging from 12 to 40 g dry weight m^{-2} day^{-1}), which is equivalent to 127 t ha^{-1} year^{-1}. Productivity was even higher at lower culture densities. In short-term experiments under summer conditions, specific growth rates of up to 60% day^{-1} were determined, which appear to be one of the highest productivity values ever reported for cultivated seaweeds (Lapointe & Ryther 1978).

Productivity of *Ulva lactuca* in intensive tank cultures (700 litres) averaged nearly 19 g dry weight m^{-2} day^{-1} (70 t ha^{-1} year^{-1} over an 18 month period (DeBusk *et al.* 1986). In aerated tank cultures (1400 litres) of the red alga *Iridaea cordata* maintained in Washington, USA, the maximum yield was 20.7 g salt-free dry weight m^{-2} day^{-1} during the summer months (Waaland 1976). The annual production was calculated as 1.95 kg m^{-2} year^{-1}, six times the production of natural populations (Fralick 1971). Intensive cultivation of *Gracilaria* has been successfully scaled up to larger systems (24 000 litres) in which a productivity of 22–25 g dry weight m^{-2} day^{-1} could be maintained over several years (Hanisak & Ryther 1984).

Intensive tank and pond cultivation systems have not so far been employed widely in Europe. In combination with sewage-treatment experiments, mixed cultures of the green algae *Enteromorpha linza*, *E. prolifera* and *Percursaria percursa* were cultivated in aerated, through-flow tank systems (6 × 400 litres) (Lehnberg & Schramm 1984; Schramm & Lehnberg 1985). Sewage enrichment varied between 0 and 40%, water exchange from 0.6 to 2 volumes day^{-1}, and stock density from 0.7 to 2 kg m^{-2}. Maximum yield of 15 g dry weight m^{-2} day^{-1} was obtained in May–June. Further examples of yields or growth obtained in cultures of unattached seaweeds are given in Table 2.

An interesting approach is the utilization of coastal deserts in either tropical or subtropical regions for intensive land-based seaweed farming, especially for the production of biofuel (Wagener 1979; Balloni *et al.* 1982). The attraction of this approach is that there would be no competition with food production, because no freshwater or arable land would be needed. Suitable areas are abundant in the tropics and subtropics. According to Wagener (1979), the total length of adequate coastlines is estimated as 25 000–30 000 km world-wide, and 1000 km in Europe.

In pilot experiments carried out in the framework of the EC Solar Energy Programme in Calabria, southern Italy, *Ulva lactuca* was cultivated in ponds (total 800 m^2 surface area) agitated with specially developed mixing boards. Over a 1 year period, daily yield varied from 7 to 24 g dry weight m^{-2} day^{-1}. The annual harvest was estimated as 67 t dry weight ha^{-1} year^{-1} (Balloni *et al.* 1982).

A special type of land-based intensive cultivation of unattached seaweeds is the so-called spray culture. The cultivation of seaweeds exposed to the air on

Table 2. Examples of growth rates and/or yield (g dry weight m^{-1} d^{-1}) of seaweeds in unattached (free-floating) culture.

Species	Yield Range (g dry weight m^{-2} day^{-1})	Average	Max.	Weight increase (day^{-1})	Remarks	Source
Intensive tank culture						
Gracilaria tikvahiae	12–46	34.8	46	Max. 60	Florida, small tanks, 20–30 vol/dry, large tanks (24 m^3)	Lapointe & Ryther (1978)
G. tikvahiae	22–25					
G. secundata				Max. 47	Sweden, tanks 2 m^3, suberged light source	
Ceramium rubrum				30		
Ectocarpus siliculosus				30		
Non-intensive tank or pond culture						
Gracilaria tikvahiae		9.7			Florida, ponds, non-aerated	Hanisak (1987)
		11.5			Florida, ponds, aerated	
		7.2			Florida, large-scale ponds	
Spray culture						
Ascophyllum nodosum				2.4	Sweden, 13 °C	Lignell & Pedersen (1986)

387

Fucus serratus			2.4		
F. vesiculosus					
Furcellaria lumbricalis			1.6		
Chondrus crispus			0.7		
Ahnfeltia plicata			0.4		
Ascophyllum nodosum	1.2–8	2.8		Deep water, 6–7°C	Rheault & Ryther (1983)
Fucus serratus	1.0–4				
Ascophyllum nodosum		1.2		Florida, outdoor	Moeller *et al.* (1984)
Gracilaria tikvahiae	0–35	20			
Ascophyllum nodosum			1.1		
In-situ cage cultures					
Gracilaria tikvahiae	0–44	13.9		Florida, lagoon	Hanisak (1987)
G. coronipifolia	2–29	21		Philippines, coral reef	Schramm (unpublished data)
Sargassum fluitans	4.2–19.1			Florida, short-term	Lapointe & Hanisak (1985)
S. natans	15.4–33.6				

trays or nets under a continuous or intermittent spray or sprinkling of seawater was probably first suggested by L. Hanic (Chapman 1973) and has been employed in experimental studies in the USA by Moeller *et al.* (1982, 1984), Rheault and Ryther (1983), and Williams (cited in Hanisak 1987), among others. In Europe, spray cultivation experiments were carried out under greenhouse conditions in Norway as well as in Sweden, partly employing an artificial light source (Indergaard *et al.* 1986; Lignell & Pedersen 1986; Haglund & Pedersen 1988). In the experiments conducted by Lignell and Pedersen (1986), seaweeds were irrigated with seawater from 40 m depth with constantly higher nutrient contents and salinities as well as stable temperatures around 6–7 °C, which may explain the higher yields and daily growth rates obtained (Table 2). In intensive tank cultivation experiments with *Gracilaria secundata* employing submerged light sources, growth rates up to 47% day^{-1} were obtained (Lignell *et al.* 1987). Indergaard *et al.* (1986) obtained comparable results using seawater from 5 and 60 m depth, in spray cultures of *Ascophyllum nodosum* and *Ahnfeltia plicata* in Norway. In contrast to the experiments in Florida, where the seaweeds became light damaged and heavily epiphytized due to the high levels of irradiance, in the Swedish experiments these problems were reduced by shading and periodic slight desiccation.

It is generally accepted that mariculture should preferably involve low energy- and labour-intensive methods and low-level technologies. Up to the present time, intensive cultivation of unattached seaweeds may demonstrate initially the potential to produce marine primary biomass. However, because of high energy costs for pumping, aeration, heating, etc., these cultivation methods are probably not yet applicable and profitable at a commercial level, either for bioenergy or for phycocolloid production. This situation may change in the future if specific algal constituents of high commercial value, such as antibiotics or other pharmaceutical substances, are found, or if cheap waste energy sources such as cooling water from power plants or heat from waste water can be utilized. Much attention has therefore been devoted to the cultivation of unattached seaweeds lying loose on the bottom of tanks or ponds of varying size without, or with only moderate, agitation and/or relatively low seawater exchange, which may be considered as a non-intensive type of cultivation. Productivity in this type of 'bottom culture' is generally considerably lower than in intensive systems. For example, in 10–20 m^2 plastic-lined, earthen ponds (0.4–0.8 m deep), without or with only moderate aeration and two volume turnovers per day, average growth rates of *Gracilaria tikvahiae* were 5–8 g dry weight m^{-2} day^{-1} or 18–29 t dry weight ha^{-1} year^{-1} (Hanisak & Ryther 1984).

In a larger pilot-scale pond (0.1 ha) without aeration, average growth rates of 7 g dry weight m^{-2} day^{-1} could be maintained in Florida only during the cooler months of the year. Growth stopped with the onset of high summer temperatures, which reached up to 40 °C in the surface layers of the ponds. In addition, serious problems were encountered with grazing by amphipods and with epiphytes such as diatoms. Frequently, the loose lying or floating plants were collected together by the wind in one corner of the pond; in this accumulated material, self-shading, nutrient depletion and anaerobic conditions during the night further reduced productivity.

More positive results were reported for low-intensive pond cultivation of *Gracilaria verrucosa* (mixed with *G. gigas* and *G. lichenoides*) together with milkfish, shrimps or crabs in brackish polyculture systems in Taiwan (Chiang 1981). In 1980, the pond area in Taiwan was more than 300 ha, producing 12 000 t dry weight annually; production was between 16 and 43 t dry weight ha^{-1} year^{-1}. Increased summer temperatures were controlled by increasing pond depth from 30–40 to 50–60 cm. Water was exchanged every 2–3 days to maintain salinities between 10 and 20‰S. In the Philippines, non-intensive pond cultivation of *Gracilaria* and *Caulerpa racemosa* var. *occidentalis* has been successfully employed on a commercial level (Trono 1981; Horstmann 1983).

In Europe, only a few attempts appear to have been made to grow unattached seaweeds in non-intensive tank or pond culture systems. On the Eastern Mediterranean coast (Israel), for example, growth experiments under non-intensive culture conditions have been made with species of *Gracilaria*, *Pterocladia capillacea*, *Hypnea musciformis* and *H. cornuta* in earthen seawater ponds, one of which received warm seawater from a power station in winter. The water exchange was less than one volume per day. The yields for unattached *Gracilaria*, *Pterocladia*, *Hypnea musciformis* and *H. cornuta* were calculated as 506, 414, 1314 and 1758 g ash-free fresh weight m^{-2} year^{-1}, respectively (Friedlander & Zelikovitch 1984).

In the northern parts of Europe, low temperatures and light levels during the winter months are generally limiting factors for non-intensive cultivation. In Kiel, northern Germany, for example, mixed cultures of green algae adapted to brackish water (*Enteromorpha linza*, *E. prolifera*, *Percursaria percursa*) from the Baltic Sea were maintained at a stocking density of 0.8 kg wet weight m^{-2} in 27 m^2 concrete basins over a year. Water exchange was 1–2 volumes per day, and only aeration sufficient to mix the water without moving the seaweeds was used. The seawater was enriched with 10% effluent from the tertiary step of an urban sewage treatment plant, equivalent to an additional 3.7 g phosphorus and 24.2 g nitrogen per day. Except for the winter months (December to March), where, at temperatures below 5 °C, no growth and nutrient uptake were observed, the average growth rate at temperatures between 8 and 23 °C was 1.8% day^{-1} (Schramm & Lehnberg 1985).

In Norway, outdoor cultures (50 m^3, two volume exchanges day^{-1}) of the unattached form (f. *aegagropila*) of the carrageenanophyte *Furcellaria lumbricalis* yielded an average specific growth rate of 0.44% over an 8 month period from August to March. However, because of low temperature and light levels from November to February, almost no growth was observed (Rueness & Tananger 1984).

Table 3. Interaction of environmental factors and system parameters affecting yield in cultures of unattached seaweeds

	Water exchange	Aeration	Carbon dioxide addition	Nutrient addition	Culture density	Water depth	Heating	Artificial light
Light	XX	XX			XX	XX		XXX
Temperature	XXX	XX				X	XXX	
Nutrient supply	XX	X		XXX	X	X		
Carbon supply	XX	XX	XXX		XX	X	X	XX
Epiphytes	XX	X	X	XX	XX	X	X	
Grazers	XX	X			X			
Water exchange	—	XX	XX	XXX	XX	X	XX	
Aeration	XX	—	XX		X	X		
Carbon dioxide addition	XX	XX	—	—	X	X		X
Nutrient addition	X	X	—		X	X		X
Culture density	X	X	X	X	—	—		XX
Water depth	X	X	X	X	—		X	X
Heating	XX	X				X	—	
Artificial light		X	X	X	XX	X		—

XXX, strong interaction; XX, medium interaction; X, moderate interaction.
Supplemented and modified from Bidwell *et al.* (1985).

The very variable results from non-intensive as well as from intensive culture systems support the statement by Bidwell *et al.* (1985, p. 88) that 'the key to an economically succesful tank cultivation system is integration of all factors to exploit physiological characteristics of the plants under cultivation and to make optimal use of free resources (sunlight, heat sinks in the sea, natural sources of nutrients, including carbon) at minimal costs.' Environmental factors and system parameters that affect yield, for example, interact to varying extents, as can be seen from Table 3.

Even more complex than the interactions shown in Table 3 would be a total assessment in which quality or economic aspects would have to be included. For example, Bidwell *et al.* (1985) emphasize that maximum levels of production are not necessarily optimal for a system. The system must be sustainable, easy to harvest and to maintain, designed to be free from competing organisms (epiphytes, grazers), and immune from diseases.

ENVIRONMENTAL AND SYSTEM VARIABLES

Among the various environmental and system variables, light and temperature appear to be the most critical, particularly in higher latitudes, as in northern or central Europe, where pronounced seasonal variations of these two key environmental factors occur. Daily global irradiation ranges from 2.2 kWh m^{-2} in northern Europe (Norwegian and Scottish coasts to 4.8 kWh m^{-2} in the Western Mediterranean (southern Iberian coasts; Palz 1984). Daily global irradiation reaches its maximum in June with 4.8 and 6.7 kWh m^{-2}, and monthly means vary by a factor of 12 from 0.2 to 2.4 kWh m^{-2} during the darkest season in December, along the northern Norwegian and southern Spanish coasts, respectively (Fig. 1). During the summer months in the north of Europe, irradiation is usually sufficient for light-saturated growth of most seaweeds. In fact, due to high solar irradiation, even detrimental effects have frequently been observed, which can easily be avoided by sun shades or an increase in water depth, culture density or agitation (see Horstmann 1983; Hansen 1984; Bidwell *et al.* 1985; Hanisak 1987). In winter, on the other hand, irradiation is mostly not sufficient in higher latitudes to sustain growth (Waaland 1976; Rueness & Tananger 1984; Schramm & Lehnberg 1985).

The use of artificial light sources in mass culture of seaweeds to maintain or increase productivity is, at present energy costs, prohibitive, although it may be cost-effective under special conditions, for example in the maintenance of seed-stock culture during winter. In intensive tank cultivation experiments in Sweden using submerged artificial light sources delivering up to 1450 μmol photons m^{-2} s^{-1}; the specific growth rate of *Gracilaria secundata* reached 47% day^{-1}, one of the highest values reported for cultivated seaweeds (Lignell *et al.* 1987).

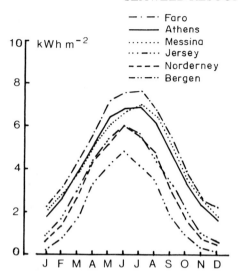

Figure 1. Monthly mean daily global irradiation in different parts of Europe

As with irradiation, temperature of the surface seawater along European coasts varies considerably with latitude and season.

Mean minimum temperatures in January and maximum temperatures in August of the surface water range from below 0 to 20 °C and above in the Baltic, from 0 to 20 °C in the German Bight, from 7 to 22 °C along the Atlantic coasts, and from 6 to 26 °C in the Mediterranean (Kuhlbrodt 1954; Gorshkov 1978; Fig. 2). Optimal temperature for productivity varies from species to species, but for surface forms it is generally in the range of the natural environmental conditions pertaining in early summer. During summer, under intensive solar irradiation, water temperatures may increase to detrimental levels, particularly in comparatively small water bodies such as land-based culture systems and in shallow sea areas, whereas at winter temperatures growth very often ceases completely. In onshore cultures of *Chondrus crispus* in Nova Scotia, for example, photosynthesis dropped off rapidly above 18 °C, and temperatures in excess of 20 °C over extended periods damaged or even killed plants (Bidwell *et al.* 1984).

Temperature control is therefore vital for sustained yield. Increase in seawater exchange rates is usually sufficient to maintain at least the ambient seawater temperature and to avoid overheating through insolation or freezing in winter (see Bidwell *et al.* 1985). Flush water may be obtained from greater depths below the thermocline, where the seawater is cooler in summer and warmer in winter compared with the surface water. Lignell and Pedersen (1986), for example, used seawater from 40 m depths with a nearly constant temperature of about 7 °C throughout the year for spray cultures in Sweden.

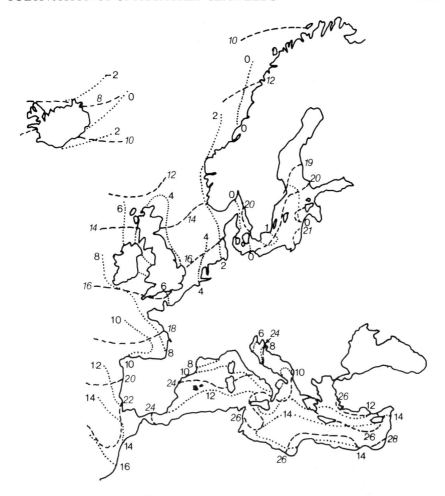

Figure 2. Mean maximum (August – – –) and minimum (January ⋯) temperature of surface seawater

In Hawaii, an OTEC-like system (Ocean Thermal Energy Conversion; Roels *et al.* 1978) was used to supply batch cultures of *Porphyra tenera* (nori) with a 15 °C mixture of nutrient-rich, cold, deep water (6 °C, 600 m depth) and warm (25 °C) surface water (Mencher *et al.* 1983). In larger culture systems, such as lagoons and culture ponds, where water exchange rates cannot easily be increased, increased water depth may help to protect the seaweeds from detrimental surface temperatures (Chiang 1981; Horstmann 1983).

For the heating of larger pond systems in Israel, cooling water from power plants has been utilized (e.g. Friedlander & Zelikovitch 1984). Another possibility is the use of waste heat sources such as municipal waste waters. In

Kiel (Baltic Sea), for example, effluents from the secondary treatment step of urban sewage have temperatures above $10\,°C$, even during the coldest months. A simple pipe system for heat exchange ($0.5\,m^2\,m^{-2}$) across the tank bottom was found to be sufficient to maintain water temperatures in $30\,m^3$ culture tanks at $2–5\,°C$, even when air temperature dropped to $-10\,°C$ (Koske et al. 1984; Schramm & Lehnberg 1985). Besides temperature control, the main purpose of water exchange is to supply nutrients as well as carbon for organic matter production, and to remove waste materials. To a certain extent, water exchange rates also restrict the development of epiphytes and grazers by flushing away these competing organisms from the seaweeds.

Lapointe and Ryther (1978) studied the effect of varying flow rates (1–30 water exchanges per day) on the growth of Gracilaria tikvahiae, with either the nutrient concentration in the cultures or nutrient loading of the inflowing seawater held constant. In both cases yield increased from 5 to 40 g dry weight $m^{-2}\,day^{-1}$ at 1–30 volume exchanges per day. Since both systems were vigorously aerated, the authors suggested that the water flow was not responsible for the effect as such, but perhaps the removal of growth-inhibiting metabolic wastes was one of the main causes for the positive effects on growth. Similarly, Fujita and Goldman (1984) observed that increase of water exchange from 5 to 20 volumes per day increased the specific growth rate (μ) of Gracilaria tikvahiae by 100%. Comparable results were obtained in similar experiments with the same species (Lapointe & Ryther 1979). Production of Ulva lactuca from Florida increased by 90–300% with increasing water exchange rates from 1 to 12 volumes day^{-1}, respectively. Further increase of the flushing rates up to 24 changes day^{-1} did not further enhance growth (DeBusk et al. 1986). In these experiments, a strong influence of water exchange on pH was observed. Fluctuation in pH between 8.6 and 9.5 (incoming seawater was at pH 8.3) occurred in the cultures at one volume exchange per day, suggesting carbon depletion. The effects of pH and carbon supply on cultivated seaweeds have been repeatedly studied. Decreased primary productivity of Gracilaria tikvahiae at high pH values (Blinks 1963; Ryther & Debusk 1982) was primarily attributed to lower levels of free carbon dioxide and an inability to assimilate bicarbonate, although later investigations showed that photosynthesis was more dependent on the concentration of bicarbonate than on free carbon dioxide (Blakeslee 1986).

The effects of pH and carbon supply on growth of Gracilaria tikvahiae were investigated in detail by DeBusk and Ryther (1984). In flow-through mode cultures, productivity increased significantly with increasing water-exchange rates when pH was acid-controlled (hydrochloric acid), although no additional carbon source was supplied. In batch-mode cultures (aerated 600 litre tanks without water exchange), pH increased to 9.5 during the day, and yields were comparatively low ($4.4\,g$ dry weight $m^{-2}\,day^{-1}$). Whereas adjustment to pH 8 with acid did not enhance productivity, addition of a carbon source (carbon dioxide, sodium bicarbonate) and pH adjustment increased yields five-fold. The authors concluded from the results that high yields in onshore cultivation of seaweeds would require either a rapid exchange of seawater or the control of pH and carbon supply. Hanisak (1987) pointed out that in land-based cultivation systems, instead of expensive pumping of seawater, it may be more cost-effective to develop other methods of pH and carbon control, such as utilization of acid wastes and recycling of carbon dioxide from combustion or fermentation processes (Hanisak 1981).

Sparging with air, no matter how vigorously, is inadequate to increase dissolved inorganic carbon, because the carbon dioxide content of air is low compared with the inorganic carbon content of seawater (28 mg carbon kg^{-1} seawater at 35‰ salinity) and dissolves relatively slowly into seawater. Significant increase in production by means of carbon dioxide addition was also observed in *Chondrus crispus* (Simpson *et al.* 1978; Bidwell *et al.* 1985). Dispersion or dissolving was more effective than bubbling or sparging with carbon dioxide. Efficiency (the amount of seaweed produced per unit carbon dioxide used) was highest at a constant pH setting of 7.7. Compared with a constant setting of pH 8.3 (= 100%), at pH 7.7 production was 228%, carbon dioxide used 183% and efficiency 125%, respectively, over a 6 month period.

Besides radiant energy and carbon, mineral nutrients control primary production to a great extent. Maximal yields are possible only when nutrients are not growth limiting. Seawater contains large enough quantities of the macronutrients magnesium, calcium, potassium and sulphate, and generally also of micronutrients, such as cobalt, molybdenum, zinc and boron, to supply the needs of the plants. The nutrient elements nitrogen and phosphorus, however, vary considerably from sea area to sea area and from season to season, and may become limiting, particularly during the summer months, and at high culture densities (e.g. Morgan *et al.* 1980; Guist *et al.* 1982). Supply of additional nutrients is therefore necessary to optimize production, but also to assure the quality of the seaweeds. Depending on the culture conditions, particularly supply of nutrients, the chemical composition of the algae, such as phycocolloid, pigment or protein content, can vary considerably (e.g. Neish *et al.* 1977; Hanisak 1979, 1983; Bird *et al.* 1981). Mean annual production of unfertilized *Hypnea musciformis*, for example, increased 4–5 times when nitrogen and phosphorus salts were added, although carrageenan content was inversely related to growth and decreased from 44.3 to 27.7%. However, carrageenan content of the fertilized material could be increased again by discontinuing fertilization for 2 weeks (Guist *et al.* 1982). Although the physiology and ecophysiology of mineral nutrition of cultivated seaweeds has been studied extensively (e.g. DeBoer *et al.* 1978; D'Elia & DeBoer 1978; Lapointe & Ryther 1979; McLachlan 1982; Dawes *et al.* 1984), more recent investigations suggest that in mass cultivation of unattached seaweeds complex relationships exist between culture density, flushing rates, agitation, carbon supply, season, epiphytism and nutrient requirements (DeBusk & Ryther 1984; Bidwell *et al.* 1985; DeBusk *et al.* 1986; Dawes 1987). Exploratory growth assays showed that in mass cultivation of unattached seaweeds, increase of water exchange rates seems to be the most effective way of increasing nutrient availability and yields. Above a minimal nutrient loading, the yield of *Gracilaria tikvahiae*, for example, was independent of nutrient loading, nutrient concentration and type of nutrient source (ammonia, nitrate), but highly dependent on flow rate (Lapoint & Ryther 1978, 1979). Thus, water exchange may compensate for nutrient depletion, especially in winter when nutrient concentrations are usually higher and growth rates are lower than in summer. In cultivation experiments with *Iridaea cordata*, doubling of seawater flow rate had the same positive effect on productivity as doubling of nutrient supply (Waaland 1976). In tropical and subtropical waters, and also in temperate seas (e.g. the Baltic) during the summer, nutrient concentrations may be so low that they become limiting to production even at maximal water exchange rates. In this instance, addition of nitrogen and phosphorus above the natural seawater levels can increase yields substantially.

At first sight, it would seem that continuous addition of nutrients is the best way to maximize yield and quality of the seaweed harvest, but in fact such practice is wasteful and not justifiable economically, because a substantial portion of the nutrients added may be lost with the flushing water. However, seaweeds have a considerable capacity to absorb nutrients rapidly at high concentration levels; these are then stored in the plants and later utilized when external nutrients are depleted (Hanisak 1979; Ryther *et al.* 1981). Pulse feeding of nutrients is a practical way of reducing fertilizing expenses. Experiments with *Chondrus crispus*, for example, showed that pulse feeding three times a week can be as effective as continuous daily addition of nutrients (Bidwell *et al.* 1985). This ability of seaweeds to store nutrients has led to the so-called 'soaking technique' in seaweed cultivation, in which after short soaking in enriched seawater the plants assimilate enough nutrients to grow at non-nutrient limited rates, even over extended periods.

Although radiant energy enhances nutrient absorption, further experiments showed little difference in production of *Chondrus crispus*, whether fertilized by day during periods of air agitation and water flushing, or by night when these were turned off and the nutrients added were thus retained in the culture tanks.

In many of the enrichment experiments with the cultivation of unattached seaweeds, expensive commercial fertilizers have been used (e.g. Waaland 1976). To reduce fertilizing costs, various alternative nutrient sources have been utilized in cultivation of unattached seaweeds. These include waste waters, such as effluents from sewage treatment plants or from mariculture systems, residues from biogas reactors, or nutrient-rich deep water.

Effluents from sewage treatment plants usually carry high loads of inorganic phosphorus and nitrogen, particularly ammonia. Some typical values for

Table 4. Nutrient loads (μmol dm^{-3}) of effluents from municipal sewage treatment plant in Kiel, Baltic Sea (Germany), servicing 270 000 inhabitants

1980–1984		Nitrite	Nitrate	Ammonia	Total nitrogen	Phosphate
Annual	Mean	236	106	40 544	40 891	6 775
Annual	Maximum	2562	1680	62 405	62 450	14 558
Annual	Minimum	0	0	15 750	15 810	1 394

average nutrient composition and loads of the final effluents from medium size municipal treatment plants are given in Table 4.

Because of the high concentration of ammonia and phosphates in sewage, even small admixtures of sewage to the seawater usually meet the nutrient demands of the seaweeds, so that no salinity effects due to dilution of the seawater occur. The suitability of municipal, industrial or agricultural waste waters as cheap nutrient sources in cultivation of unattached seaweeds has been demonstrated by several investigations outside Europe (e.g. Haines 1975; Guist & Humm 1976; Ryther *et al.* 1979; Gellenbek 1984; see also Chapter 6).

In Europe, only a few attempts have been made to utilize waste water as a nutrient source. For example, in experiments primarily aimed at sewage treatment and recycling of nutrients (Lehnberg & Schramm 1984; Schramm & Lehnberg 1984, 1985), tertiary effluents from the municipal sewage treatment plant of the city of Kiel were added (10–55%) to cultures of green algae adapted to brackish water conditions (*Enteromorpha linza, E. prolifera, E. intestinalis, Percursaria percursa*). Similarly, in southern France (Montpellier), brackish water-adapted macrophytes, predominantly the water hyacinth *Eichhornia crassipes* and the green alga *Enteromorpha intestinalis*, were grown in semi-artificial environments receiving waste waters for water purification and biomass production (Chassany de Casabianca 1982). In outdoor tank cultivation experiments with *Ulva lactuca* from the coast of Brittany, France, Houvenaghel and Mathot (1983) used urban sewage, rural run-off and liquid pig-manure as a fertilizer. Examples of the utilization of uncontrolled sewage enrichment are the lagoons of Venice, Orbetello and Lesina in Italy, where the agarophyte *Gracilaria verrucosa* is commercially harvested, or *Ulva rigida* and other seaweeds are used for biogas production (Orlandini & Favretto 1988).

Another promising approach is the recycling of nutrients within 'energy farms' or the re-use of wastes from mariculture systems. In mass cultures of *Gracilaria tikvahiae* for biogas production, for example, the nutrient-rich residues from biogas reactors have been further utilized to enrich the seaweed cultures (Hanisak 1981). In this way up to 73% of the nitrogen added was recycled. Examples for re-use of mariculture waste effluents are given by

Haines (1975) and Langton *et al.* (1977) who utilized among other alternative nutrient sources the effluents from a clam mariculture system for cultivation of *Hypnea musciformis.*

Deep water from below discontinuity layers usually contains considerably higher nutrient concentrations than surface water. The suitability of this nutrient resource for the cultivation of unattached seaweeds has been demonstrated by Haines (1975), for example, who used water from 870 m depth to grow the tropical carrageenophyte *Hypnea musciformis.* In Hawaii, Mencher *et al.* (1983) cultivated unattached *Porphyra* in mixtures of artificially upwelled seawater (OTEC system) from 600 m depth, containing 44 μmol nitrogen l^{-1}, 3.2 μmol phosphorus l^{-1} and surface water with 0.6 μmol nitrogen l^{-1} and 0.2 μmol phosphorus l^{-1}, respectively. The nutrient concentrations in seawater from 40 m depth used by Lignell and Pedersen (1986) for spray culture of various seaweeds (see Table 1) were approximately 8 μmol inorganic nitrogen l^{-1} and 0.8 μmol phosphate-phosphorus l^{-1} in July (nearly 10 μmol inorganic nitrogen l^{-1} and 0.9 μmol phosphate-phosphorus l^{-1} in January), while the surface water contained undetectable levels of both nitrogen and phosphorus in summer (9.6 μmol nitrogen l^{-1} and 0.6 μmol phosphorus l^{-1} during winter).

Closely related to nutrient supply is the infestation of seaweed cultures with epiphytes, one of the major problems and constraints to seaweed cultivation. High nutrient concentrations, particularly in combination with high levels of irradiation and increased temperatures, usually favour the development of epiphytic green (*Enteromorpha, Ulva*) and blue-green algae, but also some brown and red algae (e.g. *Ectocarpus, Ceramium*) as well as diatoms (Morgan *et al.* 1980; Bidwell *et al.* 1985; Hanisak 1987). To a certain extent, epiphytization can be controlled by manipulation of these factors. Lower light levels reduced epiphyte growth without a substantial decrease of yields in *Chondrus crispus* and *Gracilaria sjoestedtii* (Enright 1979; Hansen 1984). Studies have been made of the effects of coloured illumination; both red and green light favoured the growth of *Chondrus crispus* over green algal epiphytes (Neish *et al.* 1977). An effective method of control is to increase stocking density and agitation, probably because lower levels of light inhibit the growth of epiphytes and mechanical action removes them (Neish *et al.* 1977; Bidwell *et al.* 1985; DeBusk *et al.* 1986). Bioactive substances may be released by the host plants at higher culture densities; these may play a role in epiphyte control, but no investigations appear to have been carried out. Pulse feeding of higher levels of nutrients, instead of continuous supply, is another method of alleviating epiphyte problems, as shown, for example, in cultivation of *Gracilaria* (Hanisak 1979).

In the cultivation of intertidal forms, advantage can be taken of their adaptation to emersion. Intermittent spraying and slight desiccation of spray-cultured *Ascophyllum nodosum* not only increased production, but also reduced epiphytes like *Ulva, Enteromorpha* and *Pilayella* (Lignell &

Pedersen 1986). Similarly, *Gracilaria sjoestedtii* cultivated in raceways, when plants were exposed daily following the natural tidal cycle, showed higher production and were almost completely free of epiphyte infestation (Hansen 1984). Biological control of epiphytes has been suggested by Shacklock and Doyle (1983), who found that grazers such as the crustaceans *Gammarus lawrencianus* and *Idotea baltica* grazed selectively on *Enteromorpha* and *Ectocarpus* in *Chondrus crispus* cultures.

Herbicides for 'weed' control as tested, for example, in *Porphyra* culture (Imada & Abe 1982), do not appear to have been used in the cultivation of unattached seaweeds, except for a study on the effects of two commercial herbicides on carbon dioxide uptake rates of *Gracilaria tikvahiae* (Lloyd *et al.* 1981).

Agitation of cultures of unattached seaweeds is important for several reasons; water movement helps to break down diffusion gradients and to reduce the boundary layer on the surface of the plants, greatly influencing the exchange rates of nutrients, metabolic gases and waste products. In addition, circulation of the water is necessary to avoid temperature or chemical gradients, and to keep the seaweeds in motion, so that at higher stocking densities, in particular, individual plants are alternately exposed to light at the surface and plunged into darkness. As pointed out above, agitation may also help to remove, mechanically, sediments, epiphytes and epizoons (DeBusk *et al.* 1986). Various methods of water agitation have been tested, including circulation of the water with pumps, and the use of paddle wheels (Neish *et al.* 1977; Simpson *et al.* 1978) and mixing boards (Balloni *et al.* 1982). The most frequently used method, however, is aeration, which has been found to be trouble-free and far more energy-efficient than paddle wheels, creation of artificial waves, or pumping. The operational principle is to create circulating cells of water by rows of air bubbles rising from air pipes across the bottom of the culture tank (e.g. Lapointe & Ryther 1978; Bidwell *et al.* 1985). The effects of alternate exposure of the plants circulating with the water to maximal surface irradiation and lower light levels or darkness on the bottom of the culture tanks have been investigated by Bidwell *et al.* (1985). In *Chondrus crispus* primary production (carbon dioxide uptake) increased by 20–50% at 90–700 μmol photons $m^{-2} s^{-1}$ when light–dark cycles of about 1–1.5 min were used instead of continuous light. This interesting phenomenon may be a similar effect to that observed in higher plants which photosynthesize more efficiently when dark periods of several seconds are administered.

Costs for agitation can be reduced considerably without major sacrifices in yields through intermittent aeration (DeBusk *et al.* 1986). In tank cultures of *Ulva lactuca* (1 kg wet weight m^{-2}, 700 litres, 10 volume exchanges per day), aeration for 1 min on and 5 min off, corresponding to 4 h agitation per day, effectively reduced energy costs for aeration by 83%; however, it should be noted that production increased by only 28% when aeration was used. DeBusk *et al.* (1986) suggest that aeration time could be further reduced to daytime only, if better utilization by the seaweeds of intermittent compared with continuous light is the primary effect of aeration – a strategy also employed by Bidwell *et al.* (1985) in the cultivation of *Chondrus crispus*. Closely related to agitation and availability of radiant energy is the stocking density of the cultures. Ryther *et al.* (1979) demonstrated that specific growth rates of *Gracilaria tikvahiae* decrease exponentially with increasing stocking density (biomass per unit area). As production or yield per unit area is a product of specific growth rate and culture density, yield describes a bell-shaped curve, where at low densities the plants are unable to utilize all of the incident radiant energy, whereas at high densities self-shading reduces yield. Optimal stocking density varies from species to species and depends to a great extent on the morphology of the seaweeds and on the culture conditions (water exchange, agitation) and season (solar energy, temperature). The specific growth rate of *G. tikvahiae*, for example, was optimal (60% day^{-1}) at 0.4 kg wet weight m^{-2} stocking density, while maximum yield was obtained at 2–3 kg wet weight m^{-2} (Lapointe & Ryther 1978). Optimal stocking densities (wet weight m^{-2}) have been reported for *Hypnea musciformis* (1.9 kg), *Iridaea cordata* (2.1 kg), *Chondrus crispus* (3–4 kg), *Ulva lactuca*, *U. fasciata* (0.8 kg) and *Palmaria palmata* (3–10 kg) (Neish 1976; Waaland 1976; Simpson *et al.* 1978; Lapointe & Ryther 1978; Guist *et al.* 1982; DeBusk *et al.* 1986; Morgan *et al.* 1980). The influence of seasonal variations in solar energy on optimal stocking density has been studied in outdoor cultures of *Chondrus crispus* in France (Braud & Delépine 1980). Optimal density increased from 2.1 kg wet weight m^{-2} in January to 5 kg m^{-2} in August.

Many aspects for the critical assessment of the potential and future of aquaculture discussed by Kinne (1980) apply also to seaweed cultivation in Europe. As the basic requirements for mariculture are suitable cultivation sites (either in the sea or on land), labour and energy sources, the conditions for cultivation of seaweeds in Europe at first sight seem to be unfavourable compared with most other parts of the world, mainly for two reasons. In northern Europe, where shallow coastal areas such as embayments, fjords and archipelagos suitable for *in situ* cultivation are found, the climatic conditions (solar radiation and seawater temperature) would be favourable only during the summer. Southern Europe, on the other hand, is more favourable with regard to climatic conditions, but the traditional methods of seaweed culture in the waters along the more densely populated coastal regions would be limited. The major constraints facing potential seaweed farmers are other competitive interests and conflicting utilization of sea areas as fishing grounds, recreational areas and wildlife sanctuaries, military reserves, discharge of sewage or dumping of industrial wastes and pollutants.

In addition, the coastal areas of most European countries are either state property or belong to international waters (see Chapter 11 for legal aspects). These activities severely reduce the suitable sea area available for seaweed farming. Apart from difficulties in obtaining permission from the authorities laying claim to sea areas, other legal problems may arise from possible negative or at least unpredictable effects of culture operations on the normal functioning of the ecosystem, for example, through pollution, translocation, introduction or suppression of organisms (see Kinne 1980). Intensive cultivation of unattached seaweeds is characterized by a high level of production efficiency per unit area and control of environmental factors, including a certain independence from local climate and seawater quality. On the other hand, operating costs, energy input and technological requirements are relatively high. Comparing the world potential of marine primary biomass production, non-industrialized tropical or subtropical areas with the potential for cheap labour are more promising areas for seaweed culture at present.

There are factors, however, that may justify intensive culture of unattached seaweeds in Europe. Among these is abundant availability of cheap waste resoures such as heated or nutrient-rich waste waters, which may offer local opportunities. In addition, utilization of waste resources for intensive cultivation of seaweeds will help to reduce pollution and eutrophication of coastal ecosystems and protect natural seaweed resources.

A final consideration is that seaweeds with desirable properties (products, growth forms, productivity, etc.) will be developed by means of genetic improvement and cloning; these plants will probably be grown only under controlled conditions, such as in intensive cultivation of unattached seaweeds.

REFERENCES

Asare S.O. 1980. Animal waste as nitrogen source for *Gracilaria tikvahiae* and *Neoagardhiella baileyi* in culture. *Aquaculture* **21**: 87–91.

Augier H. 1978. Utilisation des algues et potentiel économique des végétaux marins. *Bull. Off. Nat. Pêches* (Tunisia) **2**: 249–302.

Balloni W., Florenzano G., Materassi R., Tredici M., Soeder C.J. & Wagner K. 1982. Mass cultures of algae for energy farming in coastal deserts. In *Proceedings of the 2nd E.C. Conference on Energy from Biomass*. (Eds. A. Strub, P. Chatier & G. Schleser) pp. 291–4. London: Applied Science.

Bidwell R.G.S., Lloyd N.D.H. & McLachlan J. 1984. The performance of *Chondrus crispus* (Irish moss) in laboratory simulation of environments in different locations. *Proceedings of the 11th International Seaweed Symposium*. (Eds. C.J. Bird & M. Ragan) pp. 292–4. Dordrecht: Dr. W. Junk.

Bidwell R.G.S., McLachlan J. & Lloyd N.D.H. 1985. Tank cultivation of Irish moss, *Chondrus crispus* Stackh. *Botanica Mar.* **28**: 87–97.

Bird K.T. 1988. Agar production and quality from *Gracilaria* sp. Strain G-16: Effects of environmental factors. *Botanica Mar.* **31**: 33–9.

Bird R.N.L., Chen L.C.-M. & McLachlan J. 1979. Effects of temperature, light and salinity on growth in culture of *Chondrus crispus, Furcellaria lumbricalis, Gracilaria tikvahiae* (Gigartinales, Rhodophyta) and *Fucus serratus* (Fucales, Phaeophyta). *Botanica Mar.* **22**: 521–7.

Bird K.T., Hanisak M.D. & Ryther J.H. 1981. Chemical quality and production of agars extracted from *Gracilaria tikvahiae* grown in different nitrogen enrichment conditions. *Botanica Mar.* **24**: 441–4.

Blakeslee M. 1984. Engineering aspects of carbon supply for land-based algae farms. M.S. thesis, Univ. Florida, Gainesville, USA. pp. 160.

Blakeslee M. 1986. Determination of carbon concentration effects of photosynthesis: a pH independent approach. *Nova Hedwigia* **83**: 79–94.

Blindova E.I. 1984. [Seaweed culture and its prospects.] *Ryb. Khoz.* **8**: 33–37, (in Russian).

Blinks L.R. 1963. The effect of pH upon the photosynthesis of littoral marine algae. *Phycologia* **57**: 126–63.

Braud J.P. & Delépine R. 1980. Growth response of *Chondrus crispus* (Rhodophyta, Gigartinales) to light and temperature in laboratory and outdoor tank culture. In *Proceedings of the 10th International Seaweed Symposium* (Ed. T. Levring) pp. 553–8. Berlin: De Gruyter.

Chapman A.R.O. 1973. Methods for macroscopic algae. In *Handbook of phycological methods* (Ed. J.R. Stein). Culture methods and growth measurements. pp. 87–104. Cambridge: Cambridge University Press.

Chapman V.J. & Chapman D.J. 1980. *Seaweeds and their uses.* Edn. 2. pp. 334. London: Chapman and Hall.

Chassany de Casabianca M.L. 1980. Données et problèmes écologiques concernant l'aquaculture de la biomasse végétale en milieu saumâtre. *La Technique de l'Eau et de l'Assainissement* **398**: 28–31.

Chassany de Casabianca M.L. 1982. Systèmes de production à macrophytes saumâtres sur eaux résiduaires urbaines. *La Technique de l'Eau et de l'Assainissement* **422**: 17–22.

Cheney D.P. 1984. Genetic modification in seaweeds: applications to commercial utilization and cultivation. In *Biotechnology in the Marine Sciences* (Eds. R. Colwell, E. Parker & A. Sinsky) pp. 161–175. New York: Wiley-Interscience.

Cheney D., Mathieson A. & Schubert D. 1981. The application of genetic improvement techniques to seaweed cultivation I. Strain selection in the carrageenophyte *Chondrus crispus*. In *Proceedings of the 10th International Seaweed Symposium* (Ed. T. Levring) pp. 559–67. Berlin: De Gruyter.

Chiang Y.M. 1981. Cultivation of *Gracilaria* (Rhodophyta, Gigartinales) in Taiwan. In *Proceedings of the 10th International Seaweed Symposium* (Ed. T. Levring) pp. 553–8. Berlin: De Gruyter.

Chock J.S. & Mathieson A.C. 1979. Physiological ecology of *Ascophyllum nodosum* (L.) Le Jolis and its detached ecad *scorpioides* (Hornemann) Hauck (Fucales, Phaeophyta). *Bot. Mar.* **22**: 21–6.

Dawes C.J. 1987. The biology of commercially important tropical marine algae. In *Seaweed cultivation for renewable resources* (Eds. K.T. Bird & P.H. Benson) pp. 155–190. Amsterdam: Elsevier.

Dawes C.J., Chen C.P., Jewett-Smith J., Marsh J. & Watts S.A. 1984. Effects of phosphate and ammonium levels on photosynthetic and respiratory response of the red alga *Gracilaria verrucosa*. *Mar. Biol.* Berlin **78**: 325–8.

DeBoer J.A. 1979. Effects of nitrogen enrichment on growth rate and phycocolloid content in *Gracilaria foliifera* and *Neoagardhiella baileyi* (Florideophyceae). In *Proceedings of the 9th International Seaweed Symposium* (Eds. A. Jensen & J.R. Stein) pp. 263–71. Princeton: Science Press.

DeBoer J.A. & Ryther J.H. 1977. Potential yields from a waste recycling algal mariculture system. In *The Marine Plant Biomass of the Pacific Northwest Coast* (Ed. R.W. Krauss) pp. 231–49. Corvallis: Oregon State University Press.

DeBoer J.A., Guigli H.J., Israel T.L. & D'Elia C.F. 1978. Nutritional studies of two red algae. I. Growth rate as a function of nitrogen source and concentration. *J. Phycol.* **14**: 261–66.

DeBusk T.A. & Ryther J.H. 1984. Effects of seawater exchange, pH and carbon supply on the growth of *Gracilaria tikvahiae* (Rhodophyceae) in large scale cultures. *Botanica Mar.* **27**: 357–62.

DeBusk T.A., Blakeslee M. & Ryther J.H. 1986. Studies on the outdoor cultivation of *Ulva lactuca* L. *Botanica Mar.* **29**: 381–6.

D'Elia C.F. & DeBoer J.A. 1978. Nutritional studies of two red algae. II. Kinetics of ammonium and nitrate uptake. *J. Phycol.* **14**: 266–72.

Doty M. 1979. Status of marine agronomy, with special reference to the tropics. In *Proceedings of the 9th International Seaweed Symposium* (Eds. A. Jensen & J.R. Stein) pp. 35–58. Princeton: Science Press.

Dreno J.P., Perez R. & Barbaroux O. 1984. L'algue rouge *Eucheuma spinosum*. Un essai de culture intensive en milieu enrichi. *Sci. Pêche* **348**: 10–20.

Edelstein T., Bird C.J. & McLachlan J. 1976. Studies on *Gracilaria* growth under greenhouse conditions. *Can. J. Bot.* **54**: 2275–90.

Edwards P. & Tam D.M 1984. The potential for *Gracilaria* farming in Thailand. In *Proceedings of the 11th International Seaweed Symposium* (Eds. C.J. Bird and M.A. Ragan) pp. 246–8. Dordrecht: Junk.

Enright C. 1979. Competitive interaction between *Chondrus crispus* (Florideophyceae) and *Ulva lactuca* (Chlorophyceae) in *Chondrus* aquaculture. In *Proceedings of the 9th International Seaweed Symposium* (Eds. A. Jensen & J.R. Stein) pp. 209–18. Princeton: Science Press.

Fralick J.E. 1971. The effect of harvesting *Iridaea* on a sublittoral marine plant community in Northern Washington. M.Sc. thesis. Western Washington State College, Bellingham, pp. 57.

Friedlander M. & Lipkin Y. 1982. Rearing agarophytes and carrageenophytes under field conditions in the east Mediterranean. *Botanica Mar.* **25**: 101–5.

Friedlander M. & Zelikovitch N. 1984. Growth rates, phycocolloid yield and quality of the red seaweeds, *Gracilaria* sp., *Pterocladia capillacea*, *Hypnea musciformis* and *Hypnea cornuta*, in field studies in Israel. *Aquaculture* **40**: 57–66.

Fujita R.M. & Goldman J.C. 1984. Nutrient flux and growth of the red alga *Gracilaria tikvahiae* McLachlan (Rhodophyta). *Bot. Mar.* **28**: 265–8.

Gellenbek K. 1984. Growth characteristics, nutrient uptake and reproduction of *Sargassum muticum* in free-floating culture. *J. Phycol.* **20**: Suppl. p. 4 (Abstract).

Giaccone G., Princi M., Feoli E., Locar Coassini L., Rizzi Longo L. & Tortul V. 1979. Valutazione delle risorse vegtali lagunari del basso Tirreno e sperimentazione die coltivazione controllata dell'alga rossa *Gracilaria verrucosa e di altre agarofite in Sicilia*. *Atti Conv. Scient. Nazion. Oceanografia e Fondi Marini, Roma.* **1**: 423–35.

Goldman J.C. & Ryther J.H. 1977. Mass production of algae: bioengineering aspects. In *Biological solar energy conversion* (Eds. A. Mitsui, S. Miyachi, A. SanPietro & S. Tamura). pp. 363–78. New York: Academic Press.

Gorshkov G. 1978. *World Ocean Atlas*. Vol. 2. Atlantic and Indian Ocean. Oxford: Pergamon Press.

Guerin J.M. & Bird K.T. 1987. Effects of aeration period on the productivity and agar quality of *Gracilaria* sp. *Aquaculture* **64**: 105–10.

Guist G.G. & Humm H.J. 1976. Effects of sewage effluent on growth of *Ulva lactuca*. *Florida Scientist* **39**: 267–71.

Guist G.G., Dawes C.J. & Castle J.R. 1982. Mariculture of the red seaweed *Hypnea musciformis*. *Aquaculture* **28**: 375–84.

Guist G.G., Dawes C.J. & Castle, J.R. 1985. Mariculture of the red seaweed *Eucheuma isiforme*. *Florida Scientist* **48**: 56–58.

Haglund K. & Pedersen M. 1988. Spray cultivation of seaweeds in recirculating brackish water. *Aquaculture* **72**: 181–9.

Haines K.C. 1975. Growth of the carrageenan-producing tropical red seaweed *Hypnea musciformis* in surface water, 870 m deep water, effluent from a clam mariculture system and in deep water enriched with artificial fertilizers or domestic sewage. In *Proceedings of the 10th European Marine Biology Symposium* (Eds. A.G. Persoone & E. Jaspers) pp. 207–20. Wettern: Universa Press.

Hanisak M.D. 1979. Cultivation and bioenergetics of the agarophyte *Gracilaria tikvahiae*. International Council for the Exploration of the Sea, Code Nr. C.M. 1979/F24, pp. 8.

Hanisak M.D. 1981. Recycling the residues from anaerobic digesters as a nutrient source for seaweed growth. *Bot. Mar.* **24**: 57–61.

Hanisak M.D. 1983. The nitrogen relationships of marine macroalgae. In *Nitrogen in the marine environment* (Eds. E.J. Carpenter & D.G. Capone) pp. 699–730. New York: Academic Press.

Hanisak M.D. 1987. Cultivation of *Gracilaria* and other macroalgae in Florida for energy production. In *Seaweed cultivation for renewable resources* (Eds. K.T. Bird & P.H. Bensson) pp. 191–218. Amsterdam: Elsevier.

Hanisak M.D. & Ryther J.H. 1984. Cultivation biology of *Gracilaria tikvahiae* in the United States. In *Proceedings of the 11th International Seaweed Symposium* (Eds. C.J. Bird & M.A. Ragan) pp. 295–98. Dordrecht: Junk.

Hanisak M.D. & Ryther J.H. 1986. The experimental cultivation of the red seaweed *Gracilaria tikvahiae* as an 'energy crop'. *Nova Hedwigia* **83**: 212–17.

Hanisak M.D. & Samuel M.A. 1983. The influence of major environmental factors on growth of *Gracilaria tikvahiae* (Rhodophyceae) in culture. *J. Phycol.* **19**: suppl. 6 (Abstract).

Hanisak M.D. & Samuel M.A. 1987. Growth rates in culture of several species of *Sargassum* from Florida, USA. In *Proceedings of the 12th International Seaweed Symposium* (Eds. M.A. Ragan & C.J. Bird) pp. 112–19. Dordrecht: Junk.

Hansen J.E. 1983. A physiological approach to mariculture of red algae. *J. World Maricult. Soc.* **14**: 380–91.

Hansen J.E. 1984. Strain selection and physiology in the development of *Gracilaria* mariculture. In *Proceedings of the 11th International Seaweed Symposium* (Eds. C.J. Bird & M.A. Ragan) pp. 89–94. Dordrecht: Junk.

Harlin M.M., Thorn-Miller B. & Thusby G.B. 1979. Ammonium uptake by *Gracilaria* spec. (Florideophyceae) and *Ulva lactuca* (Chlorophyceae) in closed system fish culture. In *Proceedings of the 9th International Seaweed Symposium* (Eds. A. Jensen & J.R. Stein) pp. 285–92. Princeton: Science Press.

Horstmann U. 1983. Cultivation of the green alga *Caulerpa racemosa* in tropical waters and some aspects of its physiological ecology. *Aquaculture* **32**: 361–71.

Houvenaghel G.T. & Mathot J.F. 1983. The production of marine green algae in coastal waters and their culture in ponds enriched with waste waters. In *Energy from Biomass* (Eds. A. Strub, P. Chartier & G. Schleser) pp. 308–12. London: Applied Science Publ.

Huguenin J.E. 1976a. An examination of problems and potentials for future large-scale intensive seaweed culture systems. *Aquaculture* **9**: 313–42.

Huguenin J.E. 1976b. Heat exchangers for use in culturing of marine organisms. *Chesapeake Sci.* **17**: 61–4.

Imada O. & Abe T. 1982. Application of herbicides to the culture of *Porphyra*. *Bull. Jap. Soc. Fish.* **48**: 1507–16.

Imada O. & Saito Y. 1983. Application of powdered materials to substratum of conchospores of *Porphyra*. *Bull. Jap. Soc. Fish.* **49**: 399–407.

Indergaard M., Østgaard K. & Jensen. A. 1986. Growth studies of macrolagae in microcomputer-assisted spray cultivation system. *J. Exp. Mar. Biol. Ecol.* **98**: 199–213.

Jackson G.D. 1977. Biological constraints on seaweed culture. In *Biological solar energy conversion* (Eds. A. Mitsue, S. Miyahi & A. San Pietro) pp. 437–48. New York: Academic Press.

Jackson G.D. 1980. Marine biomass production through seaweed aquaculture. In *Biochemical and photosynthetic aspects of energy production* (Ed. A. San Pietro) pp. 31–58. New York: Academic Press.

Kinne O. 1980. Aquaculture, a critical assessment of its potential and future. *Interdisciplinary Science Rev.* **5**: 24–32.

Kinne O. 1984. Realism in aquaculture—the view of an ecologist. *Biologiya Marya* **6**: 3–11.

Koske P., Ohlrogge K., Witt U. & Lenz J. 1984. The use of sewage water as heat resource for aquaculture basins: technological aspects and first results. In *Proceedings of the 1st World Symposium: Aquaculture in heated effluents and recirculation systems* (Ed. K. Tiews) pp. 347–58. Berlin: Heinemann.

Kuhlbrodt E. 1954. Klimatologie der Nordeuropäischen Gewässer. Einzelveröff. Nr. 4. *Deutscher Wetterdienst*. Hamburg: Seewetteramt.

Langton R.W., Haines K.C. & Lyon R.E. 1977. Ammonia-nitrogen production by the bivalve molluscs *Tapes japonica* and its recovery by the red seaweed *Hypnea musciformis* in a tropical mariculture system. *Helgoländer Wiss. Meeresunters.* **30**: 217–29.

Lapointe B.E. 1985. Strategies for pulsed nutrient supply to *Gracilaria* cultures in the Florida keys: interaction between concentration and frequency of nutrient pulses. *J. Exp. Mar. Biol. Ecol.* **93**: 211–22.

Lapointe B.E. & Hanisak M.D. 1985. Productivity and nutrition of marine biomass systems in Florida. In *Proceedings of the 9th Symposium Energy from Biomass and Waste*. pp. 111–26. Chicago: Inst. Gas Technol.

Lapointe B.E. & Ryther J.H. 1978. Some aspects of the growth and yield of *Gracilaria tikvahiae* in culture. *Aquaculture* **15**: 185–93.

Lapointe B.E. and Ryther J. 1979. The effect of nitrogen and seawater flow rate on the growth and biochemical composition of *Gracilaria foliifera* var. *angustissima* in mass outdoor cultures. *Bot. Mar.* **22**: 529–37.

Lapointe B.E. & Tenore K.R. 1981. Experimental outdoor studies with *Ulva fasciata* Delile. I. Interaction of light and nitrogen on nutrient uptake, growth and biochemical composition. *J. Exp. Mar. Biol. Ecol.* **53**: 135–52.

Lapointe B.E., Williams L.D., Goldman J.C. & Ryther J.H. 1976. The mass outdoor culture of macroscopic marine algae. *Aquaculture* **8**: 9–21.

Lehnberg W. & Schramm W. 1984. Mass culture of brackish-water-adapted seaweeds in sewage-enriched seawater. I. Productivity and nutrient accumulation. In *Proceedings of the 11th International Seaweed Symposium* (Eds. C.J. Bird & M.A. Ragan) pp. 276–81. Princeton: Science Press.

Lenzi M. 1985. Valutazioni sulla possibilita di realizzare reccolte e coltivazioni della rodoficea *Gracilaria confervoides* Grev. nella laguna di Orbetello. *Atti Mus. Civ. Stor. Nat. Grosseto* **6**: 17–22.

Levine H.G. & Brinkhuis B.H. 1985. Size-specific growth in *Laminaria saccharina*— criterion for genetic selection. *J. Phycol.* **21** (Suppl.): 11 (Abstract).

Lignell A. & Pedersen M. 1986. Spray cultivation of seaweeds with emphasis on their light requirements. *Botanica Mar.* **24**: 509–16.

Lignell A., Ekman P. & Pedersén M. 1987. Cultivation technique for marine seaweeds allowing controlled and optimized conditions in the laboratory and on pilot scale. *Botanica Mar.* **30**: 417–24.

Lloyd N.D.H., McLachlan J.L. & Bidwell R.G.S. 1981. A rapid infra-red carbon dioxide analysis screening technique for predicting growth and productivity of marine algae. In *Proceedings of the 10th International Seaweed Symposium* (Ed. T. Levring) pp. 461–6. Berlin: De Gruyter.

Maegawa M. & Aruga Y. 1983. Photosynthesis and productivity of the cultivated *Monostroma latissimum* population. *Umi-Mer* **21**: 164–72.

Mathieson A.C. 1982. Seaweed cultivation: A review. In *Proceedings of the 11th USA-Japan Meeting on Aquaculture* (Ed. C.J. Sinderman). New Hampshire Agric. Exper. Stn. Sci. Contrib. 959.

Mathieson A.C. & North W.J. 1982. Algal aquaculture: introduction and bibliography. In *Selected papers in phycology II*. (Eds. J.R. Rosowski & B.C. Parker); pp. 773–87. Phycol. Soc. Am.

McLachlan L. 1982. Inorganic nutrition of marine macroalgae in culture. In *Synthetic and degradative processes in marine macrophytes* (Ed. L.M. Srivastava) pp. 71–98. Berlin: De Gruyter.

Mencher F.M., Spencer R.B., Woessner J.W., Katasa S.J. & Barclay D.K. 1983. Growth of nori (*Porphyra tenera*) in an experimental Otec-aquaculture system in Hawaii. *J. World Maricult. Soc.* **14**: 458–70.

Moeller H.W., Griffin G.F. & Lee V. 1982. Aquatic biomass production on sand using seawater spray. *Int. Gas Technol. Meetings* 1982, pp. 237–48.

Moeller H.W., Garber S.M. & Griffin G.F. 1984. Biology and economics of growing seaweeds on land in a film culture. In *Proceedings of the 11th International Seaweed Symposium* (Eds. C.J. Bird & M.A. Ragan) pp. 299–302. Dordrecht: Junk.

Morgan K.C., Shacklock P.F. & Simpson F.J. 1980. Some aspects of the culture of *Palmaria palmata* in greenhouse tanks. *Bot. Mar.* **23**: 765–70.

Mumford T.F. & Waaland J.R. 1980. Progress and prospects for field cultivation of *Iridea cordata* and *Gigartina exasperata*. In *Pacific seaweed culture* (Eds. I. Abbott., M. Fester & L. Eklund) pp. 92–106. San Diego: California Sea Grant Coll. Progr. Univ. Cal.

Neish I.C. 1976. Role of mariculture in Canadian seaweed industry. *J. Fish. Res. Bd. Canada* **33**: 1007–14.

Neish I.C. 1979. Principles and perspectives of the cultivation of seaweeds in enclosed systems. In *Actas I. Algas marinas chilenas* (Ed. B. Santelices) pp. 59–74. Santiago (Chile): Subsecretaria de Pesca, Ministerio de Economia Fomento y Reconstruccion.

Neish I.C. & Knutson L.B. 1979. The significance of density, suspension and water movement during commercial propagation of macrophyte clones. In *Proceedings of the 9th International Seaweed Symposium* (Eds. A. Jensen & J.R. Stein) pp. 451–61. Princeton: Science Press.

Neish I.C., Shacklock P.F., Fox C.H. & Simpson F.J. 1977. The cultivation of *Chondrus crispus*. Factors affecting growth under greenhouse conditions. *Can. J. Bot.* **55**: 2263–71.

Norton T.A. & Mathieson A.L. 1983. The biology of unattached seaweeds. In *Progress in phycological research* Vol. 2 (Eds. F.E. Round & D.J. Chapman) pp. 333–87. Amsterdam: Elsevier.

Palz W. (Ed.) 1984. Atlas über die Sonnenstrahlung Europas. Vol. 1 & 2. Kommission der Europäischen Gemeinschaften. Köln: Verl. TüV Rheinland.

Parker H.S. 1982. Effect of simulated current on the growth rate and nitrogen metabolism of *Gracilaria tikvahiae*. *Mar. Biol.* **69**: 137–49.

Raju P.V. & Thomas P.C. 1971. Experimental field cultivation of *Gracilaria edulis* (Gmel.) Silva. *Botanica Mar.* **14**: 71–5.

Rheault R.B. & Ryther J.H. 1983. Growth, yield and morphology of *Ascophyllum nodosum* (Phaeophyta) under continuous and intermittent spray culture regimes. *J. Phycol.* **19**: 252–4.

Rice D.L. & Lapointe B.E. 1981. Experimental outdoor studies with *Ulva lactuca* Delile. II. Trace metal chemistry. *J. Exp. Mar. Biol. Ecol.* **54**: 1–11.

Roels O.A., Laurence S., Farmer M.W. & VanHemelrych L. 1978. Organic production potentials of artificial upwelling marine culture. *Process. Biochem.* **13**: 18–23.

Rueness J. & Tananger T. 1984. Growth in culture of four red algae from Norway: weight potential for mariculture. In *Proceedings of the 11th International Seaweed Symposium* (Eds. C.J. Bird & M.A. Ragan) pp. 303–7. Dordrecht: Junk.

Ryther J.H. & DeBusk T.A. 1982. Significance of carbon dioxide and bicarbonate-carbon uptake in marine biomass production. In *Energy from biomass and waste* **7**, 221–36. Inst. Gas Technol., Chicago.

Ryther J.H., DeBoer J.A. & Lapointe B.E. 1978. Cultivation of seaweeds for hydrocolloids, waste treatment and biomass for energy conversion. In *Proceedings of the 9th International Seaweed Symposium* (Eds. A. Jensen & J.R. Stein) pp.1–16. Princeton: Science Press.

Ryther J.H., Corwin N., DeBusk T.A. & Wiliams L.D. 1981. Nitrogen uptake and storage by the red alga *Gracilaria tikvahiae* (McLachlan 1979). *Aquaculture* **26**: 107–15.

Ryther J.H., DeBusk T.A. & Blakeslee M. 1984. Cultivation and conversion of marine macroalgae. *Rep. Harbor Branch Found. Inc.* pp. 88.

Santelices B., Oliger P. & Montalva S. 1981. Production ecology of Chilean Gelidiales. In *Proceedings of the 10th International Seaweed Symposium* (Ed. T. Levring) pp. 351–6. Berlin: De Gruyter.

Sauze F. 1983. Increasing the productivity of macroalgae by the action of a variety of factors. In *Energy from biomass* (Eds. A. Strub, P. Chartier & G. Schleser) pp. 324–8. Luxembourg: Comm. Europ. Commun.

Schramm W. & Lehnberg W. 1984. Mass cultivation of brackish-water adapted seaweeds in sewage-enriched seawater. II. Fermentation for biogas production. In *Proceedings of the 11th International Seaweed Symposium* (Eds. C.J. Bird & M.A. Ragan) pp. 282–7. Dordrecht: Junk.

Shacklock P.F. & Doyle R.W. 1983. Control of epiphytes in seaweed cultures using grazers. *Aquaculture* **31**: 141–51.

Shang Y.C. 1976. Economic aspects of *Gracilaria* culture in Taiwan. *Aquaculture* **8**: 1–7.

Simonetti G., Giaccone G. & Pignatti S. 1970. The seaweed *Gracilaria confervoides*, an important object for autoecologic and cultivation research in the northern Adriatic Sea. *Helgoländer wiss. Meeresunters.* **20**: 89–96.

Simpson F.J. & Shacklock P.F. 1979. The cultivation of *Chondrus crispus*. Effect of temperature on growth and carrageenan production. *Botanica Mar.* **22**: 295–8.

Simpson F.J., Neish A.C., Shacklock P.F. & Robson D.R. 1978. The cultivation of *Chondrus crispus*. Effect of pH on growth and on production of carrageenan. *Botanica Mar.* **21**: 229–35.

Smith A.H., Nichols K. & McLachlan J.F. 1984. Culture of sea moss (*Gracilaria*) in St. Lucia, West Indies. In *Proceedings of the 11th International Seaweed Symposium* (Eds. C.J. Bird & M.A. Ragan) pp. 249–251. Dordrecht: Junk.

Toft-Frederiksen O. 1987. The fight against eutrophication in the inlet of 'Odense fjord' by reaping of sea lettuce (*Ulva lactuca*). *Wat. Sci. Techn.* **19**: 81–7.

Trono G.C. Jr. 1981. Pond culture of seaweeds. In *Report of a training course on* Gracilaria *algae* (Eds. G.C. Trono & E. Ganzon-Fortes) pp. 47–50. Manila, Philipp. 1981. FAO/UNDP South China Sea Fish. Devel. Coord. Progr.

Trotta P. 1981. On the rhodophyte *Gracilaria confervoides* Grev. in Lesina lagoon:

field survey and in vitro culture. Convegno Int. 2 Fitodepurazione e impieghi delle biomasse prodotte. Parma 1981.

Turner J.W.D., Sibbald R.R. & Hemens J. 1986. Chlorinated secondary domestic sewage effluent as a fertilizer for marine aquaculture. I. Tilapia culture. II. Protein supplemented prawn culture. *Aquaculture* **53**: 133–55.

van der Meer J. 1986. Genetic contributions to research on seaweeds. In *Progress in Phycological Research* Vol. 4 (Eds. F.E. Round & D.J. Chapman) pp. 1–39. Bristol: Biopress.

Waaland J.R. 1976. Growth of the red alga *Iridaea cordata* (Turner) Bory in semi-closed culture. *J. Exp. Mar. Biol.* **23**: 45–53.

Waaland J.R. 1977. Growth and strain selection in *Gigartina exasperata* (Florideophyceae). In *Proceedings of the 9th International Seaweed Symposium* (Eds. A. Jensen & J.R. Stein) pp. 241–8. Princeton: Science Press.

Waaland J.R. 1983. Cloning marine algae for mariculture. *J. World Maricult. Soc.* **14**: 404–14.

Wagener K. 1979. Mariculture on land: A system for biofuel farming in coastal deserts. *Biomass* **1**: 145–51.

Yang S.S. & Wang C.Y. 1983. Effects of environmental factors on *Gracilaria* cultivated in Taiwan. *Bull. Mar. Sci.* **33**: 759–66.

Zablakis E. 1987. The effect of salinity on growth rate and branch morphology in tank cultivated *Grateloupia filicina* in Hawaii. *Aquat. Bot.* **27**: 187–93.

Zhang Y.J., Yang Y.X., Wang Q.Y. & Wang S.R. 1985. Studies on the breeding and genetics of *Porphyra yezoensis* Ueda. *Trans. Oceanol. Limnol.* **4**: 44–52.

ASSOCIATED TECHNICAL REPORTS

Edbom A. 1980. Investigation of the possibilities of combined production from Swedish algae. Rep. NTIS, pp. 124.

Edler L., Emmelin L. & von Wachenfeldt T. 1980. Marin biomassa: alger som energikälla. Techn. Rep. Nämden för energiproduktions forskning, Stockholm., pp. 100.

Neish A.C., & Shacklock P.F. 1971. Greenhouse experiments on the propagation of strain T-4 of Irish moss. *Techn. Rep. Nat. Res. Counc. Atlant. Reg. Lab.* **14**: 1–25.

Orlandini M. and Favretto L. 1988. Utilization of macroalgae in Italy for pollution abatement and as source of energy and chemicals. In *Proceedings of the 1st Workshop COST 48, subgroup 3* (Ed. P. Morand & E.H. Schulte) pp. 25–8. Brussels: Comm. Europ. Commun.

Schramm W. & Lehnberg W. 1985. 1. Aufnahme und Akkumulation anorganischer Nährstoffe durch benthische Großalgen aus Abwässern. 2. Untersuchungen zur Produktion und Fermentation mariner Primärbiomasse unter Verwendung von Kulturen benthischer Großalgen in abwasserangereichertem Meerwasser. pp. 1–26. Kiel: Schlußbericht MFE 0501-BMFT.

13 Conclusions and Outlooks

M.D. GUIRY[1] **and G. BLUNDEN**[2]

[1]*Department of Botany, University College, Galway, Ireland and*
[2]*School of Pharmacy and Biomedical Sciences, Portsmouth Polytechnic, UK*

So what is the future for European species of marine algae as sources of economic products? This is difficult to answer. There is no doubt that European coastal waters contain a large range of algal species, many of which have received detailed biological study. However, very few have been considered for economic utilization and it is probable that most have not been evaluated with this in mind.

The major industrial success for seaweed usage has been the development of the so-called phycocolloids. In the European context this has meant primarily alginates, as is clearly demonstrated by several chapters in this volume. Other phycocolloids, such as carrageenans and agar are also of considerable value. Agar and carrageenans are already produced in several European countries and work is in progress in others to develop new sources. Seaweed polysaccharides remain the major industrial products from marine algae, and are likely to do so, at least for the foreseeable future. However, even this cannot be taken for granted as increasing numbers of other polysaccharides, in particular those of bacterial origin, reach the marketplace. This challenge is being met, notably by the European and North American alginate companies, by the development of high-quality and high-value products for specialist uses.

The future of several of the more traditional uses of seaweeds in Europe appears somewhat bleak. Certain brown algae, in particular *Ascophyllum nodosum*, have been used in animal nutrition, but, as shown by Indergaard and Minsaas in Chapter 2, the value of such products is in doubt, particularly when related to the cost of production. The use of seaweeds in animal feedstuffs has undoubtedly diminished during the past 10 years, and this is illustrated by developments in Ireland where several factories that processed brown algae for animal use have discontinued production, leaving only one factory currently in operation.

The use of algae as a human foodstuff in Europe has always been at a low level and often associated with poor coastal communities. With the increase in affluence in these areas the traditional uses of these foods have either diminished or ceased. (A possible exception to this is the consumption of laver bread (*Porphyra* species) in South Wales.) However, with increased affluence the range of foodstuffs which has become popular has been greatly extended and in this respect there is a potential for the development of certain algae as luxury food items. The consumption of seaweeds in parts of Asia is well established and the trade in these products is considerable. To maintain this trade several species need to be cultivated, as described by Kain (Jones) in Chapter 11. Seaweed cultivation is in its infancy in Europe, but in both France and the British Isles significant work is in progress to produce algae for human food, and the prospects are encouraging.

Cultivation of algal species is the obvious way to produce good quality material in reasonably reliable quantities. However, the costs associated with cultivation are high and the products need to have a high value. This would be the case for algae sold as luxury foods, for use in cosmetic products, and as sources of fine chemicals. Of these, at the moment, the prospects for food production seem the best. Cosmetic preparations based on seaweed are established (see Roeck-Holtzhauer, Chapter 4), but it would appear that the supply of algae at present is easily met from wild stocks.

Another traditional use of seaweed, as a fertilizer, appears to have little economic future. Although the value of certain algae as organic fertilizers is not in doubt, the cost of collection, drying and transportation rules out their widespread use, in view of the availability at a lower price of other products of similar manurial value. However, the collection of seaweed and its utilization as a fertilizer by coastal communities will no doubt continue.

Algal extracts are used in agriculture and horticulture (Blunden, Chapter 3), but these are comparatively low-cost products produced from brown algae readily available from wild stocks. These extracts have been established for many years, but their use has not increased dramatically. This is no doubt partly due to the over-elaborate claims made by certain companies, but also to other factors such as lack of reproducibility of results and incomplete knowledge of the active ingredients. It is doubtful whether there will be a significant increase in the use of these products, at least in the near future. Also their price has to remain comparatively low in order to be economically viable and so the algae available for the production of the extracts will remain restricted.

With the exception of polysaccharides, the use of seaweeds as economic sources of fine chemicals has been disappointing. The vast array of compounds that has been isolated from marine algae can be appreciated from the several reviews by Faulkner (1984, 1986, 1987). Several of these compounds have been shown to have pronounced biological activity, but very few have been utilized in medicine. One exception is α-kainic acid, which is marketed in Japan as a broad spectrum anthelmintic (Murakami *et al.* 1953). Other useful materials from marine algae are available commercially, but the quantities sold are usually very small. Examples of these are the lectins isolated from, for example, *Ptilota plumosa* (Rogers *et al.* 1977) and *Codium fragile* ssp. *atlanticum* (Rogers *et al.* 1986).

For an alga to be considered for exploitation as a source of fine chemicals would require a regular and reliable supply of the plant material (as is the case with the algal sources of industrial polysaccharides). The number of algal species available in sufficiently large quantity to enable a regular supply from the wild is very restricted and, moreover, many companies probably would not consider the development of a product that was dependent on a wild source. As a result, cultivation of the desired species would probably be a prerequisite for commercial exploitation, particularly for substances for medicinal use. Although perfectly feasible, as demonstrated in earlier chapters, the commercial cultivation of marine macroalgae presents a number of problems. As a result, the attractiveness of microalgae to industry is apparent, as cultivation of these presents far fewer problems, and certain selected species are being used to produce valuable compounds (Borowitzka & Borowitzka 1988). The added attraction of microalgae as a source of fine chemicals is that it is feasible to grow the plants under controlled conditions in factories, which gives the company concerned complete control over production.

cultivation procedures for a macroalgal species not previously studied in this way. To make such expenditure worthwhile, the resulting product would have to be of high value and lead to a substantial profit over an extended period. If such a substance were found it is more likely that a concerted effort would be made to synthesize either the compound or an effective derivative of it. As a result of this, studies on algal constituents as possible model compounds for development as, for example, pharmaceutical and agrochemical products would appear to be the most likely future rather than the utilization of algal material for the commercial extraction of the desired compound. However, the latter would be necessary if, as in the case of the phycocolloids, the substances required do not lend themselves to synthesis. This would apply to high molecular weight materials such as polysaccharides and proteins.

In several coastal areas the growth of large amounts of seaweed causes problems, in particular when the algae are deposited on the beach, where they decompose causing such problems as bad odours, fouling and excessive insect activity. The removal of drift weed from resort areas is expensive for the communities concerned, but if a use could be found for the collected material this would be advantageous. Consideration has been given to using weed as substrate for conversion into products such as biogas (see Morand *et al.*, Chapter 5). The quantities of such substrates likely to be produced from the available sources of weed are low, but such a development could result in an economic product from material that is otherwise wasted. Further algal material as a source for bioconversion could be realized by growing selected species in nutrient-rich waters with the primary aim of reducing the nutrient levels (Schramm, Chapter 6). The growth of species, such as agarophytes, for the same purpose of reducing the nutrient content of polluted waters also has economic potential and this is being actively studied by several European research groups.

To assist with the exploitation of the natural resources of marine macroalgae in Europe, an action programme was proposed by Norway in 1980 under the COST action. This proposal was considered by a Working Group of Experts in 1982, was accepted by the Council of the Commission of the European Communities, and became part of the Biotechnology Action Programme (1985–1989) of the Commission (DG XII-F). The COST 48 action has been renewed under the BRIDGE programme (1990–1994).

In 1986, national delegates of the participating COST countries met to launch the research programme on the exploitation of macroalgal resources in Europe. The programme encouraged active collaboration between different research groups, encouraged the exchange of scientists between different laboratories, and financed research seminars and workshops.

The major areas of work have been divided into four subgroups (Table 1).

The COST 48 action programme has resulted in several new developments, as well as good work on the established seaweed-based products. It is too early yet to predict the outcome of the various projects, but there is an overall air of optimism among the various research groups. Let us hope the next few years will see a number of new and exciting products which owe their origins to marine algae.

Table 1. Major areas of work of the COST 48 action programme

Subgroup		Working group	
1	Intensive Cultivation and Genetic Improvement	1	Biosynthesis of algal polysaccharides
		2	Protoplast production and genetic improvement
		3	Cell and tissue culture
		4	Seaweed cultivation
2	Phycocolloids and Fine Chemicals	1	Structure/function relationships in phycocolloids
		2	Algal polysaccharide gels for biotechnology
		3	Fine chemicals: proteins from macroalgae
3	Biomass Conversion, Removal and Use of Nutrients	1	Removal and use of nutrients
		2	Seaweed fermentation
4	Natural Production and Harvesting Techniques		

REFERENCES

Borowitzka M.A. & Borowitzka L.J., eds. 1988. *Micro-algal Biotechnology*. pp. x + 477. Cambridge: Cambridge University Press.

Faulkner D.J. 1984. Marine natural products: metabolites of marine algae and herbivorous marine molluscs. *Natural Prod. Reps (R.Chem.Soc.)* **1**: 251–80.

Faulkner D.J. 1986. Marine natural products. *Natural Prod. Reps (R.Chem.Soc.)* **3**: 1–33.

Faulkner D.J. 1987. Marine natural products. *Natural Prod. Reps (R. Chem. Soc.)* **4**: 539–75.

Murakami S., Takemoto T. & Shimizu Z. 1953. The effective principle of *Digenea simplex* Aq. 1. Separation of the effective fraction by liquid chromatography. *J. Pharm. Soc. Jap.* **73**: 1026–8.

Rogers D.J., Blunden G. & Evans P.R. 1977. *Ptilota plumosa*, a new source of a blood group B-specific lectin. *Med. Lab. Sci.* **34**: 194–200.

Rogers D.J., Loveless R.W. & Balding P. 1986. Isolation and characterisation of the lectins from sub-species of *Codium fragile*. In *Lectins – Biology, Biochemistry, Clinical Biochemistry*. (Eds. T.C. Bøg-Hansen & E. Van Driessche) pp. 155–60. Berlin: Walter de Gruyter.

Index

415